Missale Ragusinum
The Missal of Dubrovnik
(Oxford, Bodleian Library, Canon. Liturg. 342)

Edited by
Richard Francis Gyug

In 1817 the Bodleian Library acquired a large part of the library of the Venetian collector Matteo Luigi Canonici (d. 1806), including several early Dalmatian manuscripts in Beneventan script, a calligraphic texthand developed in southern Italy and used between the ninth and the fifteenth centuries. One of these manuscripts, Canon. Liturg. 342, a much damaged and worn missal of the late thirteenth century from Dubrovnik ("Ragusa" *Lat.*), is the subject of the present description and edition. The Missal contains the variable mass-texts (prayers, biblical readings, and chants) for the major feasts of the ecclesiastical year, although as much as a third of its original contents are now lost.

The Missal of Dubrovnik is a unique cultural artifact when contrasted with the missals of the Roman liturgy that dictated the early modern standards for liturgical practice. It is also remarkable for its ties with other liturgical books of the Beneventan region, a meeting ground where Greeks, Latins, Slavs, Lombards, Romans, and Normans (among others) made their influence felt at different points during the medieval period. But it possesses distinctive features that arise from Dalmatian cults and contribute to the local sense of community. The Missal becomes, therefore, a tool to understand the culture and popular religion of medieval Dubrovnik within the regional tradition of the Beneventan liturgy.

Despite the lamentable state of the codex, the Missal has been frequently cited in studies of the script and liturgy of Dalmatia and the Beneventan zone, but it has never been fully edited or studied at length as a complete work. The introduction contains a summary of the regional liturgy, a codicological description, and a guide to the key features of the Missal with musical transcriptions of the most distinctive items; the text itself is presented in an edition supplemented with notes of parallel sources and musical variants.

Monumenta Liturgica Beneventana

I

General Editors

Virginia Brown
Richard F. Gyug
Roger E. Reynolds

STUDIES AND TEXTS 103

MISSALE RAGUSINUM
The Missal of Dubrovnik

(Oxford, Bodleian Library,
Canon. Liturg. 342)

EDITED WITH AN INTRODUCTORY STUDY

BY

RICHARD FRANCIS GYUG

PONTIFICAL INSTITUTE OF MEDIAEVAL STUDIES

Acknowledgment

This book has been published with the help of a grant
from the Canadian Federation for the Humanities, using
funds provided by the Social Sciences and Humanities
Research Council of Canada

CANADIAN CATALOGUING IN PUBLICATION DATA

Catholic Church
  Missale ragusinum = The missal of Dubrovnik
(Oxford, Bodleian Library, Canon. liturg. 342)

(Studies and texts, ISSN 0082-5328 ; 103)
Text in Latin; preface and introduction in English.
Includes bibliographical references.
ISBN 0-88844-103-7

1. Catholic Church — Liturgy — Texts. 2. Missals — Texts. I. Gyug, Richard,
1954- . II. Pontifical Institute of Mediaeval Studies. III. Title: The missal of
Dubrovnik. IV. Title. V. Series: Studies and texts (Pontifical Institute of Mediaeval
Studies); 103.

BX2015.A3R34 1990   264'.023   C90-093917-6

© 1990 by
Pontifical Institute of Mediaeval Studies
59 Queen's Park Crescent East
Toronto, Ontario, Canada M5S 2C4

PRINTED BY UNIVERSA, WETTEREN, BELGIUM

Contents

List of Tables

List of Musical Figures

List of Figures for the Appendix

Figures showing construction of irregular gatherings

List of Plates

Following p. 166

Preface

In addition to the numerous copies and editions of practical liturgical books that have been made in every period of church history, the editing of liturgical manuscripts for historical research purposes has a long and varied tradition of its own.[1] The publication of such historical texts began in the sixteenth century, when the liturgical codification decreed by the Council of Trent (1523-1556) prompted the study of early sources in order to produce standard and universal books. The edition of early manuscripts continued in the seventeenth and eighteenth centuries with the works of such commentators and historians as Jean Mabillon (died 1707), Giuseppe-Maria Tommasi (died 1713), Edmond Martène (died 1739), and many others whose seminal studies often remain the essential guides through the tangled ways of liturgical history.[2]

Although the writings of these pioneers provided the foundation and theoretical framework for much that followed, the modern edition of liturgical texts has been shaped by the events of more recent ecclesiastical history. In the nineteenth and twentieth centuries, the scholars of the Liturgical Movement in the Roman Catholic Church and their counterparts in other western churches applied the techniques of the historical and critical sciences to early texts in order to understand the genesis and development of the Tridentine liturgy. This academic effort concentrated on questions of form, in keeping with the contemporary emphasis on the "rubric," but it bore practical fruit of another sort in the 1960's with the liturgical reforms of the Second Vatican Council, which saw many of the general discoveries of preceding generations incorporated into the liturgy.[3] Since the Second Vatican Council, therefore, the direction of research has changed perforce. The editing of early liturgical texts no longer functions primarily as the study

---

[1] For a general survey of liturgical historiography, see Cyrille Vogel, *Medieval Liturgy: An Introduction to the Sources*, trans. and revised by William G. Storey and Niels Krogh Rasmussen (Washington, 1986), pp. 1-29; for a brief history of the liturgy, see Aimé-Georges Martimort et al., *L'Église en prière: Introduction à la Liturgie*, revised edition, 4 vols. (Paris, 1983-1984), 1: 37-94.

[2] The principal liturgists of the period are listed in Vogel, *Medieval Liturgy*, pp. 17-20.

[3] On Vatican II and the liturgy, see *Église en prière* (1983-1984), 1: 5-6 and 87-94.

of the roots of the Tridentine liturgy. It is now the task of the ecclesiastical historian to analyse the lessons of the ritual and communal lives of earlier cultures and apply them in synthesis to the sacramental functions of modern society. Although the essential instrument of the study remains the text, it is no longer the documents of the Roman tradition alone that shape the inquiry, but rather the evidence of patristic and medieval counterparts to the modern vernacular and national churches.

If the editing of liturgical texts has been a central concern with wide-ranging effects in ecclesiastical circles, for many secular historians sacred ritual has played an equal role in their reconstructions. One need not pause long over the magisterial works of Schramm, Ladner, and Kantorowicz to be struck by the importance of communal religious practice for the understanding of medieval culture.[4] But the medieval narrative or documentary source is rarely less explicit in its expression of ritual and cultic concerns than the modern historian, which is not surprising given the ecclesiastical training and environment of so many medieval authors.

Instances of the importance of ritual abound in the southern Italian and Dalmatian region that celebrated the liturgy contained in the Missal of Dubrovnik (*Missale Ragusinum*) presented in this edition.[5] For example, when Pietro Orseolo, doge of Venice, landed at Osor in Dalmatia in the year 1000 to confirm the protectorate that had been granted to him three years before by the Emperor Basil II, he was greeted with acclamations and *laudes* chanted by the clergy and people.[6] The local bishops promised to include the doge's name in future *laudes* immediately after the emperor's, thus expressing their acceptance of his new jurisdiction. Later in the same century, still within the southern Italian-Dalmatian locus of culture defined by the use of the

---

[4] E.g., Percy E. Schramm, *Kaiser, Könige, und Päpste. Gesammelte Aufsätze zur Geschichte des Mittelalters*, 4 vols. in 5 (Stuttgart, 1968-1971); Gerhart B. Ladner, *The Idea of Reform: Its Impact on Christian Thought and Action in the Age of the Fathers* (Cambridge/Mass., 1959); and Ernst Kantorowicz, *Laudes Regiae. A Study in Liturgical Acclamations and Mediaeval Ruler Worship*, with a musical study by Manfred F. Bukofzer (Berkeley, Los Angeles, 1946).

[5] Although I will discuss only a few instances directly related to the milieu that produced the thirteenth-century Missal of Dubrovnik, a similar focus on the narratives of other locales and periods would reveal incidents equally symbolic and central to the interests of other communities.

[6] [John the Deacon of Venice], "Iohannis Diaconi Chronicon venetum," p. 32 (ed. Georg H. Pertz, MGH Scriptores [Hannover, 1846; rpt. Leipzig, 1925], 7: 4-38). The incident is discussed by Kantorowicz, *Laudes Regiae*, pp. 147-148, and Victor Saxer, "L'introduction du rite latin dans les provinces dalmato-croates aux Xᵉ-XIIᵉ siècles," in *Vita religiosa, morale e sociale ed i concili di Split dei secc. X-XI*, Atti del Symposium Internazionale di Storia Ecclesiastica, Split 26-30 settembre 1978, ed. Atanazie J. Matanić, Medioevo e Umanesimo 49 (Padua, 1982), pp. 163-193 at 184-190.

Beneventan script, the regional liturgy met opposition at Monte Cassino from reformers. In 1058, as reported by Leo of Ostia in the Chronicle of Monte Cassino, Pope Stephen IX visited the abbey during his short pontificate (elected 2 August 1057, consecrated the next day, died 29 March 1058) and forbade the use of "Ambrosian" chant, which is probably a reference to the regional chant now called "Old Beneventan."[7] Pope Stephen IX, who had entered Monte Cassino in 1055 as the noted reformer Frederick of Lorraine and became abbot in 1057 shortly before his election to the papacy, was clearly no respecter of the local tradition. The Chronicle is laconic on Pope Stephen's motives, but the lack of surviving manuscript witnesses to the "Ambrosian" chant of Monte Cassino is telling evidence of the success of his prohibition. Whatever is known of the Old Beneventan rite comes principally from a series of Beneventan alternatives found transcribed after the standard Roman texts in books from Benevento, the other major centre of the regional liturgy.[8]

A century later, on the eastern shore of the Adriatic, the prerogatives of a local liturgy are expressed in a legendary incident revolving around the forced landing of Richard I, king of England, during his return from the Third Crusade.[9] In the late autumn of 1192, as his ship was being driven up the Adriatic by seasonal storms, the desperate Richard vowed to build a church worth a hundred thousand ducats on the site of his safe windfall. He found refuge on the island of Lokrum, lying just off the harbour of Ragusa (modern-day Dubrovnik) and home to a respected Benedictine community. The nearby city welcomed the king, but beseeched him to spend the promised sum on their cathedral since such a bequest would have been excessive for the monastery. He agreed, provided that Ragusa procure papal sanction for the change from the terms of his vow. Richard asked also that the citizens build a lesser church on the island out of their own funds, and permit the abbot of Lokrum to celebrate mass in the cathedral with his monks once each year on the feast of the Purification. Such incidents bind

---

[7] [Leo of Ostia], *Chronica monasterii Casinensis*, 2: 94 (ed. Hartmut Hoffmann, MGH Scriptores [Hannover, 1980], 34: 353): "Ambrosianum cantum in ecclesia ista cantari penitus interdixit." On Pope Stephen IX, see Herbert Bloch, *Monte Cassino in the Middle Ages*, 3 vols. (Cambridge/Mass., 1986), 1: 37-38. See below p. 14.

[8] The Old Beneventan liturgy is discussed below at pp. 3-12. The most exhaustive presentation of the evidence is Thomas Forrest Kelly, *The Beneventan Chant* (Cambridge, 1989); a companion volume of facsimiles will appear in the series Paléographie Musicale.

[9] Jacopo Coleti (continuing Daniel Farlati), *Illyrici sacri*, vol. 6: *Ecclesia Ragusina cum suffraganeis, et ecclesia Rhiziniensis et Catharensis* (Venice, 1800), p. 90, from a document in the archives of Dubrovnik dated 1598. To the best of my knowledge, the legend is not found in any other source.

together the more prosaic events of many a medieval account; anything less than a sympathetic and informed reading of liturgical events cannot do justice to the surroundings and concerns of most medieval writers.

The citation of ritual and cult in medieval narrative and documentary sources is matched by an abundance of practical books of the liturgy. Through the direct record of ritual in medieval missals, lectionaries, breviaries, and the like, one is permitted an indirect appreciation of the cultures that produced liturgical documents and the institutions that preserved them. Unfortunately, the potential of the sources is equalled by their often chaotic survival in uncatalogued or partially catalogued centres and by their own intractable nature. Practical books of the liturgy may be to the study of medieval communal life what a medieval court transcript or deposition is to the study of the vernaculars or administrative history, but if a knowledge of legal process and terminology is required to understand the latter, an appreciation of the former needs grounding in liturgical forms, musical notation, and local monuments, a combination of disciplines available to very few, and possessed by even fewer now that the common ecclesiastical culture of past generations has yielded to a reformed liturgical diversity.

It becomes the duty of the editor, therefore, to provide the texts of the medieval liturgy to an audience of both ecclesiastical and social historians of differing interests and backgrounds. The publication of studies of medieval liturgical books has continued within the framework established by the editors and institutions central to the Liturgical Movement (Andrieu, Dold, Duchesne, *Solesmes*, *Beuron*, etc.), with several notable successes and a few new departures. The critical editions of the Gregorian sacramentaries by Jean Deshusses, the Roman-German Pontifical of the Tenth Century by Cyrille Vogel and Reinhard Elze (completing the work initiated by Michel Andrieu), the corpus for benedictions and prefaces by Edmond Moeller, and the corpus of antiphons for the office by René-Jean Hesbert, for instance, have carried forward the study of the main features of the western liturgy and provided models and materials for the examination of liturgical diversity and regional liturgical culture.[10] None of these broadly-based editions would have been possible, however, without the concurrent study and edition of individual manuscripts from many regions. The publication of such sources has also

---

[10] Jean Deshusses, *Le Sacramentaire grégorien: Ses principales formes d'après les plus anciens manuscrits*, 3 vols., SF 16 (2nd edition), 24, 28 (Fribourg/S., 1979, 1982); Cyrille Vogel and Reinhard Elze, *Le Pontifical romano-germanique du dixième siècle*, 3 vols., ST 226-227, 269 (Vatican City, 1963, 1972); Edmond Moeller, *Corpus benedictionum pontificalium*, 4 vols., CCL 162, 162A-C (Turnhout, 1971-1979), and *Corpus praefationum*, 5 vols., CCL 161, 161A-D (Turnhout, 1980-1981); and René-Jean Hesbert, *Corpus antiphonalium officii*, 6 vols., RED, Series maior, Fontes 7-12 (Rome, 1963-1979).

continued, providing the basis for new constructs and reflections on liturgical history and medieval culture.

The present edition falls among the latter, the study and un-emended edition of a single liturgical manuscript within a distinctive regional tradition. The manuscript, now in the Bodleian Library of Oxford (Canon. Liturg. 342), hails from the Dalmatian coast, probably from the city of Dubrovnik ("Ragusa" It. and Lat., hence Missale Ragusinum), and dates most likely to the late thirteenth century. It is written in the Beneventan script and contains noted propers of the mass for the major feasts of the Temporal and Sanctoral, i.e., the texts and music of the parts of the mass that varied from day to day. With such a book, in conjunction with a shorter text for the invariable parts of the liturgy, the priest (or perhaps in this case the bishop) was equipped to celebrate mass on Sundays and the major feasts of the Christian year.

The Missal is in many respects very similar to the Tridentine missal, with texts traditional to much of the western church from at least the ninth century. It is, however, in its points of variance that its greatest interest lies: as the medieval congregation was acutely aware of the rite or use proper to its own church, so the modern historian must identify local and regional practices in order to understand the points of communal identification and conflict evident in many books of the practical liturgy. The Missal, for instance, retains features of the Old Beneventan rite abandoned at Monte Cassino in the eleventh century but still surviving in Dalmatia in the thirteenth. In particular, it contains a series of Old Beneventan Lenten gospels and a local form of the *Exultet* sung at the blessing of the Paschal candle during the Easter vigil.[11]

Despite the value of individual manuscripts such as the Missal of Dubrovnik for a fundamental knowledge of local conditions and concerns, it is only through the aggregate of sources used for the functions of ritual that the practices of local churches are fully revealed. The present edition cannot, therefore, be a definitive analysis or treatment of the thirteenth-century liturgy as practiced in Dubrovnik, nor can it provide more than partial evidence toward the study of the liturgical culture in the region defined by the use of the Beneventan script, i.e., Dalmatia and Italy between Rome and Calabria (the old Lombard duchy). Materials for the broader study of the liturgical culture of the region, already well known in paleographic, musical, and textual history, will be presented in a series of editions of individual liturgical manuscripts being published by the Pontifical Institute of Mediaeval Studies,

[11] See below pp. 72-73, for the Lenten gospels of the Old Beneventan rite copied in the Missal of Dubrovnik; and pp. 84-92 for the *Exultet.* See pp. 107-112 and 185-187 for summaries of the distinctive texts and melodies of the Missal.

the *Monumenta liturgica beneventana.* The Missal of Dubrovnik is the first volume in the series. Succeeding volumes will expand our knowledge of the regional culture by providing further texts critical for an accurate assessment of the diffusion of liturgical practices and by making available to historians of local culture or of general themes materials that will aid them in identifying liturgical issues and understanding their medieval significance.

*
*   *

I wish to acknowledge here with thanks the many who have assisted me. Permission has been granted by the Keeper of Western Manuscripts at the Bodleian Library to publish this edition of the manuscript, Canon. Liturg. 342, and print facsimiles of selected folios. The staff of Duke Humphrey's reading room at the Bodleian showed unfailing courtesy during several visits to examine the manuscript and related material. I would like to thank Dr. Bruce Barker-Benfield, in particular, for his ready and knowledgeable responses to questions on the condition and history of the codex.

Closer to home, I wish to express my gratitude to Professor Virginia Brown of the Pontifical Institute of Mediaeval Studies for her encouragement and comments, to Professor Andrew Hughes of the Faculty of Music, University of Toronto, for his counsel on musical matters and comments on the typescript, and to the many medievalists at Toronto who have answered questions and enriched this work through their insights. My thanks go also to the anonymous experts who read the book for the Department of Publications of the Pontifical Institute for their valuable comments and suggestions. Above all, I owe special thanks to Professor Roger E. Reynolds of the Pontifical Institute of Mediaeval Studies, who introduced me to the study of medieval liturgy and has read with characteristic enthusiasm and a critical eye several drafts of this edition.

Pontifical Institute of Mediaeval Studies

Abbreviations

Acta sanctorum = *Acta sanctorum quotquot toto orbe coluntur, vel a catholicis scriptoribus celebrantur quae ex latinis et graecis, aliarumque gentium antiquis monumentis collegit, digessit, notis illustravit Joannes Bollandus (1600-1681).* Ed. Jean Baptiste Carnandet. 2nd edition. 67 vols. Paris: V. Palmé, 1863-1925.

ALW = *Archiv für Liturgiewissenschaft* 1—. Abt-Herwegen-Institut für liturgische und monastische Forschung, Abtei Maria Laach. Regensburg: Pustet, 1950—. (Supersedes *JLW*).

Bibliotheca Sanctorum = *Bibliotheca Sanctorum.* 12 vols. and indices. Rome: Istituto Giovanni XXIII della Pontificia Università Lateranense, 1961-1970.

CCL = Corpus Christianorum, Series latina. Turnhout: Brepols.

CLLA = Klaus Gamber, *Codices liturgici latini antiquiores.* 2nd edition. 1 vol. in 2 parts. Spicilegii Friburgensis Subsidia 1. Fribourg/S.: Éditions Universitaires, 1968 (1st edition 1963).

DMA = *Dictionary of the Middle Ages.* Ed. Joseph R. Strayer. 12 vols. New York: Scribners, 1982-1989.

Église en prière (1961) = Aimé-Georges Martimort. With Roger Béraudy, Bernard Botte, Noële Maurice Denis-Boulet, Bernard Capelle, Antoine Chavasse, Irénée-Henri Dalmais, Benoît Darragon, Pierre-Marie Gy, Pierre Jounel, Adrien Nocent, Aimon-Marie Roguet, Olivier Rousseau, and Pierre Salmon. *L'Église en prière: Introduction à la Liturgie.* Paris: Desclée, 1961.

Église en prière (1983-1984) = Aimé-Georges Martimort. With Robert Cabié, Irénée-Henri Dalmais, Jean Évenou, Pierre-Marie Gy, Pierre Jounel, Adrien Nocent, and Damien Sicard. *L'Église en prière: Introduction à la Liturgie.* Revised edition. 4 vols. Paris: Desclée, 1983-1984.

EL = *Ephemerides Liturgicae* 1—. Rome: Centro liturgico Vincenziano, Edizioni liturgiche, 1887—. (In 2 series, *Analecta historico-ascetica* and *Ius et praxis liturgica,* since vol. 51 [1937]).

EO = *Ecclesia orans. Periodica de scientiis liturgicis.* 1—. Rome: Facultas sacrae liturgiae in Pontificio Athenaeo Anselmiano de Urbe, 1984—.

HBS = Henry Bradshaw Society Publications. London, 1891—.

Hesbert, "Tradition bénéventaine" = [René-Jean Hesbert.] "La tradition
    bénéventaine dans la tradition manuscrite." In *Le Codex 10673 de la
    Bibliothèque Vaticane. Fonds latin (XIe siècle). Graduel bénéventain.*
    Ed. Joseph Gajard. Pp. 60-465. Paléographie Musicale 14. Solemes:
    Abbaye Saint-Pierre, 1931.

Hourlier and Huglo, "Notation bénéventaine" = [Jacques Hourlier and
    Michel Huglo.] "Étude sur la notation bénéventaine." In *Le Codex
    VI.34 de la Bibliothèque capitulaire de Bénévent (XIe-XIIe siècle).
    Graduel de Bénévent avec prosaire et tropaire.* Ed. Joseph Gajard. Pp.
    70-161. Paléographie Musicale 15. Solesmes: Abbaye Saint-Pierre,
    1937.

Hourlier and Froger, *Missel de Bénévent* = Jacques Hourlier and Jacques
    Froger. *Le manuscrit VI-33 Archivio Arcivescovile Benevento. Missel de
    Bénévent (Début du XIe siècle).* Paléographie Musicale 20. Bern,
    Frankfurt: Peter Lang, 1983.

JLW = *Jahrbuch für Liturgiewissenschaft* 1-15. Münster/W.: Aschendorff,
    1921-1935. (Superseded by *ALW*.)

Loew, *Beneventan Script* = Elias Avery Loew [Lowe]. *The Beneventan
    Script. A History of the South Italian Minuscule.* 2nd edition prepared
    and enlarged by Virginia Brown. 2 vols. Sussidi Eruditi 33, 34. Rome:
    Edizioni di Storia e Letteratura, 1980 (1st edition 1914).

LQF = Liturgiegeschichtliche (since 1957, Liturgiewissenschaftliche) Quellen
    und Forschungen. Münster/W: Aschendorff, 1918–. The series Litur-
    giegeschichtliche Quellen 1-12 and Liturgiegeschichtliche Forschungen
    1-10 were united in 1928 as Liturgiegeschichtliche Quellen und
    Forschungen with Liturgiegeschichtliche Forschungen becoming vols.
    13-22. The series continued with vols. 23-31 until 1957 when the name
    was changed. Later volumes have been numbered consecutively from
    32–.

MGG = *Die Musik in Geschichte und Gegenwart. Allgemeine Enzyklopädie der
    Musik.* Ed. Friedrich Blume. 14 vols. with supplementary vols. in
    progress (vols. 15-17 to date). Kassel, Basel: Bärenreiter, 1949-1986.

MGH = Monumenta Germaniae Historica. Hannover: Hahnsche, 1826–.

MS = *Mediaeval Studies* 1–. Toronto: Pontifical Institute of Mediaeval
    Studies, 1939–.

NCE = *New Catholic Encyclopedia.* 15 vols. Vol. 16: *Supplement.* New York:
    McGraw-Hill, 1967, 1974.

New Grove Dictionary = *The New Grove Dictionary of Music and Musicians.*
    20 vols. London: Macmillan, 1980.

Paléographie Musicale = Paléographie Musicale. Les principaux manuscrits
    de chant grégorien, ambrosien, mozarabe, gallican, publiés en facsimi-

lés phototypiques. Ed. André Mocquereau (vols. 1-13, 1889-1930) and Joseph Gajard (vols. 14-19, 1931-1974). Solesmes: Abbaye Saint-Pierre, 1889—.

PL = Patrologiae cursus completus. Series latina. Ed. Jacques-Paul Migne. 221 vols. Paris: Garnier, 1844-1864.

RB = *Revue bénédictine* 1—. Abbaye de Maredsous, Belgium, 1884—.

RdCG = *Revue de chant grégorien* 1—. Grenoble: Baratier et Dardelet, 1892—.

RED = Rerum ecclesiasticarum documenta. Rome: Herder, 1950—.

Schlager, *Katalog* = Karlheinz Schlager. *Thematischer Katalog der ältesten Alleluia-Melodien aus Handschriften des 10. und 11. Jahrhunderts.* Erlanger Arbeiten zur Musikwissenschaft 2. Munich: Walter Ricke, 1965.

SE = *Sacris Erudiri: Jaarboek voor Godsdienstwetenschappen* 1—. Sint Pietersabdij, Steenbrugge. Brugge: K. Beyaert, 1948—.

SF = Spicilegium Friburgense. Textes pour servir à l'histoire de la vie chrétienne. Ed. Gérard Gilles Meerssman, Anton Hänggi, and Pascál Ladner. Fribourg/S.: Éditions Universitaires, 1957—.

ST = Studi e Testi. Vatican City: Biblioteca Apostolica Vaticana, 1900—.

Texte und Arbeiten = Texte und Arbeiten. 1. Abteilung: Beiträge zur Ergründung des älteren lateinischen christlichen Schrifttums und Gottesdienstes. Erzabtei Beuron. Beuron: Beuroner Kunstverlag, 1917—.

TU = Texte und Untersuchungen zur Geschichte der altchristlichen Literatur. Berlin: Akademie Verlag, 1883—.

Liturgical Abbreviations

all.	=	alleluia
ant.	=	antiphona
apost.	=	apostolus
Ascen.	=	Ascensio
com.	=	communio
comm.	=	commune
dom.	=	dominica
ebd.	=	ebdomada
Epiph.	=	Epiphania
epla.	=	epistola
evg.	=	evangelium
fr.	=	feria
gr.	=	graduale
hymn.	=	hymnus
int.	=	introitus
nat.	=	nativitas/natalis
oct.	=	octava
off.	=	offertorium
or.	=	oratio
Pent.	=	Pentecostes
pr.	=	prosa/prosula
ps.	=	psalmus
resp.	=	responsorium/responsum
seq.	=	sequentia
tr.	=	tractus
v.	=	versus
vig.	=	vigilia

Conspectus Siglorum

In the *conspectus siglorum* and the *apparatus parallelorum locorum* headings in small capitals have been added to direct the reader to the appropriate category of text among the following:

RL = later Roman liturgy
AMS = early mass-antiphonals
LEC = early lectionaries
SAC = early sacramentaries
GREG = Gregorian sacramentaries
GEL8 = Gelasians of the Eighth Century
AM = Ambrosian sacramentaries and missals
ES = other early sources
BEN = Beneventan books
LS = later medieval sources.

Asterisks indicate sources cited as supplements in the *apparatus parallelorum locorum*.

Dubr = Oxford, Bodleian Library, Canon. Liturg. 342.

LATER ROMAN LITURGY (= RL)

Ar* = *Antiphonale sacrosanctae Romanae ecclesiae pro diurnis horis*, ed. Solesmes, no. 820 (Paris, Rome, Tournai, 1924).

GR = *Graduale sacrosanctae Romanae ecclesiae* cum *Missae propriae Ordinis S. Benedicti*, ed. Solesmes, no. 696A (Paris, Rome, Tournai, 1952).

GR in Suppl. OSB = *Missae propriae Ordinis S. Benedicti* in *Graduale sacrosanctae Romanae ecclesiae*, ed. Solesmes, no. 696A (Paris, Rome, Tournai, 1952).

MRM = *Missale Romanum Mediolani, 1474*, ed. Robert Lippe, 2 vols., HBS 17, 33 (London, 1899, 1907).

Sources of the Roman Liturgy

Early Mass-Antiphonals (= AMS)

AMS = Ed. René-Jean Hesbert, *Antiphonale missarum sextuplex d'après le graduel de Monza et les antiphonaires de Rheinau, du Mont-Blandin, de Compiègne, de Corbie, et de Senlis* (Brussels, 1935).

Early Lectionaries (= LEC)

Alc = Cambrai, Bibliothèque Municipale, 553 (with other MSS). Ed. André Wilmart, "Le Lectionnaire d'Alcuin," *EL* 51 (1937) 136-197 (rpt. as Bibliotheca 'Ephemerides Liturgicae' 2 [Rome, 1937]).

CoP = Paris, Bibliothèque Nationale, lat. 9451. Ed. Robert Amiet, "Un 'Comes' carolingien inédit de la Haute-Italie," *EL* 73 (1959) 335-367.

Mu = Besançon, Bibliothèque Municipale, 184 (fols. 58r-74v). Ed. André Wilmart, "Le *Comes* de Muhrbach," *RB* 30 (1913) 25-69.

NapL = London, British Library, Cotton Nero D.iv. Ed. Klaus Gamber, "Die kampanische Lektionsordnung," *SE* 13 (1962) 326-352.

WuC = Würzburg, Universitätsbibliothek, M.p.th.f. 62 (fols. 2v-10v). Ed. Germain Morin, "Le plus ancien *Comes* ou Lectionnaire de l'église romaine," *RB* 27 (1910) 41-74.

WuE = Würzburg, Universitätsbibliothek, M.p.th.f. 62 (fols. 10v-16v). Ed. Germain Morin, "Liturgie et Basiliques de Rome au milieu du VII siècle d'après les listes d'évangiles de Würzburg," *RB* 28 (1911) 296-330.

Early Sacramentaries (= SAC)

Le = Verona, Biblioteca Capitolare, 85 (80). Ed. Leo Cunibert Mohlberg, Leo Eizenhöfer, and Petrus Siffrin, *Sacramentarium Veronense*, RED, Series maior, Fontes 1 (Rome, 1956).

Va = Vatican City, Biblioteca Apostolica Vaticana, Reg. lat. 316 + Paris, Bibliothèque Nationale, lat. 7193 (fols. 41r-56v). Ed. Leo Cunibert Mohlberg, Leo Eizenhöfer, and Petrus Siffrin, *Liber Sacramentorum Romanae aecclesiae ordinis anni circuli*, RED, Series maior, Fontes 4 (Rome, 1960).

Gregorian Sacramentaries (= GREG)

Ha = Cambrai, Bibliothèque Municipale, 164 (with other MSS). Ed. Jean Deshusses, "Hadrianum ex authentico ad fidem codicis Cameracensis 164," in *Le Sacramentaire grégorien: Ses principales formes d'après les plus anciens manuscrits*, 3 vols., SF 16 (2nd edition), 24, 28 (Fribourg/ S., 1979, 1982), vol. 1 pars 1.

Pa = Padua, Biblioteca Capitolare, D 47. Ed. Jean Deshusses, "Gregorianum Paduense ad fidem codicis Paduensis D 47," in *Sacramentaire grégorien*, vol. 1 pars 3.

Sp = Autun, Bibliothèque Municipale, 19*bis* (with other MSS). Ed. Jean Deshusses, "Hadrianum revisum Anianense cum supplemento," in *Sacramentaire grégorien*, vol. 1 pars 2.

Tc* = Ed. Jean Deshusses, "Additiones interpositae," in *Sacramentaire grégorien*, vol. 1 pars 4, vols. 2-3.

Z6 = Monte Cassino, Archivio della Badia, 271 (Terscriptus: lowest includes fragments of a Gregorian missal). Ed. Alban Dold, *Vom Sakramentar, Comes und Capitulare zum Missale: Eine Studie über die Entstehungszeit der erstmals vollständig erschlossenen liturgischen Palimpsesttexte in Unziale aus Codex 271 von ̀Monte Cassino*, Texte und Arbeiten 34 (Beuron, 1943).

Gelasians of the Eighth Century (= GEL8)

En = Paris, Bibliothèque Nationale, lat. 816. Ed. Patrick Saint-Roch, *Liber sacramentorum Engolismensis (Manuscrit B.N. Lat. 816. Le Sacramentaire Gélasien d'Angoulême.)*, CCL 159C (Turnhout, 1987); with the same enumeration of paragraphs as Paul Cagin and Léopold Delisle, *Le sacramentaire gélasien d'Angoulême* (Angoulême, 1919).

Ge = Paris, Bibliothèque Nationale, lat. 12048. Ed. Jean Deshusses and Antoine Dumas, *Liber sacramentorum gellonensis*, CCL 159-159A (Turnhout, 1981).

Ph* = Berlin, Deutsche Staatsbibliothek, Phillipps 1667. Ed. Odilo Heiming, *Liber sacramentorum Augustodunensis*, CCL 159B (Turnhout, 1984).

Pr* = Prague, Knihovna Metropolitní Kapitoly, O. 83. Ed. Alban Dold and Leo Eizenhöfer, *Das Prager Sakramentar*, II. *Prolegomena und Textausgabe*, Texte und Arbeiten 38-42 (Beuron, 1949).

Rh = Zürich, Zentralbibliothek, Rh 30. Ed. Anton Hänggi and Alfons Schönherr, *Sacramentarium Rhenaugiense*, SF 15 (Fribourg/S., 1970).

Sg = Sankt Gallen, Stiftsbibliothek, 348. Ed. Kunibert Mohlberg, *Das fränkische Sacramentarium Gelasianum in alamannischer Überlieferung*, 3rd edition, St. Galler Sakramentar-Forschungen 1, LQF 1-2 (Münster/W., 1971 [1918]).

AMBROSIAN SACRAMENTARIES AND MISSALS (= AM)

Sb = Bergamo, Biblioteca di S. Alessandro in Colonna, 242. Ed. Angelo Paredi and Giuseppe Fassi, *Sacramentarium Bergomense*, Monumenta Bergomensia 6 (Bergamo, 1962).

Sacr. Aribert* = Milan, Biblioteca del Capitolo metropolitano, D 3-2. Ed. Angelo Paredi, "Il Sacramentario di Ariberto," in *Miscellanea Adriano Bernareggi*, ed. Luigi Cortesi, Monumenta Bergomensia 1 (Bergamo, 1958), pp. 329-488.

STripl* = Zürich, Zentralbibliothek, C 43. Ed. Odilo Heiming, *Das Sacramentarium triplex*, Corpus Ambrosiano-Liturgicum 1, LQF 49 (Münster/W., 1968).

D3-3* = Milan, Biblioteca del Capitolo metropolitano, D 3-3. Ed. Judith Frei, *Das ambrosianische Sakramentar D 3-3 aus dem mailändischen Metropolitankapitel*, Corpus Ambrosiano-Liturgicum 3, LQF 56 (Münster/W., 1974).

OTHER EARLY SOURCES (= ES)

Co* = Paris, Bibliothèque Nationale, nouv. acq. lat. 2171. Ed. Justo Pérez de Urbel and Atilano González y Ruiz-Zorilla, *Liber commicus*, 2 vols., Monumenta Hispaniae Sacra, Serie litúrgica 2-3 (Madrid, 1950, 1955).

Corpus troporum 2/1 = Olof Marcusson, *Corpus troporum*, vol. 2: *Prosules de la messe*, pars 1: *Tropes de l'alleluia*, Studia Latina Stockholmiensia 22 (Stockholm, 1976).

F* = Göttingen, Universitätsbibliothek, Theol. 231. Ed. Gregor Richter and Albert Schönfelder, *Sacramentarium Fuldense saeculi x.*, 2nd edition with a bibliographic note by D. H. Tripp, Quellen und Abhandlungen zur Geschichte der Abtei und der Diözese Fulda 9, HBS 101 (Farnborough, 1977 [1912]).

Franz* = Adolph Franz, *Die kirchlichen Benediktionen im Mittelalter*, 2 vols. (Freiburg/Br., 1909; rpt. Graz, 1960).

PRG* = Cyrille Vogel and Reinhard Elze, *Le Pontifical romano-germanique du dixième siècle*, 3 vols., ST 226-227, 269 (Vatican City, 1963, 1972). Texts found in Monte Cassino, Archivio della Badia, 451, which is used extensively in the edition of Vogel and Elze, are cited by the separate siglum McP (see below under Beneventan sources).

Schlager, *Katalog* = Karlheinz Schlager, *Thematischer Katalog der ältesten Alleluia-Melodien aus Handschriften des 10. und 11. Jahrhunderts*, Erlanger Arbeiten zur Musikwissenschaft 2 (Munich, 1965).

SVich* = Vich, Museo Episcopal, 66. Ed. Alejandro Olivar, *El Sacramentario de Vich*, Monumenta Hispaniae Sacra, Serie litúrgica 4 (Barcelona, 1953).

Syg* = Paris, Bibliothèque Nationale, lat. 903. Facsimile edition, André
Mocquereau, *Le Codex 903 de la Bibliothèque Nationale de Paris (XIe*
siècle, Graduel de Saint-Yrieix, Paléographie Musicale 13 (Solesmes,
1925).

Vl4770 = Vatican City, Biblioteca Apostolica Vaticana, Vat. lat. 4770.
Missale (unedit.), s. xi, Abruzzi.

BENEVENTAN BOOKS (= BEN)

Bibliography for each MS in Loew, *Beneventan Script*, vol. 2: *Hand List*
of Beneventan Manuscripts.

Benevento (prefix 'Ben')

Ben29 = London, British Library, Egerton 3511 (*olim* Benevento, Biblioteca
Capitolare, VI 29). Ed. Elizabeth Peirce, *An Edition of Egerton MS.*
3511: A Twelfth Century Missal of St. Peter's in Benevento (Diss.
London, 1964).

Ben30 = Benevento, Biblioteca Capitolare, 30 (= VI 30). Missale (unedit.),
s. xiii, Benevento.

Ben33 = Benevento, Biblioteca Capitolare, 33 (= VI 33). Facsimile edition,
Jacques Hourlier and Jacques Froger, *Le manuscrit VI-33 Archivio*
Arcivescovile Benevento. Missel de Bénévent (Début du XIe siècle),
Paléographie Musicale 20 (Bern, Frankfurt, 1983).

Ben34 = Benevento, Biblioteca Capitolare, 34 (= VI 34). Facsimile edition,
Joseph Gajard, *Le Codex VI.34 de la Bibliothèque capitulaire de*
Bénévent (XIe-XIIe siècle). Graduel de Bénévent avec prosaire et tropaire,
Paléographie Musicale 15 (Solesmes, 1937).

Ben35 = Benevento, Biblioteca Capitolare, 35 (= VI 35). Graduale (unedit.),
s. xii in., Benevento.

Ben38 = Benevento, Biblioteca Capitolare, 38 (= VI 38). Graduale (unedit.),
s. xi, Benevento.

Ben39 = Benevento, Biblioteca Capitolare, 39 (= VI 39). Graduale (unedit.),
s. xi, Benevento.

Ben40 = Benevento, Biblioteca Capitolare, 40 (= VI 40). Graduale (unedit.),
s. xi, Benevento.

Dalmatia (prefix 'Da')

DaB = Berlin, Staatsbibliothek Preussischer Kulturbesitz, Lat. fol. 920. Ed.
Sieghild Rehle, "Missale Beneventanum in Berlin," *SE* 28 (1985)
469-510.

DaE = Berlin, Staatsbibliothek Preussischer Kulturbesitz, Theol. lat. quart. 278. Ed. René-Jean Hesbert, "L'Évangéliaire de Zara," *Scriptorium* 8 (1954) 177-204.

DaK = Leningrad, Sobrananie inostrannykh Rukopisei Otdela Rukopisnoi i Redkoi Knigi Biblioteki Akademii Nauk SSSR, F. no. 200 (fols. 3r-64v). Ed. Richard F. Gyug, *An Edition of Leningrad, B.A.N., F. no. 200: The Lectionary and Pontifical of Kotor* (Diss. Toronto, 1983).

DaS = Split, Kaptolski Arhiv (Riznica Katedrale), D 624 (fols. 211, 214). Ed. Klaus Gamber and Sieghild Rehle, "Fragmenta Liturgica VI.40: Fragmente eines Gregorianums in Split", *SE* 23 (1978-1979) 298-303.

DaZ = Zagreb, Metropolitanska Knjižnica, MR 166 (pp. 1-326): Missale (unedit.), s. xii, southern Italy; (pp. 327-354): Missale (unedit.), s. xiii, Dalmatia.

Monte Cassino (prefix 'Mc')

Mc127 = Monte Cassino, Archivio della Badia, 127 (pp. 9-540). Missale (unedit.), s. xi^2, Monte Cassino.

Mc426 = Monte Cassino, Archivio della Badia, 426. Missale (unedit.), s. xi^2, Monte Cassino. Mc426^1 = palimpsests and erasures.

Mc540 = Monte Cassino, Archivio della Badia, 540. Missale (unedit.), s. xi/xii, Monte Cassino. Mc540^1 = palimpsests and erasures.

Mc546 = Monte Cassino, Archivio della Badia, 546. Graduale (unedit.), s. xii/xiii, Monte Cassino.

Mc.VI = Monte Cassino, Archivio della Badia, Compactiones VI. Ed. Alban Dold, "Umfangreiche Reste zweier Plenarmissalien des 11. und 12. Jh. aus Monte Cassino," *EL* 53 (1939) 114-144.

Mc.VII = Monte Cassino, Archivio della Badia, Compactiones VII (12 fols.). Ed. Alban Dold, "Umfangreiche Reste," pp. 144-164.

Mc.VII^2 = Monte Cassino, Archivio della Badia, Compactiones VII (9 fols.). Ed. Klaus Gamber, "Fragmenta Liturgica v.29: Fragmente eines beneventanischen Missale in Montecassino," *SE* 21 (1972-1973) 241-247.

McB = Vatican City, Biblioteca Apostolica Vaticana, Borg. lat. 211. Missale (unedit.), s. xi/xii, Monte Cassino.

McO = Vatican City, Biblioteca Apostolica Vaticana, Ottob. lat. 145. Ed. Klaus Gamber and Sieghild Rehle, *Manuale Casinense*, Textus patristici et liturgici 13 (Regensburg, 1977).

McP* = Monte Cassino, Archivio della Badia, 451. Ed. Cyrille Vogel and Reinhard Elze, *Le Pontifical romano-germanique du dixième siècle*, 3 vols., ST 226-227, 269 (Vatican City, 1963, 1972). See also ES: PRG.

McV = Vatican City, Biblioteca Apostolica Vaticana, Vat. lat. 6082. Missale, s. xii, Monte Cassino. Partial edition, Alban Dold, "Die vom Missale Romanum abweichenden Lesetexte für die Messfeiern nach den Notierungen des aus Monte Cassino stammenden Cod. Vat. lat. 6082," in *Vir Dei Benedictus. Eine Festgabe zum 1400. Todestag des heiligen Benedikt*, ed. Raphael Molitor (Münster/W., 1947), pp. 293-332.

Apulia (prefix 'Pu')

PuC = Baltimore, Walters Art Gallery, W 6. Ed. Sieghild Rehle, *Missale Beneventanum von Canosa*, Textus patristici et liturgici 9 (Regensburg, 1972).

PuL = Vatican City, Biblioteca Apostolica Vaticana, Vat. lat. 7231. Missale (unedit.), s. xiii, Apulia/Dalmatia.

PuV = Vatican City, Biblioteca Apostolica Vaticana, Vat. lat. 10673. Facsimile edition, Joseph Gajard *Le Codex 10673 de la Bibliothèque Vaticane. Fonds latin (XIᵉ siècle). Graduel bénéventain*, Paléographie Musicale 14 (Solesmes, 1931).

PuZ = Lucerne, Stiftsarchiv S. Leodegar, 1912 (bifol.); Peterlingen, Comunalarchiv, S.N. (5 fols.); Zürich, Staatsarchiv, W 3 AG 19 (fasc. III); Zürich, Zentralbibliothek, Z XIV 4, nos. 1-4. Ed. Alban Dold, *Die Zürcher und Peterlinger Messbuch-Fragmente*, Texte und Arbeiten 25 (Beuron, 1934).

Other origins

Ca = Vatican City, Biblioteca Apostolica Vaticana, Barb. lat. 603. Missale (unedit.), s. xii/xiii, Caiazzo.

Esc = El Escorial, Real Biblioteca de San Lorenzo, ℞ III 1. Ed. Alban Dold, "Im Escorial gefundene Bruchstücke eines Plenarmissales," in *Spanische Forschungen der Görresgesellschaft*, 1st ser., Gesammelte Aufsätze zur Kulturgeschichte Spaniens (Münster/W., 1935), 5: 89-96.

Na1 = Florence, Biblioteca Laurenziana, 29.8. Palimpsest graduale with Laurenziana 33.31 (upper scripts are Boccaccio's autographs), s. xiii ex., Naples. An edition of the palimpsest gradual is being prepared by Virginia Brown.

Ott[1] = Vatican City, Biblioteca Apostolica Vaticana, Ottob. lat. 576 (Lower script of palimpsest). Ed. Klaus Gamber, "Fragmente eines Missale Beneventanum als Palimpsestblätter des Cod. Ottob. Lat. 576," *RB* 84 (1974) 367-372.

Ott = Vatican City, Biblioteca Apostolica Vaticana, Ottob. lat. 576. Missale (unedit.), s. xii ex., s. xiii; Benevento/Monte Cassino.

Ve = Vatican City, Biblioteca Apostolica Vaticana, Barb. lat. 699. Missale (unedit.), s. xii ex., Veroli.

Vl5100* = Vatican City, Biblioteca Apostolica Vaticana, Vat. lat. 5100. Ed. Sieghild Rehle, "Zwei beneventanische Evangelistare in der Vaticana," *Römische Quartalschrift für christliche Altertumskunde und Kirchengeschichte* 69 (1974) 182-191.

Vl10644 = Vatican City, Biblioteca Apostolica Vaticana, Vat. lat. 10644 (fols. 28r-31v). Ed. Klaus Gamber, "Fragment eines mittelitalienischen Plenarmissale aus dem 8. Jahrhundert," *EL* 76 (1962) 335-341.

Vl10645 = Vatican City, Biblioteca Apostolica Vaticana, Vat. lat. 10645 (fols. 3r-6v). Ed. Alban Dold, "Fragmente eines um die Jahrtausendwende in beneventanischer Schrift geschriebenen Vollmissales aus Codex Vatic. lat. 10645," *JWL* 10 (1930) 40-55.

Wolf = Wolfenbüttel, Herzog-August-Bibliothek, Cod. Guelf. 112 Gud. Gr. (Terscriptus: lowermost script, fols. 128-136, 139-140, 143, 145, 148). Ed. Alban Dold and Anselm Manser, "Untersuchungsergebnisse einer doppelt reskribierten Wolfenbütteler Handschrift mittels der Fluoreszenz-Photographie," *Zentralblatt für Bibliothekswesen* 34 (1917) 233-250.

LATER MEDIEVAL SOURCES (= LS)

Gs* = London, British Library, Add. 12194. Ed. Walter Howard Frere, *Graduale Sarisburiense: A Reproduction in Facsimile of a Manuscript of the Thirteenth Century* (London, 1894; rpt. Farnborough, 1966).

MWes* = *Missale ad usum ecclesie Westmonasteriensis*, ed. John Wickham Legg, 3 vols., HBS 1, 5, 12 (London, 1891, 1893, 1897).

Introduction

The Beneventan missal with musical notation now Oxford, Bodleian Library, Canon. Liturg. 342, has been recognised as an important witness to the Old Beneventan and Romano-Beneventan liturgies of southern Italy and the Yugoslavian littoral. No less an authority than the late Dom René-Jean Hesbert wrote of it:

> Ce missel, écrit au XIIIᵉ siècle sur la rive orientale de l'Adriatique, est resté sur certains points plus traditionellement bénéventain que des documents plus vieux d'un siècle ou deux, et transcrits authentiquement dans l'Italie du Sud.[1]

Although the survival in the Beneventan region of liturgical practices and texts of the early church lost or transformed elsewhere has been outlined in several excellent editions and studies, the Oxford manuscript has been neither edited fully nor studied independently.[2] Indeed, the most complete

---

[1] [René-Jean Hesbert], "La tradition bénéventaine dans la tradition manuscrite," in *Le Codex 10673 de la Bibliothèque Vaticane. Fonds latin (XIᵉ siècle). Graduel bénéventain*, ed. Joseph Gajard, Paléographie Musicale 14 (Solesmes, 1931), p. 399 n. 1.

[2] Notices of the MS appear in Falconer Madan, *A Summary Catalogue of Western Manuscripts in the Bodleian Library at Oxford* (Oxford, 1897), 4: 386; idem, *Summary Catalogue* (Oxford, 1905), 5: xvi, for a correction by Henry Marriott Bannister; Walter Howard Frere, *Bibliotheca musico-liturgica. A Descriptive Handlist of the Musical and Latin-Liturgical MSS of the Middle Ages Preserved in the Libraries of Great Britain and Ireland*, 2 vols. (London, 1901, 1932; rpt. Hildesheim, 1967), 1: 77; Elias Avery Loew [Lowe], *The Beneventan Script. A History of the South Italian Minuscule*, 2nd edition prepared and enlarged by Virginia Brown, Sussidi Eruditi 33-34 (Rome, 1980), 2: 111; idem, *Scriptura Beneventana: Facsimiles of South Italian and Dalmatian Manuscripts from the Sixth to the Fourteenth Century*, 2 vols. (Oxford, 1929), 2: pl. 94; Viktor Novak, *Scriptura Beneventana s osobitim obzirom na tip dalmatinske beneventane. Paleografijska studija* (Zagreb, 1920), p. 37; idem, "Something New from the Dalmatian Beneventana," *Medievalia et Humanistica* 14 (1962) 76-85 at 83; idem, *Latinska Paleografija*, 2nd edition (Belgrade, 1980), p. 151 n. 32c; René-Jean Hesbert, "Les dimanches de Carême dans les manuscrits romano-bénéventains," *EL* 48 (1934) 198-222 at 211; idem, "Tradition bénéventaine," passim, see index p. 471; idem, "L'Évangéliaire de Zara," *Scriptorium* 8 (1954) 177-204 at 203; [Jacques Hourlier and Michel Huglo], "Catalogue des manuscrits bénéventains notés," in *Le Codex VI.34 de la Bibliothèque capitulaire de Bénévent (XIᵉ-XIIᵉ siècle). Graduel de Bénévent avec prosaire et tropaire*, ed. Joseph Gajard, Paléographie Musicale 15 (Solesmes, 1937), p. 59; Georges Benoît-Castelli, "Le 'Praeconium Paschale'," *EL* 67 (1953) 309-334 at 320; Stephen J. P. Van Dijk, *Handlist of the Latin Liturgical Manuscripts in the Bodleian Library Oxford*

description accompanies the facsimiles of fols. 38v and 39r in E. A. Loew's *Scriptura Beneventana* (Oxford, 1929) and the most lengthy analysis is that of Hesbert in the Introduction to the facsimile edition of Vatican City, Biblioteca Apostolica Vaticana, Vat. lat. 10673 in Paléographie Musicale 14 (Solesmes, 1931).

Before consideration of the condition of the manuscript and the nature of its contents, it would be useful to outline here in some detail the distinctive liturgical history of the region of the Beneventan script, which included Italy south of Rome, Dalmatia, and the islands of the Adriatic.

LITURGICAL BACKGROUND

The liturgical history of the region before the thirteenth century shows that cultic practices developed in four distinct stages: the early regional liturgy before the eighth century; the subsequent adaptation of Greek texts under the cultural influence of the Byzantine political presence; a period during which Roman practices were adopted between the eighth and eleventh centuries, coinciding first with Carolingian incursions and later with the increased importance of Monte Cassino; and a final era when books imported by the Normans influenced the local form of the Roman liturgy.[3]

(typescript on deposit in the Bodleian, 1957), 1: 127; Joseph Gajard, *Le Graduel romain*, vol. 2: *Les sources* (Solesmes, 1957), p. 88; Albe Vidaković, "I nouvi confini della scrittura neumatica musicale nell'Europa sud-est," *Studien zur Musikwissenschaft* 24 (1960) 5-12 at 10; Klaus Gamber, "Das kampanische Messbuch als Vorläufer des Gelasianum: Ist der hl. Paulinus von Nola der Verfasser?" *SE* 12 (1961) 5-111 at 15; idem, "La liturgia delle diocesi dell'Italia centro-meridionale dal IX all'XI secolo," in *Vescovi e diocesi in Italia nel medioevo (sec. IX-XIII)*, Atti del II Convegno di Storia della Chiesa in Italia, Roma, 5-9 settembre 1961, Italia sacra: Studi e documenti di storia ecclesiastica 5 (Padua, 1964), pp. 145-156 at 147; idem, *Codices liturgici latini antiquiores*, 2nd edition, 1 vol. in 2 parts, Spicilegii Friburgensis Subsidia 1 (Fribourg/S., 1968), p. 245 n. 1; Ettore Falconi, "Frammenti di codici in beneventana nell'Archivio di Stato di Parma," *Bullettino dell'Archivio paleografico italiano* 3rd ser. 2-3 (1963-1964) 73-104 at 86-87; Elizabeth Peirce, *An Edition of Egerton MS. 3511. A Twelfth Century Missal of St. Peter's in Benevento* (Diss. London, 1964), pp. 54-55 et passim; Ivan Ostojić, *Benediktinci u Hrvatskoj i ostalim našim krajevima*, vol. 2: *Benediktinci u Dalmaciji* (Split, 1964), p. 433, pl. 452; Otto Pächt and Jonathan J. G. Alexander, *Illuminated Manuscripts in the Bodleian Library Oxford*, 3 vols. (Oxford, 1966-1973), 2: 9, no. 88; Miho Demović, *Musik und Musiker in der Republik Dubrovnik vom Anfang des 11. Jahrhunderts bis zur Mitte des 17. Jahrhunderts* (Regensburg, 1981), pp. 367-368; Josip Andreis, *Music in Croatia*, 2nd enlarged edition, trans. by Vladimir Ivir (Zagreb, 1982), p. 16; Raymund Kottje, "Beneventana-Fragmente liturgischer Bücher im Stadtarchiv Augsburg," *MS* 47 (1985) 432-437 at 434 n. 13; and Kelly, *Beneventan Chant*, pp. 45, 59, 64, 72 n. 46, 132 n. 25, 195 n. 68, and 309-310.

[3] The study of the Romano-Beneventan and Old Beneventan liturgies began with Raphaël

Old Beneventan Liturgy

The early liturgy of southern Italy, called Campanian in its origins and Old Beneventan in its diffusion, was one of several rites proper to the greater regions of the later Roman empire and the barbarian kingdoms. The few early

---

Andoyer, "L'ancienne liturgie de Bénévent," *RdCG* 20 (1912) 176-183; 21 (1913) 14-20, 44-51, 81-85, 112-115, 144-148, 169-174; 22 (1914) 8-11, 41-44, 80-83, 106-111, 141-145, 170-172; 23 (1919) 42-44, 116-118, 151-153, 182-183; 24 (1920) 48-50, 87-89, 146-148, 182-185. The subject has since received its most ample expression in the work of Solesmes: see especially Hesbert, "Tradition bénéventaine," passim; idem, "Le Répons 'Tenebrae' dans les liturgies Romaine, Milanaise et Bénéventaine," *Revue grégorienne* 19 (1934) 4-24, 57-65, 84-89; 20 (1935) 1-14, 201-213; 21 (1936) 44-62, 201-213; 22 (1937) 121-136; 23 (1938) 20-25, 41-54, 81-98, 140-143, 161-170; 24 (1939) 44-63, 121-139, 161-172; idem, "Dimanches de Carême," pp. 198-222; idem, "L''Antiphonale missarum' de l'ancien rit bénéventain," *EL* 52 (1938) 28-66, 141-158; 53 (1939) 168-190; 59 (1945) 69-95; 60 (1946) 103-141; 61 (1947) 153-210; [Jacques Hourlier and Michel Huglo], "Étude sur la notation bénéventaine," in *Le Codex VI.34 de la Bibliothèque capitulaire de Bénévent (XIᵉ-XIIᵉ siècle). Graduel de Bénévent avec prosaire et tropaire*, ed. Joseph Gajard, Paléographie Musicale 15 (Solesmes, 1937), pp. 70-161; Joseph Gajard, "Les récitations modales des 3ᵉ et 4ᵉ modes dans les manuscrits bénéventains et aquitains," *Études grégoriennes* 1 (1954) 9-45; and Jacques Hourlier and Jacques Froger, *Le manuscrit VI.33 Archivio Arcivescovile Benevento. Missel de Bénévent (Début du XIᵉ siècle)*, Paléographie Musicale 20 (Bern, Frankfurt, 1983).

More recently, others, Klaus Gamber in particular, have continued the study of the liturgy of the region: for general works with bibliographies of specialised studies, see Klaus Gamber, "Die mittelitalienisch-beneventanischen Plenarmissalien," *SE* 9 (1957) 265-285; idem, "Kampanische Messbuch," pp. 5-111; idem, "Die kampanische Lektionsordnung," *SE* 13 (1962) 326-352; idem, "Das Messbuch des hl. Paulinus von Nola," *Heiliger Dienst* 20 (1966) 17-25; idem, "Liturgia delle diocesi," pp. 145-156; idem, "Benevento, Liturgy," *DMA*, 2: 180-181; Archdale A. King, *Liturgies of the Past* (Milwaukee, 1959), pp. 57-77; idem, "Rite of Benevento," *NCE*, 2: 309; Vogel, *Medieval Liturgy*, pp. 284, 335-338; Karlheinz Schlager, "Music of the Beneventan Rite," *New Grove Dictionary*, 2: 482-484; Michel Huglo, "L'ancien chant bénéventain," *EO* 2 (1985) 265-293; and Kelly, *Beneventan Chant*, with the most complete citation of Old Beneventan MSS and texts. Victor Saxer, "Introduction du rite latin," pp. 163-193, discusses the Romano-Beneventan liturgy of Dalmatia.

A series *Miscellanea beneventana* concentrating on liturgical questions has recently begun in *Mediaeval Studies* (Toronto) with articles by Virginia Brown, "A New Beneventan Calendar from Naples: The Lost 'Kalendarium Tutinianum' Rediscovered," *MS* 46 (1984) 385-449; idem, "A New Commentary on Matthew in Beneventan Script at Venosa," *MS* 49 (1987) 443-465; idem, "A Second New List of Beneventan Manuscripts (II)," *MS* 50 (1988) 584-625; idem, "*Flores psalmorum* and *Orationes psalmodicae* in Beneventan Script", *MS* 51 (1989) 424-466; Roger E. Reynolds, "Odilo and the *Treuga Dei* in Southern Italy: A Beneventan Manuscript Fragment," *MS* 46 (1984) 450-462; idem, "A South Italian Ordination Allocution," *MS* 47 (1985) 438-444; idem, "South Italian *liturgica* and *canonistica* in Catalonia (New York, Hispanic Society of America MS. HC 380/819)," *MS* 49 (1987) 480-495; idem, "A South Italian Liturgico-Canonical Mass Commentary," *MS* 50 (1988) 626-670; Raymund Kottje, "Beneventana-Fragmente liturgischer Bücher im Stadtarchiv Augsburg," *MS* 47 (1985) 432-437; and Thomas Forrest Kelly and Herman F. Holbrook, "Beneventan Fragments at Altamura," *MS* 49 (1987) 466-479.

Many edited and unedited MSS of the Beneventan liturgy are listed with descriptions and bibliographies in *CLLA*, pp. 238-257, 465-466; of particular note are the editions by Alban

sources that survive and the handful of traces preserved in later books from
the region, including the Dalmatian coast, indicate that it shared several
features with the Old Spanish, Gallican, and Milanese or Ambrosian liturgies
of Late Antiquity and the early Middle Ages. These affinities have been
recognised since the eleventh century, at least for Old Beneventan chant,
since the musical items preserved in later Romanised manuscripts are often
titled *secundum Ambrosianum* in contrast to the surrounding Roman
material.[4]

Dold, including (with Anselm Manser) "Untersuchungsergebnisse einer doppelt reskribierten
Wolfenbütteler Handschrift mittels der Fluoreszenz-Photographie," *Zentralblatt für Bibliothekswesen* 34 (1917) 233-250; idem, "Fragmente eines um die Jahrtausendwende in
beneventansicher Schrift geschreibenen Vollmissales aus Codex Vatic. lat. 10645," *JLW* 10
(1930) 40-55; idem, *Die Zürcher und Peterlinger Messbuch-Fragmente*, Texte und Arbeiten
25 (Beuron, 1934); idem, "Im Escorial gefundene Bruchstücke eines Plenarmissales in
beneventanischer Schrift des 11. Jhs. mit vorgregorianischem Gebetsgut und dem Präfationstitel 'Prex'," in *Spanische Forschungen der Görresgesellschaft*, 1st ser., Gesammelte Aufsätze
zur Kulturgeschichte Spaniens (Münster/W., 1935), 5: 89-96; idem, "Umfangreiche Reste
zweier Plenarmissalien des 11. und 12. Jh. aus Monte Cassino," *EL* 53 (1939) 111-167; and,
idem, "Die vom Missale Romanum abweichenden Lesetexte für die Messfeiern nach den
Notierungen des aus Monte Cassino stammenden Cod. Vat. lat. 6082," in *Vir Dei Benedictus.
Eine Festgabe zum 1400. Todestag des heiligen Benedikt*, ed. Raphael Molitor (Münster/W.,
1947), pp. 293-332.
    Editions since the publication of the *CLLA* include Peirce, *Edition of Egerton MS. 3511*;
Sieghild Rehle, "Missale Beneventanum (Codex VI 33 des Erzbischöflichen Archivs von
Benevent)," *SE* 21 (1972-1973) 323-405; idem, *Missale Beneventanum von Canosa (Balti-
more, Walters Art Gallery, MS W 6)*, Textus patristici et liturgici 9 (Regensburg, 1972); idem
"Missale Beneventanum in Berlin," *SE* 28 (1985) 469-510; Klaus Gamber, "Fragmente eines
Missale Beneventanum als Palimpsestblätter des Cod. Ottob. Lat. 576," *RB* 84 (1974)
367-372; Klaus Gamber and Sieghild Rehle, *Manuale Casinense (Cod. Ottob. lat. 145)*, Textus
patristici et liturgici 13 (Regensburg, 1977); Ambros Odermatt, *Ein Rituale in beneventani-
scher Schrift. Roma, Biblioteca Vallicelliana, Cod. C 32, Ende des 11. Jahrhunderts*, SF 26
(Fribourg/S., 1980); Hourlier and Froger, *Missel de Bénévent*; and Richard F. Gyug, *An
Edition of Leningrad, B.A.N., F. no. 200: The Lectionary and Pontifical of Kotor* (Diss.
Toronto, 1983). For an updated bibliography of Beneventan MSS, including many liturgical MSS
outside the chronological limits of Gamber's catalogue or more recently discovered, see Loew,
Beneventan Script, vol. 2: *Hand List of Beneventan MSS.*; and Brown, "Second New List (II),"
pp. 584-625.
    [4] E.g., Benevento, Biblioteca Capitolare, 33 (siglum: Ben33, missale, s. xi in., Benevento;
ed. Rehle, "Missale Beneventanum," pp. 324-405; facs. ed. Hourlier and Froger, *Missel de
Bénévent*; bibl.: *CLLA*, no. 430, Loew, *Beneventan Script*, 2: 21) 68v: *Officium in parasceve
secundum Ambrosianum*; Lucca, Biblioteca Capitolare, 606 (missale, s. xii in., bibl.: *CLLA*,
no. 1417), where the Holy Thursday responsory *Lavi pedes* is called a *responsorium
Ambrosianum* (Hesbert, "'Antiphonale missarum'," *EL* 59 [1945] 92); Vatican City, Biblioteca Apostolica Vaticana, Vat. lat. 10673 (siglum: PuV, graduale, s. x/xi, Apulia, facs. ed.
Joseph Gajard, Paléographie Musicale 14; bibl.: *CLLA*, no. 470; Loew, *Beneventan Script*, 2:
155-156) for the Easter Vigil: *Lectio Hec est hereditas, que quinta est ordinata, secundum
romanum legatur hic; secundum ambrosianum legatur post Benedictionem Cerei* (Hesbert,
"'Antiphonale missarum'," *EL* 61 [1947] 158-160, 169-170); Monte Cassino, Archivio della

Lections: For the Campanian and Old Beneventan liturgies of the region, the system of lections before the eighth century is known from several sources. The Campanian epistle-list comes to us directly in the Codex Fuldensis.[5] Written ca. 546 for Victor, bishop of Capua, this famous manuscript was among the biblical and liturgical books carried to Anglo-Saxon England by Hadrian of Canterbury, abbot of the monastery of Niridan near Naples and later companion of Theodore of Tarsus and archbishop of Canterbury. The gospel-list of the Campanian liturgy was also brought to Anglo-Saxon England but is known only in later copies, including the Lindisfarne Gospels, the Codex Regius, and the marginal notes to the Gospel-book of Burchard, bishop of Würzburg.[6] Other elements of the Campanian lection system survive in later Beneventan missals, especially the fragments now in Zürich, Peterlingen, and Lucerne (henceforth = PuZ) edited by Dold, and the manuscript Benevento, Biblioteca Capitolare 33 (= Ben33) edited by Rehle and reproduced in facsimile in Paléographie Musicale 20.[7] From the evidence of these sources, the Campanian lection system is seen to have been different from the Roman at many points.

Beneventan sources retain none of the non-Roman epistles of the Codex Fuldensis, but other traces of a non-Roman system comparable to the

---

Badia, Compactiones XXII (4 fols., graduale, s. xi[1], Monte Cassino; bibl.: John Boe, "Old Beneventan Chant at Montecassino: Gloriosus Confessor Domini Benedictus," *Acta Musicologica* 55 [1983] 69-73): *Alia communio ambrosiana*; and Macerata, Biblioteca Comunale Mozzi-Borgetti, 1457, fasc. XII (1 fol., antiphonale [Dom. 2 Quadr.], s. xi, bibl.: Brown, "Second New List (II)," p. 603): *alia secundum Ambrosianum*. See also Kelly, *Beneventan Chant*, pp. 181-182.

[5] Fulda, Landesbibliothek, Bonifatianus 1; Novum testamentum, ca. 546, Capua, bibl.: *CLLA*, no. 401; Vogel, *Medieval Liturgy*, pp. 335-336. The distinctively non-Roman lections of the Codex Fuldensis have been edited and analysed several times, most recently in Gamber, "Kampanische Lektionsordnung," pp. 326-334.

[6] Lindisfarne Gospels: London, British Library, Cotton Nero D.iv; evangeliarium, ca. 700, Northumbria, bibl.: *CLLA*, no. 405. Gospel Book of Burchard: Würzburg, Universitätsbibliothek, M.p.th.f. 68; evangeliarium, s. vii[2], Italy, with a capitulare evangeliorum added in the margins, ca. 700, Northumbria; bibl.: *CLLA*, no. 407. Codex Regius: London, BL, Royal 1.B.vii; evangeliarium, s. viii, Northumbria, bibl.: *CLLA*, no. 406.

These and the other witnesses to the Campanian gospel-list—Florence, Biblioteca Laurenziana, Amiatinus 1 (Codex Amiatinus); Reims, Bibliothèque Municipale, 41, and Cambridge, Corpus Christi College, 286 (Gospel Book of St. Augustine)—are listed in *CLLA*, nos. 404-407, and Vogel, *Medieval Liturgy*, pp. 336-338.

[7] Zürich, Staatsarchiv, W 3 AG 19 (fasc. III), fols. 6-15; Zürich, Zentralbibliothek, Z XIV 4, nos. 1-4; Peterlingen, Comunalarchiv, S.N., 5 fols.; Lucerne, Stiftsarchiv S. Leodegar, 1912, 2 fols.; siglum: PuZ, missale, s. xi, Bari-type script (Apulia?); ed. Dold, *Zürcher und Peterlinger Messbuch-Fragmente*; bibl.: *CLLA*, no. 431, Loew, *Beneventan Script*, 2: 178. For Ben33, see above n. 4.

See Gamber, "Kampanische Lektionsordnung," pp. 342-352, for the reconstruction of the Campanian lection-list from the Campanian, Northumbrian, and Beneventan sources.

Gallican and Milanese liturgies are prominent. Among relict practices in
Romanised manuscripts we find lections in Ben33 drawn from the lives of
the saints instead of the Bible for the feast of Martin and the feast of Nazarius
and Celsius.[8] Ben33 and PuZ also contain remnants of the Campanian
gospel-list, again related to non-Roman liturgies (Milanese and Old
Spanish), in the choice of readings from John for the Sundays of Lent.[9] The
Old Beneventan Lenten gospels are cited indirectly in Vat. lat. 10645, a
fragmentary Beneventan missal of the eleventh century, where a nomenclature similar to that of the Milanese church survives for the Lenten Sundays:[10]
thus reference to the second week of Lent is given as *Hebdomada de
Samaritana*; presumably the other weeks of Lent were named *de Abraham*,
de caeco, and *de Lazaro* from the themes of the Sunday gospels from John.
Finally, the prophetic readings of the Easter vigil retain elements of the Old
Beneventan system in the numbering of the lection *Haec est hereditas* (Is 54:
17-55: 11), the replacement of the Roman *Audi Israel* (Bar 3: 9-38) by the
lection *Dixit Ieremias: Surgite et ascendamus* (Ier 31: 6-14), and a variant
lection from Daniel.[11]

---

[8] Ben33 118v, 125r: Klaus Gamber, "Väterlesungen innerhalb der Messe in beneventanischen Messbüchern," *EL* 74 (1960) 163-165.

[9] Ben33: Dom. 2 (Io 4: 5-42), Dom. 3 (Io 8: 12-59), Dom. 4 (Io 9: 8-38), and Dom.
5 (Io 11: 1-54). Old Beneventan Lenten gospels are also found in Leningrad, Biblioteka
Akademii Nauk, F. no. 200 (siglum: DaK, lectionarium-pontificale, s. xii, Kotor [Cattaro];
bibl.: Loew, *Beneventan Script*, 2: 50; ed. Gyug, *Edition of Leningrad, B.A.N., F. no. 200*);
and as marginalia in Berlin, Staatsbibliothek Preussischer Kulturbesitz, Lat. fol. 920 (siglum:
DaB, missale, s. xii, Kotor; ed. Rehle, "Missale Beneventanum in Berlin," pp. 469-510; bibl.:
Loew, *Beneventan Script*, 2: 24; *CLLA*, no. 477; Huglo, "Ancien chant bénéventain," pp.
288-290).

[10] Vatican City, BAV, Vat. lat. 10645, fols. 3r-6v; missale, s. xi, Bari-type; ed. Dold, "Vatic.
lat. 10645," pp. 40-55; bibl.: *CLLA*, no. 432, Loew, *Beneventan Script*, 2: 154-155. Hesbert,
"Dimanches de Carême," pp. 198-222, discusses the Lenten gospels.

[11] Roman: Dn 3: 1-50 (*Nabuchodonosor rex fecit*); Beneventan: Dn 3: 49-51 (*Angelus
domini*). The most archaic sources retaining traces of the older system for the Easter vigil are
Benevento, Biblioteca Capitolare, 38, 39, and 40 (sigla: Ben38, Ben39, Ben40; gradualia, s.
xi, Benevento, bibl.: *CLLA*, nos. 474, 476, 471; Loew, *Beneventan Script*, 2: 22); and PuV;
see also Ben33 and Macerata, Biblioteca Comunale Mozzi-Borgetti, 378 (pontificale, s. xii,
Benevento; ed. Richard F. Gyug, "A Pontifical of Benevento (Macerata, Biblioteca Comunale
'Mozzi-Borgetti' 378)," *MS* 51 [1989] 355-423; bibl.: Loew, *Beneventan Script*, 2: 55).

The replacement of Baruch by Jeremiah is found in Vatican City, BAV, Vat. lat. 4770
(siglum: Vl4770, missale, s. x ex., Abruzzi, bibl.: *CLLA*, no. 1413, Loew, *Beneventan Script*,
2: 149; Pierre Salmon, *Les manuscrits liturgiques latins de la Bibliothèque Vaticane*, vol. 2:
Sacramentaires, épistoliers, évangéliaires, graduels, missels, ST 253 [Vatican, 1969], p. 156
[no. 401]), Vat. lat. 6082 (siglum: McV, missale, s. xii/xiii, Monte Cassino; part. ed. Dold,
"Die vom Missale Romanum abweichenden Lesetexte," pp. 292-332; Virgil Fiala, "Der Ordo
missae im Vollmissale des Cod. Vat. lat. 6082 aus dem Ende des 11. Jahrhunderts," in
Zeugnis des Geistes. Gabe zum Benedictus-Jubilaeum 547-1947, Beiheft zur Benediktinische
Monatschrift 23 [Beuron, 1947], pp. 180-224; bibl.: *CLLA*, no. 455; Loew, *Beneventan*

For some feasts, later Beneventan manuscripts demonstrate their ties to the liturgies of Late Antiquity by preserving a three-lection system comparable to the early Roman and Milanese systems, with an Old Testament reading separated from the epistle by a gradual.[12] PuZ has the third lection for the masses of Quinquagesima (Gn 18: 25-33), the first and third Sundays of Lent (Ex 24: 12-34: 29 cento; Dt 1: 1, 6: 4-18), Wednesday of Holy Week (Is 62: 11-?), the Transfiguration, Lawrence (Eccli 14: 22-?), and the Sundays before and after the feast of Michael (post: Am 9: 11-? cento).[13] In Ben33, a third lection is found on the Sundays after Pentecost up to the

---

Script, 2: 152; Louis Duval-Arnould, "Un Missel du Mont-Cassin chez les chanoines du Saint-Saveur de Bologne (Vat. lat. 6082)," Rivista di Storia della Chiesa in Italia 35 [1981] 450-455), and Ottob. lat. 576 (siglum: Ott, missale, fols. 2r-220v: s. xii ex., fols. 1r-v, 221r-377v: s. xiii, bibl.: CLLA, no. 450, Loew, Beneventan Script, 2: 166; fols. 1r-v, 341r-377v [palimpsest]: CLLA, no. 437).

For the Holy Saturday lections, see Myrtilla Avery, "The Beneventan Lections for the Vigil of Easter and the Ambrosian Chant Banned by Pope Stephen IX at Montecassino," Studi Gregoriani 1 (1947) 433-458; and Hesbert, "'Antiphonale missarum'," EL 61 (1947) 155-172.

[12] The traces of a three-lection system in the Roman liturgy are discussed by Antoine Chavasse, "Le calendrier dominical romain au VIe siècle," Recherches de science religieuse 41 (1953) 96-122 at 101-105, citing the Comes and Gospel-list of Würzburg, Universitätsbibliothek, M.p.th.f. 62 (fols. 2v-10v, siglum: WuC, capitulare lectionum, s. viii; ed. Germain Morin, "Le plus ancien Comes ou Lectionnaire de l'église romaine," RB 27 [1910] 41-74; fols. 10v-16v, siglum: WuE, capitulare evangeliorum; ed. Morin, "Liturgie et Basiliques de Rome au milieu du VII siècle d'après les listes d'évangiles de Würzburg," RB 28 [1911] 296-330; bibl.: CLLA, nos. 1001, 1101; Vogel, Medieval Liturgy, pp. 339-340); see also the Comes of Leningrad, Publichnaia biblioteka, lat. Q.v.I.16 (epistolarium, ca. 772/780, Corbie; ed. Walter Howard Frere, Studies in Early Roman Liturgy, III. The Roman Epistle-Lectionary, Alcuin Club Collection 32 [Oxford, 1935], pp. 1-2; bibl.: CLLA, no. 1005; Vogel, Medieval Liturgy, p. 340); and the Comes of Alcuin (Cambrai, Bibliothèque Municipale, 553; siglum: Alc, s. ix, Cambrai; ed. André Wilmart, Le Lectionnaire d'Alcuin, Bibliotheca 'Ephemerides Liturgicae' 2 [Rome, 1937], p. 151; bibl.: Vogel, Medieval Liturgy, pp. 340-342).

Vogel, Medieval Liturgy, p. 304 (esp. n. 72), cites Radolph of Rivo (d. 1403), De canonum observantia liber, prop. 23 (Radulph von Rivo. Der letzte Vertreter der altrömischen Liturgie, ed. Kunibert Mohlberg, 2 vols., [Louvain, Münster/W., 1911-1915], 2: 139), with reference to the Old Roman custom of three readings for Christmas and its vigil; see also Giuseppe-Maria Tommasi, "Lectionarius missae iuxta ritum ecclesiae Romanae ex antiquis MSS. cod. collectus," in Opera omnia, ed. Antonius Vezzosi (Rome, 1750), 5: 321-322. Nonetheless, the early Roman system probably used three lections only for certain feasts, as has been remarked by Aimé-Georges Martimort, "A propos du nombre des lectures à la messe," Revue des sciences religieuses 58 (1984) 42-51. Later medieval continuations of a three-lection system for the masses of Christmas are found in the Dominican liturgy: see Maura O'Carroll, "The Lectionary for the Proper of the Year in the Dominican and Franciscan Rites of the Thirteenth Century," Archivum Fratrum Praedicatorum 49 (1979) 79-103.

[13] Sundays without specific readings are assumed to have had a third lection from such indicators as the lack of a gradual between the epistle and gospel: the gradual probably preceded the epistle and followed a now-lost Old Testament lection (Dold, Zürcher und Peterlinger Messbuch-Fragmente, pp. lii-lx).

fourth Sunday after the feast of Peter and Paul.[14] A fragment of a missal
preserved in Altamura provides third lections for the Sundays after Epiphany.[15] Lastly the masses of Christmas in twelfth-century Beneventan
missals from Caiazzo (Vatican City, BAV, Barb. lat. 603, = Ca) and Veroli
(Barb. lat. 699, = Ve),[16] a thirteenth-century Beneventan lectionary in
Trogir,[17] and the Dalmatian missal edited here also have the third reading.[18]

The texts of the Campanian and Old Beneventan lections are for the most
part drawn from the Vulgate; indeed, the Codex Fuldensis and the Codex
Amiatinus are authoritative early witnesses to its text.[19] Exceptions taken
from the Vetus latina are the Old Testament lessons from Jeremiah in Ben33,
and the cento from Exodus for the first Sunday of Lent in PuZ.[20]

Music: The evidence for Old Beneventan chant is scant compared to the
wealth of sources for the Old Beneventan lection system, which have been
described above as spanning several centuries and including complete lectionaries from an early period as well as special readings retained in later
books. Genuine Old Beneventan books of chant, i.e., without later Gregorian

---

[14] Ben33: Dom. 1 post Octaba Pentecosten (Act 18: 19-28); Dom. 2 (Is 44: 21-26); Dom.
3 (Is 46: 8-13); Dom. 4 (Is 43: 1-6); Dom. 1 post nat. apostolorum (Ier 7: 3-7); Dom. 2
(Ier 22: 3, 8-9); Dom. 3 (Ier 30: 1-9); Dom. 4 (Ier 30: 18-?).

[15] Altamura, Archivio Capitolare, Fondo pergamenaceo, cassetto A, Busta 3; bifolium,
missale, s. xiii, Bari-type Beneventan; facs. ed. Kelly, "Beneventan Fragments at Altamura,"
pp. 474-479; bibl.: Brown, "Second New List (II)," p. 587.

[16] Vatican City, BAV, Barb. lat. 603; siglum: Ca, missale, s. xii/xiii, Caiazzo, bibl.: *CLLA*,
no. 458, Loew, *Beneventan Script*, 2: 162: 2nd mass (Is 61: 1-2); and Barb. lat. 699; siglum:
Ve, missale, s. xii ex., Veroli, bibl.: Loew, *Beneventan Script*, 2: 162: 2nd mass (Is 61: 1-2),
3rd mass (Is 52: 6-10).

[17] Trogir, Kaptolski Arhiv (Riznica Katedrale), 2; fols. 1r-77v: s. xiii, bibl.: Loew, *Beneventan Script*, 2: 140; Antonin Zaninović, "'Prophetia cum versibus' ou 'Epistola farcita' pour la
1re messe de Noël, selon deux manuscrits de Trogir," *Revue grégorienne* 20 (1935) 81-90:
readings for the vigil and three masses of Christmas. On "farced" lections from Isaiah (9:
1-16) for the Christmas mass, see also Eugenio Costa, Jr., "Tropes et séquences dans le cadre
de la vie liturgique au moyen-âge," *EL* 92 (1978) 261-332, 440-471 at 301-304, with
reference to the practice of Catalunya and Mallorca discussed by Solange Corbin, *Essai sur
la musique portugaise au moyen âge, 1100-1385*, Collection portugaise 8 (Paris, 1952), p.
285.

[18] Oxford, Bodleian Library, Canon. Liturg. 342; siglum: Dubr; para. **1, 15** of the present
edition. A third lection (Apoc 1: 1-6) is given in McV for the Invention of Michael (Dold,
"Die vom Missale Romanum abweichenden Lesetexte," p. 306).

[19] *Biblia sacra iuxta Vulgatam versionem*, ed. Robert Weber, 2nd edition, 2 vols. (Stuttgart,
1975), 1: xxviii-xxix.

[20] Michel Huglo, "Fragments de Jérémie selon la Vetus latina," *Vigiliae christianae* 8
(1954) 83-86 at 83; and Dold, *Zürcher und Peterlinger Messbuch-Fragmente*, pp. liii-lvi, also
pp. lix-lx for Vetus latina influences on the Old Testament lesson for the Sunday after Michael
(a cento of Am 9: 11, Act 15: 16, and Is 44: 26).

influences, are represented now by only a small number of fragments and palimpsest traces.[21] For the rest, the sources of the chant are restricted principally to a series of masses included in several otherwise-Romanised manuscripts from Benevento, and to a few items for important feasts retained in books from throughout the Beneventan region.[22] The Old Beneventan calendar reconstructed from the feasts in the Old Beneventan fragments and in the manuscripts where Old Beneventan masses survive as alternatives to imported Roman masses consists of Christmas, Stephen, Palm Sunday,

[21] Thomas Forrest Kelly, "Montecassino and the Old Beneventan Chant," *Early Music History* 5 (1985) 53-83, and *Beneventan Chant*, passim, citing in particular Benevento, Biblioteca Capitolare, 35, fol. 202r-v (siglum: Ben35, graduale, s. xi, bibl.: *CLLA*, no. 478; Loew, *Beneventan Script*, 2: 21); Bari, Archivio del Duomo, S.N. (benedictio fontis, ante 1067, bibl.: Loew, *Beneventan Script*, 2: 15); and the palimpsest fols. of Rome, Biblioteca Vallicelliana, C 9 (s. xi[1], bibl.: Kelly, "Montecassino," pp. 56-61; Loew, *Beneventan Script*, 2: 127-128); Vatican City, BAV, Vat. lat. 10657 (Chartularium abbatiae S. Mariae de Mare, s. xi, bibl.: Kelly, "Montecassino," pp. 61-64; Loew, *Beneventan Script*, 2: 155); and Monte Cassino, Archivio della Badia, 361 (s. xi, bibl.: Kelly, "Montecassino," pp. 64-68; Loew, *Beneventan Script*, 2: 84).

[22] For the identification and analysis of the Old Beneventan corpus, see Andoyer, "Ancienne liturgie," *RdCG* 20 (1912)-24 (1920); and Hesbert, "'Antiphonale missarum'," *EL* 52 (1938)-61 (1947). Hesbert added the Old Beneventan masses for Christmas and St. Stephen from Ben35 to Andoyer's list; his detailed commentary extends only up to the Easter vigil. Kelly, *Beneventan Chant*, extends the study to include many new sources for the chant; see especially pp. 298-319 for a comprehensive list of manuscript sources, and pp. 250-297 for a detailed list of Old Beneventan pieces with bibliography. Other recent studies of the Old Beneventan corpus include Karlheinz Schlager, *Thematischer Katalog der ältesten Alleluia-Melodien aus Handschriften des 10. und 11. Jahrhunderts*, Erlanger Arbeiten zur Musikwissenschaft 2 (Munich, 1965), esp. pp. 21-22 (principally later Romano-Beneventan compositions); idem, "Ein beneventanisches Alleluia und seine Prosula," in *Festschrift Bruno Stäblein zum 70. Geburtstag*, ed. Martin Ruhnke (Kassel, 1967), pp. 217-225; idem, "Beneventan Rite," 2: 482-484 (with bibliography); Michel Huglo, "Les diverses mélodies du 'Te decet laus'. A propos du Vieux-romain," *Jahrbuch für Liturgik und Hymnologie* 12 (1967) 111-116; idem, "Ancien chant bénéventain," pp. 265-293; and Kelly, "Montecassino," pp. 53-83.

Romano-Beneventan sources with Old Beneventan chant are listed by Huglo, "Ancien chant bénéventain," pp. 272-280, and Kelly, *Beneventan Chant*, pp. 298-319, citing especially Ben38 and Ben40, and including the sources given in the preceding note with additions including Baltimore, Walters Art Gallery, W 6 (siglum: PuC, post 1054, Canosa, ed. Rehle, *Missale Beneventanum von Canosa*; bibl.: *CLLA*, no. 445, Loew, *Beneventan Script*, 2: 13-14); Benevento, Biblioteca Capitolare, 30 (siglum: Ben30, missale, s. xiii, Benevento, bibl.: Loew, *Beneventan Script*, 2: 20); Ben33; Benevento, Biblioteca Capitolare, 34 (siglum: Ben34, graduale, s. xi/xii, Benevento, facs. ed. Joseph Gajard, Paléographie Musicale 15; bibl.: *CLLA*, no. 475, Loew, *Beneventan Script*, 2: 21); Ben35; Ben39; Monte Cassino, Compactiones XXII; PuV; Vatican City, BAV, Ottob. lat. 145 (siglum: McO, "manuale casinense," s. xi, Benevento [from Cassinese exemplar]; ed. Gamber and Rehle, *Manuale Casinense*; bibl.: John Boe, "A New Source for Old-Beneventan Chant: The Santa Sophia Maundy in MS Ottoboni lat. 145," *Acta Musicologica* 52 [1980] 122-133; Loew, *Beneventan Script*, 2: 165); and Urb. lat. 602 (troparium, s. xi/xii and xiii, Monte Cassino; bibl.: Loew, *Beneventan Script*, 2: 170).

Maundy Thursday, the Easter vigil, Easter, the Invention of the Cross (Offertory only), the Invention of Michael (8 May), Ascension, Pentecost, John the Baptist, the apostles Peter and Paul, Lawrence, the Assumption of the Virgin, the Twelve Brothers (1 Sept.), the Exaltation of the Cross, the apostles Simon and Jude, All Saints, Martin, and the apostle Andrew. The lacuna between the masses for Stephen and Palm Sunday is an accident of survival, and undoubtedly proper texts existed for the intervening feasts at one time. The recent discovery of an Old Beneventan communion *Gloriosus confessor Domini Benedictus* for Benedict (21 March), found on a gathering with Lenten masses, helps to bridge the gap.[23]

Old Beneventan masses characteristically open with an *ingressa* without psalmody, as in the Milanese church, instead of the Roman introit and psalm verse. The other musical pieces are named as in the Roman tradition: gradual, alleluia with verse, offertory, and communion. The chant is, nonetheless, musically distinct from Gregorian chant.[24] Generally the melodies for the different pieces of the mass do not follow rigid stylistic categories, which means that the Roman distinction between the music of introits and alleluias, for instance, has no Beneventan counterpart. In that sense, Beneventan

---

[23] Boe, "Gloriosus," pp. 69-73, provides evidence by inference for the early celebration of the cult of Benedict in southern Italy, since the Old Beneventan communion of Monte Cassino, Compactiones XXII (above n. 4) is representative of a corpus that probably added few pieces after the ninth century. Cf. Antoine Chavasse, "Le sacramentaire de Monza (B. Cap. F 1/101)," *EO* 2 (1985) 3-29 at 8 n. 5, questioning the early presence of the cult in southern Italy. Previous such assumptions argue from the evidence cited by Pierre de Puniet, *Le sacramentaire romain de Gellone*, Bibliotheca 'Ephemerides Liturgicae' 4 (Rome, 1938), p. 83*, where he mistakenly attributes the mass *Aures* for Benedict to the eighth-century palimpsest sacramentary, Rome, Biblioteca Angelica, F.A. 1408 (palimpsest; sacramentarium gelasianum, ca. 800, Nonantola, later in Salerno; ed. Kunibert Mohlberg, "Un sacramentario palinsesto del secolo VIII dell'Italia centrale," *Atti della Pontificia Accademia Romana di Archeologia* 3 [1925] 391-450; bibl.: *CLLA*, no. 833; Bernard Moreton, *The Eighth-Century Gelasian Sacramentary* [Oxford, 1976], p. 195).

[24] Hesbert, "Tradition bénéventaine," pp. 451-452; Schlager, "Beneventan Rite," 2: 482-484, noting its characteristics and lack of rigid modal control; Huglo, "Ancien chant bénéventain," pp. 281-287, with remarks on similarities with Old Roman chant (282-283); and Kelly, *Beneventan Chant*, pp. 96-156.

Andoyer, "Ancienne liturgie," *RdCG* 21 (1912-1913) 45, in noting the similarity between the responsories of the Roman and Old Beneventan liturgies, hypothesised that it was indicative of a common source that had not yet developed beyond recognition. Hesbert came to a similar conclusion in his analysis of the Beneventan antiphon *Dominus Iesus postquam cenavit* of the Mandatum of Maundy Thursday in "'Antiphonale missarum'," *EL* 59 (1945) 85-92: the Roman communion for the mass of the day is textually identical and related musically. Since Hesbert convincingly argues that both antiphon and communion had existed before the adoption of Gregorian chant in southern Italy, he concludes that the two pieces represent different musical developments from an ancient source predating the divisions into Roman and Old Beneventan liturgies.

shares with Milanese chant a preference for ornamental melodies without the structure and relations between text and music that mark Gregorian chant. Both Old Milanese and Old Beneventan chants are based on limited ranges of four or five notes arranged in repetitive step-wise progressions.[25] Despite the musical differences, some of the texts of the Old Beneventan repertory have parallels in Roman books (often with variants), and many are found in the Milanese liturgy.[26] Nonetheless, some Old Beneventan texts, as many Milanese texts, are either free expositions on the theme of the feast or drawn from the lives of the saints, unlike the Gregorian corpus with its general reliance on scriptural sources.[27]

Sacramentary: Historical reference to the Sacramentary of Paulinus of Nola (d. 431) provides grounds for postulating the existence of a pre-Roman regional sacramentary.[28] The principal sources for identifying its characteristics are Ben33 and PuZ, where traces may perhaps survive in the proper prefaces of many feasts, especially during Lent when they resemble those of Milan, in the *oratio post evangelium* corresponding to the Milanese *oratio super sindonem*, and in the use of the *oratio super populum* more frequently than in Rome where it is restricted to Lent.[29] Features of the central

[25] For a musical analysis of Milanese chant, see Roy Jesson, "Ambrosian Chant," in Willi Apel, *Gregorian Chant* (Bloomington, 1958), pp. 481-482.

The step-wise progressions were considered distinctive even during the period. Aribo states: "Omnes saltatrices laudabiles, sed tamen nobis generosiores videntur quam longobardis. Illi enim spissiori, nos rariori cantu delectamur." ("Aribonis De musica," in *Scriptores ecclesiastici de musica*, ed. Martin Gerbert, 3 vols. [St. Blasien, 1784; rpt. Milan, 1931], 2: 212B). Jesson, "Ambrosian Chant," p. 481, refers the citation to Milanese chant (*longobardis* = Lombards); on the other hand, Schlager, "Beneventan Rite," 2: 483, implies that Lombardic and southern Italian are synonymous (although he does relate Old Beneventan music to very ancient indigenous Italian traditions, the probable source for both Old Beneventan and Milanese melodies).

[26] Hesbert, "'Antiphonale missarum'," *EL* 52 (1938)-61 (1947), passim, gives a detailed textual analysis of the masses before Easter; Kelly, *Beneventan Chant*, pp. 259-297, provides a list of Beneventan texts with their counterparts in other liturgies.

[27] Andoyer, "Ancienne liturgie," *RdCG* 21 (1913) 19-20; Hesbert, "Tradition béneventaine," p. 453; and Huglo, "Ancien chant bénéventain," p. 281.

[28] For the Sacramentary of Paulinus of Nola mentioned by Gennadius of Marseilles, *De viris inlustribus*, c. 48 (PL 58: 1086-1087), see Gamber, "Kampanische Messbuch," pp. 5-111, and references in *CLLA*, no. 077.

[29] Prefaces: Dold, *Zürcher und Peterlinger Messbuch-Fragmente*, pp. xli-xlii; Moeller, *Corpus praefationum*, 1: lxxxi-lxxxvii. *Oratio post evangelium*: Klaus Gamber, "Das einsame 'Oremus' vor dem Offertorium," *Heiliger Dienst* 15 (1961) 22-23; and Antoine Chavasse, "L'oraison 'Super sindonem' dans la liturgie romaine," *RB* 70 (1960) 313-323. Nine *orationes post evangelium* survive in PuZ (Dold, *Zürcher und Peterlinger Messbuch-Fragmente*, p. xli); Ben33 preserves the *orationes post evangelium* only for the Sundays after Pentecost. *Orationes super populum*: 8 in PuZ (Dold, *Zürcher und Peterlinger Messbuch-Fragmente*, p. xli).

Italian/Old Beneventan sacramentary appear also in Vat. lat. 4770, a late-tenth or early-eleventh-century missal in ordinary minuscule from the Abruzzi: it has the *oratio post evangelium*, a large number of proper prefaces, the *oratio super populum* outside Lent, and the canon set between Holy Saturday and Easter as in many Beneventan missals.[30]

Greek Influences

The first external influence on the Old Beneventan liturgy appears to have come from the Greek church due to the many political and cultural affiliations between Byzantium and the region of the Beneventan script, southern Italy and Dalmatia. Benevento itself was under Greek control intermittently from the end of the eighth to the mid ninth century, while Calabria and Apulia were Greek into the eleventh century, with Bari falling to the Normans only in 1071. Dalmatia was administered as a Byzantine theme until the tenth century, although Greek quarters and churches remained in many coastal towns long after the demise of direct political influence.[31] The first sign of a matching cultural influence is the survival of Greek manuscripts from the region.[32] But the liturgy of the Greek church also directly affected the liturgy of the Latin churches in the area: the Codex Claromontanus and the Codex Bezae of the fifth century contain the scriptures in recto-verso/Greek-Latin editions;[33] later manuscripts also attest to mixed language mass

---

[30] Vl4770: The connections with southern Italy are apparent in such physical ties as the Beneventan script of fol. 216 (*CLLA*, no. 1413; Loew, *Beneventan Script*, 2: 149; Salmon, *Manuscrits liturgiques*, 2: 156 [no. 401]).

[31] Recent studies include Vitalien Laurent, "L'Église de l'Italie méridionale entre Rome et Byzance à la vielle de la conquête normande," in *La Chiesa greca in Italia dall'VIII al XVI secolo*, Atti del Convegno Storico Interecclesiale, Bari, 30 aprile-4 maggio 1969, ed. Michele Maccarrone et al., 3 vols., Italia Sacra 20-22 (Padua, 1972-1973), 1: 5-23; and Vera von Falkenhausen, "Il monachesimo italo-greco e i suoi rapporti con il monachesimo benedettino," in *L'Esperienza monastica benedettina e la Puglia*, Atti del Convegno di Studio organizzato in occasione del xv centenario della nascita di san Benedetto, Bari, Noci, Lecce, Picciano, 6-10 ottobre 1980, ed. Cosimo Damiano Fonseca, 2 vols. (Lecce, 1983-1984), 1: 119-135.

[32] E.g., Codex Rossanensis: Rossano, Biblioteca Arcivescovile, S.N.; s. vi², bibl.: *CLLA*, no. 079c; and the works in Robert Devreesse, *Les Manuscrits grecs de l'Italie méridionale*, sᴛ 183 (Vatican City, 1955); André Jacob, "L'Evoluzione dei libri liturgici bizantini in Calabria e in Sicilia dall'VIII al XVI secolo, con particolare riguardo ai riti eucaristici," in *Calabria Bizantina. Vita religiosa e strutture amministrative*, Atti del primo e secondo Incontro di Studi Bizantini (Reggio, Calabria, 1974), pp. 47-69; and Guglielmo Cavallo, "Manoscritti italo-greci e cultura benedettina (secoli x-xii)," in *Esperienza monastica*, 1: 169-195. For Dalmatia, see Branka Pecarski, "Testimonianze artistiche, letterarie e storiche sulla liturgia greca nella Dalmazia dall'VIII al XIII secolo," in *Chiesa greca in Italia*, 3: 1237-1245.

[33] Claromontanus: Paris, Bibliothèque Nationale, gr. 107; s. v, bibl.: *CLLA*, no. 079; Vogel, *Medieval Liturgy*, p. 296. Bezae: Cambridge, University Library, Nn.2.41; s. v, bibl.: *CLLA*,

books.[34] Among the influences of the Greek liturgy on the Beneventan, the adoption of bilingual chants during Holy Week in the Good Friday ceremony for the Veneration of the Cross is perhaps the most striking and certainly indicative of a high regard for eastern custom.

Good Friday: Veneration of the Cross.[35] The chants for the Veneration of the Cross differ from other more purely Beneventan feasts. The Old Beneventan ceremony appears to have consisted of a fore-mass at terce with an adoration of the cross, another fore-mass at sext with another adoration, and then the solemn prayers followed by the Mass of the Presanctified. The Old Beneventan vespers after mass were sung, unlike Roman practice, and consisted of three psalms and the Magnificat antiphon with non-scriptural verses.

The ceremony transmitted in Beneventan manuscripts, especially Vat. lat. 10673 (= PuV), a late-tenth or early-eleventh-century mass-antiphonal in the Bari-type script, presents a collation of Roman and Old Beneventan practices, but includes several Greek antiphons with Latin translations, *O quando in cruce*, *Adoramus crucem tuam*, *Crucem tuam*, *Omnes gentes*, and *Laudamus te*, as well as the Trisagion of the Roman ceremony. Since the antiphon *O quando in cruce* is to be found also in an eleventh-century manuscript from Ravenna,[36] the common source for the versions of Benevento and Ravenna must be sought before 752 when the latter centre fell to the Lombards, ending the direct political influence of Byzantium. The antiphon was, therefore, probably brought into Italy before that date. Furthermore, since the Greek elements are superimposed on the Old Beneventan in the Good Friday

no. 079b; Vogel, *Medieval Liturgy*, p. 296. See also Paris, BN, Coislin 186 (suppl. gr. 385), a bilingual psalter (*CLLA*, no. 080).

[34] Klaus Gamber, "Die griechisch-lateinischen Mess-Libelli in Süditalien," in *Chiesa greca in Italia*, 3: 1299-1306; and Humphrey W. Codrington, *The Liturgy of St. Peter*, LQF 30 (Münster/W., 1936). Hesbert, "Tradition bénéventaine," pp. 457, cites several instances of bilingual chant in Neapolitan saints' lives of the ninth century: "Vita sancti Athanasii episcopi Neapolitani," p. 440, "Translatio sancti Athanasii episcopi Neapolitani," p. 451, and [John the Deacon of Naples], "Iohannis Diaconi Translatio sancti Severini," p. 456 (ed. Georg Waitz, MGH Scriptores rerum Langobardicarum et Italicarum saec. VI-IX [Hannover, 1878], pp. 439-459).

[35] Egon Wellesz, *Eastern Elements in Western Chant* (Oxford, Boston, 1947; rpt. Copenhagen, 1967); Andoyer, "Ancienne liturgie," *RdCG* 21 (1913) 83-85, 112-115, 144-148, 169-174; Hesbert, "Tradition bénéventaine," pp. 291-337, esp. Tables at pp. 296-297 (Old Beneventan: Ben33, Ben39, Ben40, PuV), pp. 300-301 (Romano-Beneventan: Ben34, Ben35, Ben38, Lucca 606; Roman: Ca, Monte Cassino, Archivio della Badia, 546 [siglum: Mc546, graduale, s. xii/xiii, bibl.: Loew, *Beneventan Script*, 2: 90]; McV, Ott); Hesbert, "'Antiphonale missarum'," *EL* 60 (1946) 103-135; and Kelly, *Beneventan Chant*, pp. 53-58, 194-197, 207-214.

[36] Modena, Biblioteca capitolare, O. I. 7; graduale, s. xi, bibl.: Wellesz, *Eastern Elements*, p. 68; Kelly, *Beneventan Chant*, pp. 207-209.

ceremony, and the Beneventan liturgy is unlikely to predate the sixth century, the moment of Greek influence on the Good Friday liturgy is narrowed to the seventh or early eighth centuries, perhaps during the period of Greek and Syrian popes, when bilingual practices and eastern cults played a role in the Roman liturgy.[37]

Roman Influence (1): Adoption of the Roman Liturgy

The third major period in the development of the regional liturgy is marked by the adoption of Roman prayers, lections, and chant between the eighth and eleventh centuries. Whether from some notion of centralisation, or the replacement of a less complete by a more complete system, or through the chance importation and copying of liturgical books, the Old Beneventan liturgy was largely supplanted before the mid eleventh century by texts of the Roman liturgy. In this regard, the famous injunction of Pope Stephen IX (1057-1058) that forbade Ambrosian chant at Monte Cassino in a prohibition directed against the local "non-Roman" practice was among the final steps in the replacement of the early regional liturgy.[38] The stages in the

---

[37] Vogel, *Medieval Liturgy*, p. 296: between Honorius I (625-638) and Hadrian I (772-795) there were nine eastern popes. The bilingual readings of the epistle and gospel were retained in Rome for Christmas, Easter, and the vigils of Easter and Pentecost. Other Greek ceremonies of the Roman church include the inscription of the alphabet in Greek and Latin during the dedication of a church (Vogel and Elze, *Pontifical romano-germanique*, 1: 136 [ordo 40: 26]); the litany of saints *Christe audi nos* and the melody of *Ave gratia plena* introduced by Pope Sergius I (687-701) (Wellesz, *Eastern Elements*, p. 63, citing Edmund Bishop, "The Litany of the Saints," in *Liturgica historica: Papers on the Liturgy and Religious Life of the Western Church* [Oxford, 1918], pp. 137-164); and the Trisagion of the Adoration of the Cross on Good Friday (Wellesz, *Eastern Elements*, pp. 11-13). *Ordo romanus* 27: 67-94 also contains Greek hymns for Easter week (Michel Andrieu, *Les Ordines Romani du haut moyen âge*, 5 vols., Spicilegium Sacrum Lovaniense. Études et documents 11, 23, 24, 28, 29 [Louvain, 1931-1961], 3: 362-372; Wellesz, *Eastern Elements*, pp. 63-67). Louis Brou, "Les chants en langue grecque dans les liturgies latines," *SE* 1 (1948) 165-180, 4 (1952) 226-238, gives a list of Greek ceremonies in the West. Kelly, *Beneventan Chant*, pp. 203-218, discusses the relationship between Beneventan and Byzantine chant.

[38] [Leo of Ostia], *Chronica monasterii Casinensis*, 2: 94 (ed. Hoffmann, MGH Scriptores 34: 353), as above in the Preface n. 7. See the comments of Andoyer, "Ancienne liturgie," *RdCG* 20 (1911-1912) 181-182; Hesbert, "Tradition bénéventaine," pp. 455 (interpreting the reference to mean literally "Ambrosian"); Avery, "Beneventan Lections for the Vigil of Easter," pp. 433-458; King, *Liturgies of the Past*, pp. 63, 65; *CLLA*, p. 250; Schlager, "Beneventan Rite," 2: 482-484; Boe, "Santa Sophia Maundy," pp. 123-124; idem, "Gloriosus," pp. 72-73, citing for the contrast of Gregorian and non-Roman chant the *Versi Gregorii, Ambrosii, Karoli, Paulini de Cantu Romano vel Ambrosiano*: "... non est ita intellegendum, ut cantus ambrosianus abominandus sit. Set annuente Deo, romanus cantus est preferendus pro brevitate et fastidio plebis" from Monte Cassino, Archivio della Badia, 318, pp. 244-245 (tonarium, s. xi, bibl.: Loew, *Beneventan Script*, 2: 82; Lance W. Brunner, "A Perspective on

gradual adoption of the Roman liturgy in southern Italy during the preceding centuries are not uniform for each of the elements of the mass, perhaps because its components were transmitted in separate books—sacramentaries, lectionaries, and mass-antiphonals—which often followed different courses of diffusion.

Music: Gregorian chant probably entered the region after 760 and before 839. The terminus post quem is suggested by the appearance of an Old Beneventan mass for the feast of the Twelve Brothers, a feast likely composed for the gathering of the relics of the martyr-brothers from local churches to St. Sophia in Benevento in 760;[39] and the terminus ante quem by the fabrication, on the model of what must have been newly imported Gregorian chants, of a Romano-Beneventan mass for the deposition of the relics of Bartholomew on 25 October 839, a year after their translation to Benevento from Lipari.[40] Because the chant drawn from the imported Roman books was to be preserved in the region without much contamination from later northern developments, it has been considered an important witness to early forms of Gregorian chant.[41]

the Southern Italian Sequence: The Second Tonary of the Manuscript Monte Cassino 318," *Early Music History* 1 [1981] 117-164); and Kelly, *Beneventan Chant*, pp. 25-40, esp. at 39.

The influence of Monte Cassino in cultic matters, including the provision of saints' lives and liturgies for new feasts, has been discussed in H. E. J. Cowdrey, *The Age of Abbot Desiderius. Montecassino, the Papacy, and the Normans in the Eleventh and Early Twelfth Centuries* (Oxford, 1983), pp. 39-44. Given the many close ties between Rome and Monte Cassino, the abbey may also have been the most important avenue for the entry of Roman liturgical practice into the region, especially during the eleventh century.

[39] Andoyer, "Ancienne liturgie," *RdCG* 21 (1912) 16; Hesbert, "Tradition bénéventaine," pp. 450-451; idem, "'Antiphonale missarum'," *EL* 52 (1938) 35; and Kelly, *Beneventan Chant*, p. 11. The terminus post quem was advanced by Peirce, *Edition of Egerton MS. 3511*, p. 62. The feast of the Twelve Brother-martyrs is discussed in *Acta sanctorum, Sept.*, 1: 129-155; and Agostino Amore, "Dodici Fratelli," *Bibliotheca Sanctorum*, 4: 669-670. The Twelve Brothers were in fact four groups of African martyrs celebrated on 27 August and 1 September; in 760, Duke Arechis II of Benevento translated their relics from the several sites in which they had been dispersed to the new foundation of St. Sophia in Benevento (*Acta sanctorum, Sept.*, 1: 136-138).

[40] On the translation of Bartholomew, see Ulla Westerbergh, *Anastasius Bibliothecarius, Sermo Theodori Studitae de sancto Bartholomeo Apostolo*, Studia Latina Stockholmiensia 9 (Stockholm, 1963), p. xl: elsewhere the date has been given variously as 808 (instances cited in *Acta sanctorum, Aug.*, 5: 58-59) and 832 (Boe, "Santa Sophia Maundy," p. 122 n. 2).

King, *Liturgies of the Past*, p. 63, suggests that All Saints was the last feast added to the Old Beneventan calendar. Certainly, it was celebrated on 1 November, as in the Beneventan MSS, only at a relatively late date, but the exact date of the transfer of the celebration from 13 May, if indeed it was transferred and was not a new feast altogether, cannot be fixed beyond the general acceptance of 1 November by the late eighth century (Roger E. Reynolds, "All Saints' Day," *DMA*, 1: 176).

[41] Thus the pioneering work and the continued interest of the monks of Solesmes in books

The antiquity of the form of Roman chant that was imported into the Beneventan region is emphasised by the use of the Roman psalter. In Hesbert's study of Romano-Beneventan chant, he noted a number of textual variants between Beneventan and Romano-Frankish sources among the psalmic verses of the introits.[42] In each case, the Beneventan version corresponded to the Roman psalter and the version found in St. Gall to the Gallican psalter. From comparison of other musical items of the same feasts drawn from the same psalms in both series of manuscripts, the Beneventan texts were shown to have preserved the earlier form. For instance, while the psalmic verse of the Beneventan introit *Ad te levavi* of the first Sunday of Advent is "Vias tuas Domine *notas fac* mihi et semitas tuas *edoce* me" from the Roman psalter (Ps 24) and the verse of St. Gall is "Vias tuas Domine *demonstra* mihi et semitas tuas *doce* me" from the Gallican psalter, for the gradual of the same feast both traditions have the Roman psalter reading. Since the more complex musical setting of the gradual could not be as readily adapted to a new text as the simple musical setting of the psalmic verse of an introit, Hesbert hypothesised that the Beneventan form of the introit psalm must be earlier: i.e., in Frankish territory the texts of the Roman psalter were replaced by the reading of the Gallican psalter where the melody permitted, but the Roman forms continued without change in Beneventan books uninfluenced by the Romano-Frankish reforms of the eighth to eleventh centuries.[43]

Lectionary: According to Antoine Chavasse, the Roman lectionary that circulated in central Italy and the Beneventan region represents a distinct early stage in the development of Roman lection-lists.[44] The primitive Gregorian lectionary, Type I of Chavasse, of which only the epistolary survives in the Comes of Würzburg, underwent several adaptations and local revisions during the seventh to ninth centuries. The first series of revisions persists in later copies such as the Comes of Alcuin for the epistolary and in gospel-books of Chavasse's Type II.[45] The next revision of the lectionary,

---

of the Beneventan liturgy. For the unity and distinctiveness of the Beneventan group against other witnesses of Gregorian chant, see Hesbert, "Tradition bénéventaine," pp. 153-196, esp. Figure 26, p. 190; also Gajard, "Récitations modales," pp. 9-45.

[42] Hesbert, "Tradition bénéventaine," pp. 145-151; and Kelly, *Beneventan Chant*, p. 19.

[43] Hesbert, "Tradition bénéventaine," p. 150, remarks a similar use of the Roman psalter in the Old Roman Graduals: Vatican City, BAV, Vat. lat. 5319 (s. xi/xii, Lateran [?], bibl.: *CLLA*, no. 1377), and Archivio S. Pietro, F 22 (s. xii/xiii, Rome, bibl.: Salmon, *Manuscrits liturgiques*, 2: 75-76 [no. 155]).

[44] Antoine Chavasse, "Les plus anciens types du lectionnaire et de l'antiphonaire romains de la messe," *RB* 62 (1952) 3-94; also Vogel, *Medieval Liturgy*, pp. 349-354.

[45] Type II: *CLLA*, nos. 1101-1103; see Vogel, *Medieval Liturgy*, pp. 342-343; Chavasse,

Type III, is subdivided into Class A (Beneventan and central Italian) and Class B (everywhere else), from which developed the lection-list of the Roman missal. The date of Class A is fixed to ca. 700.[46] The lection-list of Class B is distinguished by the addition of lections for the mass *Omnes gentes* of the seventh/eighth Sunday after Pentecost; this augmented list was composed at roughly the same time as the list of Class A, though perhaps closer to 740.[47]

As with the Roman source of the Beneventan mass-antiphonal, the early source of the Beneventan lectionary appears to have been common for the majority of Beneventan manuscripts and to have escaped influence from the later development of the Roman liturgy in Frankish territory. Thus, the homogeneous group of Beneventan lectionaries belonging to Class A lacks the mass *Omnes gentes* found in lectionaries of Type III from other regions (Class B) on the seventh/eighth Sunday after Pentecost. Although none of the Beneventan lectionaries predate the tenth century, the Roman lection-list (Class A) was probably adopted in the region soon after its composition, i.e., after 700, but before the lection-list of Class B had any influence, i.e., before 740.

Sacramentary: Even the most cursory general survey of the early history of Roman sacramentaries admits several genuine Roman *fontes* and a series of Frankish adaptations. The most important witnesses to the early Roman sacramentaries, all surviving only in copies prepared in later centuries outside Rome or in Frankish lands, include the Veronense or "Leonine" (an early-seventh-century copy of Roman presbyteral masses adapted for papal use),[48] the Gelasianum or Old Gelasian (a seventh-century Roman presbyteral book attested in an eighth-century Frankish copy; it is also called the Vatican sacramentary),[49] the Paduense (a ninth-century copy of the papal

---

"Plus anciens types," pp. 3-15; Type II = types Π, Λ, Σ of Theodore Klauser, *Das römische Capitulare evangeliorum*, I. *Typen*, LQF 28 (Münster/W., 1935); also the Earlier-, Martina-, and Standard-Types of Walter Howard Frere, *Studies in Early Roman Liturgy*, II. *The Roman Gospel-Lectionary*, Alcuin Club Collection 30 (Oxford, London, 1934).

[46] Chavasse, "Plus anciens types," pp. 23-28 for the date of the Class A of the Type III Lectionary; Vogel, *Medieval Liturgy*, p. 353.

[47] Chavasse, "Plus anciens types," pp. 16-17 (*Omnes gentes*), pp. 23-28 (date of Class B); and René-Jean Hesbert, "La messe 'Omnes Gentes' du VIIᵉ Dimanche après la Pentecôte," *Revue grégorienne* 17 (1932) 81-89, 170-179; 18 (1933) 1-14; idem, "Tradition bénéventaine," pp. 125-129.

[48] Verona, Biblioteca Capitolare, 85 (80); siglum: Le, s. vii in., Verona (?); ed. Leo Cunibert Mohlberg, Leo Eizenhöfer, and Petrus Siffrin, *Sacramentarium Veronense*, RED, Series maior, Fontes 1 (Rome, 1956); bibl.: Vogel, *Medieval Liturgy*, pp. 38-46; *CLLA*, no. 601.

[49] Vatican City, BAV, Reg. lat. 316 + Paris, BN, lat. 7193, fols. 41-56; siglum: Va, ca. 750,

book used in the seventh century and adapted for presbyteral use at St. Peter's),[50] the Gelasians of the Eighth Century (several manuscripts and fragments from throughout the Carolingian territories preserving formulas from sacramentaries of both the presbyteral and papal liturgies),[51] the Hadrianum with its Supplement (the papal book sent to Charlemagne by Pope Hadrian I at the end of the eighth century with the additions made by Benedict of Aniane early in the next century),[52] and the Sacramentary of Trent (a ninth-century copy of a late-seventh-century papal sacramentary modified for the use of Salzburg).[53]

Even more than the northern Frankish churches, the suburbicarian dioceses of southern Italy might be expected to have received copies of the early papal and Roman presbyteral liturgies soon after their composition. And such appears to have been the case, for the early sacramentaries are well represented in the region and among the sources used in later Romano-Beneventan missals. But the relationship between the regional liturgy and these Roman imports is even more complex than the history of the regional adoption of the Roman mass-antiphonal and lectionary, where the earliest Roman imports formed the basis for a Romano-Beneventan liturgy that was supplemented from later Roman and Frankish developments. Although the study of the transition from Old Beneventan to Romano-Beneventan sacra-

---

Chelles; ed. Leo Cunibert Mohlberg, Leo Eizenhöfer, and Petrus Siffrin, *Liber Sacramentorum Romanae aecclesiae ordinis anni circuli*, RED, Series maior, Fontes 4 (Rome, 1960); bibl.: Vogel, *Medieval Liturgy*, pp. 64-70; *CLLA*, no. 610; Antoine Chavasse, *Le sacramentaire gélasien (Vaticanus Reginensis 316). Sacramentaire presbytéral en usage dans les titres romains au VIIe siècle*, Bibliothèque de Théologie, Série 4: Histoire de la Théologie 1 (Tournai, 1958).

[50] Padua, Biblioteca Capitolare, D 47; siglum: Pa, 840-855, northern Italy (?); ed. Deshusses, "Gregorianum Paduense ad fidem codicis Paduensis D 47," in *Sacramentaire grégorien*, vol. 1 pars 3; bibl.: Vogel, *Medieval Liturgy*, pp. 92-97; *CLLA*, no. 880.

[51] For the editions and history of the Gelasians of the Eighth Century, see Vogel, *Medieval Liturgy*, pp. 70-78.

[52] Hadrianum: Cambrai, Bibliothèque Municipale, 164; siglum: Ha, ca. 811-812, Cambrai; ed. Deshusses, "Hadrianum ex authentico ad fidem codicis Cameracensis 164," in *Sacramentaire grégorien*, vol. 1 pars 1; bibl.: Vogel, *Medieval Liturgy*, pp. 80-85.

Supplementum: Autun, Bibliothèque Municipale, 19*bis*; siglum: Sp, ca. 845, Marmoutier; ed. Deshusses, "Hadrianum revisum Anianense cum supplemento," in *Sacramentaire grégorien*, vol. 1 pars 2; bibl.: Vogel, *Medieval Liturgy*, pp. 85-92, and Joseph Décréaux, *Le Sacramentaire de Marmoutier (Autun 19bis) dans l'histoire des sacramentaires carolingiens du XIe siècle*, 2 vols., Studi di Antichità Cristiana 38 (Vatican City, 1985).

[53] Trent, Museo Proviniciale d'Arte, 1590; sacramentarium gregorianum, s. ix, Tyrol; ed. Ferdinand Dell'Oro, "Il Sacramentario di Trento," in *Fontes liturgici: Libri sacramentorum*, Monumenta liturgica ecclesiae Tridentinae saeculo XIII antiquiora 2/a (Trent, 1985); bibl.: Vogel, *Medieval Liturgy*, pp. 97-102; *CLLA*, no. 724.

mentaries is yet in its infancy, the first tentative conclusions point to independent influences by several different Roman sacramentaries.[54]

The earliest source from the region is the fragmentary sacramentary-lectionary contained among the palimpsest folios of Monte Cassino, Archivio della Badia, 271 (= Z6). It is classified as a Gregorian sacramentary similar to the Paduense, i.e., a papal book adapted for presbyteral use in St. Peter's basilica and pre-dating the Hadrianum sent by Pope Hadrian I to Charlemagne.[55] The masses for the Ember days found in a ninth-century Beneventan fragment from Dalmatia have also been considered representative of the early Gregorianum.[56] A third manuscript, the twelfth-century Missal of St. Peter's of Benevento (London, British Library, Egerton 3511, olim Benevento, Biblioteca Capitolare, 29, = Ben29),[57] probably had a

---

[54] The history of pontificals in the Beneventan region follows a similar pattern, with several Roman and Frankish exemplars of comparable influence. Thus early Roman ordines are copied in Vatican City, BAV, Reg. lat. 1997 (collectio canonum, ordines; s. ix med., Chieti; bibl.: Paola Supino Martini, "Per lo studio delle scritture altomedievali italiane: la collezione canonica chietina (Vat. Reg. lat. 1997)," *Scrittura e Civiltà* 1 [1977] 133-154), and Vat. lat. 7701 (pontificale romanum, s. x, Chieti, bibl.: Loew, *Beneventan Script*, 2: 153), but are replaced in the region by more up-to-date copies of the Roman-German Pontifical of the Tenth Century and the Roman Pontifical of the Twelfth Century soon after the compositions of their archetypes: e.g., Vogel and Elze, *Pontifical romano-germanique*, 3: 65: Monte Cassino, Archivio della Badia, 451 (siglum: McP, pontificale romano-germanicum, s. xi[2], Monte Cassino, bibl.: Loew, *Beneventan Script*, 2: 87); Rome, Biblioteca Vallicelliana, D 5 (pontificale romano-germanicum, s. xi, Monte Cassino, bibl.: Loew, *Beneventan Script*, 2: 128); and Andrieu, *Ordines Romani*, 1: 176-211; *CLLA*, p. 566. Early Dalmatian copies of the Roman-German Pontifical are Dubrovnik, Franjevački Samostan Mala Braća, 5310/230/7, 8 (2 fols., s. xii, Kotor; bibl.: Loew, *Beneventan Script*, 2: 37); and DaK (above n. 9). The Roman Pontifical of the Twelfth Century is edited by Michel Andrieu, *Le Pontifical romain au moyen-âge*, 4 vols., ST 86-88, 99 (Vatican City, 1938-1941), 1: 52-71, citing Vatican City, BAV, Vat. lat. 7818 (s. xii, Chieti, bibl.: Loew, *Beneventan Script*, 2: 153), and Barb. lat. 631 (s. xi ex., Monte Cassino, bibl.: Loew, *Beneventan Script*, 2: 162); see also Macerata, Biblioteca Comunale Mozzi-Borgetti, 378 (as above n. 11), and Rome, Biblioteca Casanatense, 614 (pontificale romanum, s. xii/xiii, Benevento; bibl.: Loew, *Beneventan Script*, 2: 121; Anna Saitta Revignas, *Catalogo dei manoscritti della Biblioteca Casanatense*, vol. 6 [Rome, 1978], pp. 93-98).

[55] Monte Cassino, Archivio della Badia, 271; siglum: Z6, terscriptus: lowest is a missale gregorianum (Type II), s. vii/viii, northern Italy; ed. Alban Dold, *Vom Sakramentar, Comes und Capitulare zum Missale*, Texte und Arbeiten 34 (Beuron, 1943); bibl.: Antoine Chavasse, "Les fragments palimpsestes du Casinensis 271 (Sigle Z 6)," *ALW* 25 (1983) 9-33; *CLLA*, no. 701; Loew, *Beneventan Script*, 2: 79; Deshusses, *Sacramentaire grégorien*, 1: 45, 58-60.

[56] Split, Kaptolski Arhiv, Riznica Katedrale, D 624, fols. 211, 214; siglum: DaS, sacramentarium gregorianum (Type II), s. ix in., Split; ed. Klaus Gamber and Sieghild Rehle, "Fragmenta Liturgica VI.40: Fragmente eines Gregorianums in Split," *SE* 23 (1978-1979) 298-303; bibl: *CLLA*, no. 715; Loew, *Beneventan Script*, 2: 137. Bonifacio Baroffio and Šime Marović, "Il sacramentario-rituale di Spalato e la tradizione eucologica latina," *EO* 4 (1987) 235-241 at 235, argue that DaS derives in part from a Gelasian of the Eighth Century.

[57] London, BL, Egerton 3511 (olim Benevento, Biblioteca Capitolare, 29); siglum: Ben29, missale beneventanum, s. xii, Benevento; ed. Peirce, *Edition of Egerton MS. 3511*; bibl.: *CLLA*,

Gregorianum like the Paduense as its base to which later generations of liturgists added texts drawn from the Gelasian sacramentaries of the Eighth Century and from mixed Gelasian-Gregorian sources such as the tenth-century Sacramentary of Fulda (= F).[58]

The later Gregorian sacramentary was also influential, as were the books produced in Frankish territory. Jacques Froger concluded that the sources of Ben33 were the Hadrianum with its Supplement and a Gelasian of the Eighth Century, though not in a form directly related to any of the known witnesses of the latter tradition.[59] The circulation of later Gelasian sacramentaries in southern Italy is documented by the presence in Salerno during the Middle Ages of a copy of a Gelasian sacramentary from Nonantola.[60]

In addition to the influences of the Gregorian sacramentaries and the Gelasians of the Eighth Century, associations with the Old Gelasian and Milanese traditions have also been remarked.[61]

---

no. 452, Loew, *Beneventan Script*, 2: 53. The sources of Ben29 are discussed by Peirce, pp. 154-164.

[58] Göttingen, Universitätsbibliothek, Theol. 231; siglum: F, sacramentarium gelasianum-gregorianum, ca. 975, Fulda; ed. Gregor Richter and Albert Schönfelder, *Sacramentarium Fuldense saeculi x.*, 2nd edition with a bibliographic note by D. H. Tripp, Quellen und Abhandlungen zur Geschichte der Abtei und der Diözese Fulda 9, HBS 101 (Farnborough, 1977); bibl.: *CLLA*, no. 970.

[59] Hourlier and Froger, *Missel de Bénévent*, p. 15*.

[60] Rome, Biblioteca Angelica, F.A. 1408 (above n. 23).

[61] For common elements among Le, Va, Milanese, and Beneventan sacramentaries, see Moeller, *Corpus praefationum*, 1: lxxxiii-lxxxvii; Gamber, "Kampanische Messbuch," pp. 5-111; *CLLA*, no. 431; Dold, "Vatic. lat. 10645," p. 53, asserting that the fragment is not a mixed Gelasian-Gregorian nor a pure Gregorian (see prayer IX 3 only in Le); idem, *Zürcher und Peterlinger Messbuch-fragmente*, p. xlii, concluding that most prayers of PuZ are related to Le and Va and also to the Gelasians of the Eighth Century; and idem, "Umfangreiche Reste," p. 164, noting a considerable influence of Le and Va on Monte Cassino, Archivio della Badia, Compactiones VI (siglum: Mc.VI, missale, s. xi²), ed. Dold, "Umfangreiche Reste," pp. 114-144; bibl.: Loew, *Beneventan Script*, 2: 92) and Compactiones VII (siglum: Mc.VII, missale, s. xi/xii, ed. Dold, "Umfangreiche Reste," pp. 144-164; bibl.: Loew, *Beneventan Script*, 2: 92). The Milanese sacramentaries are listed in *CLLA*, nos. 505-535; especially the earliest MSS: Bergamo, Biblioteca di S. Alessandro in Colonna, 242 (siglum: Sb, sacramentarium, s. ix, Bergamo; ed. Angelo Paredi and Giuseppi Fassi, *Sacramentarium Bergomense*, Monumenta Bergomensia 6 [Bergamo, 1962]; bibl.: *CLLA*, no. 505); and Milan, Biblioteca Ambrosiana, A 24*bis* inf. (sacramentarium, s. ix, Biasca; ed. Odilo Heiming, *Das ambrosianische Sakramentar von Biasca*, Corpus Ambrosiano-Liturgicum 2, LQF 51 [Münster/W., 1969]; bibl.: *CLLA*, no. 515).

Two other approaches to the early history of the sacramentary have bearing on the origins of Beneventan missals. Gamber's Thesis: Gamber, "Kampanische Messbuch," pp. 5-111; and idem, "Liturgia delle diocesi," pp. 154-156; also *CLLA*, esp. pp. 106-109, 226-227, 260, 292-318, 368-428. Reversing the generally accepted direction of dependency, Klaus Gamber has suggested that the Campanian sacramentary was an influence on the Roman sacramentaries. Thus, some sacramentaries, including the books of the Roman titular churches and the most ancient Beneventan liturgical MSS, sprang directly from the reforms of the Campanian

Roman Influence (2): Adaptation of Roman Models

A second category of Roman influence is seen in its provision of models for new feasts found in neither the Old Beneventan nor early Roman calendars. While prayer texts probably entered the region in several waves, both Gregorian chant and the Roman lection-list appear to have been imported early and influenced little thereafter by external developments. The expanding calendar of the Middle Ages necessitated, however, an ever-increasing body of liturgical material: without fresh imports, new feasts in the region had to be supplied either through new compositions or the duplication of older texts. New musical compositions appeared either as original pieces of Gregorian chant or as new texts set to existing Gregorian melodies.[62]

---

book by Pope Gelasius I (492-496), while other sacramentaries, namely Va and related texts, are derived from a later reworking of the Gelasian redaction of the Campanian book by Bishop Maximianus of Ravenna (546-553). The conflation of the related books of Gelasius and Maximianus with the Sacramentary of Pope Gregory I (590-604) resulted in various mixed forms of sacramentaries, including the Gelasians of the Eighth Century. In southern Italy, the influence of the Gregorianum during the seventh and eighth centuries effectively shouldered out the earlier sources, replacing "Campanian-Gelasian" prayers except in the peripheral feasts. By this account, most southern Italian texts related to Le, Va, Milanese, and Gelasian sacramentaries of the Eighth Century are indigenous and not imported. In effect, Gamber removes a layer of influence proposed by both Peirce and Froger (above nn. 57 and 59). Gamber's view, however, has not been well received (Vogel, *Medieval Liturgy*, p. 67).

   Moreton's Thesis: see Moreton, *Eighth-Century Gelasian Sacramentary.* In his study of the Gelasian sacramentaries of the Eighth Century, Bernard Moreton made several radical suggestions about the origins of the early Roman books that may perhaps account for some of the sources of the southern Italian missals. He concluded that the roots of the compilation called the Gelasian of the Eighth Century lie in smaller Roman collections of mass-*libelli* and loose mass-sets. Specifically, in opposition to the accepted view that the eighth-century sacramentaries were conflations of the Old Gelasian and Gregorian sacramentaries, he theorised that the three major sacramentaries were composed at approximately the same time from smaller mass-*libelli* supplemented from a general stock of individual mass-sets and Gallican prayers: the Old Gelasian based on one particular collection, the Gregorian on another, and the Gelasians of the Eighth Century on both types of early collection. The early spread of mass-*libelli* of several types would explain, therefore, the lack of unanimity among the sources already cited. But Moreton's provocative suggestion is not yet widely accepted, and so long as much of the Beneventan corpus is unstudied, it will remain hypothetical as an explanation of southern Italian developments.

   [62] E.g., the composition of pieces for the new feast of Mennas described in Leo of Ostia, *Vita S. Mennatis*, ed. Giovanni Orlandi, " *Vita S. Mennatis*, opera inedita di Leone Marsicano," *Istituto Lombardo, Accademia di scienze e lettere: Rendiconti, Classe di lettere e scienze morali e storiche* 97 (1963) 467-490 at 480.

   Hesbert was the pioneer in the identification and study of Romano-Beneventan chant (see especially "Tradition bénéventaine"). But several scholars have taken up the task in the last twenty years, including Karlheinz Schlager, *Katalog*; idem, "Beneventanisches Alleluia und seine Prosula," pp. 217-225; idem, *Alleluia-Melodien*, I. *Bis 1100*, Monumenta monodica medii aevi 7 (Kassel, 1968); Kenneth Levy, " *Lux de luce*: The Origin of an Italian Sequence,"

The mass for the second Sunday of Lent is typical of this process of composition and adaptation.[63] The Sunday was originally aliturgical with a mass during its vigil doubling for the Sunday and the Saturday of the preceding Ember days; as a reflection of this arrangement, many early sacramentaries, including the Hadrianum, retain the old title *Dominica vacat* for the Sunday.[64] During the seventh century, the mass of the Ember day was firmly placed on the Saturday, and the Sunday was given its own mass. Provisions for the new mass took various forms, ranging from the adoption in Romano-Frankish sources of the mass *Reminiscere* of the preceding Wednesday to the Romano-Beneventan creation of a distinctive new mass from disparate sources and elements. Neither the text nor the melody of the Romano-Beneventan introit *Dirige me* have parallels in the Graduale Romanum (= GR).[65] The gradual *Qui confidunt,* however, is a new text set to the melody of the gradual *Miserere mihi* for the Wednesday of the third week of Lent. Although the tract *Confitemini* is found in both Roman and Beneventan books with the same melody, it is a late addition to the GR and possibly an independent conflation of text and music in both Rome and Benevento (the choice of melodies for a tract was after all quite limited).[66] The offertory *Exaltabo* found in most Beneventan books is borrowed from Ash Wednesday; the less frequently attested *Patres nostri* has a melody adapted from the Roman offertory *Confirma hoc* of Pentecost. There are also two regional communions: the distinctive text and melody of the communion *Redimet* is proper to the region and found in most Beneventan books, while the communion *Qui biberit* attested in Ben33 and the Dubrovnik missal (**145**) has a textual counterpart with a variant melody in the GR on the Friday after the third Sunday in Lent. The choice of *Qui biberit* (**145** Io 4: 13-14) is particularly appropriate for the second Sunday of Lent in the Beneventan liturgy since it echoes the Old Beneventan gospel of the day (Io 4: 5-42).

The canticle *Benedictus es* sung on the Saturday of each Ember week is a second general instance of a regional adaptation.[67] The lesson from Daniel

---

The Musical Quarterly 57 (1971) 40-61; John Boe, "Rhythmic Notation in the Beneventan Gloria Trope *Aureas Arces,*" *Musica Disciplina* 29 (1975) 5-42; idem, "The Neumes and Pater Noster Chant of Montecassino Codex 426," in *Monastica. Scritti raccolti in memoria del XV centenario della nascita di S. Benedetto (480-1980),* vol. 1, Miscellanea cassinese 44 (Monte Cassino, 1981), pp. 219-235; Brunner, "Southern Italian Sequence," pp. 117-164; and the bibliography cited in Huglo, "Ancien chant bénéventain," pp. 290-293.

[63] Hesbert, "Tradition bénéventaine," pp. 234-237.

[64] Chavasse, *Sacramentaire gélasien,* p. 229.

[65] *Graduale sacrosanctae Romanae ecclesiae* cum *Missae propriae Ordinis S. Benedicti,* ed. Solesmes, no. 696A (Paris, Tournai, Rome: Desclée, 1952) (henceforth GR).

[66] Apel, *Gregorian Chant,* pp. 323-330.

[67] Hesbert, "Tradition bénéventaine," pp. 222-224.

(Dan 3: 49-51) and an accompanying canticle were seventh-century additions to the lessons for the Saturdays of the four sets of Ember days.[68] Liturgists of the time made the addition in various ways: in the Roman tradition the lesson (Dan 3: 49-51) is followed by a canticle (Dan 3: 52-56) which continues the reading; in Romano-Beneventan books the canticle for the Saturday of the first series of Ember days (March) begins instead with Daniel 3: 56 and continues with the first quarter of the canticle *Benedicite* (Dn 3: 57-88, 56) while the remaining three quarters are distributed over the Ember days of the sixth, ninth, and twelfth months. The canticle *Benedicite* is itself common everywhere and displays no particular melodic variants in its Beneventan form.

Other Romano-Beneventan texts include the communion *Amen dico vobis* of the first Monday of Lent;[69] the musical items for the Saturday before Palm Sunday, which was aliturgical until the eighth century;[70] the mass *Converte nos* of the Saturday after Ash Wednesday in Benevento, Biblioteca Capitolare, 35 (= Ben35) and Benevento 38 (= Ben38); and the mass for Holy Thursday.[71] From the Sanctoral, the mass of Bartholomew adapts a series of Roman melodies to new texts: the introit *Gaudeamus* is based on the Roman *In voluntate*, the gradual *Exsultemus* on *Gloriosus*, the offertory *Digna promamus* on *Ave Maria*, and the communion *Beatum canimus* on *In salutari*.[72] In later centuries the process continued; thus Mercurius, a Byzantine saint translated to Benevento in 768, is represented in a twelfth or thirteenth-century manuscript from Benevento with a mass that includes metrical texts set to Gregorian melodies.[73] As well, about forty Romano-Beneventan alleluias, principally for the masses of saints, have been identified.[74] In other cases, new verses were set to melodies from earlier Roman

---

[68] Chavasse, *Sacramentaire gélasien*, p. 112.

[69] Hesbert, "Tradition bénéventaine," pp. 240-241: as the result of an effort to create a concordance between the communion and gospel texts, the communion *Amen dico vobis* appears to have been attracted to the first Monday in Lent from its original place in the mass of Mark and Marcellinus in the early Roman mass-antiphonals. Early Beneventan sources (Ben33, PuV) and many later medieval mss from other regions retain the psalmic communion *Voce mea* (Ps 3) of the early Roman mass-antiphonals, but in later Beneventan books and the Roman missal (based on the Franciscan liturgy), the evangelical communion *Amen dico vobis* is the norm.

[70] Hesbert, "Tradition bénéventaine," pp. 238-240; Kelly, *Beneventan Chant*, pp. 20-21; also Chavasse, *Sacramentaire gélasien*, pp. 226-228, for the aliturgical vigil of Palm Sunday.

[71] Hesbert, "Tradition bénéventaine," pp. 241-243, 269-275.

[72] Hesbert, "Tradition bénéventaine," pp. 450-451.

[73] Kelly, *Beneventan Chant*, p. 72 n. 50, cites Naples, Biblioteca Nazionale, XVI A 19, fol. 44; fols. 1-15: processionale, s. xii; fols. 16-48: antiphonarium, s. xii-siii, Benevento, bibl.: *CLLA* no. 482, Loew, *Beneventan Script*, 2: 105, Kelly, *Beneventan Chant*, p. 309.

[74] Schlager, *Katalog*, pp. 21-22 (nos. 53, 112, and 151 are Old Beneventan).

alleluias: thus, in southern Italy the text *Exivi* was often adapted to the music from the alleluia *Laudate*. Elsewhere *Exivi* is an alternative text for the melody of the alleluia *Cantate*, but in southern Italy the music of *Cantate* was used with the text *Qui timent* as an alternative and never with *Exivi*.[75] In general, the frequency of new compositions and regional adaptations affirms the hypothesis that Gregorian chant was brought into southern Italy at an early date, before the propers found elsewhere had been composed for the many feasts added later to the Roman calendar.

The embellishment of the chants of the mass, whether with prosulas and tropes or the addition of the sequence, followed a distinctive course in southern Italy.[76] Among the prosulas in the twelfth-century Gradual of Benevento, Biblioteca Capitolare, 34 (= Ben34), edited in facsimile in Paléographie Musicale 15, twenty-six are composed for the melismatic passages of the jubilus or alleluia-verses, nine for offertories, three for tracts, three for the responsory *Collegerunt*, and one for a gradual.[77] Most are peculiar to the region, although some are of wider distribution within Italy: thus, for instance, seven are attested also in a Bolognese manuscript of the eleventh century.[78]

Sequences, the second category of accretional text, followed a course of dispersion and adaptation analogous to that of Gregorian chant, although they were not part of the ancient Gregorian corpus. From the origin of the sequence in Carolingian France until the reform of the genre in the sixteenth century, new texts were continually being composed and older sequences modified.[79] The repertory of sequences in the twelfth-century Tonary of Monte Cassino 318, analysed by Lance Brunner, indicates that the process of adaptation and composition was especially strong in southern Italy: among the 175 sequences of Monte Cassino 318, sixty-two were regional compositions while another thirty-five are found outside the south only in other Italian centres.[80]

---

[75] Schlager, *Katalog*, melodies D 4 and D 121.

[76] A general history of tropes and sequences is presented by Costa, "Tropes et séquences," pp. 261-332, 440-471. Specific studies of Beneventan tropes are being prepared by John Boe (Tropes of the Ordinary) and Alejandro Planchart (Proper Tropes). Other texts of the genre are being published by the Corpus troporum of Stockholm; seven volumes have appeared to date (Studia Latina Stockholmiensia 21-22, 25-26, 29, 31-32 [Stockholm, 1976-1986]).

[77] Hourlier and Huglo, "Notation bénéventaine," p. 175.

[78] Rome, Biblioteca Angelica, 123; graduale, ante 1039, Bologna, bibl.: Schlager, *Katalog*, p. 261; Gajard, *Graduel romain*, 2: 119. The prosulas of PuV are listed by Hesbert, "Tradition bénéventaine," pp. 213-215.

[79] On sequences, see Apel, *Gregorian Chant*, pp. 442-464. Their early history is discussed by Richard Crocker, *The Early Medieval Sequence* (Berkeley, 1977).

[80] Brunner, "Southern Italian Sequence," p. 138, Table 4.

Norman Influences

The fourth stage in the development of the regional liturgy is marked by the introduction of Norman and northern practices. These influences may have come from several sources: certainly Cassinese clerics were frequent visitors to Rome, northern clergy were often appointed as abbots or bishops in the south, northern books were presented to Monte Cassino as the gifts of emperors and popes, and northern prelates undoubtedly brought books to such international events as the council of Urban II at Bari in 1098.[81] East Frankish elements in the southern Italian liturgy are apparent in several Cassinese missals, for instance, where the mass ordo itself is a copy of the Rhinish mass ordo of the tenth century.[82] Nonetheless, the testimony of both narrative histories and liturgical sources points to an even greater influence from Normandy and northern France.[83] Among the chroniclers, for instance,

[81] Herbert Bloch, "Monte Cassino, Byzantium, and the West in the Earlier Middle Ages," *Dumbarton Oak Papers* 3 (1946) 163-224; and idem, *Monte Cassino*, 1: 15-30, with discussion of the connections with the Ottonians. On the council of Bari, see Francesco Nitti di Vito, *La Ripresa gregoriana di Bari (1087-1105) e i suoi riflessi nel mondo contemporaneo politico e religioso* (Trani, 1942), pp. 371-453.

Imported liturgical books include an early-twelfth-century missal of Rouen brought to Troia (Naples, BN, VI G 11; bibl.: Raffaele Arnese, *I Codici notati della Biblioteca Nazionale di Napoli*, Biblioteca di Bibliografia Italiana 47 [Florence, 1967], no. 29 [pp. 21, 132-137]), and two MSS of the French royal chapel now bound in a single codex in Bari, i.e., the Gradual and Proser of Ste.-Chapelle, which formed part of the gift of Charles II of Anjou listed in the inventory of the Basilica of St. Nicholas of 1296 (Bari, Archivio della Basilica di S. Nicola, S.N.; ca. 1250, Central France; facs. ed. René-Jean Hesbert, *Le Prosaire de la Sainte-Chapelle (Manuscrit du Chapitre de Saint-Nicolas de Bari)*, Monumenta Musicae Sacrae 1 [Mâcon, 1952]; bibl.: Robert Branner, "Two Parisian Capella Books in Bari," *Gesta* 8.2 [1969] 14-19; Karen Gould, "The Sequences *De sanctis reliquiis* as Sainte-Chapelle Inventories," *MS* 43 [1981] 315-341).

For the Normans in Dalmatia, especially the incursions of Amico di Giovinazzo in the late eleventh century, see Francesco Babudri, "Il Conte Amico di Giovinazzo: la sua impresa adriatica e la marineria apulo-normanna," *Archivio Storico Pugliese* 12 (1959) 87-137; and Stjepan Gunjača, *Ispravci i dopune starijoj hrvatskoj historiji*, 4 vols. (Zagreb, 1973-1978), 3: 1-70.

[82] Josef Andreas Jungmann, *Missarum Sollemnia. Eine genetische Erklärung der römischen Messe*, 4th revised edition (Vienna, 1958), 1: 125-126, with reference to Monte Cassino, Archivio della Badia, 127 (siglum: Mc127, missale, s. xi ex., Monte Cassino; bibl.: *CLLA*, no. 458; Loew, *Beneventan Script*, 2: 70); Naples, Archivio di Stato, 4 (pontificale); and Rome, Biblioteca Casanatense, 614 (above n. 54): the three mass ordines are edited in Adalbert Ebner, *Quellen und Forschungen zur Geschichte und Kunstgeschichte des Missale Romanum im Mittelalter. Iter Italicum* (Freiburg/Br., 1896), pp. 309-313, 327-331. See also Fiala, "Ordo missae," pp. 180-224.

Brunner, "Southern Italian Sequence," pp. 139-140, discusses a comparable East Frankish influence on the sequence repertory.

[83] The religious policy of the Normans in southern Italy has been discussed in Jean Décarreaux, *Normands, papes et moines. Cinquante ans de conquêtes et de politique religieuse en Italie méridionale et en Sicilie*, (Paris, 1974); and Léon Robert Ménager, "La 'byzantini-

The Ecclesiastical History of Ordericus Vitalis includes an account of the foundation of St. Euphemia in Calabria by Norman monks and a description of the liturgy of St. Évroult practised there and in its daughter houses of Venosa, Mileto, and St. Agatha.[84] Ordericus Vitalis also mentions the passage of northern clerics through the region: for instance, we know from his history that Odo, bishop of Bayeaux, wintered in Apulia on his way to Palestine, and that Gilbert of Évreux was in Palermo in 1097.[85]

Liturgical books from the region have transmitted many instances of the new hybrid liturgy. The early appearance of the cult of Thomas of Canterbury in southern Italy has long been attributed to Norman influence.[86] Virginia Brown in a study of the Kalendarium Tutinianum of Naples found a very full list of French bishop-saints: some appear in southern Italy only in that calendar, but others, including Hilary of Poitiers, Germanus of Auxerre, Remigius of Rheims, Dionysius of Paris, Martin of Tours, and Bricius of Tours, were venerated in a wide range of calendars and martyrologies from

---

sation' religieuse de l'Italie Méridionale (ixe-xiie siècles) et la politique monastique des Normands d'Italie," *Revue d'histoire ecclésiastique* 53 (1958) 747-774, 54 (1959) 5-40; idem, "Les fondations monastiques de Robert Guiscard, duc de Pouille et de Calabre," *Quellen und Forschungen aus italienischen Archiven und Bibliotheken* 39 (1959) 1-63; also David Charles Douglas, *The Norman Achievement 1050-1100* (London, 1969), pp. 119-120; and Lynn T. White, *Latin Monasticism in Sicily* (Cambridge/Mass., 1938), pp. 47-52.

Discussions of Anglo-Norman forms in southern Italy appear in Ernst Kantorowicz, "A Norman Finale of the Exultet and the Rite of Sarum," *Harvard Theological Review* 34 (1941) 129-143; idem, *Laudes Regiae*, pp. 157-179; René-Jean Hesbert, "Les Séquences de Jumièges," in *Jumièges*, Congrès scientifique du xiiie centenaire, Rouen, 10-12 juin 1954, 2 vols. (Rouen, 1955), 2: 943-958 at 943; Gregório M. Suñol, *Introduction à la paléographie musicale grégorienne*, trans. André Mocquereau (Paris, 1935), p. 229; Francesco Terrizzi, *Missale antiquum S. Panormitanae ecclesiae (Palermo, Archivio Storico Diocesano, cod. 2)*, RED, Series maior, Fontes 13 (Rome, 1970), Intro. p. 34; David Hiley, "The Norman Chant Traditions—Normandy, Britain, Sicily," *Proceedings of the Royal Musical Association* 107 (1980-1981) 1-34; Brunner, "Southern Italian Sequence," pp. 140-142; and Brown, "New Beneventan Calendar," pp. 385-449.

Hiley, pp. 8-9, takes the opposing position that there was little influence of Norman cult on Beneventan before the mid twelfth century; a review article by Michael Altschul, "Conquests and Cultures, Norman and Non-Norman: Three Recent Studies," *Medievalia et Humanistica* ns 10 (1981) 217-222 at 217, although concerned with institutional history, questions later Norman survivals of any sort: "Insofar as a consensus may be presumed to exist, there would be few defenders of the proposition that anything authentically or exclusively Norman could be said to have survived by the mid-twelfth century in the Mediterranean world."

[84] Ordericus Vitalis, *The Ecclesiastical History*, ed. and trans. by Marjorie Chibnall, 6 vols. (Oxford, 1969-1981), 2: 100-103.

[85] Ordericus, *The Ecclesiastical History* (ed. Chibnall), 5: 34-35, 211.

[86] Charles H. Haskins, *Studies in the History of Mediaeval Science* (Cambridge/Mass., 1924), p. 186 n. 144, with reference also to older Norman saints in the calendar of Venosa (Monte Cassino, Archivio della Badia, 334).

the Beneventan region.[87] The Missal of Palermo, Archivio diocesano, cod. 2, recently edited by Francesco Terrizzi, is typical of the books of Sicily, resembling purely Norman missals more closely than it does any of the earlier representatives of the Romano-Beneventan liturgy.[88] Mixed Norman-Italian features have been identified in some of the Sicilian liturgical books now in Madrid: the thirteenth-century Sacramentary of Syracuse is particularly noteworthy for the mixture of Norman and Byzantine features in its illuminations, and the abundance of French saints in its calendar and litanies.[89]

Lance Brunner and David Hiley have both remarked that before the early twelfth century the centres of southern Italian liturgy, Benevento and Monte Cassino, appear to have resisted the adoption of sequences associated with what were, at the time, the recent conquerors of the region.[90] By the mid twelfth century, however, any such resistance had died out: a processional was copied during the twelfth century at Troia from a Normano-Sicilian exemplar;[91] and the musical pieces of a twelfth-century Cassinese troper contain a Kyrie prosula, two Sanctus tropes, and four sequence texts drawn from Norman sources.[92] To these instances may be added the hybrid ceremonies of the twelfth-century Lectionary-Pontifical of Kotor in Dalmatia (Leningrad, Biblioteka Akademii Nauk, F. no. 200, = DaK), where several practices with parallels only in Anglo-Norman sources have been introduced

[87] Geneva, Bibliothèque Publique et Universitaire, Comites latentes 195; "kalendarium tutinianum," s. xiv, Naples, ed. and facs. Brown, "New Beneventan Calendar," pp. 385-449; bibl.: Brown, "Second New List (II)," p. 599. On the French influences, see Brown, "New Beneventan Calendar," pp. 439-440.

[88] Palermo, Archivio Storico Diocesano, 2; missale, s. xii med., Palermo; ed. Terrizzi, *Missale antiquum S. Panormitanae ecclesiae.* With regard to the Norman features of the MS, Terrizzi, pp. 35-37, presents a list of saints in the litany, including several French bishops and abbots, and p. 65, remarks that the Missal of Palermo shares 86 of 117 formularies with Rouen, Bibliothèque Municipale, 274 (Y 6): ed. Henry A. Wilson, *The Missal of Robert of Jumièges,* HBS 11 (London, 1896).

[89] Madrid, Biblioteca Nacional, 52; sacramentarium, s. xiii in., Syracuse; bibl.: José Janini and José Serrano, *Manuscritos litúrgicos de la Biblioteca Nacional* (Madrid, 1969), no. 3. Other Sicilian liturgical MSS preserved in Spain are listed in Léopold Delisle, "Un livre de choeur normano-sicilien conservé en Espagne," *Journal des Savants* ns 6 (1908) 42-49; and Janini and Serrano, *Manuscritos litúrgicos,* nos. 17 (BN, 289; troparium, s. xii), 32 (BN, 678; pontificale, s. xiii), 33 (BN, 713; breviarium OFM), 34 (BN, 715; pontificale, s. xiv), and 37 (BN, 742; ordines, s. xiii): all entered the Madrid National Library from the collection of the Duke of Uceda.

[90] Brunner, "Southern Italian Sequence," pp. 141-142; Hiley, "Norman Chant Traditions," Table 6c.

[91] Naples, BN, VI G 34; processionale, s. xii, Troia, bibl.: Loew, *Beneventan Script,* 2: 102; cited in Brunner, "Southern Italian Sequence," p. 124.

[92] Vatican City, BAV, Urb. lat. 602 (above n. 22); cited in Brunner, "Southern Italian Sequence," pp. 141-142.

into an ordo for the dedication of a church from the Roman-German Pontifical.[93]

After the twelfth century, the spread of the Mendicant orders and the diffusion of their liturgical books based on the Roman liturgy of the Curia affected many local churches that had until then retained markedly regional customs.[94] The source for the liturgy of the Curia was a form of mixed Gelasian-Gregorian sacramentary, resembling the Missal of Azevedo or the Orsini sacramentary which derive directly from the Hadrianum and its Supplement with some influences from the Gelasians of the Eighth Century.[95] The reformed curial liturgy was introduced wherever the new orders established themselves, even supplanting diocesan liturgies on occasion: in Zagreb, for instance, on the edge of the Beneventan zone, the Dominican liturgy was adopted under Bishop Augustin Kažotić, OP (1303-1322).[96] Among late sources such as the Oxford manuscript, the Mendicant liturgies and their parent, the Missal of the Curia, may often have had considerable influence.

While the interplay between the older Romano-Beneventan and the new liturgies of the Mendicants is a field absolutely unstudied, the immediate connections between the Romano-Beneventan liturgy and the liturgies of neighbouring regions are also largely unexamined. The transfer of Beneventan sources, with their distinctive liturgy, to nearby centres is a phenomenon documented by both early and late evidence. The Missal of Zagreb, Metropolitanska Knjižnica, MR 166 (= DaZ), composed of Beneventan materials from southern Italy and Dalmatia, appears, for instance, to have been in the cathedral collection of Zagreb from very early in its history, perhaps even constituting one of the gifts for its foundation in the late eleventh century.[97] One need only consider the modern location of Bene-

---

[93] For DaK, see above n. 9. Anglo-Norman ceremonies include fols. 71r-v, the entrance into the church bearing the cross; 71v, the prayer *Tabernaculum hoc*; 75v, the prayer of mixing wine and water in the preparation of lustral water; 76r, the prayer *Pateant* at the aspersion of the altar; and 76r-v, the prayers during the aspersions of the interior walls and the entire ceremony of external aspersions. Cf. Vogel and Elze, *Pontifical romano-germanique*, 1: 124-173 (ordo 40).

[94] Vogel, *Medieval Liturgy*, p. 104.

[95] Azevedo missal: Rome, Archivio Lateranense, 65; s. xi-xii, ed. Manuel de Azevedo, *Vetus missale romanum monasticum Lateranense* (Rome, 1752-1754); bibl.: *CLLA*, no. 1187b. Orsini sacramentary: Vatican City, BAV, Ottob. lat. 356; sacramentarium papale, s. xiii-xiv, S. Maria in Aquiro, bibl.: Salmon, *Manuscrits liturgiques*, 2: 13-14 (no. 18).

[96] Dragutin Kniewald, "Zagrebački liturgijski kodeski xi.- xv. stoljeća," *Croatia sacra* 10 (1940) 1-128 at 126-128 for a Latin summary of the liturgical history of the diocese; and Archdale A. King, *Liturgies of the Religious Orders* (Milwaukee, 1955), p. 343.

[97] Zagreb, Metropolitanska Knjižnica (on deposit in the Nacionalna i Sveučilišna Biblioteka), MR 166; siglum: DaZ, pp. 1-326, missale, s. xii, southern Italy; pp. 327-354, missale,

ventan material in Macerata, Parma, Venice, and many other centres outside the zone of the script to realise the currency in the Adriatic region of Beneventan manuscripts.[98]

CODICOLOGICAL DESCRIPTION

Modern History

The manuscript entered the Bodleian Library in 1817 with the acquisition of the collection of the abate Matteo Luigi Canonici (1727-1806).[99] Codicological examination reveals two traces of its post-medieval history before 1817: the covers of brown calf patterned with blind tooling over wooden boards bevelled inward are similar to other bindings from the Canonici collection, and the number "112" in black ink in the middle of the lower margin of modern fol. 121r resembles the foliation found in manuscripts acquired by Canonici shortly after 1780 from the collection of the Venetian senator Jacopo Soranzo (1686-1761).[100] On the spine, the label "MISSALIS PERANTIQUI RELIQUIAE, COD. MEM. CARAC. LONGOBARD." has been added in gold letters. Sometime during the nineteenth century, many of the folios were repaired with parchment; paper pastedowns and flyleaves were added; and the leaves of the manuscript were foliated in pencil with Arabic

---

s. xiii, Dalmatia; bibl.: *CLLA*, no. 446; Loew, *Beneventan Script*, 2: 177; Andreis, *Music in Croatia*, p. 12.

[98] See the centres cited in Loew, *Beneventan Script*, vol. 2: *Hand List of Beneventan MSS.*; and Brown, "Second New List (II)," pp. 584-625. Of particular interest are items of late date that are related to medieval missals from outside the zone of the script: e.g., Dubrovnik, Dominikanski Samostan, Frag. (i) (1 fol., s. xv, bibl.: Brown, "Second New List (II)," p. 595), a late fragment containing votive masses for the seasonal commemoration of the Virgin and the mass "ad poscenda suffragia sanctorum" attributed to Innocent III, with prayers and titles corresponding to the *Missale Romanum Mediolani, 1474* (= MRM), ed. Robert Lippe, 2 vols., HBS 17, 33 (London, 1899, 1907), pp. 457-458 and 460. The masses of the Virgin and the mass attributed to Innocent III are listed by Placide Bruylants, *Les oraisons du Missel Romain*, 2 vols., Études liturgiques 1-2 (Louvain, 1952), 1: 178 (masses 533-534), 188 (mass 567).

[99] On Canonici, see Madan, *Summary Catalogue*, 4: 313-314; and Irma Merolle, *L'Abate Matteo Luigi Canonici e la sua Biblioteca* (Rome, Florence, 1958).

[100] Similar covers are found on Oxford, Bodleian Library, Canon. Liturg. 325, and Canon. Liturg. 333. See J. B. Mitchell, "Trevisan and Soranzo: Some Canonici Manuscripts from Two Eighteenth-Century Venetian Collections," *Bodleian Library Record* 8 (1967-1972) 125-135 at 133 for this style of binding, at 130 and pl. XVIa for the foliation of Soranzo's collection. Other traces of the provenance of the MS have not been forthcoming. For instance, the inventory of 1751 by Serafin Crijević [Cerva] of the important collection of the Dominican convent of Dubrovnik contains no references that may be identified with the Oxford missal (Thomas Kaeppeli and Hugues V. Shooner, *Les manuscrits médiévaux de Saint-Dominique de Dubrovnik: Catalogue sommaire* [Rome, 1965], pp. 14-29).

numerals on the upper right recto. The extent of repairs and the discrepancy between the modern foliation and the surviving earlier number on fol. 121r suggest that the manuscript was rearranged and rebound in its old covers at the time it was repaired by the Bodleian. Several library marks have been entered on the front pastedown, including the catalogue number "19428" (black ink); the shelfmarks of Henry Octavius Coxe's organisation in 1877 of the Bodleian liturgical manuscripts, "E codd: Bodl: Miscelli Liturg CCCXLII" (black ink) and "Miscel: Liturg: 342" (pencil); and the shelfmark of the reorganisation by fontes in 1887, "MS. Canon. Liturg. 342" (pencil).[101] The mark "E codd: Bodl: Miscell. Liturg. CCCXLII" (black ink) is repeated on fol. 2r.

Physical Description and Composition

Incipit: "deo nostro."
Fol. 2r incipit: "a seculo tu es" (with musical notation).
Explicit fol. 122v: "Diuina libantes misteria domine quesumus." (olim fol. 121v: "famulum tuum episcopum nostrum cum").

The folios in their present state average 250 x 165 mm. The written space of each folio is a single column of 180 x 100 mm. ruled in dry point from the hair side in 23 lines and bound on all margins by double rules; the text rules usually extend to the inner edge. Pricking survives in the outer margins of some folios.[102] To this basic preparation of each page, the scribes and rubricators of the manuscript appear to have added text, music, rubrics, initials, and capitals in the following order:[103]

The scribe using brown ink (occasionally mixed with black) wrote the texts of the prayers and lections on every rule; the texts of the musical items were written in a smaller script on every second rule where the addition of music was intended and on every rule where not.[104] Very faint traces of the titles to be added later were marked in the text and margins at this time.[105]

---

[101] The attempted organisation of the Library by subjects and the return to organisation by fontes is described by Madan, *Summary Catalogue*, 5: 843-844 (after no. 30594); and Richard W. Hunt, *Summary Catalogue* (1953), 1: xliii.

[102] Traces of the pricking may be seen on fols. 34, 66, 99, 104-116, 118-121.

[103] A nomenclature of the hierarchy of capitalisation in medieval liturgical MSS and analysis of their layout is given by Andrew Hughes, *Medieval Manuscripts for Mass and Office* (Toronto, 1982), esp. pp. 103-107.

[104] Text has been written over erasures on fols. 45r (half-word), 53v (several neumes), 72r (4 lines), 76v (one letter), 78v (one line), 80r (2 lines), 87v (2 lines and one initial), 89v (2 lines), 91r (one line of neumes), 104r (several neumes), and 113v (10 lines).

[105] Layout signs and notes for the rubricator have survived on the following fols.: 16v, 25v,

The spaces left for the addition of music were ruled next on either hair or flesh sides of the leaves between the marks of the original rules, thus creating dry-point staffs of three lines above the musical items.

The scribe then returned to brown/black ink for the addition of the clefs, the neumes, the "directs" at the end of the musical lines, and, perhaps, corrections to the texts.[106]

At this point, he changed to red ink to write the rubricated pieces, including titles, ceremonial directions, and highlights to capitals and clefs.

A slightly different shade of red ink was used for the F-lines of the musical pieces and for the large two line initials that were added, most often, in the space at the margin between the vertical double rules marking the edge of the text. Smaller one and a half line initials in the same ink begin the musical pieces; these were placed, however, at the beginning of each piece as required, whether in midline or at the left margin.

Lastly, other colours were added, in particular the yellow used for the C-lines of the musical items and as a highlight throughout, but also blue for highlights and tracings on some initials.[107]

After the text was written and each gathering prepared, the manuscript was bound and trimmed. A catchword in Beneventan, "iustitiam," survives on fol. 11v; the traces of other catchwords may be seen on fols. 29v, 44v, 60v, and

26r, 28r, 30v, 37v, 39v, 40r-v, 41r-v, 48r, 58r, 77r-v, 108r, 116v, 118v, 119r, 120r, 121r-v. Pentimenti, probably without other significance, appear on fols. 22r, 36r, and 95r.

[106] Marginal additions by the scribe on fols. 46v, 81r, and 116r correct defects in the original text.

[107] Initials and capitals in unusual positions, i.e., not at the margin, or drawn with colours other than red and highlighted with colours other than yellow, are found on fols. 2r ("M" beginning the secret, set in midline; "P" beginning the introit, with blue), 12r ("I" beginning the gospel and capitals in text, with blue), 17v ("Q" beginning the postcommunion, with black), 23v ("I" beginning the gospel, with blue), 24r ("F" beginning the secret, with blue), 30r (capitals in text, with blue), 33r ("C" beginning the collect and "F" beginning the epistle, with black), 37r ("D" beginning the collect and "T" beginning a prayer, with blue), 39v ("O" beginning a prayer, drawn with an unusual design of loops), 48v ("F" beginning the epistle and the capitals in the epistle, with blue), 49r ("X" beginning the gradual, with blue), 50r ("O" beginning the collect, with blue), 50v-51r (blue highlights on every initial and capital), 52v ("O" beginning the blessing, and "L" in "Lumen," with blue; "E" beginning "Exultet," with black and blue), 53v ("V" beginning the preface, with black and blue), 53v-54r (capitals in the preface, with blue), 62r ("M" beginning the postcommunion, set in midline), 69r ("E" beginning the first lection, with black), 71v ("G" beginning the secret, with black), 88r ("D" beginning the collect, with black), 89v ("B" beginning the collect, with black), 96v ("I" beginning the gospel, with blue), 97r (all 2-line initials, with blue and black), 108r ("P" beginning the postcommunion, set in midline), 120r ("M" beginning the secret, set in midline).

The MS in its present condition has no illustrations: the lack, however, of the gathering on which one would expect to find the ordo of the mass with its incipit "Te igitur," the most commonly historiated initial in missals, leaves the original decoration of the MS an open question.

111v, although the condition of the manuscript makes them indecipherable. At some later time, other scribes wrote in a few corrections and new texts, including a few words in the margin of the Passion of Matthew (**180** fol. 42r-v) identified as Croatian by Dr. Marica Čunčić. A different scribe has added incipits in a Beneventan hand on fols. 96v-97r and 98r. On fols. 42r-v and 88r, the additions are in a non-Beneventan hand. Large sections of faded text were carefully retraced with black ink on fols. 18r, 67v, 69r, 84r-v, 88r, 90v, 96v, 99v, and 103r-v. Apart from the short addition in Croatian, which is a sign of Dalmatian provenance, the few remaining additions are not particularly significant and suggest that the Missal was not much used or adapted for changing uses.

Later, the manuscript was much damaged by damp, probably due to improper storage or other neglect. Thus many of the folios had to have greater or lesser portions of the margins trimmed and repaired, and a few have lost areas of the written space as well.[108] The manuscript contains a modern paper flyleaf at the beginning and end, 122 numbered parchment leaves, and one unnumbered fragment between fols. 21v and 22r. The modern gatherings and foliation do not represent the original condition and order: the text is now deficient at the beginning and end, and lacks many intermediate sections.[109] The codicological evidence and a comparison of the surviving text with other Beneventan missals suggest that more than a third of the manuscript has perished (see the Appendix: Reconstruction of the Manuscript).

Script

The manuscript is written throughout in a single Beneventan hand that shows a number of regional characteristics and many features from the late

---

[108] Text has been trimmed or torn from fols. 19-21, 21ᵃ, 22, 35, 47, and 117. Stitching, probably predating the Bodleian repair of the MS with parchment strips, survives on fols. 13, 14, 52, 97, 105, and 107; the stitching has been removed and replaced with a parchment strip on fol. 81. Offsets from later printed pages have bonded with splashes of glue (?) on the parchment of fols. 23r and 36v, suggesting that the MS was once stored with interleaved printed material.

[109] The present collation of the MS with its modern parchment binding strips is i + 1^{10}, 2^8, 3^4, 4^8, 5^7, 6^8, 7^6, 8^4, 9^5, 10^6, 11^5, 12^4, 13^7, 14^9, 15^5, 16^8, 17^2, 18^6, 19^2, 20^6, 21^3 + i: the total is 123 folios. Although only 122 folios are numbered, the unnumbered fragment between fols. 21v and 22r has been included in this collation.

Apart from the fragmentary folios listed in the previous note, there are lacunae in the MS before fol. 1, and after fols. 3, 4, 18, 19, 21, 31, 33, 35, 36, 44, 46, 49, 54, 60, 66, 68, 69, 71, 74, 91, 103, 105, 107, 111, 114, 117, 119, and 121. Nor are the existing folios bound in their original order: fol. 74 is recto for verso, fols. 82-90 should follow fol. 95, fols. 107-110 should run 108, 107, 110, 109; and fol. 121 should follow fol. 122. See the Appendix for a hypothetical reconstruction of the original order and arrangement of the existing folios.

period of the script.[110] The general appearance is of an angular hand marked by the lateral compression of the bodies of many letters and the inclination to the left of the vertical strokes in some letters. Although the letter-forms follow the rules of the script with few exceptions, signs suggesting a date late in the thirteenth century are the tendency for letters not to be placed precisely on the line, thus creating a broken irregular appearance; the frequent marking of doubled-*i* with hairstrokes; a few hyphens for words split between the lines; the descent of final *r* below the line; the joining of *r* to a following *e* by a straight line without the curved shoulder of earlier periods; the occasional use of uncial *a* even in the middle of a line; and the frequent contact between letters.[111] Regional characteristics are the regular appearance of descenders hooked considerably to the left, and the distinctive ligature *fi*, which descends only slightly below the line in Dalmatian manuscripts and is marked by a large bow to the right.[112] The majuscule alphabet used for the initials and capitals mixes rustic and Beneventan elements indiscriminately; a few initials are decorated with restrained terminal flourishes.

The forms of abbreviation follow the general rules of the script, including the Beneventan forms for "autem," "eius," "pro," "que," "qui," "-ur," and "-us."[113] The general contraction sign is a horizontal, superscript line, sometimes doubled; a sign resembling a superscript *2* is used for the abbreviation of "-ur"; and, as is seen frequently in late manuscripts, abbreviations are sometimes indicated by superscript letters, e.g., "m[i]" for "mihi." The form of the Beneventan sign for an abbreviated *m*, which appears in the manuscript in an angular character resembling a superscript *7*, is also typical of the late period of the script.[114] The use of "aia" with a contraction sign for

---

[110] The basic works on the Beneventan script (Loew, *Beneventan Script*; idem, *Scriptura Beneventana*; and Brown, "Second New List (II)," pp. 584-625) are supplemented for the study of the Beneventan script in Dalmatia by Novak, *Scriptura Beneventana*; idem, "Something New from the Dalmatian Beneventana," pp. 76-85; idem, *Latinska Paleografija*, pp. 141-165; and Falconi, "Frammenti," pp. 73-110.

Falconi, "Frammenti," pp. 85-86, groups the script of Parma, Archivio di Stato, Frammenti di codici 2 (s. xiii), with the hands of the Oxford MS and the following late Dalmatian MSS: Zadar, Historijski Arhiv, Sv. 182, Poz. 4, list 4 (1 fol., graduale, s. xii, bibl.: Loew, *Beneventan Script*, 2: 174); and Zadar, Archiepiscopal Archives, S.N. (MS missing since 1918; "codex monasterii S. Grisogoni," s. xii, bibl.: Loew, *Beneventan Script*, 2: 174).

[111] Loew, *Scriptura Beneventana*, 2: pl. 94; and Falconi, "Frammenti," p. 87.

[112] On the Dalmatian features, see most recently Falconi, "Frammenti," pp. 86-87. Although similar features are found in the Bari-type of Beneventan script used in Dalmatia at an earlier stage (Loew, *Beneventan Script*, 1: 150), no one would confound the angular letter-forms of the later Dalmatian MSS with the rounded letters of MSS of the Bari-type and earlier Dalmatian developments from it (Falconi, "Frammenti," pp. 93-94).

[113] For abbreviations in Beneventan, see Loew, *Beneventan Script*, 1: 173-226.

[114] Loew, *Beneventan Script*, 1: 172.

"anima," "e̅" for "est," "ip̅e" for "ipse," and barred-*s* for "ser" are more precise indications of a date in the thirteenth century.[115] The abbreviations of "omnis," "homo," "nomen," and "anima" are particularly important criteria for dating Beneventan manuscripts:[116] although the scribe of the Oxford manuscript generally preferred "om̅is," "om̅ia," "om̅ium," "om̅i," etc., from the older system, he almost invariably used "aı̅a" and "noı̅s," etc., from the more recent convention. Since such combinations as both "om̅ibus hom̅ibus" and "om̅ibus hoı̅bus" (fol. 16v) are not uncommon, Loew suggested that the archaic forms may reflect the faithful copying of an earlier exemplar.[117]

The range of abbreviations is typical of liturgical manuscripts, and of Beneventan liturgical manuscripts in particular; they are used principally for nomina sacra and for the most frequent words of the liturgical vocabulary, especially in rubrics and titles.[118] Abbreviations of any sort are very rare in the noted musical items, probably because contractions of more than a syllable would have disturbed the syllabic relation of text and music, but also perhaps because extended melismas required even more space than the text, thus eliminating the importance of space-saving in the writing of the text itself.

Punctuation

The punctuation of the manuscript is limited for the most part to a single point on or slightly above the line for both final and medial stops. The point-and-stroke medial sign is used only occasionally; the joining of two points and a comma in a final stop found in other late Dalmatian manuscripts appears even more rarely.[119] A small hairstroke is used more frequently to

---

[115] Loew, *Beneventan Script*, 1: 175-196.

[116] Loew, *Beneventan Script*, 1: 210-213.

[117] Loew, *Scriptura Beneventana*, 2: pl. 94. (In fact, with the discovery of many more Beneventan items from Dalmatia, it now appears that the continued use of the older system of abbreviation is not as unusual as Loew thought.)

[118] The following abbreviations and contractions of more than single letters are used often: alia (*al*), alleluia (*all*), ante (*an*), antiphona (*a*), apostolus (*apls*), carissimi (*kmi*), communio/commune/commemoratio (*com*), caput (*cap*), christus (*xps*), crux (✠), deus (*ds*), dominica (*domc*), dominus (*dns*), epiphania (*epipha*), episcopus (*eps*), epistola (*epla*), euangelium (*eug*), feria (*fr*), fratres (*frs*), graduale (*gr*), gloria (*gla*), hymnus (*ym*), iohannes (*iohes*), in illo tempore (*illt*), introitus (*int/it*), lectio (*lec/l*), natale/natiuitas (*nat.*), noster (*nr*), octaua (*oct*), offertorium (*off*), omnipotens (*omips*), oratio (*or*), papa (*pp*), post (*p˙*), presta (*pra*), propheta (*ppha*), prosa (*ps*), psalmus (*ps*), quesumus (*qs*), responsus/responsorium (℟), sabbatum (*sabb*), sanctus (*scs*), secretum (*sec*), secundum (*secdm*), sempiternus (*sempt*), sequentia (*seq*), spiritus (*sps*), tractus (*tr/trc*), uersus (℣).

[119] The use of the point for all the stops is the culmination of a progressive abandonment of the other medial-signs in Dalmatian MSS (Falconi, "Frammenti," p. 87). MSS using two

indicate the shortest pauses, or sometimes word separations. Special signs for the celebrant include simple crosses for benedictions (✠) and the Beneventan interrogation sign, resembling a superscript checkmark, added regularly above the first word and after the last word of a question and highlighted with a spot of red.[120] In some lections, hairstrokes have been marked over stressed syllables. The Johannine gospels of Lent are further enhanced with several other signs designed to aid the lectors: the parts of the narrator are marked with a superscript "l"; the words of Christ with "c"; and the extra roles in the Passion by "s" or "e."[121] The punctuation, with more frequent breaks than strictly grammatical considerations would necessitate and with occasional indications of stress and performance, appears intended to facilitate the oratorical presentation of the texts.[122] The almost complete absence of medial punctuation on the line in the musical items corroborates this observation, since the performance indications of the notation itself supplant the function of punctuation.

Musical Notation

The musical items of the Oxford manuscript are noted with a fully diastematic system of clefs and neumes.[123] The neumatic notation in Beneventan manuscripts is one of many distinctive regional notations used during the early Middle Ages: most are based on similar principles and a common font of neume forms. In the regional varieties of this general type, changes of ductus and later local developments, both of which mark Beneventan notation, can produce differences of appearance as great as that which distinguishes, for instance, Beneventan script from other scripts.

---

points and a comma for the final stop include DaB, DaZ, and Zadar, Arhiv benediktinskog samostana sv. Marije, S.N. (Gregory I, *Moralia in Iob*, s. xii; bibl.: Loew, *Beneventan Script*, 2: 173).

[120] Loew, *Beneventan Script*, 1: 246 n. 1.

[121] Hesbert, "Évangéliaire," pp. 200-202, discusses the readers' signs in Berlin, Staatsbibliothek Preussischer Kulturbesitz, Theol. lat. quart. 278 (siglum: DaE, evangelistarium, s. xi ex., Zadar; ed. Hesbert, "Évangéliaire," pp. 177-204; bibl.: *CLLA*, no. 1175; Loew, *Beneventan Script*, 2: 25); for Ben33, see Hourlier and Froger, *Missel de Bénévent*, p. 11*. The symbols in Vatican MSS are presented by Henry M. Bannister, *Monumenti Vaticani di paleografia musicale latina*, Codices e Vaticanis selecti phototypice expressi, Series maior 12 (Leipzig, 1913), pp. 191-194.

[122] See the discussion on the nature of medieval punctuation in Loew, *Beneventan Script*, 1: 231.

[123] General histories of neumatic notation are presented by Suñol, *Introduction à la paléographie musicale grégorienne*; and Solange Corbin, "Neumatic Notations," *New Grove Dictionary*, 13: 128-144. Recent bibliography appears in Andrew Hughes, *Medieval Music: The Sixth Liberal Art*, 2nd edition, Toronto Medieval Bibliographies 4 (Toronto, 1980), index p. 313.

Even the earliest Beneventan manuscripts with musical notation are diastematic, with the differences in pitch indicated through the heightening of neumes relative to those that precede or follow, but without a reserved or added rule to act as a guide.[124] By the twelfth century, the general appearance of the notation had changed: the same basic neumes were drawn with greater vertical emphasis and the sharper contrast of thick and thin strokes typical also of the developed forms of the script. Apart from the general shift of aspect, some neumes underwent even greater modifications: one form, the quilisma, was no longer used; another, the liquescent virga, had been changed from a looped stroke into a variety of signs ranging from a figure resembling a *4* to a cross-like shape.[125] The indication of pitch had developed with the introduction of clefs, consistent ruling, and the use of "directs"; by the thirteenth century, a staff of three or four lines was commonly marked in red.[126]

The notation of the Oxford manuscript is closely comparable in the appearance of the neumes and in the organization of the staff to Ben34, the twelfth-century Gradual edited in facsimile in Paléographie Musicale 15. Both lack the quilisma, use a cross-like liquescent virga, and arrange the neumes about a drypoint staff of three lines; the Missal, however, uses the oriscus more frequently. Since the texts of the Missal's chants were entered on alternate rules, the staff is formed from the unused page-rule plus extra drypoint rules added above and below it; clef signs and rules in yellow and red to indicate the pitches C and F respectively are added where appropriate throughout the manuscript;[127] the clef B-flat is also marked on two occasions (**178, 369**); "directs" to the right of the coloured rules mark the pitch of the first note of the next line. The manuscript also uses "directs" to mark the final or tenor of some pieces.[128] The "directs" closing communions and offertories

---

[124] Hourlier and Huglo, "Notation bénéventaine," p. 105. Examples of this early system of notation are contained in the facsimile edition of Ben33 (Hourlier and Froger, *Missel de Bénévent*).

[125] On the quilisma, see Hourlier and Huglo, "Notation bénéventaine," pp. 143-144; on the liquescent virga, ibid., pp. 146-147. The appearance of the later system is well displayed in the facsimile edition of Ben34 (Paléographie Musicale 15).

[126] Hourlier and Huglo, "Notation bénéventaine," pp. 107-109 (custos), 110-111 (staff), 111-113 (clefs).

[127] B-flat is not marked by a coloured rule.

[128] The following noted musical items end with a custos: **22** (Int. 4r), **28** (Gr. 5r), **39** (All. 6r), **46** (Hymn. 9r), **47** (Int. 9r), **50** (Gr. 9v), **57** (Int. 11r), **63** (Off. 12v), **77** (Int. 14r), **80** (Gr. 14v), **87** (Int. 16r), **91** (All. 17r), **93** (Off. 17v), **95** (Com. 17v), **97** (Int. 18r), **119** (Gr. 23r), **120** (Tr. 23v), **122** (Off. 24r), **124** (Com. 24v), **127** (Int. 24v), **130** (Gr. 25v), **133** (Off. 26v), **145** (Com. 31r), **147** (Int. 31v), **151** (Off. 32v), **153** (Com. 33r), **175** (Int. 39r), **179** (Tr. 41v), **181** (Off. 48r), **196** (*Lancea* 51r), **199** (Ant. 51v), **201** (Ant. 51v), **212** (Com. 55r), **218** (All. 56r), **220** (Off. 56v), **222** (Com. 56v), **229** (Off. 58r), **231** (Com.

may on occasion result from an excessively faithful copying of an exemplar provided with communion and offertory verses.[129] For the psalm of the introit followed by a repeat of the introit verse, or for the alleluia verse followed by a repeat of the jubilus, the hanging "direct" probably marks the opening note of the unwritten but assumed melody to follow.

The similarity with Ben34 in the appearance of the neumes and clefs would suggest a date of the twelfth century for the Dubrovnik missal, contrary to the later indications of the script. Nonetheless, the evidence of other noted Dalmatian manuscripts datable through the analysis of their texts or scripts confirms the existence at late dates of notational forms and systems discarded long before in Italy.[130] The presence of a notational system archaic in relation to contemporary southern Italian sources is consistent with other, well-known delays in the spread of liturgical developments from southern Italy to Dalmatia.[131]

ORIGIN AND DATE

The analysis of the script of the Oxford manuscript has suggested a date in the late thirteenth century and a place of origin in Dalmatia, more specifically

---

58r), **241** (Int. 59r), **244** (All. 59v), **263** (Com. 62r), **265** (Int. 62v), **268** (All. 63r), **273** (Com. 64v), **275** (Int. 64v), **284** (Com. 66r), **286** (Int. 66r), **292** (Gr. 67v), **293** (All. 67v), **295** (Off. 68r), **299** (Int. 68v), **305** (All. 69v), **309** (Int. 70r), **312** (Gr. 71r), **313** (All. 71r), **315** (Off. 71v), **317** (Com. 71v), **348** (Int. 75v), **352** (Tr. 76r), **366** (Int. 76v), **374** (Com. 77v), **386** (Int. 78r), **395** (Off. 80r), **397** (Com. 80r), **409** (Int. 80v), **416** (Com. 81v), **425** (Off. 91v), **437** (Int. 93v), **441** (All. 94v), **445** (Com. 95v), **450** (Gr. 82r), **452** (Off. 82r), **456** (Int. 82v), **463** (Com. 83v), **473** (Com. 85v), **478** (Gr. 86v), **479** (All. 86v), **507** (Int. 89r), **511** (All. 90r), **548** (Int. 99r), **551** (Gr. 100r), **553** (Off. 100r), **557** (Int. 100r), **561** (All. 101r), **563** (Off. 101r), **565** (Com. 101v), **590** (Com. 104r), **598** (Int. 106r), **603** (Off. 108r), **605** (Com. 108r), **607** (Int. 108r), **610** (Gr. 107r), **612** (Off. 107v), **617** (Off. 110r), **634** (Off. 111v), **638** (Com. 111v), **642** (Int. 112r), **649** (All. 113r), **657** (Com. 114v), **665** (Off. 116r), **672** (All. 116v), **680** (Int. 117v), **683** (Int. 118r), **689** (Off. 119r), **691** (Com. 119r).

[129] For the communion verses of early sources, see Apel, *Gregorian Chant*, p. 311 n. 1; for offertory verses, ibid., pp. 363-375, and Carolus Ott, *Offertoriale sive versus offertorium* (Tournai, 1935).

[130] MSS postdating Ben34 (s. xi/xii), but without its notational developments, include DaB (s. xii); Dubrovnik, Franjevački Samostan Mala Braća, 5310/230/7, 8 (pontificale, s. xii, see above n. 54); and DaK (s. xii). Although the notation in DaK is generally less developed, the noted gospel on fol. 64r-v has all the features of Ben34 and the Oxford MS: clefs, rules, and directs.

[131] The adoption of liturgical practices is discussed by Saxer, "Introduction du rite latin," pp. 163-193. On the connections between culture and script, see Viktor Novak, "La paleografia latina e i rapporti dell'Italia meridionale con la Dalmazia," *Archivio Storico Pugliese* 14 (1961) 145-160. The archaic tendencies of Dalmatian cult are discussed in Hesbert, "Tradition bénéventaine," p. 399 n. 1, with reference to the Dubrovnik missal.

in Dubrovnik or Kotor according to the paleographer Viktor Novak.[132] From
the presence of a mass for the martyrs Lawrence, Peter, and Andrew, the
manuscript was considered a product of the diocese of Dubrovnik by
Bannister and Loew.[133] Later, it came to be associated with the Benedictine
monastery of St. Maria in Rožat ("in Rabiata" *Lat.*) near Dubrovnik by Van
Dijk, Ostojić, and Pächt and Alexander, but most recently Miho Demović
has challenged this attribution, quite rightly pointing out that the liturgy of
the Missal is more appropriate for a cathedral church than for a monastery.[134]

The paleographic attribution to thirteenth-century Dalmatia is general and
uncontested, but the specific dating of the manuscript from the contents of
the Missal is much less secure. Citing an inscription on the tomb of the
martyrs Lawrence, Peter, and Andrew in a church of Dubrovnik dedicated
to them, Filippo Ferrari in his *Catalogus generalis sanctorum qui in
Martyrologio Romano non sunt* (Venice, 1625) gave a date of 1249 for their
martyrdom in Kotor; Jacopo Coleti, the continuator of Daniel Farlati's
Illyrici sacri (1751-1819), later established a claim for a much earlier
martyrdom from a reference to the translation of the martyrs to Dubrovnik
in 1026 in the twelfth-century Chronicle of Miletius of Ragusa.[135] However,

---

[132] Novak, *Latinska Paleografija*, p. 151 n. 32c.

[133] Bannister's correction in Madan, *Summary Catalogue*, 5: xvi, first suggested this origin.
Loew, *Beneventan Script*, 1: 64, and *Scriptura Beneventana*, 2: pl. 94, argues the point most
fully and convincingly.

[134] Attributions to S. Maria in Rožat: Van Dijk, *Handlist*, 1: 127; Ostojić, *Benediktinci u
Hrvatskoj*, 2: 433; Pächt and Alexander, *Illuminated Manuscripts*, 2: 9; and Andreis, *Music
in Croatia*, p. 16.
   The assignment to the cathedral is given by Demović, *Musik und Musiker*, p. 368, basing
his conclusion on the rubrics citing the Palm Sunday station before the city gate (**171** fol. 37v)
and the role of the bishop in the Good Friday liturgy (**204** "*Qua finita incipiat episcopus,*" fol.
52r). As I will argue shortly, Demović is probably correct, but neither of his points is
conclusive, in particular the reference to the bishop, since monastic scribes often appear to
copy rubrics with scant attention to topicality. The famous arguments for the transmission of
MSS of the Roman-German Pontifical of the Tenth Century are based, for instance, on the
copying of the episcopal oath of obedience to the archbishops of Mainz or Salzburg, even in
books patently intended for other dioceses (e.g., McP with its oath of obedience to the
archbishop of Mainz): see Vogel and Elze, *Pontifical romano-germanique*, 3: 9.

[135] The martyrs are mentioned in *Acta sanctorum*, *Julii*, 2: 450 (7 July), citing with
scepticism the notice in Filippo Ferrari, *Catalogus Generalis Sanctorum qui in Martyrologio
Romano non sunt* (Venice, 1625), pp. 277-278 (the martyrdom at Kotor of Lawrence, Peter,
and Andrew in 1249); but, for reference to the translation of the martyrs in 1026, Coleti,
Illyrici sacri, 6: 13-16, 47, 430-432, cites the verse-chronicle of Miletius of Ragusa (1153):
   Post modicum tempus Vitale Metropolitano,
   Judice Lampridio, residentibus urbe Rhagusa
   Corpora Laurentii, sed non illius adusti,
   Andreae, Petri, non Christi discipulorum
   Coelitus ostensa, simul translata fuerunt;
   Cum quibus et Blasi constat caput esse repertum,

the date of the martyrdom of Lawrence, Peter, and Andrew is of secondary concern in the discussion of the manuscript, which may be considered to postdate 1249 on paleographic grounds alone. Other liturgical features, such as masses for the Transfiguration, Margaret, and a full series of votives, also suggest a late date for the Missal, but none of these is conclusive. Indeed, "dating by the script" remains our only recourse, no matter how problematic the exercise must be with a script as little known as the later Dalmatian Beneventana.

Equally difficult and no less critical is the localisation of the manuscript suggested by the mass for the Dalmatian martyrs. Since support for their cult in Dubrovnik is based not only on the Chronicle of Miletius but also on the existence there of a church dedicated to them, Dubrovnik has appeared the likely place of origin for the manuscript. In general, the saints afforded masses in the Missal support this attribution: important foundations in the city included churches and buildings named for Peter, Blaise, Stephen, Nicholas, Lawrence, Thomas, James, the Saviour, Clare, and Mary (the Cathedral), as well as the three Dalmatian martyrs.[136] Blaise in particular is commemorated in the diocese with an important procession; the cathedral also houses an eleventh-century reliquary of the saint.[137] Except for the Saviour and Clare, all the remaining principal patrons of Dubrovnik are represented in the Missal. On the other hand, none of the feasts preclude Kotor as the original home of the manuscript. A positive indicator, which is found in other manuscripts from Kotor, would have been a prominent place for the town's patron, Trifon (3 February).[138] Unfortunately, there is a lacuna

---

Millenus vicenus sextus cum foret annus. (Coleti, p. 13)

The questionable authenticity of Miletius, however, must cast some doubt on the chronology of the martyrs; on Miletius, see Giorgio Gozzi, *La Libera e sovrana Repubblica di Ragusa 634-1814* (Rome, 1981), p. 33.

[136] The church of Peter, Andrew, and Lawrence appears in a fifteenth-century map reproduced in Gozzi, *Repubblica di Ragusa*, plate 1 after p. 32. The churches of Dubrovnik are described by Bariša Krekić, *Dubrovnik in the 14th and 15th Centuries* (Norman, 1972), pp. 64-78, 85-88; Gozzi, *Repubblica di Ragusa*, pp. 61-63; and Coleti, *Illyrici sacri*, 6: 28-29. The modern churches of Dubrovnik are given with brief histories of their foundations in *Opći Šematizam Katoličke Crkve u Jugoslaviji cerkev v Jugoslaviji, 1974* (Zagreb, 1975), pp. 239-263.

[137] Maria Vittoria Brandi et al., "Biagio, vescovo di Sebaste in Armenia," *Bibliotheca Sanctorum*, 3: 157-170 at 160, 169; and Coleti, *Illyrici sacri*, 6: 27-28, 48-50, for the cult and its feasts. Other important feasts in Dubrovnik include the Decollation of John the Baptist (Index of Patrons in the *Bibliotheca Sanctorum*, 12: 334).

[138] On Trifon, see Agostino Amore, "Trifone e Respicio," *Bibliotheca Sanctorum*, 12: 656-657; the dedication of the cathedral of Kotor to Trifon in 1166 is described by Anton Mayer, "Catarensia," *Zbornik Historijskog Instituta Jugoslavenske Akademije* 1 (1954) 95-110. It should be noted that the liturgy of Triphon is omitted also in DaB, the Missal of Kotor, despite dedicating a fullpage miniature to the saint.

in the manuscript at the point his feast would be expected (fols. 74v-75r). Thus the attribution to Dubrovnik remains probable, but the claims of other Dalmatian cities, especially Kotor, cannot be entirely discounted.

If the general assignment to Dubrovnik is likely, the specific attribution in the literature to the Benedictine monastery of St. Maria in Rožat outside Dubrovnik is difficult to accept.[139] Not only is there no explicit mention of the monastery in the manuscript but the contents of the Missal are more suitable for secular than for monastic use. The presence of masses for Benedict and Scholastica in the Missal would be expected in a monastic rite, but the universality of their cults in both monastic and secular churches makes this evidence indecisive. The antiphon sung outside the city during the Palm Sunday procession (**171**) is a tantalising indication of use but ultimately misleading: while St. Maria was located *extra muros*, so also were the monastery of St. James, located southeast of Dubrovnik on the road to Srebreno, and the important Benedictine foundation on the nearby island of Lokrum.[140] Moreover, the procession need not have started at a monastery (even if it had, would the celebrant have been a resident of the monastery, supplied with his own missal or the bishop himself, using a diocesan book?). On the other hand, clear indication of a secular rite is the inclusion of the Genealogy of Luke followed by the hymn *Te deum* during the vigil of Epiphany (**45-46**). In secular churches and among the Dominicans, the chanting of the Genealogy of Matthew during the Christmas vigil and the

---

[139] Demović, *Musik und Musiker*, p. 368. Although Demović has presented a more likely alternative, his arguments may not be generally available: the entire issue will, therefore, be reviewed here.

The foundation of S. Maria in Rožat by monks of Monte Cassino in 1123 and its connections with the motherhouse are described by Novak, "Paleografia latina," pp. 151-152; Ostojić, *Benediktinci u Hrvatskoj*, 2: 432-435; and Bloch, *Monte Cassino*, 1: 417-418. The account of the foundation is given in the *Chronica monasterii Casinensis*, 4: 80 (ed. Hoffmann, MGH Scriptores 34: 544), where a Dalmatian noble, Savinus, requests that the abbot of Monte Cassino assist in the establishment of a Dalmatian house. The abbot responds, with special provisions for the transmission of books: "Abbas autem nichil moratus, tres de hoc monasterio ibidem fratres direxit, divinarum scripturarum codices et ecclesiasticum apparatum illis habundantissime tribuens," and a monastery is established at Rožat ("Rabiata") near Dubrovnik with papal and episcopal permission and adequate supporting staff and material.

[140] The foundation from Tremiti in 1023 of the monastery of St. Benedict (later S. Maria) on Lokrum is described in *Codice diplomatico del monastero benedettino di S. Maria di Tremiti (1005-1237)*, ed. Armando Petrucci, 3 vols., Fonti per la Storia d'Italia 98 (Rome, 1960), 2: 27-30 (no. 9); or *Codex diplomaticus regni Croatiae, Dalmatiae et Slavoniae*, 2nd edition, vol. 1, ed. Marko Kostrenčić, Jakov Stipišić, and Miljen Šamšalović (Zagreb, 1967), pp. 62-65 (no. 45). The later history of the house is given by Ostojić, *Benediktinci u Hrvatskoj*, 2: 420-430. The monastery of St. James on the road to Srebreno (*S. Jacobi de Visgniza*) is described in Ostojić, 2: 461-465. For other monasteries of Dubrovnik and its region, see Ostojić, 2: 417-486.

Genealogy of Luke at Epiphany functioned as the last lection of the third nocturn of matins before the *Te deum*. In monastic uses the Genealogy of Luke was sung on the Sunday after Epiphany, and both Genealogies followed the *Te deum* as the first of four lections of the third nocturn.[141]

Contents

The Oxford manuscript contains a missal with propers for the masses of the principal feasts of the Temporal and Sanctoral as well as masses for a Common of Saints and a series of votives. Nonetheless, it seems never to have had any of the Lenten ferias nor, since the seventeenth Sunday after Pentecost follows the eleventh Sunday after Pentecost without a break, a complete series of Sundays after Pentecost. Besides the mass-texts, it includes several other ceremonies: the Genealogy chanted during the vigil of Epiphany (**45-46**), the distribution of ashes on Ash Wednesday (**112-115**), the Palm Sunday procession (**163-174**), the Veneration of the Cross on Good Friday before the Mass of the Presanctified (**196-205**), the Blessing of the Pascal Candle on Holy Saturday (**206-208**), and a blessing of grapes (**547**). The general order of the masses is standard: Temporal followed by Sanctoral, followed by votives. Remarkable, however, is the strict separation of these elements: even the saints of Christmas week—Stephen, John, and the Innocents—usually found in the Temporal, are placed in the Sanctoral.[142]

---

[141] Hughes, *Medieval Manuscripts*, p. 62; and Joseph Pothier, "Chant de la Généalogie à la nuit de Noël," *RdCG* 6 (1897-1898) 65-71.

Witnesses to secular practice include John N. Dalton, *Ordinale Exon. (Exeter Chapter MS. 3502 collated with Parker MS. 93)*, 2 vols., HBS 37-38 (London, 1909), 1: 91; and Walter Howard Frere and Langton Brown, *The Hereford Breviary from the Rouen Edition of 1505 with Collation of MSS.*, 3 vols., HBS 26, 40, 46 (London, 1904-1915), 1: 197. Dominican practice is contained in the Ordinal of Humbert of Romans, 1254-1259 (Rome, Santa Sabina, Archivio generale dell'Ordine Domenicano, XIV.L.1; partial edition by Francisco M. Guerrini, *Ordinarium juxta ritum sacri Ordinis Fratrum Praedicatorum* [Rome, 1921], p. 15).

The Genealogy of Luke for the vigil of Epiphany is unattested in Louis Brou, *The Monastic Ordinale of St. Vedast's Abbey Arras (Arras, Bibliothèque Municipale, MS. 230 [907], of the Beginning of the 14th Century)*, HBS 86 (London, 1957); John B. L. Tolhurst, *The Monastic Breviary of Hyde Abbey, Winchester (MSS. Rawlinson Liturg. e. 1.*, and Gough Liturg. 8, in the Bodleian Library, Oxford)*, HBS 69 (London, 1932); and the Franciscan breviary (Stephen J. P. Van Dijk, *Sources of the Modern Roman Liturgy: The Ordinals by Haymo of Faversham and Related documents (1243-1307)*, 2 vols., Studia et Documenta Franciscana [Leiden, 1963]).

[142] The strict separation of Temporal and Sanctoral may be observed also in Mc127 (missale, s. xi ex.); and the Graduals cited in Hughes, *Medieval Manuscripts*, p. 135 n. 10: Paris, Bibliothèque de l'Arsenal, 110 (s. xiv, Paris); Graz, Universitätsbibliothek, IV 9 (s. xv, Neuberg); and IV 10 (s. xv, Neuberg); London, BL, Royal 2.B.iv (s. xii, St. Alban's); Lille,

Most of the masses have an introit, collect, epistle, gradual, alleluia, gospel, offertory, secret, communion, and postcommunion with the substitution of tracts for alleluias during Lent and the doubling of alleluias in the Easter season. Where masses have elements in common, as is frequently the case in the Sanctoral, only those proper to each feast are given in extenso; for the rest the celebrant is either provided with incipits for texts found in the Common of the Missal or must have been assumed capable of turning to the appropriate category in the Common without further reference.

Examination of the calendar, prayers, chants, and lections shows a preponderance of material with counterparts in the Romano-Frankish liturgy that formed the basis for later medieval and early modern practice.[143] There are, nonetheless, several peculiarities which distinguish the Dubrovnik missal as a book of the Beneventan regional form of the Roman liturgy.

1. Temporal

Third Lections for the Masses of Christmas (1, 15)

The Oxford manuscript contains two of the three Christmas masses, each of which has a reading preceding the epistle and separated from it by the gradual; the choices of lection (**1** Is 61: ?-2; **15** Is 52: 6-10) are generally appropriate prophecies of Christ's birth and coming.[144] Beneventan parallels are found in the twelfth-century missals of Caiazzo (Ca: Is 61: 1-2 for the second mass) and Veroli (Ve: Is 61: 1-2 for the second mass; 52: 6-10 for the third mass), and in a thirteenth-century lectionary of Trogir, Kaptolski Arhiv (Riznica Katedrale), 2.[145]

The custom of a third reading is ancient and perhaps derived from Old Beneventan practice in this instance, although the appearance of the same lections for Christmas in older Roman lection-lists suggests that the practice may have had another origin, i.e., the conservatism that preserved so many traditional features in Beneventan manuscripts retained in this case a feature

---

Bibliothèque Municipale, 26 (olim 599) (s. xiv, Lille); see also Hughes, p. 9, for the separation of Temporal and Sanctoral in the Cistercian and Dominican uses.

[143] A recent survey of the history and sources of the liturgy is presented by Vogel, *Medieval Liturgy*. For discussions of feasts and liturgical developments in the following pages, Martimort et al., *Église en prière*, will be cited in two editions, the revised edition in 4 volumes (1983-1984) and the earlier edition in one volume (1961).

[144] Since the first lection of the octave of Christmas (**27**) is listed only by incipit *Hec dicit dominus. Populus gentium* (Is 9: 2), a corresponding complete pericope was probably once present in the original MS, but it has been lost.

[145] For Ve and the Trogir lectionary, see above nn. 16 and 17.

found in the Roman source of the regional lection-list.[146] A less likely alternative is that the thirteenth-century Dubrovnik missal was dependent on contemporary Dominican practice (improbable since Dominican missals specify that the epistle should follow the first lection directly without an intervening chant).[147]

Second Collect and Secret for the Third Mass of Christmas (**14**, **19**)

The alternative collect *Omnipotens sempiterne deus qui hunc diem per incarnationem uerbi tui* (**14**) is found in all the early sacramentaries but absent in the Roman missal and most Beneventan missals, which dropped it along with many of the other early alternative prayers. That the Dubrovnik missal preserves the text is indicative of its conservatism.

The secret *Oblata domine munera unigeniti tui noua natiuitate* (**19**) is found in Gregorian and Beneventan sources in this position. Since the secret is unattested in the Veronese and Vatican sacramentaries and found on another feast in most of the Gelasians of the Eighth Century (the Gellone sacramentary excepted), a Gregorian source for the prayer, and thus for the mass-set, is most likely.[148]

Marian Mass within the Octave of Christmas (**26-34**)

The title and introit of the mass are missing due to the loss of leaves between fols. 4v and 5r. Nonetheless, exact parallels for the remaining texts in other Beneventan manuscripts, including twelfth-century missals from Monte Cassino (Vatican City, BAV, Vat. lat. 6082, = McV) and Kotor (Berlin, Staatsbibliothek Preussischer Kulturbesitz, Lat. fol. 920, = DaB), indicate that the mass is probably the regional Marian mass within the octave of Christmas. The fragmentary collect (**26**) appears to be the prayer from the octave in the Gregorian and Milanese sacramentaries (*Deus qui salutis*

---

[146] For the three-lection system of the early Roman liturgy, see above n. 12.

[147] Ordinal of Humbert of Romans (ed. Guerrini, *Ordinarium*, p. 151): "*In vigilia Natalis Domini. ... Lectio. Propter sion. Deinde sine intervallo legatur Epist. Paulus servus. ... In nocte. ... Lectio. Populus. Deinde sine intervallo legatur Epist. Apparuit gratia. ... In Aurora. ... Lectio. Spiritus Domini. Deinde sine intervallo legatur Epist. Apparuit benignitas. ... Ad Maiorem Missam. ... Lectio. Propter hoc sciet. Deinde sine intervallo legatur Epist. Multifarie.*"

O'Carroll, "Lectionary," p. 86, gives the Christmas lections of London, BL, Add. 23935 (Ordinal of Humbert, 1254-1263); and Ansgar Dirks, "De liturgiae Dominicanae evolutione," *Archivum Fratrum Praedicatorum* 54 (1984) 39-82 at 65, lists the Christmas lections of the Dominican liturgy before the reforms of Humbert.

[148] Gellone sacramentary: Paris, BN, lat. 12048; siglum: Ge, sacramentarium, s. viii ex.; ed. Jean Deshusses and Antoine Dumas, *Liber sacramentorum gellonensis*, CCL 159-159A (Turnhout, 1981); bibl.: *CLLA*, no. 855.

aeternae beatae mariae uirginitate fecunda Ha 82), while the secret (**32**) and
postcommunion (**34**) are adaptations of Gelasian prayers without counterpart in the Gregorian tradition. They are based on the Gelasian prayers for
the octave of Christmas with variant passages taken by the Beneventan
compiler from the feast of the Presentation in the Temple (Simeon; 2
February) contained in the Gregorian sacramentaries and the Gelasians of
the Eighth Century:[149]

Dubr 32	Va 50
SECRETA Presta quesumus omnipotens deus. ut hec munera *que oculis tue maiestatis offerimus. intercedente beata dei genitrice maria.* purificate mentis. intelligentia consequamur. per eundem.	SECRETA. Praesta, quaesumus, domine, ut per hanc munera, *qui domini Iesu Christi arcanae natiuitatis mysterio gerimus,* purificate mentes intellegentiam consequamur: per dominum.

Dubr 34	Va 52
POSTCOMMVNIO Presta quesumus omnipotens deus. *ut hec munera sacra que sumpsimus. intercedente beata dei genitrice semper uirgine maria.* perpetue nobis redemptionis conferant medicinam. per eundem.	POST COMMUNIONEM. Praesta, quaesumus, domine, *ut quod saluatoris nostri iterata solempnitate percipimus,* perpetuae nobis redemptionis conferat medicinam: per.

The octave of Christmas and the mass within the octave have complex
histories. At various periods the octave incorporated reflections of several
feasts: the Presentation, the Circumcision, a mass against pagan practices, a
Marian feast, and Christmas itself.[150] Since the prayers of the Dubrovnik
missal stress first the intercession of Mary, with reference to Christ's birth

---

[149] The texts adopted from the Gregorian Presentation mass are "munera quae oculis tuae
maiestatis offerimus" Ha 125 (Pa 105, Ge 197, Sg 186, Sb 256) and "intercedente beata
semper uirgine maria" Ha 126 (Pa 106, Ge 199, Sg 188, Sb 258). The phrases are joined to
replace corresponding passages in the Gelasian models for the prayers of the Dubrovnik
missal.

[150] Chavasse, *Sacramentaire gélasien*, pp. 211-212, 397-400, 651-654. An analysis with
different conclusions is presented by Moreton, *Eighth-Century Gelasian Sacramentary*, pp.
35-37.

and salvific role (**26**),[151] and only obliquely the Presentation and Purification (**32**),[152] they may be related to the primitive Marian feast of the ancient Gelasian, which was shifted to the feasts of 25 March and 15 August in the Vatican sacramentary and the Gelasians of the Eighth Century.[153] Nonetheless, there is no textual connection between the prayers of the Dubrovnik missal and the traces of the ancient Gelasian feast in the Bobbio missal, the Missale Gothicum, the Gelasian Annunciation, and the Gelasian Assumption.[154] Instead the prayers of the Missal are dependent on the octave and on the later Marian feast of the Presentation (2 February); therefore, their composition must postdate both the creation of the Gelasian mass of the octave, which supplanted the ancient-Gelasian Marian mass of 1 January, and the Roman (Gelasian/Gregorian) mass of the Presentation, which was composed after the introduction of Marian feasts by Pope Sergius I (687-701).

The musical items for the mass within the octave relate both to the Marian tradition of the octave itself and to the Presentation: the gradual *Diffusa est* (**28**), offertory *Offerentur regi* (**31**), and communion *Dilexisti* (**33**) are all adopted from the Roman Common for Virgins. The alleluia is not classified so readily:

---

[151] E.g., "salutis beatae mariae uirginitate fecunda, humano generi praemia praestitisti" as Ha 82.

[152] The vocabulary of the secret in offering the gifts is suitable for the Presentation: "munera que oculis tue maiestatis offerimus ... purificate mentis intelligentia consequamur."

[153] Chavasse, *Sacramentaire gélasien*, pp. 397-400, 651-654.

[154] Bobbio missal, nos. 124-128: Paris, BN, lat. 13246; s. viii, Bobbio; ed. Elias Avery Loew, *The Bobbio Missal. A Gallican Mass-Book*, 2 vols. in 3 parts, HBS 53, 58, 61 (London, 1917, 1920, 1924); bibl.: *CLLA*, no. 220. Missale Gothicum, no. 104: Vatican City, BAV, Reg. lat. 317; s. viii, Autun; ed. Leo Cunibert Mohlberg, *Missale Gothicum*, RED, Series maior, Fontes 5 (Rome, 1961); bibl.: *CLLA*, no. 210. On the feast in the ancient Gelasian, see Chavasse, *Sacramentaire gélasien*, pp. 651-654.

ge- ni-   trix   in- ter- ce-   de   pro no-

bis.

Figure 1. — **29** Alleluia. Post partum, fol. 5r.

The alleluia verse (**29**), also attested for the Marian mass within the octave
in McV and DaB, is used for the Presentation and for other masses
honouring Mary in the Roman tradition as represented in the GR. Its musical
setting in the Oxford manuscript is a variant of the standard Roman
melody.[155] For the alleluia and the closing of the verse on "no*bis*," the
repeated phrase of the Roman jubilus (DEFGEGFFDEDCE) is given only
once in the Dubrovnik missal, with the variant EG*E*F for EGFF; the variant
closing of the jubilus ends with a descent to E (EGAAAGFGFDEFFE)
instead of the Roman rise to E (EGAGEGFEDCDDE). In the verse, apart
from the numerous lesser variants on "*par*tum" (EFDEDD *GR*), "*uir*go"
(DFDE *GR*), "*inuiola*ta" (ECEGAEGFFDE *GR*), "*per*man*si*sti" (D/EFG
GR), "*de*i" (C *GR*), and "*interce*de" (FEDC/E *GR*), the GR repeats the phrase
GAABAGFGAFDE on "geni*trix*" and adds FFEGGFAGFE to close the
syllable. Although the standard melody for the text is attested everywhere,
and especially in Italian sources,[156] variants to the basic setting are found in
Beneventan, Aquitanian, and Sarum sources.[157]

The lections of the mass in the Dubrovnik missal are widespread in the
Beneventan region. Both are listed by incipit alone (**27** Is 9: 2; **30** Lc 2: 15),
the gospel at least referring to the gospel of Christmas (**5**). Presumably the
manuscript in its original state contained also the lection from Isaiah in
extenso for the first mass of Christmas, in which case both lections are
expressly chosen for the mass within the octave as echoes of the feast. Since

[155] Musical citations depend on the following conventions: the syllable on which a variant
occurs is given in italics followed by the melody of the MS; the c-clef marked in yellow by the
scribe of the MS is represented by a lower-case *c*; notes below are designated with upper-case
letters, notes above by lower-case letters. Notes more than an octave above or below *c* are
distinguished by a prime-sign (i.e., A'B'CDEFGABcdefgabc'd').

[156] Schlager, *Katalog*, no. E 164. The melody usually associated with the verse *Assumpta
est Maria* is adapted to the text *Post partum* in Vercelli, Biblioteca Capitolare, 161 (graduale,
s. xi ex., bibl.: Gajard, *Graduel romain*, 2: 149): Schlager, *Katalog*, no. E 209.

[157] Regional variants are cited in John R. Bryden and David G. Hughes, *An Index of
Gregorian Chant*, 2 vols. (Cambridge/Mass., 1969), al: C 2545 4245 E; alv: F -10-3-1
-3-5-30.

different lections for the masses of the octave, i.e., the mass of the Circumcision and a mass against paganism, are provided in the Campanian lection-lists,[158] the sources for the Marian mass within the octave in Beneventan manuscripts probably postdate the arrival of Gregorian and Gelasian books.

The drawing of chant from the Common, the musical variants in the alleluia, the unequivocal reference of the lections to Christmas masses, and the mixed sources for the prayers all point to a late composition for the Marian mass within the octave. It would appear to be a regional mass developed as a complement to the general Marian themes that are expressed in other masses of the season.

Vigil of Epiphany (35-44)

The mass for the vigil of Epiphany also contains Romano-Beneventan elements. The feast itself is not attested in the Hadrianum, the early Roman mass-antiphonals of the *Antiphonale missarum sextuplex* (= AMS),[159] or the Comes of Würzburg. Although Chavasse has hypothesised a southern Italian origin for the feast from its mention in the Campanian lection-lists, the earliest mass-set found in the Old Gelasian, the Paduense, and the Gelasians of the Eighth Century presents a relatively "late" structure of a single collect, secret, and postcommunion.[160]

The collect *Corda nostra* (36) and the secret *Tribue quesumus* (42) of the Dubrovnik missal are found in all the early sacramentaries except the Hadrianum and its Supplement, suggesting an ultimate source in either the pre-Hadrianum Gregorian sacramentaries or in the Gelasian tradition.[161] The

---

[158] Gamber, "Kampanische Lektionsordnung," p. 328 (Rm 15: 8-14; 1 Cor 8: 1-13), and p. 338 (Lc 2: 21).

[159] René-Jean Hesbert, *Antiphonale missarum sextuplex* (Brussels, 1935), from Monza, Tesoro della Basilica s. Giovanni, 109 (cantatorium, ca. 800, Monza, bibl.: *CLLA*, no. 1310); Zürich, Zentralbibliothek, Rh 30 (fols. 1v-13v, s. viii-ix, Chur, later at Rheinau, bibl: *CLLA*, no. 1325); Brussels, Bibliothèque Royale, lat. 10127-10144 (fols. 90-115, s. viii-ix, monastery of Mont Blandin in Ghent, bibl.: *CLLA*, no. 1320); Paris, BN, lat. 17436 (ca. 860-880, monastery of Saint-Corneille de Compiègne, bibl.: *CLLA*, no. 1330) and lat. 12050 (fols. 3-17; s. ix², Corbie, bibl.: *CLLA*, no. 1335); and Paris, Bibliothèque Sainte-Geneviève, lat. 111 (ca. 877-882, Saint-Denis for Senlis, bibl.: *CLLA*, no. 1322).

[160] Chavasse, *Sacramentaire gélasien*, p. 208.

[161] Among the mixed Gelasian-Gregorians, it is found in the collections with abundant alternative masses (e.g., Vatican City, BAV, Ross. 204; sacramentarium, s. xi, Niederaltaich; ed. Johannes Brinktine, *Sacramentarium Rossianum*, Römische Quartalschrift 25, Supplementheft [Freiburg/B., 1930]; bibl.: *CLLA*, no. 985) and in some later versions of the Missal of the Curia (e.g., the Orsini sacramentary, see above n. 95), but not in the Lateran missal edited by Azevedo (above n. 95) nor in the reformed books of the Mendicant orders that were to form the basis of the Roman missal.

postcommunion *Illumina quesumus* (**44**) is found in the same position and in the same form only in Beneventan sources; the text itself is drawn from the *alia* of the Hadrianum (Ha 98) and the Gellone sacramentary (Ge 112) for Epiphany. The postcommunions of the Paduense, the Gelasians, and some Beneventan books, including Ben33 and Ve, have a comparable incipit but replace the purpose clause ("ut saluatorem suum ... aprehendat") with the corresponding clause of the postcommunion of Epiphany in the Oxford manuscript (**56**), the Hadrianum (Ha 97b), and the Gelasians of the Eighth Century (En 113, Ge 110, Rh 97, Sg 105). The compiler of the Beneventan mass must have been faced with a deficient Gelasian or early-Gregorian exemplar to which he added an appropriate text from among the extras of the current Hadrianum.

The musical items for the vigil of Epiphany are drawn from the Gregorian masses for Christmas and the following Sunday, as in the GR. Only the alleluia *Multipharie* (**39**) differs:

Figure 2. — **39** Alleluia. Multipharie, fol. 6r.

The text *Multipharie* (**39**) is often proper to the octave of Christmas but is also found on the Sunday after Christmas in Ben34, and on the vigil of Epiphany in Ben33 and DaB.[162] The music is closely related to the Roman melody, except in the transposition of the setting for "deus ... nobis" up a fifth in the GR (i.e., the F-clef of the Oxford manuscript is a c-clef in the GR) and the truncated closing of the verse. While Ben34 agrees with the GR in transposing "deus ... nobis," other Beneventan sources present melodies similar to that of the Dubrovnik missal, indicating a regional type. The omission of the closing might at first glance appear as a mere space-saving device, since the normal practice is for the verse to close with a repetition of the jubilus. But a similar lack in the other Beneventan witnesses points again to a regional variant (even if Ben34 has transposed the closing up an interval throughout).[163]

While the gospel (**40** Mt 2: 19-23) is universal in the Roman tradition and unattested in the Campanian gospel-list, the epistle (**37** 2 Cor 4: 6-10), chosen perhaps for its reference to light and treasure, is unparalleled in the Roman tradition but related to a Campanian lection (*In epiphania mane*: 2 Cor 4: 3-18).[164] Since the connection between the Campanian and later Beneventan lection is not one of identity but of relation, the epistle probably represents only the parallel choice of an appropriate passage.

Genealogy (**45-46**)

The chanting of the Genealogy of Luke (**45** Lc 3: 21-4: 1) followed by the hymn *Te deum* (**46**) after the third lesson of the third nocturn of Epiphany, i.e., the ninth lesson of matins, has already been cited as a secular practice of wide diffusion (see above, pp. 40-41).

---

[162] Schlager, *Katalog*, no. G 389, lists witnesses to the melody and text.

[163] The original closing in Ben34 31v (GBdcBefe) has been supplemented by the addition in the left margin of a closing phrase comparable to the other Beneventan books.

[164] Gamber, "Kampanische Lektionsordnung," p. 328: the epistle *in ieiunio epiphaniorum* (Col 1: 9-19) differs from both Roman and later Beneventan.

tem cum bapti- za- re- tur omnis po- pu- lus. et

ie- su bapti- za- to et o- ran- te a- per- tum est ce-

lum. Et de- scen- dit spi-ri- tus sanc- tus cor-po- ra- li spe-

ci- e si- cut co- lumba in ip- sum. et uox de ce-

lo fac-ta est. Tu es fi- li- us me- us dilectus [illeg.]

in te compla- cu- it mi- chi. Et ip- se ihesus [illeg.]

e- rat in- ci- pi- ens qua-si an- no- rum tri- gin- ta ut pu-ta-

ba- tur fi- li- us io- seph. Qui fuit he-li. Qui fuit [illeg. ...] [illeg. ...

ma- that. Qui fu- it le- ui. Qui fu- it melchi. Qui fu- it ...]

iam- ne. Qui fu- it io- seph. Qui fu- it ma-tha-thi- e.

Qui fu- it a- mos. Qui fu- it na- ym.

Qui fu- it e- sli. Qui fu- it nag- ge. Qui fu- it

ma- that. Qui fu- it ma-thathi- e. Qui fu- it se- me-i.

Qui fu- it io- seph. Qui fu- it io- da. Qui fuit io- han- na. Qui fu- it re- sa.
Qui fu- it zo- ro- ba- bel. Qui fu- it sa- la- thi- el. Qui
fu- it ne- ri. Qui fu- it melchi. Qui fu- it ad- di.
Qui fu- it co- san. Qui fu- it el- mo- dan. Qui fuit her. Qui fu- it ihe- su. Qui fu- it
e- li- e- zer. Qui fu- it io- rim. Qui fu- it ma- that.
Qui fu- it le- ui. Qui fu- it sy- me- on. Qui fu- it
iu- da. Qui fu- it io- seph. Qui fu- it iona. Qui fu- it e- li- a- chym. Qui fu- it me-
le- a. Qui fu- it men- na. Qui fu- it ma- tha- tha.
Qui fu- it na- than. Qui fu- it da- uid. Qui fu- it
ies- se. Qui fu- it o- beth. Qui fu- it bo-

oz. Qui fu- it sal- mon. Qui fu- it na- a-

son. Qui fu- it a- min-a- dab. Qui fu- it a- ram. Qui

fu- it es- rom. Qui fu- it pha- res. Qui fu- it iu-

de. Qui fu- it ia- cob. Qui fu- it y- sa- ac.

Qui fu- it a- bra- he. Qui fu- it tha- re. Qui

fu- it na- chor. Qui fu- it se- ruch. Qui fu- it

ra- ga- u. Qui fu- it fa- lech. Qui fu- it he- ber.

Qui fu- it sa- le. Qui fu- it ca- y- nan.

[illeg.]

Qui fu- it ar- phax- at. Qui fu- it sem. Qui fu-

it no- e. Qui fu- it la- mech. Qui fu- it ma-thu-sa- le.

Qui fu- it e- noch. Qui fu- it ya- red. Qui fu-

it ma-la- le- hel. Qui fu- it ca- y- nan. Qui

fu- it e- nos. Qui fu- it seth. Qui fu- it a-

dam. Qui fu- it de- i. Hie- sus au- tem ple-

nus spi-ri- tu sanc- to re-gres- sus est ab ior-

da- ne. A- MEN.

Figure 3. — **45** GENEALOGIA SECVNDVM LVCAM, fols. 7r-9r.

The musical setting for the liturgical greeting and Genealogy (**45**) is more than a simple reciting tone with varying cadences at points of punctuation.[165] Often syllabic, but with numerous neumatic passages up to six notes in length, the arrangement divides into five sections characterised by the repetition of phrases corresponding to the clear textual divisions of the Genealogy. The first and last sections, "Factum est autem cum baptizaretur" (Lc 3: 21) and "Hiesus autem plenus spiritu sancto regressus est ab iordane" (Lc 4: 1), are marked by recurrent phrases on "*au*tem" (FGFEDEF). The second section up to "ut putabatur filius Ioseph" (Lc 3: 21-23) emphasises the division into clauses with the closing phrase DEFGEED for "apertum est celum," "celo facta est," "conplacuit michi" and "filius Ioseph," the latter three preceding the closing with stepwise ascending fourths (FB, DG, EA, respectively).

The bulk of the Genealogy consists of the seventy-five forebéars of Christ in the repeated form "Qui fuit" with the genitive (see Table 1). In the Dubrovnik missal, each succeeding group of nine "Qui-fuit" clauses is set to the same melody, related in its final cadence (EED) to the clausal closings of the opening verses. Each "Qui-fuit" clause within the sets of nine has a setting comparable to the corresponding clause in each of the other sets of nine. Since the larger repetition does not account for all the "Qui-fuit" clauses, the three remaining clauses are set to the same melodies as the three opening clauses of the other sets. The structure represents two levels of organisation: one, a melody repeated eight times, corresponding to a rather arbitrary textual division into sets of nine clauses; the other, a subdivision

---

[165] Apel, *Gregorian Chant*, pp. 204-208, gives a description of the recitation tones and punctuation of chanted prayers and lections; at pp. 207-208, Apel includes the *Te deum*, *Exultet*, and Eastertide Passions among the recitatives.

TABLE 1

Musical Structure of the Genealogy (**45** Lc 3: 21-4: 1) in the Dubrovnik Missal, the Missal of Kotor (DaK), and the Evangelistary of Montevergine (Vl5100)*

DaK	FGDF	AEA	AFAEGF	FAFG	ABFG	CDCFD	FBFA	AdFA	cABEFEF
Vl5100	EFCDCE	EFCE	DCFCFD	FAFG	ABFG	EGDGFGE	FBFA	AcABA	ABFGDFEFE
Dubr	DEB'D	FGDECF	FDFCFD	FGFG	ABFG	CDCGDFD	FBFA	AdGBFA	BFAGFCFD
	1	2	3	4	5	6	7	8	9
	Heli	Mathat	Levi	Melchi	Ianne	Ioseph	Mathathiae	Amos	Nahum
	Hesli	Nagge	Mahath	Mathathiae	Semei	Ioseph	Iuda	Ioanna	Resa
	Zorobabel	Salathiel	Neri	Melchi	Addi	Cosan	Elmadam	Her	Iesu
	Eliezer	Iorim	Mathat	Levi	Simeon	Iuda	Ioseph	Iona	Eliakim
	Melea	Menna	Mathatha	Natham	David	Iesse	Obed	Booz	Salmon
	Naasson	Aminadab	Aram	Esron	Phares	Iudae	Iacob	Isaac	Abrahae
	Thare	Nachor	Sarug	Ragau	Phaleg	Heber	Sale	Cainan	Arphaxad
	Sem	Noe	Lamech	Mathusale	Henoch	Iared	Malaleel	Cainan	Henos
	Seth	Adam	Dei						

* The melodic summaries of Tables 1 and 2 list only the pitches where the musical setting changes from ascending to descending or vice versa and not the steps in an ascending or descending series.

very precisely related to the basic textual division of the list of ancestors into repeated clauses.

Several musical settings for the Genealogy of Luke circulated during the Middle Ages, although southern Italian sources are limited to two basic melodies, one represented by the form of the Dubrovnik missal (see Table 1) and the other by the Missal of Caiazzo; the latter melody survives also in the modern Dominican missal (see Table 2).[166] The melody of the Dubrovnik missal, with the repetition of a different general melody over eight groups of nine and one of three, is found also in DaK (the Lectionary of Kotor) and a twelfth-century Beneventan gospel-lectionary of Montevergine (= Vl5100).[167] Within this tradition, the Oxford manuscript tends to elaborate many phrases more freely than either DaK or Vl5100.[168]

The form found in the modern Dominican missal and Ca, the twelfth-century Beneventan Missal of Caiazzo, divides the list of ancestors into six groups of eleven and a group of nine; each group is set to the same general melody with parallels between corresponding clauses. Only the final set varies: two internal melodic phrases are omitted so that the opening and

---

[166] The melodies of the Genealogies are described by Bruno Stäblein, "Evangelium," *MGG*, 3: 1618-1629 at 1622 and 1625-1627, including on 1626-1627 the general melody illustrated from Naples, BN, VI G 34, fols. 74v-77r (above n. 91), which is related in structure to the setting of the Dubrovnik missal.

[167] Evangelistarium of Montevergine: Vatican City, BAV, Vat. lat. 5100; siglum: Vl5100, s. xii; ed. Sieghild Rehle, "Zwei beneventanische Evangelistare in der Vaticana," *Römische Quartalschrift für christliche Altertumskunde und Kirchengeschichte* 69 (1974) 182-191; bibl.: *CLLA*, no. 1172; Loew, *Beneventan Script*, 2: 151.

Other Beneventan noted Genealogies are found in Benevento, Biblioteca Capitolare, 19, fol. 165r-v (breviarium, s. xii, Benevento, bibl.: *CLLA*, no. 460; Loew, *Beneventan Script*, 2: 19); Naples, BN, VI G 34, fols. 74v-77r; Rab, Nadzupski Ured, S.N. (fragments of an evangelistarium, s. xiii, Dalmatia, bibl.: Brown, "Second New List (II)," p. 611); Trogir, Kaptolski Arhiv (Riznica Katedrale), 3, fols. 13v-15v (evangelistarium, s. xiii, Trogir, bibl.: Loew, *Beneventan Script*, 2: 140); and Vienna, Universität, Institut für Österreichische Geschichtsforschung, nr. 4 (parts of an evangelistarium, s. xii, Trogir, bibl.: Loew, *Beneventan Script*, 2: 172).

[168] Variants in Clauses 8-9 of the Genealogy of Luke (see Table 1):

Dubr:	A	cd	cBAGA	BAGFGA	BAGF	G	FED	CDEFED
DaK:	A	cd	cBAGF		GA	cBA	BA	F	EF
Vl5100:	A	cd	cB	c	BA	B GF	GE DEF	EFE
	Qui	fu-	it	......		Qui	fu- it	......

While the basic upward movement A-d followed by descending phrases to the final (D, F, E, respectively) is the same, the Dubrovnik missal has a greater range (C-d) and tends toward stepwise progressions instead of jumps.

A similar embellishment of a basic melody has been noted by Hesbert, "Tradition bénéventaine," pp. 399-416, in his discussion of the melody of the *Exultet* in the Dubrovnik missal.

TABLE 2

Musical Structure of the Genealogy (Lc 3: 21-4: 1) in the Dominican Missal

Aecd	GcGA	AeG	FcGA	DBFGDED	AcG	BAcA	AcG	FcGA	AcGAEFC	DAD
1	2	3	4	5	6	7	8	9	10	11
Heli	Mathat	Levi	Melchi	Ianne	Ioseph	Mathathiae	Amos	Nahum	Hesli	Nagge
Mahath	Mathathiae	Semei	Ioseph	Iuda	Ioanna	Resa	Zorobabel	Salathiel	Neri	Melchi
Addi	Cosan	Elmadam	Her	Iesu	Eliezer	Iorim	Mathat	Levi	Simeon	Iuda
Ioseph	Iona	Eliakim	Melea	Menna	Mathatha	Natham	David	Iesse	Obed	Booz
Salmon	Naasson	Aminadab	Aram	Esron	Phares	Iudae	Iacob	Isaac	Abrahae	Thare
Nachor	Sarug	Ragau	Phaleg	Heber	Sale	Cainan	Arphaxad	Sem	Noe	Lamech
Mathusale	Henoch	Iared	Malaleel	Cainan						
				*	Aecd	Gca				
				*						
				*						
				*****	Henos	Seth	...	...		
									Adam	Dei

closing can fit the general structure. The opening and closing also vary between the two settings of the Dubrovnik missal and the Dominican missal. The tendency in both arrangements to maintain close links between textual and musical structure is best understood as a sign of common dependency on the simpler forms of liturgical recitation. From such origins, the various traditions of the melody of the Genealogy developed different solutions to the problems of setting and emphasis.[169]

Postcommunion of Epiphany (56)

The text of an alternative prayer from the Hadrianum (Ha 97) and the Gelasians of the Eighth Century (En 113, Ge 110, Rh 97, Sg 105) is used as the postcommunion of Epiphany *Presta quesumus omnipotens* (56) in the Dubrovnik missal in place of the postcommunion *Presta quesumus domine* of most other sacramentaries, including Beneventan sources and the Roman missal. The anomaly suggests a deficiency in a local exemplar: certainly the prayer appears not to have had any great circulation, although the text appears in the same position in Vat. lat. 4770, an eleventh-century missal in ordinary minuscule from the Abruzzi. Whatever the condition of the source for the Dubrovnik missal, the postcommunion ultimately must depend on the Hadrianum or the Gelasians of the Eighth Century.

Octave of Epiphany (67-76)

The mass for the octave of Epiphany follows the pattern of the Roman missal except for the gospel (72 Mt 3: 13-17): the musical items (67, 70, 71, 73, 75) and the first lection (69 Is 60: 1) are listed by incipit and borrowed from Epiphany; the prayers are all found in the Roman missal, though the origins of the collect *Deus cuius unigenitus* (68), secret *Hostias tibi* (74), and postcommunion *Celesti domine* (76) lie in borrowings in the Gelasians of the Eighth Century from the Old Gelasian formulary for Epiphany.[170] Most Beneventan manuscripts follow the Roman mass for the

---

[169] In contrast, the music of the *Liber generationis* of Matthew sung during the Christmas vigil in DaK exemplifies a different, less complex, response to the setting of a long, repetitive gospel. In DaK a simple recitation with a tenor and articulation at points of punctuation is repeated for each group of three clauses of the form *Abraham genuit Isaac.* Since each clause within the general group varies in its articulation, the music is developed beyond the simplest kind of recitation, where one would not expect any differentiation between individual clauses. The general structure may be summarised as $M_1M_2M_3$, $M_1M_2M_3$, $M_1M_2M_3$, ... (each M represents a clause and each number a variant melody).

[170] Chavasse, *Sacramentaire gélasien*, pp. 611-612. The collect is also attested in Ha 93 and Pa 64 among the extra prayers for Epiphany. The early Gregorian sacramentaries, including the Supplement of Benedict of Aniane, make no provision for the octave of Epiphany. The prayers, therefore, entered the Roman missal as some of the few prayers of

octave, but some provide a distinctive epistle (e.g., DaB and Monte Cassino, Archivio della Badia, 127 [= Mc127]), and others have proper musical selections (e.g., Ben35). The gospel of the Dubrovnik missal, which has no connection with the Roman tradition and is found at this place only in other Beneventan sources, may be a relict of the Old Beneventan liturgy: the reading, the account of Christ's baptism, is cited also in the Campanian gospel-list for a second mass of Epiphany.[171] From there, the transference to an octave without a proper gospel would be unexceptional.

Sundays after Epiphany (**57-66, 77-96**)

The masses for the three Sundays after Epiphany in the Missal are for the most part unremarkable: all the lections except the gospel for the third Sunday (**92** Lc 4: 14-22) are paralleled both in the early Roman list represented by the *Comes parisinus*[172] and in the Roman missal; all the musical pieces, except the alleluias (**61**, **81**, **91**), are also attested in the early Roman mass-antiphonals and in the Roman missal; and the prayers, except the secret of the first Sunday after Epiphany (**64** *Concede quesumus domine ut oculis tue*), are found in the Supplement to the Hadrianum based on the Gelasians of the Eighth Century.[173]

Gospel of the Third Sunday after Epiphany (**92**): In general, there is a correspondence in the Roman lectionary-antiphonary of Chavasse's Type III between the communion verse and gospel for the first and second Sundays after Epiphany, both being drawn from the same scriptural passages (see Table 3).[174] For the third Sunday, however, most sources have a communion

---

Gelasian origin via the mixed Gelasian-Gregorians such as the Sacramentarium Rossianum (s. xi, see above n. 161), or via later missals, postdating the reforms of the thirteenth century, to which local texts were added (e.g., the Orsini sacramentary, see above n. 95). Their source in the Beneventan mass may be either an early Gelasian MS or one of the later mixed sacramentaries.

[171] Gamber, "Kampanische Lektionsordnung," p. 336: *in stilla dni nocte* (Mt 3: 13); also *in stilla dni ad missa publica* (Mt 2: 1), the story of the Magi, as in the Roman missal.

[172] Paris, BN, lat. 9451; siglum: CoP, lectionarium missae, s. viii-ix, Monza (?); ed. Robert Amiet, "Un 'Comes' carolingien inédit de la Haute-Italie," *EL* 73 (1959) 335-367; bibl.: *CLLA*, no. 1210.

[173] The Sundays after Epiphany, Easter, and Pentecost, missing in the Hadrianum itself, were soon supplied by the Supplement of Benedict of Aniane (Deshusses, *Sacramentaire grégorien*, 1: 68-70).

Although the Supplement often differs in detail from the Gelasians of the Eighth Century, there are no clear indications in the prayers of the masses after Epiphany in the Dubrovnik missal to favour either tradition.

[174] Chavasse, "Plus anciens types," pp. 20-21.

Mirabantur omnes (Lc 4: 22) that does not match the usual gospel (Mt 8: 1-13) but instead relates to a gospel (Lc 4: 14-22) found on the second Sunday after Epiphany in some manuscripts of Class B of Type III.

TABLE 3 Gospels and Communions after Epiphany in the Dubrovnik Missal		
Sunday	Gospel	Communion
Dom. 1 post Epiph.	Lc 2: 42-52	Lc 2: 48-49
Oct. Epiph.	Mt 3: 13-17	Mt 2: 2
Dom. 1 post Oct.	Io 2: 1-11	Io 2: 7-11
Dom. 3 post Epiph.	Lc 4: 14-22	Lc 4: 22

In several Beneventan sources, including the Missal edited here, and in the Lateran manuscript examined by Tommasi (siglum L),[175] the gospel from Luke (Lc 4: 14-22) is said on the third Sunday, agreeing with the communion of the day (**95** Lc 4: 22). Since the same passage from Luke is read on the fifth Sunday of Advent in the Campanian lection-list,[176] the linking of gospel and communion on the third Sunday after Epiphany appears to be a Romano-Beneventan re-arrangement of the standard Roman lists, and not an Old Beneventan echo.

Alleluias (**61, 81, 91**):

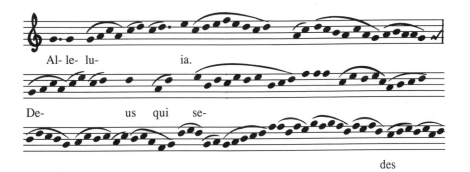

[175] Tommasi, "Lectionarius," *Opera omnia*, 5: 320; cited by Chavasse, "Plus anciens types," p. 20.
[176] Gamber, "Kampanische Lektionsordnung," p. 339.

su-   per   thro-   num   tu   iu-

di-   cas   e- quita-   tem.

Figure 4. — **61** Alleluia. Deus qui sedes, fol. 12r.

The alleluia *Deus qui sedes* (**61**) is found on the first Sunday after Epiphany only in Italian sources.[177] The text appears in the Roman missal but on another feast and with a different musical setting. As the music of the alleluia is unique and adapted to no other verse, the piece is probably a regional composition.

Al-le-   lu- ia

V. Omnis   ter-

ra a- do-   ret te   de- us et psallat

ti-   bi   psalmum di-

cat no- mi-   ni tu- o   do-   mi-

ne.

Figure 5. — **81** Alleluia. Omnis terra, fol. 14v.

The alleluia *Omnis terra adoret* (**81**) of the second Sunday after Epiphany is less unusual. While the text is not in the Roman missal among the alleluia verses, the melody is an adaptation of the setting of the alleluia *Amavit* from

---

[177] Schlager, *Katalog*, no. G 381.

the Roman Common for Doctors.[178] The combination of the text *Omnis terra adoret* and the music from the alleluia *Amavit* is attested in medieval manuscripts from many regions; perhaps the coincidence of the text of the alleluia (Ps 65: 4) with the text of the introit of the day (**77** Ps 65: 4, 65: 1-2) accounts for its universal appeal.

Figure 6. — **91** Alleluia. Timebunt gentes, fols. 16v-17r.

[178] Schlager, *Katalog*, no. E 174. The setting of the alleluias of *Omnis terra adoret* (**81**; Ben34 37v-38r) and *Amavit* of the GR differ only slightly:

Dubr:	C DEDEFGEFDDCDE E	CDFDEFGEFDDC	CDFDEFGEFDDC	E
Ben34:	C DEDEFGEFDDCDE E	CDFDEFGEFDDCDGECDFDEFGEFDDCDGEE		
GR:	C DFDEFGEFDDC DE E	CDFDEFGEFDDCEGE CDFDEFGEFDDCEGE		
	Al-le- lu-ia	....		

Dubr:	GAFGGE			DEDDC	CDE F	GAGFGG FE
Ben34:	GAFGGEE GAFGGE	FGFE		DEDDC	CDE F	GAGFGGGFE
GR:	GAGFDEE		FGFE	DEDDC		FFFGAGFG FE
	....		....	....	....	....

The chief difference between the Beneventan and Roman melodies is the Beneventan phrase GAFGGE (repeated in Ben34) for the Roman GAGFDE following the third repetition of the opening phrase (CDE/FD...DDC with a closing embellishment). Both, however, represent the general movement GAGE. Other differences between the Beneventan and Roman melodies include the incipit (Beneventan: CDED; Roman: CDFD) and the Beneventan addition of the phrase CDE before the closing sequence (FGAG...FE). The Dubrovnik missal differs from both Ben34 and the GR in omitting the final embellishment of the repeats of the opening phrase and the cadence FGFE.

The alleluia *Timebunt gentes* (**91** Ps 101: 16) of the third Sunday repeats the verse of the preceding gradual (**90** Ps 101: 16-17); in the GR it is found on the twenty-eighth Sunday after Pentecost with a related but variant melody. Although the same music is often used for other verses, this particular conjunction of music and text is found principally in Italian sources.[179]

In the Roman and Beneventan versions of the setting, the openings are similar, but instead of repeating the entire first phrase of the jubilus the Dubrovnik missal gives only a short cadence from its opening section (GAGF) and concludes the jubilus with repetitions of the same phrase.[180] Despite obvious points of similarity in the treatment of the verse among Roman and Beneventan sources, including the opening repetition of the

[179] Schlager, *Katalog*, no. E(D) 194.
[180] From GR 373-374, and Ben34 39v:

Dubr:	DFD	FGF	GAG	FABAGAcAcBGF	GAGFGDF
Ben34:*	DFDC	FGF	GAG	FABAGAcAcBGF	FABAGAcAcBGF
GR:	DFDC	FGF	GAGF	FABAGAcAcBGF	FABAGAcAcBGF
	Al-	le-	lu-	ia..........	....

Dubr:			GAGF DEF	GAGF	GAGF
Ben34:			GAGFGDEF	GFEC	CDEFGFEFED
GR:	FABAGAcAcBGF		GAGFGDEF	GFEC	CDEFGF FED
	....		....	.....	....

Dubr:	DFDC	FG	GA	AGFG	GF	FGAFGD	FGAG	GFD
Ben34:	DFDC	FGF	GA	AGFG	GF	FGAFGD	EFGF	FEC
GR:	DFDC	FGF	GAGAG	FGAGFG	FGF	FGAGFGDEFGF		FEC
	Ti-	me-	bunt	gen-	tes	no-		men

Dubr:	D		CD	D	DEFD	D DF	DECD	DEF
Ben34:	D		CD	D	DEFD	D DF	DECD	DEF
GR:	CDEFGFEDD		CB'	CDEFD	D D		DFDEC	DFGAGAGF
	tu-		um	do-	mi-	ne et	om-	nes

Dubr:	CF		FA	ABGFGAGAGFG	DFDF	CDFF
Ben34:	CF		FA	ABGFGAGAGFG	DFDF	CDF
GR:	GABcAFGAcAGF	GA		GAGFG	DFDEDCCDEFG	CDCA'
	re-	ges	ter-		re	glo-

Dubr:	F	GA	GAG		FABAGAcA
Ben34:	F	GA	GAGF		FGAGF
GR:	CD	D	FDECDFGFGAGF		FABAGAcA (repeats jubilus)
	ri-	am	tu-		am.

*Ben34 is transposed up a single note throughout, which plays havoc with the half-tones. For the sake of comparison I have transcribed the melody as if it began on D (not E as in the MS). Repeated notes have not been reproduced.

alleluia-phrase and most of the simple and neumatic syllables, Ben34 and the Dubrovnik missal form a group against the Roman setting of the GR, especially in their omission of melismas on the passage "omnes reges terre gloriam" and the lack of the closing repetition of the jubilus.

The variance between the Roman and Beneventan traditions for the Sundays after Epiphany suggests that the source for Gregorian chant in the region lacked proper alleluias for many secondary feasts, much as the Hadrianum lacked prayers for the Sundays after Epiphany and Pentecost. The response to this lack clearly seems to have sprung from a single source, accounting thus for the regional similarities in the provision of alleluias and in their musical settings.[181]

Communion of the Third Sunday after Epiphany (**95**): The choice of text (Lc 4: 22) is standard in the Roman tradition. The Beneventan musical setting differs considerably, however, from its Roman counterpart:

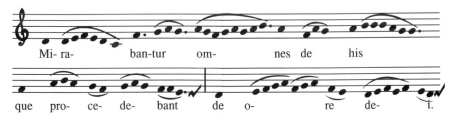

Figure 7. — **95** COMMVNIO Mirabantur omnes, fol. 17v.

The text is given a similar setting in Ben34. Since the melody is unparalleled among communions in the principal sources of early chant, it probably represents an original Romano-Beneventan composition.[182]

Secret of the First Sunday after Epiphany (**64**): Although the prayer *Concede quesumus domine ut oculis tue* (**64**) is found in several Beneventan sources as the secret for the first Sunday after Epiphany, it is attested at this position neither in the Supplement to the Hadrianum nor in the Gelasians of the Eighth Century from which the Supplement was drawn. It does appear, however, as a secret for the second Sunday after Christmas in the Gelasians, the Supplement, and the Paduense. In the Hadrianum it is used as the secret

---

[181] Apel, *Gregorian Chant*, pp. 378-381, discusses the variety among alleluias: until the eleventh century, or even later, the alleluias were not fixed in many MSS for most of the annual feasts.

[182] For melodies with a similar incipit from other categories of chant, see Bryden and Hughes, *Index*, entry D 2320 -2357 D.

for Palm Sunday and again for the Ember Saturday of September. In this case, the Beneventan tradition represented by Ben33 and Ca is based on the Gelasians and the Supplement, but an early source for the regional liturgy either provided an alternative or filled a deficiency in the idiosyncratic fashion perpetuated by the more numerous second group of Beneventan sources that includes the Dubrovnik missal.

Collect and Secret of Septuagesima (98, 104)

The collect *Preces populi* (98) and the secret *Muneribus nostris* (104) are derived from the Gregorian tradition of the Hadrianum and later Roman sacramentaries and missals; both are attested in the Vatican sacramentary and the Gelasians of the Eighth Century but on other feasts. The collect is found on the same feast in the Gelasians of the Eighth Century, but it appears there as the final prayer of the mass, the *super populum*.[183]

Ash Wednesday (112-126)

The prayers for the blessing and distribution of the ashes (112-115) on the first day of Lent are not found in the early Gregorian and Gelasian sacramentaries. Nonetheless, the prayer *Concede nobis*, which precedes the mass of the day in sacramentaries of both Gregorian and Gelasian traditions (Ha 153, Pa 127, En 276, Ge 274, Rh 193, Sg 251), is an early allusion to a ceremony before mass, probably the blessing of ashes. Later, in the Roman-German Pontifical of the Tenth Century, the prayer *Concede nobis* is explicitly the final text of the blessing of the ashes.[184] Certainly, by the thirteenth century when the Oxford manuscript was written, a series of prayers for the blessing of ashes were standard in most missals. Although identification of the opening prayer of the Dubrovnik missal (112) must be tentative due to the loss of all except three letters of the text, it probably was once the exorcism *Exorcizo te cinis* attested in several Beneventan sources.[185]

Collect of the Mass for Ash Wednesday (117): The collect *Concede nobis* (117) of the Ash Wednesday mass in the Dubrovnik missal is somewhat unusual. As has been mentioned in the discussion of the blessing of ashes, the same prayer appears in the early sacramentaries: in the Hadrianum *ad*

---

[183] The mass of Septuagesima in the Oxford MS lacks the communion and postcommunion because of damage to fol. 19r.

[184] Vogel and Elze, *Pontifical romano-germanique*, 2: 21-22 (ordo 99: 74-80).

[185] For a list of later medieval witnesses, especially the sources of the Roman missal, see Bruylants, *Oraisons*, 1: 17-18 (mass 42).

sanctam Anastasiam, i.e., at a station different from that of the mass of the day (*ad sanctam Sabinam*); and in the Paduense and the Gelasians of the Eighth Century as a separate collect before the prayers *ad missam*. The mass is provided with its own collect, *Praesta domine fidelibus*, in the early sources and in most later sources of the Roman tradition.[186] In several Beneventan missals, including Ben33 and DaB, the collect *Concede nobis* is moved to the mass, as it is in the Dubrovnik missal. In the early history of the ceremony, the two collects of the Gregorian and Gelasian sacramentaries must have created some confusion: a resolution akin to that adopted in the Beneventan books is found also in the Missal of Robert of Jumièges and the thirteenth-century Missal of Bec, where the prayer *Concede nobis* from the blessing of ashes has been adopted for the mass of the day.[187]

Sundays of Lent: Mass-sets

The prayers of the first Sunday of Lent (**128, 134, 136**) are found in both the early Gregorian sacramentaries and the Gelasians of the Eighth Century. The reading "bonis operibus" of the collect (**128**), instead of the Gelasian "bonis moribus," points, however, to a Gregorian source.[188]

In general, analysis of the prayers of the Lenten masses in the Dubrovnik missal suggests a Roman sacramentary like the Hadrianum as its original source. Only the collect *Deus qui conspiciis* (**138**) of the second Sunday and the secret *Sacrificiis presentibus* (**161**) of the fourth Sunday are common to the Hadrianum, Paduense, and Gelasians of the Eighth Century: the post-communion *Supplices te rogamus* (**146**) of the second Sunday is paralleled only in the Hadrianum;[189] the secret *Hec hostia* (**152**) of the third Sunday is found at this point in the Hadrianum and Paduense but not in the Gelasians of the Eighth Century; while the postcommunion *A cunctis* (**154**) of the third Sunday and the collect *Concede quesumus* (**156**) of the fourth Sunday are attested in the Hadrianum and the Gelasians but not the Paduense. As the common source, the Hadrianum is likely to have been the base for the Lenten prayers of the Beneventan missal. The only exception is the secret *Respice domine* (**144**), which is found in Gregorian, Gelasian, and Beneventan

---

[186] Va has two completely different collects (Va 89: *Inquoata*, 90: *Fac nos*). Later medieval missals are listed by Bruylants, *Oraisons*, 2: 39 (no. 117).

[187] Rouen, Bibliothèque Municipale, 274 (Y 6), ed. Wilson, *Missal of Robert of Jumièges*, p. 61; and Paris, BN, lat. 1105; missale, ca. 1265-1272, Bec; ed. Anselm Hughes, *The Bec Missal*, HBS 94 (London, 1963), p. 23. In the Missal of Robert of Jumièges, the second collect *Praesta* is listed as an alternative.

[188] Moreton, *Eighth-Century Gelasian Sacramentary*, pp. 55-56.

[189] See also Va 1371 among the *alia*.

traditions (both Italian and Dalmatian) as the secret of the Friday in the third week of Lent: its use in the Dubrovnik missal as the secret for the second Sunday must be counted idiosyncratic.

Musical Items of Lent

The early mass-antiphonals (AMS) do not provide a tract for Ash Wednesday. By the tenth century, however, the tract *Domine non secundum* (**120**) is widely attested for the mass.[190] The division of this tract in the Oxford manuscript into three sections by the rubric "alia" is curious: could it possibly relate to modifications of the text for the intended repetition of the tract on the second, fourth, and sixth ferias of Lent until the Wednesday of Holy Week ("per totam XLa" **120**) or is it nothing more than a reference to "verses"? The purpose of the rubric is unclear.

The mass of the first Sunday is for the most part unexceptional; only the shortened form of the tract *Qui habitat* (**131**) differs from the Roman missal. Since a similar truncated version, lacking Ps 90: 6-7, 11-16, appears in Ben34 it may represent a regional form, although the full tract is found in most Beneventan books.

Second Sunday of Lent (**137-146**): The distinctive Romano-Beneventan provision of musical pieces for the second Sunday of Lent has been re-marked.[191] With the exception of the communion *Qui biberit* (**145**), the mass of the Dubrovnik missal corresponds to the regional model.[192]

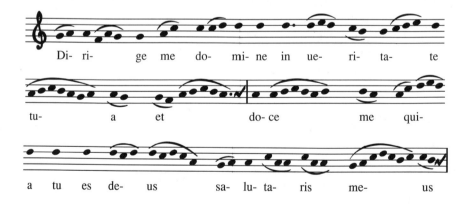

Di- ri-   ge me do- mi- ne in ue- ri- ta-   te
tu-   a   et   do- ce   me   qui-
a tu es de- us   sa- lu- ta- ris me-   us

---

[190] Apel, *Gregorian Chant*, p. 313.
[191] See above p. 22.
[192] Hesbert, "Tradition bénéventaine," Table at pp. 220-221.

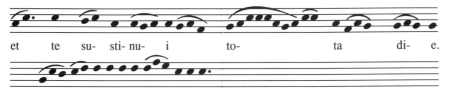

et   te   su- sti- nu- i   to-   ta   di-   e.

Ps. Ad   te   domine   leuaui.

Figure 8. – **137** INTROITVS Dirige me, fol. 27r.

The introit *Dirige me* (**137**), based on Ps 24: 5, has been set to an original
Romano-Beneventan melody.[193] Although there are similarities between the
melodic incipit and some introits and communions of the seventh mode (*In
virtute, Probasti, Dicite*) and between the closing of the antiphon on "tota
die" and the closing of the introit *Inclina* of the GR, also on "tota die," the
passages connecting either end and the structure of the antiphon as a whole
are unique. A distinguishing variant within the regional tradition is the
musical phrase on "tota die" and the corresponding psalm tone: most
manuscripts end the antiphon on "to*ta die*" with GFAG GAG G, followed
by the psalm tone of the second mode, though some have the psalm tone of
the eighth mode. A second general group ends the antiphon with *A*GFAF
GAG G; most in this group have the psalm tone of the eighth mode, but a
few adopt the psalm tone of the second mode. The Dubrovnik missal has the
setting of the second group for the explicit of the antiphon, but uses the tone
of the seventh mode, a feature paralleled only in the Tonary of Monte
Cassino 318.

Qui con-   fi- dunt   in   do-   mi- no   si-

cut   mons   sy-   on   non   com- mo-ue-   bi-   tur

in   e-   ter-   num .   V. Qui-a   non   de-

re- lin- quet

---

[193] Hesbert, "Tradition bénéventaine," pp. 235-236, presents the following analysis.

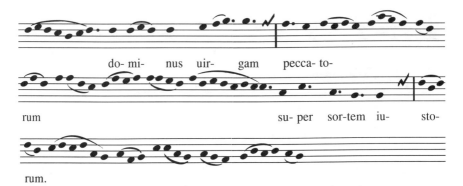

do- mi-   nus uir- gam   pecca- to-

rum   su- per sor-tem iu-   sto-

rum.

Figure 9. − **140** GRADVALE Qui confidunt, fols. 27v-28r.

The gradual of the second Sunday of Lent is a Romano-Beneventan adaptation of the text *Qui confidunt* (**140**) to the melody of the gradual *Miserere mihi* for the Wednesday of the third week of Lent in the GR.[194] Since the structure of the psalmic respond is similar in *Miserere mihi* and *Qui confidunt*, the adaptation of the melody involves few dislocations:

Dubr	GR
Qui confidunt in domino,	Miserere mihi domine,
sicut mons syon;	quoniam infirmus sum;
non commouebitur in eternum.	sana me Domine.

On the other hand, the differences in syllabification and grammatical forms between the second verses *Conturbata sunt omnia* (GR) and *Quia non derelinquet* (**140**) are reflected in melodic repetitions and omissions in the adapted arrangement of the latter.[195]

The prosula on the melisma of "Memento" in the tract *Confitemini* (**141**) of the Missal is found also in Ben34: text and melody are inserted in both manuscripts after the full melisma on "Memento."[196] The text of the prosula is non-biblical and reminiscent of many prayers, including the canon of the mass, in its vocabulary and structure. Although the tract itself is found in the Roman tradition with the same melody, the Dubrovnik missal and Ben34 show common variants against the Roman melody on "domino quoniam bonus" and "misericordia" (see the *apparatus musicus*).

[194] Hesbert, "Tradition bénéventaine," p. 236.

[195] Roman verse: "Conturbata sunt omnia ossa mea: et anima mea turbata est valde" with variants in the long melismas on "derelin*quet*" Dubr] "conturba*ta*" GR; "pecca*torum*" Dubr] "ossa me*a*" GR; and the omission in the Dubrovnik missal of the melisma in the GR on "anima me*a*."

[196] Costa, "Tropes et séquences," p. 304, remarks on the unusual southern Italian practice of troping the tracts of Lent.

... Prosa. Me-men- to que-su- mus rex xpi- ste fa- mu-los-

que tu- os et nos e- ri- pi- as a mor- te a- ni- me at-

que te po- scen- ti- bus.

Figure 10. — **141** PROSA Memento, fol. 28v.

The offertory *Exaltabo te* (**143**), a straight-forward adoption of the Roman offertory of Ash Wednesday, is the choice of most Beneventan books for the second Sunday of Lent.[197] The transposition of the melody down a fifth in the Dubrovnik missal compared to the GR should be considered of merely graphic significance. The apparent variants between the minor and major thirds on "susce*pi*sti" (B′DFDB′] FAcAF GR), and "*me nec*" (B′D] FA GR) probably suggest only that the Beneventan cantor understood B′-flat for the B′-natural of the manuscript, since the scribe rarely marks B-flat, even when otherwise expected. The clef is implied, however, from the transposition of the melody up a fifth in Ben34, as in the GR. In the latter instances, the need for an accidental has been removed without damaging the intervals of the melody, while the ambiguity of the Oxford manuscript has been avoided.[198]

The communion *Qui biberit* (**145**) will be discussed in the following section.

Communions of Lenten Sundays (**145, 153, 162**)

The communion *Passer inuenit* (**153** Ps 83: 4-5) of the third Sunday is

[197] Hesbert, "Tradition bénéventaine," p. 236: approximately a third of the sources give the offertory *Patres nostri* arranged to the melody of *Confirma hoc* of Pentecost.

[198] Hesbert, "Tradition bénéventaine," p. 210: "Mais comme les manuscrits bénéventains n'ont pas l'habitude d'indiquer les bémols, il n'est pas étonnant qu'on ait pu le chanter sans qu'il fût écrit." Apel, *Gregorian Chant*, pp. 157-165, argues that the basis for such transpositions lay in the need to accommodate pre-existing chromatics: thus, the Oxford MS could represent a copy of an early stage when accidentals were not marked since the purpose of the notation was more mnemonic than instructive. But, given the fact of regional transmission and development, it may represent instead a legitimate variant based on differences arising in the adaptation of oral to written traditions where earlier graphic ambiguities took on canonical status. In either event, the notation would have the same appearance, only its interpretation would differ.

shared with the Roman tradition. Its melody, however, presents several
regional variants:

Figure 11. − **153** COMMVNIO Passer inuenit, fol. 32v.

The melody is classified in the second mode with its final on A in the GR
and Ben34. In the Dubrovnik missal, however, the music is at points a fifth
lower and at other points a fourth lower, presenting some alterations in the
melody and modality. The final on e in the Oxford manuscript and its
ambitus (with exceptions) from E-e place it in the third mode.[199] The Roman
transcription using both B-flat and B-natural is perhaps a graphic attempt to
provide a structure admissible to medieval theorists for a chromatic formula
with E-flat that existed before the development of notation.[200] In the Oxford
manuscript, however, the scribes found different solutions. The phrase on

---

[199] The identification of the mode of the Romano-Beneventan melody is given by Hesbert,
"Tradition bénéventaine," pp. 212-213, citing PuV and Montpellier, Bibliothèque Universitaire (Faculté de Médicine), H 159 (tonarium, s. xi, Dijon; facs. ed. André Mocquereau,
Antiphonarium tonale missarum, XIᵉ siècle, 2 vols., Paléographie Musicale 7-8 [Solesmes,
1901]; bibl.: *CLLA*, no. 1365).

[200] Apel, *Gregorian Chant*, p. 159.

"pul*los*" (B♭dc) in the GR, which would have been E♭GF in the Oxford manuscript, has been written FAG to preserve the relation of pitches, thus representing a difference of a fourth between the Roman and Beneventan traditions. Other phrases show transpositions of a fifth to reposition the pitch E on B (e.g., "de*us*": FEF] cBc GR). The transpositions also produce several variants, as in the opening "*Passer*," where the Roman notation cf would require f-sharp to be equivalent to the GB of the Dubrovnik missal. In this instance, the transposition up a fourth in Ben34, to ce, points to a regional melody, which begins with an ascending major third. The many variants between the Beneventan and Roman traditions may, in such cases, be differing responses to the need to represent pre-existing melodies with later notational systems.

Evangelical communions: The communion *Qui biberit* (**145** Io 4: 13-14) of the second Sunday of Lent and *Lutum fecit* (**162** Io 9: 11) of the fourth Sunday both correspond to the distinctive, Old Beneventan gospels of their respective Sundays (**142**, **159**). The same agreement is found in Ben33, which also retains the Old Beneventan gospels. Other Beneventan sources have the communion *Redimet* with a Romano-Beneventan setting for the second Sunday.[201] In most Beneventan sources, and in the Roman missal, *Qui biberit* is the communion of the Friday after the third Sunday of Lent. The Beneventan version, however, including the communions of the second Sunday in Ben33 and the Dubrovnik missal, presents variants both textually and musically.[202] While the text of the communion in the Oxford manuscript agrees with the Roman version in reading "dabo ei" instead of the Beneventan "dabo vobis," its musical setting is in agreement throughout with the Beneventan variants on "aquam," "dabo," "Dominus," "fiet in eo fons aquae," and "vitam."[203]

The communion *Lutum fecit* (**162**) of the fourth Sunday in Ben33 and the Dubrovnik missal is attested elsewhere in Beneventan and Roman sources on the Wednesday after the fourth Sunday of Lent.[204] The Beneventan musical setting, however, is regional and differs from the standard Roman melody:

Lu-   tum fe-   cit   ex   pu-   to   do-   mi-

---

[201] Hesbert, "Tradition bénéventaine," pp. 220, 237.
[202] Hesbert, "Tradition bénéventaine," p. 227.
[203] See the *apparatus musicus* **145**, for the points of difference vs. the GR.
[204] Hesbert, "Tradition bénéventaine," p. 229.

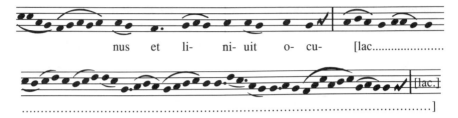

nus   et   li-   ni- uit   o- cu-   [lac.....................

[lac.]

....]

Figure 12. — **162** commvnio Lutum fecit, fol. 35v.

The Romano-Beneventan setting of the communion exists in two versions: one attested primarily in Cassinese sources, the other in manuscripts from Benevento itself. Ben34 (fol. 94r) presents both incipits:

Dubr:	DFGA	G
Monte Cassino (Ben34):	DFGA	G
Benevento (Ben34 in marg.):	FGAB	A
	Lu-	tum

In this instance, the Dubrovnik missal follows the Cassinese version. Considering the prominent role of Monte Cassino and its dependent Tremiti in the foundation and supply of the important Benedictine monasteries in Rožat and on the island of Lokrum near Dubrovnik, the association with Monte Cassino instead of Benevento is to be expected.[205]

Lenten Gospels (**142, 150, 159**)

The gospels from John for the Sundays of Lent are a distinguishing feature of the Old Beneventan liturgy that links it to the Gallican liturgies of western Europe (see Table 4).[206] Despite the general similarities, regional characteristics distinguish the gospel-lists of the Beneventan, Milanese, and Old Spanish lectionaries; indeed, there are variants among the few Beneventan sources themselves.

For the first and second Sundays of Lent, the Dubrovnik missal agrees with all the cited sources. The fragmentary condition of the manuscript for the gospels of the third and fourth Sundays, which contain the principal regional variants, makes further comparison inconclusive. In general, the Beneventan sources, including the Oxford manuscript, are related to the Milanese list for the gospels *de Abraham* (Milan: Io 8: 31-59; Ben.: Io 8: 12-59) and *de caeco* (Milan: Io 9: 8-38; Ben.: Io 9: 1-38) of the third and

---

[205] See above p. 40, for the relations between Monte Cassino and the monasteries of Lokrum and Rožat.

[206] Hesbert, "Dimanches de Carême," p. 211, with discussion of the Oxford ms.

| TABLE 4 | | | | | | |
| Lenten Sunday Gospels in the Milanese, Old Spanish, and Beneventan Liturgies | | | | | | |

| | AM: Sb | ES: Co | BEN | | | |
			Ben33	DaK	Dubr	PuZ
Dom. 2	Io 4: 5-42	4: 5-42	4: 5-42	4: 5-42	4: 5-42	lac.
Dom. 3	Io 8: 31-59	9: 1-38	8: 12-59	8: 12-30	8: []48-59	8: 12-22[]
Dom. 4	Io 9: 8-38	7: 14-30	9: 1-38	9: 1-38	9: []8-38	lac.
Dom. 5	Io 11: 1-46	11: 1-46	11: 1-54	11: 1-46	lac.	lac.

fourth Sundays; the order of the Old Spanish gospels is reversed. But the apparent connection between the Dubrovnik missal and the Milanese source for the fourth Sunday of Lent, where both read Io 9: 8-38 instead of the lection Io 9: 1-38 of Ben33, DaB (inc.), and DaK, is rendered meaningless by the lack of the folio in the Oxford manuscript that once contained the incipit. Similarly, the incipit of the gospel for the third Sunday (Ben.: Io 8: 12; Milan: Io 8: 31) is also lacking. The ultimate source for the lections of the Beneventan sources is, of course, the readings from John in the Campanian gospel-lists: the close similarities between the Campanian list—Dom. 1 (Mt 4: 1-11), Dom. 2 (Io 4: 5-42), Dom. 3 (Io 8: 12-59), Dom. 4 (Io 9: 1-38)—and the later Beneventan sources highlights the continuity of tradition in the region, especially compared to the significant, though slight, variants noted in the lists from other regions.[207]

Palm Sunday Processions (163-174)

The processions and blessing of palms that developed from patristic origins in fourth-century Jerusalem are not found in the early sacramentaries of the Gregorian tradition. They are taken into it, however, by the eleventh or twelfth century when the Lateran missal was compiled, probably from a mixed Gelasian-Gregorian sacramentary drawing on the references to the ceremony in the Gelasians of the Eighth Century and in the Roman-German Pontifical of the Tenth Century.[208] Although the ceremony is everywhere

---

[207] The Campanian list is given by Gamber, "Kampanische Lektionsordnung," pp. 346-352.

[208] Chavasse, *Sacramentaire gélasien*, pp. 234-235; Terence Bailey, *The Processions of Sarum and the Western Church*, Studies and Texts 21 (Toronto, 1971), pp. 16-17, 115-117, 166-171; *Église en prière* (1961), pp. 713-733; *Église en prière* (1983-1984), 4: 84-85.

marked by a stational character consisting of processions to the place where the palms are blessed, their distribution, the return to the church for the mass of the day, and the mass itself, the diversity among regional traditions is very pronounced, especially during the entrance into the church where mass is to be said. Some sources require a ceremony related to the entrance into a church before its dedication; others a variety of prayers and hymns: in particular, the hymn *Gloria laus* attributed to Theodulph of Orleans (d. 821) is cited frequently.[209] In this regard, even the Beneventan sources display adaptations to local geography: thus the ordo for the ceremony at Monte Cassino (McV) with its stational references to the churches of Benedict, Martin, and Stephen differs from the ordines of Apulia and Benevento (PuV; Ben34, Ben35, Ben39).[210]

The manuscript in its present condition lacks the early parts of the Palm Sunday blessing of palms, including the blessing itself. The ceremony begins in the middle of the responsory *Collegerunt* (**163**) sung in procession; lacunae before and after fol. 36r-v make it impossible to determine whether the processional chants on the folio were intended for the procession to the place where the palms were to be blessed, or for the returning procession, or for both. In the GR, the responsory *Collegerunt* precedes the blessing, the antiphons *Pueri Hebraeorum portantes* and *Pueri Hebraeorum vestimenta* are sung during the distribution of the palms, and other antiphons follow during the procession to the church. Among Beneventan and related sources, *Collegerunt* precedes the blessing of palms in some cases (Ben30; McV) and follows in others (Ben38; Paris, BN, nouv. acq. 1669).[211] The ceremony closes in the Dubrovnik missal with a series of prayers to be said before the entrance into the city and the church.

The processional chants in the Oxford manuscript are for the most part close to the Roman tradition textually and musically. Regional features are apparent only in the prosulas of the responsory *Collegerunt* (**163**) and the melody of the antiphon *Cum audisset populus* (**168**).

[lac.] Prosa. Templum et   lo- cum et   ci- ui- ta-   tem re- gnumque

[209] Edmond Martène, *De antiquis ecclesiae ritibus*, 2nd edition (Antwerp, 1737), 3: 196-223; cf. Aimé-Georges Martimort, *La documentation liturgique de Dom Edmond Martène. Étude codicologique*, ST 279 (Vatican City, 1978), pp. 465-468; and idem, "Additions et corrections à la documentation liturgique de Dom Edmond Martène," *EO* 3 (1986) 81-105.

[210] Hesbert, "Tradition bénéventaine," p. 249-251.

[211] Paris, BN, nouv. acq. 1669; missale, s. xiii, Gubbio; see Hesbert, "Tradition bénéventaine," p. 249-263, Table at 252-253.

Figure 13. − **163** RESP. <Collegerunt>, fol. 36r.

The responsory *Collegerunt* (**163**) is universally attested with this melody for the processions of Palm Sunday.[212] Distinctively Beneventan are the prosula *Templum et locum* set to the melisma at the end of the first chanting of the verse "Ne forte veniant Romani et tollant nostrum locum et gentem" and the prosula *Xpistus moriturus* set to the melisma from the following phrase "Ab illo." Both prosulas are found in Beneventan manuscripts from Benevento and Veroli (Ben30, Ben34, Ben35, Ben38, Ben39, Ve).

[212] Bailey, *Processions*, p. 167.

Figure 14. − **168** ANTIPHONA Cum audisset, fol. 36v.

The antiphon *Cum audisset* (**168**) is sung in both Roman and Beneventan traditions during the processions of Palm Sunday. Unlike the other processional antiphons, however, it shows several textual variants between the two traditions and is set to a different melody in each.[213] The Dubrovnik missal contains the Beneventan melody for the antiphon but is cut short before the points where the distinctive Beneventan textual variants are normally found. The Beneventan melody, while differing from the Roman setting of the same verse, is closely related to that of the antiphon *Cum appropinquaret*, common to both traditions though missing in the Oxford manuscript, and thus probably represents a regional adaptation of an available melody.

For the other processional antiphons, there are numerous minor variants. The Missal is particularly idiosyncratic in its presentation of several textual differences against the common text found in both the GR and Ben34: in the antiphon *Occurrunt* (**164**), the Dubrovnik missal reads "regem regum" for "ore gentes" and "sonant" for "tonant";[214] and in the antiphon *Pueri hebreorum* (**165**), "tollentes" for "portantes."[215]

---

[213] Hesbert, "Tradition bénéventaine," pp. 256-258; Bryden and Hughes, *Index*, entry G 240-2 0254 G.

[214] In the reading "laude" for "laudem," the Oxford MS and Ben34 agree against the GR.

[215] Ben35 gives only the incipit: "Pueri hebreorum"; see Vogel and Elze, *Pontifical romano-germanique*, 2: 48 l. 24 (ordo 99: 186), for the reading "tollentes."

Although what little the Oxford manuscript preserves of the processions and the blessing of palms is unremarkable, with the exception of the regional prosulas to the responsory *Collegerunt* (**163**) and the Romano-Beneventan melody for the antiphon *Cum audisset* (**168**), the entrance into the city is noteworthy for several unique features. The ceremony is structured about two "Gallican" benedictions (**169**, **172**), the first followed by a short alternative blessing (**170**) and a responsory (**171**), the second by an antiphon (**173**) and a prayer to be said during the entrance into the church and choir (**174**). The blessing of palms, which was contained in the lost folios, probably took place outside the city since the responsory *Ingrediente* (**171**) after the first benediction of the entrance-way (**169**) is explicitly to be performed "in ingressu ciuitatis," according to the rubric.[216]

The benediction *Domine iesu christe qui introitum* (**169**) is attested in the early benedictionals and later pontificals. From its origin as an *oratio in introitu monasterii* in the Gellone (Ge 2859) and Phillipps sacramentaries (Ph 1878),[217] it spread as part of the Gallican list of monastic prayers into the northern versions of the Roman-German Pontifical.[218] Although the southern Italian version of the Roman-German Pontifical does not transmit the prayer, it had entered the region by the eleventh century when it appears in the Collectarium of Vatican City, BAV, Ottob. lat. 145 (= McO), written for the use of Santa Sofia in Benevento but produced from a Cassinese exemplar.[219] The prayer is clearly appropriate for recitation at the entrance

---

[216] Cf. Vogel and Elze, *Pontifical romano-germanique*, 2: 51 (ordo 99: 191): "*cum intraverint portas civitatis omni populo cantante* Kyrie eleison, *primus scolae imponat responsum*: Ingrediente." Although the stational reference in an examplar may mention the city gates, geographic specificity in any dependent ordo must, of course, be considered with caution.

[217] Berlin, Deutsche Staatsbibliothek (Öffentliche Wissenschaftliche Bibliothek), Phillipps 1667; siglum: Ph, sacramentarium, s. viii/ix, east Frankish; ed. Odilo Heiming, *Liber sacramentorum Augustodunensis*, CCL 159B (Turnhout, 1984); bibl.: *CLLA*, no. 853.

[218] Vogel and Elze, *Pontifical romano-germanique*, 2: 360-361 (ordo 210), from Bamberg, Staatliche Bibliothek, Lit. 53, fol. 134r (pontificale, siglum: B, ca. 1012-1014, Bamberg); Eichstätt, Bistumsarchiv, "Pontificale Gundecarianum II," fol. 136v (siglum: G, ca. 1057-1075); and Vienna, Österreichische Nationalbibliothek, 701, fol. 134r (siglum: T, pontificale, s. xi¹, St. Alban's of Mainz). Also in Adolph Franz, *Das Rituale von St. Florian aus dem zwölften Jahrhundert* (Freiburg/Br., 1904), pp. 99-100; and Max Josef Metzger, *Zwei karolingische Pontifikalien vom Oberrhein*, Freiburger Theologische Studien 17 (Freiburg/Br., 1914), p. 80*. The text is found in one MS of the Supplement to the Hadrianum as an *oratio in introitu portae* (Tc 441*): Cologne, Bibliothek des Metropolitankapitels, 137 (s. ix ex., Cologne, bibl.: Deshusses, *Sacramentaire grégorien*, p. 37; *CLLA*, no. 746).

[219] On McO, see above n. 22. The benediction probably entered the region through a Gelasian of the Eighth Century or a later mixed sacramentary, e.g., F 2803 where it appears as a monastic prayer *in introitu claustri*.
Variants within the tradition provide no clear indication of the antecedent for the version in the Oxford missal (compared with Tc 441*, McO 129, F 2803, and Vogel and Elze,

into the city and has been adapted to that use in the Dubrovnik missal by the replacement of the phrase "domus istius" of earlier sources with the reference "istius ciuitatis." As will be seen with the longer benediction before the doors of the church, the compiler of the ordo for the Palm Sunday procession was not in the least averse to adopting and modifying suitable texts from other ceremonies or general lists.

The alternative blessing *Tuere quesumus* (**170**) is not found among edited sources. In structure at least it corresponds to the standard Roman formula for a bidding-prayer; the vocabulary is less usual but not without parallel in prayers of the Roman tradition. Although the origin of the prayer must remain obscure, it likely represents a local composition for the feast or perhaps a much-modified adaptation of a little-known and late composition in the universal sacramentary tradition.

Prayer before the Church (**172**): Among the most striking features of the Dubrovnik missal is the prayer *Deus cuius filius non rapinam* (**172**) to be said before the doors of the church during the Palm Sunday procession. E. A. Loew printed a transcription of part of the prayer with the facsimiles of fols. 38v and 39r in his *Scriptura Beneventana* (vol. 2, plate 94); he could find, however, no parallel for the text. With the appearance of numerous liturgical editions and concordances since the publication of Loew's work in 1929, some sources for the prayer can now be traced, even if no exact counterpart for the entire composition has yet been found.

The prayer opens addressing the Father and qualifying the reference with a relative clause based on Phil 2: 6 describing the relation of Father and Son:

> Deus cuius filius *non rapinam arbitratus est; esse se equalem deo* tibi patri sed essentialiter tecum gloriam possidet per naturam.

Pontifical romano-germanique, ordo 210 [from mss B, G, and T; see the preceding note for the sigla]): introitum] in introitu *B,G,T*; portarum] *om. McO*; et ualuas] ualuas *B,G,T* ualua *McO* saluans *Tc,F*; dum] dumque *F* dum in *McO*; splendore] splendorem *T*; totidem] -que *F,McO*; apostolorum nomina] nomina apostolorum *McO*; prompsisti] promsisti *B,G,T* promisisti *Tc,F* premisisti *McO*; dicens] *om. Tc,McO,F,B,G,T*; lauda deum tuum syon] *om. Tc,McO,F,B,G*; quoniam] quia *Tc,F,B,G* qui *McO*; benedixit] et benedixit *Tc* benedixisti *McO*; filios tuos] -is -is *B,T*; te quesumus] quesumus *T*; omnes fines] -ibus -ibus *McO*; istius ciuitatis] domus istius *G,T* domus istius sanctae Mariae *B* domus istius sancti ill. *McO* domus istius sanctae Mariae et sancti Petri *Tc* monasterii istius *F*; velociter] ut velociter *Tc,F,B,G,T*; eos] seruos tuos *F*; defendat] descendat *MaC*; illos] eos *B*; in ea] interius *omnes*; ore] ore *ante corr. T* opere *Tc,B,G,T*; dominus noster] dominus noster Iesus Christus *McO,B,G*; Qui cum ...] per *McO*.

The agreements between the Dubrovnik prayer and the *Pontifical romano-germanique* (ms T, i.e., Vienna, Österreichische Nationalbibliothek, 701, fol. 134r) at "prompsisti," "lauda deum tuum syon," "quoniam," "ore," and "dominus noster," are tantalising but cannot be considered conclusive demonstrations of relation.

The prayer continues with a series of relative clauses describing the sacrifice of the Son, beginning with a gloss on Phil 2: 6-7 ("semetipsum exinaniuit. formam serui suscipiens"). The epistle for the day in the Dubrovnik missal is Phil 2: 5-11 as in the Roman lection-list but not the Campanian list, which has 2 Cor 11: 19-31.[220] The lection of the older system did not survive among later Beneventan sources. Clearly, the prayer before the doors of the church in the Oxford manuscript must be classified as a Romano-Beneventan composition postdating the adoption of the Roman lection in the region.

After the glosses on Phil 2: 6-7, for that is what clauses such as "Non enim mundus poterat expiari a crimine nisi pretiosus sine crimine sanguis mundi domini manasset ex latere" may be considered in form and vocabulary, the author of the prayer reflects on the divinity of Christ in a series of florid phrases describing in very ornate language the luxury Christ himself spurned for his entry into Jerusalem. Although many of the more recondite words have counterparts only among prefaces and benedictions of Gallican origin,[221] I have not been able to identify a specific source for the passage. The ornaments are stripped from the prose once again when the author returns to the image of Christ's entry into Jerusalem:

> Sed uili indumentorum accinctus uelamine. *sedens super pullum asine. filium subiugalis.* celorum dominus iter carpebat puluereum. ... Nam *turba que precedebat et que sequebatur.*

The italicised words are more closely related to Mt 21: 5 ("sedens super asinam et pullum filium subiugalis") and 21: 9 ("turbae autem quae praecedebant et quae sequebantur") than to the other evangelists. The gospel narrative of the entry into Jerusalem was not read during the mass of the day but rather before the blessing of palms. Although some early witnesses cite either Mark (Mc 11: 1-10) or Luke (Lc 19: 29-38),[222] most later Roman books draw the gospel from Matthew.[223] The scriptural references are connected and followed by commentary replete with echoes of the exegetical

---

[220] Gamber, "Kampanische Lektionsordnung," p. 331.

[221] Words attested only, or more frequently, in Moeller, *Corpus benedictionum pontificalium*, than in the *Concordances et tableaux pour l'étude des grands sacramentaires*, ed. Jean Deshusses and Benoît Darragon, Spicilegii Friburgensis Subsidia 11-14 (Fribourg/S., 1982-1983), include "rutilat" (9 references *Corpus*; 1 ref. *Concordances*), "columna nubis" (3; 1), "quadrigera" (1; 0), "purpurato" (2; 0), "uernabat" (3; 0), and "fimbriis" (3; 0).

[222] E.g., Vogel and Elze, *Pontifical romano-germanique*, 2: 42-53 (ordo 99: 166, 202).

[223] E.g., Haymo of Faversham, *Ordo missalis* (ed. Van Dijk, *Sources*, 2: 234); and Ben30, Ben38, Lucca 606, and McV, among regional MSS listed by Hesbert, "Tradition bénéventaine," pp. 252-253. Andrieu, *Ordines Romani*, 5: 165-166 (ordo 50: 23.8), gives gospels from both Matthew and Mark, indicating the sharp division between the two traditions at this point.

tradition such as "salubribus exemplis," "typicis misteriorum documentis," "figurabatur," and "typicabat."[224]

All the preceding phrases were linked relative clauses or parenthetical statements related to the opening reference to the Father ("Deus cuius"). With the next clause, beginning "quem totis precordiis suppliciter exoramus," the invocation is completed and the dependent purpose clauses introduced. The first group of requests are related in language to the corpus of benedictions and prefaces but otherwise unparalleled:

> ut dignetur hanc propitius ingredi domum. et benedictionis sue gratiam in ea inmensa pietate multiplicet. Omniumque charismatum dona. sancti spiritus tribuente conferat maiestate. Aera iocundis temperet astris. terrarum germina. tranquillo imbre fecundet.

The requests that follow are, however, adaptations of two benedictions of the Gallican collection contained in the Gelasians of the Eighth Century and later in the Roman-German Pontifical of the Tenth Century. In the Gellone (Ge 2820, 2821), Rheinau (Rh 1255, 1256),[225] and Phillipps sacramentaries (Ph 1846, 1847) the two form separate halves of a *benedictio domus*; the same arrangement is continued in later pontificals.[226] The entry of the blessings into Italy is undocumented, since neither the Italian copies of the Roman-German Pontifical nor the later Beneventan missals contain them, but their appearance in a modified form in the Dubrovnik missal provides indirect evidence for the circulation of the list of benedictions in southern Italy.

The text of the Missal differs at several points from both sacramentary and pontifical traditions. For instance, the phrase "frumenti scilicet uini et olei" is transferred from the second to the first section of the prayer. Other variants appear to be the result of the adaptation of the text from the blessing of a

---

[224] Cf. *Biblia sacra cum glossa ordinaria et interlineari ... et Postilla Nicholai Lyrani*, 7 vols. (Lyons, 1545), 5: 64A, C.

[225] Zürich, Zentralbibliothek, Rh 30, fols. 27r-165r; siglum: Rh, s. viii ex., Chur; ed. Anton Hänggi and Alfons Schönherr, *Sacramentarium Rhenaugiense*, SF 15 (Fribourg/S., 1970); bibl.: *CLLA*, no. 802.

[226] E.g., Freiburg/Br., Universitätsbibliothek, 363 (pontificale, s. ix, Oberrhein; ed. Metzger, *Zwei karolingische Pontifikalien*; bibl.: *CLLA*, no. 1551); Donaueschingen, Fürstlich Fürstenbergische Hofbibliothek, olim 192 (sold to an undisclosed buyer in 1982; pontificale, s. ix ex., St. Gallen; ed. Metzger, *Zwei karolingische Pontifikalien*; bibl. *CLLA*, no. 1552); and Vogel and Elze, *Pontifical romano-germanique*, 2: 355 (ordo 191: 1-2; from Bamberg, Staatliche Bibliothek, Lit. 53, fol. 133r; and Eichstätt, Bistumsarchiv, "Pontificale Gundecarianum II," fol. 135r-v). The blessings are found also in the mixed Gelasian-Gregorian sacramentaries, although not in exactly the same form: e.g., F 2769, 2768 with the order reversed and alternative prayers added for the blessing of a house.

house to a prayer before a church. Thus the closing lines of the first section have been omitted in the Oxford manuscript ("et infra pariaetes domus istius angelus lucis tuae inhabitet" Rh 1255) and a new clause referring to the theme of the prayer has been added to the closing of the second section ("Populumque suum cum omnibus ad se pertinentibus suo pretioso sanguine tueatur").

The ceremony of the Palm Sunday procession ends with an antiphon *Turba multa* (**173**), common also to the Roman tradition, and a prayer *Ascendat oratio nostra* (**174**) that appears to be unparalleled. The vocabulary of the prayer suggests an origin in a text related to the Gelasians of the Eighth Century, especially in the connection of "uacua" and "postulatio," which is found in the Gellone sacramentary (Ge 1229) but nowhere among the Gregorian sacramentaries. But this remains a hypothetical relation and could be explained as a late composition echoing earlier phrases.

Mass of Palm Sunday (**175-184**)

The mass of Palm Sunday is Roman and Gregorian throughout: the lections (**177, 180**) follow the model of the *Comes parisinus* and the early Roman sources, not the lections of the Campanian lists (2 Cor 11: 9-31; Mc 14: 1- 15: 27; Io 21: 1-11);[227] the musical items are common to the early Roman mass-antiphonals;[228] and the prayers are attested in Roman books from the Hadrianum through the twelfth-century Lateran missal to the *Missale Romanum Mediolani, 1474* (= MRM) and the Pian missal (1570). Of some significance for determining the sources of the Dubrovnik missal is the fact that different secrets and postcommunions are found in the Gelasians of the Eighth Century and some mixed Gelasian-Gregorians,[229] and a different postcommunion in the Paduense. In this case, the Hadrianum must be understood as the ultimate source for the mass-set of the Missal.

Good Friday (**191-205**)

The ordo for Good Friday in the Oxford manuscript is deficient at the beginning and commences in the middle of the solemn prayers (**191-195**)

---

[227] Gamber, "Kampanische Lektionsordnung," pp. 349-350.

[228] Only the tract *Deus deus meus respice* (**179**) differs from the standard Roman tract in its omission of several verses (Ps 21: 18, 19, 22, 24, 32, *add.* GR). The omission of verses is not an unusual feature in the medieval transmission of tracts: the variants in the witnesses of AMS 73b attest to the practice. In the Beneventan region itself, some MSS omit the extra verses (Ben30, Ben39) while others retain them (Ben29, Ben34, Ben38, DaB, McV, Ott, PuV).

[229] E.g., F 625-631.

that come after the gospel of the Mass of the Presanctified. The prayers are
followed by the Adoration of the Cross (**196-203**), consisting of the three
major reproaches (**196**), the exposure of the cross (**197**), the adoration of
the cross by each order in turn while antiphons are sung (**198-199**), the
hymn *Pange lingua* (**200**), the minor reproaches (**201**), a prayer (**202**), and
the deposition of the cross (**203**).[230] Only the antiphon *Crucem tuam* (**199**)
is Beneventan. For the rest, the elements are common to sources from many
regions: the distinctive Beneventan adorations of the cross during fore-
masses at terce and sext have no counterpart in the Dubrovnik missal.[231]
After the adoration of the cross, the Mass of the Presanctified continues
(**203-205**).[232]

[230] The reproaches are discussed by Johann Drumbl, "Die Improperien in der lateinischen
Liturgie," *ALW* 15 (1973) 68-100; Hermann A. P. Schmidt and Helmut Hucke, *Hebdomada
sancta*, 2 vols. (Rome, Freiburg/Br., Barcelona, 1956-1957), 2: 796, 940-943.

[231] Hesbert, "Tradition bénéventaine," pp. 296-297, 300-301 (Tables: Old Beneventan and
Romanised MSS); Kelly, *Beneventan Chant*, pp. 53-58, 88-89, 170-171.

Some features are unusual, though not unknown: for instance, the prayer *Domine iesu
christe adoro te* (**202**) appears in Frankish sources first in the ninth century and, among
Beneventan sources, in Vat. lat. 7818, a twelfth-century pontifical of Chieti (fol. 11r-v:
Andrieu, *Pontifical romain*, 1: 52-61; and above n. 54). The prayer is given by André Wilmart,
"Prières médiévales pour l'adoration de la croix," *EL* 46 (1932) 22-65 at 24 (prayer of the
ninth century). Also, the rubric specifying that the Greek and Latin formulas of the reproaches
should be sung alternately by a pair of singers and the choir ("*et respondeant duo de choro.
Agios ... Chorus interim respondeat.* Sanctus ...") is paralleled by the directions of Sarum,
Rheinau, and the Dominican *Ordinarium* to have the formulas sung by two deacons and the
choir, unlike the Roman use of two choirs: for Sarum, see Hughes, *Medieval Manuscripts*, p.
261; for Rheinau, see Zürich, Zentralbibliothek, Rh 80 (liber ordinarius, s. xii in.; ed. Anton
Hänggi, *Der Rheinauer Liber Ordinarius*, SF 1 [Fribourg/S., 1957], p. 129 ll. 25-27); for the
Dominican liturgy, see the Ordinal of Humbert of Romans (ed. Guerrini, *Ordinarium*, p. 173).

Finally, the communion *Hoc corpus* (**203**) is absent from most Roman sources, indeed the
Pontifical of William Durand prohibits its use on Good Friday: Andrieu, *Pontifical romain*,
3: 586 (lib. 3, ordo 3: 24). The text and music are, however, standard for the fifth Sunday
of Lent (AMS 67b).

[232] Descriptions of the Good Friday liturgy are presented by Hughes, *Medieval Manuscripts*,
pp. 248-249; O. B. Hardison, *Christian Rite and Christian Drama in the Middle Ages*
(Baltimore/Md., 1965), pp. 128-134; *Église en prière* (1961), pp. 698-700; and *Église en
prière* (1983-1984), 4: 61-63.

fi-   ca-   mus. Ve- ni- te   om-nes   a-   do- re-

mus   xpi- sti   re- sur-rec- ti-   o- nem. Ps. Deus   misereatur   nobis.

Figure 15. – **199** ANTIPHONA Crucem tuam adoramus, fol. 51r-v.

The antiphon *Crucem tuam adoramus* (**199**) of the Oxford manuscript is related in text and music to the Beneventan translation of the Greek antiphon Τόν σταυρόν.[233] In Beneventan manuscripts preserving the Old Beneventan structure of the Good Friday liturgy, the antiphon was one of four *troparia* presented in Greek and Latin. In the early Roman mass-antiphonals, the antiphon preserves a different text:

> Crucem tuam adoramus Domine et sanctam resurrectionem tuam laudamus et glorificamus ecce enim propter crucem venit gaudium in universo mundo. *Psalm.* Deus misereatur nostri (AMS 78b).

Later Roman sources present the text with a musical setting that is considerably more elaborate than the Beneventan version. The melody of the Dubrovnik antiphon is in agreement with other Beneventan sources; textually, however, the psalm verse has its counterpart only in the Roman tradition.[234] In the Missal, the psalm of the Roman tradition has been set to the Romano-Beneventan melody of the closing "Euouae" ("seculorum Amen").

Holy Saturday (**206-208**)

The ceremony for the blessing of lights and the Paschal candle on Holy Saturday (**206-208**) is cut off in the middle of the *Exultet* (**208**) by the loss of several folios, probably once containing masses for Easter and the first three following Sundays as well as the rest of the Holy Saturday liturgy. Nonetheless, what survives in the Oxford manuscript shows much that is

---

[233] Schmidt and Hucke, *Hebdomada sancta*, 2: 795, 943-946; Wellecz, *Eastern Elements*, pp. 28-29; Hesbert, "Tradition bénéventaine," pp. 309-313; and Kelly, *Beneventan Chant*, pp. 207-214, 266.

[234] Among Beneventan sources, the psalms *Laudate* or *Cantate* are expected instead of the Roman *Deus misereatur.* The text of the antiphon in the Missal agrees with other Beneventan sources, except Ben35, which has "venite gentes" instead of "venite omnes," the Beneventan norm.

noteworthy. Although the opening blessing of lights *Domine deus pater omnipotens* (**206**) is found among the series of benedictions in the Gelasians of the Eighth Century (Ge 2848; Ph 1867) and the tenth-century mixed Gelasian-Gregorian Sacramentary of Fulda (F 2774), it was not usually added to the Holy Saturday service until the fourteenth century when it entered the Roman missal via the Missal of the Curia.[235] Among Beneventan books, the blessing is given on Holy Saturday only in Ben29 and Ve, although the text is a later addition in the latter missal. The presence of the benediction in the Dubrovnik missal is further indication of the late date for the composition of the manuscript.

The blessing of the Paschal candle *Exultet iam angelica turba* (**207-208**) is in origin a Gallican custom found first in the early Gallican missals and ordines but soon adopted during the ninth century into the Romano-Frankish liturgy through the Supplement to the Hadrianum.[236] While the melody of the *Exultet* probably developed later and exists in several regional forms, a distinct version of the text as well as of the musical setting circulated in the Beneventan region.[237] The Beneventan melody, whether set to the text

---

[235] Bruylants, *Oraisons*, 2: 134-135 (no. 489); also Haymo of Faversham, *Ordo missalis* (ed. Van Dijk, *Sources*, 2: 245 l. 9); but not in the Dominican Ordinal of Humbert of Romans (ed. Guerrini, *Ordinarium*, p. 176).

The earliest source to place the blessing of the new fire on Holy Saturday is the Prague sacramentary (Pr 96.1): Prague, Knihovna Metropolitní Kapitoly, O. 83 (siglum: Pr, s. viii; bibl.: *CLLA*, no. 630; ed. Alban Dold and Leo Eizenhöfer, *Das Prager Sakramentar*, II. *Prolegomena und Textausgabe*, Texte und Arbeiten 38-42 [Beuron, 1949]). In the pontifical tradition, the benediction is found first in Vogel and Elze, *Pontifical romano-germanique*, 2: 57-58 (ordo 99: 217), as a general blessing for the kindling of lights on Holy Thursday; during the twelfth century, it was adopted for the Holy Saturday liturgy in the Roman pontifical: Andrieu, *Pontifical romain*, 1: 238 (ordo 32: 3).

[236] Gallican sources: Loew, *Bobbio Missal*, no. 1027; Mohlberg, *Missale Gothicum*, no. 225; Vatican City, BAV, Pal. lat. 493 (s. viii¹; ed. Leo Cunibert Mohlberg, Leo Eizenhöfer, and Petrus Siffrin, *Missale Gallicanum Vetus*, RED, Series maior, Fontes 3 [Rome, 1958], nos. 132-134; bibl.: *CLLA*, nos. 212-214).

The origins of the *Exultet* are discussed by Vogel, *Medieval Liturgy*, p. 171; Chavasse, *Sacramentaire gélasien*, pp. 101-106; Jordi M. Pinell, "La benedicció del ciri pasqual i els seus textos," in *Liturgica Cardinali I. Schuster in memoriam*, 2 vols., Scripta et documenta 7, 10 (Montserrat, 1956-1958), 2: 1-119; Schmidt and Hucke, *Hebdomada sancta*, 2: 639-645, 824-826, 948-949; Benoît-Castelli, "'Praeconium Paschale'," pp. 309-334, concerning the writing of the Norman setting over the erased melody of the *Exultet* in a Franciscan missal of ca. 1230-1250: Naples, Biblioteca Nazionale, VI G 38 (bibl.: Arnese, *Codici notati*, no. 42 [pp. 151-159]); Joseph Gajard, "Le Chant de l'Exultet," *Revue grégorienne* 29 (1950) 50-69; [André Mocquereau], "Le Cursus et la psalmodie (1)," in *Le Codex 121 de la Bibliothèque d'Einsiedeln. X^e-XIe siècle. Antiphonale missarum s. Gregorii*, Paléographie Musicale 4 (1893-1896), pp. 25-204 at 171-196; and Andrieu, *Ordines Romani*, 3: 301-305.

[237] The Beneventan sources and practices of the Holy Saturday liturgy are presented by Guglielmo Cavallo, *Rotoli di Exultet dell'Italia meridionale. Exultet 1, 2, Benedizionale dell'Archivio della cattedrale di Bari. Exultet 1, 2, 3 dell'Archivio capitolare di Troia* (Bari,

of the Romano-Frankish "Vulgate" or the regional "Vetus Itala," is characterised by the repetition of formulas found also in other recitatives with
regional Beneventan melodies.[238] Although the text of the *Exultet* in the
Dubrovnik missal (**207-208**) follows the Romano-Frankish tradition,[239] the
melody remains a much elaborated version of the Beneventan *Exultet*:

1973); *CLLA*, pp. 254-257, nos. 485-499; and Kelly, *Beneventan Chant*, pp. 46-48, 59-60.
Earlier studies include Myrtilla Avery, *The Exultet Rolls of South Italy*, 2 vols. (Princeton,
1936); and Hesbert, "Tradition bénéventaine," pp. 337-446 (*Exultet*: 375-423).

[238] Hesbert, "Tradition bénéventaine," pp. 416-417.

[239] Schmidt and Hucke, *Hebdomada sancta*, 2: 639-645 (Vulgate), 824-826 (Vetus Itala).

na- ta   ful-go-   re et   ma-gnis po- pu- lo- rum

uo-ci- bus   hec au-   la   re- sul-   tet.

Qua-propter   a- stanti- bus   uo- bis fra- tres   ka- ris- si-

mi. ad tam mi-ram sanc-ti   hu- ius lu- mi-nis   cla-

ri- ta-   tem. u- na me-cum que-so   de- i   om-ni-

po- ten- tis mi- se- ri-   cor- di- am   in- uo-

ca- te. Vt   qui   non   me-is   me- ri- tis in- tra le-

ui- ta-   rum nu- merum di- gna-tus   est a- gre-   ga- ri

lu- mi-nis su- i gra-ti- am   in- fun- dens. ce- re- i   hu-

ius lau-dem im- ple-   re   pre- ci- pi- at. Per

do- mi- num no- strum   ie-   sum chri- stum fi- li-   um su-

um. ui- uen- tem   se- cum at- que   re- gnan-   tem in u- ni-

ta- te spi-ri- tu sanc- ti de- us. Per om-ni- a se- cu-

la se- cu- lo- rum. A- men.

Do-mi- nus uo- bis- cum. Et cum spi- ri- tu tu- o.

Sur- sum cor- da. Ha- be-mus ad do- mi- num. Gra-

ti- as a- ga- mus do- mi-no

de- o no- stro. Di- gnum et iu- stum est.

Ve- re qui-a di- gnum et iu- stum est. per

chri-stum do- mi- num no- strum.

Vt in- ui-si- bi-lem de- um pa- trem om-ni- po- ten-

tem. fi- li- um-que e- ius u- ni-ge- ni- tum do- mi- num no- strum

ie- sum chri- stum. to- to cor- dis ac mentis

af- fec- tu. et uo- cis mi- ste-ri- o per-

so- ne- mus. Qui pro no- bis e- ter- no pa- tri

a- de de- bi- tum sol- uit. et ue- te- ris pi- a- cu- li

cau- ti- o- nem. pi- o cru-o- re de-

ter- sit. Hec sunt e- nim fe- sta pa- sca- li- a gau- di-

o- rum. in qui-bus ue- rus il- le a- gnus oc- ci- di-

tur. e- ius- que san- guis po- sti-bus

con- se- cra- tur. In qui- bus pri- mum pa- tres no- stros

fi- li- os i- sra-hel. e- duc-tos de e- gyp- to ru-

brum ma- re. sic- co ue- sti-gi- o tran- si- re

fe- ci- sti. Hec i- gi- tur nox est que pec-

ca- to- rum te- ne- bras co- lum-ne il- lu- mi- na-ti- o-

ne pur- ga- uit. Hec nox est que ho- di- e

per u- ni- uer- sum mun- dum. In xpi-sto cre-den- tes a ui-

ti- is se- cu- li se- gre-ga- tos. et ca- li- gi- nem pec-

ca- to- rum red- dit gra- ti- e so- ci- at

sanc- ti- ta- tem. Hec nox est in qua de- struc-

tis uin-cu- lis mor- tis xpistus ab in- fe- ris

uic- tor a- scen- dit. Ni- chil

e- nim no- bis na- sci pro- fu- it. ni- si re- di- mi

pro- fu- is- set. O mi- ra cir-

ca nos tu- e pi- e- ta- tis di- gna- ti- o. O in- e-

sti-ma- bi- lis di- lec-ti- o ca- ri- ta- tis. ut ser- uum

re- di- me-res fi- li- um tra- di- di-

sti. O cer-te ne- ces-sa- ri- um a- de

pec-ca- tum. quod xpi-sti mor- te de-

le- tum est. O fe- lix cul- pa. que ta- lem ac

tan- tum me- ru- it ha- be- re re-

dem- pto- rem. O be- a- ta nox. que so- la

me-ru- it sci- re tempus et ho- ram. in qua

christus ab in- fe- ris re- sur- rex-

it. Hec nox est de qua scri- ptum est. et nox

ut di- es il- lu- mi- na- bi- tur. et nox il- lu- mi- na- ti- o

me-a in de- li- ci- is me- is. Hu-

ius i- gi- tur sancti- fi- ca- ti- o noc- tis.

fu- gat sce- le- ra. cul- pas la- uat. et red-

dit in- no- centi- am lap- sis. me-stis le- ti- ti- am.

fu- gat ho- di- a. con- cordi- am pa- rat et cur-

uat im- pe- ri- a.

Figure 16. — **207-208** BENEDICTIO CEREI Exultet iam angelica turba, fols. 52v-54v.

The entire composition is divided into two general parts: a prologue and a preface-like prayer for the blessing of the Paschal candle. Since the *Exultet*, although using forms of the cursus of medieval recitation throughout, is neither written in verse nor constructed on a form as repetitive as the Genealogies,[240] the arrangement of repeated melodic elements follows only general patterns based on the structure of the prayer. Thus, while the first clauses of the prologue begin with the ascending progression FGB, followed by a recitation on G and long melismas on the accentuated closings,[241] the order of the elements from "quapropter astantibus" to the end of the prologue varies with the use of a different opening on "quapropter"; the repetition of a lesser melisma at "omnipotentis" (BABAGFGFGF), "leuitarum," "huius laudem," "iesum," "filium," "uiuentem," and "sancti"; and the omission of the long melisma on the closing words "agregari" and "sancti deum." Furthermore, the doxology uses A instead of G as the reciting tone between inflections.[242] The same compositional elements are repeated with variants

[240] See above pp. 49-57.

[241] E.g., "amississe caligine": GFGBAcdccBAGAGFGAGAGFEF

[242] The loose structure of the prologue is evident in a tabular comparison of its elements (A = opening FGB; B = linking passage GA ... FGG; C = long melisma; D = lesser melisma; v = variants):

A	B	C
Exultet	iam angelica	turba celorum;
A	B	
exultent	diuina mysteria;	
A	B	C
et pro tanti	regis uictoria tuba	intonet salutaris;
A	B	C
gaudeat se	tantis tellus	irradiata fulgoribus;
A	B (v)	C
et eterni	regis	splendore illustrata;
A (v)	B (v)	C
totius orbis	se sentiat	amississe caligine;
A	B	
Letetur et	mater ecclesia	
	B	C
	tanti luminis	adornata fulgore;
A	B	C
et magnis	populorum uocibus	hec aula resultet;
A	B	C
Quapropter	astantibus uobis	fratres karissimi;
A	B	C
ad tam miram	sancti huius	luminis claritatem;

throughout the blessing, the principal distinction being the tenor on A instead of G, which is used in the prologue until the doxology.[243]

A	B (v)	D
una mecum	queso dei	omnipotentis
A	B (v)	C
mise-	ricordi-	am inuocate;
A	B	D
Vt qui me	non meis meritis	intra leuitarum
	B (v)	D (v)
	numerum dignatus	est agregari;
A (v)	B (v)	D
luminis sui	gratiam infundens,	cerei huius laudem
		C
		implere precipiat;

[243] Hesbert, "Tradition bénéventaine," pp. 399-417, has transcribed the *Exultet* of the Dubrovnik missal and listed all the compositional elements and their variants in different accentual environments. Hesbert also notes the similarities between its melody and the melodies of other Beneventan MSS, which are occasionally identical (e.g., "totius orbis se sentiat": FAGGGFFGGG) but more often differ in the greater elaborations of the setting in the Dubrovnik missal (e.g., "secu*la*": FGBcdcBcBAGABAGF Dubr] GAGAGF Benevento). Huglo, "Ancien chant bénéventain," pp. 289-290, pl. II, links the melody of the *Exultet* in DaB with the melody of the *Exultet* in the Oxford MS, i.e., the "mélodie de Raguse." Comparison of the Kotor melody (DaB) with the Oxford MS and the other Beneventan MSS cited by Hesbert shows, however, that the melody in DaB is more closely related to southern Italian sources than to the Dubrovnik melody:

Ben:	F	FA	G	G	F	FG	G	G	GA	AG
DaB:	F	A	G	A	F	FG	G	G	GA	AG
Dubr:	FG	B	A	GA	F	FG	G	G	c	BBAGFGA
	Ex-	ul-	tet	iam	an-	ge-	li-	ca	tur-	ba

Ben:	F	GAG	F	F	A	G	G	GA	AG
DaB:	F	GAG	F	F	A	G	G	GA	AG
Dubr:	F	GAGFE	F	FG	B	A	G	G	A
	ce-	lo-	rum,	ex-	ul-	tent	di-	ui-	na

Ben:	F	GA	G	F	F	F	A	G	G	G
DaB:	F	GA	G	F	F	G	A	G	G	A
Dubr:	F	FG	G	G	F	G	BB	A	G	A
	my-	ste-	ri-	a	et	pro	tan-	ti	re-	gis

Ben:	F	FG	G	G	G	F	G	F	GAGAGF
DaB:	F	FG	G	G	G	F	G	F	GAGAGF
Dubr:	F	FG	G	G	FA	G	G	F	GABcdccBAGAGF
	ui-	cto-	ri-	a	tu-	ba	in-	to-	net

Ben:	GA	GAG	F	F
DaB:	GA	GG	F	F
Dubr:	FGA	GAG	FGFE	F
	sa-	lu-	ta-	ris ... .

Sundays after Easter (**209-223**)

Due to the lack of several folios before fol. 55r, the manuscript contains only the fourth and fifth Sundays after Easter, and the former begins with the closing of the gospel (**209**). The lections are Roman. With the exception of the secret *Suscipe domine fidelium* of the fifth Sunday (**221**), all the prayers are also common to the early books of both Gregorian and Gelasian traditions, entering the Roman missal through the Supplement, since the Hadrianum itself made no provision for the Sundays following the feasts of Epiphany, Easter, and Pentecost. There are few textual indications favouring either tradition as the source for the mass-sets of the Dubrovnik missal,[244] but the secret *Suscipe domine fidelium* (**221**) is attested for the fifth Sunday in the Supplement, the Paduense, and some but not all of the Gelasians (Sg 750), increasing the probability of a Gregorian or Gelasian-Gregorian source for the mass-sets.

Among the musical items, only the alleluias of the fifth Sunday (**217, 218**) are unusual.

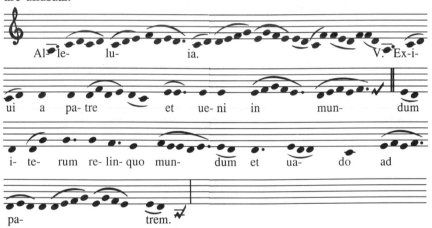

Figure 17. — **217** Alleluia. Exiui a patre, fols. 55v-56r.

The longer melismas of the Oxford MS are without parallel in DaB; in general the versions of Benevento and Kotor (DaB) are only slightly different. Nonetheless, since at those points of variance DaB corresponds often to the melody of the Dubrovnik missal (e.g., "*pro re*gis"), the melody of Kotor may represent a basic "Dalmatian" melody much enhanced in the later Oxford MS.

[244] E.g., in **211**, the Missal reads "cognouimus" with Va, the fourteenth-century Missal of the Curia (above n. 95), MRM, and the Roman missal of 1570 against "cognoscimus" of the Gelasians of the Eighth Century and Sp (Bruylants, *Oraisons*, 2: 114 [no. 409]); in **213**, the MS agrees with the later Roman missals against the Gelasians and Sp in reading "Adesto nobis" for "Adesto" alone (Bruylants, *Oraisons*, 2: 19 [no. 34]). Such evidence points to the diffusion and influence of later medieval Roman texts in the region.

The text of the verse *Exiui* (**217** Io 16: 28) is drawn from the gospel of the day in both Roman and Romano-Beneventan traditions (**219** Io 16: 23-30). The musical setting of the text in the Beneventan sources differs, however, from its Roman counterpart, suggesting the independence of the regional development. The Beneventan melody is in fact an adaptation of the setting of the alleluia *Surrexit Christus qui creavit* of the GR, although among early mass-antiphonals the melody is found with many different verses, especially *Laudate dominum.*[245]

Figure 18. – **218** Alleluia. Vsque modo, fol. 56r.

The text of the second alleluia *Vsque modo* (**218** Io 16: 24) is also drawn from the gospel (**219** Io 16: 23-30). While the verse is found on other feasts in some early manuscripts and in Roman books such as the early printed missals from Venice cited in the second volume of MRM,[246] it appears to be attested for the fifth Sunday after Easter primarily in Beneventan sources. The melody is an adaptation of the setting of the alleluia with the verse *Post partum* of the GR. Unlike the majority of the unusual alleluia verses of the Dubrovnik missal, which are specifically Romano-Beneventan, the adaptation of *Vsque modo* to the *Post partum* melody has parallels in several Aquitainian

[245] Schlager, *Katalog*, no. D 4.
[246] E.g., Schlager, *Katalog*, nos. E 164, G 382 (different melody); and MRM 2: 334, 336. The second volume of MRM contains comparative texts from other early printed missals.

manuscripts as well as Beneventan sources.[247] In general, through some as-yet-undefined historical link, the Gregorian music of Aquitaine and the Beneventan region share melodic variants distinguishing them from northern European sources:[248] the alleluia *Vsque modo* of the Oxford manuscript may be considered further evidence of that connection.

Rogation Days (**224-240**)

The Dubrovnik missal contains masses for the Rogation days of the second and third weekdays (Monday and Tuesday) before the vigil of Ascension. Two penitential occasions regularly fall in the Easter season: the major litany on the feast of Mark (25 April), originally of Roman origin replacing the pagan *robigalia*, and the lesser litanies or Rogation days of Gallican origin celebrated on the three days before Ascension, replacing the pagan *ambarvalia*.[249] The processions and mass of the major litany of the Roman custom were gradually adopted by the Gallican churches with the spread of books of the Roman liturgy in the eighth and ninth centuries. Nonetheless, the Rogation days continued to be observed and entered the Roman missal through the hybrid Romano-Frankish liturgy, although the three distinct mass-sets of the Gallican liturgy were gradually dropped in favour of simply repeating the Roman mass of the major litany (as the Oxford manuscript does for the musical items). Of course, the process left many traces of the earlier mass-sets in sources from the transitional periods. Thus, the Gelasians of the Eighth Century in conflating the traditions adopt the Gregorian series of processional prayers and the Gregorian mass of the major litany (Ha 466-475; Ge 890-899) but retain processional prayers and mass-sets for two more days (Ge 900-921): presumably the prayers for the major litany doubled for the first Rogation day.[250]

---

[247] Schlager, *Katalog*, no. E 164, with *Usquemodo* in thirteen Graduals from Aquitaine, including Paris, BN, lat. 903, fol. 84v (siglum: Syg, ca. 1031, St.-Yrieix; facs. ed. André Mocquereau, *Le Codex 903 de la Bibliothèque Nationale de Paris (XIᵉ siècle, Graduel de Saint-Yrieix)*, Paléographie Musicale 13 [Solesmes, 1925]; bibl.: Gajard, *Graduel romain*, 2: 96). The Beneventan sources containing the verse (Ben39, McV, Ve) are not among those tabulated by Schlager.

[248] Hesbert, "Tradition bénéventaine," p. 190, fig. 26.

[249] Bailey, *Processions*, pp. 52-58, 95-98; *Église en prière* (1961), pp. 725-726; and *Église en prière* (1983-1984), 4: 73.

[250] The tenth-century Fulda sacramentary (F) continues the Gelasian tradition but is more explicit: it has prayers and a mass for the major litany with directions to repeat them on the first rogation day (*In laetania maiore et in II. feria rogationum* F 861-871) and separate sets for the second and third days (*In letania minore. feria III. in rogationibus* F 915-925; *Feria IIII* F 926-935).

Mass-sets: Beneventan sources also reflect varying moments in the development of the liturgy of the Rogation days. Ben33, for instance, has the Gregorian processional prayers and mass of the major litany followed by the mass for the second day of the Rogations from the Gelasian tradition,[251] and the mass for the third day found in the tenth-century Sacramentary of Monza.[252] The prayers of the Dubrovnik missal fall into a different Beneventan group, which includes Ben29 and DaB. Generally, the three missals use the Gregorian texts for the first mass and Gelasian texts for the second, but the choice and order of the prayers are distinctive. The Gregorian postcommunion *Pretende nobis domine* (**232**) of the first mass is listed as an alternative in the Hadrianum (Ha 475) and the Gellone sacramentary (Ge 899) and as a *super populum* in the Fulda sacramentary (F 871); the prayer was dropped altogether in the later Roman missals.[253] The three Beneventan missals appear to depend on another tradition attested in the Sacramentary of Rheinau (Rh 575) that assigns the prayer as the sole postcommunion. The prayers of the second mass follow the Gellone sacramentary except for the collect *Presta quesumus omnipotens deus ut qui iram* (**234**), which is usually assigned to the prayers during the procession in the Gelasian sacramentaries (Ge 901, Ph 709, Rh 570, F 928).

Lections: The epistles and gospels of the two Rogation masses (**226, 228, 235, 236**) are unparalleled in the Roman lection-lists. Since the lections are attested in other Beneventan missals but not in the Campanian lection-lists, the choice of readings would appear to be a later regional development.

Vigil of Ascension (**241-249**)

The vigil of Ascension is among the secondary series of feasts added to the Roman propers only after the seventh century.[254] The relative lateness of the feast is demonstrated in the variety of treatments it receives in the early books of the liturgy: the vigil is lacking altogether in the Campanian lection-lists, the Comes of Würzburg, the early Gregorian sacramentaries (Ha, Pa), the

---

[251] Only the postcommunion *Quesumus omnipotens deus ut ad te toto corde* (Ben33 92v) is unparalleled.

[252] Monza, Biblioteca capitolare, f. 1/101, at nos. 369-371; sacramentarium, s. ix/x, Bergamo; ed. Alban Dold and Klaus Gamber, *Das Sakramentar von Monza*, Texte und Arbeiten, Beiheft 3 (Beuron, 1957); bibl.: *CLLA*, no. 801; and Chavasse, "Sacramentaire de Monza," pp. 3-29.

[253] Bruylants, *Oraisons*, 1: 48 (mass 104).

[254] *Église en prière* (1961), p. 713; and *Église en prière* (1983-1984), 4: 73.

Supplement, and in two of the earliest mass-antiphonals (AMS);[255] among other early books, it presents numerous variants. Later Roman books depend either on the Gelasian mass of the vigil or adopt the mass-set of the preceding Sunday.[256] Apart from the epistle (**243** Eph 4: 7-13), which is taken from the Common of later Roman lection-lists,[257] and the gospel (**245** Io 17: 1-11) drawn from the early Roman lection-lists (CoP 223), the proper mass of the Dubrovnik missal exhibits several distinctive solutions to the need for a vigil-mass.

Collect: The secret (**247**) and postcommunion (**249**) follow the vigil mass of the Gelasian sacramentaries, but the collect *Deus cuius filius* (**242**) found in several Beneventan missals differs. The prayer is listed for the mass of the feast itself either as an alternative (Ha 503), a postcommunion (Va 578) or a *super populum* in Gelasian and Gregorian sources.[258]

Musical Items: While the introit *Omnes gentes* (**241**) is found on the vigil in two of the earliest mass-antiphonals (AMS 101*bis*), it did not remain proper to the feast in later sources. In the GR, it is found with the same melody and psalm tone on the seventh Sunday after Pentecost, although Ps 46: 3 begins the verse instead of Ps 46: 4 of the Oxford manuscript and the early sources. The other musical items are unrelated to the pieces of the vigil mass in the early mass-antiphonals. Unlike the later Roman use of the mass of the preceding Sunday, the author of the Missal drew instead on the mass of the feast itself: the alleluia *Ascendit* (**244**), the offertory *Ascendit* (**246**) and the communion *Psallite* (**248**) are all proper to Ascension in the Roman sources. Other Beneventan sources are not unanimous in following this scheme: only the Dubrovnik missal, for instance, repeats the communion *Psallite* (**248**) of Ascension on the vigil as well.[259]

---

[255] Chavasse, *Sacramentaire gélasien*, pp. 245-246; Hesbert, *Antiphonale missarum sextuplex*, p. lxv.

[256] Haymo of Faversham, *Ordo missalis* (ed. Van Dijk, *Sources*, 2: 255); Bruylants, *Oraisons*, 1: 48-49 (mass 105).

[257] Haymo of Faversham, *Ordo missalis* (ed. Van Dijk, *Sources*, 2: 255); and MRM 232. Since Ben33 95v and McV 163v both have Act 2: 41-47, the epistle Eph 4: 7-13 of DaB, PuC, and the Oxford MS (**243**) probably represents the influence of later medieval Roman books.

[258] Bruylants, *Oraisons*, 1: 49 (mass 106).

[259] Ben33 96v, Ben34 177v, and DaB 163r have the distinctive communion *Non pro his rogo*. PuC 513 has the communion *Pacem meam*; the early Roman mass-antiphonals (*Feria IIII post Pentecosten* AMS 109) have the same text elsewhere but two alternatives for the vigil (*Pater cum essem* and *Non vos relinquam* AMS 101*bis*). The Old Beneventan communion *Pacem meam* for Ascension (Ben40 71v) is textually different from PuC (Andoyer, "Ancienne liturgie," *RdCG* 22 [1914] 142; Kelly, *Beneventan Chant*, p. 283).

Offertory of Ascension (**251**)

The mass of Ascension (**250-254**) in the Oxford manuscript is incomplete, lacking the folio(s) with the collect, epistle, alleluias, gospel, and the beginning of the offertory. Nonetheless, unlike the purely Roman introit, secret, communion, and postcommunion,[260] what survives of the offertory (**251**) distinguishes it from the Roman tradition:

Figure 19. – **251** OFFERTORIVM <Viri galilei>, fol. 61r.

The text of the offertory (Act 1: 11) is drawn from the Roman epistle for the feast and repeats the introit (**250**). Although the Vatican edition of the GR has the offertory *Ascendit* (Ps 46: 6) with a different melody, and Hesbert has argued that *Ascendit* was the earlier text,[261] medieval Roman sources are as likely to have one as the other.[262]

Secret (**262**) *and Postcommunion* (**264**) *of the Vigil of Penetecost*

The secret *Munera domine quesumus oblata* (**262**) is attested for the vigil of Pentecost in the Gregorian sacramentaries and later Roman missals but in none of the Gelasians.[263] Its presence in the Dubrovnik missal and other

---

[260] The postcommunion *Presta quesumus omnipotens et misericors deus* (**254**), attested in both Gregorian and Gelasian repertories, is more closely related to later witnesses of the traditions: thus, the Dubrovnik missal and MRM 234 read "Praesta quaesumus" for "Praesta *nobis* quaesumus" of most sources; and both the Oxford MS and the Missal of the Curia read "affectu" where most have "effectu" (Bruylants, *Oraisons*, 2: 239 [no. 841]).

[261] Hesbert, *Antiphonale missarum sextuplex*, p. lxvi.

[262] Carolus Ott, *Offertoriale sive versus offertorium* (Paris, 1935), no. 102; AMS 102a-b (Hesbert, *Antiphonale missarum sextuplex*, p. lxv n. 5, citing sources with both offertories); even Haymo of Faversham, *Ordo missalis* (ed. Van Dijk, *Sources*, 2: 255) and MRM 234 have the offertory *Viri Galilaei*.

  In Beneventan sources, this offertory appears to be the norm: among the Beneventan MSS with musical items for Ascension examined for this edition, only Ve and DaZ do not have the offertory *Viri Galilaei*.

[263] Bruylants, *Oraisons*, 1: 51-52 (mass 109). The prayer is repeated on the feast in the Gregorian sources; the Gelasians have the same secret for Pentecost but provide proper texts for the vigil (*Virtute sancti spiritus* Va 626, Ge 1015; *Hostias populi* Va 633, Ge 1023).

Beneventan books reinforces the suggestion of a Gregorian source for the sacramentary at the base of the Roman prayers of the Beneventan corpus.[264]

The postcommunion *Mentes nostras* (**264**) is certainly a composition of the Roman tradition but is nowhere else found as the postcommunion for the vigil of Pentecost except in Beneventan sources. Among both the Gregorian sacramentaries and the Gelasians of the Eighth Century, the prayer is cited as the postcommunion of the third feria during the week of Pentecost, but in both the Veronese sacramentary and the Vatican Gelasian the prayer is listed on Pentecost itself: in the Veronese as an alternative (Le 223) and in the Vatican Gelasian as the secret (Va 639). Since the masses of Pentecost week were seventh-century additions to the Roman sacramentary,[265] the liturgists of the period evidently sought suitable thematic material from among earlier alternatives: thus, *Mentes nostras*, an early Pentecostal prayer, became proper to the third feria in later Roman books. A parallel process of supplementing the original Roman source of the Romano-Beneventan sacramentary saw the adoption of *Mentes nostras* for the vigil in Beneventan sources. In this case, however, the Roman source of the regional sacramentary appears to have lacked not only ferial masses but also the vigil mass for Pentecost.

Pentecost (**265-274**)

Although the mass of Pentecost in the Dubrovnik missal is entirely Roman, the second alleluia *Dum complerentur* with its prosula (**269**) and the secret *Virtute sancti spiritus* (**272**) are regional modifications to the Roman mass.

---

[264] Among the Beneventan sources that I have examined, only PuC 530 has the Gelasian secret *Virtute* instead of the Gregorian doublet *Munera*.

[265] For Pentecost week, see Chavasse, *Sacramentaire gélasien*, pp. 247-251, 595-604; and *Église en prière* (1961), pp. 722-725.

stes pro-missus ce- los spi-ri- tus ad- ue-   ni- ens i- gnis in

e- gni-ma- te. Bis-se- nos si- mul co- mo-ran-tes   do- mi- ni re-ple-

uit ple-ni- ter di- sci-pu- los. Lin- guis ef- fan-tur   om-ni- bus xpi-

sti sa- cra nec-non ma-gna-li-   a. E- rant   om- nes pa-

ri- ter di-   cen- tes.

Figure 20. – **269** Alleluia. Dum complerentur dies *cum prosula*, fol. 63r-v.

Pentecost is one of the few feasts in the early mass-antiphonals (AMS 106) to have fixed alleluias.[266] Since the only hint of earlier divergence is the substitution of *Haec dies* for *Veni sancti spiritus* in the Antiphonal of Mont-Blandin,[267] the appearance of a different alleluia in most Beneventan sources is all the more remarkable, emphasising again the early date of the Gregorian exemplar used in the region. The prosula is found in several other Beneventan manuscripts, all from Benevento itself.[268]

The text of the Beneventan verse (Act 2: 1), drawn from the first lection (**267** Act 2: 1-11), is certainly appropriate; in the GR, the same text and melody are found on the following Saturday, restating the theme of Pentecost week. While the melodic lines of both Beneventan and Roman versions of the alleluia are very similar, the relation with the text underlay varies at several points, corresponding as follows:

Dubr: Dum   comple- ren-   tur   dies.
GR: Dum complerentur   di-   es   pen-   te-   costes.

---

[266] Apel, *Gregorian Chant*, p. 379.

[267] Hesbert, *Antiphonale missarum sextuplex*, p. lxvii (Brussels, Bibliothèque Royale, 10127-10144).

[268] I.e., Ben34, Ben38, Ben39, Ben40. See also Olof Marcusson, *Corpus troporum*, vol. 2: *Prosules de la messe*, pars 1: *Tropes de l'alleluia*, Studia Latina Stockholmiensia 22 (Stockholm, 1976), no. 23.6, p. 51, citing Ben34 and Paris, BN, lat. 776 (graduale, Gaillac, bibl.: Gajard, *Graduel romain*, 2: 93).

Dubr: Pentecostes [+ prosa]   Erant omnes pariter   dicentes.
GR: Erant omnes   pariter   sedentes.[269]

The music is an adaptation of the setting for the alleluia with the verse *Iustus ut palma*, one of the most frequently adapted melodies in the corpus of alleluias.[270]

The secret *Virtute sancti spiritus* (**272**) of Pentecost is attested in several Beneventan sources, including the Dubrovnik missal, but is evidently a borrowing from the Gelasian mass of the vigil of Pentecost (Va 626, Ge 1015). Table 5 compares the choice of secrets for Pentecost and its vigil in the Gregorian, Gelasian, and Beneventan traditions:

TABLE 5 Secrets of the Vigil and Feast of Pentecost			
Feast	GREG: Ha	SAC: Va, GEL8: Ge	BEN
Vigil of Pentecost Pentecost Sunday	Munera dne Munera dne	Virtute Munera dne	Munera dne Virtute

The prayer is not found in any of the Gregorian sacramentaries nor even in the mixed Gelasian-Gregorians. Faced with the repetition of the secret *Munera domine* (**262**) for both the vigil and feast in the Hadrianum (Ha 521, 531), the author of the Beneventan source appears to have looked elsewhere for an appropriate alternative, in this case finding it on the vigil in a book of the Gelasian tradition: why *Virtute sancti spiritus* was substituted for the secret of Pentecost instead of being retained on the vigil remains unexplained.

Ember Days: Saturday (**275-285**)

The Dubrovnik missal provides only a single mass for Pentecost week: the Saturday mass of the Ember days. The relation between Pentecost week and the Ember days of the "fourth" month is among the many unsettled issues of early medieval liturgical development.[271] The Ember days, with their own

---

[269] The melody of "pente*costes*" in the GR has no counterpart in Dubr; similarly, the extra syllables of "erant om*nes pariter*" of Dubr require several additional notes when compared to "pariter" of the GR. The long melisma on "*erant omnes*" of the GR is the setting of the prosula *Pentecostes promissus* in Dubr; in Ben34, the same melisma is the setting for "*pentecostes*" and then repeated after the alleluia as the setting of the prosula.

[270] Schlager, *Katalog*, no. D 38.

[271] G. G. Willis, *Essays in Early Roman Liturgy*, Alcuin Club Collections 46 (London,

penitential masses, had been celebrated on the fourth, sixth, and seventh days
of Pentecost week from the time of their institution. By the seventh century,
however, masses had been composed for the weekdays relating to Pentecost
itself and are found in all the early liturgical books except the Vatican
Gelasian, which retains the older disposition. The new masses were not
entirely independent of the old texts, especially in the choice of lections;
nonetheless, the custom in Gallican churches by the end of the seventh
century was to retain the proper masses of the Ember days by transferring
them to another week after Pentecost.[272] The Roman reformers of the
eleventh century sought with some success to reinstitute the practice of the
coincidence of Ember days and Pentecost week, but the evidence of many
regional texts indicates that the celebrations continued to be separate for
several centuries. The fluidity of the tradition during the four centuries from
the seventh to the eleventh when the basic sources for the local forms of the
Roman liturgy were being transmitted means regional variants must be
expected. The mass of the Dubrovnik missal does not surprise in this regard.

Prayers: The mass-set of the Missal is thoroughly penitential in its themes.
The collect *Deus qui tribus* (**277**) is common to both Gregorian and Gelasian
traditions and usually found on this day but occasionally on other Ember
days (Va 1049); the secret *Sollemnibus ieiuniis* (**283**) is a Gelasian text
adopted from the Wednesday mass of the Ember days; and the postcommunion *Sumptum quesumus* (**285**) has counterparts only in the Gelasians
and Beneventan books. The mass-set is clearly dependent on the mass of an
earlier Gelasian or Gelasian-Gregorian sacramentary, although the idiosyncratic adoption of the secret (**283**), found in no other source on this feast
(to the best of my knowledge), suggests the dependency is perhaps several
steps removed.

Lections: The epistle (**278** Rm 5: 1-5) is the standard lection in Roman
sources from every stage of the tradition, while the gospel (**281** Mc 1: 21-34)
is unattested elsewhere. Nonetheless, the stories of Christ's teaching in the

---

1964), pp. 68-72; *Église en prière* (1961), pp. 722-725, 740, 743; *Église en prière*
(1983-1984), 4: 73; Chavasse, *Sacramentaire gélasien*, pp. 247-251, 595-604; and Hesbert,
Antiphonale missarum sextuplex, pp. lxviii-lxx.

[272] For the Ember days following the third Sunday after Pentecost in the Gelasians of the
Eighth Century, see Ge 1094-1115 and the Sacramentary of Sankt Gallen, Stiftsbibliothek,
348, nos. 875-894 (siglum: Sg, s. viii/ix, Chur/Sankt Gallen; ed. Kunibert Mohlberg, *Das
fränkische Sacramentarium Gelasianum in alamannischer Überlieferung*, 3rd edition, St.
Galler Sakramentar-Forschungen 1, LQF 1-2 [Münster/W., 1971; 1st ed. 1918]; bibl.: *CLLA*,
no. 830); see also Andrieu, *Ordines Romani*, 5: 101 (ordo 50: 14).

synagogue, casting out a spirit, and curing Simon's mother related in the gospel of Mark from the Dubrovnik missal are the same "pentecostal" stories found in the more widely spread gospel of Luke (4: 38-43) of the later medieval Roman tradition.[273]

Musical Items: In contrast to the penitential origin and emphasis of the prayers, the chants for the Saturday of the Ember days continue the pentecostal themes introduced by the epistle and gospel. The introit *Karitas dei* (**275**) is standard in Roman sources of every period. The tract *Laudate* (**280**), an exception to the emphasis on pentecostal themes, is found at this point in later Roman sources and on Holy Saturday and the Ember Saturdays of Advent, Lent, and September in the early mass-antiphonals. The offertory *Emitte* (**282**) is suitable for the feast and generally attested for it in medieval manuscripts.[274] The communion *Non uos relinquam* (**284**) of the Oxford manuscript is found on this feast in the early mass-antiphonals and some later manuscripts,[275] although it appears on a different feast in the GR.

The alleluia *Karitas dei* (**279**) is more distinctively Romano-Beneventan:

Figure 21. — **279** Alleluia. Karitas dei, fol. 65r.

---

[273] E.g., Vogel and Elze, *Pontifical romano-germanique*, 2: 136 l. 36 (ordo 99: 451); Haymo of Faversham, *Ordo missalis* (ed. Van Dijk, *Sources*, 2: 260 l. 3). The older penitential gospel was Mt 20: 29-34 (*Église en prière* [1961], p. 724).

[274] Hesbert, *Antiphonale missarum sextuplex*, p. lxxi n. 3, cites 104 MSS with *Emitte*, sixty-one with *Domine*, and forty-five others split among eight different texts; Hesbert argues that the offertory *Domine salutis* of the GR and the early mass-antiphonals (AMS 111) was the original text of the Ember day that came to be supplanted by the offertory *Emitte* from the vigil of Pentecost.

[275] E.g., Hänggi, *Rheinauer Liber Ordinarius*, p. 171 l. 27.

The text (Rm 5: 5) corresponds to the standard introit for the day (**275**) and is drawn from the epistle (**278** Rm 5: 1-5). In other regions the same text was arranged with the melody of the alleluia with the verse *Confitebuntur*;[276] the Dubrovnik melody, however, is proper to the text and found almost exclusively in Beneventan sources.[277]

Sundays after Pentecost (**286-302**)

Several irregularities mark the Temporal of the Dubrovnik missal for the Sundays after Pentecost, where the choice of Sundays and the texts of the masses are particularly unusual. Only parts of the first Sunday (**286-288**), all of a mass probably for the eleventh Sunday (**289-298**), and part of the seventeenth Sunday (**299-302**) survive. In addition one may assume there were texts on the lost folios that included perhaps one Sunday between the first and eleventh, and perhaps one after the seventeenth. The titles are not explicit: the first mass is labelled "Dominica I," which is either the first Sunday after Pentecost or the first after its octave (either system can be found in medieval liturgical books); the second mass lacks a label; and the third mass is titled "Dominica XVII" but contains the texts found elsewhere for the nineteenth or twentieth Sundays after Pentecost.

Classified by the arrangement of the Sundays after Pentecost, most Beneventan books form a homogeneous group, corresponding to Class A of Chavasse's Type III. Nonetheless, even the fragmentary survival of the Sundays after Pentecost in the Dubrovnik missal is adequate to demonstrate that it does not fit clearly into either Class A or Class B, the later and more widely diffused system, but falls somewhere between the two. Tables 6 and 7 compare the masses of the Sundays after Pentecost of the Missal with the usual prayers, lections, and chant of Classes A and B.

The Dubrovnik missal shows affinities with Class A in the agreement of epistle, gospel, and chant for the eleventh Sunday after Pentecost. But it also has the epistle (**288** 1 Io 4:2-20) of the first Sunday typical of Class B. Unattested in either class, the introit (**286** Ps 30) for the first Sunday is a unique adoption of the Roman introit for Wednesday in the third week of Lent (AMS 56). The texts of the seventeenth Sunday in the Missal represent a linked group in both classes: it is, however, unusual to find the texts on the seventeenth Sunday and not on the nineteenth or twentieth as in Classes A and B respectively.

---

[276] Schlager, *Katalog*, no. F 220, exclusively in Italian sources.

[277] Schlager, *Katalog*, no. G 256: the verse *Lux perpetua* is also set to the same melody in Ben34 163v; the only MS with the melody from outside the region is the Tonary of Montpellier, fol. 67r (above n. 199).

TABLE 6 Lections and Chant for the Sundays after Pentecost		
Dubr	Class A (Chavasse)	Class B (Chavasse)*
DOM. 1 Int. Ps 30 Epla. 1 Io 4: 2-20	( ) ( )	( ) Dom. 2
DOM. ? (11/12) Int. Ps 67 Gr. Ps 27 Off. Ps 29 Com. Prov 3 Epla. 2 Cor 3: 4-9 Evg. Lc 18: 9-14	Dom. 11 Dom. 11 Dom. 11 Dom. 11 Dom. 11 Dom. 11	Dom. 12 Dom. 12 Dom. 12 Dom. 12 Dom. 13 Dom. 12
DOM. 17 Int. Eccli 36 Epla. Eph 4: 23-28	Dom. 19 Dom. 19	Dom. 20 Dom. 20

* Chavasse, "Plus anciens types," pp. 12-13; unfilled parentheses ( ) indicate that the text of Dubr is not found in Chavasse's lists.

TABLE 7 Prayers for the Sundays after Pentecost*							
Dubr	GREG			GEL8		BEN	
	Pa	Ha	Sp	Ge	Sg	Ben33	McO
DOM. 1 **287**	Dom. vacat 496	Dom. vacat 553	Dom. 3 1135	Ebd. 4 1116	Ebd. 4 895	Dom. 1 post oct. 126r	Dom. 4 post oct. 375
DOM. ? **290** **296** **298**	Dom. 5 post oct. apost. 591 592 593	 [ ] [ ] [ ]	Dom. 11 1159 1160 1180	Ebd. 12 1332 1334 1336	Ebd. 12 1047 1049 1051	 ( ) ( ) ( )	Dom. 6 post apost. 398 ( ) ( )
DOM. 17 **300**	 ( )	 [ ]	Dom. 18 1180	Ebd. 21 1543	Ebd. 21 1261	Dom. 3 post s. Angeli 133r	Dom. 1 post s. Angeli 437

* Unfilled parentheses ( ) indicate that the prayer of Dubr is not found in the source being compared; unfilled brackets [ ] that the Sunday is omitted.

The mass-sets follow the Roman model of the Hadrianum (Ha 553) and its Supplement (Sp 1135) for the collect *Deprecationem nostram* (**287**) of the first Sunday after Pentecost; in the Gelasians of the Eighth Century, the text falls instead on the fourth Sunday after Pentecost (Ge 1116). For the second mass-set (**290, 296, 298**), the Supplement and Gelasians are in agreement although the Sunday is identified as the eleventh after Pentecost in the Supplement (Sp 1159) and the twelfth in the Gelasians (Ge 1332).[278] The collect *Da quesumus* (**300**) of the seventeenth Sunday after Pentecost is found in the Supplement on the eighteenth Sunday (Sp 1180) and in the Gelasians on the twenty-first Sunday after Pentecost (Ge 1543): again, the Oxford manuscript follows more closely the Gregorian tradition.

The choice of Sundays requires explanation. The surviving titles are numbered by reference to the Sundays after Pentecost or its octave: the first, perhaps the eleventh, and the seventeenth. According to the enumeration by the "Gregorian" sections of some early sacramentaries, where the Sundays are numbered following the principal feasts of the season and not Pentecost itself, the mass of the first Sunday retains its title, but the mass of the seventeenth Sunday corresponds to the mass found elsewhere on the Sunday after the feast of the Archangel.[279] Given the absence of a title for the second mass of the Missal, there can be no guarantee of its place in either system of enumeration, but the epistle (**291** 2 Cor 3: 4-9) is found in some manuscripts of Class B on the first Sunday after the feast of Lawrence, i.e., the thirteenth after Pentecost in other books of Class B. To these masses for the Sundays after Pentecost and after the feasts of Lawrence and the Archangel, one may add also masses for the Sundays after the feast of the apostles and the feast of Martin, which would correspond to the texts on the missing folios after the first and seventeenth Sundays. The feast of Martin was not widely used in the enumeration of Sundays, but it does appear in Ben33 and in Vatican City, BAV, Ottob. lat. 296, a gospel-book in Beneventan script of the Bari-type.[280] The Gospel-book is also one of the rare instances of a similar abbreviated list of Sundays after Pentecost: in its case, however, the references are explicitly to gospels for the Sunday *post octavam*, and four

---

[278] Since the other mass-sets of the Dubrovnik missal appear most closely related to those in the Supplement, I have chosen to follow the enumeration of the Supplement for the missing title in the Missal.

[279] Chavasse, "Plus anciens types," pp. 12-13, presents a Table of the Sundays after Pentecost for Classes A and B with the enumeration by both "Gregorian" sections and weeks after Pentecost.

[280] Vatican City, BAV, Ottob. lat. 296; evangelistarium, s. xi, bibl.: *CLLA*, no. 1177; Loew, *Beneventan Script*, 2: 166; Salmon, *Manuscrits liturgiques*, 2: 48-49 (no. 87). Gamber, *CLLA*, p. 465, identifies the Gregorian section *post s. Martini* as a distinctive Beneventan feature.

Sundays *post octavam apostolorum, post s. Laurentii, post s. Angeli,* and *post s. Martini.*

The "Gregorian" sections had an organisational advantage because they supplied invariable masses for Sundays between the fixed feasts of the Sanctoral, but the need for flexible arrangements for the varying number of Sundays between the moveable feast of Pentecost and the fixed feast of the apostles led to several different systems. These variants are central to Chavasse's grouping of Roman lectionaries,[281] but his classification follows the choice of lections not the system of titles: thus, sources of Type III, subdivided into Classes A and B by the presence or absence of the mass *Omnes gentes* on the seventh/eighth Sunday after Pentecost, use either "Gregorian" sections or continuous numbering regardless of classification. The difference in practice was real (masses may fall on different Sundays depending on the year and on which enumeration the book in use followed) but seems to have affected little the general sequence of mass-texts among books within each classification. Certainly, the system of "Gregorian" sections, which may have made some sense in Ottob. lat. 296, where fixed Sundays were identified and given special treatment, makes much less sense in the Oxford manuscript, where the number of each Sunday is determined by Pentecost: what would have been the point of retaining a division based on the Sanctoral while applying an enumeration derived from the Temporal? The Sundays do not seem in themselves to have been of such importance that their significance would survive the change to continuous numbering after Pentecost used in the Dubrovnik missal: yet this appears to be the case. The irregularity remains a puzzle.

Conclusion

The general influences on the Beneventan liturgy have left their marks on the Temporal of the Dubrovnik missal: to this extent it is very clearly a book of the regional liturgy, with traces of Old Beneventan, early Romano-Beneventan, and later Romano-Frankish texts. As the preceding comparisons and discussions based on the *apparatus parallelorum locorum* show, the majority of prayers have counterparts in both Gregorian and Gelasian sacramentaries; most lections are found in the early lectionaries and in the Roman missal; and, with the notable exception of the alleluias, the repertory of musical items is common to most of the earliest antiphonals of the mass. Nonetheless, the use of distinctive texts with parallels in only one or another of the early sacramentaries, lectionaries, or mass-antiphonals reveals that the

---

[281] Chavasse, "Plus anciens types," passim.

stock of liturgical material available to the compiler of a missal in Dalmatia in the thirteenth century was the product of several layers of influence and adoption.

Old Beneventan: At first glance, the traditional categories of the Old Beneventan sacramentary appear to be unrepresented: there are no *orationes post evangelium*, no prefaces to compare with those of early Beneventan sources, such as PuZ and Ben33, and only one *oratio super populum*, which is Roman in origin.[282] For the most part, the prayers without exact Roman parallel do not possess the stylistic traits of any non-Roman liturgy.[283] Those that do, in particular the benedictions of Palm Sunday (**169, 172**), are based on Gallican sources that circulated primarily through the Gelasians of the Eighth Century. Of course, the similarities in vocabulary and structure between the prayers of PuZ, presumably pure Old Beneventan, and the Roman corpus of the Gelasian sacramentaries must qualify any purely stylistic search for Old Beneventan prayers. There appears to be no reason to seek the prolixities and metaphors of the Gallican liturgy in the Old Beneventan corpus; one should expect instead the more sober and precise language of the early Roman sacramentaries.

The Temporal of the Missal retains none of the Old Beneventan masses of the manuscripts from Benevento.[284] However, as Hesbert has noted, it does have a distinctive musical setting for the *Exultet* (**207-208**) based on the melody found in other Beneventan sources.[285] The similar elaboration of the setting for the Genealogy of Luke (**45**) has regional parallels but cannot be considered indigenous, despite the antiquity of other recitatives in the Beneventan tradition.[286]

The retention of Old Beneventan lections in the Temporal of the Oxford manuscript is particularly noticeable: the gospels from John for the Sundays of Lent are a distinguishing feature of the Old Beneventan liturgy that associate it with the other early rites of western Europe. Unlike the musical pieces of the few masses that survived as alternatives to Roman masses in the mass-antiphonals of Benevento, the Johannine gospels continued to be copied as the proper lections for the Sundays of Lent in several Beneventan centres. The combined witness of the Dubrovnik missal and the recently-

---

[282] I.e., *Inclinantes se domine* (**126**) from Ash Wednesday, found on the same day in Ha 157, Pa 131, and the Roman missal, but elsewhere in the Gelasians of the Eighth Century.
[283] The style of Gallican prayers is described by Jungmann, *Missarum Sollemnia*, 1: 62-63.
[284] Huglo, "Ancien chant bénéventain," pp. 272-280.
[285] Hesbert, "Tradition bénéventaine," pp. 399-416.
[286] Hesbert, "Tradition bénéventaine," pp. 416-417.

discovered lection-lists of Kotor in DaB and DaK reinforce the long-held thesis that Dalmatian cult was particularly resistant to change in this regard.[287]

The survival of a three-lection system is another traditional feature, although the Missal gives a prophetic lesson only for the masses of Christmas (**1**, **15**). The evidence in the early Roman lectionaries for a similar system on certain central feasts points both to the connections between the liturgies of Rome and southern Italy and to the conservatism of the Beneventan churches.

Roman Influences: For the prayers of the Missal, the first Roman substrate was probably a Gregorian sacramentary related to, but predating, the Hadrianum sent to the Carolingian court in 783. The masses of the central feasts are entirely Gregorian: Christmas, the Sunday after Christmas, Epiphany, Septuagesima, Sexagesima, Quinquagesima, the Sundays of Lent except the second Sunday, the first Rogation mass, and Ascension. A number of other feasts are Gregorian with minor variants: the mass of Ash Wednesday, the vigil and feast of Pentecost, and the first Sunday after Pentecost. Moreover, the absence of counterparts in the Gelasians of the Eighth Century for the secret of Christmas (**19**), the mass of Septuagesima (**98**, **104**), the *super populum* of Ash Wednesday (**126**), the postcommunion of the second Sunday of Lent (**146**), the secret of the third Sunday (**152**), the secret and postcommunion of Palm Sunday (**182**, **184**), the secret of the vigil of Pentecost (**262**), and the collect of the first Sunday after Pentecost (**287**), all found in the Hadrianum, are best accounted for by postulating a Gregorian base.

The exception of the second Sunday of Lent is important for dating the Gregorian source for the masses of the Missal. Although it has the normal Gregorian collect (**138**) and the postcommunion of the Hadrianum (**146**), the secret (**144**) is unique to the feast. The mass of the Dubrovnik missal was, therefore, probably compiled originally for a Gregorian source lacking a mass for the Sunday, i.e., one that predated the seventh century when a general mass for the second Sunday of Lent was instituted. The variant secret of Pentecost is also an important exception to the Gregorian base: in this case, the variant has counterparts in other Beneventan sources and represents a regional modification borrowed from early Gelasian sacramentaries.[288]

Since the source for the Romano-Beneventan sacramentary has no exact counterpart among surviving manuscripts, it cannot be defined precisely,

---

[287] E.g., Hesbert, "Tradition bénéventaine," p. 399, quoted above, p. 1.
[288] See above p. 101.

although the sacramentaries used as supplements to the Gregorian base are highlighted in the texts of the Dubrovnik missal. The major prayers of the Temporal not found in the Gregorian source are the masses after Epiphany, Easter, and Pentecost, which are omitted in the Hadrianum, but the Missal also contains other adapted prayers and some original texts. The Paduense and Gelasians of the Eighth Century, representing the second, supplemental influence on the Romano-Beneventan corpus, are the principal sources for the masses of the vigil of Epiphany, the Sundays after Epiphany, including the octave, the Sundays after Easter, the vigil of Ascension, and the Ember Saturday after Pentecost. On the other hand, the Sundays after Pentecost show more signs of relation to the Supplement to the Hadrianum than to the Gelasians of the Eighth Century.

Romano-Beneventan prayers distinctive either for their placement or their unique texts include the secret (**32**) and postcommunion (**34**) of the Marian mass within the octave of Christmas, the postcommunion (**44**) of the vigil of Epiphany, the secrets for the octave (**74**) and first Sunday (**64**) after Epiphany, the prayers for the Ash Wednesday ceremony (**112-114**), the secret (**144**) of the second Sunday of Lent, the prayers said during the Palm Sunday processions (**169, 170, 172, 174**), the prayer before the Cross (**202**), the *benedictio ignis novi* (**206**), the second Rogation mass (**234, 238, 240**), the collect (**242**) of the vigil of Ascension, the postcommunion (**264**) of the vigil of Pentecost, the secret of Pentecost (**272**), and the secret (**283**) of the Ember Saturday after Pentecost.

For the musical items, the source for the majority of texts and melodies of the Dubrovnik missal is clearly Roman, but of a regional variety. In common with other Beneventan manuscripts, the list of musical items has been augmented for lesser feasts and masses that were without provision in the Gregorian source of the Beneventan mass-antiphonal. Thus, the mass for the second Sunday of Lent (**137-145**), which was formed to fill the gap in the original book left by the aliturgical *Dominica vacat* after the Ember Days of Lent, has a unique introit (**137**) and gradual (**140**) and the communion *Qui biberit* (**145**) drawn from another feast. Similarly, the Roman source must have lacked proper alleluias for many feasts since there are a number of Romano-Beneventan alleluias with regional texts or melodies in the Dubrovnik missal.[289] The later development of regional prosulas (**141, 163**) is also indicative of the local activity required to fill out areas neglected in earlier books.

[289] Romano-Beneventan alleluias of the Temporal are nos. **29, 39, 61, 81, 91, 217, 218, 269,** and **279**.

The lection-list of the Temporal parallels less closely the two waves of
Roman influence apparent from consideration of the sources of the prayers.
The most notable exception is the continued presence of the Old Beneventan
Lenten gospels, but the lections also show fewer traces of the division
between Gregorian feasts and feasts taken from the Gelasians of the Eighth
Century or from the Supplement that is evident in the prayers. In general,
the readings for the central feasts have counterparts in both the Comes of
Würzburg, which corresponds most closely to the Hadrianum, and the
Comes of Muhrbach and Paris, which correspond to the Gelasian sacramentaries. But the selections for the lesser feasts are Romano-Beneventan,
including the epistles for the Mass within the octave of Christmas (**27**), the
vigil of Epiphany (**37**), and the first and second Rogation masses (**226, 235**);
for the gospels, the octave of Epiphany (**72**), the third Sunday after Epiphany
(**92**), the Rogation masses (**228, 236**), and the Ember Saturday after
Pentecost (**281**) have regional lections. Moreover, several lections not found
in the early lectionaries have parallels in later Roman missals, suggesting late
influences on the Temporal of the Dubrovnik missal.[290] The distinction to be
drawn from the lections, therefore, is less between Gregorian and Gelasian
than between early Roman and later.

Later Influences: Although the Missal, compiled in the latter half of the
thirteenth century, could be expected to show signs of later developments
and influences on its Romano-Beneventan liturgy, in fact, apart from a
handful of late Roman lections and the adoption of northern texts for the
Palm Sunday benedictions (**169, 172**), perhaps via the Roman-German
Pontifical of the Tenth Century,[291] there is little evidence in the Temporal for
influences post-dating the tenth century.[292]

The Marian mass within the octave of Christmas (**26-34**) is the only late
regional addition to the calendar of the Temporal, although its elements are

---

[290] The later Roman lections are the gospel of the Marian mass within the octave of
Christmas (**30**), the epistle of the octave of Epiphany (**69**), and the lections of the Sundays
after Pentecost (**288, 291, 294, 301**).

[291] The texts may have entered the region even earlier since they also circulated in the
Gelasians of the Eighth Century.

[292] Of course, the distinction between *fons formalis* and *fons materialis* must be kept in
mind. Many texts may well have enjoyed their greatest circulation in the later mixed
Gelasian-Gregorian sacramentaries, or even in the much later missals of the Mendicant orders.
Thus a "Gelasian" influence can only be considered direct if the text does not appear in later
witnesses: a demonstration often problematic as long as so many later sources remain
unstudied. Nonetheless, the checks provided by consideration of the relation between the
Dubrovnik missal and other Beneventan sources offer some degree of surety for the discussion
of the regional liturgy.

more closely dependent on the Roman tradition than were the pieces of the mass for the second Sunday in Lent.

2. Sanctoral

The Sanctorals of the early liturgies, Old Beneventan, Gelasian, and Gregorian, are less developed and less stable than their corresponding Temporal cycles. The homogeneity of the Temporal in any group of sources is consequently not so marked in the Sanctoral. The same phenomenon of late development that created such variety in the alleluias of the Temporal, or the masses of the Ember days and the Rogations, for instance, is at work in encouraging a proliferation of local variants in the Sanctoral. For this reason, the divergences and peculiarities of the Dubrovnik missal and of other Beneventan manuscripts are more frequent in the masses of the Sanctoral but less striking than the points of difference already cited for the Temporal: more frequent due to the development in isolation of masses for feasts not found in the early liturgical books, less striking because diversity is the norm in this instance.

The variety in the Sanctoral of any medieval liturgical book, and especially later medieval sources, has practical consequences for the study of regional liturgies. Not only does it limit confidence in the conclusions of analysis so long as many later witnesses remain unstudied, but it also reduces the utility of a point-by-point consideration of texts not common to every branch of the Roman tradition. For example, where the dependence of one tradition on another in the Temporal could be understood through examination of the relatively few variant texts, many more prayers, lections, and musical pieces in the Sanctoral are at odds with one or another of the early sources.[293] Thus, bowing to considerations of economy and clarity, I will use a different method to examine the contents of the Sanctoral. First, the general patterns of its composition and source dependence will be considered; then the masses and individual items proper to the region or absent in the standard sources of the liturgy will be listed with brief comments. Of course, the hope remains that many of these texts will be placed more securely as the details of later medieval liturgical development become clearer; for the moment, however, it must suffice to identify the more distinctive pieces and provide a cursory and all-too-hypothetical guide to their importance and history.

---

[293] E.g., in the Temporal, 68 of 97 prayers (70%) are Gregorian vs. 45 of 110 (41%) in the Sanctoral; and 43 of 57 (75%) of the lections in the Temporal are found in MRM vs. 26 of 61 (43%) in the Sanctoral.

Prayers of the Sanctoral

The basis for studying the Sanctoral of the Dubrovnik missal will be a breakdown of the masses by source. Since the pattern varies for the prayers, lections, and musical items, the sources will be considered separately for each category, beginning with the prayers. Summaries of the information concerning the prayers presented in the *apparatus parallelorum locorum* are listed in separate tables according to the origins of the texts (Tables 8-14).

The fifty-three mass-sets of the Sanctoral, including the blessing of grapes (**547**), which is not part of the eucharistic liturgy, contain 110 prayers. Due to deficiencies of the manuscript and the citation of only a single collect for many of the feasts, only twenty-eight masses, or just over half the total, have all three prayers: a collect, secret, and postcommunion. Of the rest, two masses have two prayers; twenty-two masses have a single prayer; and one mass, the feast of Nicholas, has none. Since some mass-sets are common to both Gregorian and Gelasian traditions, their witness is of secondary importance in understanding the development of the Beneventan missal. The twelve common mass-sets are cited in Table 8. In each case, the relation of the prayer to the Hadrianum, Paduense, four Gelasians of the Eighth Century, Beneventan manuscripts, and other relevant sources is listed.

Although the prayers in the common mass-sets account for only sixteen of the 110 prayers of the Sanctoral, the small size of the set belies the extent of the similarities between the masses of the Dubrovnik missal and masses of the Roman tradition, whether Gregorian, Gelasian, or a mixture:[294] in fact, a further fourteen prayers from other feasts are also common to both Gregorian and Gelasian traditions.[295] The thirty common prayers, slightly less than a third of the total, are for the most part taken directly into later medieval missals and the Roman missal. Exceptions are the blessing of grapes (**547**) and the collects for Sebastian (**326**), Agatha (**338**), and Alexander, Eventus and Theodolus (**420**). The blessing of grapes, though found in some early printed missals, is more often copied in pontificals;[296] the collect for Sebastian disappears in the Roman missal where the feast is conflated with the following feast for Fabian (**327**) and provided with the mass of the latter;[297] and the collect for Alexander, Eventus, and Theodolus

---

[294] Fifty-three of the 110 prayers of the Sanctoral have counterparts in MRM.

[295] I.e., **310**, **318**, **322**, **385**, **410**, **415**, **429**, **436**, **448**, **464**, **466**, **472**, **476**, and **558**; two more are common to both Pa and the Gelasians of the Eighth Century (**419**, **578**) but not Ha.

[296] Missals: MRM 2: 302. Pontificals: Vogel and Elze, *Pontifical romano-germanique*, 2: 371 (ordo 226); Andrieu, *Pontifical romain*, 1: 264 (ordo 45); 2: 454 (ordo 40); 3: 540 (lib. 2, ordo 27).

[297] Bruylants, *Oraisons*, 1: 75-76 (mass 179).

Feast		GREG	GEL8	Misc	BEN
Felix	**324**	Ha,Pa	En,Ge,Sg,Rh		Ben,Da,Mc,Ott,Ve
Marcellus, Pope	**325**	Ha,Pa	En,Ge,Sg,Rh		Ben,Da,Mc,Ott,Ve
Sebastian	**326**	Ha,Pa	En,Ge,Sg,Rh	AM: Sb	Ben,Da,Mc,Ott,Ve
Fabian	**327**	Ha,Pa	En,Ge,Sg		Ben,Da,Mc,Ott,Ve
Vincent	**332**	Ha,Pa	En,Ge,Sg,Rh	AM: Sb	Ben,Da,Mc,Ott,Ve
Agatha	**338**	Ha,Pa	En,Ge,Sg,Rh		Pu
Alexander, Eventus and Theodolus	**420**	Ha,Pa	En,Ge	MRM v.2	Ben,Mc,Ott,Ve
John the Baptist	**438**	Ha,Pa	En,Ge,Sg,Rh		Ben,Mc,Ott,Pu,Ve
	444	Ha,Pa	En,Ge,Sg,Rh		Ben,Mc,Ott,Pu,Ve
	446	Ha,Pa	En,Ge,Rh,Sg		Ben,Mc,Ott,Pu,Ve
Stephen, Pope	**535**	Ha,Pa	En,Ge,Sg,Rh		Ben,Mc,Ott,Ve
Blessing of Grapes	**547**	Ha	Ge,Rh	AM: Sb	Ben,Mc
Vigil of Lawrence	**549**	Ha,Pa	En,Ge,Sg,Rh		Ben,Mc,Ott,Ve
	554	Ha,Pa	En,Ge,Sg,Rh		Ben,Mc,Ott,Pu,Ve
	556	Ha,Pa	En,Ge,Sg,Rh		Ben,Mc,Ott,Ve
Tiburtius	**567**	Ha,Pa	En,Ge,Sg		Ben,Mc,Ott,Ve

TABLE 8
Sanctoral: Mass-sets Common to Gregorian and Gelasian Sources*

* In the following tables, Beneventan manuscripts are cited in groups by place of origin: Ben = Benevento, Da = Dalmatia, Mc = Monte Cassino, Pu = Apulia, Ca = Caiazzo, Ve = Veroli. Manuscripts without established origins are cited by their full sigla. The origin references are used as prefixes to the individual citations in the *apparatus parallelorum locorum*, where the complete list of comparable sources for each text may be found.

(**420**) also appears in mixed Gelasian-Gregorian sacramentaries (F 898) and some printed missals if not the standard Roman missal.[298]

The collect for Agatha (**338**) points more clearly to a Gelasian origin: the Gregorian text is an alternative following the mass (Ha 131, Pa 111), whereas the Gelasian books give it as the first collect (En 209, Ge 201, Rh 151, Sg 189). In this case, the Gregorian collect *Deus qui inter* (Ha 128)

[298] Missals: MRM 2: 195. Moreton, *Eighth-Century Gelasian Sacramentary*, pp. 105-106, notes that only the collect is common to both Gregorian and Gelasian sacramentaries. However, since the Oxford MS gives only the collect, and since it contains major textual variants not present in either tradition, the immediate source of the prayer must be considered undefined.

became the collect of the Roman missal, while the alternative was dropped.[299]
The Dubrovnik missal also follows the Gelasian sacramentaries in several
distinguishing textual variants:

> 338 Indulgentiam nobis domine beata agathe martira imploret. que *tibi grata
> extitit; uirtute martirii.* et merito *castitatis.* Per.

> tibi grata] *ut Ge, Rh*, tibi grata semper *Ha*, grata semper *Sg*   extitit uirtute martirii] *ut Ge, Rh,
> Sg*, existit *Ha*, exstitit *Pa*   castitatis] *ut Ge, Rh, Sg*, et tuae professione uirtutis *add. Ha.*

The prayer is attested among Beneventan books only in the Dubrovnik missal
and the Missal of Canosa (Baltimore, Walters Art Gallery, W 6, = PuC). In
the latter source, though given as the collect for the mass, it presents the
textual variants of the Gregorian text. The appearance of the prayer in
Dubrovnik is, therefore, unusual and suggests the restricted influence of a
Gelasian source at some point in the composition of the collection forming
the basis of the Missal.

More telling for the history of the sources of the Missal are lists of the
masses entirely proper only to one or the other principal tradition. Table 9
contains the five Gregorian mass-sets that differ from the Gelasians in at least
one element.

These five Gregorian masses contain fifteen of the prayers of the Sanctoral
that may be attributed to Gregorian sources, including one proper to the
Paduense.[300] There are a further thirty: twenty-six that have parallels in both
the Hadrianum and Paduense, and four found in the Hadrianum. Discounting
for the moment the prayers common to both Gregorian and Gelasian
sources, there are sixteen prayers that may be considered "pure" Gregorian
texts without counterparts in the Gelasians of the Eighth Century.[301]

A second group of mass-sets derives from Romano-Frankish or Gelasian
sources. Table 10 lists the nine masses that correspond throughout to the

---

[299] Bruylants, *Oraisons*, 1: 82 (mass 198).

[300] I.e., *Concede quesumus omnipotens deus* (578) as Pa 621 and the Sacramentary of Trent
701 (above n. 53): see Moreton, *Eighth-Century Gelasian Sacramentary*, pp. 125-126; and
Chavasse, *Sacramentaire gélasien*, pp. 390-397, for the Marian masses, esp. 392 for the
Assumption, where he concludes that the prayer originates in a Roman sacramentary such as
Pa.

[301] I.e., **330**, **331** (Agnes), **377** (Annunciation), **417*** (Philip and James), **434*** (Vigil of
John the Baptist), **453***, **455*** (John and Paul), **462** (Vigil of Peter and Paul), **482***, **484***
(Commemoration of Paul), **531** (Chains of Peter), **564** (Lawrence), **569** (Vigil of the
Assumption), **578***, **584***, **586*** (Assumption). Although **578*** is attested in Pa and the
Gelasians of the Eighth Century but not in Ha, it is included in this list due to its probable
Gregorian origin (see the preceding note). Entries with a single asterisk are listed in Table
9. The prayers common to both traditions (not including **547**, the blessing of grapes) are listed
above at n. 295 and Table 8.

TABLE 9 Sanctoral: Mass-sets from Gregorian Sources					
Feast		GREG	GEL8	BEN	
Philip and James	410	Ha,Pa	En,Ge,Sg,Rh	Ben,Mc,Ott,Pu,Ve	
	415	Ha,Pa	En,Ge,Sg,Rh	Ben,Mc,Ott,Pu,Ve	
	417	Ha,Pa	(En,Ge,Sg)	Ben,Mc,Ott,Ve	
Vigil of John the Baptist	429	Ha,Pa	En,Ge,Sg,Rh	Ben,Mc,Ott,Pu,Ve	
	434	Ha,Pa	(En,Ge,Sg,Rh)	Ben,Mc,Pu,Ve	
	436	Ha,Pa	En,Ge,Sg,Rh	Ben,Mc,Ott,Ve	
John and Paul	448	Ha,Pa	En,Ge,Sg,Rh	Ben,Mc,Ott,Ve	
	453	Ha,Pa	(En,Ge,Sg,Rh)	Ben,Mc,Ott,Pu,Ve,Vl10645	
	455	Ha,Pa	(En,Ge,Sg,Rh)	Ben,Mc,Ott,Ve,Vl10645	
Commemoration of Paul	476	Ha,Pa	En,Ge,Sg,Rh	Ben,Mc,Ott,Ve	
	482	Ha,Pa	(En,Ge,Sg,Rh)	Ben,Mc,Ott,Ve	
	484	Ha,Pa	( )	Ben,Mc,Ott,Ve	
Assumption	578	(Ha),Pa	En,Ge,Rh,Sg	Ben,Mc,Ott	
	584	Ha	( )	Ve	
	586	Ha	( )	Ben,Mc,Ott,Pu,Ve	

* In all the remaining tables parentheses ( ), whether filled or unfilled, indicate a prayer for the feast different from that of Dubr; brackets [ ] show that the feast itself is absent in the source being compared. A siglum between either parentheses or brackets indicates that the prayer of Dubr appears on a different feast in the source being considered: thus (Ha) signifies that the Hadrianum has prayers for the feast, but the comparable text is found on another day; while [Ha] indicates that the Hadrianum lacks the feast but has a comparable prayer elsewhere. Where the column is a comparison with a single edition or text, then an equal sign = signifies the presence of the same text on the same feast; where the column is a comparison with a category of sources, e.g., GREG or GEL8, the relevant texts are listed by their sigla in each field.

Gelasians of the Eighth Century but do not match the Gregorian sacramentaries for every prayer.

The Gelasian masses contain fifteen prayers without exact counterparts in the Gregorian sacramentaries. Other Romano-Frankish texts found on feasts not entirely Gelasian are the collect of Agnes (**328**), the collect for Agatha (**338**),[302] the secret of the Annunciation (**383**), and the collect for the vigil of the apostles Peter and Paul (**457**). Two prayers are paralleled in both the Paduense and the Gelasians but not the Hadrianum: the first, the collect *Deus*

---

[302] See above pp. 114-115.

TABLE 10
Sanctoral: Mass-sets from the Gelasians of the Eighth Century

Feast		GREG	GEL8	ES: F	BEN
Stephen	310	Ha,Pa	En,Ge,Sg,Rh	=	Ben,Ca,Mc,Ott,Ve
	316	( )	En,Ge,Sg,Rh	=	Da,Pu
	318	Ha,Pa	En,Ge,Sg,Rh	=	Ben,Ca,Da,Mc,Ott,Pu,Ve
Conversion of Paul	334	[ ]	En,Sg	=	Ben,Da,Mc,Ott,Ve
Chair of Peter	349	[Ha,Pa]	En,Ge,Sg,Rh	=	Ben,Da,Mc,Ott,Ve
	355	[Ha,Pa]	En,Ge,Sg,Rh	=	Ben,Ve
	357	[ ]	En,Ge,Sg,Rh	=	Ve
George	387	( )	En,Ge,Sg	=	Ben,Mc,Pu
	396	( )	En,Ge,Sg	( )	Ben,Mc,Ott,Pu
	398	(Pa)	En,Ge,Sg	=	Ben,Mc,Ott,Pu
Vitalis	399	( )	En,Ge,Sg	=	
Invention of the Cross	419	Pa	En,Ge,Sg,Rh	=	Ben,Mc,Ott,Pu,Ve
	426	( )	En,Ge,Sg,Rh	=	Ben,Mc,Ott,Pu,Ve
Peter and Paul	466	Ha,Pa	En,Ge,Sg,Rh	=	Ben,Mc,Ott,Pu,Ve
	472	Ha,Pa	Ge,Sg,Rh	=	Ben,Mc,Ott,Pu,Ve
	474	( )	En,Ge,Sg,Rh	( )	Ben,Mc,Ott,Pu,Ve
James	523	[Ha]	En,Ge,Sg,Rh	=	Ben,Mc,Ott,Pu,Ve
	527	[ ]	En,Ge,Sg,Rh	=	Ben,Mc,Ott,Pu,Ve
	529	[ ]	En,Ge,Sg,Rh	=	Ben,Mc,Ott,Pu,Ve
Machabees	532	[ ]	En,Ge,Sg	=	Ben,Mc,Ott,Ve

qui in preclara (**419**) of the Invention of the Cross, is generally considered a Gelasian prayer;[303] the second, the collect of the Assumption (**578**), is probably a Gregorian text.[304] Thus, twenty prayers of the 110 in the Sanctoral are of sure Gelasian origin.

These Romano-Frankish masses fall into two general groups depending on whether or not any prayers of the mass-set are common to both Gregorian and Gelasian traditions. Masses without common texts may be further subdivided into feasts with counterparts in the Gregorian calendar and those

---

[303] Ge 944, Rh 564, Sg 743, Pa 421 (Moreton, *Eighth-Century Gelasian Sacramentary*, pp. 134-135; and Chavasse, *Sacramentaire gélasien*, pp. 351-357).

[304] See above n. 300.

without parallel. In general, Romano-Frankish feasts without parallel in early Gregorian sources have left greater traces in later medieval Roman books, undoubtedly because the Gregorian calendar was enhanced for these feasts by the adoption of masses directly from the Gelasian sacramentaries without any need to supplant pre-existing Gregorian masses. This observation certainly holds true for the Dubrovnik missal. The Romano-Frankish masses for the Conversion of Paul (**334**), the Chair of Peter (**349, 355, 357**), the Invention of the Cross (**419, 426**), the apostle James (**523, 527, 529**), and the Machabees (**532**) are the same masses that eventually make their way into the Roman missal via mixed Gelasian-Gregorian sacramentaries, such as the fourteenth-century Missal of the Curia and earlier corrected copies of the supplemented Hadrianum.[305]

The other Gelasian prayers and masses, those for feasts found also in the Hadrianum, are without exception not taken into the Roman missal. Nonetheless, the Gelasian secret for Stephen (**316**), collect and postcommunion of George (**387, 398**), collect of Vitalis (**399**), and collect for the vigil of the apostles Peter and Paul (**457**) are all attested in Gelasian-Gregorian sacramentaries of the "eccentric" tradition represented by the Fulda sacramentary (= F).[306] Only the secret for George (**396**) and the postcommunion of the apostles Peter and Paul (**474**) are not found in the Fulda sacramentary. For these two prayers, one need only consider the variety in choice of prayers and feasts among the "eccentric" sacramentaries to realise that some witnesses of the type may have carried the prayers. The Romano-Beneventan source of the Dubrovnik missal, therefore, was perhaps dependent in part on such a sacramentary for the additions to its Gregorian base and not directly on the Gelasians of the Eighth Century.[307]

Related to the Gregorian and Gelasian masses are three masses that draw all their prayers from the two Roman traditions but are not clearly dependent on one or the other. Table 11 lists the relevant masses.

Again remarkable is the presence in the Fulda sacramentary of every prayer except the postcommunion of the vigil of the apostles Peter and Paul

---

[305] E.g., the mass for the Conversion of Paul (**334**) is found in Cambrai, Bibliothèque Municipale, 162-163 (Hadrianum cum Suppl., s. ix², Saint-Vaast d'Arras; bibl.: *CLLA*, no. 761; ed. Deshusses, *Sacramentaire grégorien*, 1: 690, no. 40*).

[306] Vogel, *Medieval Liturgy*, pp. 102-104, describes the categories of Gregorian sacramentaries with Gelasian additions, based on Emmanuel Bourque, *Études sur les sacramentaires romains*, 2 parts in 3 vols., Studi di Antichità Cristiana 20, 25 (Vatican City, Quebec, 1948-1958), 2: 444-472.

[307] Of course, the mixed sacramentary in question need not have been composed north of the Alps: the influence of a Gelasian sacramentary on an earlier Gregorian book may have taken place in a southern Italian centre.

TABLE 11				
Sanctoral: Mass-sets of Mixed Gregorian and Gelasian Origin				
Feast	GREG	GEL8	ES: F	BEN
Agnes **328**	( )	En,Ge,Sg,Rh	=	( )
330	Ha,Pa	(En,Ge,Sg,Rh)	=	Ben,Da,Mc,Ott,Pu,Ve
331	Ha,Pa	(En,Ge,Sg,Rh)	=	Ben,Da,Mc,Ott,Pu,Ve
Annunciation **377**	Ha	( )	=	Ben,Mc
383	( )	En,Ge,Sg	=	Ben,Da,Mc,Ott,Pu
385	Ha,Pa	En,Ge,Sg,Rh	=	Ben,Da,Mc,Ott,Pu,Ve
Vigil of Peter				
and Paul **457**	( )	En,Ge,Sg,Rh	=	Ben,Mc,Ott,Pu,Vl10645
462	Ha,Pa	(En,Ge,Sg,Rh)	=	Ben,Mc,Ott,Ve
464	Ha,Pa	En,Ge,Sg,Rh	(=)	Ben,Mc,Ott,Pu,Ve

(**464**), which is found there on the feast itself. In the Fulda sacramentary, however, the masses are scarcely stable: each is provided with both Gregorian and Gelasian prayers as propers and alternatives. The idiosyncratic choice of individual prayers from each tradition in the Oxford manuscript reflects a process of trimming, condensation, and abbreviation from the overflowing abundance of an "eccentric" mixed Gelasian-Gregorian model. Indeed, since the mass-sets in their simplest form appear elsewhere principally in Beneventan books (with the exception of the collect of Agnes), the selection was likely to have been made at an early point in the general development of the Romano-Beneventan missal. The many Beneventan counterparts to the masses of the Dubrovnik missal derived without variant from the Gregorian or Gelasian traditions are not unexpected, but parallels among less easily classified "mixed" masses point to a regional source, perhaps a southern Italian form of the Gelasian-Gregorian sacramentaries of the tenth and eleventh centuries.

Other groups of distinctive masses are those composed of Gelasian or Gregorian prayers adapted from other feasts (Table 12).

Not all the prayers in these mass-sets are Gregorian or Gelasian: some prayers are unique,[308] others are found in later Romano-Frankish sources,[309] one is related to the Milanese liturgy,[310] and some are proper to the feasts

---

[308] I.e., the collect and postcommunion of the Dalmatian martyrs Lawrence, Peter, and Andrew (**486, 494**); see also Table 14.

[309] I.e., the mass of Matthias (**359, 362, 364**), the collect and secret of Benedict (**367, 373**), and the postcommunion of All Saints (**591**): see also Table 13.

[310] I.e., the collect of Mark (**401**).

TABLE 12					
Sanctoral: Prayers Adapted from Gregorian and Gelasian Sources					
Feast		GREG	GEL8	Misc	BEN
Thomas	308	(Ha,Pa)	(En,Ge,Sg,Rh)		Mc,Ott,Pu
Silvester, Pope	320	(Tc)	(En,Ge,Sg,Rh)		( )
	322*	Ha,Pa	En,Ge,Sg,Rh		Ben,Da,Mc,Ott,Ve
	323	( )	(Ge,Sg)		( )
Matthias	359**	Tc	[ ]	ES: F	Ve
	362**	Tc	[ ]	ES: F	Ve
	364	Tc,[Ha]	[En,Ge]	ES: F	( )
Benedict	367**	[ ]	( )	ES: F	Ben,Da,Mc,Ott,Pu,Ve
	373**	[ ]	( )	ES: F	Ben,Da,Mc,Ott,Pu,Ve
	375	[Ha,Pa]	(En,Ge,Sg)		(Ben)
Mark	401**	[ ]	[ ]	AM:Sacr. Aribert	Ben,Mc,Pu
	406	[Ha,Pa]	[En,Ge,Sg,Rh]		(Ben)
	408	[Ha,Pa]	[En,Ge,Sg,Rh]		(Ben)
Lawrence, Peter and Andrew	486**	[ ]	[ ]		[ ]
	492	[Pa,Tc]	[En,Ge,Sg]		[ ]
	494**	[ ]	[ ]		[ ]
Apollenaris	517	[ ]	[En,Ge,Sg,Rh]		Ben,Mc,Ott
Invention of Stephen	536	[Ha,Pa]	[En,Ge,Sg]		Ben,Mc,Ott,Ve
	539	[Ha,Pa]	[En,Ge,Sg,Rh]		Ben,Mc,Ott
	540	[Ha,Pa]	[En,Ge,Sg,Rh]		Ben,Mc,Ott,Ve
Vigil of the Assumption	569	Ha	( )		Ben,Mc,Ott,Ve
	574	( )	(En,Ge,Sg,Rh)		Ben,(Mc),Pu
	576	( )	(En,Ge,Sg,Rh)		Ben,Mc,Ott,Pu
All Saints	589	Tc, [Ha,Pa]	[En,Ge,Sg]		Ben,Mc,Ott,Ve
	591**	Tc	[ ]	ES: F	Pu,Ve

* Common to Gregorian and Gelasian sources.
** Without Gregorian or Gelasian sources except in modified copies of GREG, i.e., Tc (Tables 13-14).

in the early sources.[311] Three masses have corresponding feasts in the Gregorian sacramentaries (Thomas, Silvester, and the vigil of the Assumption), and one additional mass has counterparts in the Gelasians of the Eighth Century (Benedict). Obviously, the remaining feasts are either so much less ancient or less widely celebrated that the adaptation of prayers is not unusual.[312] But if we assume that a feast in the Missal composed of adapted prayers indicates an omission in the regional exemplar, a closer look at certain Gregorian and Gelasian feasts may shed light on the history of the early Romano-Beneventan sacramentary.

Thomas (**308**): The feast of Thomas is attested with a different mass in the Vatican Gelasian (Va 1088-1090), the Gelasians of the Eighth Century (Ge 1757-1761), the Comes of Muhrbach,[313] and in later mixed sacramentaries (Tc 301*-303*); it is absent altogether from the Hadrianum, Paduense, Comes of Alcuin, Comes of Würzburg, and the early mass-antiphonals. The Beneventan source for the Dubrovnik missal, McV, and the twelfth-century Beneventan missal of Vatican City, BAV, Ottob. lat. 576 (= Ott), which have adapted the same Gregorian-Gelasian text for the feast, was likely composed before the Gelasians of the Eighth Century had circulated widely in the region: otherwise the Gelasian proper texts would have been chosen. In this case, the earliest source for the Romano-Beneventan sacramentary would appear to have been a Gregorian book predating the Gelasians of the Eighth Century and the mixed Gelasian-Gregorian sacramentaries of later centuries; this source lacked the feast of Thomas but contained the prayers used to the form the mass when the feast eventually entered the regional calendar.

Silvester (**320, 322, 323**): The feast of Silvester is among the oldest in the Sanctoral;[314] it is found in the Comes of Würzburg, the early mass-antiphonals, and most early sacramentaries from the Veronese (Le 1161-1163) to the Hadrianum (Ha 79-81) and the Gelasians of the Eighth Century (Ge, Sg 73-75), though not in the Vatican Gelasian. Despite the wide diffusion of the feast, the mass-sets present several variants: Moreton concluded that

---

[311] I.e., the secret of Silvester (**322**), and the collect for the vigil of the Assumption (**569**).

[312] Even the feast of Apolenaris (**517**), though found in the early mass-antiphonals, WuC, and the Comes of Muhrbach (see the following note), has no proper mass in the early sacramentaries, which suggests a relatively late date for its composition (Hesbert, *Antiphonale missarum sextuplex*, p. xcix).

[313] Besançon, Bibliothèque Municipale, 184, fols. 58r-74v; siglum: Mu, capitulare lectionum, s. viii ex.; ed. André Wilmart, "Le *Comes* de Muhrbach," *RB* 30 (1913) 25-69; bibl.: *CLLA*, no. 1226.

[314] Hesbert, *Antiphonale missarum sextuplex*, pp. lxxxiv-lxxxv.

the standard set found in the Hadrianum and some of the Gelasians was not the only mass-set circulating for the feast among the early Roman collections of *libelli*.[315] Since the mass of the Dubrovnik missal is paralleled in no other sacramentary, it may bear witness to the early confusion of prayers, although the lack of parallels for the collect (**320**) and postcommunion (**323**) even among Beneventan sources suggests that the Missal is truly individual in this instance.

Vigil of the Assumption (**569, 574, 576**): Despite provision of proper texts in both the Gregorian sacramentaries and the Gelasians of the Eighth Century, the mass for the vigil of the Assumption cannot be considered among the oldest feasts. The feast of Assumption itself was only introduced to the west in the late seventh century; the differences between the Gregorian and Gelasian masses and the absence of the feast in three of the six early mass-antiphonals point to its late composition.[316] The vigil must be even later, for it is not found in the early mass-antiphonals, the Vatican Gelasian, or the Comes of Würzburg, which otherwise make provision for the feast. The mass of the Dubrovnik missal reflects this late development: while the collect (**569**) is adopted from the Hadrianum, the secret (**574**) is a borrowing of the Gelasian secret for the feast itself (Ge 1349), and the postcommunion (**576**) comes from the Gelasian Birth of the Virgin (Ge 1432). The exemplar was evidently only poorly equipped for the vigils of late feasts: some Beneventan missals, including our Dalmatian missal, eventually adopted the collect of the Hadrianum. But at least one early source, which lies at the base of the mass in Ben33, Ben30, and the Dubrovnik missal and has left traces in the postcommunion of other Beneventan manuscripts, created its own mass with a proper secret and postcommunion drawn from related feasts in an early Gelasian sacramentary that was perhaps akin to the Vatican Gelasian in its lack of a mass for the vigil.

The masses for Thomas, Silvester, and the vigil of the Assumption point each to a different influence on the early Beneventan sacramentary: the composition of the mass for Thomas suggests a Gregorian book predating the Gelasians of the Eighth Century and the mixed Gelasian-Gregorian

---

[315] Moreton, *Eighth-Century Gelasian Sacramentary*, p. 103.

[316] The feast of the Assumption is discussed by Moreton, *Eighth-Century Gelasian Sacramentary*, pp. 125-126; *Église en prière* (1961), pp. 756-758; *Église en prière* (1983-1984), 4: 151-152; and Hesbert, *Antiphonale missarum sextuplex*, pp. lxxx-lxxxii. For the vigil, see Moreton, *Eighth-Century Gelasian Sacramentary*, pp. 151-152. The several additions to the early calendar of the Gregorian sacramentaries are summarised in Deshusses, *Sacramentaire grégorien*, 3: 60-63.

sacramentaries of later centuries ; the mass of Silvester must be considered idiosyncratic; and the vigil of the Assumption is best explained by composition from an early Gelasian sacramentary somewhat like the Vatican Gelasian. The feast of Benedict is also representative of particular influences on the Beneventan liturgy, though much later ones.

Benedict (**367, 373, 375**): The feast of Benedict is found in neither the Hadrianum nor the Paduense; the cult, however, is attested in the *communicantes* of the Bobbio missal among Gallican books, in the early calendars on 21 March, and in a proper mass for Benedict on 11 July in the Gelasians of the Eighth Century.[317] The Gelasian mass became eventually the principal Roman mass, but among other Romano-Frankish books a second mass was found on 21 March.[318] The second mass was gradually replaced by new masses for the vigil and feast, including the mass of the Fulda sacramentary and many later French sources, which resembles the Dubrovnik mass in its collect (**367**) and secret (**373**).[319] The mass of Benedict represents, therefore, the later effects of the Romano-Frankish liturgy. For the postcommunion (**375**), however, the missal is without parallel among Beneventan sources and departs from the mass of the Fulda sacramentary. In a tradition of such fluidity, the eccentricity of the manuscript is noteworthy but scarcely remarkable.

Consideration of the mass of Benedict has pointed to another layer in the composition of the Dubrovnik missal, i.e., texts of later medieval composition. While some new feasts were given prayers adapted from the Gregorian-Gelasian corpus (see Table 12), others were adopted whole from later sources: the nine masses of this category are listed in Table 13.

All these feasts, except that of Benedict which has just been discussed, are without counterparts in the early Gregorian and Gelasian sacramentaries. Whatever influences early copies of the Roman sources may have had on the Beneventan corpus, the composers of regional sacramentaries felt free to

---

[317] Moreton, *Eighth-Century Gelasian Sacramentary*, pp. 15-16, and Vogel, *Medieval Liturgy*, p. 73, consider the reference in the Gelasians to be indicative of a monastic source for the Gelasians of the Eighth Century.

The cult of Benedict is studied by Jean Deshusses and Jacques Hourlier, "Saint Benoît dans les livres liturgiques" in *Le Culte et les reliques de saint Benoît et de sainte Scholastique*, Studia Monastica 21 (Montserrat, 1979), pp. 143-204; and Réginald Grégoire, *Prières liturgiques médiévales en l'honneur de saint Benoît, de sainte Scholastique et de saint Maur*, Studia Anselmiana 54 (Rome, 1965).

[318] Chavasse, "Sacramentaire de Monza," p. 8 n. 5, corrects the false attribution of the mass *Aures* of 21 March to Rome, Biblioteca Angelica, F.A. 1408 (cf. Bourque, *Études*, 2: 166 n. 5; Deshusses and Hourlier, "Saint Benoît," pp. 163-164; and above n. 23).

[319] Deshusses and Hourlier, "Saint Benoît," pp. 165-166.

Table 13 Sanctoral: Later Mass-sets					
Feast		GREG	GEL8	Misc	BEN
Blaise	337	[ ]	[ ]	MRM v.2	[ ]
Scholastica	340	[ ]	[ ]	ES: F	Ben,Da,Mc,Ott
	345	Tc	[ ]	ES: F MRM v.2	Ben,Da,Mc,Ott,Pu,Ve
	347	Tc	[ ]	ES: F MRM v.2	Ben,Da,Mc,Ott,Pu,Ve
Matthias*	359	Tc	[ ]	ES: F	Ve
	362	Tc	[ ]	ES: F	Ve
	364	[Ha],Tc	[En,Ge]	ES: F	( )
Benedict*	367	[ ]	( )	ES: F MRM v.2	Ben,Da,Mc,Ott,Pu,Ve
	373	[ ]	( )	ES: F	Ben,Da,Mc,Ott,Pu,Ve
	375	[Ha,Pa]	(En,Ge,Sg)	( )	(Ben)
Margaret	496	[ ]	[ ]	LS: MWes	[ ]
Mary Magdalen	508	[ ]	[ ]	MRM	( )
	514	[ ]	[ ]	MRM	Mc
	516	[ ]	[ ]	MRM	( )
Vigil of James	519	[ ]	[ ]	ES: F	(Mc)
Transfiguration	542	[ ]	[ ]	ES: SVich MRM v.2	Ben,Mc,Ott,Pu,Ve
	545	[ ]	[ ]	ES: SVich MRM v.2	Ben,Mc,Ott,Pu,Ve
	546	[ ]	[ ]	ES: SVich MRM v.2	Ben,Mc,Ott,Pu
All Saints*	589	[Ha],Tc	[En,Ge,Sg]		Ben,Mc,Ott,Ve
	591	Tc	[ ]	ES: F	Pu,Ve

* Also listed under adapted prayers (Table 12).

draw on later masses of the Romano-Frankish tradition for new feasts and even for the replacement of feasts such as All Saints found in the Old Beneventan calendar. Among the three prayers with parallels in the Gregorian and Gelasian sacramentaries,[320] only the postcommunion of Benedict (375) appears to be a regional, and probably unique, adaptation: the two other adapted prayers and the remaining seventeen texts are more likely dependent on later Romano-Frankish sources, since ready counterparts are found in augmented Gregorians, the Fulda sacramentary, the Sacramentary of Vich (= SVich),[321] the Missal of Westminster (= MWes),[322] and later printed missals.

A first group of prayers—the masses of Scholastica (340, 345, 347) and Matthias (359, 362, 364), the collect and secret of Benedict (367, 373), and the collect of the vigil of James (519)—is paralleled in sacramentaries of the mixed Gelasian-Gregorian tradition. Indeed, since the postcommunion of Matthias (364) and the collect of the vigil of James (519) are not found in other Beneventan sources, the particular influence of a mixed sacramentary on the Dubrovnik missal seems probable, above and beyond the general effect on southern Italy of later sacramentaries of the "eccentric" group, such as the Fulda sacramentary or other mixed sacramentaries.

A second group of prayers has parallels in early Roman missals printed in Venice (MRM, v. 2) but not in MRM itself and in neither the Pian (1570) nor Clementine missals (1604). Since, apart from the collect of Blaise (337),[323] among these prayers the secret and postcommunion of Scholastica (345, 347), the collect of Benedict (367), and the mass of the Transfiguration (542, 545, 546) are widely attested in Beneventan sources, they may represent particular regional developments that were discarded in the general process of condensation that produced the Roman missal from the more prolix local Italian sources of the later Middle Ages. Several feasts with unusual sources bear closer examination:

Margaret (496): The collect *Deus qui beatam Margaritam* (496) is found elsewhere only in English missals among the sources consulted for this

---

[320] I.e., postcommunion of Matthias (364), postcommunion of Benedict (375), and the secret of All Saints (589).

[321] Vich, Museo Episcopal, 66; siglum: SVich, sacramentarium, s. xi, Vich; ed. Alejandro Olivar, *El Sacramentario de Vich*, Monumenta Hispaniae Sacra, Serie litúrgica 4 (Barcelona, 1953); bibl.: *CLLA*, no. 960.

[322] John Wickham Legg, *Missale ad usum ecclesiae Westmonasteriensis*, 3 vols., HBS 1, 5, 12 (London, 1891, 1893, 1897).

[323] The incipits of the Dubrovnik missal and the Venetian edition (MRM 2: 178) differ, but the prayer is clearly related and has no other counterpart.

edition.[324] Without exhaustive soundings in later medieval liturgical manuscripts, it is impossible to tell if the prayer indeed travelled more widely, but
for the moment its appearance here indicates a connection between the
English and Dalmatian churches, perhaps via the Norman intermediaries of
southern Italy.

Mary Magdalen (**508, 514, 516**): Among the recent feasts of the Dubrovnik
missal, apart from the collect for Matthias (**364**) and the secret for All Saints
(**589**), both drawn from the common stock of Gregorian-Gelasian prayers,
only the mass of Mary Magdalen has exact counterpart in the later medieval
Roman missal. Although the feast of the Magdalen is first mentioned in the
Martyrology of Bede and a mass-set (*Deus qui beate Marie Magdalene
penitentiam*; *Accepta*; *Auxilientur*) dates from the ninth century, the cult is
unattested in most early sacramentaries and calendars.[325] From the mid
eleventh century, as the re-dedication of Vézelay to the saint and its
emergence as a pilgrimage centre provided impetus for the development of
the cult, dedications and devotion to Mary Magdalen grew apace with the
spread of monastic reform from Cluny and its daughter houses. While French
and northern liturgical books tend to reproduce a mass-set first attested in
the tenth-century Sacramentary of St. Aubin of Angers,[326] a separate tradition
developing from the tenth century in Italian and East Frankish liturgical
books was to form the basis for the mass-set in the fourteenth-century Missal
of the Roman Curia (*Beate Marie Magdalene quaesumus*; *Munera nostra*;
Sumpto domine), from which the mass entered the later Roman missal.[327]

---

[324] E.g., MWes 2: 871; William G. Henderson, *Missale ad usum percelebris ecclesiae
Herefordensis* (Leeds, 1874; rpt. Farnborough, 1969), p. 286; John Wickham Legg, *The
Sarum Missal Edited from Three Manuscripts* (Oxford, 1916), p. 292. For the cult, see
Joseph-Marie Sauget and Maria Chiara Celletti, "Marina (Margherita), santa, martire di
Antiochia di Pisidia," *Bibliotheca Sanctorum*, 8: 1150-1165; the distribution of the cult in
southern Italy is indicated by the calendars cited in Brown, "New Beneventan Calendar," pp.
410-411: two feasts are given for Margaret, 18 July ("Sancte Marine uirginis") and 20 July
("Sancte Margarite uirginis").

[325] Victor Saxer and Maria Chiara Celletti, "Maria Maddalena, santa," *Bibliotheca Sanctorum*, 8: 1078-1107; and Saxer, *Le culte de Marie Madeleine en occident des origines à la fin
du moyen âge*, Cahiers d'archéologie et d'histoire 3, ed. René Louis (Paris, 1959).

[326] Angers, Bibliothèque Municipale, 92 (missale, s. x, Angers; bibl.: Saxer, *Culte*, no. M
8): *Largire*, *Hanc nostre*, *Sanctificet.*

[327] Bruylants, *Oraisons*, 1: 120 (mass 340), citing the fourteenth-century Missal of the
Curia (i.e., Avignon, Bibliothèque Municipale, 100, and the Orsini sacramentary, as above n.
95), the Sacramentarium Rossianum (s. xi, see above n. 161), MRM, and the Roman missals
of 1570 and 1604.

Saxer and Celletti, "Maria Maddalena," *Bibliotheca Sanctorum*, 8: 1091-1092, cite also two
tenth-century sacramentaries of Essen and Modena; Saxer, *Culte*, pp. 367-370, edits the secret
Munera nostra and the postcommunion *Sumpto domine* from Angers 92 (see the preceding

The prayers of the Dubrovnik missal (**508, 514, 516**) belong to the latter Italian tradition.

Transfiguration (**542, 545, 546**): During the thirteenth century, when the Oxford manuscript was written, the feast of the Transfiguration was celebrated throughout the west, but before the twelfth century it appears to have had a much more restricted range, with the first references to the feast concentrated in Spanish sources and the first masses found in Catalan and Beneventan sources of the eleventh century.[328] Since the mass in the Missal (**542, 545, 546**) is found in several other Beneventan manuscripts and in Venetian printed missals (MRM 2: 220-221) with a parallel elsewhere only in the eleventh-century Sacramentary of Vich, it is likely representative of an early tradition supplanted in the Roman missal by a mass developed in Romano-Frankish territory.

A final category of masses consists of those proper to the region or to the Dubrovnik missal itself. Apart from the few prayers in masses otherwise Gregorian or Gelasian, and the adapted prayers without counterpart, the missal also contains three masses that may be considered Beneventan (the mass of Elias may in fact be Old Beneventan) and two others without apparent parallel. The unique and regional masses are listed in Table 14.

The fragmentary prayer for an unidentified martyr (**319**) falls after the mass for Stephen (26 December) and before the mass for Silvester (31 December) but is not immediately appropriate for the other expected masses of Christmas week: John the Evangelist was not martyred; and the Innocents, though martyrs, are excluded by the singular reference of the prayer ("cuius martirio"). Since the Old Beneventan mass-antiphonals are deficient between the feast of Stephen and Lent, and the Campanian lection-lists are not explicit between the Innocents and the feast of the Circumcision, the Old Beneventan calendar is unhelpful at this point. Considering the special links between southern Italy and the Anglo-Norman kingdom, it is tempting to see the collect as part of the later medieval feast of Thomas of Canterbury, who was martyred in 1162, canonised in 1173, and venerated very soon after in southern Italy.[329] Unfortunately, this identification cannot be confirmed since

---

note); Paris, Bibliothèque de l'Arsenal, 160 (missale, s. xv ex., Utrecht: for the use of Leyden); Paris, BN, lat. 2295 (sacramentarium, s. xii, Cahors), BN, lat. 2301 (sacramentarium, s. xii², Arles), and BN, lat. 9433 (sacramentarium gelasianum, s. xi in., Echternach: prayers of feast added in s. xii, bibl.: *CLLA*, no. 920).

[328] The origins and spread of the feast are described by Richard W. Pfaff, *New Liturgical Feasts in Later Medieval England* (Oxford, 1970), pp. 13-39.

[329] Hugh Farmer, "Tommaso Beckett, arcivescovo di Canterbury, santo, martire," *Biblio-*

TABLE 14				
Sanctoral: Unique or Regional Mass-sets				
Feast	GREG	GEL8	Misc	BEN
Martyr (?) 319				
Gregory. 365	( )	( )		Ben,Da,Mc,Ott,Pu
Lawrence, Peter and Andrew 486 492 494	[ ] [Pa,Tc] [ ]	[ ] [En,Ge,Sg] [ ]		[ ] [ ] [ ]
Felicitas 495	( )	( )		( )
Elias 498 504 506	[ ] [ ] [ ]	[ ] [ ] [ ]		Vl10645 ( ) ( )
Chains of Peter 531 533 534	Ha ( ) ( )	[ ] [ ] [ ]		Ben,Mc,Ott,Ve Ben,Mc,Ott Ben,Mc,Ott
All Souls 593	[ ]	[ ]	(MRM)	( )

the text of the prayer is not found in the standard Roman mass for Thomas of Canterbury.[330]

Gregory (**365**): The collect for Gregory (**365**) is attested in a wide range of Beneventan sources but nowhere else. The feast is not found in the Vatican Gelasian or the Paduense but does appear in the Hadrianum, the Prague sacramentary (= Pr),[331] and the Gelasians of the Eighth Century, though with three different mass-sets; among the mass-antiphonals, the feast is relatively stable but not considered ancient;[332] lections for the feast are found in the Comes of Muhrbach, but in neither the Comes of Alcuin nor the Comes of Würzburg. The obvious conclusion from the spotty character of the evidence is that the feast was a late introduction into the Roman calendar, postdating the seventh-century development of the cult, but predating the eighth-century

theca Sanctorum, 12: 598-605. The spread of the cult to southern Italy is attested in several Beneventan calendars and martyrologies (Brown, "New Beneventan Calendar," pp. 420-421).

[330] Bruylants, *Oraisons*, 1: 9 (mass 18), citing the fourteenth-century Missal of the Curia (above n. 327), and later Roman missals (MRM, Pian missal of 1570, and Clementine missal of 1604).

[331] For the Prague sacramentary (= Pr), see above n. 235.

[332] Hesbert, *Antiphonale missarum sextuplex*, p. xc; also the variant offices cited in Hesbert, *Corpus antiphonalium officii*, 1: 120.

copies of the major early sacramentaries.[333] The southern Italian range of the collect from the Missal (365) supports this conclusion and suggests that the Roman exemplar, lacking the feast, was made more complete through the addition of a new composition or the adoption of an older prayer. This is further evidence for the use of a sacramentary like the Paduense, which lacked the feast, or, perhaps, for the presence of a feast of Gregory in the Old Beneventan calendar.

Lawrence, Peter, and Andrew (**486, 492, 494**): The feast of Lawrence, Peter, and Andrew, the Dalmatian martyrs, has been discussed in considering the origin and provenance of the manuscript.[334] Apart from the reference to their martyrdom in the twelfth-century Chronicle by Miletius of Ragusa, early evidence for the cult of the martyrs consists of a church dedicated to them in Dubrovnik and the mass of the Dubrovnik missal itself. The secret *Suscipe domine quesumus munera* (**492**) is found among the masses of the Common in the Vatican Gelasian (Va 1118), the Gelasians of the Eighth Century (Ge 1822), the Paduense (Pa 834), and later mixed Gelasian-Gregorians (Tc 3270); it is applied also to the feast of Zoticus, Irenaeus, and Iacinthus in the eighth-century Gelasians (Ge 216, Sg 203). Its use on a comparable feast in the Missal is, therefore, not surprising. The collect *Deus qui hodiernam diem* (**486**) and postcommunion *Vt accepta* (**494**), however, are not so readily placed: they may be either original compositions after general Roman models or adaptations of later medieval texts as yet unpublished.

Felicitas and her seven sons (**495**): The collect for Felicitas and her seven sons (**495**) is unique to the best of my knowledge, although Felicitas and her sons were the objects of special devotion in the city of Benevento itself. One version of their Passion relates that Archbishop Ursus, elected in 833, was responsible for the translation of their relics and the dedication of their church in Benevento on 10 July.[335] The feast itself represents a conflation of the two Roman masses for Felicitas (23 November) and the Seven Brothers

---

[333] Moreton, *Eighth-Century Gelasian Sacramentary*, p. 103; seventh-century evidence for the cult is given by Pierre Jounel, "Le culte de saint Grégoire le Grand," *EO* 2 (1985) 195-209.

[334] See above pp. 38-39.

[335] *Acta sanctorum, Julii*, 3: 5-26; also the references to the three medieval *passiones* in [Albert Poncelet], *Bibliotheca hagiographica Latina antiquae et mediae aetatis*, 2 vols. and Supplement (Brussels, 1898-1911; rpt. 1949), 1: 429-430 (nos. 2853-2855); and Filippo Caraffa and Maria Chiara Celletti, "Felicita e VII Figli, santi, martiri di Roma," *Bibliotheca Sanctorum*, 5: 605-611. Felicitas is acknowledged as mother of the seven brothers in the *passiones* and in most martyrologies; nonetheless, the feast of 10 July is rarely associated with her.

(10 July), related in the martyrologies but usually distinguished in the liturgy. The feast of the Seven Brothers is among the oldest of the Roman calendar, provided with the same mass in both the Gregorian and eighth-century Gelasian sacramentaries, a proper mass in the early mass-antiphonals, and lections in the Comes of Würzburg and Muhrbach.[336] The feast of Felicitas on 23 November is not as widely attested, lacking masses in the early antiphonals and the Comes of Muhrbach and Alcuin, although attested in the Veronese sacramentary, the Vatican Gelasian, the Gregorian sacramentaries, the Gelasians of the Eighth Century, and the Comes of Würzburg: the mass of Felicitas in the sacramentaries is less homogeneous than the mass of the Seven Brothers.[337]

The Beneventan treatment of the feasts of Felicitas and the Seven Brothers is distinctive, perhaps deriving from the special veneration attached to the feast of 10 July in Benevento. Instead of suppressing one or the other, or including both in separate feasts, the two cults are linked to form a single celebration and mass by turning the "seven brothers" into Felicitas and her "seven sons." While the collect of the Dubrovnik missal seems to have no counterpart in other Beneventan sources, the title for the feast appears in Ben33 and in the calendar of PuC, the latter citing it on the same day as another distinctive Beneventan feast, the assumption of Elias.[338] Since the prayers of Ben33 for the feast are entirely Roman, i.e., referring only to the martyrs but not to Felicitas, the Dalmatian collect with its simple pun on the relation between blessed Felicitas and perpetual felicity is a unique composition: whether local or a relict of a special Beneventan cult cannot be determined.

Elias (**498, 504, 506**):[339] The connections between the Beneventan region and the eastern churches is highlighted by the appearance of a mass for Elias

---

[336] The masses are discussed by Moreton, *Eighth-Century Gelasian Sacramentary*, pp. 102, 112; and Hesbert, *Antiphonale missarum sextuplex*, pp. xcviii-xcix. A mass is found also in Le (396-399), though not in Va.

[337] For the Seven Brothers, only the mass-set of Le had differed; for the mass-set of Felicitas, the collect *Praesta quaesumus omnipotens* is found in the Gregorian sacramentaries and the Gelasians of the Eighth Century (Ha 757, Pa 759, Ge 1641, Sg 1351) but not in Va; the secret *Munera tibi* is common to the Gelasians (Va 1071, Ge 1642, Sg 1352) but differs in the Gregorians; and the final prayers fall into two groups: *Praesta domine* (Va 1072, Ge 1643) and *Supplices te* (Ha 759, Pa 761, Ge 1644, Sg 1353). Le differs throughout.

[338] Ben33 113v-114v: "S. Felicitatis et filiorum eius" (mass as Roman mass except for the Alleluia). PuC (p. 39): "vi. Id. [Iulii] Passio sce felicitatis et septem filiorum eius. et assumptio sci helie precursoris dni." See also Brown, "New Beneventan Calendar," pp. 410-411: 10 July, *Sancte Felicitatis cum filiis suis*, but without references on 23 November (cf. Brown, pp. 418-419).

[339] Tarsicio Stramare, Francesco Spadafora, and Francesco Negri Arnoldi, "Elia, profeta," *Bibliotheca Sanctorum*, 4: 1022-1039.

(**498, 504, 506**). Before its adoption by the Carmelites in 1551, the feast, though common in the east, is found elsewhere in the west only in a fragmentary eleventh-century missal in Beneventan script of the Bari-type (Vat. lat. 10645), in the early-eleventh-century Missal of the Abruzzi (Vat. lat. 4770),[340] and in the Gallican Masses of Mone.[341] Both Vat. lat. 4770 and the Masses of Mone present texts different from the prayers in the Beneventan missals. Even in the Oxford manuscript and the Vatican fragment, however, only the collects (**498**) are in agreement: the secrets (**504**) differ; and the mass in the Vatican fragment is deficient at the end, thus lacking a postcommunion for comparison. Although the feast of Elias is unrepresented in the Old Beneventan mass-antiphonals and the Campanian lection-lists, the appearance of a prayer for such a distinctive feast in two Beneventan missals so widely separated in origin and date of composition implies an early antecedent for the text, perhaps even an Old Beneventan mass. Both the secret (**504**) and postcommunion (**506**) are unattested elsewhere.

Chains of Peter (**531, 533, 534**): The feast of the Chains of Peter is a Gregorian feast given a full mass in the Hadrianum and Paduense and a citation in the title to the feast of the Machabees in the Gelasians of the Eighth Century.[342] The absence of the feast in the early mass-antiphonals and the Comes of Muhrbach, Alcuin, and Würzburg suggests that the mass of the Gregorian sacramentaries is a late addition to the calendar; it developed, however, into the principal feast of the day, supplanting by stages the Gelasian feast of the Machabees until only the collect of the latter feast (**532**) remains in the Oxford manuscript. The Missal also has the Gregorian collect (**531**) for the feast of the Chains of Peter but gives regional texts for the secret and postcommunion (**533, 534**). Most Beneventan missals reproduce the Gregorian mass,[343] but the few witnesses to different prayers may indicate the regional composition of a mass based on the passing reference in the Gelasians of the Eighth Century. Early Beneventan liturgists, faced with evidence for a feast but no mass-set, were forced to provide their own prayers.

---

[340] Hesbert, "Dimanches de Carême," p. 200.

[341] Karlsruhe, Badische Landesbibliothek, Augiense 253, fol. 96; sacramentarium, ca. 630-640, Burgundy; ed. Leo Eizenhöfer, "Die Mone-Messen," in Mohlberg, Eizenhöfer, and Siffrin, *Missale Gallicanum Vetus*, pp. 61-91, 135-138 (Elias at pp. 88-89); bibl.: *CLLA*, no. 203.

[342] I.e., Sg (Mohlberg, *Fränkische Sacramentarium*, p. 159): "Kalendas Augustas. Statio ad sanctum Petrum ad Uincula quando catenae eius osculantur. Ipso die natale Machabaeorum."

[343] E.g., Ben33 115v, in addition to the entire Gelasian mass of the Machabees.

All Souls (**593**): The mass of All Souls is a late medieval development.[344] Despite its establishment by Odilo of Cluny (d. 1048) and the diffusion of the commemoration with the spread of the Cluniac order, many local liturgies lack any mention of the feast well into the later Middle Ages. The three masses of the Roman missal date only to the sixteenth century, although a single mass with the texts of the first mass of the Roman missal is found earlier in the Dominican missal and the Missal of the Curia.[345] The collect of the Dubrovnik missal (**593**) has a counterpart with some variants among the votive masses of MRM.

Two distinctive prayers are found in the other masses of the Sanctoral: the collect of Mark (**401**) is shared only with the Milanese Sacramentary of Aribert,[346] PuC, and McO; and the postcommunion of Lawrence (**566**) is found elsewhere only among Milanese sacramentaries.[347] The relatively few references to prayers of the Milanese tradition are particularly important reminders of the early connections between the regions. While the prayers may be late adoptions, there remains the possibility that they predate the pervasive influence of the Roman and Romano-Frankish liturgies, especially since the feast of Lawrence is among the most ancient in the calendar.[348]

Adapted prayers without counterparts in other Beneventan manuscripts are also significant, if only to help identify local tendencies within the regional liturgy. To this category belong the collect and postcommunion of Silvester (**320, 323**), the postcommunion of Benedict (**375**), the secret and postcommunion of Mark (**406, 408**), and the secret of the Dalmatian martyrs (**492**).[349]

---

[344] Roger E. Reynolds, "All Souls' Day," *DMA*, 1: 177; Augustine Cornides, "All Souls' Day," *NCE*, 1: 319.

[345] Bruylants, *Oraisons*, 1: 159 (mass 464); and the Ordinal of Humbert of Romans for Dominican practice (ed. Guerrini, *Ordinarium*, p. 208).

[346] Milan, Biblioteca del Capitolo metropolitano, D 3-2; s. xi in., Milan; ed. Angelo Paredi, "Il Sacramentario di Ariberto," in *Miscellanea Adriano Bernareggi*, ed. Luigi Cortesi, Monumenta Bergomensia 1 (Bergamo, 1958), pp. 329-488; bibl.: *CLLA*, no. 530.

[347] E.g., Sb 1053; Milan, Biblioteca del Capitolo metropolitano, D 3-3; siglum: D 3-3, s. ix ex.; cloister of San Simpliciano, Milan; ed. Judith Frei, *Das ambrosianische Sakramentar D 3-3 aus dem mailändischen Metropolitankapitel*, Corpus Ambrosiano-Liturgicum 3, LQF 56 (Münster/W., 1974), no. 1086; bibl.: *CLLA*, no. 510; and Zürich, Zentralbibliothek, C 43; siglum: STripl, ca. 1010-1030, St. Gallen; ed. Odilo Heiming, *Das Sacramentarium triplex*, Corpus Ambrosiano-Liturgicum 1, LQF 49 (Münster/W., 1968), no. 2287; bibl.: *CLLA*, no. 535. Further sources are cited in Frei, *Ambrosianische Sakramentar*, p. 525 (no. 1086).

[348] The collect (**558**) and secret (**564**) of Lawrence are both Gregorian; the mass is discussed by Moreton, *Eighth-Century Gelasian Sacramentary*, pp. 129-130.

[349] See above Table 12.

Lections

Due to the varying histories of the separate books containing the prayers and lections of the mass, the epistles and gospels of the Sanctoral are even less dependent on the Romano-Frankish tradition than the prayers are. As demonstrated, the prayers of the Sanctoral present a mixture of Gregorian and Gelasian sources in a proportion not unrepresentative of the "eccentric" mixed sacramentaries of the later Middle Ages, with regional traditions manifest principally in mass-sets composed for local or late feasts. The Sanctoral lection-list of the Dubrovnik missal, on the other hand, is the product of a more individual history, i.e., analysis uncovers fewer parallels with the general history of the Roman lectionary. Thus, while we have seen that lacunae in the Gregorian corpus of prayers were filled directly from Gelasian collections, suggesting that the diffusion of new cults accompanied the spread of successive sacramentaries, the lections of the Dubrovnik missal for the new feasts introduced through the Gelasians of the Eighth Century or the mixed sacramentaries often do not match the readings of the Comes of Muhrbach, the lectionary corresponding most closely to the Gelasian sacramentaries. The divergence between the Dalmatian and Gelasian lection-lists implies the late arrival of the latter, at a point well after the new feasts of the Gelasian sacramentary had become established in regional practice.[350]

Roman (see Table 15): Eight of the thirty-two masses with lections have exact counterparts in both early and late Roman lection-lists: Stephen (**311, 314**), Philip and James (**411, 413**), the vigil and feast of John the Baptist (**430, 432, 439, 442**), the vigil and feast of Peter and Paul (**458, 460, 467, 470**), and the vigil and feast of Lawrence (**550, 552, 559, 562**). Although the epistle for the mass of Silvester (**321**) differs from the lection of the Roman missal, it also is unquestionably Roman, since it is found in the Comes of Alcuin, Würzburg, and Paris.[351] Similarly, the gospel for the Commemoration of Paul (**480**) is found in both early and late lection-lists, although the epistle (**477** 2 Tim 4: 1-8) differs. In each case, the feast is very ancient and central to the early calendar.

Discussion of the relation between the Dubrovnik missal and the early Roman lectionaries is complicated by the fragmentary condition of the

---

[350] Demonstration that a regional lectionary for the Gelasian feasts developed simultaneously with the introduction of Gelasian sacramentaries in southern Italy must be sought first in the shared witness of Beneventan sources. Nonetheless, any conclusion from such analysis is probable at best since the Romano-Beneventan lectionary may represent with equal plausibility the adoption of an imported idiosyncratic lection-list that has left little trace outside the region.

[351] Mu 7 has the feast but a different epistle (Eccli 44: 16-17).

TABLE 15 Sanctoral: Sources of Lections					
Feast	RL:	LEC			BEN
	MRM	Wu	Mu	CoP	
Nicholas 303	( )	[ ]	[ ]	[ ]	Mc
306	( )	[ ]	[ ]	[ ]	Mc
Stephen 311	=	=	=	( )	Ben,Ca,Da,Mc,Ott,Pu,Ve
314	=	=	=	=	Ben,Ca,Da,Mc,Ott,Pu,Ve
Silvester 321	( )	=	( )	=	Ben,Da,Mc,Ott
Conversation of Paul 335	=	[ ]	=	[ ]	Ben,Da,Mc,Ott,Ve
336	( )	[ ]	( )	[ ]	Ben,Da,Mc,Ott
Scholastica 341	( )	[ ]	[ ]	[ ]	Ben,Da,Mc,Ott
344	( )	[ ]	[ ]	[ ]	Ben,Da,Mc,Ott,Pu
Chair of Peter 350	( )	[ ]	( )	[ ]	Ben,Da,Mc,Ott
353	( )	[ ]	( )	[ ]	Ben,Da,Mc,Ott
Matthias 361	( )	[ ]	[ ]	[ ]	(Ben)
Benedict 368	( )	[ ]	( )	[ ]	Ben,Da,Mc,Ott
371	( )	[ ]	( )	[ ]	Ben,Da,Mc,Ott,Pu
Annunciation 378	=	[ ]	=	=	Ben,Da,Mc,Pu
381	=	[ ]	=	=	Ben,Da,Mc,Pu,Ve
George 388	( )	[ ]	[ ]	[ ]	Ben
391	( )	[ ]	[ ]	[ ]	Ben,Da,Mc
392	( )	[ ]	[ ]	[ ]	(Ben,Da),Mc,Ott
393	( )	[ ]	[ ]	[ ]	
Mark 402	( )	[ ]	[ ]	[ ]	(Ben,Pu,Ve)
404	( )	[ ]	[ ]	[ ]	Ben,Da,Ott
Philip and James 411	=	( )	=	=	Ben,Mc,Ott,Pu,Ve
413	=	=	=	=	Ben,Da,Mc,Ott,Pu,Ve
Invention of the Cross 421	( )	[ ]	( )	[ ]	Ben,Mc,Ott,Pu
424	( )	[ ]	( )	[ ]	Ben,Da,Mc,Ott,Pu
Vigil of John the Baptist 430	=	=	=	=	Ben,Mc,Ott,Pu,Ve
432	=	=	=	=	Ben,Da,Mc,Ott,Pu,Ve
John the Baptist 439	=	=	=	=	Ben,Da,Mc,Ott,Pu,Ve
442	=	=	=	=	Ben,Da,Mc,Ott,Pu,Ve
John and Paul 449	( )	( )	( )	( )	Ben,Mc,Ott
Vigil of the Apostles 458	=	=	=	=	Ben,Mc,Ott,Pu,Ve,Vl10645
460	=	=	=	=	Ben,Da,Mc,Ott,Pu,Ve

TABLE 15 (cont'd) Sanctoral: Sources of Lections					
Feast	RL:	LEC			BEN
	MRM	Wu	Mu	CoP	
Peter and Paul **467**	=	=	=	=	Ben,Mc,Pu,Ve
470	=	=	=	=	Ben,Da,Mc,Ott,Pu,Ve
Commemoration of Paul **477**	( )	( )	( )	( )	Ben,Mc,Ott,Ve
480	=	=	=	=	Ben,Da,Mc,Ott,Ve
Lawrence, Peter, **487**	[ ]	[ ]	[ ]	[ ]	[Ben]
and Andrew **490**	[ ]	[ ]	[ ]	[ ]	[Da]
Elias **499**	[ ]	[ ]	[ ]	[ ]	[Ben],Vl10645
502	[ ]	[ ]	[ ]	[ ]	[Ben],Da,Vl10645
Mary Magdalen **509**	( )	[ ]	[ ]	[ ]	( )
512	=	[ ]	[ ]	[ ]	(Ben),Da,Mc,Ve
Vigil of James **520**	[ ]	[ ]	[ ]	[ ]	( )
521	[ ]	[ ]	[ ]	[ ]	Mc,Ott
James **525**	=	[ ]	( )	[ ]	Ben,Da,Mc,Ott,Ve
Invention of Stephen **537**	( )	[ ]	[ ]	[ ]	(Ben)
538	( )	[ ]	[ ]	[ ]	Ben,Mc,Ott
Transfiguration **543**	( )	[ ]	[ ]	[ ]	Ben,Da,Mc,Ott
544	( )	[ ]	[ ]	[ ]	Ben,Da,Mc,Ott,Pu,Ve
Vigil of Lawrence **550**	=	=	=	=	Ben,Mc,Ott,Pu,Ve
552	=	=	=	=	Ben,Da,Mc,Ott,Pu,Ve
Lawrence **559**	=	=	=	=	Ben,Da,Mc,Ott,Pu,Ve
562	=	=	=	=	Ben,Da,Mc,Ott,Pu,Ve
Vigil of the Assumption **570**	=	[ ]	[ ]	[ ]	Ben,Mc,Ott
572	( )	[ ]	[ ]	[ ]	Ben,Da,Mc,Ott,Pu,Ve
Assumption **579**	=	[ ]	=	[ ]	Ben,Da,Mc,Ott,Pu,Ve
582	=	[ ]	=	[ ]	Ben,Da,Mc,Ott,Pu,Ve
All Saints **587**	( )	[ ]	[ ]	[ ]	Ben,Da,Mc,Ott,Pu
All Souls **594**	=	[ ]	[ ]	[ ]	Pu
597	( )	[ ]	[ ]	[ ]	(Ben)

Sanctoral in the Oxford manuscript and its numerous late feasts, both of which reduce the number of common texts. The general absence of correspondences between the Missal and the early lectionaries is, however, less important in the comparison than are the similarities in the shared feasts. Once the field is narrowed to include only the common feasts, the identity between the Missal and the early Roman lection-lists, represented by WuC and WuE, is remarkable, with variants only for the epistles of Philip and James (**411**),[352] the Commemoration of Paul (**477**), and John and Paul (**449**).[353] Moreover, the variance throughout between the Roman lections attested in the Dubrovnik missal and the lections cited in the early Campanian lists is clear evidence that the basis for the later Beneventan lection-system of the Sanctoral was an early Roman lectionary and not the indigenous Campanian list.[354]

Romano-Frankish: Several lections point to the secondary influence of a later Romano-Frankish lection system. The epistle for the Conversion of Paul (**335**) is found in the Comes of Muhrbach and the Roman missal; the gospel (**336**), however, differs.[355] The epistle for Philip and James (**411**) agrees with the later Comes of Muhrbach and Paris but differs from the Comes of Würzburg and Alcuin. The diversity of the Roman lection systems for the Marian feasts of the Annunciation (**378, 381**) and Assumption (**579, 582**), which are seventh-century additions to the Roman Sanctoral, is also reflected in the Dubrovnik missal.[356] For the Annunciation, the epistle and gospel of the Missal are paralleled in the Comes of Paris and Muhrbach, and in the Roman missal, but the feast is omitted in the Comes of Würzburg, and a different epistle is given in the Comes of Alcuin. The lections of Assumption are found in the Comes of Muhrbach, the gospel-list of Würzburg, and the Roman missal, but in neither the Comes of Alcuin and Paris nor the

[352] The choice of lection differs also in Alc; Mu and CoP agree, however, with the Dubrovnik missal.

[353] A gospel for John and Paul is lacking in the Oxford MS. WuC has two epistles for John and Paul (126, 127): the latter becomes the choice of the other early epistle-lists (Mu, Alc, CoP) and eventually of the Roman missal. The variants between the Missal's readings for John and Paul (**449**) and the Commemoration of Paul (**477**) and the Roman epistles for those feasts point to another possible distinction among the early sources of the Romano-Beneventan lection-list: not only did the Roman lection-lists in general enter the region separately from the corresponding Gelasian sacramentary, but the Roman epistolary and evangelistary may also have followed different courses.

[354] Cf. Gamber, "Kampanische Lektionsordnung," pp. 326-352, for the Campanian lections.

[355] See above n. 353 for other discrepancies between epistles and gospels which suggest separate sources for the Romano-Beneventan epistolary and evangelistary.

[356] See above p. 122.

epistle-list of Würzburg. Thus, for the feast of Philip and James and the Marian feasts, the Beneventan lectionary appears to have been dependent on the tradition represented by the Comes of Muhrbach, the lectionary corresponding to the Gelasian sacramentaries of the Eighth Century, although the exact source might have been any one of the later witnesses to the Roman lections that predate the earliest Beneventan sources.

Nonetheless, the agreement between the Oxford manuscript and the Romano-Frankish lists breaks down for the lections of another series of Gelasian feasts—the Conversion of Paul (**335, 336**), the Chair of Peter (**350, 353**), Benedict (**368, 371**), the Invention of the Cross (**421, 424**), and James (**525**)—since the epistle for the Conversion of Paul (**335**) is the only lection paralleled in the Comes of Muhrbach.[357] None of the feasts is represented in either the Hadrianum or the Comes of Würzburg. The variants between Romano-Beneventan sources and the Gelasian lectionaries for these feasts are crucial to understanding the adoption of Romano-Frankish practice in the region. Assuming that independent lections would not have been selected if a model had been on hand, the distinctive Romano-Beneventan lections probably predate the entry of Gelasian lectionaries into the region but postdate the adoption of the feasts themselves via the Gelasian sacramentaries.[358] The points of agreement cited in the previous paragraph are less telling, particularly in a late source such as the Dubrovnik missal, because generations of liturgical copies could have resulted easily in the casual substitution of one lection for another, i.e., the replacement of the Romano-Beneventan lections by the lections of northern books for the new feasts of the Gelasian sacramentaries.

Later Roman: Most of the remaining feasts of the Sanctoral provided with lections are later or regional and therefore without parallel in the early lection-lists. The feasts of George (**388, 391-393**) and Mark (**402, 404**) are exceptions: both are common to the early sacramentaries, Gregorian and Gelasian, but neither is given specific lections in the early Roman lection-

---

[357] The feast of James is not provided with an epistle in the Missal; the gospel, however, corresponds to the later medieval tradition of the Franciscan missal (Haymo of Faversham, *Ordo missalis* [ed. Van Dijk, *Sources*, 2: 290]) and the Roman missal. Since the epistle of the vigil (**520**) in the Oxford MS is given as the epistle of the feast in Mu and the Roman missal, the Dubrovnik missal probably intended the same lection for the epistle of the feast.

[358] The summary of the sources for the prayers of the Sanctoral contained in Table 10 reinforces the probability of differing histories for the sacramentaries and lectionaries at the base of the Romano-Beneventan missal: the Conversion of Paul, the Chair of Peter, the Invention of the Cross, and James are provided with prayers from the Gelasian tradition, although only the epistle for the Conversion of Paul (**335**) has any parallel in the early lection-lists.

lists. The regional tradition, therefore, specified its own readings, which are also found in the Common of the Roman missal. No clear explanation exists for the extraordinary three gospels for George (**391** Io 15: 5-11 *Ego sum uitis uos palmites*; **392** Io 15: 1-4 *Ego sum uitis uera*; **393** Mc 13: 33-37 *Videte uigilate*), but some relation to the *Commune sanctorum tempore paschali* is possible. Later medieval office books frequently place the Easter Common in the Sanctoral at the end of the spring feasts.[359] While to the best of my knowledge the practice is unattested in missals, and certainly rubrics setting off the Easter Common would be expected even in office books, the Oxford manuscript may represent an attempt at such an organisation of the Easter feasts, or perhaps a confused copying of a more explicit version. Since the gospel that is given by incipit for the feast of Mark (**404** Io 15: 1) follows the gospels for George (**391-393**) and corresponds to the second gospel of the three, the possibility of a seasonal Common is reinforced. One must wonder, however, for whom the third lection was intended. Despite its many lacunae, the Dubrovnik missal was never a complete missal: could it have been based on a more complete source that did include an Easter Common in the Sanctoral?

Several individual lections of the Missal derive from the later Roman liturgy. The gospel of the feast of Mary Magdalen (**512**) is common to the Roman missal and several Beneventan sources; the epistle, however, is not only unparalleled in the Roman and Beneventan sources for the feast but appears to be an entirely unprecedented pericope. In a second case, since the later Roman and Beneventan gospel for James (**525**) differs from the early witness of the Comes of Muhrbach, the choice of the Beneventan lection would appear to be a reference to the later Roman gospel; alternatively, the Beneventan lection itself may be the regional pericope at the base of the later medieval Roman reading. In a third instance, the epistle of the vigil of the Assumption (**570**) agrees with the Roman missal but with none of the earlier sources; the gospel of the same feast (**572**) is regional, i.e., it has its exact counterpart only in Beneventan manuscripts, though also attested in the Roman tradition on other Marian feasts.[360] Since the Roman epistle for the vigil is not found as widely in the region as the Beneventan gospel, and then only in missals of the twelfth or later centuries,[361] the selection of the epistle is likely a later Roman influence on an indigenous mass. Lastly, although the gospel for the later medieval feast of All Souls (**597**) is found on a different feast in the Roman missal, the epistle (**594**) is Roman. The late date of the

---

[359] Hughes, *Medieval Manuscripts*, pp. 188, 238.

[360] E.g., the Birth of the Virgin in MRM 8.

[361] I.e., Ben29, Mc127, McV, Ott.

Oxford manuscript is evident from the agreement with the Roman missal in this instance where other Beneventan sources differ.[362]

Regional Feasts: The mass for the martyrs Lawrence, Peter, and Andrew is a local feast, restricted to the Dalmatian coast. Since the earliest reference to the martyrs places them in the eleventh century, the feast must date to well after the introduction of Romano-Frankish books into the region: the choice of lections from the Roman Common is scarcely surprising (**487** Eccli 44: 10-15; **490** Lc 21: 9). The feast of the Transfiguration is also a later feast not current generally until the twelfth century, but distinctive due to the early witness of its celebration in southern Italy.[363] Thus, the absence of parallels in the early lection-lists is natural, and a lack of counterpart in the Roman missal not unexpected. In fact, the epistle of the Dubrovnik missal (**543**) and other Beneventan books is shared with Venetian printed missals, reinforcing the hypothesis of local regional variants of the Roman liturgy suggested by some prayers of the Sanctoral.[364] The regional mass for the vigil of James is complicated by its relation to the feast of the saint: the epistle (**520**), which is found in the Roman tradition on the feast, probably does double duty for both vigil and feast in the Oxford manuscript; since the gospel for the vigil of James (**521** Mc 10: 35-40) relates the same incident as the gospel for the feast (**525** Mt 20: 20-23), it is an obvious choice. Finally, the lections (**499, 502**) for the feast of Elias are also regional. The celebration of the feast is rare in the west before the fifteenth century. Nonetheless, the parallels in an eleventh-century Vatican missal in a Beneventan script of the Bari-type (Vat. lat. 10645) indicate that the mass and its lections had a long tradition in the region.

The debts and parallels with the Roman lection-lists, early and late, make up less than half the readings of the Sanctoral (25 of 59; 42%). To a basic core of Gregorian feasts concentrated on the saints of Christmas week (Stephen, Silvester), apostles (Philip and James, Peter and Paul), John the Baptist, and Lawrence, the early Beneventan books added the Marian feasts of the Annunciation, Assumption, and, later, the vigil of the Assumption. The course of the development is reflected in the degree of agreement between the earliest lections of the Dubrovnik missal and the early Roman lection-lists. But, as clearly as the basis for the Romano-Beneventan

---

[362] Other feasts of wide diffusion in the later Middle Ages but with distinctive regional lections are Scholastica (**341, 344**), Matthias (**361**), the Invention of Stephen (**537, 538**), and All Saints (**587**). The lections for Scholastica, Matthias, and the Invention of Stephen are paralleled in the Roman Common.

[363] See above p. 127; Pfaff, *New Liturgical Feasts*, pp. 13-39.

[364] See above p. 125, and Dubrovnik, Dominikanski Samostan, Frag. (i), cited above n. 98.

lection-lists was Roman, so also the differences between the lections of the
Missal and the mixed Gelasian-Gregorian lists of the Comes of Muhrbach
and Paris reinforce the thesis that Roman practices were adopted in the
region at an early date, probably during the eighth century, after the adoption
of the Marian feasts but before the Gelasian feasts of the Conversion of Paul,
the Chair of Peter, Benedict, the Invention of the Cross, and James entered
the Roman calendar. After these Gelasian feasts were added also to the
Beneventan calendar via the sacramentary tradition, local liturgists, lacking
a comparable lection-list except for the Marian feasts, were forced to supply
their own readings. Thus, these feasts became fixed with regional lections. In
addition, there are other Gelasian feasts in the Dubrovnik missal which show
signs of conformity with the mixed Gelasian-Gregorian lection-lists, but the
late date of the manuscript may account for this influence. For later feasts,
such as Mary Magdalen, no local tradition, whether imported earlier or
indigenous, ruled against the adoption of contemporary Roman practices.
Lastly, purely regional feasts and some regional modifications of feasts with
various later medieval traditions account for several lections in the Sanctoral.

Musical Items

Analysis of the distribution and selection of chant for the sung portions
of the masses of the Sanctoral is complicated by several factors. First, each
mass is supplied with as many as five items instead of only three prayers or
two lections. Second, whereas the history of the adoption of the Roman
sacramentaries sufficed as a framework within which to understand the
selection of prayers, for the musical items structural developments must be
considered in addition to historical influences. In particular, the discussion
must take account of the later accretions to the mass, including the assimi-
lation of alleluias into individual masses and the provision of prosulas, tropes,
and sequences. Lastly, the analysis must proceed with regard for both music
and text: thus, the text of the alleluia *Confitebuntur* (**389**) appears in the GR,
the early mass-antiphonals, the Oxford manuscript, and other Beneventan
sources on the feast of George, but the Beneventan musical setting is
unrelated to the Roman melody. It is evident that, whatever common history
the verse may have had, its melody developed along different lines. Despite
these necessary qualifications, a comparison of layers of influence, the
method used for the study of the prayers and lections of the Sanctoral, yields
similar conclusions when applied to the musical items.

Gregorian Masses (1): The earliest source for the musical items of the
Sanctoral was a mass-antiphonal corresponding at many points to the Roman

lectionary influential in the history of the early Romano-Beneventan lectionary (see Table 16). The Gregorian or Roman heart of the Sanctoral, consisting of masses for Stephen (**309-317**), Agnes (**329**), Philip and James (**409-416**), the vigil and feast of John the Baptist (**428-445**), John and Paul (**447-454**), the vigil and feast of Peter and Paul (**456-473**), the Commemoration of Paul (**475-483**), and the vigil and feast of Lawrence (**548-565**), all with parallels in the early mass-antiphonals edited by Hesbert (AMS), is only slightly more extensive than the Gregorian core of the lection-list.[365]

TABLE 16					
Sanctoral: Musical Items from Gregorian Sources**					
Feast		RL: GR	AMS	Misc	BEN
Stephen	309 Int.	=	=		Ben,Ca,Mc,Ott,Pu,Ve
	312 Gr.	=	=		Ben,Ca,Da,Mc,Ott,Pu,Ve
	313 All.	=	=		Ben,Ca,Da,Mc,Ott,Pu,Ve
	315 Off.	=	(=)		Ben,Ca,Da,Mc,Ott,Pu,Ve
	317 Com.	=	=		Ben,Ca,Da,Mc,Ott,Pu,Ve
Agnes	329 All.	( )	( )		Ben,Da,Mc,Ott
Philip and James	409 Int.	=	=		Ben,Mc,Ott,Pu,Ve
	412 All.*	(=)	( )		Ben,Mc,Ott
	414 Off.*	=	=		Ben,Mc,Ott,Pu,Ve
	416 Com.	=	=		Ben,Mc,Ott,Pu,Ve
Vigil of John	428 Int.	=	=		Ben,Mc,Ott,Pu,Ve
the Baptist	431 Gr.	=	=		Ben,Mc,Ott,Pu,Ve
	433 Off.*	=	=		Ben,Mc,Ott,Pu,Ve
	435 Com.*	=	=		Ben,Mc,Ott,Pu,Ve
John the Baptist	437 Int.	=	=		Ben,Mc,Ott,Pu,Ve
	440 Gr.	=	=		Ben,Mc,Ott,Pu,Ve
	441 All.	( )	( )		Ben,Mc,Ott
	443 Off.	=	=		Ben,Mc,Ott,Pu,Ve
	445 Com.	=	=		Ben,Mc,Ott,Pu,Ve
John and Paul	447 Int.	=	=		Ben,Mc,Ott,Ve
	450 Gr.	=	=		Ben,Mc,Ott,Ve
	451 All.	=	( )		(Ben)
	452 Off.	=	=		Ben,Mc,Ott,Ve
	454 Com.	=	=		Ben,Mc,Ott,Ve,Vl10645

[365] The feast of Agnes is not provided with lections in the Oxford MS, and the lections for John and Paul do not correspond to the selections of the Roman lection-lists.

Feast			RL: GR	AMS	Misc	BEN
						TABLE 16 (cont'd) Sanctoral: Musical Items from Gregorian Sources**

Feast			RL: GR	AMS	Misc	BEN
Vigil of Peter	456	Int.	=	=		Ben,Mc,Ott,Pu,Ve,Vl10645
and Paul	459	Gr.*	=	=		Ben,Mc,Ott,(Pu),Ve
	461	Off.*	=	=		Ben,Mc,Ott,Pu,Ve
	463	Com.	=	(=)		Ben,Mc,Ott,Pu,(Ve)
Peter and Paul	465	Int.	=	=		Ben,Mc,Ott,Pu,Ve
	468	Gr.	=	=		Ben,Mc,Ott,Pu,Ve
	469	All.	( )	=	MRM v.2	Ben,Mc,Ott,Pu,Ve
	471	Off.	=	=		Ben,Mc,Ott,Pu,Ve
	473	Com.	=	(=)		Ben,Mc,Ott,Pu,(Ve)
Commemoration	475	Int.	=	=		Ben,Mc,Ott,Ve
of Paul	478	Gr.	=	=		Ben,Mc,Ott,Ve
	479	All.	=	( )		Ben,Ve
	481	Off.*	=	=		Ben,Mc,Ott,Ve
	483	Com.	=	=		Ben,Mc,Ott
Vigil of Lawrence	548	Int.	=	=		Ben,Mc,Ott,Pu,Ve
	551	Gr.	=	=		Ben,Mc,Ott,Pu,Ve
	553	Off.	=	=		Ben,Mc,Ott,Pu,Ve
	555	Com.*	=	=		Ben,Mc,Ott,Pu,Ve
Lawrence	557	Int.	(=)	(=)		Ben,Mc,Ott,Pu
	560	Gr.	=	=		Ben,Mc,Ott,Pu,Ve
	561	All.	=	( )		Ben,(Mc),(Ott),Ve
	563	Off.	=	=		Ben,Mc,Ott,Pu,Ve
	565	Com.	=	=		Ben,Mc,Ott,Pu,Ve

* In this and the following tables an asterisk indicates pieces given by incipit without musical notation.

** Although the Table does not show melodic variants, minor variants are given in the *apparatus musicus* and major variants or different melodies are transcribed in full in the Introduction following this Table. Parentheses filled with an equal sign indicate that the feast is found in the same source being compared but the item is proper to another feast in that source.

Among the masses judged Gregorian from their similarities to the masses of the early antiphonals, several regional or local features are apparent, particularly in the lack of stability among the alleluias, where even the earliest feasts of the calendar show considerable diversity.[366] Thus, the alleluias of the Dubrovnik missal for Agnes (**329**), Philip and James (**412**),[367] John the

[366] Apel, *Gregorian Chant*, p. 380.

[367] *Pretiosa*, given in incipit; the full verse and melody are found on the preceding feast of George (**389**) (see below pp. 155-156).

Baptist (**441**), John and Paul (**451**), the Commemoration of Paul (**479**), and Lawrence (**561**) are not found in the early mass-antiphonals. While some of the variant alleluias have textual counterparts elsewhere in the GR,[368] or even on the feast itself,[369] only the alleluia *Hec est uera fraternitas* (**451**) for John and Paul is found on the feast with the same melody in the later GR. The evidence suggests that the primitive Roman source for Romano-Beneventan chant lacked even the few alleluias found in the earliest surviving mass-antiphonals. Eventually supplied by regional liturgists, the texts of individual verses sometimes parallel selections made in other regions, but the variant musical settings indicate that their origins are ultimately different.

As consideration of the alleluias makes clear, even the central Gregorian feasts are not entirely uniform. The variant pieces will be transcribed and considered each in turn.

---

[368] E.g., *Pretiosa* (**389, 403, 412**) for Philip and James.

[369] E.g., *Laurentius* (**561**) with a variant melody; the alleluia *Beatus vir* is given in AMS 136 for Lawrence.

tum　me- um　al- le-

lu- ia.

Figure 22. — **315** OFFERTORIVM Elegerunt apostoli stephanum, fol. 71v.

The text of the offertory for Stephen in the early mass-antiphonals *In virtute* (AMS 12) is replaced in Beneventan sources and later Roman missals by the text *Elegerunt* of the Oxford manuscript. Nonetheless, the Beneventan offertory has a musical setting different from the later Roman setting, although both Roman and Beneventan melodies are in the eighth mode (final G, ambitus C-d).[370] The earliest reference to the text *Elegerunt* is found in the ninth-century Antiphonal of Senlis as *Item Offitio de sancto Stephano* on the fourth Ides of September (AMS 148 *bis*).[371] Hesbert, noting in this source other traces of the Gallican liturgy, postulates a Gallican origin for the Roman offertory.[372] Whatever the ultimate shared origin of the Romano-Frankish and Romano-Beneventan witnesses to the offertory text, the varying melody suggests that the musical settings had separate histories from an early period.

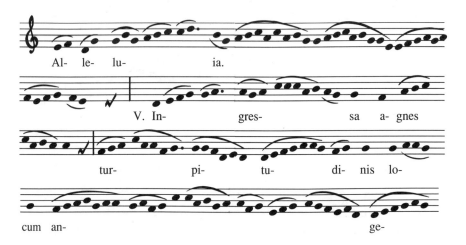

Al- le- lu-　　ia.

V. In-　　gres-　　sa　a- gnes

tur-　　pi-　tu-　　di- nis lo-

cum an-　　　　　　　ge-

---

[370] Incipits: CDCDDEFDEF *Benevento*] CDFFEFGAEC GR.

[371] See above n. 159 for the Antiphonal of Senlis (Hesbert, *Antiphonale missarum sextuplex*, pp. xxiii-xxiv).

[372] Hesbert, "'Antiphonale missarum'," *EL* 52 (1938) 143-145.

lum   do- mi-   ni   prē- pa- ra-   tum   in-

ue- nit.

Figure 23. — **329** Alleluia. Ingressa agnes, fol. 72v.

The alleluia verse *Ingressa agnes* (**329**) for the mass of Agnes is derived
from an antiphon of the office and found principally in Beneventan sources;
it is seen elsewhere only in an eleventh-century Bolognese manuscript in the
Angelica.[373] Although the verse is regional, the melody is adapted from the
universal setting of the alleluia with the verse *Adducentur*.[374]

Al- le-   lu-   ia.

V. Mul- ti   gau- de-bunt sanc- ti si- cut sol

an- te do- mi- num   re-ful-gen-   ti- bus   in   ce- lum ex- ul- tat ut cum

do- mi- no   a- stra   si- de- ra   ce- li- que et ma- ri- a   col- lau- dan-

tes   de- um in se- de ce- le-sti- a re-   gnant   cum do- mi- no. V. Ex

u-   te- ro   se- nec- tu- tis et   stē-   ri-

---

[373] Rome, Biblioteca Angelica, 123 (above n. 78); and [Jacques Hourlier and Michel
Huglo], "Notice descriptive sur le manuscrit," in *Le Codex VI.34 de la Bibliothèque capitulaire
de Benevent (XIᵉ-XIIᵉ siècle)*, ed. Jospeh Gajard, Paléographie Musicale 15 (Solesmes, 1937),
p. 165.
[374] Schlager, *Katalog*, no. E 203.

Figure 24. — **441** Alleluia. V. Multi gaudebunt, V. Ex utero *cum prosula*, fol. 94r-v.

The alleluia for John the Baptist contains the verse *Ex utero* and two prosulas: *Multi gaudebunt* as an exordium set to the repetition of the jubilus, and *Iohannes baptista* on the melisma at "Iohannes." The verse *Ex utero* (or *De utero*) is a distinctive regional text adapted to the melody of the alleluia *Iustus ut palma*.[375] The exordium prosula is found in southern French mass-antiphonals as well as in Italian sources;[376] but the intercalated prosula *Iohannes baptista* is attested only in sources from Benevento itself.[377]

The musical items for the feasts of John and Paul (**447-454**) and the vigil of Peter and Paul (**456-463**) are unremarkable, except that the alleluia *Hec est uera fraternitas* of the former (**451**) and the communion *Symon iohannis diligis* of the latter (**463**) follow the later medieval tradition of the GR instead of the selections of the early Roman mass-antiphonals.[378] In the GR, the

---

[375] Schlager, *Katalog*, no. D 38; also Corpus troporum 2/1, nos. 16, 40.5, 40.7, with the prosulas.

[376] *French*: Paris, BN, lat. 776 (Gaillac); BN, lat. 1084 (Aurillac); BN, lat. 1118 (Auch); and *Italian*: Oxford, Bodleian Library, Douce 222 (s. xi, Novalese; bibl.: Gajard, *Graduel romain*, 2: 88); Rome, Biblioteca Angelica 123 (Bologna); Vl4770 (Abruzzi).

[377] I.e., Ben34, Ben35, Ben39, Ben40.

[378] John and Paul: Hesbert, *Antiphonale missarum sextuplex*, p. xcvii; AMS 120 with the alleluia *Gaudete iusti* in three MSS and the indication *Quale volueris* in the Antiphonal of Mont-Blandin (above n. 159). Vigil of Peter and Paul: Hesbert, *Antiphonale missarum sextuplex*, pp. xcvii-xcviii; AMS 121 with the communion *Tu es Petrus*; in AMS, the vigil and feast of Peter are without reference to Paul.

Dubrovnik missal, and other Beneventan sources, the communions of the vigil (**463**) and feast (**473** *Tu es petrus*) reverse the order presented in the early mass-antiphonals. Since the communions of the GR and Oxford manuscript correspond to the gospels that are assigned to the vigil (**460** Io 21: 15-19) and the feast (**470** Mt 16: 13-19) in all the early lection-lists, the witness of the early mass-antiphonals is particularly curious: later manuscripts may have transferred the communions to achieve a sought-after balance of gospel and communion. Certainly, it seems unlikely that the early antiphonals would be unanimous in creating an unbalanced arrangement if it had not existed historically.

Figure 25. — **469** Alleluia. Beatus es symon, fol. 85r.

The alleluia *Beatus es symon* (**469** Mt 16: 17) for the feast of Peter and Paul is drawn from the traditional Roman gospel for the feast (**470** Mt 16: 13-19); the same verse is found in two of the early mass-antiphonals,[379] other Beneventan sources, and an early Venetian printed missal (MRM 2: 206). In two other early mass-antiphonals and the GR, the verse *Tu es Petrus*, also from the gospel (Mt 16: 18), is preferred.[380] From its origins as an alternative to the text eventually taken into the GR, the verse *Beatus es symon* spread widely, but its melodic tradition is among the most fluid: the verse is set to

---

[379] AMS 122b: the Antiphonals of Compiègne and Corbie (above n. 159).

[380] AMS 122b: the Antiphonal of Mont-Blandin and the Cantatorium of Monza (above n. 159).

five different melodies in various sources.[381] The verse *Beatus es symon* is adapted in the Oxford manuscript to the setting of the verse *Benedictus es domine*, a combination of text and melody restricted to Italian sources.[382]

Figure 26. — **479** Alleluia. Magnus sanctus paulus, fol. 86v.

The alleluia *Magnus sanctus paulus* (**479**) for the Commemoration of Paul in the Dubrovnik missal and other Beneventan sources is found in the GR for the Conversion of Paul (25 January) with a different melody.[383] The alleluia for the Commemoration is *Gaudete* in the early mass-antiphonals of Monza,

---

[381] Schlager, *Katalog*, p. 32, melodies with the text are nos. D 27 (*Dies sanctificatus*), D 46 (*Posuisti domine*), D 90 (Frankish: *Beati estis*), F 228 (*Diligam te*), and G 302 (*Benedictus es domine*); all except D 90 are melodies of wide distribution with numerous adapted verses.

[382] Schlager, *Katalog*, no. G 302, cites Beneventan sources and other Italian MSS: Ivrea, Biblioteca Capitolare, 60, fol. 103v (s. xi, Pavia; bibl.: Gajard, *Graduel romain*, 2: 54); Milan, Biblioteca Ambrosiana, E 68 sup., fol. 57r (s. xi, S. Abbondio in Como; bibl.: Gajard, *Graduel romain*, 2: 71; *CLLA*, no. 1349); Monza, Biblioteca Capitolare, c. 12/75, fol. 64r (s. xi in., Monza; bibl.: Gajard, *Graduel romain*, 2: 76), and c. 13/76, fol. 130v (s. xi, Monza; bibl.: Gajard, *Graduel romain*, 2: 76); Oxford, Bodl., Douce 222, fol. 27v, and Misc. Lit. 366, fol. 28r (s. xi, Brescia; bibl.: Gajard, *Graduel romain*, 2: 89); and Vercelli, Biblioteca Capitolare, 161, fol. 82v.

[383] The melody of the GR is adapted from the setting of *Dies sanctificatus* (Schlager, *Katalog*, no. D 27).

Mont-Blandin, Corbie, and Senlis, with *Caeli enarrant* in the Gradual of
Compiègne (AMS 123). In later manuscripts, the feast was supplied with
more specific texts, including the verses *Magnus sanctus paulus* of the Oxford
manuscript and *Sancte Paule apostole* of the GR. The verse of the Missal, like
the alleluia *Beatus es symon* (**469**) for the feast of the apostles, is found in
several regions with various musical settings.[384] Even in the Beneventan zone,
the text is given at least two arrangements: the melody of *Dies sanctificatus*,
attested in the GR and in a late-eleventh-century Cassinese missal (Monte
Cassino, Archivio della Badia 540, = Mc540),[385] and the melody of *Spiritus
paraclitus* found in the Dubrovnik missal. In southern Italy, this melody is
used for the verses *Spiritus paraclitus* and *Magnus sanctus paulus*; outside the
region the melody is found with the verse *Spiritus paraclitus* in the Tonary
of Montpellier (Montpellier H 159, fol. 57r).[386]

Figure 27. – **561** Alleluia. Laurentius bonum opus, fol. 101r.

[384] Schlager, *Katalog*, nos. D 27 (*Dies sanctificatus*), D 47 (*Spiritus paraclitus*), D 77 (*Iusti
epulentur*), and D 79 (*Non vos me elegistis*).

[385] Monte Cassino, Archivio della Badia, 540; siglum: Mc540, missale, s. xi/xii; bibl.:
CLLA, no. 458b; Lowe, *Beneventan Script*, 2: 89; Gajard, *Graduel romain*, 2: 74.

[386] Schlager, *Katalog*, no. D 47.

Although the early mass-antiphonals lack an alleluia for Lawrence (AMS 136), the verse *Levita Laurentius bonum opus* of the GR and its variant *Laurentius bonum opus* (**561**) of the Dubrovnik missal are universal for the feast in later sources. As was the case with the preceding alleluias *Beatus es symon* (**469**) and *Magnus sanctus paulus* (**479**), the texts are set to many different melodies.[387] The melody of the verse in the Oxford manuscript is based on the setting of the alleluia with the verse *Laetamini in domino;*[388] found outside Italy in the Tonary of Montpellier (Montpellier H 159, fol. 67v), the melody is adapted to several verses in Italian manuscripts. The combination with the verse *Laurentius bonum opus* is attested, however, only in southern Italian sources.[389]

The choice of the introit *Probasti domine* (**557**) for the feast of Lawrence in the Missal and most other Beneventan sources differs from the Roman tradition, which has *Probasti domine* with the same melody for the octave of Lawrence, and *Confessio et pulchritudo* for the feast (AMS 136). The Dubrovnik missal lacks the octave, but in Ben33 the introit of the octave is given by reference to the feast (*Probasti domine*), while in Ben34 it is listed in incipit as *Confessio et pulchritudo*, although with reference to the Friday of the first week of Lent. Evidently, the Gregorian exemplar for the Romano-Beneventan mass-antiphonal did not know the introit *Confessio* for the feast of Lawrence. Since the masses of both feast and octave are stable in the Roman tradition, the early exemplar at the base of the Romano-Beneventan books probably belonged to another, otherwise unattested branch of the Gregorian tradition.

Gregorian Masses (2): The second layer of Roman influence consists of a series of feasts also given proper masses in the early mass-antiphonals but corresponding less closely to their counterparts in the Dubrovnik missal (see Table 17). The group includes the feasts of the Annunciation (**376-384**), George (**386-397**), the Invention of the Cross (**418-427**), and the Assumption of Mary (**577-585**). For the lection-list of the Oxford manuscript,

---

[387] Schlager, *Katalog*, nos. D 38 (*Iustus ut palma*), D 115 (*Nonne cor nostrum*), G 274 (*Laetabitur justus*), G 284 (*Laetamini in domino*), and G 351 (*In die resurrectionis*); the base-melody for the text is G (D) 270.

[388] Schlager, *Katalog*, no. G 284.

[389] See the *apparatus parallelorum locorum*, and also Rome, Biblioteca Vallicelliana, C 52, fol. 117r (s. xii, Nursia; bibl.: Gajard, *Graduel romain*, 2: 123; *CLLA*, no. 1377b). Several Beneventan sources add the alleluia "Beatus laurentius orauit et dixit domine iesu christe deus de deo miserere mei serui tui" (Schlager, *Katalog*, no. D 280): this verse is found in Ben33 118v, Ben34 217v, Ben35 139r, Ben38 123r, Ben39 144r, and Ben40 111r; in all except Ben33 the verse *Laurentius bonum opus* is also given.

the Marian feasts had been added via a mixed lectionary of the Gelasian-Gregorian, Romano-Frankish liturgy, while the Invention of the Cross and the feast of George were provided with regional lections. In general, the presence or absence of the Marian masses and the masses for George and the Invention of the Cross is important in dating and defining the earliest comparative sources. In this regard, the Comes of Würzburg and the Comes of Muhrbach represent separate, distinct stages in the development of the lection system from Roman to Romano-Frankish (for the sacramentaries, from Gregorian to mixed Gelasian-Gregorian). Similarly the early mass-antiphonals (AMS) mark several steps in the integration of the Roman and Frankish liturgies, the simplest already more advanced than the Comes of Würzburg or the Hadrianum, for instance, but less developed than the Comes of Muhrbach or the Fulda sacramentary.[390]

TABLE 17					
Sanctoral: Musical Items from Romano-Frankish Sources					
Feast			RL: GR	AMS	BEN
Annunciation	376	Int.*	(=)	=	Ben,Da,Mc,Ott,Pu,Ve
	379	Gr.*	(=)	=	Ben,Da,Mc,Pu
	380	Tr.	( )	( )	Ben,Da,Mc,Ott,Pu,Ve
	382	Off.*	=	=	Ben,Da,Mc,Ott,Pu,Ve
	384	Com.*	=	=	Ben,Da,Mc,Ott,Pu,Ve
George	386	Int.	=	=	Ben,Mc,Ott,Ve
	389	All.	=	=	Ben,Mc,Ott
	390	All.	(=)	( )	Ben,Mc,Ott
	394	Seq.	( )	( )	(Ben)
	395	Off.	=	=	Ben,Mc,Ott,Ve
	397	Com.	=	(=)	Ben,(Mc)
Invention of the Cross	418	Int.	=	=	Ben,Mc,Ott,Pu,Ve
	422	Gr.*	(=)	=	(Ben,Pu)
	423	All.	=	( )	Ben,Mc,Pu,Ve
	425	Off.	(=)	( )	Ben,Mc,(Pu),Ve
	427	Com.	( )	( )	Ben
Assumption	577	Int.	=	( )	(Ben),Ve
	580	Gr.	=	=	Ben,Mc,Ott,Pu,Ve
	581	All.	( )	( )	Ben,Mc,Pu
	583	Off.*	(=)	=	Ben,Mc,Ott,Pu,Ve
	585	Com.*	(=)	=	Ben,Mc,Ott,Pu,Ve

[390] E.g., the distinctively Gelasian feast of the Invention of the Cross is found in the Antiphonal of Compiègne (above n. 159, AMS 97 *bis*), whereas the equally distinctive mass for James is not; both masses are provided with lections in Mu.

The Marian masses have already been described as late additions to the
Gregorian calendar dating to the seventh century.[391] The introit *Rorate* (**376**)
and gradual *Tollite* (**379**) of the Annunciation, given in incipit,[392] are
common to Beneventan sources and the Antiphonal of Senlis (AMS 33a). The
remaining early antiphonals have the introit *Vultum tuum*, which is found in
the later Roman Common. The divergence in traditions for the seventh-
century feast points to the early date of the Romano-Beneventan exemplar,
although the offertory *Ave maria* (**382**) and the communion *Ecce uirgo
concipiet* (**384**), given in incipit with reference to a now-lost portion of the
manuscript, are standard in both the early mass-antiphonals and the GR. The
tract *Ave maria* (**380**) is a distinctive regional chant.

A- ue ma- ri- a gra- ti- a
ple- na do- mi- nus te-
cum. Be- ne- dic- ta tu
in- ter mu- li- e-
res. Et be- ne- dic- tus
fruc- tus uen- tris tu- i.

Figure 28. — **380** TRACTVS Ave maria, fol. 78r.

The text of the tract *Ave maria* (**380**) is attested in the GR as an alleluia
verse, and among Venetian printed missals as the tract for the feast (MRM 2:
191).[393] The melody is similar to the Beneventan setting of the tract *Adducen-*

---

[391] See above pp. 122, 136; summarised in Deshusses, *Sacramentaire grégorien*, 3: 60-63.
[392] The full versions are absent from the Oxford MS as presently constituted. Both were
probably contained among the masses for Advent, as in the GR.
[393] Apel, *Gregorian Chant*, p. 313, speculates that the tract *Ave Maria* assigned in tenth-

tur (**661**) for the Common of a Virgin, also found in McV and Ben34 for Agnes. Although the melody of *Ave Maria* has a range from D to c (only once going to e on "*gratia*," and once to d in the melisma on "*mulieres*"), the related music of *Adducentur* frequently uses the range D-d, and both melodies open and close on G, as do other tracts of the eighth mode. The standard phrases of the Gregorian tracts of the eighth mode are, however, not repeated in the Beneventan melodies, except for the closing cadences.[394]

The mass for the Assumption of Mary (**577-585**), like the mass for the Annunciation, is a later addition to the Roman calendar that forms the core of the primitive Gregorian mass-book. As a result, there are several discrepancies between the early mass-antiphonals and the later GR: only the gradual *Propter ueritatem* (**580**) is common to all sources. The Dubrovnik missal has the introit *Gaudeamus* (**577**), which is standard for the feast in the GR and in some regional manuscripts (Vat. lat. 4770, Ve),[395] but not found in the majority of Beneventan sources and the early mass-antiphonals, a discrepancy that points, as many other features have, to the later Roman influences on the Dubrovnik missal. The offertory *Offerentur* (**583**) and communion *Dilexisti iustitiam* (**585**) represent the opposite process, i.e., the retention of regional features. Both pieces, cited by incipit and referring to the Marian mass within the octave of Christmas (**31, 33**),[396] are found in Beneventan sources and the three early mass-antiphonals that have the feast; the GR relegates the texts and melodies to the Common and selects instead the more appropriate offertory *Assumpta est* and communion *Optimam partem*. Although later Roman sources may have influenced the choice of introit in the Oxford manuscript, less specific items were retained for the offertory and communion.

The distinction between the Romano-Beneventan mass-antiphonal and the later medieval books of Gregorian chant is clear also in the alleluia *O quam beata* (**581**) of the Assumption.

Al-   le-   lu- ia.

---

century sources to the feast of Gabriel was originally proper to the Annunciation. However, the Roman and Beneventan texts vary ("inter mulieres" *Ben*] "in mulieribus" *GR*), and the melodies are unrelated.

[394] See Apel, *Gregorian Chant*, p. 320, for the standard phrases of the eighth mode; *Ave Maria* closes on Apel's G_n.

[395] The melody and text are attested elsewhere in Ben34 49v (Agatha) and 237r (All Saints) and the early mass-antiphonals (AMS 30: Agatha).

[396] See above pp. 45-46.

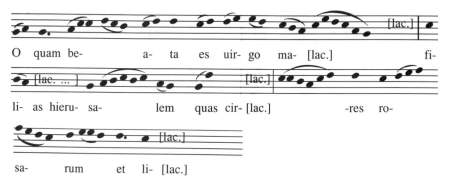

O   quam be-   a- ta   es   uir- go ma- [lac.]   fi-

li- as hieru- sa-   lem   quas cir- [lac.]   -res ro-

sa-   rum   et   li- [lac.]

Figure 29. − **581** Alleluia. O quam beata, fol. 103r.

The circulation of this particular combination of text and melody is restricted to southern Italian sources, although the melody is found occasionally in the region with other verses.[397] The musical items of the mass of the Assumption in the Dubrovnik missal, apart from its exceptional adoption of the later Roman introit, indicate that the Gregorian source for the Romano-Beneventan mass-antiphonal clearly resembled the early mass-antiphonals even in its lack of an alleluia, a lack that was filled with a local composition.

Since the feast of George, though early and attested in the Hadrianum and some Gelasian sacramentaries, is provided with different prayers in each tradition and not witnessed at all in the early lectionaries, it is probably a late-seventh-century addition to the Roman calendar.[398] As discussed in relation to the extraordinary triple gospel of the feast, the mass for George in the Missal may represent an attempt to provide a *Commune sanctorum tempore paschali*.[399] Certainly, among the musical items, the introit *Protexisti* (**386**) is repeated in incipit for the following feast of Mark (**400**); the second alleluia *Pretiosa* (**390**) is given in incipit for Mark (**403**) and Philip and James (**412**); the offertory *Confitebuntur* (**395**) is cited by incipit for both subsequent feasts (**405, 414**); and the communion *Ego sum uitis uera* (**397**) is paralleled in Mark (**407**), also in incipit. Both the introit and offertory are common to the GR and the early mass-antiphonals as well as to other Beneventan sources; the communion, however, is proper instead to the feast

---

[397] Schlager, *Katalog*, no. G 373.

[398] Hesbert, *Antiphonale missarum sextuplex*, p. xci, remarks that the Roman church jointly dedicated to Sebastian and George dates to the pontificate of Leo II (682-683); Moreton, *Eighth-Century Gelasian Sacramentary*, p. 103, concludes from the independent prayer traditions that the feast is late.

[399] See above p. 138.

of Vitalis in the GR and the early mass-antiphonals (AMS 95). In the Dubrovnik missal, the feast of Vitalis follows George and is provided with a collect (**399**); the lack of other proper texts suggests that the rest of the mass may have been drawn from the preceding Easter Common represented by the mass for George. The text of the alleluia *Confitebuntur* (**389**) is also paralleled in the GR and the early mass-antiphonals, although the melody is unrelated.

Figure 30. – **389** Alleluia. Confitebuntur, fol. 78v.

The text is frequently attested with other musical settings,[400] but the combination of text and music found in the Oxford manuscript finds counterpart only among Italian sources, especially Beneventan manuscripts where the melody is found as well with the verses *Cantate domino, Cernentibus discipulis,* and *Repleti sunt apostoli.*[401]

---

[400] Cf. Schlager, *Katalog*, nos. D 27, E 205, G 271, G 376.
[401] Schlager, *Katalog*, no. F (D) 220.

Figure 31. — **390** Alleluia. Pretiosa, fols. 78v-79r.

The melody of the second alleluia *Pretiosa* (**390**) has a much wider
circulation, being found throughout Italy and Germany; the Italian sources
sometimes set the verse *Universae angelorum* to the same melody.[402] The text
has an even greater currency: with other musical settings, it is cited from
several regions and enters the GR in the Common.[403]

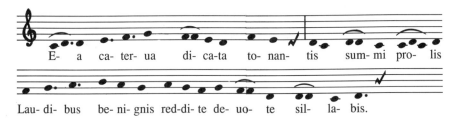

Figure 32. — **394** SEQVENTIA Ea caterua, fol. 80r.

The sequence *Ea caterua* (**394**) for the feast of George, given in incipit
with a musical setting, is a regional text and melody found elsewhere only
in Benevento and intended there for the feast of Mark.[404] If the mass for
George is indeed an unspecific copy of an Easter Common, the assignment
of the sequence to George may be understood as part of the muddle of
Commons and Propers. Instead of coming before the gospel, the sequence
is found after the last of the gospels for George (**393**) in the Oxford
manuscript. This curious placement supports the suggestion that some
confusion lies behind its designation among the texts of the mass for George.

   The Invention of the Cross, originally a Frankish feast adopted into the
Roman liturgy via the Gelasian sacramentaries, is found in the ninth-century

---

[402] Schlager, *Katalog*, no. G 282.

[403] Cf. Schlager, *Katalog*, nos. D 28, E 200; the text is omitted from AMS.

[404] Ben38 70v-71r, Ben39 66r, and Ben40 46r-47r; also Brunner, "Southern Italian
Sequence," p. 131 (Table 3, no. 81); and *Analecta hymnica medii aevi*, ed. Guido Maria
Dreves, Clemens Blume, and Henry M. Bannister, 55 vols. (Leipzig, 1886-1922), 53:
291-293.

Antiphonal of Compiègne (AMS 97 *bis*). The introit *Nos autem gloriari* (**418**), common to the Compiègne antiphonal, the GR, and several Beneventan sources, is also given in the Missal as the introit for the votive mass for the cross (**693**). For the gradual *Christus factus* (**422**), listed by incipit without musical setting, and found elsewhere in the manuscript on Holy Thursday (**189**) and in the votive mass for the cross (**696**) with the melody of the GR, the only parallel is the Compiègne antiphonal. Most Beneventan sources and the GR have instead the alleluia *Dicite in gentibus* appropriate for the Paschal season. The parallels between the Compiègne antiphonal and the Dubrovnik missal, however, are not continued for the remaining chants: the alleluia *Dulce lignum* (**423**) is found in the GR and other Beneventan sources with the same melody (Compiègne: AMS 97 *bis*: *Dominus regnavit a ligno*); the offertory *Protege* (**425**) is common to the Beneventan sources, proper to the Exaltation of the Cross in the GR, and lacking in the early mass-antiphonals;[405] and the communion *Per sanctam crucem* (**427**) is regional.

Figure 33. — **427** COMMVNIO Per sanctam crucem, fol. 91v (see Plate 6).

The text *Per sanctam crucem* is cited in incipit in Ben35, Ben38, and Ben40, but its musical setting is found only in the Oxford manuscript.[406] Even the texts and melody of the Old Beneventan mass for the Invention are entirely unrelated.[407]

---

[405] Since Beneventan sources supply the same offertory for the Exaltation (*Protege*: Ben33 122r, Ben34 234v), the chants of the Roman and Beneventan masses probably developed independently to provide for prayer-sets introduced into the Roman liturgy through the Gelasian sacramentaries. In this case, the Roman source developed along the lines of greater specificity with different texts for the offertories of the Exaltation and the Invention.

[406] Cf. Bryden and Hughes, *Index*, entry C 2524 2057, for similar melodic incipits, principally antiphons.

[407] Invention communion *Crucem tuam* in Ben40 124v (= Antiphon *Crucem tuam* of Good Friday: Andoyer, "Ancienne liturgie," *RdCG* 22 [1913-1914] 144; Huglo, "Ancien chant bénéventain," p. 278; and Kelly, *Beneventan Chant*, pp. 51, 78 n. 79, 81-82, 87 n. 104, and 266).

Later Roman Masses: Musical items from four masses in the Dubrovnik missal are paralleled in the GR, but without counterpart in the early mass-antiphonals (Table 18). Other individual items for masses shared with the later GR are the introit *Vir dei benedictus* (**366**) for Benedict and the introit *Protexisti* (**400**) for Mark.

TABLE 18 Sanctoral: Musical Items for Later Masses (1. Roman)					
Feast			RL: GR	AMS	BEN
Conversion of Paul	**333**	Int.*	=	[=]	Ben,Da,Mc,Ott
Chair of Peter	**348**	Int.	=	[=]	Ben,Da,Mc,Ott,Ve
	351	Gr.	=	[ ]	Ben,Ve
	352	Tr.	=	[ ]	Ve
	354	Off.*	(=)	[=]	(Ben,Pu)
	356	Com.*	=	[=]	(Ben,Pu),Ve
Chains of Peter	**530**	Int.*	=	[=]	Ben,Mc,Ott,Ve
All Souls	**592**	Int.*	=	[ ]	Ben,Ott,Pu
	595	Gr.*	( )	[ ]	Ben,Ott,(Pu)
	596	Tr.*	=	[ ]	( )

Among the pieces listed in Table 18 all except the introit, gradual, and tract for the Chair of Peter (**348**, **351**, **352**) are given in incipit. In most instances the GR and the Oxford manuscript simply repeat appropriate items found elsewhere in the early mass-antiphonals: the introit *Scio cui credidi* (**333**) for the Conversion of Paul is taken from the Commemoration of Paul (**475**); the offertory *Inueni dauid* (**354**) for the Chair of Peter repeats a text from the Commons of both the GR and the Dubrovnik missal (**653**), although the GR has the offertory *Tu es Petrus* on the feast; and lastly the communion *Tu es Petrus* (**356**) for the Chair of Peter and the introit *Nunc scio* (**530**) for the Chains of Peter are adoptions in the Roman missal and Dubrovnik missal from the earlier mass for the apostles Peter and Paul (**465**, **473**).

The mass for All Souls (**592-596**) is less dependent on the early Roman tradition. While the introit *Requiem* (**592**) and the tract *Absolue* (**596**) are proper to the feast in the GR, neither has counterpart in the early mass-antiphonals; for the gradual *Conuertere anima mea* (**595**), unattested in the Roman tradition, parallels are found in other Beneventan sources. Although each of the musical items of the mass are given in incipit, the full noted texts are lacking from the manuscript in its present condition.

Apart from the unnoted gradual *Conuertere* (**595**) of All Souls, the gradual *Exaltent* (**351**) and tract *Tu es petrus* (**352**) for the Chair of Peter are the only distinctive musical items among the later Roman masses.

Figure 34. – **351** GRADVALE Exaltent eum, fol. 75v.

The text of the gradual *Exaltent* with its verse *Confiteantur* (**351** Ps 106: 32, 31) is given in the GR for the same feast but is without parallel in the early mass-antiphonals. As with many late texts and melodies, the musical setting of the gradual is presented with regional variants. The regional melodies of the Dubrovnik missal and Ben34 are related in general arrangement despite the transposition up a fifth throughout in the former. In this instance, the transposition is a graphic device to represent the full interval of the incipit given by B♭-C in Ben34. Since the scribe of the Oxford manuscript rarely marks B-flat, the transposition of the incipit to E-G became necessary to preserve the relation of the initial interval and subsequent pitches.[408]

---

[408] I.e., EG of the Oxford MS is represented by B♭c in the earlier Ben34.

Figure 35. — **352** TRACTVS Tu es petrus, fol. 76r.

Although the tract *Tu es petrus* (**352**) for the Chair of Peter is also found in the GR on the same feast with a similar melody, the arrangement of the text with the melody is considerably different. Since *Tu es Petrus* is among the more recent tracts of the second mode, i.e., it is not present in the early mass-antiphonals, perhaps the discrepancies between the Roman and Dalmatian settings indicate an independent composition of the text and music in the Beneventan zone.[409]

Later Roman Masses (Adapted): While the music of only four feasts post-dating the early mass-antiphonals is shared with later Roman sources, many more late feasts are given regional masses composed of elements drawn from the Roman Common or other similar feasts (see Table 19). The feasts themselves fall into two categories: eight masses with wide circulation in later sources, most eventually taken into the GR, and the local/regional masses of the Dalmatian martyrs (**485-493**) and Elias (**497-505**).[410] The introit *Protexisti* (**400**) for Mark is the sole item with an exact counterpart in the GR, although several pieces are found on the same feasts in other later missals.[411]

---

[409] Apel, *Gregorian Chant*, p. 323, lists the earliest tracts of the second mode; also pp. 326-327, for a tabular analysis of the standard phrases of *Tu es Petrus*.

[410] The three late feasts of wide diffusion with unique texts or melodies—Nicholas, Benedict, and Mary Magdalen—are discussed in the next section (Table 20).

[411] Exact parallels in the Venetian early printed missals (MRM, vol. 2), perhaps indicative of local Italian or Adriatic practice, are found for the tract *In columbe* (**343**) for Scholastica,

TABLE 19					
Sanctoral: Musical Items for Later Masses (2. Adapted)					
Feast			RL: GR	AMS	Misc	BEN
Scolastica	**339**	Int.*	=	[=]		Ben,Da,Mc,Ott,(Pu)
	342	Gr.*	(=)	[=]		Ben,Da,Mc,Ott,(Pu)
	343	Tr.*	(=)	[ ]	MRM v.2	Ben,Da,Mc,Ott
	346	Com.	(=)	[=]		Ben,Da,Mc,Ott
Matthias	**358**	Int.*	(=)	[=]	(MRM v.2)	Ben
	360	Gr.*	(=)	[=]		Ben
	363	Com.*	(=)	[=]		Ben
Mark	**400**	Int.*	=	[=]		Ben,Mc,Ve
	403	All.*	(=)	[ ]		Ben,Mc
	405	Off.*	(=)	[=]	MRM v.2	Ben,Mc,(Pu)
	407	Com.*	(=)	[=]		Ben,Mc
Lawrence, Peter,	**485**	Int.*	[=]	[=]		[Ben]
and Andrew	**488**	Gr.*	[=]	[=]		[Ben]
	489	All.*	[=]	[ ]		[Ben]
	491	Off.*	[=]	[=]		[Ben,Pu]
	493	Com.*	[=]	[=]		[Ben,Pu]
Elias	**497**	Int.*	[=]	[=]		[Ben]
	500	Gr.*	[=]	[=]		[Ben]
	501	All.*	[=]	[ ]		[Ben]
	503	Off.*	[=]	[=]		[Ben]
	505	Com.*	[=]	[=]		[Ben,Pu]
Vigil of James	**518**	Int.*	=	[=]	MRM v.2	(Ben),Mc,Ott
James	**522**	Int.*	=	[=]	MRM v.2	Ben,Mc,Ott,(Pu),Ve
	524	Gr.*	(=)	[=]		(Ben),Mc,Ott,(Pu)
	526	Off.*	=	[=]	MRM v.2	(Ben),Mc,(Pu)
	528	Com.*	(=)	[=]		(Ben)
Transfiguration	**541**	Int.*	(=)	[=]		Ben,Mc,Ott,Pu,Ve
Vigil of the	**568**	Int.*	(=)	[=]		Ben,Mc,Ott,Pu
Assumption	**571**	Gr.*	(=)	[=]		Ben,Mc,Ott,(Pu)
	573	Off.*	(=)	[=]		Ben,Mc,(Ott),Pu,Ve
	575	Com.*	(=)	[=]		Ben,Mc,Pu
All Saints	**588**	Off.	(=)	[=]		Ben,Mc,Ott
	590	Com.	(=)	[=]		(Ben),Ve

Most of the adapted items for the later masses are given in incipit; only the communion *Simile est regnum* (**346**) for Scholastica, and the offertory *Letamini* (**588**) and communion *Gaudete* (**590**) for All Saints are written in extenso with neumes. Among the texts given by incipit, those paralleled in the Common would have been found readily.[412] Their presence in the Common is indicative also of their likely origin: many of the texts for these masses are found in the Roman Common, from which generally appropriate pieces were used freely to provide music for masses absent in early sources or introduced via non-musical liturgical texts.[413] As with the Gelasian feasts introduced via sacramentaries but requiring a local selection of lections, so also later feasts were often provided with musical items from the Common when prayers, lections, or a calendar entry had been the medium for the diffusion of a cult. The regional feast of Elias (**497-505**) and the local feast of the Dalmatian martyrs (**485-493**) are heavily dependent on the musical items of the Common: the exceptions are the gradual *Ecce quam bonum* (**488**) and alleluia *Hec est uera fraternitas* (**489**) for the Dalmatian martyrs taken from the feast of John and Paul,[414] and the introit *Da pacem* (**497**) for Elias taken from the seventeenth Sunday after Pentecost (**299**).[415]

Some musical items listed in incipit are not found in extenso elsewhere in the manuscript: undoubtedly the damage to the codex has removed the expected antecedent (or Common text) for the introit *Dilexisti iustitiam*, which is found in incipit for Scholastica (**339**), the vigil of the Assumption (**568**), and the Common of a Virgin (**669**). Similarly, the incipits of the offertory *Exultabunt sancti* (**491**) and the communion *Iustorum anime* (**493**) for the Dalmatian martyrs probably refer to pieces once found among the leaves lost between fols. 111v and 112r after the incipit of the introit

---

the offertory *Confitebuntur* (**405**) for Mark, the introit *Ego autem* (**518**) for the vigil of James, and the introit *Michi autem* (**522**) and offertory *Nimis honorati* (**526**) for the feast of James.

[412] I.e., **339** (= **669**), **342** (= **671**), **358** (= **598**), **360** (= **601**), **363** (= **605**), **485** (= **641**), **500** (= **601**), **501** (= **629**), **503** (= **652**), **518** (= **598**), **541** (= **683**), **568** (= **669**), **571** (= **671**), **573** (= **673**), and **575** (= **675**). The music for the mass of Mark (**400-407**) is supplied from the mass of George (**386-398**), reinforcing the identification of the latter as an "Easter common" (above pp. 138, 154-155).

[413] I.e., **339**, **342**, **346**, **358**, **360**, **363**, **403**, **405**, **407**, **485**, **491**, **493**, **500**, **501**, **503**, **505**, **518**, **524**, **528**, **541**, **568**, **571**, **573**, **575**, **588**, and **590** have counterparts in the Roman Common.

[414] The texts given in incipit are referred specifically to the earlier feast by the rubric "in sanctorum iohannis et pauli"; the compiler of the Missal was evidently aware the texts were not in the Common and so required special identification.

[415] The marginal rubric by a different hand referring to the seventeenth Sunday after Pentecost, and the later addition in the lower margin of the text in extenso, point to the difficulties encountered by later users of the Missal when confronted by a text not in the Common.

Sapientiam (**641**) for the Common of Martyrs. The neumed text for the communion *Beatus seruus* (**505**) of Elias, also not to be found in extenso in the present manuscript, was probably among the Common texts for a confessor-not-priest, which have been lost between fols. 114v and 115r. On the other hand, three of the four musical items for the later Gelasian feast of James marked in incipit but not given in the Common (**522-528**) may never have been attested in the manuscript, since the entry of the four incipits does not appear to have been the work of the original scribe. Perhaps the later additions assume access to a Roman book, where the pieces are usually paralleled in the Common and on the feasts of Andrew and Thomas.[416]

Two of the musical items from the masses otherwise taken from the Common are distinctive, although they are both adaptations of items from other earlier masses of the Beneventan corpus. The tract *In columbe* (**343**) for Scholastica is listed by incipit, referring to the feast of Benedict (**370**); the text is also found in Venetian missals (MRM 2: 189) for the feast of Benedict.[417] The alleluia *Pretiosa* (**403**) for Mark, also listed by incipit, is a repetition of the Romano-Beneventan text and melody of the alleluia for George (**390**).[418]

Regional Masses: Three masses of the Sanctoral of the Dubrovnik missal are clearly regional compositions (see Table 20). Each of the feasts has a counterpart in later Roman sources, but the majority of the musical items are distinctive, either unattested outside the region or set to regional melodies.

None of the early liturgical sources makes provision for the feast of Nicholas. Furthermore, despite evidence for the cult from the ninth century, in particular the *Vita* composed ca. 880 by John the Deacon of Naples and the liturgy of the office composed ca. 960 by Reginald of Eichstätt, the full veneration of the saint blossoms only after the late eleventh century with the translation of his relics from Myra to Bari in 1087.[419] The cult developed

---

[416] Introit (**522**): Roman mass for Andrew; gradual (**524**): Common; offertory (**526**): Thomas; communion (**528**): Common. The communion *Amen dico uobis* (**528**) is found elsewhere in the Oxford MS as the communion for the Commemoration of Paul (**483**): considering the lack of parallels for the other pieces of the mass of James, the repetition of the communion may be more accidental than deliberate. The introit (**522**) and offertory (**526**) are attested on the same feast in the early Venetian printed missals (MRM, vol. 2): could the corrector of the MS have had on hand a book of Venetian practice? Or did the practice known to the corrector of the MS represent a Dalmatian use later adopted in Venice? Unfortunately, neither question can be answered from the evidence of the Dubrovnik missal.

[417] See below pp. 170-171, for transcription and discussion of the tract (**370**) for Benedict.

[418] See above pp. 155-156.

[419] The *Vita s. Nicolai* by John the Deacon of Naples is listed in *Bibliotheca hagiographica Latina*, 2: 890-891. For the office, see Charles William Jones, *The Saint Nicholas Liturgy and Its Literary Relationships* (Berkeley, 1963); on the translation, Nitti di Vito, *Ripresa grego-*

TABLE 20
Sanctoral: Musical Items for Regional Masses

Feast			RL: GR	AMS	Misc	BEN
Nicholas	304	Gr.	( )	[ ]		Na1
	305	All.	( )	[ ]		Ben
	307	Off.	( )	[ ]		Na1
Benedict	366	Int.	(=)	[ ]	MRM v.2	Ben,Da,Mc,Ott,Pu
	369	Gr.	( )	[ ]		Ben,Da,Mc,Ott,Pu
	370	Tr.	( )	[ ]	MRM v.2	Ben,Da,Mc,Ott
	372	Off.	( )	[ ]		Ben,Da,Mc,Ott,Pu
	374	Com.	( )	[ ]	MRM v.2	Ben,Da,Mc,Ott,Pu
Mary Magdalen	507	Int.	(=)	[=]		(Ben)
	510	Gr.	(=)	[=]		(Ben,Pu)
	511	All.	(=)	[ ]		(Ben)
	513	Off.*	(=)	[=]		(Ben),Mc,(Pu)
	515	Com.	(=)	[ ]		( )

quickly thereafter, becoming a standard feature in liturgical sources after the twelfth century. As with many feasts of the later Middle Ages, the texts vary greatly from region to region: the mass of the Oxford manuscript is no exception, with the surviving gradual *O beate nicolae* (**304**) and offertory *O beate pastor* (**307**) paralleled only in the palimpsest mass-antiphonal recently reconstructed by Virginia Brown (Florence, Biblioteca Laurenziana, 29.8 = Na1, with Laurenziana, 33.31),[420] and the alleluia *Beate confessor* (**305**) attested elsewhere only in Ben38.

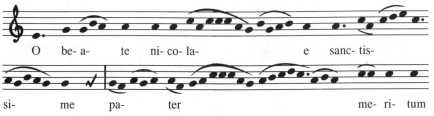

O be- a- te ni- co- la- e sanc- tis-
si- me pa- ter me- ri- tum

riana, pp. 147-308. For later masses of Nicholas, see Hänggi, *Rheinauer Liber Ordinarius*, pp. 37-38; in Haymo of Faversham, *Ordo missalis* (ed. Van Dijk, *Sources*, 2: 271), only prayers are cited for the mass of Nicholas: the chant must be taken from the Common. Bruylants, *Oraisons*, 1: 68-69 (mass 156), lists different masses in the twelfth-century Lateran missal edited by Azevedo (above n. 95) and later Roman missals.

[420] Florence, Biblioteca Laurenziana, 29.8; siglum = Na1, palimpsest gradual with Laurenziana 33.31 (upper scripts are Boccaccio's autographs), s. xiii ex., Naples; bibl.: Loew, *Beneventan Script*, 2: 41-42. The palimpsest texts have been edited by Virginia Brown, "Boccaccio in Naples: The Beneventan Liturgical Palimpsests of the Laurentian Autographs (MSS 29.8 and 33.31)" (forthcoming).

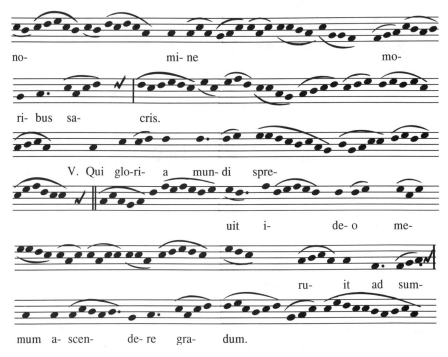

no- mi- ne mo-

ri- bus sa- cris.

V. Qui glo-ri- a mun-di spre-

uit i- de- o me-

ru- it ad sum-

mum a- scen- de- re gra- dum.

Figure 36. — **304** GRADVALE O beate nicolae, fol. 69r-v (see Plates 2, 3).

The text of the verse *Qui gloria mundi spreuit* of the gradual (**304**) is echoed in an antiphon of the office:

> *Gloriam mundi sprevit* cum suis oblectationibus et *ideo meruit* provehi *ad summum* sacerdotii *gradum.*[421]

The ultimate source for both antiphon and gradual probably lies in the account of the choice of Nicholas as bishop in the *Vita sancti Nicholai* by John the Deacon.[422] The melody is unrelated to any in the standard Gregorian repertory.[423]

---

[421] The italics are my own. The text is printed by Jones, *Saint Nicholas Liturgy*, p. 20; and found also in Hesbert, *Corpus antiphonalium officii*, 2: 12 (Zürich, Zentralbibliothek, Rh 30) and 2: 55 (Benevento, Biblioteca Capitolare 21; antiphonale monasticum, s. xii; bibl.: Loew, *Beneventan Script*, 2: 20).

[422] Jones, *Saint Nicholas Liturgy*, p. 42, identifies the *Vita* as the source for the bulk of the cursus of the Nicholas liturgy, although he cites in addition the use of other legends for various hymns and proses.

[423] The melodic incipit of the gradual (E 3758 5853 A) is without parallel in Bryden and Hughes, *Index*.

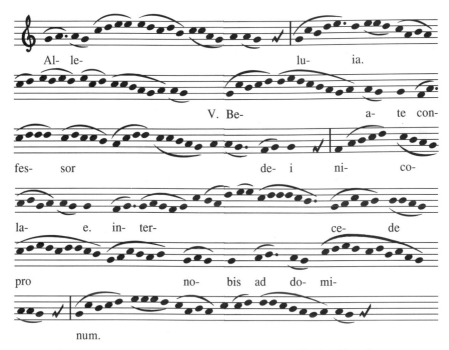

Figure 37. — **305** Alleluia. Beate confessor dei, fol. 69v (see Plate 3).

The alleluia *Beate confessor dei* (**305**) is found also in Ben38. Despite a minor variant in the incipit of the Beneventan manuscript ("Beate confessa dei" Ben38), the two texts and melodies are otherwise similar. The verse repeats the opening phrase of a responsory of the office but is for the most part more closely related to prayer texts in vocabulary and structure.[424] The ties between the responsory *Confessor Dei* and the Beneventan region are particularly marked: a legend added to John the Deacon's *Vita sancti Nicolai* relates the story of how the responsory was composed in Bari.[425] The melody of the alleluia is a regional composition without parallel elsewhere.[426]

The offertory *O beate pastor* (**307**) is found elsewhere only in the four-teenth-century Neapolitan gradual of the Laurentian autographs (Na1), indicating that the offertory is a late addition to the Romano-Beneventan

---

[424] Cf. Jones, *Saint Nicholas Liturgy*, p. 21: "*Responsoria II*: Confessor Dei Nicholaus nobilis pro genere." The responsory is cited in Hesbert, *Corpus antiphonalium officii*, 2: 12, 55.

[425] Brussels, Bibliothèque Royale, lat. 1960-1962, fols. 63v-66v; s. xiii, partial ed., *Catalogus codicum hagiographicorum Bibliothecae Regiae Bruxellensis*, 3 vols. (Brussels, 1886-1889), 1: 320-322; trans. Jones, *Saint Nicholas Liturgy*, pp. 57-62.

[426] Schlager, *Katalog*, no. G 403.

corpus. From its use of the otherwise uncommon phrase "miraculi corusci," the surviving fragment of the text can be related to the *Vita* by John the Deacon, in particular to the praise of Nicholas and his works read from the *Vita* during the office.[427] The musical setting is without parallel in the Roman tradition.[428]

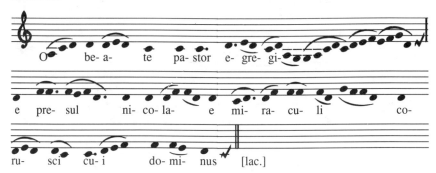

Figure 38. — **307** OFFERTORIVM O beate pastor, fol. 69v (see Plate 3).

The non-biblical texts of the musical items for the mass of Nicholas show the continued strength of the regional taste for texts and phrases drawn from outside the Bible, in contrast with the Roman predilection for scriptural texts.[429] Of course, due to the late date of the feast and the limited number of parallels in other Beneventan sources, it is very unlikely that the texts from the *Vita* used in the Missal were parts of the Old Beneventan corpus.

The development of the mass-sets for the feast of Benedict has already been discussed.[430] The diversity noted in the spread of several masses and varying texts is paralleled in the musical items of the feast: only the introit *Vir dei benedictus* (**366**) is found in the GR with the same melody. The texts of the tract *In columbe* (**370**) and communion *Hodie dilectus* (**374**) are attested in early printed missals from Venice (MRM 2: 189), but not in the GR or the early mass-antiphonals. The gradual *Repletus* (**369**) and the offertory *Intempesta* (**372**) are not found in any of the standard Roman books. Nonetheless, since the entire mass is paralleled in Beneventan sources from each of the major areas of the script, including DaB, Ben34, and McV, the musical items constitute a development of wide circulation in the region. The appearance, however, of the same items in southern French sources such as the eleventh-century Gradual of Saint-Yrieix (Paris, BN, lat. 903, = Syg)

---

[427] Jones, *Saint Nicholas Liturgy*, p. 28 (VI Lectio).
[428] Cf. Bryden and Hughes, *Index*: no entries for A 3575 3575.
[429] Huglo, "Ancien chant bénéventain," p. 281.
[430] See above p. 123.

is indication that the mass was not restricted to the Beneventan area. Since the connections between southern Italy and southern France have been well documented for musical variants and repertory, the coincidence is not surprising.[431]

Although the introit *Vir dei benedictus* (**366**) is found in the GR, the Roman psalm verse (*Secundum nomen tuum*) is replaced in some Beneventan sources by the verse *Beatus vir qui timet* (Ben34) and in the Oxford manuscript by the verse *Recessit igitur scienter*. As with the alleluia verse *Ingressa agnes* (**329**) and the gradual (**304**) and offertory (**307**) of Nicholas, the source for the verse *Recessit igitur* in the Dubrovnik missal was an antiphon of the office, in this case drawn from the life of Benedict in the *Dialogues* of Pope Gregory I.[432]

Re- ple- tus sanc- to spi- ri- tu be- a- tus be- ne- dic- tus in- ter mul- ta mi- ra- cu- la que fe- ce- rat su- sci- ta- uit pu- e- rum. V. Il- lu- si- o- nem re- gis co- gno-

[431] Hesbert, "Tradition bénéventaine," p. 190, fig. 26 (comparison of variants). The Romano-Beneventan mass *Vir Dei Benedictus* is discussed by Hourlier and Huglo, "Notice descriptive," p. 165, citing Rome, Biblioteca Angelica 123, Vl4770, and other MSS; see also Boe, "Gloriosus," p. 71 n. 4.

[432] Gregory I, *Dialogues*, lib. 2, prol. 1 (ed. Adalbert de Vogüé, *Grégoire le Grand. Dialogues*, trans. Paul Antin, 3 vols, Sources chrétiennes 251, 260, 265 [Paris, 1978-1980], 2: 126 ll. 14-15): "Recessit igitur scienter nescius et sapienter indoctus." The antiphon is listed by Hesbert, *Corpus antiphonalium officii*, 2: 210, 243, 245.

Figure 39. — **369** GRADVALE Repletus sancto spiritu, fol. 77r (see Plate 4).

The text of the gradual *Repletus sancto spiritu* (**369**), based on a miracle of Benedict related in the *Dialogues*,[433] is found outside the Beneventan region only in southern French sources such as Syg; moreover, despite distinctive variants in the musical settings of each region, the melodies are related.[434] Among Beneventan sources, the musical settings of the Oxford manuscript and Ben34 are similar except for the transposition up a fifth in Ben 34.

---

[433] Gregory I, *Dialogues*, lib. 2, c. 32 *De mortuo suscitato* (ed. de Vogüé, 2: 226-231).
[434] Bryden and Hughes, *Index*, citing the incipits for Syg (D 3537 5753 F) and Ben34 (a 3530 3785 c).

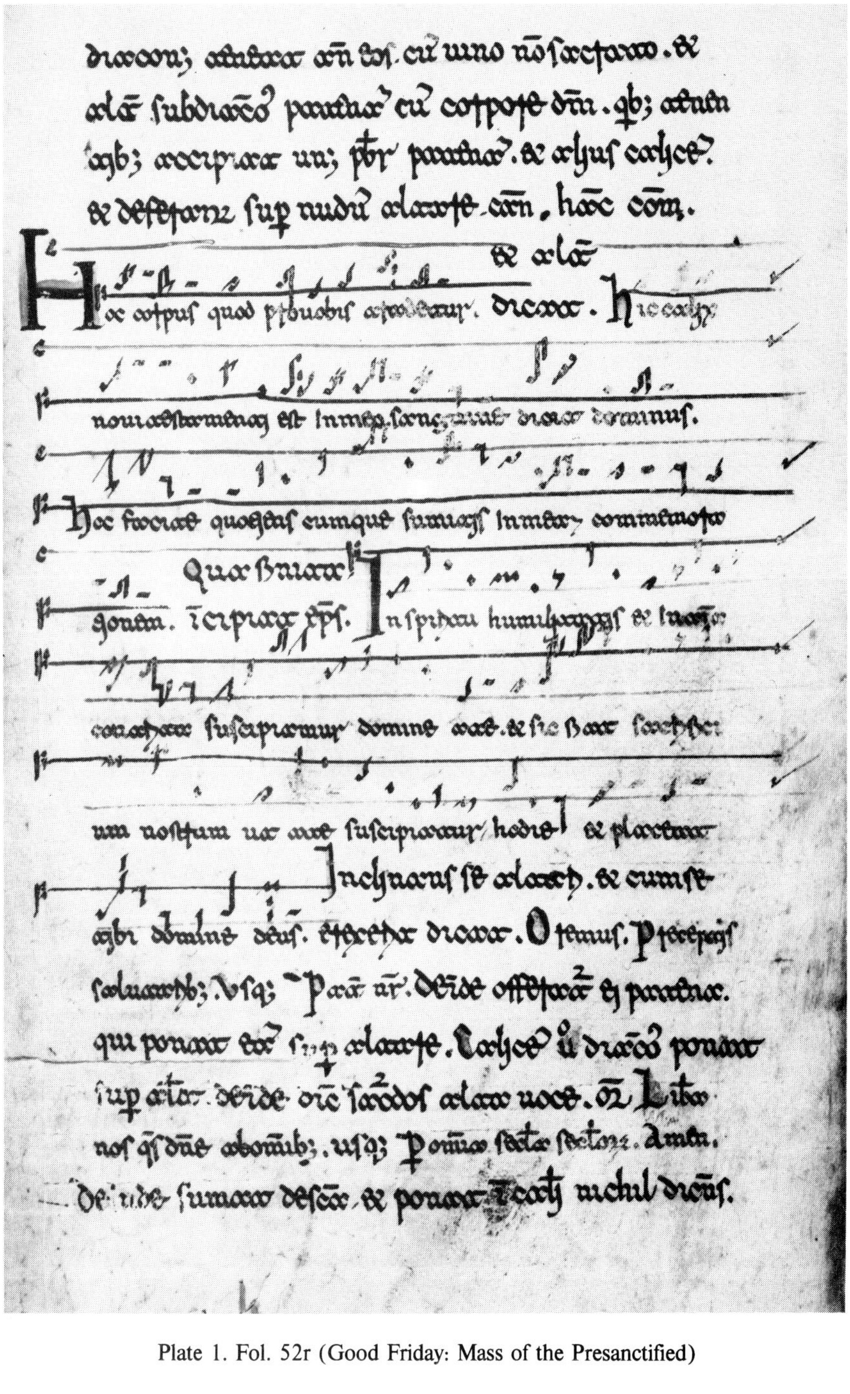

Plate 1. Fol. 52r (Good Friday: Mass of the Presanctified)

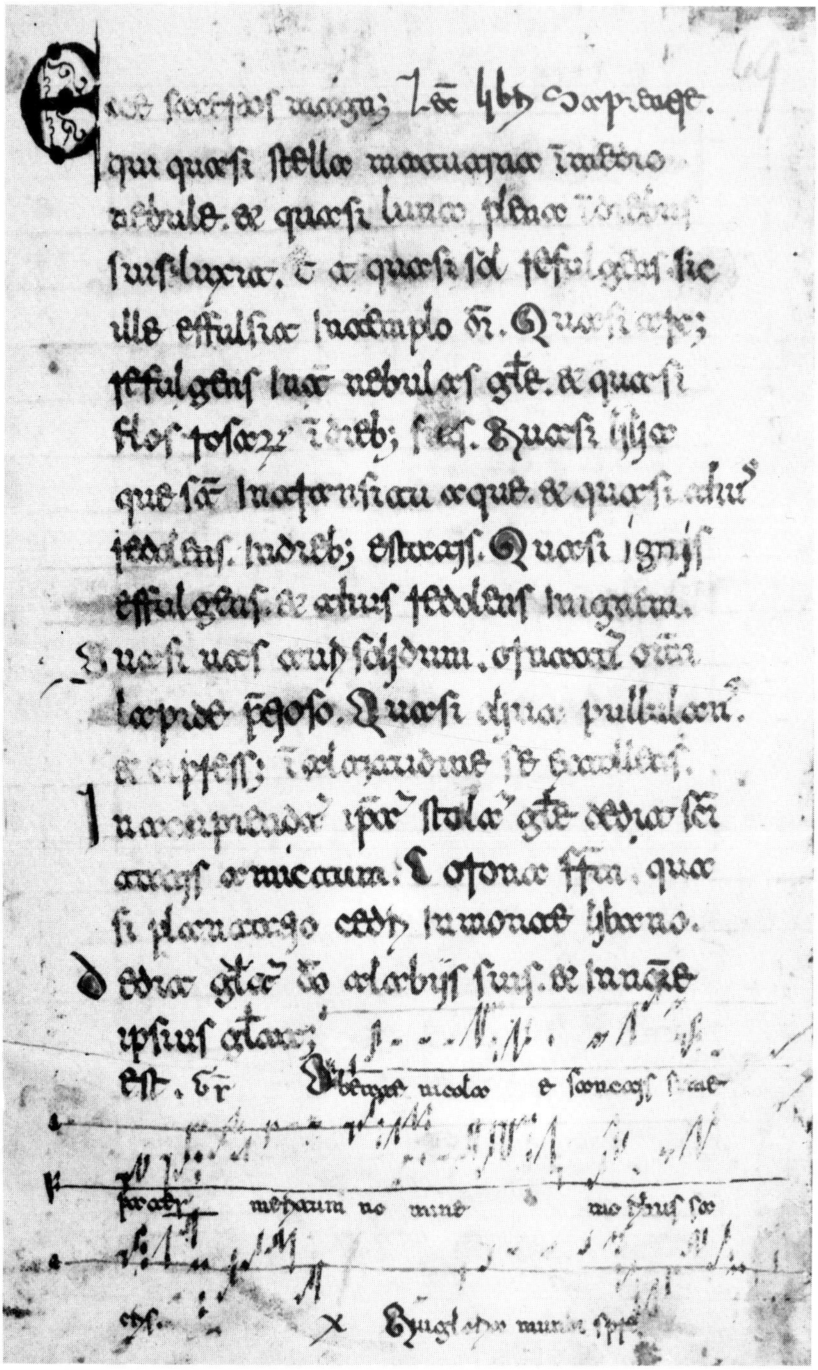

Plate 2. Fol. 69r (Mass of Nicholas)

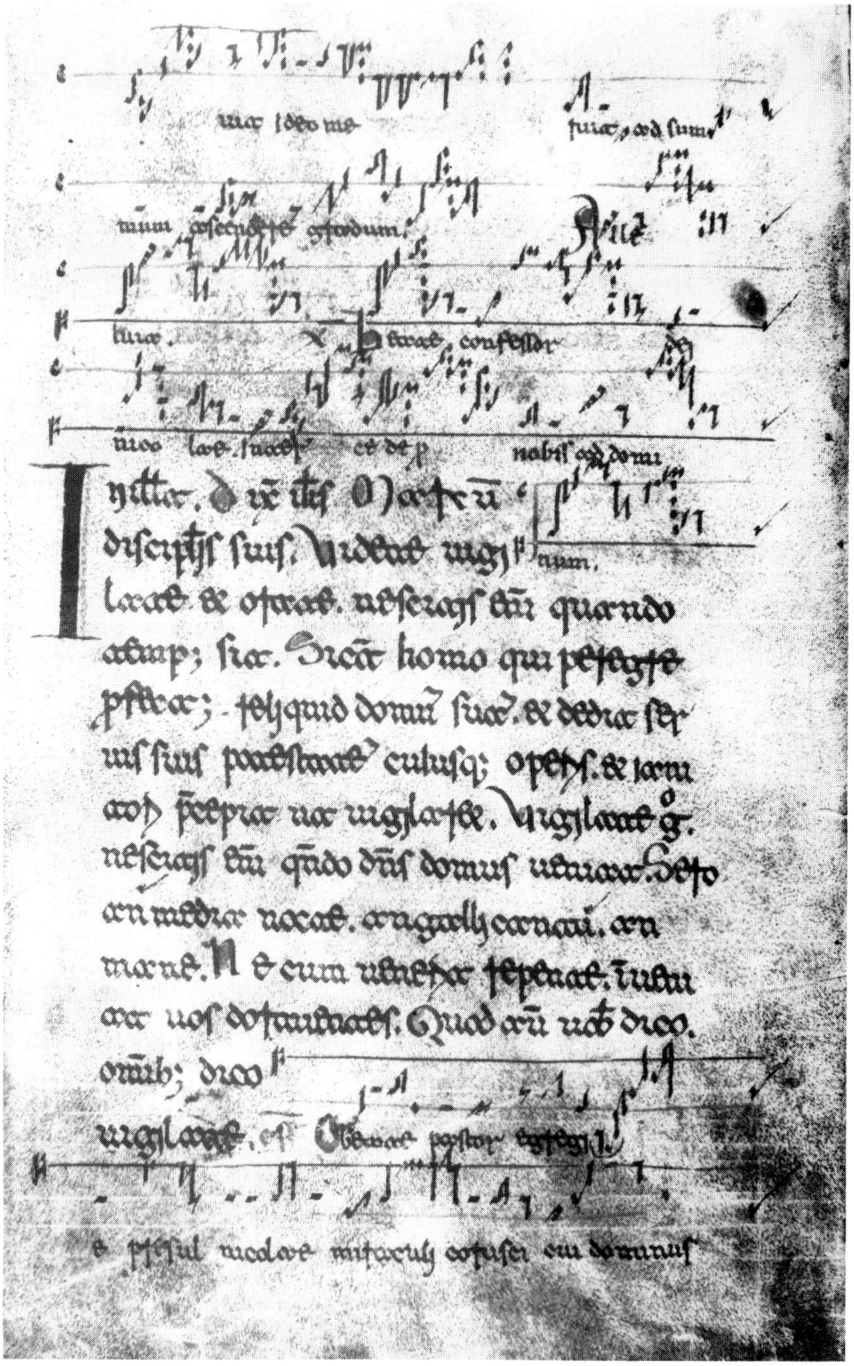

Plate 3. Fol. 69v (Mass of Nicholas, cont'd)

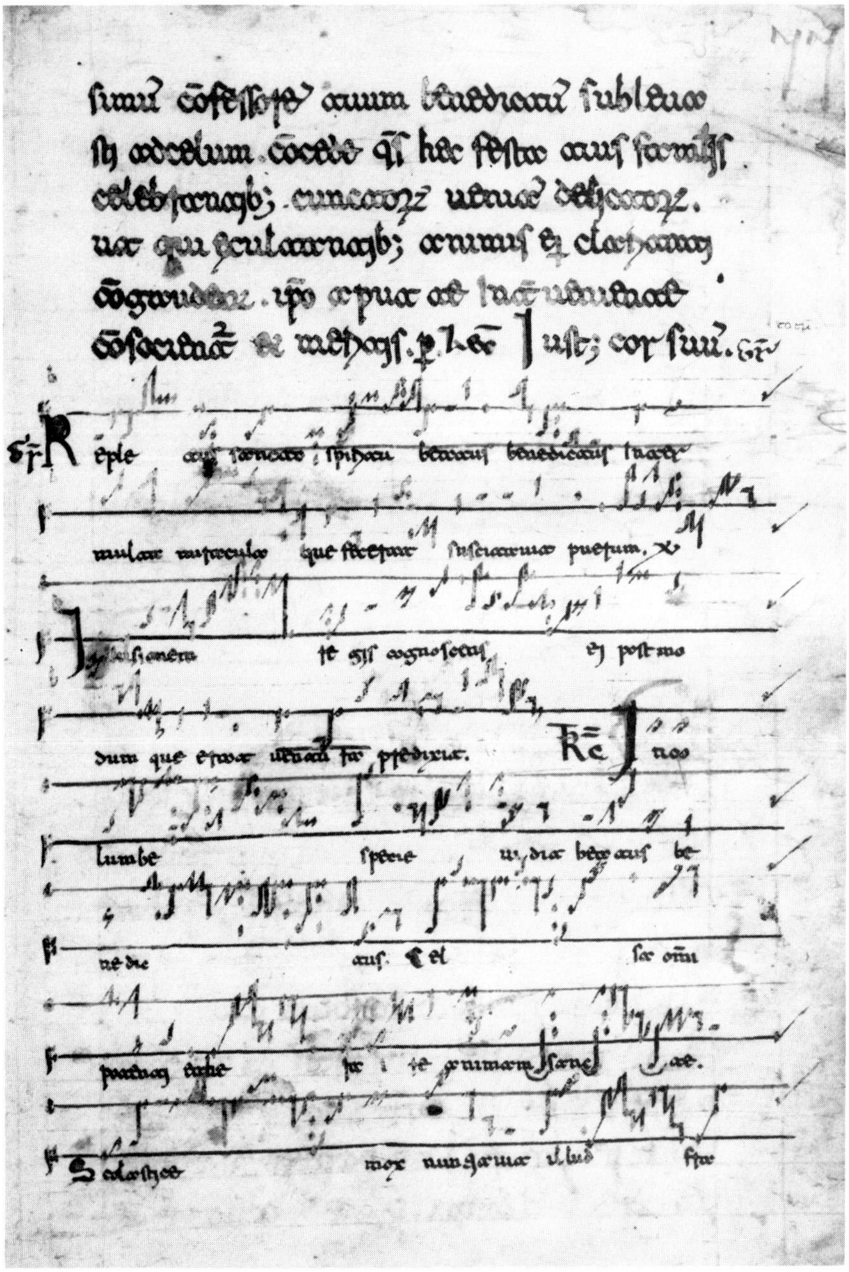

Plate 4. Fol. 77r (Mass of Benedict)

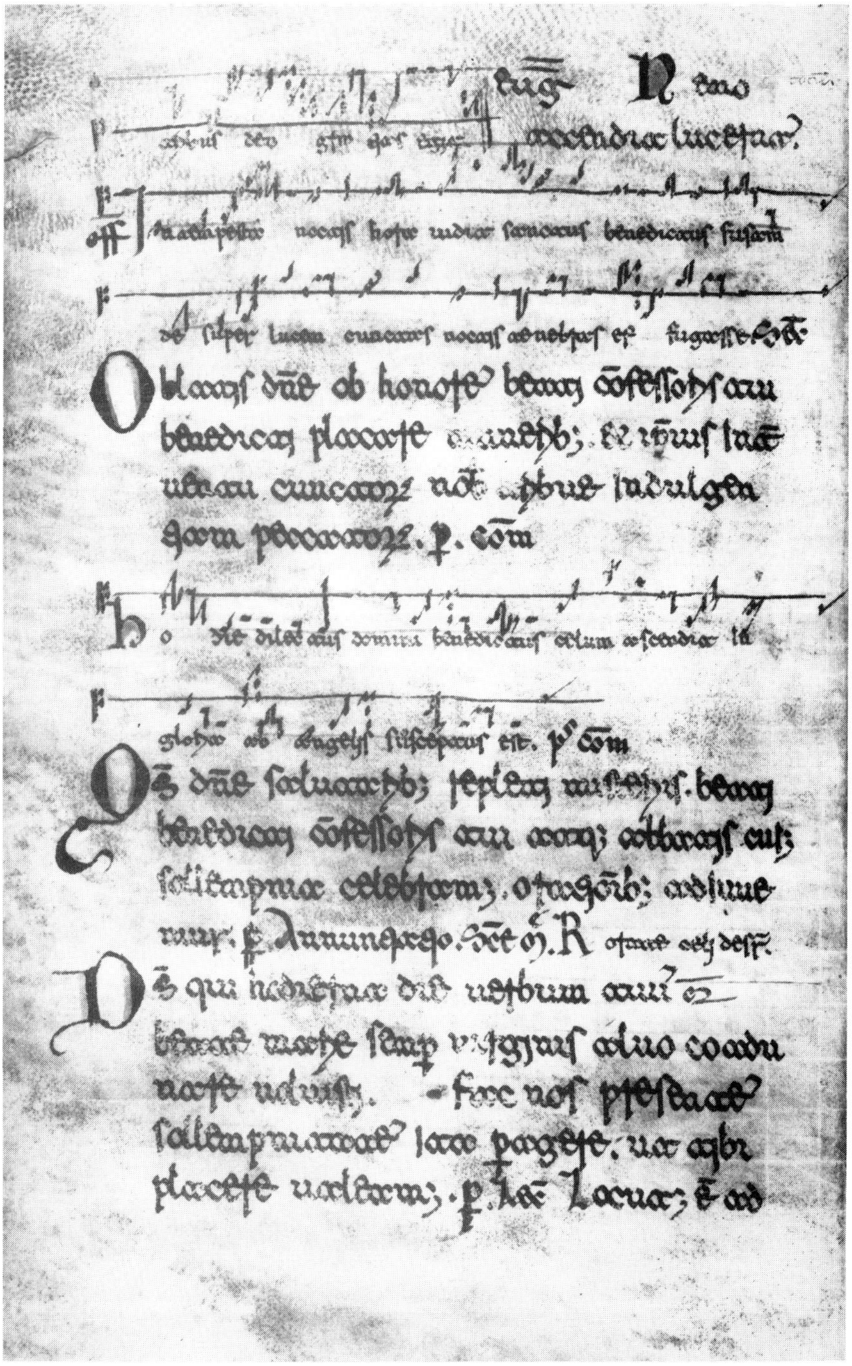

Plate 5. Fol. 77v (Mass of Benedict, cont'd; and the Mass of the Annunciation)

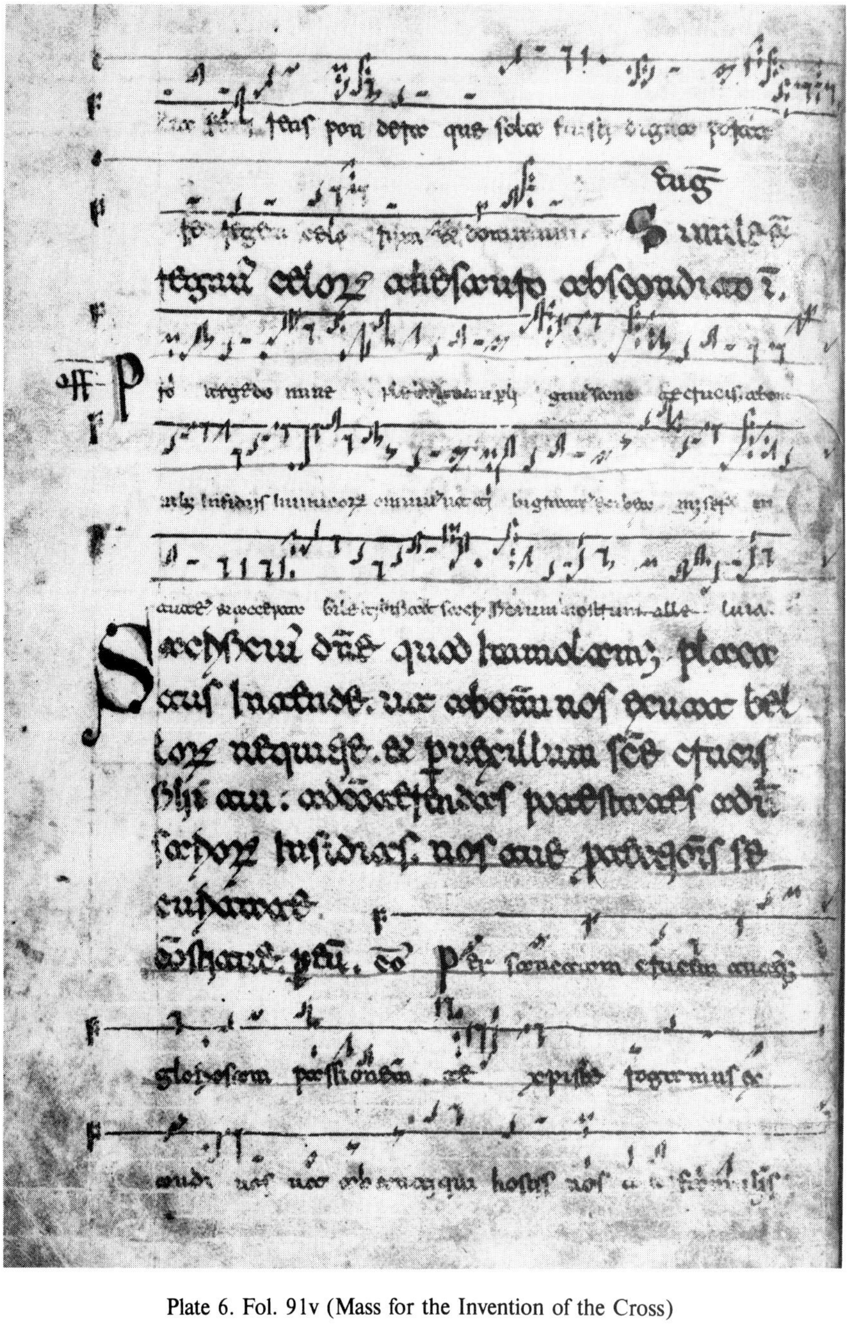

Plate 6. Fol. 91v (Mass for the Invention of the Cross)

te.   Scho-   la-   sti-
ce   mox   nun-   ti-   a-   uit
il-   lud   fra-   tri-   bus
de-   o   gra-   ti-   as   e-
git.

Figure 40. – **370** TRACTVS In columbe, fol. 77r-v (see Plates 4, 5).

The text of the tract *In columbe* (**370**), adapted freely from the *Dialogues* of Gregory I,[435] is found in Beneventan sources, southern French manuscripts, and the early printed missals of Venice (MRM 2: 189). The melody of the Beneventan tract is an adaptation of the early tract *Commovisti* of the eighth mode.[436]

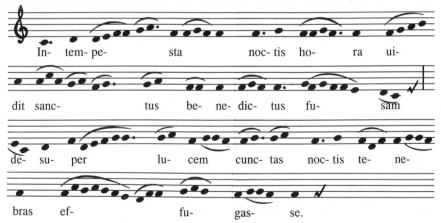

In-   tem- pe-   sta   noc- tis ho-   ra   uidit sanc-   tus   be- ne- dic- tus   fu-   sam
de- su-   per   lu-   cem   cunc- tas noc- tis te- ne-
bras   ef-   fu-   gas- se.

Figure 41. – **372** OFFERTORIVM Intempesta noctis hora, fol. 77v (see Plate 5).

[435] Cf. Gregory I, *Dialogues*, lib. 2, c. 34 (ed. de Vogüé, 2: 234 ll. 4-8): "vidit eiusdem sororis suae animam, de eius corpore egressam, *in columbae specie* caeli secreta penetrare. Qui tantae eius gloriae congaudens, omnipotenti Deo in hymnis et laudibus gratias reddidit, eiusque obitum *fratribus denuntiavit.*"

[436] The same melody is adapted to the tracts *Exurge* and *Magnificat* (Bryden and Hughes, *Index*, entry E 3585 58,10,8 G); Syg 56 has a different incipit (G 2420 2057 G).

The text of the offertory *Intempesta* (**372**), found in Beneventan and southern French sources, is adopted from a responsory of the office based on the *Dialogues* of Gregory I.[437] Although Ben34 is arranged a fifth higher than the setting of the Oxford manuscript, their melodies represent a regional composition distinct even from its southern French counterpart.[438]

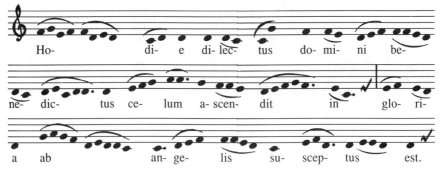

Figure 42. — **374** COMMVNIO Hodie dilectus, fol. 77v (see Plate 5).

The communion *Hodie dilectus* (**374**) is another borrowing from the office, although in this case without directly quoting the *Dialogues*.[439] The melodies of the southern French and Beneventan settings of the communion are related; each, however, has distinctive regional variants apparent in the similarity of the melodies of the Dubrovnik missal and Ben34 compared to Syg.[440]

While the prayers of the Missal for the feast of Mary Magdalen belong to a clearly defined Italian tradition (**508**, **514**, **516**),[441] most of the chants are more widely attested. The gradual *Propter ueritatem* (**510**) from the Assumption and Birth of Mary in the early mass-antiphonals (AMS 140, 144*bis*) is standard for the feast of the Magdalen in later medieval sources;[442] the introit *Cognovi* (**507**) and the offertory *Diffusa* (**513**) are frequently attested alternatives drawn from the Common to replace the standard introit *Gaudeamus* and offertory *Angelus*.[443] The alleluia *Dilexisti* (**511**) and communion *Optimam partem* (**515**) are more unusual regional compositions.

[437] Gregory I, *Dialogues*, lib. 2, c. 35 (ed. de Vogüé, 2: 236 ll. 19-20): "subito intempesta noctis hora respiciens, vidit fusam lucem desuper cunctas noctis tenebras exfugasse." For the responsory of the office, see Hesbert, *Corpus antiphonalium officii*, 2: 212-213, 245.

[438] Cf. Bryden and Hughes, *Index*, entry G 2457 9575 c (Ben34 55r); entry D 3253 5235 E (Syg 57).

[439] Hesbert, *Corpus antiphonalium officii*, 2: 212-213, 245.

[440] Bryden and Hughes, *Index*, entry F 2-10-3 -1-3-5-3 (Ben34 55r); entry c -10-3-1 -3-5-3-1 E (Syg 57).

[441] See above pp. 126-127.

[442] Saxer, *Culte*, p. 291.

[443] Saxer, *Culte*, p. 292.

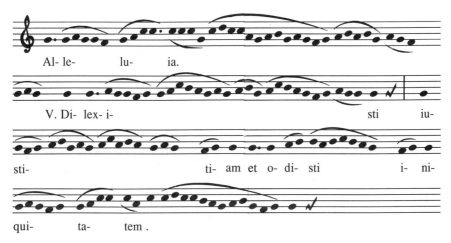

Figure 43. — **511** Alleluia. Dilexisti iustitiam, fol. 90r.

The text of the alleluia verse *Dilexisti* (**511**), unattested in the early mass-antiphonals, is drawn from the later Roman Common. Its musical setting, however, adapts the melody that usually accompanies the verse *Dilexi quoniam*: the setting of *Dilexisti* to this melody is regional and found elsewhere only in Benevento.[444]

Figure 44. — **515** COMMVNIO Optimam partem, fol. 96r.

The communion *Optimam partem* (**515**) is an idiosyncratic use found at this point in none of the sources considered for this edition. The same verse (Lc 10: 42) is commonly noted, however, for the feast of the Assumption, although without parallel in the early mass-antiphonals. The music of the communion in the Dubrovnik missal appears to be a unique setting of

[444] Ben35 179r, Ben38 165v (Schlager, *Katalog*, no. G 307).

Optimam partem to the melody of the communion *Posuisti domine*, which was widely used in the early mass-antiphonals for feasts of the Sanctoral.[445]

3. Common and Votives

The Common and votives of the Dubrovnik missal are more closely tied to the Roman tradition of the later Middle Ages than either the Temporal or Sanctoral, especially for the sung parts of the mass and the lections. The late date of the manuscript becomes most apparent in areas where the differences between the early and late Roman sources are greatest. Thus, because the Temporal was relatively fixed from an early date, there are only minor differences between the masses of the Hadrianum, for instance, and the Franciscan missal of the thirteenth century; for the Sanctoral, although the growth of the calendar was more marked, a central core of feasts and observances is shared in sources early and late. But the Common and votives were less stable than the Temporal or Sanctoral, with considerable differences among the early sources both in the list of feasts and in the individual choice of prayers, musical pieces, and lections for each feast. Instead of developing or expanding on a regional solution to compensate for the lack of elaborate Commons in the early sources of the Romano-Beneventan liturgy, the Oxford manuscript displays many points of relation to the later medieval Roman Common, either through direct influence or perhaps through a parallel history of adopting appropriate elements from the primitive core of the early Roman Sanctoral.

Musical Items

The similarities between the later GR and the Dubrovnik missal compared to the early sources are particularly striking for the sung parts of the mass and a notable contrast to the numerous regional pieces and arrangements of the Temporal and Sanctoral. Whereas the feasts of the Temporal not provided for in the early Roman exemplar of the Romano-Beneventan mass-antiphonal were given regional masses early on, probably as soon as the individual feasts became current in the region, the absence of a developed Common in the early Roman mass-antiphonals had less effect on the regional liturgy.[446]

---

[445] I.e., AMS 20, 114, 118b, 137, 144, 147, 148b, 154, 163, 167; also in the Common of the GR.

[446] Among the early mass-antiphonals, only the Antiphonals of Corbie and Senlis (above n. 159) have any masses for the Common, and they are restricted to four sets for the vigil and feast of a bishop (AMS 170-171 *quat*); the early mass-antiphonals also have a series of unspecified alleluias, probably functioning as a Common (AMS 199).

Despite the lack of early models, which has been the evident cause of great diversity in other areas such as the alleluias, the similarities between the Dubrovnik missal and the GR may be accounted for in two ways: either as a direct influence of later Roman sources (quite possible in the thirteenth century when the Oxford manuscript was written) or as the chance consequence of a similar process of compilation. In other words, just as the Common was formed in the GR from the primitive Sanctoral, so also the Common of the Dubrovnik missal is drawn from the primitive Sanctoral of the early Roman sources.

Regardless of the exact process, the result is that among the forty-eight musical items of the Common and votives of the Missal, all except six are found in the later Roman Common.[447] Of the six distinctive choices, two are found in the Roman Sanctoral (**627, 634**);[448] and the remaining four are either regional or medieval developments of wider circulation which were not adopted in the GR.

Figure 45. – **619** COMMVNIO Vos qui secuti, fol. 110r.

The communion *Vos qui secuti* (**619**) for the Common of Apostles is a text found in the same mass in the GR and attested for other feasts in the early

---

[447] The forty-two Roman pieces include the gradual *Posuisti* (**626**), absent from some later medieval missals such as the Franciscan missal and MRM, but appearing in the early mass-antiphonals on a different feast and in the GR with the same melody.

[448] The gradual *Exaltent* (**627**) for the Common of a Martyr is given in incipit; the same text appears in extenso for the Chair of Peter (**351**) with the Roman melody in a regional form (above p. 159, fig. 34).

mass-antiphonals (AMS 160). The melody, however, is regional without close parallel in the Roman corpus.[449]

Figure 46. — **649** Alleluia. Elegit te dominus, fols. 112v-113r.

Although the alleluia with the verse *Elegit te dominus* (**649**) for the Common of a Confessor-bishop is without parallel in the later medieval GR, the text appears in the early mass-antiphonals (AMS 132) and was found in many regions. In the Beneventan region at least two melodies were used: the unique setting of Ben39 and the melody of the Dubrovnik missal, adapted from the setting of the verse *Redemptionem*.[450] The association of verse and melody is not restricted, however, to the Missal and other regional books: instances of the combination are found from France and Germany.[451]

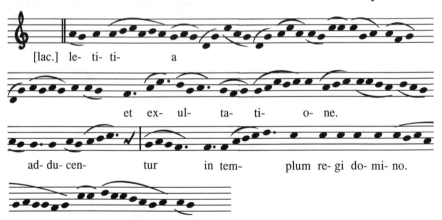

Figure 47. — **661** TRACTVS <Adducentur>, fol. 115r.

---

[449] Bryden and Hughes, *Index*, entry D 2305 3230 E, mode 4 (Ben34 28v).

[450] Schlager, *Katalog*, nos. D 134 and G 253 (Ben39) with variant melodies; D 28 (*Redemptionem*) with the same melody.

[451] Schlager, *Katalog*, no. D 28.

The incipit of the tract (**661**) for the Common of a Virgin-martyr is lost. While the tract *Audi filia* of the Roman Common concludes with the same verse (Ps 44: 11-16), the Romano-Beneventan tract *Adducentur* (Ben34) is an abbreviated text (Ps 44: 15-16) with a different musical setting. Since the melody of the explicit of the tract in the Oxford manuscript follows the Romano-Beneventan model, the text was most likely similar also, beginning with "Adducentur" instead of the Roman "Audi filia."

Figure 48. − **686** GRADVALE Benedictus es domine, fol. 118r-v.

The gradual *Benedictus es domine* with the verse *Benedicite* (**686**) for the votive mass in honour of the Trinity is related to the standard Roman gradual *Benedictus es Domine* for the feast of the Trinity but with a different verse.[452] Neither the verse *Benedicite* nor its musical setting have exact parallels in the GR, although elements of the melody are related to other Roman graduals of the fifth mode, including the gradual *Benedictus es Domine* with the verse

---

[452] *Benedictus* is given by Bryden and Hughes, *Index*, entry D 3757 5378 F; for the verse *Benedicite*, see entry F 4764 6724.

Benedictus.[453] Nonetheless, the verse of the Dubrovnik missal cannot be considered regional because the same combination of verses and melodies is attested in the Sarum Gradual (Gs) and the Gradual of Saint-Yrieix (Syg) in addition to several Beneventan sources: evidently the medieval tradition of the gradual *Benedictus es Domine* was exceptionally fluid.[454]

Lections

The lections of the Common in the Dubrovnik missal are for the most part found also in the later medieval Roman Common. The few exceptions absent from the Roman Common are the gospel *Facta est contentio* (**602** Lc 22: 24-30) for the vigil of an apostle, paralleled in the Roman Sanctoral; the gospel *Conuocatis* (**611** Mt 10: 1-18) for the vigil of apostles, found on another feast among Venetian printed missals (MRM 2: 356); and the gospel *Si quis uult* (**631** Lc 9: 23-27) for the Common of a Martyr, attested in the Comes of Muhrbach. Indeed, although only the Comes of Muhrbach and the epistle-list of Würzburg among the early lectionaries have readings for a series of Common masses, and the selection of masses is more limited than in the Oxford manuscript,[455] ten of the sixteen lections for the Common and votives in the Dubrovnik missal are found in the Commons of the early lectionaries.

Prayers

The Common of the Dubrovnik missal finds no precedent in the earliest sacramentaries: the Hadrianum makes no provision for a Common; and, although the Paduense and the Gelasians of the Eighth Century have several masses, the texts and their order differ from the list of the Oxford manuscript.[456] It is only with the Supplement to the Hadrianum, which in its

---

[453] Cf. *Constitues eos* in the GR for a similar melodic incipit to both gradual and verse.

[454] Eugène Cardine, *Graduel neumé* (Solesmes, n.d.), p. 288: "texte très variable."

[455] E.g., Mu has lections for the following masses: "In vig. unius sacerd." (158), "It. in nat. ubi supra" (159), "In vig. unius conf. siue mart." (160), "It. natal. ubi supra" (161), "natl. plurimorum sanctorum" (162), "In natl. plurimorum mart." (163), "In natl. virginum" (164), "Explicit de sanctorum."

[456] Cf. the Gellone sacramentary (Ge 1762-1842), followed by a series of votives, masses for the dead, benedictions, etc.: "Denunc. nal. unius martyrum" (1762-1763), "Denuntiatio cu. reliquie ponende s. mart." (1764), "In uigl. unius sci. siue cofr. siue mar." (1765-1769), "In nal. unius martyru." (1770-1779), "In nal. unius confessoris" (1780-1788), "In nal. plurimoru. scorum." (1789-1793), "In nal. plurimor. scorum." (1794-1796), "It. alia mis. plurim. scor." (1797-1800), "Item alia mis. in nali. plr." (1801-1807), "In nal. plurimorum martyrum" (1808-1812), "Item alia mis. in nal. plurimr. mar." (1813-1816), "In nal. plurimoru. martyrum" (1817-1820), "Item in nal. plurimoru. martyr." (1821-1828), "Mis. in

simple outlines scarcely hints at the later medieval elaboration of the
Common, that the central core of prayers and masses of the Roman
Common first became defined.[457] But from these origins the Common took
on many regional forms and adopted even in the Roman missal a much
augmented list of prayers and votive masses. Thus, despite several shared
feasts, the correspondences between the Common prayers of the Dubrovnik
missal and the Supplement to the Hadrianum are surprisingly few (see Table
21). The Common of the Oxford manuscript is present in the Supplement
only in a very embryonic state: differences in the list of feasts can be seen
most clearly in the greater specificity of the Missal, with its distinctions
between the vigils and feasts of apostles, and the addition of Common masses
for a confessor-bishop and a virgin-not-a-martyr.

The second stage in the development of the later Roman Common is
noteworthy for an exuberant diversity of masses and feasts in the layer of
sacramentaries developing out of the conflation of the Gregorian and
Gelasian sacramentaries during and after the ninth century. As Deshusses has
remarked in his edition of the Gregorian sacramentary, the process was
personal: "chaque rédacteur a puisé comme il l'a voulu aux sources dont il
disposait."[458] Among the proliferation of mixed sacramentaries, the Fulda
sacramentary of the tenth century, for instance, has an abundance of votives
but almost no provision for Common masses.[459] In the case of the Dubrovnik
missal, however, the instances of correspondences in the choice of feasts are
complete, with no mass of the Dubrovnik Common unrepresented in
Romano-Frankish sources of the Gregorian tradition (see Table 21, references to Tc). Many counterparts among individual prayers are also evident,
especially in the shared prayers of the vigil of several apostles (**608-615**), the
confessor-bishop (**643**, **658**), the virgin-martyr (**668**) and the dedication
(**681**), and in the use of the *missa Alcuini* for the vigil of an apostle
(**599-606**). There are also numerous Common prayers found on different

---

uigl. uirginum" (1829-1832), "In natale uirginu. siue martyra" (1833-1838), "Mis. in basilicis
mar." (1839-1842).

The Common of the Sacramentary of St.-Gallen is related but considerably shorter (Sg
1460-1513).

The Common of the Paduense is also shorter but contains a different selection of prayers
(Pa 818-848): "In uigilia unius sancti" (818-821), "In natale unius sancti" (822-828; 825 =
Ge 1773; 827 = Ge 1784), "In uigilia plurimorum sanctorum" (829-831), "In natale
plurimorum sanctorum" (832-836; 834 = Ge 1822), "In uigilia uirginum" (837-839; 837 =
Ge 1829; 838 = Ge 1830), "In natale unde supra" (840-843; = Ge 1834-1837), "In basilicis
martyrum" (844-848; 844 = Ge 1839; 848 = Ge 1842).

[457] Bruylants, *Oraisons*, 1: 169.

[458] Deshusses, *Sacramentaire grégorien*, 2: 26.

[459] F 1779-2905 are votives and special masses; F 2906-2909 are common.

TABLE 21				
Prayers of the Common				
Feast	GREG		RL: MRM	Misc	BEN
	Sp	Tc			
VIGIL OF AN APOSTLE					
599 Concede	[ ]	Missa Alcuini	( )	[ES: F]	Ben,Da,Mc,Ott,Ve
604 Accepta	[ ]	Missa Alcuini	( )	[ES: F]	Ben,Da,Mc,Ott,Ve
606 Presta	[ ]	Missa Alcuini	( )	[ES: F]	Ben,Da,Mc,Ott,Ve
VIGIL OF SEVERAL APOSTLES					
608 Concede	[ ]	=	=	SAC: Va (GEL8: Ge)	(Ben),Da,Ott,Ve
613 Muneribus	[ ]	=	=	SAC: Va (GREG: Pa) (GEL8: Ge)	(Ben,Mc),Ott,Ve
615 Quesumus	[ ]	(birth)	(birth)	(SAC: Va) [GREG: Ha] (GEL8: Ge)	(Ben,Da),Mc,(Ott,Pu),Ve
BIRTH OF AN APOSTLE					
616 Da nobis	( )	( )	(=)	(SAC: Le,Va) (GEL8: Ge)	Mc,Ott,Pu
[lac.]					
BIRTH OF SEVERAL APOSTLES					
618 Munera	=	=	=	[GREG: Ha] (GEL8: Ge)	(Ben),Mc,Pu,(Ve)
620 Sumpto	( )	(vigil)	(vigil)	(SAC: Le,Va) (GEL8: Ge)	(Ott),Pu,(Ve)
BIRTH OF A MARTYR					
622 Deus qui hunc	( )	( )	( )		( )
623 Deus qui nos	( )	( )	=	[GREG: Pa] (GEL8: Ge)	Ben,Mc,Ott
635 Grata tibi	( )	( )	( )		( )
636 Vt nostre	( )	( )	( )		( )
639 Tua sancta	( )	( )	( )		( )
640 Presta	( )	(vigil)	( )	[SAC: Va] [GREG: Pa] (GEL8: Ge)	( )
BIRTH OF SEVERAL MARTYRS					
[lac.]					

Feast	GREG		RL: MRM	Misc	BEN
	Sp	Tc			
CONFESSOR AND BISHOP					
643 Da quesumus	[ ]	=	=	[SAC: Le,Va] [GREG: Ha] [GEL8: Ge]	Da,Mc,Ott,Pu,Ve
644 Deus qui	[ ]	( )	( )		( )
654 Hostias	[=]	( )	(=)	[SAC: Va] [GREG: Pa] [GEL8: Ge] [AM: Sb]	Mc,Ott
655 Sicut	[ ]	( )	( )		(Ben),Mc,Pu
658 Presta	[=]	=	=	GREG: Z6 [Ha,Pa] [GEL8: Ge]	(Ben),Mc,Ott,Pu
659 Purificent	[ ]	(=)	(=)	[SAC: Va] [GREG: Ha] [GEL8: Ge]	(Mc,Ott)
CONFESSOR-NOT-A-PRIEST [lac.]					
VIRGIN-MARTYR					
666 Sacris	( )	(=)	(=)	(GREG: Pa) (GEL8: Ge)	Mc,Ott
668 Adiuuent	( )	=	( )	GREG: Pa GEL8: Ge	Da,Mc,Ott,(Pu),Ve
VIRGIN-NOT-A-MARTYR					
670 Deus qui nos	[ ]	(=)	( )	[GREG: Pa] [GEL8: Ge]	Mc,Ott,(Pu),Ve
674 Hec hostia	[ ]	( )	(=)	[GREG: Ha,Pa] [GEL8: Ge] [AM: Sb]	(Ben),Mc,Ott,Ve
676 Sanctificet	[ ]	(=)	(=)	[SAC: Le] [GREG: Ha,Pa] [GEL8: Ge]	Da,Mc,Ott

TABLE 21 (cont'd)
Prayers of the Common

TABLE 21 (cont'd) Prayers of the Common					
Feast	GREG		RL: MRM	Misc	BEN
	Sp	Tc			
SEVERAL VIRGINS 677 Sanctarum	[ ]	( )	( )	[SAC: Le,Va] (GREG: Pa) GEL8: Ge	Da,Mc,Ott
678 Intende	[ ]	( )	=	[SAC: Le,Va] (GEL8: Ge] [AM: Sb]	Mc,Ott
679 Supplices	[ ]	( )	(=)	GREG: [Ha],(Pa) (GEL8: Ge)	Mc,Ott
DEDICATION OF A CHURCH 681 Deus qui	( )	=	=	GREG: Ha	Da,Mc,Pu
682 Deus qui nobis [lac.]	=	=	=	GEL8: Ge	Ben,Da,Mc,Ott,Pu,Ve

feasts in the later Gregorian sacramentaries and the Missal but omitted in the Supplement.[460]

The later medieval tradition of the Roman Common, represented by the Franciscan missal and MRM, provides few new developments with influences on the Missal beyond those advanced among the Romano-Frankish sacramentaries of the Gregorian tradition. Indeed, the later sources drop the *missa Alcuini* for the vigil of an apostle (**599-606**) and lack other prayers found in the Gregorian Commons and the Oxford manuscript.[461] On the other hand, several prayers of the Missal with counterparts in the later Common are absent from the Romano-Frankish masses, although in each case an equivalent is found in the Temporal or Sanctoral of the Gregorian tradition and not in the Common itself (**654, 674, 679**).

Despite their Romano-Frankish heritage, the prayers of the Dubrovnik missal are not without distinctive elements. In particular, the collect *Da nobis* (**616**) for the Common of an Apostle appears to be a regional prayer used

---

[460] I.e., **615, 620, 640, 659, 666, 670,** and **676.**
[461] I.e., **640, 668, 670, 676,** and **677.**

TABLE 22 Prayers of the Votives					
Feast	GREG		RL: MRM	Misc	BEN
	Sp	Tc			
TRINITY					
684 Omnipotens	[ ]	Missa Alcuini	=	ES: F	Ben,Da,Mc,Ott,Pu,Ve
690 Sanctifica	[ ]	Missa Alcuini	=	ES: F	Ben,Da,Mc,Ott,Pu,Ve
692 Proficiat	[ ]	Missa Alcuini	=	ES: F	Ben,Da,Mc,Ott,Pu,Ve
HOLY CROSS					
694 Deus qui	[ ]	Missa Alcuini	=	ES: F	[Ben],Mc,Ott,Pu,Ve
[lac.]					
HOLY SPIRIT					
698 Munera	[ ]	( )	=	[GREG: Ha] [GEL8: Ge]	[Ben],Da,[Pu]
700 Sancti	[ ]	=	=	[VAC: Va] [GREG: Ha] [GEL8: Ge]	[Ben],Da,[Pu]
APOSTLES					
701 Exaudi	[ ]	(=)	( )	[GREG: Ha] [GEL8: Ge]	[Ben]
702 Munus	[ ]	(=)	(=)	[GREG: Ha] [ES: F]	[Ben]
703 Quos	[ ]	( )	(=)	[GREG: Ha] [GEL8: Ge]	[Ben],[Pu]
MARTYR					
704 Presta	[ ]	( )	[ ]		Mc,[Ott]
705 Suscipe	[ ]	( )	[=]	[SAC: Va] [GEL8: Ge]	[Ben],Mc,[Ott]
706 Beati	[ ]	( )	[ ]	[SAC: Va] [GREG: Ha] [GEL8: Ge]	Mc,[Ott]
SEVERAL MARTYRS					
707 Infirmitatem	[ ]	=	[ ]	[GREG: Ha] [GEL8: Ge]	( )
708 Purificent	[ ]	(=)	[ ]	[GREG: Ha] [GEL8: Ge]	[Ben],Mc,[Ott]
709 Vt tuis	[ ]	( )	[ ]		Mc,[Ott]

TABLE 22 (cont'd) Prayers of the Votives				
Feast	**GREG**		**RL: MRM**	**Misc**	**BEN**
	Sp	Tc			
CONFESSORS					
710 Exaudi	[ ]	[ ]	[ ]	[SAC: Le] [GREG: Ha] [GEL8: Ge]	( )
711 Hostias	[ ]	[ ]	[ ]	[SAC: Le] [GREG: Ha] [GEL8: Ge]	[Ben],[Pu]
712 Beati	[ ]	[=]	[ ]	[GREG: Pa] [GEL8: Ge]	Mc,[Ott]
VIRGINS					
713 Tribue	[ ]	[ ]	[ ]	[ ]	( )
714 Hec hostia	[ ]	[ ]	[=]		[Ben],Mc,[Ott,Ve]
715 Sanctificet	[ ]	[ ]	[=]	[SAC: Le] [GREG: Ha] [GEL8: Ge]	Mc,[Ott]
ALL SAINTS					
716 Concede	[ ]	( )	[ ]		Da,Mc,Ott
717 Munera	[ ]	=	[=]	[GREG: Ha] [GEL8: Ge]	[Ben],Da,Mc,Ott
718 Maiestati	[ ]	=	[ ]		Da,Mc,Ott
FOR THE SAINTS WHOSE RELICS ARE HELD					
719 Propitiare	[ ]	Missa Alcuini	=	[ ]	( )
720 Oblatis	[ ]	(=)	(=)	[GREG: Ha] [GEL8: Ge]	[Ben],[Pu],Ve
721 Diuina	[ ]	Missa Alcuini	=		[Pu]
GENERAL MASS					
722 Pietate	[ ]	=	=		Da,Mc,Ott
723 Deus qui	[ ]	=	=		Da,Mc,Ott
724 Sumpta	[ ]	=	=		Da,Mc,Ott
FOR A PRIEST					
725 Concede	[ ]	( )	[ ]	[ES: F] [LS: MWes]	
726 Suscipe [lac.]	[ ]	(=)	[ ]	[AM: STripl]	

here only in Beneventan sources. The Common of a Martyr (**622-640**) is also probably local: the collect *Deus qui hunc diem* (**622**) is a unique conflation of two prayers of the early Roman sacramentaries (Ha 594 + 701; Ge 1188 + 1469); the secrets *Grata tibi* (**635**) and *Vt nostre* (**636**) are unparalleled; and the postcommunion *Tua sancta* (**639**) is a variant of a Roman prayer. Only the second collect *Deus qui nos* (**623**) and the second postcommunion *Presta quesumus domine* (**640**) are close to Gregorian models. Other more general regional features are evident in the series of prayers given for the same feast in Beneventan sources but found elsewhere in other sources.[462]

The votives share an important characteristic with the Common: both are witness to the position of the Missal as a late representative of Gregorian traditions not in the direct line of the Roman missal (see Table 22). No early sacramentary has a list of votive masses similar to the selection in the Oxford manuscript, nor do the later medieval missals of the Roman tradition match the selection in every instance. Although the Hadrianum and its Supplement are ill-supplied with votive masses, some modified Gregorian sacramentaries contain comparable lists.[463] The parallels between the Dubrovnik missal and the later Gregorian sacramentaries, whether the prayers fall on the same mass or elsewhere, also outnumber the instances where the later Roman missals and the Missal agree against the modified Gregorian sources.[464]

Although the votive masses were composed and developed later than other divisions of the missal, the unique and regional prayers of the Dubrovnik votives are relatively few: the collect *Presta quesumus* (**704**) for the mass in honour of a martyr, the postcommunion *Vt tuis* (**709**) for several martyrs, and the collect *Concede quesumus* (**716**) for all saints are found only in Beneventan sources; the collect *Tribue nos* (**713**) for several virgins is perhaps unique, without parallel among the texts examined for this edition.

CONCLUSION

The liturgical history of the Beneventan region, and of Dalmatia in particular, is reflected in the mixture of sources for the prayers, lections, and chant of the masses found in the Dubrovnik missal. In seeking to demonstrate of the

---

[462] I.e., **615**, **616**, **620**, **654**, **655**, **666**, **670**, **674**, **676**, and **679**.

[463] E.g., Deshusses, *Sacramentaire grégorien*, 3: 25-26 (Mainz, Seminarbibliothek, 1; s. ix ex., St.-Alban de Mayence); 3: 43-45 (Leningrad, Publichnaia biblioteka, lat. Q.v.I.41; ca. 870, St.-Amand).

[464] I.e., prayers of the Dubrovnik missal are found in Tc, but not MRM, on two occasions (**707**, **718**), and the Missal and Tc share several texts on different feasts (**701**, **708**, **712**, **726**). By contrast, the Missal equals MRM, but not Tc, on only one occasion (**698**), and the Missal and MRM share texts on four (**703**, **705**, **714**, **715**).

extent of this correspondence between the regional liturgy and its local manifestation in the Missal, I have concentrated on the points either of variance with the received texts of the Roman tradition or of agreement with one or another of the roots of that Roman tradition. The results are summarised readily: while the Missal remains faithful to the earlier tradition of the Old Beneventan liturgy at certain key points, for the most part it follows the regional adaptations of the Roman liturgy and often bears the marks of the Romano-Frankish liturgy of the later Middle Ages. Evidence for the effects of later medieval liturgical developments, such as the spread of the papal liturgy with the rise of the Mendicant orders, is not lacking, but the extent of these influences cannot be confirmed without more precise knowl-edge about the sources of the new liturgies and the course of their diffusion.

The Old Beneventan and Romano-Beneventan features of the Missal have been known since Hesbert's analysis of the manuscript during the course of his studies of the regional liturgy; these practices include the Old Beneventan lections of Lent, the Romano-Beneventan chants for the second Sunday of Lent, and the distinctive *Exultet*.[465] The present examination of the manu-script and its contents has shown further that the Missal is a complex witness to a local branch of the Beneventan tradition. In particular, its parallels with the early printed missals of Venice confirm a meeting in Dalmatia of the Beneventan liturgy with the Venetian branch of the Roman liturgy, an association that has been suggested both by the dispersion of Beneventan items in northern Adriatic centres and by the recent discovery of late fragments of other texts comparable to the early printed missals.[466] Further particular influences are implicit in the comparisons with the Beneventan sources of Dalmatia, Apulia, Monte Cassino, and Benevento contained in the *apparatus parallelorum locorum*, although clarification of their relationships must await continued study of the local practices of the regional liturgy.

The Dubrovnik missal, like every medieval liturgical book, lies at the end of a process of composition that implies selection and choice. In this sense, it is witness to the liturgy of a particular church in a particular period: it has some features common to most books of the Roman liturgy, others appro-priate to Beneventan sources, and still others that are idiosyncratic or local. Of course, many nuances of the local use must elude us; undoubtedly some significant features fall into this category. The very date of composition and place of origin of the manuscript are less clear than earlier studies have

---

[465] Hesbert, "Tradition bénéventaine," passim; musical items of the Old Beneventan liturgy listed in Huglo, "Ancien chant bénéventain," pp. 272-280; and Kelly, *Beneventan Chant*, pp. 250-297.

[466] See above pp. 28-29.

concluded, and the connections with contemporary sources are only hinted at. But the characteristics of the Missal, whether considered in isolation or as part of the development of the liturgy, emphasise the range of influences on the local liturgy in one medieval church.

RULES OF THE EDITION

The edition of early liturgical texts is scarcely standardised. Nonetheless, some guidelines used in successful editions and others sought by students of the field are generally accepted. The criteria for texts edited from manuscripts, particularly from a single source, include not only the faithful transcription of text but also some rendering of the conscious and meaningful non-literary signs indicated by the layout of the manuscript itself. Thus, for instance, headings and directives in red in the manuscript should be set off in some way in the edition; so also attention must be paid to the hierarchy of scripts and capitalisation that carried considerable meaning for the contemporary users of the book. Such *desiderata*—a strict fidelity to medieval intention preserved in an intelligible modern typography—form the basis for the rules followed in this edition.

The texts of the prayers and musical items have been transcribed fully. The extended readings from the Old and New Testament in the lections have been indicated only by incipit and explicit, with reference in the text to the omitted passage and in the *apparatus textualis* to variants vs. the Vulgate. Abbreviations are expanded silently except for the "response"- sign, "R," which is rendered *Resp.* since the expansion could be one of several similar forms, i.e., "responsum, responsorium, respondendum," etc. The orthography of the manuscript has been retained. No distinction is made between vocalic and consonantal *u/v*: lower-case *u* and *v* are both represented by *u*, the upper-case forms by *V*. As in the manuscript, classical *ae* and *oe* are invariably written *e*; the caudate-*e* is not used in the manuscript.

Physical defects or illegible passages have been supplied in angle brackets from parallel texts in other sources; no text has been added where the manuscript is whole and none is missing (despite the temptation to gloss the occasional laconic titulus). Lacunae are noted in the text between square brackets, with other codicological comments given in the *apparatus textualis*; folio breaks are indicated by vertical slashes in the text with the relevant folios noted in the margin.

The text has not been emended; in every instance, the reading is that of the manuscript with expanded abbreviations. The reader should be alert, therefore, to a number of infelicities and local constructions:

Orthographic variants are frequent. Some are simply alternatives,[467] and others are medieval,[468] while further instances may be regional, including the interchangeable use of *b* and consonantal-*u* (*v*) in the future and perfect tenses,[469] and the occasional intrusive or dropped *h*.[470] Proper names also give rise to many peculiarities.[471] The practice of copying from dictation, or at least sounding the words as they were copied, leads to several aural confusions, e.g., (162) "ex puto" for "ex sputo."[472] Of course, some variants are undoubtedly mistakes, e.g., omitted,[473] doubled,[474] and reversed letters or words.[475] Sometimes also the scribe has omitted or confused the signs of

[467] E.g., the omission of *s* after *ex-* (100 "exurge" for "exsurge," passim); *i* for *y* (136 "misteriis" for "mysteriis"); the use of *e* for *ae* and *oe* (3 "uite" for "uitae"); or 543 "caligoso" for "caliginoso" (2 Petr 1: 19).

[468] E.g., 44 "aprehendat" for "apprehendat"; 134 "solempniter" for "sollemniter" or "quadragessimalis" for "quadragesimalis"; 211 "comercia" for "commercia"; 483 "centumplum" for "centuplum"; and 546 "transferi" for "transferri."

[469] E.g., 132 "mandauit" for "mandabit" (Mt 4: 6); 550 "laudabit" for "laudauit" (Eccli 51: 8); 611 "appropinquabit" for "appropinquauit" (Mt 10: 7); 621 "Letabitur iustus in domino et sperauit in eo et laudabuntur omnes recti corde" (Ps 63: 11); and 625 "cibauit" for "cibabit" (Eccli 15: 3).

[470] E.g., 139 "habundetis" for "abundetis" (1 Thess 4: 1); and 515 "que non auferetur hab ea in eternum" (Lc 10: 42).

[471] E.g., the spelling of Luke in the accusative as either "Lucam" or "Lucan"; also 24 "LECTIO EPISTOLE BEATI. PAVLI. APOSTOLI AD GALTHAS"; and 243 "LECTIO EPISTOLE BEATI PAVLI APOSTOLI AD PHESIOS."

[472] See also 311, 432, and 665 "addextris" for "a dextris."

[473] E.g., 8 "suffrantibus" for "suffragantibus"; 32 "ut [per?] hec munera que oculis tue maiestatis offerimus intercedente beata dei genitrice maria purificate mentis intelligentia consequamur"; 56 "ut saluatoris mundi stella duce [nativitas?] manifestata mentibus nostris reueletur semper et crescat"; 193 "ut agnita ueritatis tue [luce?] que christus est a suis tenebris eruantur"; 213 "ut [per?] hec que fideliter sumpsimus et purgemur a uitiis et a periculis omnibus exuamur"; 394 "Ea" for "Eia"; and 527 "Oblationes populi tui domine quesumus beati apostoli iacobi [passio?] conciliet." Other omissions are clearly intentional from their repetition, e.g., the headings before 309 "IN SANCTI STEPHANI PROTOMARTIRIS" for "IN NATALE"; 320 "IN SANCTI SILVESTRI PAPE," etc.; and perhaps 719 "PRO QUORVM RELIQVIAE HABENTVR" for "PRO SANCTIS."

The secret for the votive Mass in Honour of All Saints (717) presents a confusion of texts that results from a misunderstood composition: 717 "Munera tibi ... offerimus que ut tuo sint grata conspectui beate marie uirginis omniumque ordinum ... quesumus intercessionibus adiuuari semper et ubique mereamur." The prayer is cited in several Beneventan MSS with occasional variants, e.g., "que ut *et* tuo" in Ott. It appears to be composed from the conflation of clauses from two Gregorian prayers (incipit: Ha 634 + explicit Ha 611) with some modifications. In particular, where Ha 611 reads "adiuuantur," the Dubrovnik missal has "quesumus intercessionibus adiuuari semper et ubique mereamur."

[474] E.g., 207 "amississe" for "amisisse"; and 535 "Deus qui nos annua beati stephani martiris tui atque pontificis annua sollemnitate letificas" for the repetition of "annua."

[475] I.e., 103 "spall<ere>" for "psall<ere>"; 134 "epulamur" for "epularum"; 269 "egnimate" for "enigmate"; and 629 "usque ihc" for "usque hic."

abbreviation;[476] in a few cases, the rubricator has added inappropriate titles or omitted capitals.[477]

More interesting are consistent grammatical features that do not follow standard classical usage.[478] Of course, strict adherence to classical paradigm is not every medieval writer's greatest virtue; nor is it even one of the more important in the case of liturgical texts. Many supposed faults should in this sense be understood in melodic or poetic terms, or as traces of vulgar Latin or echoes of the developing vernaculars. Such features are on occasion biblical, e.g., (**175**) "unicornuorum" (Ps 21: 22) for "unicornuum"; other instances are attested in the regional liturgical corpus, e.g., (**4**) "et precinxit se uirtutem" found in Ben34 and one gradual of the AMS but otherwise given as "uirtute" in the GR and most early graduals.[479] These variants cover a wide range of grammatical and linguistic features, such as the tendency in vulgar Latin to drop the final-*m* that may have influenced the copyist at several points.[480] Plural inflections are found in the manuscript for collective nouns,

---

[476] I.e., **146** "qui nos" for "quos," where a stroke through the descender of "q" indicates "qui" and the "-uos" must now be read "nos" for sense; **297** "redundabut" for "redundabunt"; **408** "depcamur" for "deprecamur"; **654** "cofessoris" for "confessoris"; and **694** "cocede" for "concede." The omission of the sign of abbreviation may also be responsible for some instances of the missing final-*m* listed below in n. 480.

[477] I.e., **74** "-ui tecum" with "Q" omitted; **557** "- xaudi" with the "E" omitted; and **586** "SECRETA" for "POSTCOMMVNIO."

[478] The studies of Christine Mohrmann have defined the development of a Christian Latin and its liturgical uses, e.g., "Le latin liturgique" in *L'Ordinaire de la messe*, ed. Bernard Botte and Christine Mohrmann, Études liturgiques 2 (Paris, Louvain, 1952), pp. 29-48; and her collected papers in *Études sur le latin des chrétiens*, 3 vols., Storia e Letteratura, Raccolta di Studi e Testi 65, 87, 103 (Rome, 1956, 1965). The features of vulgar Latin are presented by Veikko Väänänen, *Introduction au latin vulgaire*, Bibliothèque française et romane, Série A: Manuels et études linguistiques 6 (Paris, 1963).

[479] See also **178** "Tenuisti manum dextere mee" as in Ben34 and DaB for "dexteram meam" of the GR; and **475** "in illo die" as Ben33 and Ben34 for "in illum diem" of the GR. Other regional variants are remarked in the following notes.

[480] I.e., **16** and **598** "ante conspectu" for "conspectum" (perhaps the preposition does not govern the classical case in these instances); **85** "dum gustasset architriclinus aqua uinum factum" found in two graduals of the AMS unlike the more widely spread "aquam" of the Vulgate and GR; **145** "Qui biberit aqua" for "aquam"; **155** "conuentu facite" for "conuentum"; **180** "remissione" for "remissionem" (Mt 26: 28); **196** "Aceto namque siti mea potasti" as Ben34 for "sitim meam" of the GR; **207** "totius orbis se sentiat amississe caligine" for "caliginem"; **252** "et ad uitam perueniamus eterna" for "eternam"; **303** "altitudine" for "altitudinem" (Eccli 50: 11); **304** "Qui gloria mundi spreuit" for "gloriam"; **315** "Elegerunt apostoli stephanum leuita" for "leuitam" and "quem lapidauerunt iudei orante" for "orantem"; **388** "angustia" for "angustiam" (Sap 5: 3); **478** "in apostolatu" as Ben33 and Ben34 for "in apostolatum" of the GR; **582** "sola" for "solam" (Lc 10: 40); **595** "Quia eripuit anima" for "animam" (Ps 114: 8); **657** "mensura" for "mensuram"; and **660** "sapientia" for " sapientiam" (Ps 36: 30). Although one may suspect that some instances are due to the omission of a sign of abbreviation for the final-*m*, the number of examples suggests that a more significant rule

e.g., **(57)** "uirum quem adorant multitudo angelorum."[481] The vocative is sometimes given a nominative form.[482] Other forms appear with changes of declension or gender,[483] perhaps representing on occasion modifications of case or declension due to attraction.[484] The parallels between the halves of chiastic constructions are sometimes faulty by classical standards,[485] and there are other disagreements with antecedents.[486] For such reasons, cases do not follow classical rules in every instance,[487] and consistencies are not always

of language is involved. The omission of final-*m* in vulgar Latin is discussed by Väänänen, *Introduction au latin vulgaire*, pp. 69-70.

[481] See also **173** "Turba multa que conuenerant ad diem festum clamabant domino"; and **205** "*Et sic cum silentio communicent omnes. et post paululum unusquisque priuatim cum silentio cantent uesperum. et sic uadant ad commedendum qui uolunt.*"

[482] E.g., **283** "sua nos dominus misterio congruentes" for "domine" (Väänänen, *Introduction au latin vulgaire*, p. 118).

[483] E.g., **297** "de primitiis frugum tuorum" for "tuarum." "Misericordia" is very frequently cited, but in a few instances it appears to be treated as a neuter-plural noun: **80** and **351** "Confiteantur domino misericordia eius" for "misericordiae"; and **364** "misericordiam quam deposcit et que precatur humiliter" with "que" for "quam." In other instances, abstract nouns in the neuter plural are treated as feminine singulars in -*a*; this was a feature in the decline of the neuter in vulgar and late Latin (Väänänen, *Introduction au latin vulgaire*, pp. 108-109): e.g., **151** "Iustitie domini recte letificantes corda. et dulciora super mel et fauum nam et seruus tuus custodit eam" for the omission of "iudicia" before "dulciora" and the pronoun "eam" for the usual "ea" ("iudicia"); **362** "Deus qui proditoris apostate ruinam. ne apostolorum tuorum numerus sacratus careret beati mathie electione supplesti presentia munera sanctifica et per eam nos gratie tue uirtute confirma" with "eam" for "ea" ("munera"); **474** "insignia que corporalibus officiis exequitur"; **532** "et multiplici nos suffragia consoletur" for "suffragio"; and **567** "Beati tiburtii nos domine foueat continuata presidia."

[484] I.e., **123** "quibus ipsius uenerabilis sacramentis celebramus exordium" for "sacramenti"; **134** "Sacrificium domine quadragessimalis initiis solempniter immolamus" for "initii"; **136** "et a uetustate purgatos in misteriis salutaris faciat transire consortium" for "misterii"; **206** "BENEDICTIO IGNI NOVI" for "IGNIS"; **274** "Sancti spiritus domine quesumus corda nostra mundet infusio. et suis roris intima aspersione fecundet" for "sui"; **546** "ut diuini pasti alimoniis. in eius mereamur membra transferi" for "diuinis"; and **615** "Quesumus domine salutaribus repletis misteriis" for "repleti." In **584** "quam etsi pro conditionis <carnis migrasse> cognoscimus" for "conditione" may represent a similar process, although it remains conjectural since damage to the folio requires that two key words be supplied from parallel passages in other missals.

[485] E.g., **146** "qui nos tui reficis sacramentis" for "tuis"; **196** "*posito ante ea oratorium*" for "oratorio"; **263** "Vltimo festiuitatis diem dicebat hiesus" for "die"; **283** "sua nos dominus misterio congruentes" for "suo"; **426** "ut ab omni nos exuat bellorum nequitie" for "ab omni ... nequitia"; and **474** "ut apostolicis petri et pauli natalis insignia" for "apostolici ... natalis."

[486] E.g., **315** "quem lapidauerunt iudei orante et dicentes" for "orantem et dicentem"; and **595** "Conuertere anima meam" for "mea" (Ps 114: 7).

[487] I.e., **80** "Confiteantur domino misericordia eius et mirabilia eius filios hominum" for "filiis"; **200** "*Per unumquemque uersus*"; **207** "in unitate spiritu sancti" for "spiritus"; **223** "Tribue nobis domine celestis mense uirtutem satiatis" for "uirtute"; **277** "ut nos famulos tuos non exurat flammas uitiorum" for "flamma"; **289** "ipse dabit uirtutem et fortitudinem plebis sue" for "plebi"; **301** "Renouamini spiritus mentis uestre" for "spiritu" (Vulgate); **316** "que beati stephani martiris tui commemoratione gloriosa depromit" for "commemoratio"; **401**

maintained for number and person.[488] A few readings follow neither linguistic nor liturgical developments but present instead peculiarities that change the sense of otherwise traditional passages. In the tract of the first Sunday of Lent, for instance, the psalmic verse, and most liturgical uses, read "scuto circumdabit te veritas eius" (Ps 90: 5), whereas the Dubrovnik missal has "scuto circumdabit me ueritas eius" (**131**).[489]

Since, as I have argued, the punctuation relates the oratorical rules by which the text was presented, it has been retained: points, semi-colons, commas, and question marks correspond to the stop, lesser pauses, and interrogation sign. Where the manuscript occasionally lacks punctuation at the end of a text before a large initial, it has been added to conform to modern usage: the larger size of the initial in such cases would have served to notify the medieval reader of a final stop and new paragraph, as our modern punctuation does. The presence of initials has dictated the division into paragraphs, although the continuous numbering in Arabic numerals is my own. Directional rubrics are reproduced as italics, titles as small capitals, and headings preceding new mass-texts as centred capitals. This is a slight departure from the manuscript, which indicates titles, directions, and headings as rubricated texts without further differentiation.

The medieval distinction between pieces said by the celebrant and items sung by the choir was made by letter-size; the use of a smaller font for the musical items reproduces the practice of the manuscript itself. Not all musical texts were noted however: sections with neumes have been indicated by placing the passage between eighth notes. Since the transcription of neumatic notation is fraught with difficulties of interpretation, the ideal at this stage of understanding is still reproduction by facsimile, at least for disputed points

---

"qui unigeniti tui meruit fieri euangelicus predicaturo" for "predicator"; **429** "ut familiam tuam per uiam salutis incedat" for "familia tua"; **553** "ut detur locum uoci mee in celo" for "locus"; **563** "sanctitas et magnificentiam in sanctificatione eius" for "magnificentia"; and **704** "ut nos beati illius. martiris tui interuentione gloriosa commendet" for "interuentio."

[488] E.g., **206** "sicut illuminasti moysem ita illuminare corda nostra et sensus nostros" for "illumines"; **211** "Deus qui nos per huius sacrificii ueneranda comercia unius summe diuinitatis participes effecti" for "effecisti"; **275** "per inhabitantes spiritum eius in nobis" for "inhabitantem"; **309** "quia seruus tuus exercebantur in tuis iustificationibus"; and **434** "Munera domine oblata sanctifica et intercedente beato iohanne baptista nos per hec a peccatorum maculis emundet" for "emunda."

[489] See also **7** "ut sicut homo unigenitus idem refulsit et deus sic nobis hec eterna substantia conferat quod diuinum est" where most parallels read "terrena" for "eterna"; **120** "et propitius esto peccatis nostri propter nomen tuum" with the genitive of the personal pronoun instead of the more common pronomial adjective "nostris" (GR); **365** "ut illius quoque eodem aput te optinente mereamur subsequi quo peruenit" for "illuc" as in most Beneventan MSS; **544** "assumpsit" for "assumit" (Mc 9: 1); and **680** "hic do<mus dei> est et portas celi" for "porta" (Gn 28: 17, GR, Ben34).

if not for the line of the melody. The gap between manuscript and edition for musical notation is, to my mind, so much more conjectural than the same inevitable gap in the edition of Latin text that the utility of a transcription is limited.

But, if edition of the music must remain less than ideal, ignoring it altogether is certainly no better. For this edition, the noted passages have been compared to the corresponding melodies of the GR (Desclée, no. 696A).[490] The *apparatus musicus* citing musical variants depends on several conventions. The syllable on which a variant occurs is given in italics followed by the melody of the manuscript; the c-clef marked in yellow by the scribe of the manuscript is represented by a lower-case *c*; notes below by upper-case letters, notes above by lower-case letters. Notes more than an octave above or below *c* are distinguished by a prime-sign (A′B′CDEF-GABcdefgabc′d′). All other phrases are equivalent to the corresponding passages in the GR; thus, the general melody of the manuscript may be reconstructed with the aid of a modern edition. Nonetheless, since the comparisons do not include repeated notes, variants in the relation of musical to textual phrases (i.e., same melody but different syllables), or graphic differences such as the choice of neumes, the musical paleographer must still have recourse to facsimiles or the original.

For the most striking pieces, however,—those unattested in Roman sources or sharply variant—full transcriptions and brief comments have been provided in the introduction. The Beneventan neumes of the manuscript on F and C-rules are transcribed into simple note-heads on a five-line staff. Line breaks are indicated with a vertical bar; checkmarks before the bars are used for the directs of the manuscript. Compound neumes are represented by series of notes connected by slurs; these have been added below the notes for descending neumes and above in all other cases. Liquescent neumes are distinguished by a point after the modified note.

The sources cited in the *apparatus parallelorum locorum* have been selected to show the biblical origins of each piece and any similar texts in the early books of the Roman, Milanese, and Beneventan liturgies. Where equivalent texts have been found on the same feast, the paragraph or folio number follows the siglum without distinction. Where, however, equivalent

---

[490] *Graduale sacrosanctae Romanae ecclesiae* cum *Missae propriae Ordinis S. Benedicti*, ed. Solesmes, no. 696A (Paris, Tournai, Rome: Desclée, 1952). Gradual 696A differs from other editions of the GR principally in its supplement containing masses for Benedictine feasts and in some individual features of pagination. With the aid of an index, therefore, the comparisons of the *apparatus musicus* are applicable also to other Roman graduals of the series edited by Solesmes.

texts are found only at other points in the source, citations are given in parentheses. Thus, for instance, in the *apparatus* for the postcommunion *Satiasti domine* (**11**) of the Nativity, the Hadrianum is cited as "Ha 47," i.e., with the same prayer on the same feast, but the Veronese sacramentary is cited as "Le (746)," i.e., with a comparable text but on a different feast. Where there are many such references in a single source to similar items on different feasts, the note has been restricted in some cases to the first citation in the Temporal or Sanctoral and a citation from the Common.

The biblical source of an item is listed first. It is followed by comparisons with the later medieval and Tridentine liturgies (heading RL) as contained in the Graduale Romanum (no. 696A, GR) and the *Missale Romanum Mediolani, 1474* (MRM), which has been reprinted by the Henry Bradshaw Society with a second volume of citations from other early printed missals. These books of the later Roman liturgy have been cited as standards to isolate immediately the most unusual regional pieces. The list of parallels continues with the earliest sources of the liturgy: the Veronese (Le) and Vatican (Va) sacramentaries (under the heading SAC), the early mass-antiphonals (AMS), and the Comes of Würzburg (WuC, WuE), Muhrbach (Mu), Paris (CoP), and Alcuin (Alc) for the lectionary (heading LEC). Among Gregorian sacramentaries (GREG), the sources compared throughout are the Hadrianum (Ha), Paduense (Pa), the lowest script of Monte Cassino 271 (Z6), and the Supplement (Sp). Gelasians of the Eighth Century (GEL8) include the Angoulême (En), Gellone (Ge), Rheinau (Rh), and St.-Gallen (Sg) sacramentaries. For the Ambrosian liturgy (AM), the Sacramentary of Bergamo (Sb) is used. Vat. lat. 4770 (Vl4770), an early witness from the Abruzzi, provides comparisons with central Italian practice. Other texts cited only as supplements in particular instances include Gregorian variants from several manuscripts (Tc), the Phillipps (Ph), Triplex (STripl), Fulda (F) and Vich (SVich) sacramentaries, the Liber commicus (Co), Schlager's catalogue of alleluias, and the Graduals of Sarum (Gs) and Saint-Yrieix (Syg). Sources less frequently used are listed in the *conspectus siglorum*.

The Beneventan manuscripts cited include every edited manuscript known to me and all the principal unedited manuscripts from the major Beneventan centres. The references to similar texts on different feasts are not exhaustive for the unedited manuscripts. In order to emphasise geographical groupings within the Beneventan zone, the sigla for Beneventan manuscripts from each centre are identified by prefixes: Mc for Monte Cassino, Da for Dalmatia, Pu for Apulia, and Ben for Benevento. Not all the sources have been so tractable: Ottob. lat. 576, for instance, defies location and has been cited as Ott. Since some of the localisations are tentative, the reader is asked to treat them as tools, more-or-less accurate, but amenable to further refinement.

MISSALE RAGVSINVM

Editorial Symbols and Abbreviations

TEXT

| = folio break
[ ] = codicological information
lac. = lacuna
< > = lacuna with supplied text
... = omitted lections, compared in *apparatus lectionum* vs. *Biblia sacra iuxta Vulgatam versionem* (= *Vulgata*), ed. Robert Weber, 2nd edition, 2 vols. (Stuttgart, 1975).
♪...♪ = items with musical notation
1 ... paragraphs enumerated with Arabic numerals

APPARATUS

(MUSICALIS, PARALLELORUM LOCORUM, TEXTUALIS)

add. = addere (with inflexions)
App. = Appendix
corr. = corrigere/correctio
dext. = dexter
expl. = explicere
inc. = incipere
inf. = inferior
lin. = linea
Intro. = Introductio (esp. reference to musical figures)
m. v. = minores variationes
marg. = margo
n. m. = neumae musicae
om. = omittere
recent.= recentior
ref. = referre
sinist.= sinister
trans. = transponere
var. = varia
al*le*luia = melodic variants cited by italicised syllable where different in whole or part from the *Graduale Romanum* (= GR), ed. Solesmes, no. 696A (Paris, Tournai, Rome, 1952)
A′B′CDEFGABcdefgabc′d′ = musical pitches, where F and c are the coloured rules of the MS
See the *Conspectus siglorum* for abbreviations of manuscripts and editions. Abbreviations of liturgical terms precede the Introduction.

\<SECVNDA MISSA NATIVITATIS DOMINI\>

1

1r [*lac.*] |deo nostro.

2

GRADVALE ♪ Benedictus qui uenit in nomine domini deus dominus et illuxit nobis. VERSVS A domino factum est et est mirabile in oculis nostris. ♪

3

LECTIO EPISTOLE BEATI PAVLI APOSTOLI. AD TITVM [3: 4-7]. Karissime. Apparuit benignitas et humanitas ... spem uite eterne in \<christo\> iesu domino nostro.

4

1v ♪ Alleluia. D\<ominus regna\>uit decorem \<induit\> |induit dominus fortitudinem et precinxit se uirtutem. ♪

---

1 *lac. ante 1r*

---

2 do*mini*: BdcBAdcBA   do*mino*: dcAcdeBcdedcdecAcAFAFAGFAFGAcdB-cAcdfc   no*stris*: cABcAFGABcdecAGBAF

4 *do*minus[2]: FGFEFG   fortitudi*nem*: DFCFDEDC   uirtu*tem*: GAGA-GEFGFEDEFD

---

1 Is 61: 2. LEC: Mu 3, WuC 6, CoP 8. BEN: Ca 4v (Is 61: 1-2 *Spiritus domini super me*), Ve 10r-v.

2 Ps 117: **26, 27, 23**. RL: GR 31, MRM 18. AMS 10. ES: Vl4770 2r. BEN: Ben29 26r, Ben33 2v, Ben34 15v, Ca 4v, Mc127 345, Mc540 42, Mc546 13-14, McV 18r, Ott 17r, Ve 10v.

3 Tit 3: **4-7**. RL: MRM 18. LEC: Mu 3, WuC 3, CoP 7. ES: Vl4770 2r. BEN: Ben29 25v-26r, Ben33 2v, Ca 4v, DaK 6v, Mc127 345, Mc540 42, McV 18r-v, Ott 17r, Ve 10v.

4 Ps 92: **1**. RL: GR 31-32, MRM 18. AMS 10. ES: Vl4770 2r. BEN: Ben29 26r, Ben33 2v-3r, Ben34 15v, Ca 5r, Mc127 345, Mc540 42, Mc546 14, McV 18v, Ott 17r, Ve 10v.

5

SEQVENTIA SANCTI EVANGELII SECVNDVM LVCAM [2: 15-20]. In illo tempore. Pastores loquebantur ad inuicem ... ad illos.

6

OFFERTORIVM ♪ Deus enim <firmaui>t orbem terre qui non com<mouebi-
2r tur> parata sedes tua deus ex tunc |a seculo tu es. ♪

7

SECRETA Munera nostra quesumus domine natiuitatis hodierne mysteriis apta proueniant. ut sicut homo unigenitus idem refulsit et deus.
sic nobis hec eterna substantia conferat quod diuinum est. per eundem.

8

SECRETA DE SANCTA ANASTASIA. Accipe quesumus domine munera
dignanter oblata. et beate anastasie suffrantibus meritis. ad nostre
salutis auxilium prouenire concede. per.

9

COMMVNIO ♪ Exulta filia syon lauda filia hierusalem ecce rex tuus uenit sanctus
et saluator mundi. ♪

---

5 hoc uerbum quod dominus ostendit] hoc verbum quod factum est quod fecit
Dominus et ostendit *Vulgata* (2: 15)

---

6 *Deus*: GFGF   firma*uit*: ... F (*ut vid.*)   *non*: GAcAGFG   *tunc*: GAGAF.

9 *Exulta f*ilia: EFGDEFEFG   *sanctus*: GEFE   *et*: FG   *saluator*: E ... GA

---

5 Lc 2: 15-20. RL: MRM 18. LEC: Mu 3, WuE 297, CoP 9. ES: Vl4770 2r. BEN:
Ben29 26r (Lc 2: 15-21), Ben33 3r, Ca 5r, DaE 3v, DaK 7r, Mc127 346, Mc540
42, McV 18v, Ott 17v, Ve 10v-11r.

6 Ps 92: 1-2. RL: GR 32, MRM 18. AMS 10. ES: Vl4770 2r. BEN: Ben29 26r, Ben33
3r, Ben34 16r, Mc127 346, Mc540 42-43, Mc546 14, McV 18v, Ott 17v, Ve 11r.

7 SAC: Va 7. RL: MRM 18. GREG: Ha 44, Pa 12. GEL8: En 2, Ge 10, Rh 10, Sg 11.
ES: Vl4770 2r. BEN: Ben29 26r-v, Ben33 3r, Mc127 346, Mc540 43, McV 18v-19r,
Ott 18r, Ve 11r.

8 RL: MRM 19. SAC: Le (759). GREG: Ha 43, Pa 11. GEL8: En 8, Ge 17, Rh 15, Sg
16. ES: Vl4770 2r. BEN: Ben29 26v, Ben33 3r, Mc127 346, Mc540 43, McV 19r,
Ott 18r, Ve 11r.

9 Zach 9: 9. RL: GR 32, MRM 19. AMS 10. ES: Vl4770 2v. BEN: Ben29 26v, Ben33
3r, Ben34 16v, Mc127 346, Mc540 43, Mc546 14, McV 19r, Ott 18r, Ve 11r.

10

POSTCOMMVNIO Huius nos domine sacramenti nouitas semper natalis instauret. cuius natiuitatis singularis humanam reppulit uetustatem. Qui tecum.

11

POSTCOMMVNIO DE SANCTA ANASTASIA. Satiasti domine familiam tuam muneribus sacris. eius quesumus semper interuentione nos refoue. cuius sollemnia celebramus. per.

IN DIE SACRE NATIVITATIS.

12

2v ♪ Puer natus est nobis et filius dat<us est> |nobis cuius imperium super humerum eius et uocabitur nomen eius magni consilii angelus. PSALMVS Cantate domino canticum nouum quia. ♪

13

ORATIO Concede quesumus omnipotens deus. ut nos unigeniti tui noua per carnem natiuitas liberet. quos sub peccati iugo, uetusta seruitus tenet. per eundem.

---

12 no*bis*[2]: AG   *eius*[1]: cABcBcBA   *eius*[2]: cdcBA   *con*silii: Ac

---

10 RL: MRM 19. SAC: Va 4. GREG: Ha 48, Pa 16. GEL8: En 17, Ge 23, Rh 21, Sg 22. AM: Sb (150). ES: Vl4770 2v. BEN: Ben29 26v, Ben33 3r, Mc127 346, Mc540 43, McV 19r, Ott 18r, Ve 11r.

11 RL: MRM 19. SAC: Le (746). GREG: Ha 47, Pa 15. GEL8: En 10, Ge 19, Rh 17, Sg 18. AM: Sb (13, 1670). ES: Vl4770 2v. BEN: Ben29 26v, Ben33 3r, Mc127 346, Mc540 43, McV 19r, Ott 18r, Ve 11r.

12 Is 9: 6, Ps 97: 1. RL: GR 33, MRM 19. AMS 11a. ES: Vl4770 2v. BEN: Ben29 26v, Ben33 3r, Ben34 16v, Mc127 346-347, Mc540 43, Mc546 15, McV 19r, Ott 18r, PuC 334, Ve 11r.

13 RL: MRM 19. SAC: Va 6. GREG: Ha 49, Pa 17. GEL8: En 21, Ge 26, Rh 24, Sg 25. AM: Sb (98, 116). ES: Vl4770 2v (add. alia manu). BEN: Ben29 26v, Ben33 3r, Mc127 347, Mc540 43, McO 220, McV 19r, Ott 18r, PuC 335, Ve 11r.

14

ALIA ORATIO Omnipotens sempiterne deus. qui hunc diem. per incarnationem uerbi tui. et partum beate marie semper uirginis consecrasti. da populis tuis in hac celebritate consortium. ut qui tua gratia sunt redempti. tua adoptione sint filii. per eundem.

15

LECTIO YSAYE PROPHETE [52: 6-10]. Hec dicit dominus. Propter hoc 3r sciet populus meus ... |... salutare dei.·,

16

GRADVALE ♪ Viderunt omnes fines terre salutare dei nostri iubilate deo. omnis terra. VERSVS Notum fecit dominus salutare suum ante conspectu gentium reuelauit iustitiam suam. ♪

17

LECTIO EPISTOLE BEATI PAVLI APOSTOLI AD HEBREOS [1: 1-12]. Fratres. 3v Multipharie ... |... amictum mu- [*lac.*]

---

15 supra montes] super montes *Vulgata* (52: 7)   redemit Ierusalem ... in oculis omnium gentium *om. Dubr* (52: 9-10)

17 multisque modis] et multis modis *Vulgata* (1: 1)   tanto melior est] est *om. Vulgata* (1: 4)   uirga] et virga (1: 8)

---

16 o*mnis*: cABcBAGABAG   *f*ecit: c   *d*ominus: dcAcdcBcdBAFAcd-cAcdcBcdAFABGBcBcGFAFAGFAFGAcdef   *suum*: AcAcABA *con*-spectu: cd

---

14 SAC: Va 17. GREG: Ha 58, Pa 24. GEL8: En 19, Ge 25, Rh 23, Sg 24. AM: Sb 103. BEN: McO 221.

15 Is 52: 6-10. LEC: Mu 4, CoP 11. BEN: Ve 11r-v.

16 Ps 97: 3-4, 2. RL: GR 33-34, MRM 20. AMS 11a. ES: Vl4770 3r. BEN: Ben29 27r, Ben33 3v, Ben34 17v, Ben35 (1r: var.), Ca 5v, Mc127 348, Mc540 44, Mc546 15, McV 19v, Ott 19r, PuC 337, Ve 11v-12r.

17 Heb 1: 1-12. RL: MRM 19-20. LEC: Alc 4, Mu 4, WuC 4, CoP 10. ES: Vl4770 2v-3r. BEN: Ben29 26v-27r, Ben33 3v, Ca 5v, DaK 7r, Mc127 347-348, Mc540 43-44, McV 19r-v, Ott 18v-19r, PuC 336, Ve 11v.

18

4r [*lac.*] | ♪ -ratio. sedis tue. ♪

19

SECRETA Oblata domine munera. unigeniti tui noua natiuitate sanctifica. nosque a peccatorum nostrorum maculis emunda. per eundem.

20

COMMVNIO ♪ Viderunt omnes fines terre salutare dei nostri. ♪

21

POSTCOMMVNIO Presta quesumus omnipotens deus. ut natus hodie,
saluator mundi. sicut diuine nobis regenerationis est auctor. ita et
immortalitatis sit ipse largitor. qui tecum uiuit.

---

18 *lac. inter 3v-4r*

---

18 se*dis*: FEAGFGAG

20 Vi*d*erunt: GEF   saluta*re de*i: FDFAG

---

18 Ps 88: 15. RL: GR 35 (*Tui sunt caeli*), MRM 20. AMS 11b. ES: Vl4770 3r-v. BEN:
Ben29 27v, Ben33 3*bis*r, Ben34 19v, Ca 6r, Mc127 349, Mc540 45, Mc546 16,
McV 20r, Ott 19v, PuC 340, Ve 12r.

19 RL: MRM 20. GREG: Ha 50, Pa 18. GEL8: En (131), Ge 28, Rh (115), Sg (123).
AM: Sb (287). ES: Vl4770 3v. BEN: Ben29 28r, Ben33 3*bis*r, Ca 6r, Mc127 349,
Mc540 45, McV 20r, Ott 19v, PuC 341, Ve 12r.

20 Ps 97: 3. RL: GR 35, MRM 20. AMS 11b. ES: Vl4770 3v. BEN: Ben29 28r, Ben33
3*bis*r, Ben34 20v, Ca 6r, Mc127 349, Mc540 45, Mc546 16, McV 20r, Ott 19v,
PuC 343, Ve 12v.

21 RL: MRM 21. SAC: Le (1271), Va 18. GREG: Ha 53, Pa 19. GEL8: En 20, Rh 28,
Sg 30. AM: Sb 111. ES: Vl4770 3v. BEN: Ben29 28r, Ben33 3*bis*v, Ca 6v, Mc127
349, Mc540 46, McV 20r, Ott 19v, PuC 344, Ve 12v.

DOMINICA POST NATIVITATEM DOMINI.

22

♪ Dum medium silentium tenerent omnia et nox in suo cursu medium iter haberet omnipotens sermo tuus domine de celis a regalibus sedibus uenit. PSALMVS Dominus regnauit decorem. ♪

23

4v |ORATIO Omnipotens sempiterne deus; dirige actus nostros. in bene-placito tuo. ut in nomine dilecti filii tui. mereamur bonis operibus habundare. Qui tecum.

24

LECTIO EPISTOLE BEATI. PAVLI. APOSTOLI AD GALTHAS [4: 1-7]. Fratres. Quanto tempore heres paruulus est. ... heres per deum.

25

GRADVALE ♪ Speciosus forma pre filiis hominum diffusa est gratia in labiis tuis. ♪

---

24 a seruo] servo *Vulgata* (4: 1)   et actoribus est] est et actoribus (4: 2)
quoniam autem estis filii dei] dei *om.* (4: 6)   iam non est] iam non es (4: 7)

25 tuis] tu...is *ante corr. per rasuram*

---

22 *re*galibus: AB   *se*dibus: Bc

25 for*ma pre*: dBcdecdcdcAcB   *fili*is: BdcABdc   diffu*sa*: BGAcGFD   *est*:
EF   *gratia*: GBABAGAcBAcGF   *in*: G   *labiis*: BGABcGFGFEGAGAc

---

22 Sap 18: 14-15, Ps 92: 1. RL: GR 44-45, MRM 27. AMS 17. ES: Vl4770 (8r). BEN:
Ben29 33r, Ben33 6v, Ben34 30v-31r, Ben35 2r-v, Ca 9v, DaB 18r, Mc127 23,
Mc540 52-53, Mc546 21, McV 23v, Ott 26v, Ve 16r.

23 RL: MRM 27. GREG: Ha 85, Pa 52, Sp 1093. GEL8: En (91), Ge (91), Rh (77),
Sg (85). ES: Vl4770 (8r). BEN: Ben29 33r, Ben33 6v, Ca 9v, DaB 18r, Mc127 24,
Mc540 53, McO 240, McV 24r, Ott 26v, Ve (20r).

24 Gal 4: 1-7. RL: MRM 27. LEC: Alc (12), Mu 9, WuC 26, CoP 25. ES: Vl4770
(8r-v). BEN: Ben29 33r-v, Ben33 6v, Ca 10r, DaB 18r, Mc127 24, Mc540 53, McV
24r, Ott 26v-27r, Ve 16r.

25 Ps 44: 3. RL: GR 45-46, MRM 27. AMS 17. ES: Vl4770 (8v). BEN: Ben29 33v,
Ben33 6v-7r, Ben34 31r, Ben35 2v, Ca 10r, DaB 18r-v, Mc127 24, Mc540 53,
Mc546 21-22, McV 24r, Ott 27r, Ve 16r-v.

\<MISSA SANCTE MARIE INFRA OCTAVAM\>

26

5r *[lac.]* |uite suscipere. Dominum nostrum.

27

LECTIO YSAYE PROPHETE [9: 2]. Hec dicit dominus. Populus gentium.

28

GRADVALE ♪ Diffusa est gratia in labiis tuis propterea benedixit te deus in eternum. VERSUS Propter ueritatem et mansuetudinem et iustitiam et deducet te mirabiliter dextera tua. ♪

29

♪ Alleluia. VERSVS Post partum uirgo inuiolata permansisti dei genitrix intercede pro nobis. ♪

---

26 *lac. inter 4v-5r*

---

28 *Diffusa*: DEFA   *est*: GAF   *benedi*xit: GABcd   *in*²: FGFDFGAFEF *e*ter*num*: GFAGF   *ueri*ta*tem*: cdcAcGAcdcAcBcdcd   *mansuetudi*nem: dcdcBdedcefecdecAcdcAcBcAGF   iustiti*am*: cBdfcdc   *deducet*: cd   *mira*-bi*liter*: cB   tu*a*: cAcAcAFGABcdecAGBAF

29 *Vide Intro. p. 45*

---

26 RL: MRM (29 *Deus qui salutis*). SAC: Va (993). GREG: Ha (82), Pa (49), Sp (1090). GEL8: En (69), Ge (67), Rh (62), Sg (67). AM: Sb (181). ES: Vl4770 (3v). BEN: Ben29 32r, 32v, Ca 9v, DaB 17v, Mc127 355, Mc540 52, McO 238, McV 23v, Ott 25v-26r, Ve (16r).

27 **Is 9: 2.** RL: MRM (2: 336). LEC: WuC (5). ES: Vl4770 (3v-4r). BEN: Ben29 32r, 32v-33r, DaB 18r, DaK 9r (Is 9: 2, 6-7), Mc127 355, Mc540 52, McV 23v, Ott 26r.

28 **Ps 44: 3, 5.** RL: GR ([69]-[70]). RL: MRM (324, 444, 2: 167, 2: 247). AMS (16*bis*, 33a, 23*bis*). ES: Vl4770 (4r). BEN: Ben29 32r, Ben33 (11v), Ben34 29v, DaB 18r, Mc127 355, Mc540 52, McV 23v.

29 RL: MRM (455). BEN: Ben29 32r, Ben33 (119v), Ben34 (220v), Ben38 (125r-v), Ben39 (146v-147r), DaB 18r, Mc127 355, Mc540 52, McV 23v. Var. (melodia): RL: GR ([77]), ES: Schlager, *Katalog* E 164, E 209, Syg (48), LS: Gs (r).

30

SECVNDVM. LVCAM [2: 15]. In illo tempore. Pastores loquebantur ad
·inuicem.

31

OFFERTORIVM ♪ Offerentur regi uirgines proxime eius offerentur tibi in letitia
5v et exultatione addu|centur in templum regi domino. ♪

32

SECRETA Presta quesumus omnipotens deus. ut hec munera que oculis
tue maiestatis offerimus. intercedente beata dei genitrice maria. purificate mentis. intelligentia consequamur. per eundem.

33

COMMVNIO ♪ Dilexisti iustitiam et odisti iniquitatem propterea uncxit te deus
deus tuus. ♪

34

POSTCOMMVNIO Presta quesumus omnipotens deus. ut hec munera
sacra que sumpsimus. intercedente beata dei genitrice semper uirgine
maria. perpetue nobis redemptionis conferant medicinam. per eundem.

---

31 Offe*rentur*[1]: E   *regi*[1]: A   uir*gines*: FE   pro*xime*: E   e*ius*: FGFDED
regi[2]: EFGAGFECD

---

33 F-*clavis*] c-*clavis trans.* GR *passim*   Dilexi*sti*: EDEDC   *iu*stitiam: D   *et*:
G   o*di*sti: AGA   *prop*terea: EC   unc*xit*: GA   *tu*us: FAGFGFE

---

30 Lc 2: 15. RL: MRM (18, 456). BEN: Ben29 32r, 33r, Ben33 (3r), Ca (5r), DaB
18r, DaE (3v), Mc127 355, Mc540 52, McV 23v, Ott 26r-v, Ve (10v-11r).

31 Ps 44: 15-16. RL: GR ([54]), MRM (446). AMS (16*bis*, 23*bis*, 140). ES: Vl4770
(3r). BEN: Ben29 32r, Ben 33 (11v, 120r), Ben34 30r, DaB 18r, Mc127 355,
Mc540 52, McV 23r.

32 BEN: DaB 18r, Mc127 356, Mc540 52, McV 23v, Ott 26v. Var.: RL: MRM (32),
SAC: Va (50), GEL8: Ge (78), Rh (73), Sg (78), ES: Vl4770 (11r), AM: STripl (319),
BEN: Ben29 (33r), Ca (9v).

33 Ps 44: 8. RL: GR ([71]), MRM (446). AMS (33b, 140). BEN: Ben33 (17v, 120v),
Ben34 (219v-220r), DaB 18r.

34 BEN: Ben29 33r, DaB 18r, Mc127 356, Mc540 52, McV 23v. Var. ("ut ...
maria"): SAC: Va (52), GEL8: Ge (80), Rh (75), Sg (80), BEN: Ca (9v), Ott (26r).

VIGILIA EPIPHANIE.

35

INTROITVS Lux fulgebit hodie.

36

ORATIO Corda nostra quesumus domine; uenture festiuitatis splendor illustret. quo et mundi huius tenebris carere ualeamus. et perueniamus ad patriam claritatis eterne. per.

37

AD CORINTHIOS [2 Cor 4: 6-10]. Fratres. Deus qui dixit de tenebris
6r lucem splendescere. ... |... manifestetur.

38

GRADVALE ♪ Speciosus forma. VERSVS Eructauit cor. ♪

39

♪ Alleluia. VERSVS Multipharie olim deus loquens in prophetis nouissimis diebus istis locutus est nobis in filio suo. ♪

---

37 illuxit] qui inluxit *Vulgata* (4: 6)   iesu christi] Christi Iesu (4: 6)   habentes] habemus (4: 7)   derelinquimur humiliamur sed non confundimur] derelinquimur (4: 9)   christi iesu] Iesu (4: 10)   uita iesu christi] vita Iesu (4: 10) corpore nostro] corporibus nostris (4: 10)

---

38 Speci*osus*: B   for*ma*: dB   *cor*: Bcdeded

39 *Vide Intro. p. 48*

---

35 Is 9: 2. RL: GR (30), MRM (17). BEN: Ben34 (15r-v), Ca 10v, Ve 17v.

36 SAC: Va 57. GREG: Pa 55. GEL8: En 97, Ge 97, Rh 83, Sg 91. ES: Vl4770 9v. BEN: Ben29 34r, Ben33 7r, Ca 10v, DaB 20r, Mc127 357-358, Mc540 55, McO 241, McV 25r, Ott 27v, Ve 17v.

37 2 Cor 4: 6-10. BEN: Ben29 34r, Ben33 7r-v, DaB 20r, Mc127 358, Mc540 55-56, Mc.VII 2, McV 25r-v, Ott 27v-28r.

38 Ps 44: 3, 2. RL: GR 56 (vide 45-46), MRM 30 (ref.), 2: 23. BEN: Ben29 34r, Ben33 (6v-7r), Ben34 (31r), Ca (10r), DaB 20r, Mc127 358, Mc540 56, Mc.VII 2, McV 25v, Ott 28r.

39 Heb 1: 1. RL: GR (49-50), MRM (29). BEN: Ben33 7v, Ben34 (31v), Ben35 (2v), Ca (10r), DaB 20r-v, Mc127 358, Mc540 56, Mc546 22, McV 25v.

40

SECVNDVM MATHEVM [2: 19-23]. In illo tempore. Defuncto herode.
6v ecce angelus domini in somnis apparuit. ioseph ... |... quoniam
nazareus uocabitur.

41

OFFERTORIVM Deus enim firmauit orbem.

42

SECRETA Tribue quesumus domine. ut eum presentibus immolemus
sacrificiis et sumamus. quem uenture sollemnitatis, pia munera prolo-
quuntur. Dominum nostrum.

43

COMMVNIO ♪ Tolle puerum et matrem eius et uade in terram iuda defuncti sunt
enim qui querebant animam pueri. ♪

44

POSTCOMMVNIO Illumina quesumus domine populum tuum. et splen-
7r dore gratie tue cor eius semper accende. |ut saluatorem suum, et
incessanter agnoscat. et ueraciter aprehendat. Qui tecum.

---

40 consurgens] surgens *Vulgata* (2: 21)

---

43 ter*ram*: ABcdBAB   de*functi*: GcB   *enim*: ede   *qui*: cB

---

40 Mt 2: 19-23. RL: MRM 30. LEC: Mu 10, WuE 298, CoP 28. ES: Vl4770 9v-10r.
BEN: Ben29 34r-v, Ben33 7v, Ca 10v, DaB 20v, DaE 9v, Mc127 358, Mc540 56,
Mc.VII 2, McV 25v, Ott 28r, Ve 17v.

41 Ps 92: 1. RL: GR (32), MRM 30 (ref.), 2: 23. BEN: Ben29 34v, Ben33 7v, Ben34
(31v), Ben35 (3v), Ca 10v, DaB 20v, Mc127 358, Mc540 56, Mc546 22, Mc.VII
2, McV 25v, Ott 28r, Ve 17v (add. alia manu).

42 SAC: Va 58. GREG: Pa 56. GEL8: En 98, Ge 98, Rh 84, Sg 92. BEN: Ben29 34v,
Ben33 7v, Ca 10v, DaB 20v, Mc127 358, Mc540 56, Mc.VII 2; McV 25v, Ott 28r,
Ve 17v.

43 Mt 2: 20. RL: GR 56 (vide 46), MRM 30 (ref.), 2: 23. BEN: Ben29 34v, Ben33
7v, Ben34 (31v), Ben35 (3v), Ca 10v, DaB 20v, Mc127 359, Mc540 56, Mc546
22-23, Mc.VII 2, McV 25v, Ott 28v.

44 GREG: Ha (98: Epiph.). GEL8: Ge (112, 125), Rh (107), Sg (115). AM: STripl
(370). BEN: Ben29 34v, Ca 10v, DaB 20v, Mc127 359, Mc540 56-57, Mc.VII 2,
McV 25v, Ott 28v. Var. (post "ut saluatorem"): SAC: Va 60, GREG: Pa 57, GEL8: En
100, Ge 100, Rh 86, Sg 94, AM: Sb 195, BEN: Ben33 7v, Ve 17v.

45

♪ Dominus uobiscum. Et cum spiritu tuo. GENEALOGIA DOMINI NOSTRI IESV
CHRISTI. SECVNDVM LVCAM [3: 21-4: 1]. Factum est autem cum baptizaretur
7v-8v, 9r omnis populus. ... |... regres|sus est ab iordane. AMEN. ♪

46

YMNVM ANGELORVM ♪ Te deum laudamus.·, ♪

MISSA IN DIE EPIPHANIE.

47

♪ Ecce aduenit dominator dominus et regnum in manu eius et potestas et
imperium. PSALMVS Deus iudicium. ♪

48

ORATIO Deus qui hodierna die, unigenitum tuum, gentibus stella duce;
reuelasti. concede propitius; ut qui iam te ex fide cognouimus. usque
ad contemplandam speciem tue celsitudinis perducamur. per eundem.

49

LECTIO YSAYE PROPHETE [60: 1-6]. Hec dicit dominus. Surge illumi-
9v nare ierusalem. ... |... annuntiantes.

---

49 consurgent] surgent *Vulgata* (60: 4)

---

45 *Vide Intro. p. 49*

46 *Te*: D   *deum*: FG   *laudamus*: GFGABAG.

47 *do*minator: D   *et*[1]: DF

---

45 Lc 3: 21-4: 1. BEN: Ca 10v-11r (cum neumis musicis), DaB 20v-21v (cum n.
m.), DaK 62r-63v (cum n. m.), Ve 17v-18r, Vl5100 4v-5v (cum n. m.).

46 RL: GR (141*, 144*, 147*). BEN: Ca 11r, Ve 18r, cf. Vl5100 14v.

47 Mal 3: 1, 1 Par 29: 12, Ps 71: 1. RL: GR 57, MRM 31. AMS 18. ES: Vl4770 10r.
BEN: Ben29 34v, Ben33 7v, Ben34 32r, Ben35 4r, Ca 11r, DaB 21v, DaZ 338,
Mc127 359, Mc540 57, Mc546 23, Mc.VII 3, McV 25v, Ott 28v, PuC 376 (ps.
var.), Ve 18r.

48 RL: MRM 31. GREG: Ha 87, Pa 58. GEL8: En 101, Ge 101, Rh 87, Sg 95. AM:
Sb (113). ES: Vl4770 10r. BEN: Ben29 34v, Ben33 7v, Ca 11r, DaB 21v, DaZ 338,
Mc127 359, Mc540 57, Mc.VII 3, McO 242, McV 26r, Ott 28v, PuC 377, Ve 18r.

49 Is 60: 1-6. RL: MRM 31. LEC: Alc 14, Mu 11, WuC 19, CoP 29. ES: Vl4770 10r.
BEN: Ben29 34v-35r, Ben33 7v, Ca 11r-v, DaB 21v-22r, DaK 9v, DaZ 339-340,
Mc127 359, Mc540 57, Mc.VII 3, McV 26r, Ott 28v-29r, PuC 378, Ve 18r-v.

50

GRADVALE ♪ Omnes de saba uenient aurum et thus deferentes et laudem domino annuntiantes. VERSVS Surge illuminare ierusalem quia gloria domini super te orta est. ♪

51

10r ♪ Alleluia. VERSVS Vidimus stellam e|ius in oriente et uenimus cum muneribus adorare dominum. ♪

52

SECVNDVM MATHEVM [2: 1-12]. Cum natus esset iesus in bethleem 10v iude. ... |... in regionem suam.

53

OFFERTORIVM ♪ Reges tharsis et insule munera offerent reges arabum et saba dona adducent et adorabunt eum omnes reges terre omnes gentes seruient ei. ♪

---

52 uidimus stellam] vidimus enim stellam *Vulgata* (2: 2)   at illi dixerunt] ei *add.* (2: 5)

---

50 *Om*nes: FGAGAcdcAGFG   sa*ba*: AcdecAGcdcA   deferen*tes*: cdcA
et[2]: Ac   lau*dem*: c   annuntian*tes*: FGAGAcdcAFAGAGF   *su*per: c
te: AGAG

51 *A*lleluia: DC ... GFGEDFGAGCDFDFEFDFDEFD

53 *munera*: FGBAGAGFGF   sa*ba*: cdcAGcdcAGF

---

50 Is 60: 6, 1. RL: GR 57-58, MRM 31. AMS 18. ES: Vl4770 10r. BEN: Ben29 35r, Ben34 33r-v, Ben35 4r, Ca 11v, DaB 22r, DaZ 340, Mc127 359, Mc540 57, Mc546 23, Mc.VII 3, McV 26r, Ott 29r, PuC 379, Ve 18v.

51 Mt 2: 2. RL: GR 58, MRM 31. AMS 18. ES: Vl4770 10r. BEN: Ben29 35r, Ben34 33v, Ben35 4r, Ca 11v, DaB 22r, DaZ 340, Mc127 359, Mc540 57, Mc546 24, Mc.VII 3, McV 26r, Ott 29r, PuC 380, Ve 18v.

52 Mt 2: 1-12. RL: MRM 31-32. LEC: Mu 11, WuE 298, CoP 30. ES: Vl4770 10r-v. BEN: Ben29 35r-v, Ca 11v, DaB 22r-v, DaE 10r, DaK 9v-10r, DaZ 340-342, Mc127 359-360, Mc540 57-58, Mc.VII 3, McV 26r-v, Ott 29r-v, PuC 381, Ve 18v-19r.

53 Ps 71: 10-11. RL: GR 59, MRM 32. AMS 18. ES: Vl4770 10v. BEN: Ben29 35v, Ben34 34r-v, Ben35 5v-6r, Ca 11v-12r, DaB 22v, DaZ 342, Mc127 360-361, Mc540 58, Mc546 24, Mc.VII 3, McV 26v, Ott 29v, PuC 382, Ve 19r.

54

SECRETA Ecclesie tue quesumus. domine. dona propitius intuere. quibus iam non aurum thus et mirra defertur. sed quod idem mune-
11r ribus declaratur. |immolatur et sumitur. Dominus noster.

55

COMMVNIO ♪ Vidimus stellam eius in oriente et uenimus cum muneribus adorare dominum. ♪

56

POSTCOMMVNIO Presta quesumus omnipotens deus. ut saluatoris mundi stella duce, manifestata. mentibus nostris reueletur semper et crescat. per eundem.

DOMINICA .I. POST. EPIPHANIA.

57

♪ In excelso throno uidi sedere uirum quem adorant multitudo angelorum psallentes in unum ecce cuius imperii nomen est in eternum. PSALMVS Iubilate deo omnis terra psalmum. ♪

---

55 *stellam*: FA

57 ado*rant*: AG

---

54 RL: MRM 32. GREG: Ha 88, Pa 59. GEL8: En 105, Ge 103, Rh 89, Sg 97. AM: Sb (188, m. v.). ES: Vl4770 10v. BEN: Ben29 35v-36r, Ca 12r, DaB 22v, DaZ 342-343, Mc127 361, Mc540 58, Mc.VII 3, McV 26v, Ott 29v, PuC 383 (m. v.), Ve 19r.

55 Mt 2: 2. RL: GR 59, MRM 32. AMS 18. ES: Vl4770 11r. BEN: Ben29 36r, Ben33 8r, Ben34 35r, Ben35 6r, Ca 12r, DaB 22v, DaZ 343, Mc127 361, Mc540 58-59, Mc546 24, Mc.VII 3, McV 27r, Ott 29v, PuC 385, Ve 19r.

56 GREG (ut "alia"): Ha 97. GEL8 (ut "alia"): En 113, Ge 110, Rh 97, Sg 105. AM: Sb (192). ES: Vl4770 11r. BEN: McO 245. Var. (post "ut saluatoris"): RL: MRM 32, BEN: Ben29 36r, Ben33 8r, Ca 12r, DaB 22v, Mc127 361, Mc.VII 3, McV 27r, Ott 30r, PuC 386, Ve 19r. Var. (ante "ut saluatoris"): SAC: Va (60), GREG: Pa (57), GEL8: En (100), Ge (100), Rh (86), Sg (94), BEN: Ben33 (7v), DaZ 343, Ve (17v).

57 Ps 65: 1-2. RL: GR 64, MRM 32 (ps. var.). AMS 19a. BEN: Ben29 36v, Ben33 8r, Ben34 36r, Ben35 6r, Ca 12r, DaB 23r, Mc127 25, Mc540 59, Mc546 24 (ps. var.), McV 27v, Ott 30r, Ve (20r).

58

ORATIO Vota quesumus domine supplicantis populi, celesti pietate prosequere. ut et que agenda sunt uideant. et ad implenda que uiderint conualescant. per.

59

AD ROMANOS [12: 1-5]. Fratres. Obsecro uos per misericordiam dei. 11v ... |... alterius menbra.

60

GRADVALE ♪ Benedictus dominus deus israhel qui facis mirabilia magna solus 12r a seculo. VERSVS Suscipiant montes pacem populo tuo et colles |iustitiam. ♪

61

♪ Alleluia. Deus qui sedes super thronum tu iudicas equitatem. ♪

---

59 bene placens] placens *Vulgata* (12: 2)   et unicuique] unicuique (12: 3)

---

60 *is*rahel: dc   *qui*: FA   mira*bi*lia: GAc   so*lus*: BdcAGAGAGAcAc-BAcGF   secu*lo*: AcdecAcedcBGAGABcBcdcAGABAG   *pa*cem: decde-decdfcedecABcdBdcBGAcBcAcBcAFGdedGAGABcdfdfegfgfdfefdcde   *populo*: dfdfdedgfegfded   *tu*o: cf   *colles*: cdecdedecdfdcdededcAGAGBAGAG iu*stitiam*: GAcdcAGBGAGFGdfdfdfdcAGBAG

61 *Vide Intro. p. 59*

---

58 RL: MRM 33. GREG: Ha (86), Pa 66, Sp 1096. GEL8: En 114, Ge 113, Rh 98, Sg 106. ES: Vl4770 11r. BEN: Ben29 36v, Ben33 8r, Ca 12r, DaB 23r, Mc127 25, Mc540 59, McO 246, McV 27v, Ott 30r, Ve (21r).

59 Rm 12: 1-5. RL: MRM 33. LEC: Alc 15, Mu 12, WuC 20, CoP 31. ES: Vl4770 11r. BEN: Ben29 36v-37r, Ben33 8r, Ca 12r, DaB 23r, Mc127 25-26, Mc540 59, McV 27v, Ott 30r, Ve (20r).

60 Ps 71: 18, 3. RL: GR 64-65, MRM 32. AMS 19a. ES: Vl4770 11r-v. BEN: Ben29 37r, Ben33 8r, Ben34 36r, Ben35 6r-v, Ca 12r-v, DaB 23r-v, Mc127 26, Mc540 59, Mc546 24-25, McV 27v, Ott 30r-v, Ve (20r).

61 Ps 9: 5. RL: GR (331: m. v.), MRM (262). ES: Schlager, *Katalog* G 381. BEN: Ben33 8r, Ben34 36v, Ben35 6v, Ca 12v, DaB 23v, Mc127 26, Mc540 59-60, Mc546 25, McV 28r, Ott 30v.

62

SECVNDVM MATHEVM [Lc 2: 42-52]. In illo tempore. Cum factus esset
12v iesus annorum duodecym. ... |... gratia apud deum et homines.

63

OFFERTORIVM ♪ Iubilate deo omnis terra. Iubilate deo omnis terra. Seruite
domino in letitia intrate in conspectu eius in exultatione. quia dominus ipse est
deus. ♪

64

13r |SECRETA Concede quesumus domine. ut oculis tue maiestatis munus
oblatum et gratiam nobis deuotionis optineat. et effectum beate
perennitatis acquirat. per.

65

COMMVNIO ♪ Fili quid fecisti nobis sic ego et pater tuus dolentes querebamus
te. et quid est quod me querebatis nesciebatis quia in his que patris mei sunt
oportet me esse. ♪

---

62 hierusolymam] in Hierosolymam *Vulgata* (2: 42)   uenerunt autem iter] autem
om. (2: 44)   reuersi sunt] regressi sunt (2: 45)   audientes ... interrogantes eos]
audientem ... interrogantem (2: 46)   et etate] aetate (2: 52)

---

63 *omn*is[1]: AG   *terr*a[1]: FAcedcAcBGBGBABcGFGF   iubi*late*[2]: AcAcd-
cAGFAcAGAcAcedcAcedcdcABAGAGFAFAcAcG   *terr*a[2]: FAcedcAc-
BGBGFGF   Ser*ui*te: AcAc   *ei*us: cedcBABA   do*min*us: dcBA

65 *fe*cisti: GE   nescie*bat*is: Ac   *qui*a: A   *in*: A   o*port*et: FG

---

62 Lc 2: 42-52. RL: MRM 33. LEC: Mu 12, WuE 298, CoP 32. ES: Vl4770 11v. BEN:
Ben29 37r-v, Ben33 8r-v, Ca 12v, DaB 23v, DaE 11v, Mc127 26, Mc540 60, McV
28r, Ott 30v-31r, Ve (20r-v).

63 Ps 99: 2-3. RL: GR 66, MRM 33. AMS 19b. ES: Vl4770 11v. BEN: Ben29 37v,
Ben33 8v, Ben34 36v, Ben35 7r-v, Ca 12v, DaB 23v-24r, Mc127 26, Mc540 60,
Mc546 25, McV 28r, Ott 31r, Ve (20v).

64 RL: MRM (28, 141, 289). GREG: Ha (313, 718), Pa (53), Sp (1094). GEL8: En
(93), Ge (93), Rh (79), Sg (87). BEN: Ben29 37v, Ben33 (7r), DaB 24r, Mc127
26-27, Mc540 60, McV 28r-v, Ott 31r.

65 Lc 2: 48-49. RL: GR 66-67, MRM 34. AMS 19b. ES: Vl4770 11v. BEN: Ben29 37v,
Ben33 8v, Ben34 37r, Ben35 7v, Ca 12v, DaB 24r, Mc127 27, Mc540 60-61,
Mc546 25-26, McV 28v, Ott 31r, Ve (20v).

66

POSTCOMMVNIO Supplices te rogamus omnipotens deus. ut quos tuis reficis sacramentis. tibi etiam placitis moribus dignanter deseruire concedas. per.

OCTAVA EPIPHANIE.

67

INTROITVS Ecce aduenit.

68

Deus cuius unigenitus in substantia nostre mortalitatis apparuit. presta quesumus; ut per eum quem similem nobis foris agnouimus. intus reformari mereamur. Qui tecum.

69

LECTIO [Is 60: 1]. Surge illuminare ierusalem.

70

GRADVALE Omnes de saba. VERSVS Surge.

---

66 RL: MRM 34. GREG: Ha (149), Pa 68, Sp 1098. GEL8: En 118, Ge 118, Rh 102, Sg 110. AM: Sb (357). ES: Vl4770 11v. BEN: Ben29 37v, Ben33 8v, Ca 13r, DaB 24r, Mc127 27, Mc540 61, McV 28v, Ott 31r, Ve (21v).

67 Mal 3: 1. RL: GR 67 (vide 57), MRM 34. AMS (18). BEN: Ben29 37v, Ben33 (7v), Ben34 (32r), Ca 13r, DaB 24v (ref.), Mc127 363, Mc540 62, Mc546 158, McV 28v, Ott 32r, Ve 19r.

68 RL: MRM 34. SAC: Va (62). GREG: Ha (93), Pa (64). GEL8: En 120, Ge 121, Rh 104, Sg 112. ES: Vl4770 12r. BEN: Ben29 37v, Ca 13r, DaB 24v, Mc127 363, Mc540 62, McV 28v, Ott 32r, Ve 19r.

69 Is 60: 1. RL: MRM 34. BEN: Ben29 (34v-35r), Ben33 8v, Ca (11r-v), DaK 10r, McV (26r), Ott (28v-29r), Ve (18r-v).

70 Is 60: 6, 1. RL: GR 67 (vide 57-58), MRM 34. AMS (18). ES: Vl4770 (10r). BEN: Ben29 37v (ref.), Ben34 (33r-v), Ca 13r, DaB 24v (ref.), Mc127 (359), Mc540 62 (ref.), McV (26r), Ott (29r), Ve (18v).

71

Alleluia. VERSVS Vidimus stellam.

72

13v |MATHEVM [3: 13-17]. In illo tempore. Venit iesus a galilea in iordanem ad iohannem. ut baptizaretur ab eo. ... complacui ipsum audite.

73

OFFERTORIVM Reges tharsis.

74

SECRETA Hostias tibi domine, pro nati filii tui apparitione deferimus; suppliciter exorantes. ut sicut ipse est nostrorum munerum auctor. ipse sit misericors et susceptor. -ui tecum.

75

Vidimus stellam.

---

72 sic nos enim decet] sic enim decet nos *Vulgata* (3: 15)   iesus confestim] confestim (3: 16)   aperti sunt celi] aperti sunt ei coeli (3: 16)   descentem ... et manentem] descendentem ... uenientem (3: 16)   de celo] de caelis (3: 17) ipsum audite] *om.* (3: 17)

71 Mt 2: 2. RL: GR 67 (vide 58), MRM 34. AMS (18). ES: Vl4770 (10r). BEN: Ben29 37v (ref.), Ben34 (33v), Ca 13r, DaB 24v (ref.), Mc127 (359), Mc540 62 (ref.), McV (26r), Ott (29r), Ve (18r).

72 Mt 3: 13-17. LEC: NapL 5. BEN: Ben29 38r-v, Ca 13r, DaB 25r, DaE 13r, DaK 10r-v, Mc127 363-364, Mc540 63, McV 29r, Ott 32r-v.

73 Ps 71: 10. RL: GR 67 (vide 59), MRM 34. AMS (18). ES: Vl4770 (10v). BEN: Ben29 37v (ref.), Ben34 (34r-v), Ca 13r, DaB 24v (ref.), Mc127 (360-361), Mc540 63 (ref.), McV (26v), Ott (29v), Ve (19r).

74 RL: MRM 35 (m. v.). SAC: Va (64). GEL8: Ge (115), Rh 105, Sg 113. ES: Vl4770 12r. BEN: Ben29 38v, Ca 13r, DaB 25r, Mc127 364, Mc540 63, McV 29r, Ott 32v, Ve 19v.

75 Mt 2: 2. RL: GR 67 (vide 59), MRM 35. AMS (18). ES: Vl4770 (11r). BEN: Ben29 37v (ref.), Ben33 (8r), Ben34 (35r), Ca 13r, DaB 24v (ref.), Mc127 (361), Mc540 63 (ref.), McV (27r), Ott (29v), Ve (19r).

76

POSTCOMMVNIO Celesti domine quesumus lumine semper et ubique nos preueni. ut misterium cuius nos participes esse uoluisti. et puro cernamus intuitu. et digno percipiamus affectu. per.

DOMINICA .I. POST OCTAVAM

77

14r | ♪ Omnis terra adoret te deus et psallat tibi psalmum dicat nomini tuo altissime. PSALMVS Iubilate deo omnis terra psalmum. ♪

78

ORATIO Omnipotens sempiterne deus; qui celestia simul et terrena moderaris. supplicationes populi clementer exaudi. et pacem tuam nostris concede temporibus. per.

79

AD ROMANOS [12: 6-16]. Fratres. Habentes donationes secundum 14v gratiam ... |... consentientes.

---

77 deo *add. inter lin. manu beneventana*

79 diligentes honore invicem *om. Dubr fortasse per homeotel.* (12: 10)   id ipsum invicem sentientes *om. Dubr* (12: 16)

---

77 *ti*bi: GF   *di*cat: EGA   Ps.: AGA ... AFGAGE

---

76 RL: MRM 35. SAC: Va (67). GREG: Ha (459). GEL8: En 122, Ge 124, Rh 106, Sg 114. AM: Sb (201). ES: Vl4770 12r-v. BEN: Ben29 38v, Ca 13r, DaB 25r, Mc127 364, Mc540 63, McV 29r-v, Ott 32v, Ve 19v-20r.

77 Ps 65: 4, 65: 1-2. RL: GR 67, MRM 35. AMS 21a. ES: Vl4770 13r. BEN: Ben29 38v, Ben34 37r-v, Ben35 8r-v, Ca 13r, DaB 25r, Mc127 27, Mc540 63, Mc546 26, McV 29v, Ott 32v, Ve (20v-21r).

78 RL: MRM 35. GREG: Ha (922), Sp 1099. GEL8: En 129, Ge 134, Rh 113, Sg 121. AM: Sb 207. ES: Vl4770 13r. BEN: Ben29 38v, Ca 13v, DaB 25v, Mc127 27, Mc540 63, McO 247, McV 29v, Ott 32v, Ve (22r).

79 Rm 12: 6-16. RL: MRM 35-36. LEC: Mu 14, WuC 21, CoP 38. ES: Vl4770 13r. BEN: Ben29 38v-39r, Ca 13v, DaB 25v, Mc127 27, Mc540 63-64, McV 29v, Ott 32v-33r, Ve (21r).

80

GRADVALE ♪ Misit dominus uerbum suum et sanauit eos et eripuit eos de interitu eorum. VERSVS Confiteantur domino misericordia eius et mirabilia eius filios hominum. ♪

81

♪ Alleluia. VERSVS Omnis terra adoret te deus et psallat tibi psalmum dicat nomini tuo domine.·, ♪

82

15r SEQVENTIA SANCTI EVANGELII SECVNDVM IOHANNEM [2: 1-11]. |In illo
15v tempore. Nuptie facte sunt in chana galilee. ... |... discipuli eius.

83

OFFERTORIVM ♪ Iubilate deo uniuersa terra iubilate deo uniuersa terra psalmum dicite nomini eius. uenite et audite me et narrabo uobis omnes qui timetis deum quanta fecit dominus anime mee alleluia. ♪

---

82 uocatus est autem iesus ibi] vocatus est autem et Iesus *Vulgata* (2: 2)   quid michi et tibi] est *add.* (2: 4)   dicit eis iesus] et dicit eis Iesus (2: 8)   aqua uinum factum] aquam vinum factam (2: 9)   nesciebat] non sciebat (2: 9) auserant] haurierant (2: 9)   tu autem seruasti] tu servasti (2: 9)

---

80 sana*uit*: cAcAGF   *eos*[2]: cedcAGAcdcB   eorum: cdcBA   Confite*antur*: cAcAcAcAcdcAc   misericordi*a*: dcBdedcefecdedBcdcAc   *eius*[2]: cecA-GAcdcB   homi*num*: cAcAFGAcdecAGBAF

81 *Vide Intro. p. 60*

83 iubi*late*[2]: cAcGFDCDCDCDFGAGAFGAGAcBcdcd   *terra*[2]: FAcAGB-GAcAGABcB   *psal*mum: FG   nomini: FGAFGAGBdc   *me*: ABA] *om.* GR   *omnes*: FGAGABAGAGBdc   *do*minus: GF   anime: DFGFDGE-FAcG

---

80 Ps 106: 20-21. RL: GR 68, MRM 36. AMS 21a. ES: Vl4770 13r. BEN: Ben29 39r, Ben33 9r, Ben34 37v, Ben35 8v, Ca 13v, DaB 25v-26r, Mc127 27, Mc540 64, Mc546 26, McV 29v, Ott 33r, Ve (21r).

81 Ps 65: 4. ES: Schlager, *Katalog* E 174, Syg 35. BEN: Ben29 39r, Ben34 37v-38r, Ben35 8v-9r, Ca 13v, DaB 26r, Mc127 27-28, Mc540 64, Mc546 26-27, McV 30r, Ott 33r, Ve (21r).

82 Io 2: 1-11. RL: MRM 36. LEC: Mu 14, WuE 299, CoP 39. ES: Vl4770 13v. BEN: Ben29 39r-v, Ben33 9r, Ca 13v-14r, DaB 26r, DaE 13v, Mc127 28, Mc540 64-65, McV 30r, Ott 33r-v, Ve (21r-v).

83 Ps 65: 1-2, 5, 16. RL: GR 69-70, MRM 36. AMS 21b. ES: Vl4770 13v. BEN: Ben29 39v, Ben33 9r, Ben34 38r-39r, Ben35 9r-v, Ca 14r, DaB 26r-v, Mc127 28, Mc540 65, Mc546 27, McV 30r, Ott 33v, Ve (21v).

84

SECRETA Oblata domine, munera, sanctifica. nosque per hec a peccatorum nostrorum maculis emunda. per dominum.

85

COMMVNIO ♪ Dicit dominus implete ydrias aqua et ferte architriclino. dum
16r gustasset architriclinus aqua uinum fac|tum dicit sponso seruasti bonum uinum usque adhuc. hoc signum fecit ihesus primum coram discipulis suis. ♪

86

POSTCOMMVNIO Augeatur in nobis domine quesumus, tue uirtutis operatio. ut diuinis uegetati sacramentis. ad eorum promissa capienda. tuo munere preparemur. per.

DOMINICA .III.

87

♪ Adorate deum omnes angeli eius audiuit et letata est syon. et exultauerunt filie iude. PSALMVS Dominus regnauit exultet. ♪

---

85 archi*tri*clinus: AGA   *aqua*²: AG   *dicit*: ABGABcA   *adhuc*: BcA

87 *et*¹: cB

---

84 RL: MRM 36. GREG: Ha (50), Pa 73, Sp 1100. GEL8: En 131, Ge 136, Rh 115, Sg 123. AM: Sb 209. ES: Vl4770 13v. BEN: Ben29 39v, Ben33 9r, Ca 14r, DaB 26v, Mc127 28, Mc540 65, McV 30r, Ott 34r, Ve (22v).

85 Io 2: 7-11. RL: GR 70, MRM 36. AMS 21b. ES: Vl4770 13v. BEN: Ben29 39v, Ben33 9r, Ben34 39r, Ben35 9v, Ca 14r, DaB 26v, Mc127 28, Mc540 65, Mc546 27, McV 30r-v, Ott 34r, Ve (21v).

86 RL: MRM 36. SAC: Va (1263). GREG: Pa 74, Sp 1101. GEL8: En 133, Ge 138, Rh 117, Sg 125. AM: Sb 211. ES: Vl4770 13v-14r. BEN: Ben29 39v, Ben33 9r, Ca 14r, DaB 26v, Mc127 28-29, Mc540 65, McV 30v, Ott 34r, Ve 22v.

87 Ps 96: 7-8, 96: 1. RL: GR 70-71, MRM 37. AMS 26. ES: Vl4770 17r. BEN: Ben29 39v, Ben33 10r, Ben34 39r, Ben35 9v-10r, Ca 14r, DaB 26v, Mc127 29, Mc540 65, Mc546 28, McV 30v, Ott 34r, Ve (22r).

88

ORATIO Omnipotens sempiterne deus, infirmitatem nostram propitius respice. atque ad protegendum nos. dexteram tue maiestatis extende. per dominum.

89

16v AD ROMANOS [12: 16-21]. Fratres. Nolite esse prudentes. ... |... sed uince in bono malum.

90

GRADVALE ♪ Timebunt gentes nomen tuum domine et omnes reges terre gloriam tuam. VERSVS Quoniam edificauit dominus syon et uidebitur in maiestate sua. ♪

91

17r ♪ Alleluia. VERSVS |Timebunt gentes nomen tuum domine et omnes reges terre gloriam tuam. ♪

---

89 sed prouidentes] providentes *Vulgata* (12: 17)   et si esurierit] sed si esurierit (12: 20)   si hoc enim faciens] si *om.* (12: 20)

---

90 *tuum*: AGAcAGAG   *om*nes: AGA   *reges*: Ac   *terre*: BdcBA   *uide*-*bitur*: cBcAcAGAcAcBAcGAGF

91 *Vide Intro. p. 61*

---

88 RL: MRM 37. GREG: Pa 94, Sp 1102. GEL8: En 171, Ge 176, Rh 134, Sg 155. ES: Vl4770 17r. BEN: Ben29 39v, Ben33 10r, Ca 14r, DaB 26v, Mc127 29, Mc540 66, McO 248, McV 30v, Ott 34r, Ve (22v).

89 Rm 12: 16-21. RL: MRM 37. LEC: Mu 15, WuC 22, CoP 45. ES: Vl4770 17r. BEN: Ben29 39v-40r, Ben33 10r, Ca 14r, DaB 26v-27r, Mc127 29, Mc540 66, McV 30v, Ott 34r-v, Ve (22r).

90 Ps 101: 16-17. RL: GR 71-72, MRM 37. AMS 26. ES: Vl4770 17r. BEN: Ben29 40r, Ben33 10r, Ben34 39r-v, Ben35 10r, Ca 14r-v, DaB 27r, Mc540 66, Mc546 28, McV 30v, Ott 34v, Ve (22r).

91 Ps 101: 16. RL: GR (373-374: m. v.), MRM (290). ES: Schlager, *Katalog* E (D) 194, Vl4770 (13v). BEN: Ben29 40r, Ben33 10r, Ben34 39v, Ben35 10r, Ca 14v, DaB 27r, Mc127 29, Mc540 66, Mc546 28, McV 30v, Ott 34v, Ve (22r). Var. (melodia): ES: Syg (249), LS: Gs (167).

92

SEQVENTIA SANCTI EVANGELII SECVNDVM LVCAM [4: 14-22]. In illo
17v tempore. Regressus iesus in uirtute spiritus in galileam. ... |... de ore
ipsius.

93

OFFERTORIVM ♪ Dexterra domini fecit uirtutem dexterra domini exaltauit me
non moriar sed uiuam. et narrabo opera domini. ♪

94

SECRETA Hec hostia domine quesumus. mundet nostra delicta. et
sacrificium celebrandum. subditorum tibi corpora, mentesque sanctificet. per.

95

COMMVNIO ♪ Mirabantur omnes de his que procedebant de ore dei. ♪

---

92 de illo per uniuersam regionem] per universam regionem de illo *Vulgata* (4: 14)
ysaye prophete] prophetae Esaiae (4: 17)   misit me sanare contritos corde]
misit me (4: 18)

---

93 A' *inc.*] E *inc.* GR *(F-clavis]* c-*clavis trans.* GR *passim*)   *ui*uam: DFC
ope*ra*: DEGFGFE   domi*ni*: DFEDED

95 *Vide Intro. p. 63*

---

92 **Lc 4: 14-22.** LEC: WuE (299). BEN: Ben29 40r-v, Ben33 10r-v, DaB 27r-v,
Mc127 29-30, Mc540 66-67, McV 30v-31r, Ott 34v-35r.

93 **Ps 117: 16-17.** RL: GR 72, MRM 38. AMS 26. ES: Vl4770 17v. BEN: Ben29 40v,
Ben33 10v, Ben34 39v-40r, Ben35 10r-v, Ca 14v, DaB 27v, Mc127 30, Mc540 67,
Mc546 28, McV 31r, Ott 35r, Ve (22v).

94 RL: MRM 38 (m. v.). GREG: Ha (24), Pa 95, Sp 1103. GEL8: En 173, Ge 178,
Rh 136, Sg 157. AM: Sb (399, 1455). ES: Vl4770 17v. BEN: Ben29 40v (m. v.),
Ben33 10v, Ca (18v), DaB 27v, Mc127 30, Mc540 67, McV 31r, Ott 35v, Ve (23r).

95 **Lc 4: 22.** RL: MRM 38. AMS 26. ES: Vl4770 17v. BEN: Ben29 40v, Ben33 10v,
Ben34 40r, Ben35 10v, Ca 14v, DaB 27v, Mc127 30, Mc540 67, Mc546 28-29,
McV 31r, Ott 35r, Ve (22v). Var. (melodia): RL: GR 73, ES: Syg 43, LS: Gs 24.

96

POSTCOMMVNIO Quos tantis domine, largiris uti misteriis. quesumus. ut effectibus nos eorum ueraciter aptare digneris. per.

DOMINICA IN SEPTVAGESSIMA.

97

18r ♪ Circumdederunt me gemitus mortis dolores |inferni circumdederunt me. et in tribulatione mea. inuocaui dominum et exaudiuit de templo sancto suo uocem meam. PSALMVS Diligam te domine. ♪

98

ORATIO Preces populi tui quesumus domine; clementer exaudi. ut qui iuste pro peccatis nostris affligimur. pro tui nominis gloria. misericorditer liberemur. per.

99

AD CORINTHIOS [1 Cor 9: 24-10: 4]. Fratres. Nescitis quod hi qui in
18v stadio ... |... christus.

---

99 omnis enim] omnis autem *Vulgata* (9: 25)   aherem] aerem (9: 26)

97 *circ*umdederunt[2]: cB   *templo*: AB   Ps.: FAcdBcAGAF

---

96 RL: MRM 38. SAC: Va (1266). GREG: Pa 96, Sp 1104. GEL8: En 175, Ge 180, Rh 138, Sg 159. ES: Vl4770 17v. BEN: Ben29 40v, Ben33 10v, Ca 14v, DaB 27v, Mc127 30, Mc540 67, McV 31r, Ott 35r, Ve (23r).

97 Ps 17: 5-7, 17: 2. RL: GR 73-74, MRM 40. AMS 34. ES: Vl4770 19v-20r. BEN: Ben29 55v, Ben30 18v, Ben33 18r, Ben34 56r, Ben35 24v, Ca 15v, DaB 40v, Mc127 34, Mc540 87, Mc546 40, McV 40v-41r, Ott 50v-51r, Ve 35v.

98 RL: MRM 41. SAC: Va (1173: var.). GREG: Ha 144, Pa 118. GEL8: En (255), Ge (252), Rh (180), Sg (233). AM: Sb 265. ES: Vl4770 20r. BEN: Ben29 55v, Ben30 18v, Ca 15v, DaB 40v-41r, Mc127 34, Mc540 87-88, McV 41r, Ott 51r, Ve 35v.

99 1 Cor 9: 24-10: 4. RL: MRM 41. LEC: Alc 29, Mu 19, WuC 34, CoP 63. ES: Vl4770 20r. BEN: Ben29 55v-56r, Ben30 18v-19r, Ben33 18r, Ca 15v, DaB 41r, DaK 12r-v, Mc127 34-35, Mc540 88, McV 41r, Ott 51r, Ve 35v-36r.

100

GRADVALE ♪ Adiutor in oportunitatibus in tribulatione sperent in te qui nouerunt te. VERSVS Quoniam non derelinquis querentes te domine. Quoniam non in finem obliuio erit pauperum patientia pauperum non peribit in eternum exurge domine non preualeat homo. ♪

101

TRACTVS ♪ De profundis clamaui ad te domine domine exaudi uocem meam. Fiant aures ♪ [*lac.*]

102

19r [*lac.*] | [Mt 20: 16] -uissimi primi. et primi <nouissimi. m>ulti enim sunt uocati <pauci uero electi.>

103

♪ Bonum est confi<teri domino.> et spall- ♪ [*lac.*]

---

100 domine. Quoniam non] erit pauperum patientiam pauperum non *ante corr. per rasuram*

102 *lac. inter 18v-19r*   *19r: frag. 6 ll.*

---

100 *Adiutor*: GBcGAcAGAcBABcB   *in*[1]: B   *in*[2]: G   tri*bulatio*ne: GE-GABcBAGAcAFGcABG   *qui*[1]: E   no*uerunt*: EFA   *non*[1]: BcAGAcG-cABGAFE   *derelin*quis: EDFA   *do*mine[1]: EFGAcGAFGBABAGAEFE-FEFGFGcAGAGE   *non*[2]: BcdBcBcAcBcABAGBcefdBdecAcBcAGBGBcGA-cAGFD   *pau*perum[1]: FG   *non*[3]: B   *per*ibit: B   *ex*urge: A   *non*[4]: B
101 domi*ne*[1]: GFBAGAGAGAcABGF   *domi*ne[2]: FGFG   *uo*cem: FGBABA   *me*am: BcGcAGABGFAcABG

103 *Bonum est con*fiteri: GBAFG

---

100 Ps 9: 10-11, 19-20. RL: GR 74-75, MRM 41. AMS 34. ES: Vl4770 20r. BEN: Ben29 56r, Ben30 19r-v, Ben33 18r, Ben34 56r-v, Ben35 24v-25r, Ca 15v-16r, DaB 41r, Mc127 35, Mc540 88, Mc546 40-41, Mc.VI 12, McV 41r, Ott 51r-v, Ve 36r.

101 Ps 129: 1-2. RL: GR 75-76, MRM 41. AMS 34. ES: Vl4770 20r. BEN: Ben29 56r, Ben30 19v, Ben33 18r, Ben34 56v-57r, Ben35 25r-v, Ben38 1r, Ca 16r, DaB 41r-v, Mc127 35, Mc540 88, Mc546 41-42, Mc.VI 12, McV 41r-v, Ott 51v, PuV 1, Ve 36r.

102 Mt 20: 16. RL: MRM 41-42 (Mt 20: 1-16 *Simile est regnum caelorum homini*). LEC: Mu 19, WuE 302, CoP 64. ES: Vl4770 20r-v. BEN: Ben29 56r-57r, Ben30 19v-20v, Ben33 18v, Ca 16r, DaB 41v-42r, DaE 24r, DaK 12v-13r, Mc127 35-36, Mc.VI 12, McV 41v-42r, Ott 51v-52r, Ve 36r-v.

103 Ps 91: 2. RL: GR 76, MRM 42. AMS 34. ES: Vl4770 20v. BEN: Ben29 57r, Ben30 20v, Ben33 18v, Ben34 57r-v, Ben35 25v, Ben38 1r-v, Ca 16r, DaB 42r, Mc127 36, Mc546 42, Mc.VI 12, McV 42r, Ott 52r, PuV 1, Ve 36v.

104

Muner<ibus nostris quesumus domine precibusque> susc<eptis et celestibus nos munda> mi- [*lac.*]

<DOMINICA IN SEXVAGESIMA>

105

19v [*lac.*] | ♪ -bliuisceris tribulationem <nostram? adhesit in terra uen>ter noster. ex<urge domine adiuua nos et libera nos.> PSALMVS Deus <aurib>us nostris. ♪

106

[*lac.*] omnia [*lac.*]

107

20r [*lac.*] | [Lc 8: 8-15] Et aliud cecidit in terram bonam. ... hi sunt. qui
20v audiu-[*lac.*] | in bonam terram. ... in patientia.

---

105 *19v: frag. 6 ll.*

107 *lac. inter 19v-20r*   *20r: frag.*   Quod autem] Qui autem *Vulgata* (8: 12)
lac. Dubr. (8: 12-15)   *20v: frag.*

---

105 obliui*sce*ris: A   tri*bu*lationem: F

---

104 RL: MRM 42. SAC: Le (1124), Va (762). GREG: Ha 145, Pa 119. GEL8: En (71), Ge (69, 84), Rh (64), Sg (69). AM: Sb (183). ES: Vl4770 20v. BEN: Ben29 57r, Ben30 20v, Ben33 18v, Ca 16v, DaB 42r, Mc127 36, Mc.vi 12, McV 42r, Ott 52r, Ve 36v.

105 Ps 43: 24-26, 43: 2. RL: GR 77 (Ps 43: 23-26, 43: 2 *Exurge quare obdormis*), MRM 42. AMS 35. ES: Vl4770 24r. BEN: Ben29 57r, Ben30 21r, Ben34 57v-58r, Ben35 25v-26r, Ben38 1v, Ca 16v, DaB 42r, Mc127 36, Mc546 42, Mc.vi 13, McV 42r, Ott 52v, PuV 2, Ve 36v-37r.

106 RL: MRM 42 ("Deus qui conspicis quia ex nulla nostra actione confidimus concede propitius ut contra aduersa *omnia*"). GREG: Ha 147, Pa 121. GEL8: En 256, Ge 253, Rh 181, Sg 234. AM: Sb (2). BEN: Ben29 57r, Ben30 21r, Ca 16v, DaB 42r, Mc127 36, Mc.vi 13, McO 276, McV 42r, Ott 52v, Ve 37r.

107 Lc 8: 8-15. RL: MRM 44 (Lc 8: 4-15 *Cum autem turba plurima*). LEC: Mu 20, WuE 302, CoP 69. ES: Vl4770 25r-v. BEN: Ben29 58v-59r, Ben30 23r-24r, Ca 17r-v, DaB 43v, DaE 26r, DaK 14r-v, Mc127 38-39, Mc540 89, Mc.vi 13, McV 43r-v, Ott 53v-54r, Ve 38r.

108

OFFERTORIVM ♪ Perfice gressus meos in semitis tuis ut non moueantur uestigia
mea inclina aurem tuam et exaudi uerba <mea. mirifica> misericordias tuas qui
sal- ♪ [*lac.*]

<DOMINICA IN QVINQVAGESIMA>

109

21r | ♪ Esto michi in deum protectorem et in locum refugii ut saluum me facias.
quoniam firmamentum meum et refugium meum es tu et propter nomen tuum
dux michi eris et enutries me. PSALMVS In te domine ♪ [*lac.*]

110

Preces populi tui quesumus domine; cle<menter> exaudi. atque a
pe<ccatorum uinculis> absol-[*lac.*]

111

21v [*lac.*] |[1 Cor 13: 3-8] omnes. facultates meas. et si tradidero ...
lingue cessabunt. <siue scientia destruetur. ex parte> enim [*lac.*]

---

109 *21r: frag. 8 ll.*

111 *21v: frag. 13 ll.*

---

108 Perfi*ce*: E   mouean*tur*: DEF   *uesti*gia: CEFD   *in*clina: E   tu*am*:
E   exau*di*: EG   miri*fica*: E   *mise*ricordias: EGE   *qui*: E

109 E*sto*: DEF   *in*¹: F   *lo*cum: GF   *sal*uum: EG   *fir*mamentum: AB
*et*³: D

---

108 Ps 16: 5-7. RL: GR 79-80, MRM 44. AMS 35. ES: Vl4770 25v. BEN: Ben29 59r,
Ben30 24r, Ben33 (131v), Ben34 58v, Ben35 26v, Ben38 2r-v, Ca 17v, DaB
43v-44r, Mc127 39, Mc540 89, Mc546 43-44, Mc.VI 13, McV 43v, Ott 24r, PuV
3, Ve 38r.

109 Ps 30: 3-4, 30: 2. RL: GR 80-81, MRM 45. AMS 36a. ES: Vl4770 25v. BEN: Ben29
59r, Ben30 24v, Ben34 59r-v, Ben35 27r, Ben38 2v-3r, Ca 18r, DaB 44r, Mc127
40, Mc540 89, Mc546 44, Mc.VI 14, McV 43v, Ott 54v, PuV 4, Ve 39r.

110 RL: MRM 45. GREG: Ha 150, Pa 124. GEL8: En 263, Ge 259, Rh 187, Sg 240.
ES: Vl4770 25v. BEN: Ben29 59r, Ben30 24v, Ca 18r, DaB 44r, Mc127 40, Mc540
89, Mc.VI 14, McO 277, McV 43v, Ott 54v, Ve 39r.

111 1 Cor 13: 3-8. RL: MRM 45 (1 Cor 13: 1-8 *Si linguis hominum loquar*). LEC:
Alc 31, Mu 22, WuC 36, CoP 73. ES: Vl4770 25v-26r. BEN: Ben29 59r-v, Ben30
24v-25v, DaB 44r-v, DaK 14v-15v, Ca 18r, Mc127 40-41, Mc540 89-90, Mc.VI 14,
McV 42v-43r, Ott 54v-55r, PuZ I.Ep, Ve 39r-v.

\<FERIA .IV. CINERVM IN CAPITE IEIVNII\>

112

21ᵃr   [*lac.*] |-sor- (?) [*lac.*]

113

Deus qu\<i non mortem sed penitentiam de\>sideras \<peccatorum. fragilitatem\> condic-[*lac.*]

114

21ᵃv   [*lac.*] |que \<iuste postulauerun\>t. ef\<ficaciter tribuas. et concessa\> perpetua \<stabilitate. et manere intac\>ta de-[*lac.*]

115

22r |ANTIPHONA ♪ Immutemur habitu in cin\<ere et cilicio\> ieiunemus et ploremus an\<te dominum\> quia multum misericor\<s est dimittere\> peccata nostra deus \<noster.\> ♪

---

112 *lac. inter 21v-21ᵃr*   *21ᵃr: frag. 4 ll.*

114 *21ᵃv: frag. 4 ll.*

115 *22r: frag.*

---

115 ha*bitu*: AGBGA   ie*iunemus*: ABcBAGA   *et*: AGAG   mi*sericors*: FGFE   *no*stra: GABAG   *deus*: FGAFGFE

---

112 ES: Franz 1: 465. BEN: Ben29 45v ("Exorcizo te cinis ... *sordibus emundes.* Per"), Mc127 42, Mc540 92, Mc.VII² 5v-6r, McV 45r, Ott 56r-v.

113 RL: MRM 47. BEN: Ben30 28r, Ca 19v, DaB 45v, Mc127 42, Mc540 92, Mc.VI 15, Mc.VII² 6r, McP 99: 75, McV 45r, Ott 56v, Ve 40v.

114 RL: MRM 47 (*Deus qui humiliatione*). BEN: Ben30 28v-29r, DaB 45v-46r, Mc.VII² 6r, Mc127 43, Mc540 92, McP 99: 76. McV 45r-v, Ott 57r.

115 **Ioel 2: 13**. RL: GR 85, MRM 48. AMS 37a. BEN: Ben30 28v, Ben34 61v-62r, Ben35 28r-v, Ben38 4v, Ca 19v, DaB 46r, Mc127 43, Mc540 92, Mc.VI 15, Mc.VII² 6r, McV 45r, Ott 57r, Ve 40v.

\<MISSA. FERIA .IV.\>

116

♪ Misereris omnium domine et \<nichil odisti\> eorum que fecisti dissimul\<ans peccata\> hominum propter peniten\<tiam et par\>ce nobis quia tu \<es dominus\> deus noster. PSALMVS Mis- ♪ [*lac.*]

117

Concede nobis domine presidi\<a militie\> christiane; sanctis inchoare \<ieiuniis. ut\> contra spirituales nequitias \<pugnaturi\> continentie muniamur \<auxiliis.\> per dominum.

118

22v   LECTIO IOHELIS PROPHETE [2: 12-19]. [*lac.*] |conuertimini ad me ...
23r   [*cum lacunis*] ... dixit populo |suo. ecce ego mittam. ... in gentibus. Ait dominus omnipotens.

---

118 *22v: frag.*   et fletu] et in fletu *Vulgata* (2: 12)   ignoscat deus] ignoscat (2: 14)   parce populo] populo (2: 17)   frumentum uinum] frumentum et vinum (2: 19)   replebimini eis] replebimini eo (2: 19)

---

116 *do*mine: AGA   *fe*cisti: FGEF   pe*ni*tentiam: dcB   *deus*: FAGAFE-DEFAFGFE   *no*ster: DEFEF

---

116 Sap 11: 24-25, 27, Ps 56: 2. RL: GR 87, MRM 48. AMS 37a. ES: Vl4770 26v. BEN: Ben29 60v, Ben30 29r, Ben33 19r, Ben34 62r, Ben35 28v, Ben38 4v, Ca 19v, DaB 46r, Mc127 43, Mc540 92-93, Mc546 47, Mc.VI 15, McV 45v, Ott 57r-v, PuV 6, Ve 41v.

117 RL: MRM (48 *Benedictio cinerum*). SAC: Le (207), Va (631, 654). GREG: Ha (153), Pa (127). GEL8: En (276), Ge (274), Rh (193), Sg (251). AM: Sb (271). ES: Vl4770 (26v). BEN: Ben29 60v, Ben30 (27r-v), Ben33 19r, Ca (19v), DaB 46r, Mc127 43, Mc540 93, Mc.VI (15), McV 45v, Ott 57v, Ve (41v).

118 Ioel 2: 12-19. RL: MRM 49. LEC: Alc 32, Mu 23, WuC 37. ES: Vl4770 26v-27r. BEN: Ben29 60v-61r, Ben30 29r-30r, Ben33 19r-v, Ca 20r, DaB 46r-v, Mc127 43-44, Mc540 93, Mc.VI 15, McV 45v-46r, Ott 57v-58r, Ve 41v.

119

GRADVALE ♪ Miserere mei deus miserere mei quoniam in te confidit anima mea. VERSVS Misit de celo et liberauit me dedit in opprobium conculcantes me. ♪

120

Per totam XLa. ♪ Domine non secundum peccata nostra facias nobis neque 23v secundum iniquitates no|stras retribue nobis. ALIA Domine ne memineris iniquitatum nostrarum antiquarum cito nos anticipet misericordia tua quia pauperes facti sumus nimis. ALIA Adiuua nos deus salutaris noster. et propter gloriam nominis tui domine libera nos. et propitius esto peccatis nostri propter nomen tuum. ♪

121

MATHEVM [6: 16-21]. In illo tempore. Dixit iesus discipulis suis. Cum 24r ieiunatis, nolite fieri. sicut ypochrite tristes. ... |... cor tuum.

---

121 exterminant] demoliuntur *Vulgata* (6: 16)   et ubi fures] ubi fures (6: 19) thesaurizate uobis] thesaurizate autem vobis (6: 20)   ubi est enim] ubi enim est (6: 21)

---

119 de*us*: FDFGFDFGFDCEDEDC   confi*dit*: DFDFGFDED   *celo*: AFA-BAGAFGAcBcAcAGcAcGcdcAFGAcBc   op*pro*brium: AFGAcBcAcAGAB-FEGAFDFEGAGAFDFGFABGFEGAGA   concul*cant*es: GAGAGAFABG-FEFGABA

120 Domi*ne*: CDCDEDCDCDEDCDFEFED   *secundum*[1]: CDCDCB'   *re-tri*bue: FGEFE   anti*quarum*: DFEDE   paupe*res*: E   *facti su*mus: E *ni*mis: DC   tu*i*: D   li*bera*: DFEDED   *tuum*: GFGFDEFAGAFDEFD

---

119 Ps 56: 2, 4. RL: GR 88, MRM 49. AMS 37b. ES: Vl4770 27r. BEN: Ben29 61r, Ben30 30r, Ben33 19v, Ben34 62r-v, Ben35 28v, Ben38 4v-5r, Ca 20r, DaB 46v, Mc127 44, Mc540 93, Mc546 47, Mc.VI 15, McV 46r, Ott 58r, PuV 6-7, Ve 42r.

120 Ps 102: 10, 78: 8-9. RL: GR 89-90, MRM 49. BEN: Ben29 61r (add. alia manu in marg.), Ca 20r, DaB 46v, Mc127 52*bis* (manu recent.), Mc546 160 (manu recent.), McV 46r (manu recent.), Ve 42r.

121 Mt 6: 16-21. RL: MRM 49-50. LEC: Mu 23, WuE 302. ES: Vl4770 27r. BEN: Ben29 61r-v, Ben30 30r-v, Ben33 19v, Ca 20r-v, DaB 46v, Mc127 44, Mc540 93-94, Mc.VI 15, McV 46r, Ott 58r, Ve 42r.

122

OFFERTORIVM ♪ Exaltabo te domine quoniam suscepisti me nec delectasti inimicos meos super me domine clamaui ad te et sanasti me. ♪

123

SECRETA Fac nos quesumus domine his muneribus offerendis; conuenienter aptari. quibus ipsius uenerabilis sacramentis, celebramus exordium. per dominum.

124

24v |COMMVNIO ♪ Qui meditabitur in lege domini die ac nocte dabit fructum suum. in tempore suo. ♪

125

POSTCOMMVNIO Percepta nobis domine prebeant sacramenta subsidium. ut et tibi grata sint nostra ieiunia. et nobis proficiant ad medellam. per.

---

122 A′ *inc.*] E *inc.* GR (F-*clavis*] c-*clavis trans.* GR *passim*)   domi*ne*[1]: DED quoni*am*: DFGFEFEDED   su*per*: FDGFGFCDEFEDEDCFEFEDEF-DEDC   domi*ne*[2]: DCDCA′   *cla*maui: DA′   sa*nas*ti: FDCDF-DCDECFDF

124 medi*tabitur*: ABcB   *in*: B   le*ge*: cA   di*e*: AF   da*bit*: AG   fruc-*tum*: GAG   *suum*: EFGFEFEDEFEF   tempo*re*: GDFGA

---

122 Ps 29: 2-3. RL: GR 90, MRM 50. AMS 37b. ES: Vl4770 27r. BEN: Ben29 61v, Ben30 30v, Ben33 19v, Ben34 62v-63r, Ben35 28v-29r, Ben38 5r, Ca 20v, DaB 46v, Mc127 44, Mc540 94, Mc546 47, Mc.VI 15, McV 46r, Ott 58r-v, PuV 7, Ve 42r-v.

123 RL: MRM 50. SAC: Va 91. GREG: Ha 155, Pa 129. GEL8: En 278, Ge 276, Rh 195, Sg 253. ES: Vl4770 27v. BEN: Ben29 61v, Ben30 30v, Ben33 19v-20r, Ca 20v, DaB 47r, Mc127 44, Mc540 94, Mc.VI 15, McV 46r, Ott 58v, Ve 42v.

124 Ps 1: 2-3. RL: GR 90-91, MRM 50. AMS 37b. ES: Vl4770 27v. BEN: Ben29 61v, Ben30 30v, Ben33 20r, Ben34 63r, Ben35 29r, Ben38 5r-v, Ca 20v, DaB 47r, Mc127 45, Mc540 94, Mc546 47-48, Mc.VI 15, McV 46r, Ott 58v, PuV 7, Ve 42v.

125 RL: MRM 50. SAC: Va (252). GREG: Ha 156, Pa 130. GEL8: En 280, Ge 278, Rh 197, Sg 255. ES: Vl4770 27v. BEN: Ben29 61v, Ben30 31r, Ben33 20r, Ca 20v, DaB 47r, Mc127 45, Mc540 94, Mc.VI 15, McV 46r, Ott 58v, Ve 42v.

126

SVPER POPVLVM. ORATIO Inclinantes se domine maiestati tue. propitius intende. ut qui diuino munere sunt refecti. celestibus semper nutriantur auxiliis. per.

DOMINICA CAPVT .XL.

127

♪ Inuocauit me et ego exaudiam eum eripiam eum et glorificabo eum longitudine dierum adimplebo eum. PSALMVS Qui habitat. ♪

128

Deus qui ecclesiam tuam, annua quadragessimali obseruatione purificas. presta familie tue. ut quod a te obtinere abstinendo nititur; hoc
25r bonis operibus |exequatur. per.

129

AD CORINTHIOS [2 Cor 6: 1-10]. Fratres. Hortamur uos ne in uacuum
25v gratiam dei recipiatis. ... |... omnia possidentes.

---

129 adiuui te] adiuvavi te *Vulgata* (6: 2)

---

127 Inuoca*uit*: A   e*go*: B   e*x*audiam: B   ad*im*plebo: B

---

126 RL: MRM 50. SAC: Le (485). GREG: Ha 157, Pa 131. GEL8: En (285), Ge (283), Rh (202), Sg (260). ES: Vl4770 27v. BEN: Ben29 61v, Ben30 31r, Ben33 20r, Ca 20v, DaB 47r, Mc127 45, Mc540 94, Mc.VI 15, McV 46r-v, Ott 31r, Ve 42v.

127 Ps 90: 15-16, 90: 1. RL: GR 93-94, MRM 55. AMS 40a. ES: Vl4770 30r. BEN: Ben29 65v, Ben30 31r, Ben33 22r, Ben34 64v-65r, Ben35 30r, Ben38 6v, Ca 22v, DaB 49v, Mc127 50, Mc540 99, Mc546 50, McV 49r, Ott 62r-v, PuV 10, PuZ III.a.

128 RL: MRM 56. GREG: Ha 166, Pa 136. GEL8: En 297, Ge 296, Rh 213, Sg 271. ES: Vl4770 30r. BEN: Ben29 65v, Ben30 31r, Ben33 22v, Ca 22v, DaB 49v, Mc127 50, Mc540 99, McO 278, McV 49r, Ott 62v, PuZ III.1.

129 2 Cor 6: 1-10. RL: MRM 56. LEC: Alc 34, Mu 27, WuC 39, CoP 81. ES: Vl4770 30r. BEN: Ben29 65v-66r, Ben30 31v-32r, Ben33 22v, Ca 22v, DaB 49v-50r, DaK 16r-v, Mc127 50-51, Mc540 99-100, McV 49r-v, Ott 62v.

130

GRADVALE ♪ Angelis suis mandauit de te ut custodiant te in omnibus uiis tuis.
VERSVS In manibus portabunt te ne unquam offendas ad lapidem pedem tuum. ♪

131

TRACTVS ♪ Qui habitat in adiutorio altissimi in protectione dei celi commorabi-
tur. Dicet domino susceptor meus es et refugium meum deus meus sperabo in
26r eum. |Quoniam ipse liberauit me de laqueo uenantium et a uerbo aspero.
Scapulis suis obumbrabit tibi et suppennis eius sperabis. Scuto circumdabit me
ueritas eius non timebis a timore nocturno. ♪

132

SECVNDVM MATHEVM [4: 1-11]. In illo tempore. Ductus est iesus in
26v desertum ab spiritu. ut temptaretur a diabolo. ... |... ministrabant ei.

133

OFFERTORIVM ♪ Scapulis suis obumbrabit tibi dominus et suppennis eius
sperabis. scuto circumdabit te ueritas eius. ♪

---

132 solo pane uiuit] pane solo vivet *Vulgata* (4: 4)   mandauit] mandabit (4: 6)
hec omnia tibi] haec tibi omnia (4: 9)   procidens] cadens (4: 9)   *Cum
signis ad legendum (vide Intro. p. 35)*: l, ✚

---

130 *su*is: cAcAGBGAB   tu*is*:   dcdedcecefdcAGABcdcdededecABcA
por*ta*bunt: edcBcAGBGAcdedecefdcAGAcAGAdfefede   of*fen*das: ecedcA-
cAcdedcedcdA

131 *celi*: CFD   commo*rabi*tur: GDGFGFD   re*fu*gium: DFEFEFAGFEDE
*spera*bo: FEFGED   *ip*se: DFGAFEGFEDEFEF   as*pe*ro: DC   *Scapu*-
lis: F   *spe*rabis: DFE   *non*: DE

133 suppen*nis*: B   e*ius*: cBABAGAG   *spera*bis: BABcAcdcd   u*eritas*:
GBAGAcdc

---

130 Ps 90: 11-12. RL: GR 94, MRM 56. AMS 40a. BEN: Ben29 66r, Ben30 32r, Ben34
65r, Ben35 30r, Ben38 6v-7r, Ca 22v-23r, DaB 50r, Mc127 51, Mc540 100,
Mc546 50, McV 49v, PuV 10.

131 Ps 90: 1-5. RL: GR 95-98 (Ps 90: 1-7, 11-16), MRM 56. AMS 40a. ES: Vl4770
30r-v. BEN: Ben29 66r, Ben30 32r-v, Ben33 22v-23r, Ben34 65r-66v, Ben35
30r-31r, Ben38 7r-v, Ca 23r, DaB 50r-v, Mc127 51, Mc540 100-101, Mc546
50-52, McV 49v-50r, Ott 63r-v, PuV 10-12.

132 Mt 4: 1-11. RL: MRM 56-57. LEC: Mu 27, WuE 302, CoP 82. ES: Vl4770 30v.
BEN: Ben29 66v, Ben30 32v-33r, Ben33 23r, Ca 23r-v, DaB 50v, DaE 29r, DaK
16v, Mc127 51-52, Mc540 101-102, McV 50r, Ott 63v-64r.

133 Ps 90: 4-5. RL: GR 98-99, MRM 57. AMS 40b. ES: Vl4770 30v. BEN: Ben29 66v,
Ben30 33r, Ben33 23r, Ben34 66v-67r, Ben35 31r, Ben38 8r, Ca 23v, DaB 50v,
Mc127 52, Mc540 102, Mc546 52, McV 50v, Ott 64r, PuV 12-13.

134

27r SECRETA Sacrificium domine quadragessimalis in|itiis, solempniter immolamus te domine deprecantes. ut cum epulamur restrictione carnalium. a noxiis quoque uoluptatibus temperemur. per.

135

COMMVNIO ♪ Scapulis suis obumbrabit tibi et suppennis eius sperabis scuto circumdabit te ueritas eius. ♪

136

POSTCOMMVNIO Tui nos domine sacramenti libatio sancta restauret. et a uetustate purgatos. in misteriis salutaris faciat transire consortium. per.

DOMINICA .II.

137

♪ Dirige me domine in ueritate tua et doce me quia tu es deus salutaris meus et te sustinui tota die. PSALMVS Ad te domine leuaui. ♪

---

135 *Scapulis suis*: GAcBcBABA   *ob*umbrabit: G   sup*pen*nis: Bc   *circum-dabit*: FGAGAFAGFEFGFG

137 *Vide Intro. p. 66*

---

134 RL: MRM 57. SAC: Va 106. GREG: Ha 167, Pa 137. GEL8: En 300, Ge 297, Rh 215, Sg 273. ES: Vl4770 30v-31r. BEN: Ben29 66v-67r, Ben30 33v, Ben33 23r, Ca 23v, DaB 50v, Mc127 52, Mc540 102, McV 50v, Ott 64r.

135 Ps 90: 4-5. RL: GR 99, MRM 57. AMS 40b. ES: Vl4770 31r. BEN: Ben29 67r, Ben30 33v, Ben33 23v, Ben34 67r, Ben35 31r-v, Ben38 8r, Ca 23v, DaB 50v, Mc127 52, Mc540 102, Mc546 52, McV 50v, Ott 64r, PuV 13.

136 RL: MRM 57. GREG: Ha 168, Pa 139. GEL8: En 303, Ge 299, Rh 217, Sg 275. ES: Vl4770 31r. BEN: Ben29 67r, Ben30 33v, Ben33 23v, Ca 23v, DaB 50v-51r, Mc127 52, Mc540 102, McV 50v, Ott 64r.

137 Ps 24: 5, 24: 1. BEN: Ben29 73v, Ben30 33v, Ben33 29v, Ben34 74v-75r, Ben35 36r, Ben38 14v, Ca 29v, DaB 59v, Mc127 67, Mc540 118, Mc546 60, McV 58r, Ott 75r-v, Ve 47r-v. Vide Hesbert, "Tradition bénéventaine," pp. 220-221 (Table).

138

ORATIO Deus qui conspicis omni nos uirtute destitui. interius exterius-
27v que custodi. ut et ab omnibus aduersitatibus muni|amur in corpore.
et a prauis cogitationibus mundemur in mente. per.

139

AD THESALONICENSES [1 Thess 4: 1-7]. Fratres. Rogamus uos et
obsecramus in domino iesu. ... in sanctificatione. In christo iesu
domino nostro.

140

28r GRADVALE ♪ Qui confidunt in domino sicut |mons syon non commouebitur
in eternum. VERSVS Quia non derelinquet dominus uirgam peccatorum super
sortem iustorum. ♪

---

139 et habundetis] ut abundetis *Vulgata* (4: 1)   scientes] scitis (4: 2)   suum]
vestrum suum (4: 4)   et ne quis] ut ne quis (4: 6)   unusquisque] in negotio
(4: 6)   in his omnibus] de his omnibus (4: 6)   prediximus] et praediximus
(4: 6)   inmunditiam] inmunditia (4: 7)

---

140 *Vide Intro. p. 67*

---

138 RL: MRM 71. GREG: Ha 202, Pa 174. GEL8: En 363, Ge 352, Rh 258, Sg 319.
AM: Sb (212). ES: Vl4770 37r. BEN: Ben29 73v, Ben30 33v, Ben33 29v, Ca 29v,
DaB 59v, DaS 5, Mc127 67, Mc540 118, McO 310, McV 58r, Ott 75v, Ve 47v.

139 1 Thess 4: 1-7. RL: MRM 71. LEC: Alc 46, Mu 34, WuC 50, CoP 101. ES:
Vl4770 37r. BEN: Ben29 73v-74r, Ben30 33v-34r, Ben33 30r, Ca 29v-30r, DaB 59v,
DaK 17v, Mc127 67-68, Mc540 118, McV 58r-v, Ott 75v, Ve 47v.

140 Ps 124: 1, 3. BEN: Ben29 74r, Ben30 34v, Ben33 30r, Ben34 75r, Ben35 36r,
Ben38 14v-15r, Ca 30r, DaB 59v-60r, Mc127 68, Mc540 118, Mc546 60, McV
58v, Ott 75v, Ve 47v.

141

TRACTVS ♪ Confitemini domino quoniam bonus quoniam in seculum misericordia eius. Quis loquetur potentias domini auditas faciet omnes laudes eius.
28v Beati qui custodiunt iudicium |et faciunt iustitias in omni tempore. Memento.
PROSA Memento quesumus rex xpiste famulosque tuos et nos eripias a morte
anime atque te poscentibus. Nostri domine in beneplacito populi tui uisita nos
in salutari tuo. ♪

142

SECVNDVM IOHANNEM [4: 5-42]. In illo tempore. Venit iesus in
29r-30v ciuitatem samarie. que dicitur sichar. ... |... quia hic est uere saluator
mundi.·,

---

142 dederat] dedit *Vulgata* (4: 5)   iesus autem] Iesus ergo (4: 6)   at iesus
dicit ei] dicit ei Iesus (4: 7)   quo utuntur] coutuntur (4: 9)   puteum istum]
puteum (4: 12)   bibit ex eo] ex eo bibit (4: 12)   quam ego dabo] quam dabo
(4: 14)   dicit ei mulier] respondit mulier et dicit (4: 17)   hunc quem] nunc
quem (4: 18)   ut uideo] video (4: 19)   ueniet hora] venit hora (4: 23)
Messias ueniet] Messias venit (4: 25)   et uidete] videte (4: 29)   quem non
scitis] quem vos nescitis (4: 32)   quattuor messe] quatuor menses (4: 35)   et
ut] ut et (4: 36)   labores] laborem (4: 38)   *Cum signis ad legendum (vide
Intro. p. 35)*: l, ✶

---

141 *Pr.* Memento ... poscentibus.: *vide Intro. p. 69*   domi*no*: DEFEFEDED
quoniam[1]: CDEFGFED   *bo*nus: DEC   *misericordi*a: FGEFEDCDCE
Quis: D   *loquetur*: DFGFDEFEDFGFEGAGEFGEFDEFED   *auditas*:
DE   *faciet*: DCDEFGFEFGF   *om*nes: FGEFED   *laudes*: E   *Beati*:
FGAGAGFGFECDCDEFEDEDECDEFEDCDED   *iudici*um: DFEDED
iusti*tias*: DCDEFGFEGF] ju*stitiam GR*   *in*[2]: F   *omni*: FGEFEDCE
Me*mento*: GAGFGAGABGFAGABGFAGAGFAGAGFAGAGFDED   *tu*i:
DFEDE   *nos*: FEFGF   *sa*lutari: FGEFE

---

141 Ps 105: 1-4. RL: GR 113-114 (om. Prosula), MRM 71 (om. Pr.). BEN: Ben29
74r (om. Pr.), Ben30 34v (om. Pr.), Ben33 30r (om. Pr.), Ben34 75r-v (cum Pr.),
Ben35 36r-v (cum Pr.), Ben38 15r (cum Pr.), Ca 30r (om. Pr.), DaB 60r (om. Pr.),
Mc127 68 (om. Pr.), Mc540 118-119 (om. Pr.), Mc546 61 (om. Pr.), McV 58v
(om. Pr.), Ott 75v-76r (om. Pr.), Ve 47v-48r (om. Pr.).

142 Io 4: 5-42. RL: MRM (94-95). AM: Sb 92v-94r. ES: Co 142-144. BEN: Ben33
30r-31r, DaB 60r (add. inc. in marg.), DaE (34v), DaK 18r-19v.

143

31r OFFERTORIVM ♪ Exaltabo te domine quoniam su|scepisti me nec delectasti inimicos meos super me domine clamaui ad te et sanasti me. ♪

144

SECRETA Respice domine propitius ad munera que sacramus. ut et tibi grata sint; et nobis salutaria. semper existant. per.

145

COMMVNIO ♪ Qui biberit aqua quam ego dabo ei dicit dominus fiet in eo fons aque sallientis in uitam eternam. ♪

146

POSTCOMMVNIO Supplices te rogamus omnipotens deus. ut qui nos tui reficis sacramentis. tibi etiam placitis moribus dignanter deseruire concedas. per.

---

143 A' *inc.*] E *inc.* GR (F-*clavis*] c-*clavis trans.* GR *passim*)   domi*ne*[1]: DED quoni*am*: DFGFEFEDED   *cla*maui: DA'   sa*na*sti: FDCDFDCDECFDF

145 a*qua*: EF   *quam*: DE   *da*bo: GAcBcdc   do*minus*: EGFE   *fi*et: EAB   *eo*: ABA   *fons*: ABcBA   *in*[2]: E   *ui*tam: FEFEFA   eternam: AcGFGAG

---

143 Ps 29: 2-3. RL: GR (90), MRM (50, 273). AMS (37b). BEN: Ben29 74v, Ben33 31r, Ben34 75v (62v), Ben38 15v, DaB 60v, Mc127 69, Mc540 119, Mc546 61, McV 59r, Ott 76v, PuV (7).

144 RL: MRM (95). GREG: Ha (249), Pa (222). GEL8: En (448), Ge (434), Sg (383). AM: Sb (375, 380). ES: Vl4770 (49r). BEN: Ben29 (93r), Ben33 (43v), Ca (41r), Mc127 (99), Mc540 (149), McV (73v), Ott (97v).

145 Io 4: 13-14. RL: GR (136), MRM (95). AMS (58). ES: Vl4770 49r). BEN: Ben29 (93r), Ben33 31r, Ben34 (88r-v), Ben35 (44r), Ben38 15v, Ca (41r-v), DaB (76v), Mc127 (99), Mc540 (149), Mc546 (94), McV (73v), Ott (97v), PuV (23-24).

146 RL: MRM 71. SAC: Va (1371). GREG: Ha 204, Pa (68), Sp (1098). GEL8: En (118), Ge (118), Rh (102), Sg (110). AM: Sb 357, STripl 753. ES: Vl4770 37r. BEN: Ben29 74v, Ben30 35v, Ben33 31r-v, Ca 30r, DaB 60v, DaS 5, Mc127 69, Mc540 119, Mc.VI 21, McV 59r, Ott 76v, Ve 48r.

DOMINICA .III.

147

♪ Oculi mei semper ad dominum quia ipse euellet de laqueo pedes meos respice
31v |in me et miserere mei quoniam unicus et pauper sum ego. PSALMVS Ad te
domine leuaui. ♪

148

ORATIO Quesumus omnipotens deus; uota humilium respice. atque ad
protegendum nos; dexteram tue maiestatis extende. per.

149

AD EPHESIOS [5: 1-7]. Fratres. Estote immitatores dei ... Nolite ergo
effici-[*lac.*]

150

32r [*lac.*] |[Io 8: 48-59] -derunt igitur iudei et dixerunt ei. Nonne bene
32v dicimus ... |... exiuit de templo.

---

149 semetipsum] se ipsum *Vulgata* (5: 2)   pertinet] pertinent (5: 4)   Propter
hoc] Propter haec (5: 6)

150 *lac. inter 31v-32r*   iudicet] iudicat *Vulgata* (8: 50)   cognoui eum] novi
eum (8: 55)   uidit] et vidit (8: 56)   *Cum signis ad legendum (vide Intro.
p. 35)*: 1, ✶

---

147 *euellet*: dfefeded   *in*: Bd   mise*r*ere: GAc   Ps.: GcBcd ... dfedcAG

---

147 Ps 24: 15-16, 24: 1. RL: GR 123, MRM 84. AMS 53. ES: Vl4770 43v. BEN: Ben29
84r, Ben30 35v, Ben33 37v, Ben34 82r, Ben35 40r, Ben38 20r, Ca 36r, DaB 68v,
Mc127 84, Mc540 134, Mc546 67, McV 66v, Ott 87r, PuZ v.a, Ve 55v.

148 RL: MRM 84. GREG: Ha 229, Pa 202. GEL8: En 411, Ge 389, Rh 294, Sg 355.
ES: Vl4770 43v. BEN: Ben29 84r, Ben30 35v, Ben33 37v, Ca 36r, DaB 68v-69r,
Mc127 84, Mc540 134, McO 311, McV 66v, Ott 87r, PuZ v.1, Ve 55v.

149 Eph 5: 1-7. RL: MRM 84 (Eph 5: 1-9). LEC: Alc 53, Mu 41, WuC 56, CoP 115.
ES: Vl4770 43v. BEN: Ben29 84r-v, Ben30 35v-36v, Ben33 37v, Ca 36r, DaB 69r,
DaK 19v, Mc127 84-85, Mc540 134-135, McV 66v, Ott 87r-v, PuZ v.Ep, Ve 55v.

150 Io 8: 48-59. Cf. RL: MRM (114 Io 8: 12-20). AM: Sb 103v-104v (Io 8: 31-59).
BEN: Ben33 38r-39r (Io 8: 12-59 *Ego sum lux mundi*), DaB 69v (add. inc. in
marg.), DaK 19v-20v (Io 8: 12-30), PuZ v.Ev (Io 8: 12-22).

151

OFFERTORIVM ♪ Iustitie domini recte letificantes corda. et dulciora super mel et fauum nam et seruus tuus custodit eam. ♪

152

SECRETA Hec hostia domine quesumus. emundet nostra delicta. et sacrificium celebrandum; subditorum tibi corpora mentesque sanctificet. per.

153

COMMVNIO ♪ Passer inuenit sibi domum et turtur nidum ubi reponat pullos
33r suos altaria tua domine uirtutum rex meus et deus │meus beati qui habitant in domo tua in seculum seculi laudabunt te. ♪

154

POSTCOMMVNIO A cunctis nos domine reatibus et periculis propitiatus absolue. quos tantis misteriis tribuis esse participes. per.

---

151 Iustiti*e*: FGAGA   *et*[1]: FE   *fa*uum: FDEFGFDCD   cu*stodit eam*:
AGAGFDFAGFAGF

153 *Vide Intro. p. 70*

---

151 **Ps 18: 9-12.** RL: GR 126, MRM 85. AMS 53. ES: Vl4770 44r. BEN: Ben29 85r, Ben30 37v, Ben33 39r, Ben34 82v-83r, Ben35 40v-41r, Ben38 20v-21r, Ca 36v, DaB 70r, Mc127 86, Mc540 136, Mc546 68, McV 67v, Ott 88v, PuV 17, Ve 56v.

152 RL: MRM 85. GREG: Ha 230, Pa 203. GEL8: En (173), Ge (178), Rh (136), Sg (157). AM: Sb (399). ES: Vl4770 44r. BEN: Ben29 85r, Ben30 37r-38r, Ben33 39r, Ca 36v, DaB 70r, Mc127 86, Mc540 136, McV 67v, Ott 88v, Ve 56v.

153 **Ps 83: 4-5.** RL: GR 126-127, MRM 85-86. AMS 53. ES: Vl4770 44r. BEN: Ben29 85v, Ben30 38r, Ben33 39r, Ben34 83r-v, Ben35 41r, Ben38 21r, Ca 36v-37r, DaB 70r, Mc127 86, Mc540 136, Mc546 68-69, McV 67v, Ott 88v, PuV 17-18, Ve 56v.

154 RL: MRM 86. SAC: Va (231). GREG: Ha 231, Pa 204. GEL8: En 415, Ge 393, Rh 298, Sg 359. ES: Vl4770 44r. BEN: Ben29 85v, Ben30 38r, Ben33 39r, Ca 37r, DaB 70r, Mc127 86, Mc540 136, McV 67v, Ott 88v, Ve 56v.

DOMINICA .IIII.

155

INTROITVS ♪ Letare iherusalem et conuentu facite omnes qui diligitis eam gaudete cum letitia qui in tristitia fuistis ut exultetis et satiemini ab uberibus consolationis uestre. PSALMVS Letatus sum in his que dicta sunt. ♪

156

ORATIO Concede quesumus omnipotens deus. ut qui ex merito nostre actionis affligimur. tue gratie consolatione respiremus. per.

157

33v   AD GALATHAS [4: 22-31]. Fratres. Scriptum est quoniam abraham | duos filios ... liberauit.·,

158

GRADVALE [*lac.*]

---

157 in monte] a monte *Vulgata* (4: 24)   filiis suis] filiis eius (4: 25)   clama] exclama (4: 27)   erit heres] heres erit (4: 30)   christus nos] nos Christus (4: 31)

---

155 *Letare*: GcABAG   conuen*tu*: cBAcABAG   *qui*: A   *di*ligitis: A   *in*: GA   *tristitia*: A   exulte*tis*: dB   sa*ti*emini: Acdcd   *u*beribus: GA conso*la*tionis: AG   Ps.: FAcdBcAG

---

155 **Is 66: 10-11, Ps 121: 1.** RL: GR 138-139, MRM 99. AMS 60. ES: Vl4770 51r. BEN: Ben29 96r, Ben30 38r, Ben33 45r, Ben34 89v, Ben35 45r, DaB 79r, Mc127 104, Mc540 153, Mc546 75, McV 75v, Ott 100v, PuV 25, Ve 64v.

156 RL: MRM 99. GREG: Ha 256. GEL8: En 458, Ge 443, Sg 391. ES: Vl4770 51r. BEN: Ben29 96r, Ben30 38r, Ben33 45r, DaB 79r, Mc127 104, Mc540 154, McO 312, McV 76r, Ott 100v, Ve 64v.

157 **Gal 4: 22-31.** RL: MRM 99-100. LEC: Alc 60, Mu 48, WuC 62, CoP 129. ES: Vl4770 51r-v. BEN: Ben29 96r-v, Ben30 38v-39r, Ben33 45v, DaB 79r-v, DaK 20v-21r, Mc127 104-105, Mc540 154, Mc.VI 25, McV 76r, Ott 100v-101r, Ve 64v.

158 Cf. RL: MRM 100 (*Laetatus sum*), AMS 60, ES: Vl4770 51v, BEN: Ben30 39, Ben33 45v, Ben34 89v-90r, Mc127 105, Mc540 154, PuV 25-26.

159

34r, 34v-35v [*lac.*] |[Io 9: 8-38] -ne hic est, qui sedebat, et mendicabat? ... |... adorauit eum.

160

OFFERTORIVM ♪ Laudate dominum quia benignus est psallite nomini eius quoniam suauis est omnia quecumque uoluit fecit in celo et in terra. ♪

161

SECRETA Sacrificiis presentibus quesumus domine, intende placatus. ut deuotioni nostre proficiant ad salutem. per.

162

COMMVNIO ♪ Lutum fecit ex puto dominus et liniuit ocu- ♪ [*lac.*]

---

159 *lac. inter 33v-34r*   similis eius est] simile est eius *Vulgata* (9: 9)   ille autem] ille (9: 9)   tibi oculi] oculi tibi (9: 10)   quidam ex phariseis] ex Pharisaeis quidam (9: 16)   qui sabbatum] quia sabbatum (9: 16)   qui viderat *om. Dubr* (9: 18)   uidet] videat (9: 21)   qui cecus fuerat] qui fuerat caecus (9: 24)   cum essem cecus] caecus cum essem (9: 25)   *35r: frag. 19 ll.*   es] sis (9: 28)   oculos meos] meos oculos (9: 30)   *lac. Dubr* (9: 34-36)   *35v: frag.*   *Cum signis ad legendum (vide Intro. p. 35):* 1, ✠

---

160 domi*num*: DC   *est*[1]: DEFECDFD   nom*ini*: CE

162 *Vide Intro. p. 71*

---

159 Io 9: 8-38. RL: MRM (106-107). AM: Sb 113v-115r. BEN: Ben33 45v-46v (Io 9: 1-38 *Preteriens dominus Iesus uidit hominem cecum*), DaB 79v (add. inc. in marg.), DaE (40v), DaK 21r-22v.

160 Ps 134: 3, 6. RL: GR 140-141, MRM 101. AMS 60. ES: Vl4770 51v-52r. BEN: Ben29 97r-v, Ben30 40r, Ben33 46v, Ben34 90r-91r, Ben35 45r-v, DaB 80r, Mc127 106, Mc540 155, Mc546 76, Mc.VI 25, McV 76v, Ott 102r, PuV 26-27, Ve 65v.

161 RL: MRM 101. SAC: Le (1326), Va (1138). GREG: Ha 257, Pa 231. GEL8: En 460, Ge 445, Rh (1021), Sg 393. AM: Sb (54). ES: Vl4770 52r. BEN: Ben29 97v, Ben30 40v, Ben33 46v, DaB 80r, Mc127 106, Mc540 155, Mc.VI 25, McV 76v, Ott 102r, Ve 65v.

162 Io 9: 11. RL: MRM (108). AMS (63b). BEN: Ben29 (103r), Ben33 46v, Ben34 (94r), Ben35 (48r), DaB (85r), Mc127 (115), Mc540 (164), Mc546 (79), McV (81r), Ott (108r), PuV (31). Vide Hesbert, "Tradition bénéventaine," p. 229. Var. (melodia): RL: GR (146), ES: Syg (106), Vl4770 (55v), LS: Gs (68).

<DOMINICA IN PALMIS>

163

36r [*lac.*] | PROSA ♪ Templum et locum et ciuitatem regnumque perdiderunt simul et suam gentem. VERSVS Vnus autem ex ipsis cayphas nomine cum esset pontifex anni illius prophetauit dicens. Expedit uobis <ut unus> moriatur. homo pro populo et non tota gens pereat. PROSA Xpistus moriturus ut saluaret suum populum. Ab illo ergo die cogitauerant interficere eum dicentes. Ne forte. ♪

164

ANTIPHONA ♪ Occurrunt turbe cum floribus et palmis redemptori obuiam et uictori triumphanti digna dant obsequia filium dei regem regum predicant. et in
36v lau|de xpisti uoces sonant per nubila osanna. ♪

165

ANTIPHONA ♪ Pueri hebreorum tollentes ramos oliuarum obuiauerunt domino clamantes et dicentes osanna in excelsis. ♪

---

163 *lac. inter 35v-36r*

---

163 *Pr.* Templum ... gentem, Xpistus ... populum: *vide Intro. pp. 74-75*   *ip*sis: EGF   *ponti*fex: ED   illi*us*: A'B'CB'A'G'   *ut u*nus: EF   *mo*riatur: ED   po*pu*lo: CDEFEDE   *et*⁴: DCA'CDE   to*ta*: EFG   *pereat*: DFE-DCD   (*Pros.* Xpistus: AFAGEDFGEDFECD] *ut inc.* Ab GR)   *Ab*: DEFG-FED   *il*lo: D

164 *Occur*runt: CDFE   flo*ribus*: BcB   uic*tori*: Gcd   *digna*: cd   *dant*: cBA   obse*quia*: BA   *filium*: AcBAG   *predic*ant: GAGF   *et*³: A   *in*: GF   lau*de*: ABc   *xpi*sti: cdc   uo*ces*: AB   so*nant*: G   *nubi*la: FGAFE   *osanna*: EFGcBAcAG

165 *Pue*ri: FD   hebre*orum*: FGA   *o*sanna: E   excel*sis*: DAGFD

---

163 Io 11: 49-50, 53. RL: GR 166-167 (*Collegerunt* om. Prosula), MRM 129 (om. Pr.). AMS (213b om. Pr.). ES: Vl4770 67r, 70r (om. Pr.). BEN: Ben29 117r (om. Pr.), Ben30 44v-45v (cum Pr.), Ben34 105v-106v (cum Pr.), Ben35 54v-55r (cum Pr.), Ben38 32v-33r (cum Pr.), Ben39 9v-10r (cum Pr.), Mc127 139 (om. Pr.), Mc540 188 (om. Pr.), McP 99: 165 (om. Pr.), McV 93r (om. Pr.), Ott 127r-v (om. Pr.), PuV 45-46 (om. Pr.), Ve 81v (cum Pr.). Vide Hesbert, "Tradition bénéventaine," pp. 252-253 (Table).

164 RL: GR 174-175, MRM 133. ES: Vl4770 66r, 70r. BEN: Ben30 50r, Ben34 107r, Ben35 55v, Ben38 34r, Ben39 10r, Mc127 142, McP 99: 185, McV 95r, Ott 130v, PuV 45, Ve 82r (inc.), 83v (add. in marg.).

165 RL: GR 170, MRM 132. ES: Vl4770 66r, 70r. BEN: Ben30 49v, Ben34 107v, McP 99: 185, Ve 82r (add. in marg.), 83v.

166

ANTIPHONA ♪ Pueri hebreorum uestimenta prosternebant in uia et clamabant dicentes. osanna <filio dauid> benedictus qui uenit in nomine domini. ♪

167

ANTIPHONA ♪ Cum angelis et pueris fideles inueniamur triumphatori mortis clamantes osanna in excelsis. ♪

168

ANTIPHONA ♪ Cum audisset populus quia hiesus uenit hierusolimam. Acceperunt ramos palmarum. exierunt ei obuiam et clama- ♪ [*lac.*]

169

37r | *Sequitur* ORATIO. Domine iesu christe qui introitum portarum ierusalem et ualuas sanctificasti. dum splendore gemmarum duodecim totidem apostolorum nomina presignasti. Et qui per organum propheticum prompsisti dicens. lauda ierusalem dominum. lauda deum tuum syon. quoniam confortauit seras portarum tuarum. benedixit filios tuos in te. Te quesumus ut ponas omnes fines istius ciuitatis pacem. Velociter currens interius sermo tuus. adipe frumenti satiet eos. Spiritus sanctus defendat illos. ut numquam eis nocere preualeat

---

169 *lac. inter 36v-37r*

---

166 *Pue*ri: FD   hebre*o*rum: FGA   *in*[1]: FE   cla*mab*ant: GFED   di-
*cen*tes: E   *in nomine domini*: FEFGFDCDAGF

167 fi*del*es: e   inue*nia*mur: ABA   cla*man*tes: B   *o*sanna: B   excel*sis*:
GdedcBA

168 *Vide Intro. p. 76*

---

166 RL: GR 170, MRM 132. ES: Vl4770 66r, 70r. BEN: Ben30 49v-50r, Ben34 107v, McP 186, Ve 82r (add. in marg.).

167 RL: GR 175, MRM 133. BEN: Ben34 107v, McP 99: 188.

168 Io 12: 12-13. RL: GR 172-173 (melodia var.), MRM 133. ES: Vl4770 66v, 70r. BEN: Ben34 107r-v, Ben35 56r, Ben38 33v-34r, Ben39 10v, Mc127 137, Mc540 187, McP 99: 191, McV 92v, Ott 126r-v, PuV 44-45, Ve 82v-83r. Vide Hesbert, "Tradition bénéventaine," pp. 256-257. Cf. RL: GR 171 (Ant. *Cum appropinquaret*: melodia eadem).

169 GREG: Tc (441*). GEL8: Ge (2859), Ph (1878). ES: F (2803), PRG (210). BEN: McO (129).

inimicus. Sed omnes habitantes in ea. uoce, corde et ore decantent dicentes. Magnus dominus noster. et magna uirtus eius. et sapientie eius non est numerus. Qui cum patre eiusdem.

170

ALIA ORATIO Tuere quesumus hunc populum tuum deus. et spirituali munitione ciuitatem istam circunda. ut tui nominis gloriatio. super nos fulgeat in eternum. per in unitate eiusdem.

171

37v |*In ingressu civitatis. RESP.* ♪ Ingrediente domino in sanctam ciuitatem. Hebreorum pueri resurrectionem uite pronuntiantes. Cum ramis proce<d>entes osanna clamabant in excelsis. VERSVS Cumque audissent quia uenit hiesus hierusolimam. exierunt obuiam ei. ♪

172

Ante regiam ecclesie. ORATIO Deus cuius filius, non rapinam arbitratus est; esse se equalem deo tibi patri sed essentialiter tecum gloriam possidet per naturam. Qui semetipsum exinaniuit. formam serui suscipiens. filius uero tuus esse non desiit. Sed ut seruum redimeret dominus angelorum. seruilium uulnerum, pertulit passionem. Cuius
38r liuore sanati sumus. Non enim |mundus poterat expiari a crimine. nisi pretiosus sine crimine sanguis. mundi domini manasset ex latere. O ineffabili mirabilique modo. singulariter stupenda clementia. Deum quem celi celorum capere non poterant. angusto uoluit crucis coartari sub stipite. Qui sedet super cherubin et thronus eius rutilat in columna nubis. paruissimi pecudis, quadrigera uehebatur a poplite. Non aureis

---

171 ci*ui*tatem: DFGEFE   Hebreo*rum*: G   resur*recti*onem: DEDC   excelsis: FDFE   Cum*que*: DEFGF   *audissent quia uenit hiesus*: FGAGFE] *audisset populus quod Jesus veniret* GR

---

170 Non inveni.

171 RL: GR 177-178, MRM 134. BEN: Ben30 50v, Mc127 142, McP 99: 191, McV 95r, Ott 131r, Ve 83v.

172 Non inveni, sed "Tribuat nobis de rore ... ysaac et iacob," vide GEL8: Rh (1255), Ge (2820); ES: F (2769), Franz 1: 607-608, PRG (191: 1); et "Augeat famulis suis ... prestare dignetur," vide GEL8: Ge (2821), Rh (1256); ES: F (2768), Franz 1: 607-608, PRG (191: 2). 38v-39r ed. E. A. Loew, *Scriptura Beneventana*, pl. 94.

petalis spumantia frena rigebant. nec indicus pendulo lapis micabat sub phalere. Non purpurato gemmeus uernabat ordo sub tegmine. nec fucatis ostro fimbriis radiantia. fila fluebant. qua seculi arridens pompa, altitudo mundana tumescit. Sed uili indumentorum accinctus uelamine. sedens super pullum asine, filium subiugalis. celorum dominus

38v iter carpebat puluereum. Quatinus nos, et sue man|suetudinis tam salubribus exemplis imbueret. et typicis misteriorum documentis ostenderet. quemammodum per stultitiam insontis asini; gentilis populi figurabatur simplicitas. Super quam iesus dominus noster, diuino more, gubernandam presidens; ad illam celestem ierusalem pergens in qua pax summe permanet uisionis. cotidie electorum animas secum intrare permittit. Nam turba que precedebat et que sequebatur. duorum typicabat personam populorum. Quia ex utraque plebe. iudayca scilicet que precesserat; et gentili que per omne sequitur tempus. osanna filio dei sine fine proclamatur. Quem totis precordiis suppliciter exoramus. ut dignetur hanc propitius ingredi domum. et bene ✠ dictionis sue gratiam in ea, inmensa pietate multiplicet. Omniumque charismatum dona, sancti spiritus tribuente conferat maies-

39r tate. Aera iocundis temperet |astris. terrarum germina, tranquillo imbre fecundet. Tribuat nobis de rore celi abundantiam. et de pinguedine terre uite substantiam. frumenti, scilicet uini et olei. Et desideria uoti nostri; ad effectum sue miserationis perducat. Introitum uero nostrum. bene ✠ dicere et sancti ✠ ficare dignetur. sicut benedicere dignatus est domum abrahe ysaac, et iacob. Augeat famulis suis pacem ac sanitatem. letitiam cunctis, et benignitatem. ab homine, usque ad pecus prestare dignetur. Populumque suum, cum omnibus ad se pertinentibus suo pretioso sanguine tueatur. Iesus christus dominus noster. qui tecum uiuit et regnat in unitate eiusdem spiritus sancti deus. per omnia secula seculorum. Amen.

173

In ingressu ecclesie. can. ANT. ♪ Turba multa que conuenerant ad diem

39v festum clamabant domino benedictus qui uenit in nomine |domini osanna in excelsis. ♪

---

173 *Tur*ba: E mul*ta*: E *festum*: AG *do*mino: E *benedictus*: FE *u*enit: EF *in*[1]: G nomi*ne*: FE *domi*ni: DEDC *o*sanna: E *e*xcelsis: GAG

---

173 RL: GR 175, MRM 133. BEN: Ben38 32v, McP 99: 185, Ve 82r (add. in marg.).

174

Item ORATIO *in ingressu ecclesie. et in choro.* Ascendat oratio nostra usque ad thronum claritatis tue, domine. et non uacua reuertatur ad nos postulatio nostra. per.

ITEM AD MISSAM.

175

INTROITVS ♪ Domine ne longe facias auxilium tuum a me ad defensionem meam aspice libera me de ore leonis et a cornibus unicornuorum humilitatem meam. PSALMVS Deus deus meus respice. ♪

176

ORATIO Omnipotens sempiterne deus; qui humano generi ad imittandum humilitatis exemplum. saluatorem nostrum carnem sumere, et crucem subire fecisti. concede propitius; ut et patientie ipsius habere documenta. et resurrectionis eius, consortia mereamur. per.

177

40r AD PHILIPENSES [2: 5-11]. Fratres. Hoc enim sentite ... |... in gloria est dei patris.

---

177 exaltauit illum] illum exaltavit *Vulgata* (2: 9)   nomen quod est super] nomen super (2: 9)   flectatur] flectat (2: 10)   terrestrium] et terrestrium (2: 10)   dominus noster] Dominus (2: 11)   *40r*: ego p
 (presbyter *ut vid.*) *add. alia manu in marg. superiori*

---

175 *defensionem*: GEGABcB   *cornibus*: AG   *unicor*nuorum: ABAGAB humi*litatem*: ABcBcBABcBA   Ps.: GAGc ... cBGAcBAG

---

174 Non inveni.

175 Ps 21: 20, 22, 21: 2. RL: GR 178, MRM 134. AMS 73a. ES: Vl4770 67r, 70r. BEN: Ben29 117v, Ben30 50v-51r, Ben34 108v, Ben35 57v, Ben38 35v, Ben39 13r-v, DaB 99v, Mc127 142, McV 95r, Ott 131r, PuC 426, PuV 47, Ve 84r.

176 RL: MRM 134. SAC: Va 329. GREG: Ha 312, Pa 281. GEL8: En 558, Ge 566, Rh 373, Sg 463. ES: Vl4770 70r. AM: Sb (501). BEN: Ben29 117v, Ben30 51r, DaB 99v, DaS 11, Mc127 142, McO 314, McV 95r, Ott 131r, PuC 427, Ve 84r.

177 Phil 2: 5-11. RL: MRM 135. LEC: Alc 76, Mu 62, WuC 75, CoP 159. ES: Vl4770 67r, 70r. BEN: Ben29 117v-118r, Ben30 51r-v, DaB 99v-100r, DaK 24v, Mc127 142, McV 95r-v, Ott 131r-v, PuC 428, Ve 84r, Wolf 136r.

178

GRADVALE ♪ Tenuisti manum dextere mee et in uoluntate tua deduxisti me et
40v   cum gloria assumpsisti me. VERSVS Quam bonus israhel |deus rectis corde mei
autem pene moti sunt pedes pene effusi sunt gressus mei quia zelaui in peccatoribus pacem peccatorum uidens. ♪

179

TRACTVS ♪ Deus deus meus respice in me quare me dereliquisti. Longe a salute
41r   mea. Verba delictorum meorum deus meus cla|mabo per diem nec exaudies in
nocte et non ad insipientiam michi. Tu autem in sancto habitas laus hisrahel in
te sperauerunt patres nostri sperauerunt et liberasti eos. Ad te clamauerant et
salui facti sunt in te sperauerunt et non sunt confusi. Ego autem sum uermis et
41v   non homo oprobrium hominum et ab|iectio plebis. Omnes qui uidebant me
aspernabantur me locuti sunt labiis et mouerunt caput. Sperauit in domino eripiat
eum saluum faciat eum quoniam uult eum. ♪

---

178 *ma*num: DGEG   me*e*: FDCDFDCDCEDEDC   *et*[1]: C] *om. GR*   uo-
*lunta*te: E   de*du*xisti: E   glori*a*: EGAFEFGFDCEDEDCDFEFDEFDFC
as*sum*psisti: E   *me*[2]: DEFGFGAGEFABGFAGAGE   *Quam*: EFDG *V.
scripsit cum B*♭ *ut GR (vide Intro. p. 36)*   *de*us: AGAGAFGAB♭cAG-
FB♭AGAB♭AGAG   *rect*is: FEFDEFGcAcAGB♭Ac   *m*ei: DA   au*tem*:
GE   pe*ne*[1]: E   *mot*i: EFGFEFGAcAcAGAB♭AGAGB♭Ac   pe*ne*[2]:
C   *in*[2]: GD   peccatori*bus*: GEFEFEFAGEFD   peccato*rum*: GEFAG-
FDCDEFE   *uid*ens: FDFCEFGEFAGAcGFDGFAGAFE

179 De*us*[1]: CDCA'CDCDEDCDCDEDCDFEFEDED   de*us*[2]: D   *in*[1]: DE
me[2]: FEF   de*re*liquisti: CE   *mea*: DFDEDCEDEFGDCDED   *delic*-
torum: D   me*or*um: FDEDFGFEFGDCFEDFDC   *de*us[3]: FE   *nec*: D
insi*pientiam*: EFGAGDGF   *au*tem: FGFDFGAFEGFEDEFEFDEFEDE
habi*tas*: CDEDEDFGDC   *hisra*hel: DEF   *no*stri: DFEDE   libe*ra*sti:
CE   *eo*s: DC   clama*ue*runt: DFEFEFAGFEDE   *et non sunt*: GCD
sum: DFG   *uerm*is: GA   opro*brium*: DE   *ab*iectio: CD   uide*bant*:
GF   a*spernaban*tur: DCGAGDFDAGFEDEDCD   *labi*is: DCDEFGFEF
*mo*uerunt: CD   *do*mino: GD

---

178 Ps 72: **24, 1-3**. RL: GR 179-180, MRM 135. AMS 73a. ES: Vl4770 67r, 70r. BEN:
Ben29 118r, Ben30 51v-52r, Ben34 109r, Ben35 57v-58r, Ben38 35v-36r, Ben39
13v, DaB 100r, Mc127 142, Mc546 81, McV 95v, Ott 131v, PuV 47-48, Ve 84r-v.

179 Ps 21: **2-9**. RL: GR 180-183 (Ps 21: 2-9, 18, 19, 22, 24, 32), MRM 135. AMS
73b. ES: Vl4770 70r-v. BEN: Ben29 118r, Ben30 52r, Ben34 109r-110v, Ben35
58r-v, Ben38 36r-v, Ben39 13v, DaB 100r-v, Mc127 142-143, Mc546 81-82, McV
95v-96r, Ott 132r-133r, PuC 429, PuV 48-49, Ve 84v-85r.

180

PASSIO DOMINI NOSTRI IESV CHRISTI SECVNDVM MATHEVM [26: 1-27: 66].
In illo tempore. Dixit iesus discipulis suis. Scitis quia post biduum
42r-44v, 45r pasca fiet. ... |... scripture prophetarum. [*lac.*] |es. nam et loquela tua
45v-46v, 47r ... |... cyreneum, uenientem [*lac.*] |-tes de monumentis. ... zebedei.
47v *Hic incipe euangelium.* Cum sero autem factum esset. ... |... cum
custo<dibus.>

181

♪ Improperium <exspectauit cor meum. et mi>seria<m. et sustinui qui simul
48r mecum contristaretur. et non fuit. consolantem me quesi>|ui et non inueni et
dederunt in escam meam fel et in siti mea potauerunt me aceto. ♪

---

180 habebitis ... habebitis] habetis ... habetis *Vulgata* (26: 11)   *42r:* uspomenu
negovo (?) (*i.e.* in memoriam eius [?] *in lingua croatica*) add. in marg. dext., *manu
sec. XV-XVI*   die azimorum] azymorum (26: 17)   discipulis suis] discipulis
(26: 20)   *42v:* u isti (*i.e.* in eundem *in lingua croatica*) *et* equas (*ut vid.*) add. in
marg. dext.; Talesni (*ut vid., i.e.* corporalis *in lingua croatica*) add. in marg. sinist.
intingit] intinguit (26: 23)   de eo] de illo (26: 24)   tradetur] traditur (26: 24)
illis] eis (26: 26)   effundetur] effunditur (26: 28)   remissione] remissionem (26: 28)   filii] filiis (26: 37)   discipulos suos] discipulos (26: 40)
tradetur] traditur (26: 45)   tradet] tradit (26: 46)   missi a principibus] a
principibus (26: 47)   et amputauit] amputauit (26: 51)   *lac. inter 44v-45r:*
tunc discipuli ... ex illis *lac. Dubr* (26: 56-73)   continuo egressus] egressus (26:
75)   fleuit] ploravit (26: 75)   hoc est ager sanguinis] ager sanguinis (27: 8)
et tunc] tunc (27: 9)   habebant] habebat (27: 16)   barabas qui propter
omicidium missus fuerat in carcerem] Barabbas (27: 16)   uobis dimittam]
dimittam vobis (27: 17)   eo] illo (27: 19)   eum] illum (27: 19)   huius]
eius (27: 25)   pretorium] praetorio (27: 27)   uestimenta sua clamidem]
chlamydem (27: 28)   et arundinem in dextera eius *add. corr. in marg. sinist.
Dubr* (27: 29)   flexu] flexo (27: 29)   cyreneum uenientem] cyreneum
(27:32)   *lac. inter 46v-47r:* nomine ... et exeun- *lac. Dubr* (27: 32-53)   *47r-v:*
frag. 18 ll. Cum signis ad legendum (vide Intro. p. 35): l, ✠ , S, e

---

181 *Im*properium: DEFGFED   *mi*seriam: cdcBABcBAB   *meam*: ABc-
BAGF   *fel*: AGAGABcBAG   *po*tauerunt: B

---

180 Mt 26: 1-27: 66. RL: MRM 136-141. LEC: Mu 62, WuE 304, CoP 160. ES:
Vl4770 70v-74r. BEN: Ben29 118r-124r, Ben30 52r-62r, Ben33 59r-v, Ca 43r-44r,
DaB 100v-104v, DaE 51v, DaK 24v-30r, Mc127 143-152, McV 96r-100r, Ott
133r-138v, Ve 85r-88v.

181 Ps 68: 21-22. RL: GR 184, MRM 141. AMS 73b. ES: Vl4770 74r. BEN: Ben29
124r, Ben30 62r-v, Ben34 110v-111r, Ben35 58v-59r, Ben38 37r-v, Ben39 14r-v,
Ca 44r-v, DaB 104v, Mc127 152, Mc546 83, McV 100r, Ott 138v, PuC 431, PuV
49, Ve 88v.

182

SECRETA Concede quesumus domine. ut oculis tue maiestatis munus oblatum. et gratiam nobis deuotionis optineat. et effectum beate perhennitatis acquirat. per.

183

COMMVNIO ♪ Pater si non potest hic calix transire nisi bibam illum fiat uoluntas tua. ♪

184

POSTCOMMVNIO Per huius domine operationem misterii. et uitia nostra purgentur. et iusta desideria compleantur. per.

FERIA .V. IN CENA DOMINI.

185

♪ Nos autem gloriari oportet in cruce domini nostri ihesu xpisti. in quo est salus uita et resurrectio nostra per quem saluati et liberati sumus. PSALMVS Deus misereatur. ♪

---

183 tran*si*re: B   uolun*tas tu*a: BAGAG

185 *au*tem: EFGFDFC   glo*ri*ari: E   *in*[1]: GE   no*stri*: FE   *ihe*su: FE
*li*berasti: GF   Ps.: AGAFGAGE

---

182 RL: MRM 141. GREG: Ha 313, Pa 282. GEL8: En (93), Ge (93), Rh (79), Sg (87). ES: Vl4770 74r. BEN: Ben29 124r, Ben30 62v, Ben33 (7r), Ca 44v, DaB 104v, DaS 11, Mc127 152, McV 100r, PuC 432, Ve 88v.

183 Mt 26: 42. RL: GR 184, MRM 141. AMS 73b. ES: Vl4770 74r. BEN: Ben29 124r, Ben30 62v, Ben34 111r, Ben35 59v, Ben38 37v, Ben39 14v, Ca 44v, DaB 104v, Mc127 152, Mc546 83, McV 100r, Ott 138v, PuC 434, PuV 50, Ve 88v.

184 RL: MRM 141. SAC: Va (1524). GREG: Ha 314, Pa (54, 578). GEL8: En (95), Ge (95, 1528), Rh (81), Sg (89). AM: Sb (44, 308). ES: Vl4770 74v. BEN: Ben29 124r, Ben30 62v-63r, Ben33 (7r), Ca 44v, DaB 104v, DaS 11, Mc127 152, McV 100r, PuC 435, Ve 88v.

185 Gal 6: 14, Ps 66: 2. RL: GR 195-196, MRM 156. AMS 77a (ps. var.). ES: Vl4770 83v. BEN: Ben29 132v, Ben30 63r, Ben33 63r, Ben34 115r (112v), Ben35 61v, Ben39 18r, Ben40 4r, Ca 51v, DaB 112r, Mc127 166, Mc546 88, McV 107r, Ott 150v, PuC 436, Ve 98r.

186

Dicat Gloria in excelsis.

187

48v | ORATIO Deus a quo et iudas proditor reatus sui penam. et confessionis sue latro premium sumpsit. concede nobis tue propitiationis effectum. ut sicut in passione sua iesus christus dominus noster diuersa utrique intulit stipendia meritorum. ita nobis ablato uetustatis errore, resurrectionis sue gratiam largiatur. Qui tecum.

188

LECTIO EPISTOLE BEATI PAVLI APOSTOLI AD CORINTHIOS [1 Cor 11: 49r 20-32]. Fratres. Conuenientibus uobis in unum. ... | ... damnemur.

189

49v GRADVALE ♪ Xpistus factus est pro nobis obediens | usque ad mortem mortem autem crucis. VERSVS Propter quod et deus exaltauit illum et dedit illi nomen quod est super omne nomen. ♪

---

188 quod pro uobis tradetur] pro vobis *Vulgata* (11: 24)   bibitis ... bibitis] bibetis ... bibetis (11: 25-26)   annuntiabitis] adnuntiatis (11: 26)   et biberit] vel biberit (11: 27)   corpus domini] corpus (11: 29)   infirmi] infirmes (11: 30)   cum autem iudicamur] dum iudicamur autem (11: 32)

---

189 us*que* ad: GBAGA   au*tem*: cABcBAGABAG   *de*us: c   il*lum*: dcAcdcdcGcefgfdecBcBdecedcedcBA

---

186 RL: MRM 156. BEN: Ben29 182v, Mc127 166, Mc546 88, Ve 98r.

187 RL: MRM 156. SAC: Va (396). GREG: Ha 328, Pa 299. GEL8: En 642, Ge 633, Rh 397, Sg 514. AM: Sb 483. ES: Vl4770 83v-84r. BEN: Ben29 132v, Ben30 63v, Ben33 63r, Ca 52r, DaB 112r-v, Mc127 166, McV 107r, Ott 150v, PuC 437, Ve 98r.

188 1 Cor 11: 20-32. RL: MRM 156-157. LEC: Alc 83, Mu 66, WuC 82, CoP 169. ES: Vl4770 84r. BEN: Ben29 133r-v, Ben30 63v-64v, Ben33 64v-65r, Ca 52r, DaB 112v, DaK 30r, Mc127 166-167, McV 107r-v, Ott 150v-151v, PuC 438, Ve 98r.

189 Phil 2: 8-9. RL: GR 196, MRM 157. AMS 77a. ES: Vl4770 84r. BEN: Ben29 133v, Ben30 64v-65r, Ben33 64v, Ben34 115r-v, Ben35 61v, Ben39 18r-v, Ben40 4r, Ca 52r, DaB 113r, Mc127 167, Mc546 88, Mc.vi 32, McV 107v, Ott 151v, PuC 439, Ve 98r-v.

190

SEQVENTIA SANCTI EVANGELII SECVNDVM IOHANNEM [13: 1-6]. In illo tempore. Ante diem festum pasce ... ergo ad symonem [*lac.*]

<FERIA .VI. IN PARASCEVE>

191

50r [*lac.*] |-uitate deposita. et errantium corda resipiscant. et ad ueritatis tue redeant unitatem. per eundem.

192

Oremus; et pro perfidis iudeis. ut deus et dominus noster, auferat uelamen de cordibus eorum. ut et ipsi agnoscant iesum christum dominum nostrum.

193

Hic non flectent genua. Oremus. Omnipotens sempiterne deus. qui etiam iudaycam perfidiam a tua misericordia non repellis. exaudi

---

190 cor] corde *Vulgata* (13: 2)　　misit] mittit (13: 5)　　peluim] pelvem (13: 5)　　*Cum signis ad legendum (vide Intro. p. 35):* 1

191 *lac. inter 49v-50r*

---

190 Io 13: 1-6. RL: MRM 157 (Io 13: 1-15). LEC: Mu 66, WuE (304), CoP 170. ES: Vl4770 84r-v. BEN: Ben29 133v-134r, Ben30 65r-66r, Ben33 65v-66r, Ca 52r-v, DaB 113r-v, DaE 67r, Mc127 167-168, Mc.VI 32, McV 107v-108r, Ott 151v-152r, Ve 98v.

191 RL: MRM 169 (*Omnipotens sempiterne deus qui salvas omnes*). SAC: Va 413. GREG: Ha 351, Pa 316. GEL8: En 672, Ge 661, Rh 417, Sg 533. AM: Sb 517. ES: Vl4770 91r. BEN: Ben33 72v, Ca 56r, DaB 122v, Mc127 187, McP 99: 323, McV 116v-117r, Ott 165r-v, Ve 103r. Vide Hesbert, "Tradition bénéventaine," pp. 291-337.

192 RL: MRM 169. SAC: Va 414. GREG: Ha 352, Pa 317. GEL8: En 673-674, Ge 662, Rh 418, Sg 534. AM: Sb 518. ES: Vl4770 91r. BEN: Ben33 72v, Ca 56r, DaB 122v, Mc127 187, McP 99: 324, McV 117r, Ott 165v, Ve 103r.

193 RL: MRM 169. SAC: Va 415. GREG: Ha 353, Pa 318. GEL8: En 675, Ge 663, Rh 419, Sg 535. AM: Sb 519. ES: Vl4770 91r. BEN: Ben33 72v, Ca 56r, DaB 122v, Mc127 187-188, McP 99: 325, Mc.VI 33, McV 117r, Ott 165v, Ve 103r-v.

preces nostras, quas tibi pro illius populi obcecatione deferimus. ut
agnita ueritatis tue que christus est; a suis tenebris eruantur. per
eundem.

194

Oremus; et pro paganis. ut deus omnipotens; auferat iniquitatem de
cordibus eorum. et relictis idolis suis; conuertantur ad deum uiuum et
uerum. et unicum filium eius iesum christum dominum nostrum.

195

Flectate. Leuate. Oremus. Omnipotens sempiterne deus; qui non
mortem peccatorum, sed uitam semper inquiris. suscipe propitius
orationem nostram. et libera eos ab idolorum cultura. et aggrega
ecclesie tue sancte. ad laudem et gloriam nominis tui. per eundem.

196

50v *Finitis uero orationibus preparetur crux retro altare | et sustentata hinc
et inde; a duobus clericis. posito ante ea oratorium. in cuius laudes
dicant latores.* ♪ Popul meus quid feci tibi aut in quo contristaui te responde
michi. Quia eduxi te de terra egipti. Parasti crucem saluatori tuo. ♪ *et respondeant duo de choro.* ♪ Agios o theos. Agios ischiros. Agios athanatos.
eleyson ymas. ♪ *Chorus interim respondeat.* ♪ Sanctus deus. Sanctus fortis.
Sanctus et immortalis miserere nobis. ♪ *et latores.* ♪ Quia eduxi te per

---

196 fe*ci*: D   contri*sta*ui: FE   *te*[1]: FED   re*sponde*: EGFED   mi*chi*: ED
te[2]: ED   e*gipti*: E   *tu*o[1]: FE   Agi*os*[1,2]: FGFED   *Agios*[3]: FAGA-
GAG   e*ley*son: ABcBAG   *y*mas: FE   San*ctus*[1,2]: FGFED   *Sanctus*[3]:
FAGAGAG   mi*serere*: ABcBA   *no*bis: FE   *te*[3]: ED

---

194 RL: MRM 169. SAC: Va 416. GREG: Ha 354, Pa 319. GEL8: En 676-677, Ge 664,
Rh 420, Sg 536. AM: Sb 520. ES: Vl4770 91r. BEN: Ben33 72v, Ca 56r, DaB
122v-123r, Mc127 188, McP 99: 326, Mc.VI 33, McV 117r, Ott 165v, Ve 103v.

195 RL: MRM 170. SAC: Va 417. GREG: Ha 355, Pa 320. GEL8: En 678, Ge 665, Rh
421, Sg 537. AM: Sb 521. ES: Vl4770 91r. BEN: Ben33 72v, Ca 56r, DaB 123r,
Mc127 188, McP 99: 327, McV 117r, Ott 165v, Ve 103v.

196 RL: GR 211-214 (rubr. var.), MRM 170-171 (rubr. var.). AMS 78b (rubr. var.).
ES: Vl4770 92r-v. BEN: Ben34 117v-118r, Ben35 65r, Ben39 22r, Ben40 12r, Ca
56r-v, Mc127 188-189, McP 99: 330, Mc546 91-92, McV 119v, Ott 166r-v, PuV
55, Ve 103v.

desertum quadraginta annis et manna cibaui te et introduxi in terram satis optimam. Parasti crucem. ♪ *et illi ut supra. in tertio dicant latores.* ♪ Quid
51r ultra debui facere tibi et non feci. Ego quidem | plantaui te uineam meam speciosissimam. Et tu facta es michi nimis amara. Aceto namque siti mea potasti. Et lancea aperuisti latus saluatori tuo. ♪ *et respondeant ut supra.* ♪ Agios. ♪ *et in choro.* ♪ Sanctus deus. ♪

197

Finitis uersibus. discoperiant latores crucem. dicentes alta uoce. ♪ Ecce lignum crucis in quo salus mundi pependit. Venite adoremus. ♪ *Et cum dixerint* Venite adoremus. *mox omnes in choro flexis genibus adorent crucem. et surgentes dicant.* PSALMVM. Beati immaculati. *et per tres uersus eadem antiphona repetatur.* Ecce lignum.

198

Interea ueniens sacerdos cum ministris et incenso stent ante ipsam crucem. et adoratam deosculentur eam. deinde ceteri per ordinem. et adorauerint cantando antiphonam hanc.

199

♪ Crucem tuam adoramus domine. Et sanctam resurrectionem tuam glorifica-
51v mus. Venite omnes adore|mus christi resurrectionem. PSALMVS Deus misereatur nobis. ♪

---

196 *qua*draginta: E *et²*: E ci*b*aui: FE *te⁴*: EDFE introdu*x*i: FE
*in te*rram: EDE *satis*: DCFE *optimam*: DEDEDFE debu*i*: DE
facere: EDC *et³*: DE plan*t*aui: FE *te⁵*: DC ui*neam*: DCDC
specio*sis*simam: GF *Et⁴*: CDC *a*mara: GFEDC Ace*to*: DEF
siti: EFE *Et⁵*: CDC *lan*cea: DEFG la*tus*: DE tu*o²*: FE
Agi*os⁴*: FGFED San*ctus⁴*: FGFED

197 *li*gnum: DFEC sa*lus*: A *mundi*: GAGFE *pe*pendit: F Veni*te*: GFDEDC

199 *Vide Intro. p. 82*

---

197 RL: GR 211 (om. ps.), MRM 170. AMS 78b. ES: Vl4770 (91v), 92v. BEN: Ben35 65r-v, Ben40 11v, Ca 56v, McP 99: 330, Ve 103v. Var.: BEN: Ben34 117v (ante *Populus meus*), Ben39 21v, Mc127 188, Mc546 91, McV 117v, Ott 166r.

198 RL: MRM 170. BEN: Ca 56v, Mc127 188, McV 117v. Var.: BEN: McP 99: 330.

199 Ps 66: 2. RL: GR 217 ("Venite ... resurrectionem" om., melodia var.), MRM 171 (var.: "Venite ... resurrectionem" om.). AMS 78b. ES: Vl4770 (91v), 92v. BEN: Ben34 115v (ps. *Laudate.*), Ben35 65v (ps. *Laudate*), Ben40 11r (ps. *Laudate*), McP 99: 334, McV 119r, Ott 166v (var.), PuV 56 (ps. var.), Ve 103v-104r.

200

Et per unumquemque uersus, eadem antiphona repetatur. Quibus expletis tres clerici uenientes ante crucem, incipiant YMNVM. Crux fidelis. *et in choro similiter.* Crux fidelis. *et illi ante crucem.* Pange lingua. *Per ordinem et per unumquemque uersum, semper a choro repetatur.* Crux fidelis. *Et postea cantent hos uersos. usquedum adoratur crux.*

201

♪ Ego propter te flagellaui egiptum cum primogenitis suis. Et tu me flagellatum tradidisti. RESP. Popule meus. VERSVS Ego te eduxi de egipto demerso pharaone in mare rubrum. Et tu me tradidisti principibus sacerdotum. RESP. Popule meus. Ego ante te aperui mare. Et tu aperuisti lancea latus meum. Popule meus. ♪

202

ITEM ORATIO. Domine iesu christe adoro te in crucem.

203

Qua salutata ab omnibus, et reposita in loco suo. duo presbiteri, et duo subdiaconi. intrent in secretarium ubi positum fuerat corpus domini.
52r *quod pridie remansit. ponentes illud in patena. et sub\diaconus teneat ante eos, cum uino non sacrato. et alter subdiaconus patenam cum corpore domini. quibus tenentibus accipiat unus presbiter patenam. et*

---

201 G *inc.*] C *inc.* GR (c-*clavis*] F-*clavis trans.* GR *passim*)   egiptum: B
tradidisti[1]: cBABAG   egipto: B   principi*bus sacerdotum*: BcBABAG
latus meum: cBABAG

---

200 RL: GR 218-221, 222-225, MRM 172-173. AMS 78b. ES: Vl4770 91v-92r, 92v. BEN: Ca 56v, McP 99: 334, Mc127 189, Mc546 94, McV 120r, Ott 166v (ante *Crucem tuam*), PuV 57-58, Ve 104r.

201 RL: GR 214-217, MRM 171. BEN: Ben34 118r-119r, Ben39 22r-23r, Ben40 12r-v, Mc127 189, Mc546 92-94, McV 119v-120r, PuV 55-56. Vide Drumbl, "Improperien," pp. 68-100.

202 Vat. lat. 7818 11r-v (Andrieu, *Pontifical romain*, 1: 53). Vide Wilmart, "Prières médiévales," pp. 22-65.

203 RL: GR (Com.: 155, [104]), MRM 173 (rubr. var.), (116: Com.). AMS (67b: Com.). BEN: Ben33 (66r-v: Com.), Ben34 (98v-99r: Com.), Ben38 (4r-v: Com.), Ca 56v, McP 99: 335 (Com. om.), Mc127 189 (var.), McV 120r (var.), PuC (445: Com.).

alius calicem. et deferant super nudum altare, cantando hanc COMMV-
NIONEM. ♪ Hoc corpus quod pro uobis tradetur. ♪ *et alter dicat.* ♪ Hic calix
noui testamenti est in meo sanguine dicit dominus. Hoc facite quotienscumque
sumitis in meam commemorationem. ♪

204

Qua finita incipiat episcopus. ♪ In spiritu humilitatis et in anima contrita
suscipiamur domine ad te. et sic fiat sacrificium nostrum ut a te suscipiatur hodie
et placeat tibi domine deus. ♪ *Inclinans se altari, et cum se erexerit dicat.*
Oremus. Preceptis salutaribus. *Vsque* Pater noster. *Deinde offeratur ei
patena. qui ponat eam super altare. Calicem uero diaconus ponat super
altare. deinde dicat sacerdos alta uoce.* ORATIONEM. Libera nos quesumus
domine ab omnibus. *usque* Per omnia secula seculorum. Amen.

205

52v *Deinde sumat de sancta, et ponat in calici nichil dicens.* | *nisi secrete
aliquid dicere uoluerit.* Pax domini. *non dicatur. quia oscula non se-
cuntur. Et sic cum silentio communicent omnes. et post paululum
unusquisque priuatim cum silentio cantent uesperum. et sic uadant ad
commedendum qui uolunt.*

IN SABBATO SANCTO.

206

BENEDICTIO IGNI NOVI. ORATIO Domine deus pater omnipotens.
exaudi nos lumen indeficiens. tu es sancte conditor omnium luminum.

---

203 fa*ci*te: AG   *quoti*enscumque: GB

204 *Vide Ar 365 (om. GR).*   *a*nima: F   *contrita*: FDEFDCDC   *fi*at:
FAGA   susci*pi*atur: C   *hodie*: DFCG'   *do*mine[2]: DC   *de*us: FED

---

204 RL: Ar 365, MRM 173-174 (m. v.). BEN: Ben39 25r (m. v.), Ben40 14v (m. v.),
DaB 123r (m. v.), Ott 166v (m. v.), Ve 104r (m. v.). Var.: BEN: Ben33 72v, Ben38
43r, Ca 56v-57r, Mc127 189, McP 99: 335, McV 120r.

205 RL: MRM 174 (var.). BEN: Ben33 72v (rubr. var.), Ben38 43r, Ben40 14v (m.
v.), Ca 57r (var.), DaB 123r (m. v.), Mc127 189 (var.), McP 99: 335 (var.), McV
120r (var.), Ott 166v (var.), Ve 104r (var.).

206 RL: MRM 174-175. GEL8: Ge (2848), Pr 96.1. ES: F (2774). BEN: Ben29 159r,
Ben38 45v (var.), McP (99: 217), Ve 104r (manu recent.).

bene ✳ dic domine hoc lumen quod a te sanctificatum atque
bene ✳ dictum est. tu illuminasti omnem mundum; ut ab eo lumine
accendamur et illuminemur igne claritatis tue. sicut illuminasti moysem; ita illuminare corda nostra et sensus nostros. ut ad uitam eternam
peruenire mereamur. per dominum.

207

BENEDICTIO CEREI. *Ter dicat.* ♪ Lumen xpisti. Deo gratias. EXVL-
TET iam angelica turba celorum. exultent diuina mysteria et pro tanti regis
53r uictoria tuba intonet salutaris. Gaudeat se tan|tis tellus irradiata fulgoribus. et
eterni regis splendore illustrata. totius orbis se sentiat amississe caligine. Letetur
et mater ecclesia tanti luminis adornata fulgore. et magnis populorum uocibus
hec aula resultet. Quapropter astantibus uobis fratres karissimi. ad tam miram
sancti huius luminis claritatem. una mecum queso dei omnipotentis misericordiam inuocate. Vt qui me non meis meritis intra leuitarum numerum dignatus est
agregari luminis sui gratiam infundens. cerei huius laudem implere precipiat. Per
53v dominum nostrum | iesum christum filium suum. uiuentem secum atque regnan-
tem in unitate spiritu sancti deus. Per omnia secula seculorum. Amen. ♪

208

♪ Dominus uobiscum. Et cum spiritu tuo. Sursum corda. Habemus ad dominum. Gratias agamus domino deo nostro. Dignum et iustum est. ♪
♪ Vere quia dignum et iustum est. per christum dominum nostrum. Vt inuisibi-
lem deum patrem omnipotentem. filiumque eius unigenitum dominum nostrum
iesum christum. toto cordis ac mentis affectu. et uocis misterio personemus. Qui
pro nobis eterno patri ade; debitum soluit. et ueteris piaculi cautionem. pio

---

207 uocibus] uocibus uocibus *ante corr.*

---

207 *Vide Intro. p. 85*

208 *Vide Intro. p. 87*

---

207 RL: MRM 176. GREG: Sp 1021. GEL8: En 733, Ge 677, Rh 424, Sg 538. ES:
Vl4770 93r, 99v-100r. BEN: Ben29 159r-160r, Ben33 76v, Ca 57r, DaB 123r-v,
Mc127 190, McP 99: 347, McV 120v-121r, Ott 167r-v, PuV 70, Ve 104r. Ed.
Hesbert, "Tradition bénéventaine," pp. 399-400.

208 RL: MRM 176-177. GREG: Sp 1022. GEL8: En 734, Ge 678, Rh 425, Sg 539.
ES: Vl4770 100r-v. BEN: Ben29 160r-162v, Ben33 76v-77v (var.), Ca 57r-58r, DaB
123v-125r, McP 99: 347, McV 121r-122v, Ott 168r-171r, Ve 104r-v. Ed. Hesbert,
"Tradition bénéventaine," pp. 400-401.

54r cruore detersit. Hec sunt enim festa pascalia gaudi|orum. in quibus uerus ille agnus occiditur. eiusque sanguis postibus consecratur. In quibus primum patres nostros filios israel. eductos de egypto rubrum mare. sicco uestigio transire fecisti. Hec igitur nox est que peccatorum tenebras. columne illuminatione purgauit. Hec nox est que hodie per uniuersum mundum. in xpisto credentes a uitiis seculi segregatos. et caliginem peccatorum reddit gratie sociat sanctitatem. Hec nox est in qua destructis uinculis mortis. xpistus ab inferis uictor ascendit. Nichil enim nobis nasci profuit. nisi redimi profuisset. O mira circa nos tue

54v pietatis digna|tio. O inestimabilis dilectio caritatis. ut seruum redimeres filium tradidisti. O certe necessarium ade peccatum. quod xpisti morte deletum est. O felix culpa. que talem ac tantum meruit habere, redemptorem. O beata nox. que sola meruit scire tempus et horam. in qua christus ab inferis resurrexit. Hec nox est de qua scriptum est. et nox ut dies illuminabitur. et nox illuminatio mea in deliciis meis. Huius igitur sanctificatio noctis. fugat scelera. culpas lauat. et reddit innocentiam lapsis. mestis letitiam. fugat hodia. concordiam parat et curuat imperia.♪ *Hic ponantur .V. grana incensi in modum crucis.* [*lac.*]

\<DOMINICA .IV. POST PASCHA\>

209

55r [*lac.*] | [Io 16: 14] -bit quia de meo accipiet. et annuntiabit uobis.

210

OFFERTORIVM Iubilate deo uniuersa. *Dominica .I. post epiphania.*

---

209 *lac. inter 54v-55r*

210 Dominica ... epiphania *add. inter lin.*

---

209 Io 16: 14. RL: MRM 228-229 (Io 16: 5-14 *Vado ad eum*). LEC: Mu 82, WuE 306, CoP 214. ES: Vl4770 133v. BEN: Ben29 189r-v, Ben30 97v-98r, Ben33 90r, Ca 74v, DaB 159r-v, DaE 91v, Mc127 237-238, McV 160v-161r, Ott 246r-v, Ve 119r-v.

210 Ps 99: 2 (vide **63** supra: **Ps 99: 2-3**). RL: GR 270, MRM 229. AMS 90. ES: Vl4770 133v. BEN: Ben29 189v, Ben30 98r, Ben33 90r, Ben34 151r (38r-39r), Ben35 86v, Ben38 68v, Ben39 (56r), Ben40 45r, Ca 74v, DaB 159v, Mc127 238, McV 161r, Ott 246v, Ve 119v.

211

SECRETA Deus qui nos per huius sacrificii ueneranda comercia. unius summe diuinitatis participes effecti. presta quesumus. ut sicut tuam cognouimus ueritatem. sic eam dignis moribus assequamur. per.

212

COMMVNIO ♪ Cum uenerit paraclitus spiritus ueritatis ille arguet mundum de peccato et de iustitia et de iudicio alleluia alleluia. ♪

213

POSTCOMMVNIO Adesto nobis domine deus noster. ut hec que fideliter sumpsimus. et purgemur a uitiis et a periculis omnibus exuamur. per.

DOMINICA .V.

214

♪ Vocem iocunditatis annuntiate et audiatur alleluia. nuntiate usque ad extremum terre liberauit dominus populum suum alleluia alleluia. PSALMVS Iubilate deo seruite. ♪

---

212 ueri*ta*tis: cdcd   *ille arguet mundum*: AedefefecdedcBcd   peccato ... *ad finem*: F ... F] G ... G *trans.* GR *passim*

214 Vo*cem*: FDGED   *iocunditatis*: FGAcB   *annun*tiate: GB   au*di*atur: AcG   al*le*luia[1]: DGE   nunti*ate*: FG   *ad*: B   extremum: BcBcBcedcB ter*re*: BdcBAGAG   alle*lui*a[2]: GFE   Ps.: GABcAGABG

---

211 RL: MRM 229. SAC: Va 553. GREG: Pa 412, Sp 1121. GEL8: En 924, Ge 927, Rh 556, Sg 728. AM: Sb (647). ES: Vl4770 133v-134r. BEN: Ben29 189v, Ben30 98r, Ben33 90r, Ca 74v, DaB 159v, Mc127 238, McV 161r, Ott 246v, Ve 119v.

212 Io 16: 8. RL: GR 270, MRM 229. AMS 90. ES: Vl4770 134r. BEN: Ben29 189v-190r, Ben30 98r, Ben33 90r, Ben34 151r, Ben35 86v, Ben38 68v, Ben39 (56r), Ben40 45r, Ca 74v-75r, DaB 159v, Mc127 238, McV 161r, Ott 246v, Ve 119v.

213 RL: MRM 229. SAC: Le (556-557), Va 555. GREG: Pa 414, Sp 1122. GEL8: En 926, Ge 929, Rh 558, Sg 730. AM: Sb 664. ES: Vl4770 134r. BEN: Ben29 190r, Ben30 98r-v, Ben33 90r, Ca 75r, DaB 159v, Mc127 238, McV 161r, Ott 246v, Ve 119v.

214 Is 48: 20, Ps 99: 2. RL: GR 270-271, MRM 229 (ps. var.). AMS 91. ES: Vl4770 134r. BEN: Ben29 190r, Ben30 98v (ps. var.), Ben33 90v, Ben34 151r-v, Ben35 86v, Ben38 68v, Ben39 (56r), Ben40 45r, Ca 75r, DaB 159v, Mc127 238 (ps. var.), McV 161r, Ott 246v, Ve 119v-120r.

215

55v ORATIO | Deus a quo bona cuncta procedunt. largire supplicibus. ut cogitemus te inspirante que recta sunt. et te gubernante eadem faciamus. per.

216

BEATI IACOBI APOSTOLI [1: 22-27]. Karissimi. Estote factores uerbi. et non auditores. ... ab hoc seculo.·,

217

56r ♪ Alleluia. VERSVS Exiui a patre et ueni in mun|dum iterum relinquo mundum et uado ad patrem. ♪

218

♪ Alleluia. VERSVS Vsque modo non petistis quicquam in nomine meo petite et accipietis. ♪

---

216 in lege perfecte libertatis] in lege perfecta libertatis *Vulgata* (1: 25)   et immaculatum] inmaculatum (1: 27)

---

217 *Vide Intro. p. 93*

218 *Vide Intro. p. 94*

---

215 RL: MRM 229. SAC: Va 556. GREG: Pa 424, Sp 1123. GEL8: En 944, Ge 949, Rh 568, Sg 748. ES: Vl4770 134r. BEN: Ben29 190r, Ben30 98v, Ben33 90v, Ca 75r, DaB 159v-160r, Mc127 238, McO 346, McV 161r, Ott 246v, Ve 120r.

216 Iac 1: 22-27. RL: MRM 229-230. LEC: Alc 111, Mu 84, WuC 97, CoP 218. ES: Vl4770 134r. BEN: Ben29 190r, Ben30 98v-99r, Ben33 90v, Ca 75r-v, DaB 160r, Mc127 238, McV 161r-v, Ott 246v-247r, Ve 120r.

217 Io 16: 28. RL: GR 272 (melodia var.), MRM 230. ES: Schlager, *Katalog* D 4. BEN: Ben29 190r-v, Ben34 (150r), Ben35 86r, Ca 75v, DaB 160r, Mc127 239, McV 160v, Ott 247r.

218 Io 16: 24. RL: MRM (2: 334, 336). ES: Schlager, *Katalog* E 164, Syg 168-169. LS: Gs 130 (melodia var.). BEN: Ben39 (57r), Ve 120r.

219

SEQVENTIA SANCTI EVANGELII SECVNDVM IOHANNEM [16: 23-30]. In illo
tempore. Dixit iesus discipulis suis. Amen amen dico uobis. si quid
56v petieritis patrem ... | ... quia a deo existi.

220

OFFERTORIVM ♪ Benedicite gentes dominum deum nostrum et ob<audite>
uoci laudis eius qui posuit ani<mam> meam ad uitam et non dedit commoueri
pedes meos. benedictus dominus qui non amouit deprecationem meam et
misericordiam suam a me alleluia. ♪

221

SECRETA Suscipe domine fidelium preces cum oblationibus hostiarum.
ut per hec pie deuotionis officia. ad celestem gloriam transeamus. per.

222

COMMVNIO ♪ Cantate domino alleluia cantate domino et benedicite nomen
eius. bene nuntiate de die in die salutare eius. alleluia alleluia. ♪

---

219 ueniet] venit *Vulgata* (16: 25)   de patre meo] de patre (16: 25)   in illo
die] illo die (16: 26)   a deo exiui] ego a deo exivi (16: 27)   discipuli] discipuli
eius (16: 29)

---

220 be*ne*dictus: F   a*mo*uit: DFC   deprecatio*nem*: DF   me*am*²: FCD
al*le*luia: CFGFECDFDFGFG

---

222 D *inc.*] A *inc.* GR (F-*clavis*] c-*clavis trans.* GR *passim*)   *no*men: DFEF
*be*ne: AGAEFGFG   nun*ti*ate: FC   sa*lu*tare: DC

---

219 Io 16: 23-30. RL: MRM 230. LEC: Mu 84, WuE 306, CoP 219. ES: Vl4770
134r-v. BEN: Ben29 190v, Ben30 99r-100r, Ben33 90v, Ca 75v, DaB 160r-v, DaE
92v, Mc127 239, McV 161v, Ott 247r-v, Ve 120r.

220 Ps 65: 8-9, 20. RL: GR 272-273, MRM 230. AMS 91. ES: Vl4770 134v (var.:
"Benedictus" ad finem om.). BEN: Ben29 190v, Ben30 100r (var.), Ben33 90v,
Ben34 152v (93v-94r), Ben35 87v, Ben38 69v, Ben39 (58r), Ben40 45v, Ca 75v,
DaB 160v, Mc127 239, McV 161v-162r, Ott 247v, Ve 120r.

221 RL: MRM 230. GREG: Ha (402, 743), Pa 425, Sp 1124. GEL8: En (1649), Ge
(1603), Sg 750. ES: Vl4770 134v. BEN: Ben29 190v, Ben30 100r, Ben33 90v, Ca
75v, DaB 160v, Mc127 239-240, McV 162r, Ott 247v, Ve 120r.

222 Ps 95: 2. RL: GR 273, MRM 230. AMS 91. ES: Vl4770 134v. BEN: Ben29
190v-191r, Ben30 100r, Ben33 90v-91r, Ben34 152v, Ben35 87v, Ben38 69v,
Ben39 (58r-v), Ben40 45v, Ca 75v, DaB 160v, Mc127 240, McV 162r, Ott 247v,
Ve 120r-v.

223

57r POSTCOMMVNIO Tribue nobis domine celestis mense uirtutem sa|tiatis. et desiderare que recta sunt. <et de>siderata percipere. per.

TEMPORE ROGATIONIS FERIA .II.

224

♪ Exaudiuit de templo sancto suo uocem meam alleluia et clamor meus in cons<pectu eiu>s introiuit in aures eius alleluia alleluia. PSALMVS Diligam te domine. ♪

225

ORATIO Presta quesumus omnipotens deus. ut qui in afflictione nostra de tua pietate confidimus. contra aduersa omnia tua protectione muniamur. per.

226

BEATI PETRI APOSTOLI [1 Petr 5: 6-11]. Karissimi. Humiliamini sub 57v potenti manu dei. ... | ... imperium in secula seculorum. Amen.

---

226 et uigilate] vigilate *Vulgata* (5: 8)   in fide] fide (5: 9)   eandem passionem] eadem passionum (5: 9)   fraternitati uestre] vestrae fraternitati (5: 9)   et confirmabit] confirmabit (5: 10)   gloria et imperium] imperium (5: 11)

---

224 *meam*: DEGFED   *et clamor*: EFGAG   *in²*: E   *eius²*: GFED   Ps.: AGAFGAGE

---

223 RL: MRM 230. SAC: Le (543), Va 560. GREG: Pa 427, Sp 1125. GEL8: En 948, Ge 954, Sg 752. AM: Sb 669. ES: Vl4770 134v. BEN: Ben29 191r, Ben30 100r, Ben33 91r, Ca 75v, DaB 160v, Mc127 240, McV 162r, Ott 247v, Ve 120v.

224 Ps 17: 7, 17: 2. RL: GR 282, MRM 231. AMS 94a. ES: Vl4770 127v. BEN: Ben29 191r, Ben33 91v, Ben34 161v, Ben35 95v-96r, Ben38 74r, Ben39 65v, Ben40 50v, Ca 75v-76r, DaB 160v, Mc127 390, McV 162r, Ott (255r), PuC 464, Ve 120v.

225 RL: MRM 231. GREG: Ha 472, Pa 405. GEL8: En 965, Ge 895, Sg 719. AM: Sb 703. ES: Vl4770 127v-128r. BEN: Ben29 191r, Ben33 (92r), Ca 76r, DaB 160v, Mc127 390, McO 355, McV 162r, Ott 253v, PuC 465, Ve 120v.

226 1 Petr 5: 6-11. RL: MRM (260). BEN: Ben29 191r, DaB 160v-161r, Mc127 390, McV 162r, Ott 253v.

227

♪ Alleluia. VERSVS Confitemini domino et inuocate nomen eius annuntiate <inter gen>tes opera eius. ♪

228

SECVNDVM MARCVM [2: 13-17]. In illo tempore. Cum egressus esset iesus ad mare omnis turba ueniebat ad eum ... peccatores.

229

58r OFFERTORIVM | ♪ Confitebor domino nimis in ore meo et in medio multorum laudabo eum qui assistit ad dexterram pauperis ut saluam faceret a persequentibus animam meam alleluia. ♪

230

SECRETA Hec munera domine quesumus et uincula nostra absoluant iniquitatis. et tue misericordie dona concilient. per.

---

228 leui] Levin *Vulgata* (2: 14)   manducat] manducat et bibit (2: 16)

---

227 D *inc.*] A *inc.* GR (F-*clavis*] c-*clavis trans.* GR *passim*)   domi*no*: DC   *et*: EC   *inuocate*: DEGFGFDC   annunti*ate*: DAGFDGFECDFD   *gen*tes: [*lac.*] GAFD   o*pera*: D   *eius*: DFDFGFGAFCFED

229 me*o et*: cAGAG   *dex*terram: BdBd   pau*peris*: AGA   per*sequentibus*: GcdBcB   *animam*: AGdcA   *meam*: GAGF   *alle*luia: GAGcdcdcAFG-FAGAcdcA

---

227 Ps 104: 1. RL: GR (376), MRM (291). AMS 94a. ES: Vl4770 128r. BEN: Ben29 191r, Ben34 162r, Ben35 96r, Ben38 74r-v, Ben39 65v-66r, Ben40 50v, Mc127 390, McV 162v, Ott (255v), Ve 120v.

228 Mc 2: 13-17. BEN: Ben29 191r-v, DaB 161r, Mc127 390-391, McV 162v, Ott 253v-254r.

229 Ps 108: 30-31. RL: GR 283, MRM 232. AMS 94b. ES: Vl4770 128r. BEN: Ben29 191v, Ben33 92r, Ben34 162r-v, Ben35 96r-v, Ben38 74v, Ben39 67r-v, Ben40 50v-51r, Ca 76v, DaB 161r, Mc127 391, McV 162v, Ott (255v), PuC 469, Ve 121r.

230 RL: MRM 232. SAC: Va (1050). GREG: Ha 473, Pa 406. GEL8: En 966, Ge 896, Sg 720. AM: Sb 722. ES: Vl4770 128r. BEN: Ben29 191v, Ben33 92r, Ca 76v, DaB 161r, Mc127 391, McV 162v, Ott 254r, PuC 470, Ve 121r.

231

COMMVNIO ♪ Petite et accipietis querite et inuenietis pulsate et aperietur uobis omnis enim qui petit accipit et qui querit inuenit pulsanti aperietur alleluia. ♪

232

POSTCOMMVNIO Pretende nobis domine quesumus misericordiam tuam. ut que uotis expetimus. conuersatione tibi placita consequamur. per.

FERIA .III.

233

INTROITVS Exaudiuit.

234

Presta quesumus omnipotens deus. ut qui iram tue indignationis agnouimus. misericordie tue indulgentiam consequamur.

235

PETRI APOSTOLI [1 Petr 3: 8-15]. Karissimi. Omnes unanimes in fide 58v estote | compatientes. ... in cordibus uestris.

---

235 neque maledictum] vel maledictum *Vulgata* (3: 9)   sequatur] persequatur (3: 11)   ad preces] in preces (3: 12)   patiamini] patimini (3: 14)   beati eritis] beati (3: 14)

---

231 pul*san*ti: DFGFEFGFG   *allelu*ia: CFAGAFGFEGFGECDEFGFEDE-FEDE

---

231 **Lc 11: 9-10**. RL: GR 284, MRM 232. AMS 94b. ES: Vl4770 128v. BEN: Ben29 191v, Ben33 92r, Ben34 162v, Ben35 96v, Ben38 74v-75r, Ben39 67v, Ben40 51r, Ca 76v, DaB 161v, Mc127 391, McV 162v, Ott (256r), PuC 471, Ve 121r.

232 SAC: Le (554). GREG: Ha 475, Pa (872). GEL8: En 978, Ge 899, Rh 575. ES: Vl4770 (128v). BEN: Ben29 191v, DaB 161v, Mc127 391, McV 162v, Ott 254r.

233 **Ps 17: 7**. RL: GR 282, MRM 231. AMS 94a. ES: Vl4770 (127v). BEN: Ben29 191v, Ben34 (161v), Ben35 (95v-96r), Ben38 (74r), Ben39 65v, Ben40 (50v), Ca 76v, DaB 161v, Mc127 391, McV 163r, Ott (255r), PuC 464, Ve 121r.

234 GREG: Ha (859), Pa (949). GEL8: En (971), Ge (901), Rh (570). BEN: Ben29 191v, DaB 161v, Mc127 391, McV 163r.

235 **1 Petr 3: 8-15**. RL: MRM (263). BEN: Ben29 192r, DaB 161v, Mc127 391, McV 163r, Ott 254r-v.

236

SECVNDVM MARCVM [4: 35-40]. In illo tempore. Cum sero esset
59r factum. dixit iesus discipulis suis. transeamus contra. ... | ... obediunt
ei?

237

OFFERTORIVM Confitebor domino.

238

SECRETA Quesumus domine nostris placare muneribus. quoniam tu
eadem tribuisti ut placareris. per.

239

Petite.

240

POSTCOMMVNIO Propitiare domine iniquitatibus nostris. et exorabilis
tuis esto supplicibus. ut concessa uenia quam precamur. perpetuo
misericordie tue munere gloriemur. per.

---

236 in naui erant] erat in navi *Vulgata* (4: 36)   nauim] navem (4: 37)

---

236 Mc 4: 35-40. RL: MRM (2: 364). BEN: Ben29 192r-v, DaB 161v-162r, Mc127
391-392, McV 163r, Ott 254v-255r.

237 Ps 108: 30. RL: GR 283, MRM 232. AMS 94b. ES: Vl4770 (128r). BEN: Ben29
(191v), Ben34 (162r-v), Ben35 (96r-v), Ben38 (74v), Ben39 (67r-v), Ben40
(50v-51r), Ca (76v), DaB 162r, Mc127 (391: ref.), McV (162v), Ott (255v), PuC
469.

238 SAC: Va (1335). GREG: Tc (2479, 2494). GEL8: En (2222), Ge 906, Rh
(1239). BEN: Ben29 192v, Ben33 92r-v, DaB 162r, Mc127 392, McV 163v, Ott
255r.

239 Lc 11: 9. RL: GR 284, MRM 232. AMS 94b. ES: Vl4770 (128v). BEN: Ben29
(191v), Ben34 (162v), Ben35 96v), Ben38 (74v-75r), Ben39 (67v), Ben40 (51r),
Ca (76v), DaB 162r, Mc127 (391: ref.), McV (162v), Ott (256r), PuC 471.

240 GREG: Ha (882). GEL8: En (1952), Ge 911. AM: Sb (697: m. v.). BEN: Ben29
192v, DaB 162r, Mc127 392, McV 163v, Ott 255r.

VIGILIA ASCENSIONIS.

241

♪ Omnes gentes plaudite manibus iubilate deo in uoce exultationis. PSALMVS Subiecit populos. ♪

242

59v ORATIO Deus cuius filius in alta celorum potenter ascen│dens; cap-
tiuitatem nostram; sua duxit uirtute captiuam. tribue quesumus. ut
dona que suis participibus contulit. largiatur et nobis. Iesus christus.

243

LECTIO EPISTOLE BEATI PAVLI APOSTOLI AD PHESIOS [4: 7-13]. Fratres.
Vnicuique nostrum data est gratia; secundum mensuram ... plenitudi-
nis christi domini nostri.

244

♪ Alleluia. VERSVS Ascendit deus in iubilatione et dominus in uoce tube. ♪

---

243 adimpleret] impleret *Vulgata* (4: 10)   quidem prophetas ... apostolos]
quidem apostolos ... prophetas (4: 11)   agnitionem] agnitionis (4: 13)

---

241 Ps.: FGFGABAGFABGFGFDFGF

244 *deus*: GAGEGFG   iubi*latio*ne: GAGAFDEGFD   domi*nus*: ABGE-
GABFDFDGFEGAFGEFDFGFE

---

241 Ps 46: 2, 46: 4. RL: GR (336: ps. var.), MRM (266: ps. var.). AMS 101*bis*. ES:
Vl4770 140r (ps. var.). BEN: Ben29 192v (ps. var.), Ben33 95v, Ben34 177r, Ben35
107r-v, Ben38 88v, Ben39 85v-86r, Ben40 66v, Ca 76v, DaB 162r, Mc127 392,
McV 163v, Ott 256r, PuC 506, Ve 121r.

242 SAC: Va (578). GREG: Ha (503: Ascen.), Pa (447). GEL8: Ge (985), Rh (598),
Sg (780). AM: Sb (685). BEN: Ben29 192v, Ben33 95v, DaB 162r, Mc127 392, McV
163v, Ott 256r, PuC 507, Ve (122v).

243 Eph 4: 7-13. RL: MRM 232. LEC: Alc 114. BEN: DaB 162r, Mc127 392, PuC
508.

244 Ps 46: 6. RL: GR (286), MRM (234). AMS (102a). ES: Vl4770 140v. BEN: Ben33
96r, Ben34 177r, Ben35 107v, Ben38 88v-89r, Ben39 86r, Ben40 67r, Ca 77r,
Mc127 (394), PuC 509, Ve 121v.

245

60r | SECVNDVM IOHANNEM [17: 1-11]. In illo tempore. Subleuatis oculis
60v iesus ... | ... uenio.

246

OFFERTORIVM ♪ Ascendit deus in iubilatione et dominus in uoce tube alleluia. ♪

247

SECRETA Sacrificium domine, pro filii tui supplices uenerabili nunc
quam preuenimus ascensione deferimus. presta quesumus. ut et nos
per ipsum his commerciis sacrosanctis. ad celestia consurgamus. per.

248

COMMVNIO ♪ Psallite domino qui ascendit super celos celorum ad orientem
alleluia. ♪

---

245 ut et filius] et *om. Vulgata* (17: 1)   facerem] faciam (17: 4)   claritate]
claritatem (17: 5)   et nunc] nunc (17: 7)

---

246 *de*us: ABcdcAGABAB   tu*be*: EGF   al*lelu*ia: GAGFGEFD-
FGFAGFDGFGFD

248 *su*per: Acdc   *o*rientem: DFGA

---

245 Io 17: 1-11. RL: MRM 232-233. LEC: Mu 86, WuE 306, CoP 223. ES: Vl4770
140v. BEN: Ben29 193r-v, Ben33 96r, Ca 77r, DaB 162r-v, DaE 97v, Mc127
392-393, McV 163v-164r, Ott 256v, Ott¹ 9, PuC 510, Ve 121v.

246 Ps 46: 6. RL: GR (287), MRM (235). AMS (102a). ES: Vl4770 140v. BEN: Ben29
193v, Ben33 96r, Ben34 177r-v, Ben35 107v, Ben38 89r, Ben39 86v, Ben40 67r-v,
Ca 77r, DaB 162v, Mc127 393, McV 164r, Ott 256v, Ott¹ 10, PuC 511, Ve (122v).

247 SAC: Va (574). GEL8: Ge 973, Rh 587, Sg 768. AM: Sb (682). ES: Vl4770 140v.
BEN: Ben29 193v, Ca 77r, DaB 162v, Mc127 393, McV 164r, Ott 256v, Ott¹ 11,
PuC 512, Ve 121 (m. v.).

248 Ps 67: 33-34. RL: GR (287), MRM (234). AMS (102b). ES: Vl4770 (141v). BEN:
Ben29 (194v-195r), Ben33 (97r), Ben34 (182r), Ben35 (110r-v), Ben38 (93r),
Ben39 (91r), Ben40 (71r), Ca (78r), DaB (164r), Mc127 (395), McV (165v), Ott
(258r), PuC (523), Ve (122v).

249

POSTCOMMVNIO Tribue quesumus domine. ut per hec sacramenta que sumpsimus. illuc tendat nostre deuotionis affectus. quo tecum est nostra substantia. Iesus christus.

IN DIE ASCENSIONIS.

250

♪ Viri galilei quid ammiramini aspicientes in celum alleluia quemammodum uidistis eum ascendentem in celum. ita ♪ [*lac.*]

251

61r [*lac.*] | ♪ -tem in celum. alleluia. ♪

252

SECRETA Suscipe domine munera que pro filii tui gloriosa ascensione deferimus. et concede propitius. ut et a presentibus periculis liberemur. et ad uitam perueniamus eterna. per.

---

251 *lac. inter 60v-61r*

---

250 a*spicientes*: cdA   *in*[1]: c   *al*leluia: AG   ui*distis*: c   *in*[2]: ABc
ce*lum*[2]: B

251 *Vide Intro. p. 98*

---

249 SAC: Va (584). GEL8: Ge 975, Rh 589, Sg 770. AM: Sb 674. ES: Vl4770 140v. BEN: Ben29 193v, Ben33 96v, Ca 77r, DaB 163r, Mc127 393, McV 164r-v, Ott 257r, PuC 514, Ve 122r.

250 Act 1: 11. RL: GR 285-286, MRM 233. AMS 102a. ES: Vl4770 140v-141r. BEN: Ben29 193v, Ben33 96v, Ben34 178v, Ben35 108r, Ben38 89v, Ben39 87v, Ben40 68r, Ca 77r, DaB 163r, DaZ 352, Mc127 393, McV 164v, Ott 257r, PuC 515, Ve 122r.

251 Act 1: 11. RL: MRM 234 (*Viri Galilaei*). AMS 102b. ES: Syg 180, Vl4770 141v. LS: Gs 133-134. BEN: Ben29 194v, Ben33 97r, Ben34 180v-181r, Ben35 110r, Ben38 92v-93r, Ben39 90r-v, Ben40 70v-71r, Ca 78r, DaB 164r, Mc127 395, McV 165r-v, Ott 258r, PuC 520, Ve (121v).

252 RL: MRM 234. GREG: Ha 498, Pa 441. GEL8: Ge 979, Rh 593, Sg 774. AM: Sb (672). ES: Vl4770 141v. BEN: Ben29 194v, Ben33 97r, Ca 78r, DaB 164r, Mc127 395, McV 165v, Ott 258r, PuC 521, Ve 122v.

253

COMMVNIO Psallite domino.

254

POSTCOMMVNIO Presta quesumus omnipotens et misericors deus. ut que uisibilibus misteriis sumenda percepimus. inuisibili consequamur affectu. per.

VIGILIA PENTECOSTES

255

Fiant letanie pro introitu. deinde dicat. Gloria in excelsis deo.

256

ORATIO Presta quesumus omnipotens deus ut claritatis tue super nos splendor effulgeat. et lux tue lucis corda eorum qui per gratiam tuam renati sunt. spiritus sancti illustratione confirmet. per in unitate.

257

ACTVVM APOSTOLORVM [19: 1-8]. In diebus illis. Cum apollo esset
61v corinti. ... | ... de regno dei.

---

257 et paulus] ut paulus *Vulgata* (19: 1)   dixit] dixitque ad eos (19: 2)   at illi dixerunt] at illi (19: 2)   ille autem ait] ille vero ait (19: 3)   in baptismate iohannis] in Ioannis baptismate (19: 3)   uenturus est] venturus esset (19: 4) erant enim] erant autem (19: 7)   fere uiri] viri fere (19: 7)

---

253 Ps 67: 33. RL: GR 287, MRM 234. AMS 102b. ES: Vl4770 141v. BEN: Ben29 194v-195r, Ben33 97r, Ben34 182r, Ben35 110r-v, Ben38 93r, Ben39 91r, Ben40 71r, Ca 78r, DaB 164r, Mc127 395, McV 165v, Ott 258r, PuC 523, Ve 122v.

254 RL: MRM 234 (m. v.). SAC: Le 172. GREG: Ha 501, Pa 444. GEL8: Ge 982, Rh 596, Sg 777. AM: Sb (690). ES: Vl4770 141v. BEN: Ben29 195r, Ben33 97r, Ca 78r, DaB 164r, Mc127 395, McV 165v, Ott 258r, PuC 524, Ve 122v.

255 RL: GR 290, MRM 237-238 (m. v.). AMS 105. ES: Vl4770 143v (m. v.). BEN: Ben29 197r, Ben33 98r, Ben38 95r (rubr. var.), Ben40 74v (m. v.), DaB 166v, Mc127 244, McV 167v, Ott 259v, Ve 130r, Vl10645 4v.

256 RL: MRM 238. GREG: Ha 520, Pa 460. GEL8: Ge 1014, Rh 614, Sg 799. AM: Sb (765). ES: Vl4770 143r. BEN: Ben29 197v, Ben33 98r (m. v.), Ca 79v, DaB 166v, Mc127 244, McO 365, McV 167v, Ott 259v, PuC 525, Ve 130r.

257 Act 19: 1-8. RL: MRM 238. LEC: Alc 117, Mu 89, CoP 230. ES: Vl4770 143v. BEN: Ben29 197v, Ben33 98r-v, Ca 79v-80r, DaB 166v, DaK 39r, Mc127 244, McV 167v-168r, Ott 259v-260r, PuC 526, Ve 130r.

258

Alleluia. VERSVS Confitemini. *In sabbato sancto.*

259

TRACTVS Laudate dominum omnes gentes.

260

SECVNDVM IOHANNEM [14: 15-21]. In illo tempore. Dixit iesus discipu-
62r lis suis. Si diligitis me mandata mea seruate. ... | ... ei meipsum.

261

OFFERTORIVM ♪ Emitte spiritum tuum et creabuntur et renouabis faciem terre.
sit gloria domini in secula alleluia. ♪

262

SECRETA Munera domine quesumus oblata sanctifica. et corda nostra
sancti spiritus illustratione emunda. per in unitate eiusdem.

---

258 In sabbato sancto *add. inter lin.*

260 quia qui non] quia non *Vulgata* (14: 17)   nescit eum] nec scit (14: 17)
cognoscetis] cognoscitis (14: 17)   uos relinquam] relinquam vos (14: 18)
uidebitis] videtis (14: 19)

---

261 *tu*um: FGBGA   cre*a*buntur: Bdc   *renouabis*: GAcdBdcAdBcdcdcAGA
*faci*em: GAdBdc   glo*ria*: cd   domi*ni*: B   alle*lu*ia: G

---

258 Ps 106: 1. RL: GR 290, MRM 238. AMS 105. ES: Vl4770 143v-144r. BEN: Ben29
197v, Ben33 98v, Ben34 184r (122r), Ben35 111r, Ben38 95v, Ben39 94r, Ben40
75r, Ca 80r, DaB 166v, Mc127 244, McV 168r, Ott 260r, Ve 130r.

259 Ps 116: 1. RL: GR 290, MRM 238. AMS 105. ES: Vl4770 144r. BEN: Ben29 197v,
Ben33 (29r), Ben34 (74r), Ca 80r, DaB 166v, Mc127 244, McV 168r, Ott 260r,
Ve 130r.

260 Io 14: 15-21. RL: MRM 238-239. LEC: Mu 89, WuE 307, CoP 231. ES: Vl4770
144r. BEN: Ben29 197v-198r, Ben33 98v, Ca 80r, DaB 166v-167r, DaE 101v, DaK
39r-v, Mc127 244-245, McV 168r, Ott 260r, PuC 528, Ve 130r-v.

261 Ps 103: 30-31. RL: GR 290-291, MRM 239. AMS 105. ES: Vl4770 144r. BEN:
Ben29 198r, Ben33 98v, Ben34 184r-v, Ben35 111v, Ben38 96r-v, Ben39 94r-v,
Ben40 75r-v, Ca 80r, DaB 167r, Mc127 245, McV 168r, Ott 260r, PuC 529, Ve
130v.

262 RL: MRM 239. GREG: Ha 521, Pa 461. GEL8: Ge (1029), Rh (623), Sg (812).
ES: Vl4770 144r. BEN: Ben29 198r, Ben30 (108v), Ben33 98v, Ca 80r, DaB 167r,
Mc127 245, McV 168r, Ott 260r, PuC (539), Ve 130v.

263

COMMVNIO ♪ Vltimo festiuitatis diem dicebat hiesus qui in me credit flumina de uentre eius fluent aque uiue. hoc autem dixit de spiritu quem accepturi erant credentes in eum alleluia alleluia. ♪

264

62v POSTCOMMVNIO Mentes nostras quesumus domine diuinis reparet | sacramentis. quia ipse est remissio. omnium peccatorum. per eiusdem.

DOMINICA SANCTI PENTECOSTES.

265

♪ Spiritus domini. repleuit orbem terrarum alleluia. et hoc quod continet omnia scientiam habet uocis alleluia. alleluia alleluia. PSALMVS Exurgat deus. ♪

266

ORATIO Deus qui hodierna die corda fidelium sancti spiritus illustratione docuisti. da nobis in eodem spiritu recta sapere. et de eius semper consolatione gaudere. per eiusdem.

---

263 dice*bat*: cBA   hie*sus*: BcdAG   *me*: dede   *de*: c   flu*ent*: FA
*a*que: AGAcBA   *hoc*: BcA   *au*tem: d   spiri*tu*: c   ac*cep*turi: AG
cre*dentes*: FAc   *in*²: cBGABAG   *alle*luia: FAGcded

265 *al*leluia¹: AG   *omnia*: GAB   scien*ti*am: dB   *ha*bet: Bd   alle*luia*³:
cBcAB

---

263 Io 7: 37-39. RL: GR 291, MRM 239. AMS 105. ES: Vl4770 144r. BEN: Ben29 198r, Ben33 98v, Ben34 184v, Ben35 111v-112r, Ben38 96v, Ben39 94v, Ben40 75v, Ca 80r-v, DaB 167r, Mc127 245, McV 168r-v, Ott 260r, PuC 531, Ve 130v.

264 RL: MRM (245). SAC: Le (223), Va (639). GREG: Ha (537), Pa (479). GEL8: Ge (1043), Sg (827). ES: Vl4770 (146r). BEN: Ben29 198r, Ben33 98v, Ca (82r), DaB 167r, Mc127 245, McV 168v, Ott 260r-v, PuC 532, Ve (132v).

265 Sap 1: 7, Ps 67: 2. RL: GR 292-293, MRM 239 (ps. var.). AMS 106. ES: Vl4770 144r-v. BEN: Ben29 198r, Ben30 106r-v, Ben33 99r, Ben34 185r, Ben35 112r-v, Ben38 97r, Ben39 95r-v, Ben40 76r, Ca 80v, DaB 167r-v, Mc127 245, McV 168v, Ott 260v, PuC 533, PuL 71v-72r, Ve 130v.

266 RL: MRM 240. GREG: Ha 526, Pa 466, Z6 xv.1. GEL8: Ge 1028, Rh 621, Sg 810. AM: Sb (763). ES: Vl4770 144v. BEN: Ben29 198v, Ben30 106v, Ben33 99r, Ca 80v, DaB 167v, Mc127 245, McO 366, McV 168v, Ott 260v, PuC 534, PuL 72r, Ve 130v.

267

LECTIO ACTVVM APOSTOLORVM [2: 1-11]. In diebus illis. Cum com-
63r plerentur dies pentecostes. ... | ... magnalia dei.∶,

268

♪ Alleluia. VERSVS Emitte spiritum tuum et creabuntur et renouabis faciem
terre. ♪

269

♪ Alleluia. VERSVS Dum complerentur dies. PROSA Pentecostes promissus
63v celos spiritus adue|niens ignis in egnimate. Bissenos simul comorantes domini
repleuit pleniter discipulos. Linguis effantur omnibus xpisti sacra necnon
magnalia. Erant omnes pariter dicentes. ♪

---

267 omnes discipuli] omnes *Vulgata* (2: 1)   uariis linguis] aliis linguis (2: 4)
sub celo est] sub caelo sunt (2: 5)   mirabantur ad inuicem] mirabantur (2: 7)
ecce omnes] omnes ecce (2: 7)   linguam nostram] lingua nostra (2: 8)
iudeam] et Iudaeam (2: 9)   eos loquentes] loquentes eos (2: 11)

---

268 spiri*tum*: FD   crea*bun*tur: ABGEGABFDFDGFEGAFGEFDFGEF
renouabis: DEFE   ter*re*: ABAGFABAGEGAFEFGFE

269 *Vide Intro. p. 99*

---

267 Act 2: 1-11. RL: MRM 240. LEC: Alc 118, Mu 90, WuC 106, CoP 232, Z6
XV.Ep. ES: Vl4770 144v. BEN: Ben29 198v-199r, Ben30 106r-107v, Ben33 99r, Ca
80v, DaB 167v, DaK 39v-40r, Mc127 245-246, McV 168v-169r, Ott 260v-261r,
PuC 535, PuL 72r-v, Ve 130v-131r.

268 Ps 103: 30. RL: GR 293, MRM 240. AMS 106. ES: Vl4770 144v. BEN: Ben33 99r,
Ben34 187v, Ben35 112v, Ben38 97v, Ben39 95v, Ben40 77r, Ca 80v, McV (173v),
PuC (527), Ve 131r.

269 Act 2: 1. RL: GR (305-306: om. Prosula, melodia m. v.), MRM (250: om. Pr.).
ES: Schlager, *Katalog* D 38, Vl4770 144v (Pr. var.). BEN: Ben29 199r, Ben30 107v,
Ben33 99r, Ben34 187r-v (cum Pr.), Ben35 112v-113r, Ben38 97v, 99r (cum Pr.),
Ben39 95v-96r (cum Pr.), Ben40 77r (cum Pr.), Ca 80v, DaB 168r, Mc127 246,
McV 169r, Ott 261r, PuC 536, PuL 73r.

270

SEQVENTIA SANCTI EVANGELII SECVNDVM IOHANNEM [14: 23-31]. In illo tempore. Dixit iesus discipulis suis. Si quis diligit me sermonem meum
64r seruabit. ... | ... sic facio.

271

OFFERTORIVM ♪ Confirma hoc deus quod operatus es in nobis a templo tuo quod est in ierusalem. tibi offerunt reges munera alleluia. ♪

272

SECRETA Virtute sancti spiritus domine munera nostra continge. ut quod sollempnitate presenti tuo nomine dicauit. et intelligibile nobis faciat et eternum. per in unitate eiusdem.

273

COMMVNIO ♪ Factus est repente de celo sonus aduenientis spiritus uehementis ubi erant sedentes alleluia. et repleti sunt omnes spiritu sancto loquentes
64v ma|gnalia dei alleluia alleluia. ♪

---

270 mansionem] mansiones *Vulgata* (14: 23)   sermonem meum] sermones meos (14: 24)

---

271 *Confirma hoc*: A'CDEFGEAGAFG   *quod*[1]: E   *operatus*: EGF-DFGAGF   *es*: FE   *no*bis: AcGF   *a tem*plo: FGAG   *ti*bi: E   *re*ges: E   *mu*nera: EGF   *al*leluia: AGAFBABGA

273 repen*te*: A   *uehemen*tis: B   *lo*quentes: cBcd   *magnali*a: ABcBAB-cAG   *alleluia*[1]: GcBdcA

---

270 Io 14: 23-31. RL: MRM 241-242. LEC: Mu 90, WuE 307, CoP 233, Z6 xv.Ev. ES: Vl4770 144v-145r. BEN: Ben29 199r-v, Ben30 107v-108v, Ben33 99r-v, Ca 80v-81r, DaB 168r, DaE 102v, DaK 40r, Mc127 246-247, McV 169r, Ott 261r, PuC 537, PuL 73r-73v, Ve 131r-v.

271 Ps 67: 29-30. RL: GR 295-296, MRM 242. AMS 106. ES: Vl4770 145r. BEN: Ben29 199v, Ben30 108v, Ben33 99v, Ben34 189v-190r, Ben35 114v-115r, Ben38 98v-99r, Ben39 97v-98r, Ben40 79r-v, Ca 81r, DaB 168r, Mc127 247, McV 169r-v, PuL 73v, Ve 131v.

272 SAC: Va (626: vig.). GEL8: Ge (1015), Rh (616), Sg (801). AM: Sb (757). ES: Vl4770 145r. BEN: Ben29 199v, Ben33 99v (m. v.), DaB 168r-v, Mc127 247, McV 169v, Ott 261r-v, PuC (530), PuL 73v.

273 Act 2: 2, 4. RL: GR 296, MRM 242. AMS 106. ES: Vl4770 145r. BEN: Ben29 199v, Ben30 109r, Ben33 99v, Ben34 191r, Ben35 115r, Ben38 99r, Ben39 98r-v, Ben40 79v, Ca 81r, DaB 168v, Mc127 247, McV 169v, Ott 261v, PuC 541, PuL 74r, Ve 131v.

274

POSTCOMMVNIO. ORATIO Sancti spiritus domine quesumus corda nostra mundet infusio. et suis roris intima aspersione fecundet. per in unitate eiusdem.

SABBATO DE TEMPORALIA.

275

♪ Karitas dei diffusa est in cordibus uestris alleluia per inhabitantes spiritum eius in uobis alleluia alleluia. PSALMVS Domine deus salutis mee. ♪

276

Dicat. Gloria in excelsis deo. *Et* Credo in.

277

ORATIO Deus qui tribus pueris mitigasti flammas ignium. concede propitius. ut nos famulos tuos non exurat flammas uitiorum. per.

278

PAVLI APOSTOLI AD ROMANOS [5: 1-5]. Fratres. Iustificati igitur ex fide. 65r ... | ... qui datus est nobis.

---

278 per fidem] fide *Vulgata* (5: 2)   in gratia ista] in gratiam istam (5: 2)

---

275 *Karitas dei*: GBcBA   *in*: E   *per*: EGE   in*habitan*tes: FGAcA-GAFGA   Ps.: GABcAGABG

---

274 RL: MRM 242. SAC: Va (650). GREG: Ha 531, Pa 465. GEL8: Ge 1033, Rh 627, Sg 816. ES: Vl4770 145r. BEN: Ben29 199v, Ben30 109v, Ben33 99v-100r, Ca 81r, DaB 168v, Mc127 247, McV 169v, Ott 261v, PuC 542, PuL 74r, Ve 131v.

275 **Rm 5: 5, Ps 87: 2**. RL: GR 304 (ps. var.), MRM 249. AMS 111. BEN: Ben29 204r, Ben30 116v, Ben33 102v, Ben34 193r-v, Ben35 117r, Ben38 101v, Ben39 101v, Ben40 81v-82r, Ca 84r, Mc127 254, McV 173r, Ott 265v, Ve 134v.

276 RL: GR 306 (*Gloria*), MRM 249 (*Gloria*). BEN: Ben29 206r (add. alia manu beneventana).

277 RL: MRM 251. SAC: Va (1049). GREG: Ha 550, Pa 492. GEL8: En (1610), Ge 1058, Rh (1014), Sg 841. BEN: Ben29 206r, Ben30 121r, Ben33 103v, Ca (2v), Mc127 257, McV 174v, Ott 267v, Ve (137v).

278 **Rm 5: 1-5**. RL: MRM 251-252. LEC: Mu 102, WuC 123. BEN: Ben29 206r, Ben30 121r-v, Ben33 103v, DaK 40v, Mc127 257-258, McV 175r, Ott 267v.

279

♪ Alleluia. VERSVS Karitas dei diffusa est in cordibus uestris per spiritum sanctum qui datus est nobis. ♪

280

TRAVTUS Laudate dominum. *In sabbato sancto.*

281

SECVNDVM MARCVM [1: 21-34]. In illo tempore. Ingressus iesus in
65v sinagogam sabbati. et docebat. ... | ... sciebant eum.

282

OFFERTORIVM Emitte spiritum tuum.

283

SECRETA Sollemnibus ieiuniis expiatos. sua nos dominus misterio congruentes. hoc sacro munere efficiat. quia tanto nobis salubrius adheret. quanto id deuotius sumpserimus. per.

---

281 docebat] eos *add.* Vulgata (1: 21)   stupebant omnes] stupebant (1: 22) sinagoga] synagoga eorum (1: 23)   uenisti ante tempus torquere nos] venisti perdere nos (1: 24)   iesus dicens ei] ei Iesus dicens (1: 25)   de homine] ab eo (1: 26)   quirerent] conquirerent (1: 27)   que doctrina] quae doctrina haec (1: 27)   recumbebat] decumbebat (1: 30)   de ipsa] de illa (1: 30)   afferrebant omnes] afferrebant ad eum omnes (1: 32)   ianuas] ianuam (1: 33)

---

279 *Vide Intro. p. 103*

---

279 Rm 5: 5. ES: Syg 187 (melodia var.). BEN: Ben29 206r, Ben33 103v, Ben34 194r, Ben35 117r, Ben38 101v, Ben39 101v, Ben40 82r, Ca 84r, Mc127 258, McV 175r, Ott 267v.

280 Ps 116: 1. RL: GR 307, MRM 252. AMS (79b). BEN: Ben29 206r, Ben30 121v, Ben33 (29r), Ben34 (74r), Ott 267v.

281 Mc 1: 21-34.

282 Ps 103: 30. RL: GR (290-291), MRM (239, 2: 277). AMS (105). BEN: Ben29 (198r), Ben33 (98v), Ben34 194r, Ben38 101v, Ben39 101v, Ca (80r), Mc127 (245), McV (168r), Ott (260r), Ve (130v).

283 SAC: Va (657). GEL8: Ge (1098), Sg (879). ES: Vl4770 (150r). BEN: Ben33 (104r), Ca (85v), Ve (136r).

284

66r COMMVNIO ♪ Non uos relinquam orfanos ueni|am ad uos alleluia et gaudebit cor uestrum alleluia alleluia. ♪

285

POSTCOMMVNIO Sumptum quesumus domine uenerabile sacramentum. et presentis uite subsidium nos foveant et eterne. per.

DOMINICA .I.

286

INTROITVS ♪ Ego autem in domino sperabo exultabo et letabor in tua misericordia quia respexisti humilitatem meam. PSALMVS In te domine speraui non confundar. ♪

287

Deprecationem nostram quesumus domine benignus exaudi. et quibus supplicandi prestas effectum. tribue defensionis auxilium. per.

---

284 orfanos: AB   uos alleluia: AFGBAGAG] vos iterum alleluia GR   alleluia²: FGAcdcdfecedc   alleluia³: GcABcBAGABAG

286 quia: FA

---

284 Io 14: 18. RL: GR (303), MRM (248). AMS 111. BEN: Ben29 206v, Ben33 104r, Ben34 194r, Ben35 117r, Ben38 101v, Ben39 101v-102r, Ca 84v, Mc127 258, McV 175r, Ott 268r, Ve 135r.

285 SAC: Va (674). GEL8: Ge 1114, Rh 676, Sg 893. BEN: Ben30 122v, Ben33 (104v).

286 Ps 30: 7-8, Ps 30: 2. RL: GR (132), MRM (89). AMS (56). BEN: Ben33 (41r), Ben34 (85r-v).

287 RL: MRM (103). GREG: Ha 553, Pa 496, Sp (1135). GEL8: En (998), Ge (1116), Rh (678), Sg (895). AM: Sb (393). ES: Vl4770 152v. BEN: Ben29 206v, Ben30 (125v), Ben33 126r, Ca (89v), Mc127 258, McO (375), McV (176r), Ve (139v).

288

LECTIO EPISTOLE BEATI IOHANNIS APOSTOLI [1 Io 4: 9-20]. Karissimi. In
66v hoc apparuit caritas dei in nobis. ... | ... quomodo potest dilige- [*lac.*]

<DOMINICA .XI.>

289

67r | ♪ Deus in loco sancto suo deus qui habitare facis unanimes in domo ipse dabit
uirtutem et fortitudinem plebis sue. PSALMVS Exurgat deus et dissipentur. ♪

290

ORATIO Deus qui omnipotentiam tuam parcendo maxime et miserando
manifestas. multiplica super nos misericordiam tuam. ut ad tua
promissa currentes. celestium bonorum facias esse consortes. per.

---

288 misit in hunc mundum] misit Deus in mundum *Vulgata* (4: 9)   prior dilexit]
dilexit (4: 10)   sicut deus] si sic Deus (4: 11)   cognoscimus] intellegimus
(4: 13)   filium suum] Filium (4: 14)   manet in eo] in eo manet (4: 15)   ipse
in eo] ipse in Deo (4: 15)   credimus] credidimus (4: 16)   fiduciam] fiduciam
habeamus (4: 17)   penam non habet] poenam habet (4: 18)   perfectus in
caritatem] perfectus in caritate (4: 18)   deum quoniam prior] quoniam Deus
prior (4: 19)   qui autem non diligit] qui enim non diligit (4: 20)   quem uidet]
quem vidit (4: 20)   non uidet] non vidit (4: 20)

289 *lac. inter 66v-67r*

---

289 san*c*to: AG   *ha*bitare: AGA] *in*habitare GR   *et*: AB   forti*tudinem*:
AcBGBAGAG   *plebis*: GAcBcdcABc   *sue*: GAG   Ps.: GcBcdfedcAG

---

288 1 Io 4: 9-20. RL: MRM 254-255 (1 Io 4: 8-21). BEN: Ben29 206v-207r, Ben30
122v-123v, Ca (88r-v: dom. 1 post oct. Pent.), Mc127 258-259, McV 175r-v, Ott
268v, Ve 138r.

289 Ps 67: 6-7, 36, Ps 67: 2. RL: GR 347-348, MRM 272. AMS 183. ES: Vl4770
175v. BEN: Ben29 217v, Ben30 144r, Ben34 253r, Ben35 160r, Ben38 143v, Ben39
182r-v, Ben40 145v, Mc127 275, McV 220v, Ott 278v, Ve 146r.

290 RL: MRM 270. SAC: Va (1198). GREG: Pa 591, Sp 1159. GEL8 (dom. 12): En
1179, Ge 1332, Rh 767, Sg 1047. AM: Sb (727). ES: Vl4770 178r. BEN: Ben29 217v,
Ben30 142r-v, Mc127 275, McO 398, McV 220v, Ott 278v, Ve 146r.

291

AD CORINTIOS [2 Cor 3: 4-9]. Fratres. Fiduciam talem habemus per
67v christum ad deum. ... | ... iustitie in gloria.

292

GRADVALE ♪ In deo sperauit cor meum et adiutus sum et refloruit caro mea
et ex uoluntate mea confitebor illi. VERSVS Ad te domine clamaui deus meus ne
sileas ne discedas a me. ♪

293

♪ Alleluia. VERSVS Te decet ymnus deus in syon et tibi reddetur uotum in
hierusalem. ♪

294

LVCAM [18: 9-14]. In illo tempore. Dicebat iesus ad eos, qui in se
68r confidebant tanquam iusti. ... | ... exaltabitur.

---

291 littera sed spiritu] litterae sed Spiritus *Vulgata* (3: 6)   non possint filii israel
intendere] non possent intendere filii Israel (3: 7)

294 orabat dicens] orabat *Vulgata* (18: 11)   homines] hominum (18: 11)
amen dico uobis] dico vobis (18: 14)

---

292 *cor*: GAGAG   me*a*: FDFGFGDEDCD   *confite*bor: BcAdcBAGF
illi: GFGFGFAGAGF   clama*ui*: dcAcdcdcAcdfgfdecAcBdecedcedcBA
*si*leas: cAcdef

293 Al*leluia*: GAdBcdcBdcdBdfdcdcGcAGABAG   *no*tum: BcdcBcdfdcgfed
hierusa*lem*: dAdedcfdcAGABAG

---

291 **2 Cor 3: 4-9**. RL: MRM 273 (dom. 12 post Pent.). LEC: Mu 124 (ebd. 13). BEN:
Ben29 218r, Ben30 142v, Mc127 275-276 (dom. 10 post oct. Pent.), McV
220v-221r, Ott 278v (dom. 10 post oct. Pent.), Ve 146v (dom. 12 post oct. Pent.).

292 **Ps 27: 7, 1**. RL: GR 348, MRM 272. AMS 183. ES: Vl4770 176r. BEN: Ben29
218r, Ben30 145r, Ben33 (43r), Ben34 253r (87v), Ben35 160r, Ben38 143v,
Ben39 182v, Ben40 145v, Mc127 276, McV 221r, Ott 278v, Ve 146r.

293 **Ps 64: 2**. RL: GR (346), MRM 271. AMS (177). BEN: Ben29 218r, Ben30 143r,
Ben34 (252r-v), Ben35 172r, Ben38 156r, Ben40 161v-162r, Mc127 276, McV
221r, Ott 278v, Ve (145r).

294 **Lc 18: 9-14**. RL: MRM 271. LEC: Mu 120 (ebd. 12), WuE 311 (ebd. 7 post
Apost.), CoP 314 (ebd. 5 post Apost.). ES: Vl4770 178v. BEN: Ben29 218r-v, Ben30
143r-v, DaE 166r, Mc127 276, McV 221r, Ott 278v-279r, Ve 146v.

295

OFFERTORIVM ♪ Exaltabo te domine quoniam suscepisti me nec delectasti inimicos meos super me domine clamaui ad te et sanasti me. ♪

296

SECRETA Tibi domine sacrificia dicata reddantur. que sic ad honorem nominis tui deferenda tribuisti. ut eadem fieri remedia nostra prestares. per.

297

COMMVNIO ♪ Honora dominum de tua substantia et de primitiis frugum tuorum ut impleantur orrea tua saturitate et uino torcularia redundabut. ♪

298

68v Quesumus domine deus noster. ut quos diuinis reparare | non desinis sacramentis. tuis non destituas benignus auxiliis. per.

---

295 A′ inc.] E inc. GR (F-clavis] c-clavis trans. GR passim)   domine: DED
quoniam: DFGFEFEDED   sanasti: FDCDFDCDECFDF

297 impleantur: Ac   saturitate: GAGFGAGFGF   uino: AGAEFG
torcularia: DF   redundabut: FGABGABAG

---

295 Ps 29: 2-3. RL: GR 349 (vide 90), MRM 273. AMS 183. ES: Vl4770 176r. BEN: Ben29 218v, Ben30 145v, Ben33 (19v, 31r), Ben34 253v, (62v-63r), Ben35 160r, Ben38 143v, Ben39 182v, Ben40 145v, Mc127 276, McV 221v, Ott 279r, Ve 146v.

296 RL: MRM 271. SAC: Va (1199). GREG: Pa 592, Sp 1160. GEL8 (dom. 12): En 1181, Ge 1334, Rh 769, Sg 1049. ES: Vl4770 178v. BEN: Ben29 218v, Ben30 143v, Mc127 276, McV 221v, Ott 279r, Ve 146v.

297 Prov 3: 9-10. RL: GR 349, MRM 273. AMS 183. ES: Vl4770 176r. BEN: Ben29 218v, Ben30 (145v), Ben34 253v, Ben35 160r-v, Ben38 143v-144r, Ben39 182v, Ben40 145v, Mc127 276, McV 221v, Ott 279r, Ve 146v.

298 RL: MRM 271. SAC: Va (1200). GREG: Pa 593, Sp 1161. GEL8 (dom. 12): En 1183, Ge 1336, Rh 771, Sg 1051. AM: Sb (206). ES: Vl4770 178v. BEN: Ben29 218v, Ben30 143v-144r, Mc127 277, McV 221v, Ott 279r, Ve 146v.

DOMINICA .XVII.

299

♪ Da pacem domine sustinentibus te ut prophete tui fideles inueniantur et exaudi preces seruorum tuorum et plebis tue israhel. PSALMVS Letatus sum in his que dicta. ♪

300

Da quesumus domine populo tuo diabolica uitare contagia. et te solum dominum pura mente sectari. per.

301

LECTIO EPISTOLE BEATI PAVLI APOSTOLI AD EPHESIOS [4: 23- 28]. Fratres. Renouamini spiritus mentis uestre. ... patienti.

302

GRADVALE [*lac.*]

---

301 et nolite] nolite *Vulgata* (4: 27)   operando] operando manibus (4: 28)

---

299 *do*mine: ABA   tu*i*: GF   ex*audi*: FABAGAG   *seruorum*: FG   *tuorum*: GFGAGAG   ple*bis*: AGFDED   Ps.: FGAcAGFD

---

299 Eccli 36: 18, Ps 121: 1. RL: GR 372-373, MRM 290. AMS 193. ES: Vl4770 200r. BEN: Ben29 231r, Ben30 192r, Ben34 259v, Ben35 163r, Ben38 147v, Ben39 186r, Ben40 148v-149r, Mc127 297, McV 231r, Ott 290v, Ve 154r.

300 RL: MRM 280. SAC: Le (78), Va (1226). GREG: Sp 1180. GEL8: En (1406), Ge (1543), Rh (890), Sg (1261). ES: Vl4770 202v. BEN: Ben29 231r, Ben30 (193v), Ben33 133r, Mc127 297, McO 437, McV 231r, Ott 290v, Ve 154v.

301 Eph 4: 23-28. RL: MRM 291. LEC: Alc 183, Mu (139: ebd. 20), WuC 232, CoP 371. ES: Vl4770 202v. BEN: Ben29 231r, Ben30 192r-v, Mc127 297, McV 231r, Ott 290v, Ve (155r).

302 Cf. *Laetatus sum*: RL: GR 373, MRM 290, BEN: Ben29 231r, Mc127 297, McV 231r, Ott 290v.

\<IN NATALE SANCTI NICOLAI CONFESSORIS\>

303

69r | LECTIO LIBRI SAPIENTIE [Eccli 50: 6-13]. Ecce sacerdos magnus qui quasi stella ... in accipiendam ipsam stolam glorie dedit sanctitatis amictum. Corona fratrum. quasi plantatio cedri in monte libano. Dedit gloriam deo a labiis suis. et in nomine ipsius gloriatus est.

304

GRADVALE ♪ O beate nicolae sanctissime pater meritum nomine moribus sacris.
69v VERSVS Qui gloria mundi spre|uit ideo meruit ad summum ascendere gradum. ♪

305

♪ Alleluia. VERSVS Beate confessor dei nicolae. intercede pro nobis ad dominum. ♪

306

MARCVM [13: 33-37]. In illo tempore. Dixit iesus discipulis suis. Videte uigilate et orate. ... uigilate.

307

OFFERTORIVM ♪ O beate pastor egregie presul nicolae miraculi corusci cui dominus [*lac.*]

---

303 *lac. inter 68v-69r* luxit] lucet *Vulgata* (50: 6)   refulgens] effulgens (50: 8) inter nebulas] in nebulam (50: 8)   suis] veris (50: 8)   redolens in ignem] ardens in igni (50: 9)   cipressus] gyrus (50: 11)   altitudine] altitudinem (50: 11)   extollens] tollens (50: 11)

306 precepit ut uigilaret] praecipiat ut vigilet *Vulgata* (13: 34)

---

304 *Vide Intro. p. 165*

305 *Vide Intro. p. 167*

307 *Vide Intro. p. 168*

---

303 Eccli 50: 6-13. BEN: Mc127 339 (inc.), McV 15r.

304 Na1 24r/19v.

305 BEN: Ben38 164v (= ES: Schlager, *Katalog* G 403).

306 Mc 13: 33-37. RL: MRM (436, 440). BEN: Mc127 339, Ve (190r).

307 Na1 24r/19v.

\<IN NATALE SANCTI THOME\>

308

70r [*lac.*] | passione. nobis proficiant ad medelam. per.

IN SANCTI STEPHANI PROTOMARTIRIS

309

♪ Etenim sederunt principes et aduersus me loquebantur et iniqui persecuti sunt me adiuua me domine deus meus quia seruus tuus exercebantur in tuis iustificationibus. PSALMVS Beati immaculati. ♪

310

ORATIO. Da nobis quesumus domine imitari quod colimus. ut discamus et inimicos diligere. quia eius natalicia celebramus; qui nouit etiam pro persecutoribus exorare. Dominum nostrum.

311

LECTIO ACTVVM APOSTOLORVM [6: 8-10, 7: 54-59]. In diebus illis. 70v Stephanus plenus gratia ... | ... obdormiuit in domino.

---

308 *lac. inter 69v-70r*

311 esset Stephanus] esset *Vulgata* (7: 55)   addextris] a dextris (7: 55) stantem a dextris uirtutis dei] a dextris stantem Dei (7: 56)   uoce magna dicens] voce magna (7: 59)   dixissiset] dixisset (7: 59)

---

309 domi*ne*: GF   *tu*is: ABGF   Ps.: FGABAGFD

---

308 RL: MRM (301, 393 *Perceptis domine sacramentis*). SAC: Le (320), Va (945). GREG: Ha (769), Pa (773). GEL8: En (1443, 1527), Ge (1576, 1663), Rh (915), Sg (1291, 1370). AM: Sb (880, 1125). BEN: Ben33 (113r, 123v: var.), Mc127 341, Mc540 38, Mc.VII^2 2r, McV 16v, Ott 14r, PuC (674).

309 Ps 118: 23, 86, 23, Ps 118: 1. RL: GR 36, MRM 21. AMS 12. ES: Vl4770 4r. BEN: Ben29 28r, Ben33 3*bis*v, Ben34 21r, Ca 6v, Mc127 349, Mc540 46, Mc546 17, McV 20r-v, Ott 20r, PuC 345, Ve 13r.

310 RL: MRM 21. GREG: Ha 62, Pa 25. GEL8: En 42, Ge 42, Rh 38, Sg 41. AM: Sb 141. ES: F 72, Vl4770 4r. BEN: Ben29 28r, Ben33 3*bis*v, Ca 6v, Mc127 349, Mc540 46, McO 227, McV 20v, Ott 20r, Ve 13r.

311 Act 6: 8-10, 7: 54-59. RL: MRM 21. LEC: Alc 5, Mu 5, WuC 8, CoP 13. ES: Vl4770 4v. BEN: Ben29 28r-v, Ben33 3*bis*v, Ca 6v-7r, DaB 14r, DaE 6r, DaK 7r-v, Mc127 349-350, Mc540 46-47, McV 20v, Ott 20r-v, PuC 347, Ve 13r.

312

GRADVALE ♪ Sederunt principes et aduersus me loquebantur. et iniqui perse-
71r cuti sunt me. VERSVS Adiuua me domine deus meus sal|uum me fac propter
misericordiam tuam. ♪

313

♪ Alleluia. VERSVS Video celos apertos et hiesum stantem a dextris uirtutis
dei. ♪

314

SECVNDVM MATHEVM [23: 34-39]. In illo tempore. Dicebat iesus turbis
iudeorum. et principibus sacerdotum. Ecce ego mitto ad uos prophetas
71v ... | ... in nomine domini.

315

OFFERTORIVM ♪ Elegerunt apostoli stephanum leuita plenum fide et spiritu
sancto quem lapidauerunt iudei orante et dicentes domine hiesu accipe spiritum
meum alleluia. ♪

---

314 iusti abel] Abel iusti *Vulgata* (23: 35)   congregari] congregare (23: 37)
relinquetur] relinquitur vobis (23: 38)

312 Sede*runt*: GF   *prin*cipes: FGB   *me*¹: cdcABA   *me*²: FGAGAcdcA-
FAGAGF   domi*ne*: dcAcdcdcAcefdecAcBdecedcedcBA

313 *Alleluia*: DFGFGEDFGAGCDFDEFD   uir*tu*tis: DFGAFDGFEDCD

315 *Vide Intro. p. 143*

---

312 Ps 118: 23, 86, 6: 5. RL: GR 36-37, MRM 22. AMS 12. ES: Vl4770 4v. BEN:
Ben29 28v, Ben33 3*bis*v, Ben34 21r-v, Ca 7r, DaB 14r, Mc127 350, Mc540 47,
Mc546 17, McV 20v, Ott 20v, PuC 348, Ve 13r-v.

313 Act 7: 56. RL: GR 37, MRM 22. AMS 12. ES: Vl4770 4v. BEN: Ben29 28v, Ben33
3*bis*v, Ben34 21v, Ca 7r, DaB 14r, Mc127 350, Mc540 47, Mc546 17-18, McV
20v-21r, Ott 20v, PuC 349, Ve 13v.

314 Mt 23: 34-39. RL: MRM 22. LEC: Mu 5, WuE 297, CoP 14. ES: Vl4770 4v-5r.
BEN: Ben29 28v-29r, Ben33 3*bis*v-4r, Ca 7r-v, DaB 14r-v, DaE 6r, DaK 7v-8r,
Mc127 350, Mc540 47, McV 21r, Ott 20v-21r, PuC 350, Ve 13v.

315 Act 6: 5, 7: 58. RL: MRM 22. ES: Vl4770 5r. BEN: Ben33 4r, Ben34 22r-v, Ca
7v, DaB 14v, Mc127 350, Mc540 47, Mc546 18, McV 21r, Ott 21r, PuC 351, Ve
13v. Var. (melodia): RL: GR 37-38, ES: Syg 23, LS: Gs 16.

316

Grata tibi domine sint munera quesumus deuotionis hodierne. que beati stephani martiris tui commemoratione gloriosa depromit. per.

317

COMMVNIO ♪ Video celos apertos et hiesum stantem a dextris uirtutis dei. domine hiesu accipe spiritum meum et ne statuas illis hoc peccatum quia nesciunt quid faciunt. ♪

318

POSTCOMMVNIO Auxilientur nobis sumpta misteria. et intercedente beato stephano martire tuo. sempiterna [*lac.*]

<IN NATALE MARTIRIS>

319

72r [*lac.*] | -isti;(?) concede quesumus; ut eius pia intercessione adiuuemur in celis. cuius martirio gloriamur in terris. per.

IN SANCTI SILVESTRI PAPE.

320

Misericordiam tuam domine nobis quesumus interueniente beato siluestro confessore tuo atque pontifice clementer impende. et nobis peccatoribus ipsius propitiare suffragiis. per.

---

319 *lac. inter 71v-72r*

---

317 *et*[1]: cB   *dei*: BcABG   *hoc*: FG

---

316 SAC: Le (700), Va 33. GEL8: En 43, Ge 44, Rh 40, Sg 43. ES: F 74. BEN: DaZ 327, PuC 352.

317 **Act 7: 56, 59-60.** RL: GR 38, MRM 22. AMS 12. ES: Vl4770 5r. BEN: Ben29 29r, Ben33 4r, Ben34 22v, Ca 7v, DaB 14v, DaZ 327, Mc127 351, Mc540 48, Mc546 18, McV 21r, Ott 21r-v, PuC 354, Ve 13v.

318 RL: MRM 22. SAC: Va (1241). GREG: Ha 64, Pa 28. GEL8: En 45, Rh 42, Sg 45. ES: F 76, Vl4770 5r. BEN: Ben29 29r, Ben33 4r, Ca 7v, DaB 14v-15r, DaZ 327, Mc127 351, Mc540 48, McV 21r, Ott 21v, PuC 355, Ve 13v.

319 Non inveni.

320 GREG: Tc (3318, 3334, 3645). GEL8: En (1574, 1652), Ge (1708, 1785), Rh (1043), Sg (1413, 1480). AM: Sb (1085).

321

EPISTOLA [Hebr 7: 23] *retro .I. folium.* Plures facti sunt sacerdotes.

322

ORATIO SECRETA Sancti tui nos domine quesumus ubique letificent. ut dum eorum merita recolimus. patrocinia sentiamus. per.

323

POSTCOMMVNIO Sumptum domine celestis remedii sacramentum ad perpetuam nobis prouenire gratiam. beatus siluester pontifex optineat. per.

IN SANCTI FELICIS.

324

Concede quesumus omnipotens deus. ut ad meliorem uitam sanctorum tuorum exempla nos prouocent. quatinus beati felicis cuius sollempnia agimus. etiam actus imitemur. per.

IN SANCTI MARCELLI. PAPE.

325

Preces populi tui quesumus domine clementer exaudi. ut beati marcelli martiris tui atque pontificis. meritis adiuuemur. cuius passione letamur. per.

---

321 Hebr 7: 23. RL: MRM (2: 349). LEC: Alc 10, WuC 14, CoP 20. BEN: Ben29 31v, DaB 19r, Mc127 356, Mc.VII² 2v, McV 24v, Ott 25v.

322 RL: MRM 29. GREG: Ha 80, Pa 47, Sp (1234). GEL8: En 78, Ge 74, Rh 69, Sg 74. BEN: Ben29 32r, Ben33 6r, DaB 19r, Mc127 356, Mc.VII² 2v, McV 24v, Ott 25v, Ve 17r.

323 GEL8: En (1576), Ge (1710), Sg (1415).

324 RL: MRM 305. GREG: Ha 99, Pa 69. GEL8: En 124, Ge 127, Rh 108, Sg 116. ES: Vl4770 12v. BEN: Ben29 43v (m. v.), DaB 29v, Mc127 364, Mc540 70, McV 33r, Ott 37r-v, Ve 24r (m. v.).

325 RL: MRM 306. GREG: Ha 102, Pa 75. GEL8: En 135, Ge 146, Rh 119, Sg 127. AM: Sb (10). ES: Vl4770 14r. BEN: Ben29 44r, Ben33 9r, DaB 30r, Mc127 365, Mc540 71, Mc.VI 1, McO 251, McV 33r, Ott 38r, Ve 24v.

IN SANCTI SEBASTIANI.

326

72v Deus qui beatum sebastianum martirem tuum | uirtute constantie in passione roborasti. ex eius nobis imitatione tribue pro amore tuo prospera mundi despicere. et nulla eius aduersa formidare. per.

IN SANCTI FABIANI.

327

Infirmitatem nostram respice omnipotens deus. et quia nos pondus proprie actionis grauat. beati fabiani martyris tui atque pontificis intercessio gloriosa nos protegat. per.

IN SANCTE AGNES.

328

Crescat in nobis domine quesumus semper sancte iocunditatis effectum. et beate agne uirginis ac martire tue, ueneranda festiuitas augeatur.

329

♪ Alleluia. VERSVS Ingressa agnes turpitudinis locum angelum domini preparatum inuenit. ♪

---

329 *Vide Intro. p. 144*

---

326 GREG: Ha 111, Pa 84. GEL8: En 156, Ge 161, Rh 125, Sg 142. AM: Sb 221. BEN: Ben29 45r, Ben33 10v, DaB 31r, Mc127 366, Mc540 71, Mc.VI 4, McV 33v, Ott 39r, Ve 25v.

327 RL: MRM 308. GREG: Ha 108, Pa 81. GEL8: En 151, Ge 156, Sg 138. AM: Sb (871). BEN: Ben29 45r, Ben33 10v, DaB 31r, Mc127 366, Mc540 71-72, Mc.VI 4, McO 252, McV 33v, Ott 39v, Ve 25v.

328 SAC: Va 822 (m. v.). GEL8: En 162, Ge 167, Rh 128, Sg 147. ES: F 164.

329 ES: Schlager, *Katalog* E 203. BEN: Ben34 45r, Ben35 13v, DaB 32r, Mc127 367, Mc540 73, Mc546 159, McV 34r, Ott 40v.

330

SECRETA Hostias domine quas tibi offerimus; propitius suscipe. et intercedente beata agnete martira tua. uincula peccatorum nostrorum absolue. per.

331

POSTCOMMVNIO Refecti cibo potuque celesti deus noster. te supplices
73r exoramus. ut | in cuius commemoratione percepimus. eius muniamur et precibus. per.

IN SANCTI VINCENTII.

332

Adesto supplicationibus nostris quesumus domine. ut qui ex iniquitate nostra reos nos esse cognoscimus. beati uincentii martiris tui intercessione liberemur. per.

IN CONVERSIONE SANCTI PAVLI APOSTOLI.

333

INTROITVS Scio cui credidi.

---

330 RL: MRM 309. GREG: Ha 115, Pa 88. GEL8: En (385), Ge (370), Rh (774), Sg (337). AM: Sb (332). ES: F 166, Vl4770 16v. BEN: Ben29 46r, Ben30 2v, Ben33 11v, DaB 32v, Mc127 367, Mc540 73, Mc.VI 5, McV 34r-v, Ott 40v, PuC (606), Ve 26v.

331 RL: MRM 309. SAC: Le (724). GREG: Ha 116, Pa 90. GEL8: En (56), Ge (54), Rh (51), Sg (54). AM: Sb 231. ES: F 170 (alia), Vl4770 17r. BEN: Ben29 46r, Ben30 3r, Ben33 11v, DaB 32v, Mc127 367, Mc540 73, Mc.VI 5, McV 34v, Ott 40v-41r, PuC (366), Ve 27r.

332 RL: MRM 310. GREG: Ha 117, Pa 91. GEL8: En 167, Ge 173, Rh 131, Sg 152. AM: Sb 233. BEN: Ben29 46r, Ben33 11v, DaB 32v, Mc127 367, Mc540 73, Mc.VI 6, McV 34v, Ott 41r, Ve 27r.

333 2 Tim 1: 12. RL: GR 417-418, MRM 310. AMS (123). BEN: Ben29 46v, Ben30 3r, Ben33 (112r), Ben34 (207v), DaB 33r, Mc127 367, Mc540 74, Mc546 30, McV 34v, Ott 41v.

334

ORATIO Deus qui uniuersum mundum beati pauli apostoli predicatione docuisti. da nobis quesumus. ut qui eius hodie conuersionem colimus. per eius ad te exempla gradiamur. per.

335

LECTIO ACTVVM APOSTOLORVM [9: 1-22]. In diebus illis. Saulus adhuc
73v-74r spirans ... | hic est christus.

336

SECVNDVM LVCAM [16: 1-8]. In illo tempore. Dixit iesus discipulis suis parabolam hanc. Homo quidam erat diues ... prudentiores filii- [*lac.*]

\<IN SANCTI BLASII\>

337

75r | POSTCOMMVNIO Te deum saluatorem nostrum; suppliciter exoramus. ut intercessione beati blasii martiris tui atque pontificis. ab omnibus diabolicis liberemur insidiis. per.

---

335 *73v, 74v, 74r (N.B.: 74v ante 74r legendum est; vide App.)* et discipulos] et caedis in discipulos *Vulgata* (9: 1) principes] principem (9: 1) petit] petit ab eo (9: 2) ierusalem] in Ierusalem (9: 2) iesus nazarenus] Iesus (9: 5) tu persequeris durum est tibi contra stimulum /73v/ calcitrare et tremens ac stupens dixit domine quid me uis facere et dominus ad eum] tu persequeris (9: 5) obstupefacti] stupefacti (9: 7) discipulus] quidam discipulus (9: 10) et uade] vade (9: 11) nomine ananiam] Ananiam nomine (9: 12) ad illum] ad eum (9: 15) ego ostendam] ego enim ostendam (9: 16) pati pro nomine meo] pro nomine meo pati (9: 16) domum] in domum (9: 17) dominus iesus misit me] Dominus misit me Iesus (9: 17) continuo ingressus] continuo (9: 20) sinagogas] synagogis (9: 20) aduceret] duceret (9: 21)

336 uocauit illum dominus suus] vocavit illum *Vulgata* (16: 2)

337 *lac. inter 74r-75r (N.B.: 74r post 74v legendum est; vide App.)*

---

334 RL: MRM 310. GEL8: En 181, Sg 169. ES: F 180. BEN: Ben29 46v, Ben30 3r, DaB 33r, Mc127 367-368, Mc540 74, Mc.VI 7, McV 35r, Ott 41v, Ve 27v.

335 **Act 9: 1-22.** RL: MRM 311-312. LEC: Mu 15.8. ES: Vl4770 (167r-v). BEN: Ben29 46v-47v, Ben30 3r-5r, Ben33 (112r-v), DaB 33r-34r, Mc127 368-369, Mc540 74-76, Mc.VII^2 3v, McV 35r-v, Ott 41v-42v, Ve 27v-28r.

336 **Lc 16: 1-8.** RL: MRM (268). BEN: Ben29 47v-48r, Ben30 5r, DaB 34r, Mc127 369, Mc540 76-77, Mc.VII^2 3v, McV 35v, Ott 42v.

337 RL: MRM 2: 178 ("Spiritalis participatione sacramenti *te deum ... insidiis*").

IN SANCTE AGATHE.

338

Indulgentiam nobis domine beata agathe martira imploret. que tibi grata extitit; uirtute martirii, et merito castitatis. per.

IN SANCTE SCOLASTICE VIRGINIS.

339

Dilexisti iustitiam.

340

Deus qui beate uirginis tue scolastice animam, ad ostendendam innocentie uitam. in columbe specie, celum penetrare fecisti. concede nobis ipsius meritis. innocenter uiuere. ut ad eadem mereamur gaudia peruenire. per.

341

LECTIO [2 Cor 10: 17]. Qui gloriatur in domino.

342

GRADVALE Dilexisti iustitiam.

---

338 RL: MRM (442). SAC: Va 832. GREG: Ha 131 (m. v.), Pa 111 (m. v.), Sp (1240). GEL8: En 209, Ge 201, Rh 151, Sg 189. BEN: PuC 398 (m. v.).

339 Ps 44: 8. RL: GR 438, MRM (441). AMS (3, 101). ES: Vl4770 21r (vide 219v). BEN: Ben29 50r-v, Ben33 15r, Ben34 51r, Ben35 21r, DaB 36v, Mc127 374, Mc540 81, Mc.VI 11, McV 38r, Ott 45v, PuC (766).

340 GREG: Tc 3446 (Missa Alcuini). ES: F 209. BEN: Ben29 50v, DaB 36v, Mc127 374, Mc540 81, Mc.VI 11, McV 38r, 271r, Ott 45v-46r.

341 2 Cor 10: 17. RL: MRM (443). ES: Vl4770 21r (vide 219v). BEN: Ben29 50v, DaB 36v, Mc127 374, Mc540 81, McV 38r, Ott 46r.

342 Ps 44: 8. RL: GR ([52]), MRM (444). AMS (3, 101). ES: Vl4770 21r (vide 219v). BEN: Ben29 50v, Ben33 15r, Ben34 51r, DaB 36v, Mc127 374, Mc540 81, Mc546 36, McV 38r, Ott 46r, PuC (769).

343

TRACTVS In columbe.

344

EVANGELIVM [Mt 13: 44]. Simile est regnum celorum thesauro.

345

SECRETA Suscipe quesumus domine ob honorem sacre uirginis tue scolastice munus oblatum. et quod nostris meritis assequi non ualemus. eiusdem suffragantibus meritis largire propitius. per.

346

COMMVNIO ♪ Simile est regnum celorum homini negotiatori querenti bonas
75v margaritas inuenta una pretiosa de|dit omnia sua et comparauit eam. ♪

347

POSTCOMMVNIO Quos celesti domine refectione satiasti. beate quesumus scolastice uirginis tue meritis. a cunctis exime propitiatus aduersis. per.

---

346 pretiosa] pretiosa margarita *ante corr. (ut* GR)

---

346 nego*ti*atori: A   *inuen*ta: Acdcd   pretio*s*a: GA   compa*r*auit: GAcA

---

343 RL: MRM (2: 189). BEN: Ben29 50v, Ben34 (54v), DaB 36v, Mc127 374, Mc540 81, McV 38r, Ott 46r.

344 Mt 13: 44. RL: MRM (445). BEN: Ben29 50v, DaB 36v, DaE (150r), Mc127 374, Mc540 81, Mc.VI 11, McV 38r, Ott 46r, PuC (771).

345 RL: MRM 2: 179. GREG: Tc 3447 (Missa Alcuini). ES: F 210. BEN: Ben29 50v, Ben33 15r, DaB 36v, Mc127 374, Mc540 82, Mc.VI 11, McV 38r, 271r, Ott 46r, PuC 402, Ve 32r.

346 Mt 13: 45-46. RL: GR ([66], 115**), MRM (446). AMS (16*bis*, 23*bis*, 28, 127, 153). BEN: Ben29 50v, Ben33 15r, Ben34 (30v: m. v.), DaB 36v, Mc127 374, Mc540 82, McV 38r, Ott 46r.

347 RL: MRM 2: 179. GREG: Tc 3448 (Missa Alcuini). ES: F 211. BEN: Ben29 50v, Ben33 15r, DaB 36v, Mc127 374, Mc540 82, McV 38r, 271r, Ott 46r, PuC 403, Ve 32r.

CATHEDRA SANCTI PETRI.

348

♪ Statuit ei dominus testamentum pacis et principem fecit eum ut sit illi sacerdotii dignitas in eternum. Misericordias tuas domine. ♪

349

Deus qui beato petro apostolo tuo collatis clauibus regni celestis animas ligandi atque soluendi, pontificium tradidisti. concede propitius. ut intercessionis eius auxilio a peccatorum nostrorum uinculis liberemur. per.

350

LECTIO [Eccli 44: 16]. Ecce sacerdos magnus.

351

GRADVALE ♪ Exaltent eum in ecclesia plebis et in cathedra seniorum laudent eum. VERSVS Confiteantur domino misericordia eius et mirabilia eius filiis hominum. ♪

---

348 *prin*cipem: FGA   *in*: DEFGEFGA   Ps.] Memento domine David GR (*eadem melodia*)

351 *Vide Intro. p. 159*

---

348 **Eccli 45: 30, Ps 88: 2.** RL: GR 408 (vide [3], [32]: ps. var.), MRM 319 (ps. var.). AMS (22, 171 *ter*). BEN: Ben29 51v, Ben30 13r, Ben33 (9r), Ben34 (41r), DaB 37v, Mc127 375, Mc540 83, Mc546 160, McV 38v, Ott 48r, Ve 32v.

349 RL: MRM 319. SAC: Va (918). GREG: Ha (598: m. v.), Pa (545). GEL8: En 238, Ge 234, Rh 167, Sg 217. AM: Sb (982). ES: F 224. BEN: Ben29 51v, Ben30 13r (m. v.), DaB 37v, Mc127 375 (m. v.), Mc540 83 (m. v.), McO 261, McV 38v, Ott 48r (m. v.), Ve 32v.

350 **Eccli 44: 16.** RL: MRM (433). BEN: Ben29 51v, DaB 37v, Mc127 375, Mc540 83, McV 38v, Ott 48r.

351 **Ps 106: 32, 31.** RL: GR 408-409 (melodia var.), MRM 320. ES: Syg 53. LS: Gs 182. BEN: Ben29 52r, Ben34 (244v-245r), Ve 33r.

352

76r | TRACTVS ♪ Tu es petrus et super hanc petram edificabo ecclesiam meam. Et porte inferi non preualebunt aduersus eam et tibi dabo claues regni celorum. Et quodcumque ligaueris super terram erit ligatum et in celis. Et quodcumque solueris super terram erit solutum et in celis. ♪

353

EVANGELIVM [Io 21: 15]. Dixit iesus petro. Symon iohannis diligis me.

354

OFFERTORIVM Inueni dauid.

355

SECRETA Ecclesie tue domine quesumus. preces et hostias beati petri apostoli comendet oratio. ut quod pro illius gloria celebramus; nobis prosit ad ueniam. per.

356

COMMVNIO Tu es petrus.

357

Letificet nos domine munus oblatum. ut sicut in apostolo tuo petro; te mirabilem predicamus. sic per illum tue sumamus indulgentie largitatem. per.

---

352 *Vide Intro. p. 160*

---

352 **Mt 16: 18-19**. RL: GR 409-410 (m. v.), MRM 320. ES: Syg 53. LS: Gs 182. BEN: Ve 33r-v.

353 **Io 21: 15**. RL: MRM (346). BEN: Ben29 52r, Ben30 14r-v, Ben33 (110v-111r), DaB 37v, Mc127 375, Mc540 83, McV 38v, Ott 48r.

354 **Ps 88: 21**. RL: GR ([9]-[10], [34]), MRM (415). AMS (16a, 170). BEN: Ben33 (6r, 116r), Ben34 (28v), PuC (759).

355 RL: MRM 320. SAC: Le (318), Va (919). GREG: Ha (605), Pa (549). GEL8: En 239, Ge 235, Rh 168, Sg 218. ES: F 225. BEN: Ben33 (113r), Ve 33v.

356 **Mt 16: 18**. RL: GR 412, MRM 320. AMS (121). BEN: Ben33 (112r), Ben34 (207r), PuC (582), Ve 33v.

357 RL: MRM 320. SAC: Va (920). GEL8: En 241, Ge 237, Rh 170, Sg 220. ES: F 227. BEN: Ve 33v.

IN SANCTI MATHIE APOSTOLI

358

INTROITVS Ego autem sicut.

359

ORATIO Deus qui beatum mathiam. apostolorum tuorum collegio
76v sociasti. tri│bue quesumus. ut eius interuentione. tue semper circa nos
uiscera pietatis sentiamus. per.

360

GRADVALE Iustus ut.

361

EVANGELIVM [Io 15: 1 vel 5]. Ego sum uitis.

362

ORATIO SECRETA Deus qui proditoris apostate ruinam, ne apostolorum
tuorum numerus sacratus careret. beati mathie electione supplesti.
presentia munera sanctifica. et per eam nos gratie tue uirtute confirma.
per.

363

COMMVNIO Magna est gloria eius.

364

POSTCOMMVNIO Percipiat domine quesumus populus tuus intercedente
beato mathia apostolo tuo misericordiam quam deposcit. et que
precatur humiliter. indulgentiam consequatur et pacem. per.

---

358 Ps 51: 10. RL: GR (448: vig.), MRM (403, 2: 181: vig.). AMS (154). BEN: Ben30
190r, Ben33 (4r), Ben34 (22v-23r).

359 RL: MRM 320. GREG: Tc 3449. ES: F 228. BEN: Ve 33v.

360 Ps 91: 13. RL: GR (448: vig., vide [2]), MRM (403). AMS (154). BEN: Ben30
191r, Ben33 (4v, 138v), Ben34 (23r).

361 Io 15: 1 vel 5. RL: MRM (405). BEN: Ben33 (92v, 138v).

362 GREG: Tc 3450. ES: F 229. BEN: Ve 33v.

363 Ps 20: 6. RL: GR (448: vig., vide [2]), MRM (404). AMS 155. BEN: Ben30 192r,
Ben33 (4v, 123v), Ben34 (24r).

364 GREG: Ha (932), Tc 3454. GEL8: En (1975), Ge (1655). ES: F 231.

IN SANCTI GREGORII. PAPE.

365

Deus qui frumenta tui eloquii beatum pontificem tuum gregorium.
esurientibus populis dispertire fecisti. concede tuis famulis toto mentis
affectu. seruare quod docuit. ut illius quoque eodem aput te optinente,
mereamur subsequi quo peruenit. per.

IN SANCTI BENEDICTI.

366

♪ Vir dei benedictus mundi gloriam despexit et reliquit quoniam dei spiritus erat
cum eo. VERSVS Recessit igitur scienter. ♪

367

77r Omnipotens sempiterne deus. qui hodierna die beatis|simum confesso-
rem tuum benedictum subleuasti ad celum. concede quesumus hec
festa tuis famulis celebrantibus, cunctorum ueniam delictorum. ut qui
exultantibus animis eius claritati congaudent. ipso aput te interueniente consocientur et meritis. per.

368

LECTIO [Eccli 39: 6]. Iustus cor suum.

---

368 totum *add. in marg. dext.*

---

366 *Vir*: EGA   *quo*niam: EFGABABc   *dei*²: B   V.: GABcBGAcBAG

---

365 BEN: Ben30 15r, Ben33 15v, DaB 38v, Mc127 377, Mc540 84, Mc.VII 7, McO
262, McV 39r, Ott 48v, PuC 404.

366 RL: GR in Suppl. OSB (27, oct.: ps. var.), MRM 2: 188. ES: Vl4770 23v. BEN:
Ben34 54r, Ben35 23r, DaB 39r, Mc127 378, Mc540 85, Mc546 37, Mc.VII 9, McV
39v, Ott 49v, PuC 407 (ps. var.).

367 RL: MRM 2: 188. ES: F 252, Vl4770 23v. BEN: Ben29 54v, Ben30 15r-v, Ben33
16v (m. v.), DaB 39r-v, Mc127 378, Mc540 85, McV 39v, Ott 49v, PuC 408, Ve
34v (m. v.).

368 Eccli 39: 6. RL: MRM (411). BEN: Ben29 54v, DaB 39v, DaK 11r, Mc127 378,
Mc540 85, McV 39v, Ott 49v.

369

GRADVALE ♪ Repletus sancto spiritu beatus benedictus inter multa miracula que fecerat suscitauit puerum. VERSVS Illusionem regis cognoscens ei postmodum que erat uentura predixit. ♪

370

TRACTVS ♪ In columbe specie uidit beatus benedictus. Celsa omnipotenti
77v ethera ire animam sancte. Scolastice mox nuntiauit illud fra|tribus deo gratias egit. ♪

371

EVANGELIVM [Lc 11: 33]. Nemo accendit lucernam.

372

OFFERTORIVM ♪ Intempesta noctis hora uidit sanctus benedictus fusam desuper lucem cunctas noctis tenebras effugasse. ♪

373

SECRETA Oblatis domine ob honorem beati confessoris tui benedicti placare muneribus. et ipsius interuentu cunctorum nobis tribue indulgentiam peccatorum. per.

---

371 totum *add. in marg. dext.*

---

369 *Vide Intro. p. 169*

370 *Vide Intro. p. 170*

372 *Vide Intro. p. 171*

---

369 ES: Syg 56, Vl4770 23v. BEN: Ben34 54r-v, Ben35 23r, DaB 39v, Mc127 378, Mc540 86, Mc546 37, McV 39v-40r, Ott 49v, PuC 410 (m. v.).

370 RL: MRM 2: 189. ES: Syg 56, Vl4770 23v. BEN: Ben29 (50v), Ben34 54v, Ben35 23r-v, DaB 39v, Mc127 378, Mc540 86, Mc546 38-39, Mc.VII 9, McV 40r, Ott 49v.

371 Lc 11: 33. RL: MRM (436, 440). BEN: Ben29 54v, Ben33 17r, DaB 39v-40r, DaK 11r-v, Mc127 378, Mc540 86, Mc.VII 9, McV 40r, Ott 49v-50r, PuC 411.

372 ES: Syg 57 (melodia var.), Vl4770 24r. BEN: Ben34 55r, Ben35 23v, DaB 40r, Mc127 378, Mc540 86, Mc546 38, Mc.VII 9, McV 40r, Ott 50r, PuC 412.

373 ES: F 253, Vl4770 24r. BEN: Ben29 55r, Ben30 15v, Ben33 17r, DaB 40r, Mc127 378, Mc540 86, Mc.VII 9, McV 40r, Ott 50r, PuC 413 (m. v.), Ve 34v.

374

COMMVNIO ♪ Hodie dilectus domini benedictus celum ascendit in gloria ab angelis susceptus est. ♪

375

POSTCOMMVNIO Quesumus domine salutaribus repleti misteriis. beati benedicti confessoris tui atque abbatis cuius sollempnia celebramus. orationibus adiuuemur. per.

ANNVNTIATIO. SANCTE MARIE.

376

Rorate celi desuper.

377

ORATIO Deus qui hodierna die uerbum tuum beate marie semper uirginis aluo coadunare uoluisti. fac nos presentem sollempnitatem ita peragere; ut tibi placere ualeamus. per.

378

78r LECTIO [Is 7: 10]. Locutus est ad | achaz.

---

374 *Vide Intro. p. 172*

---

374 RL: MRM 2: 189. ES: Syg 57 (melodia var.), Vl4770 24r. BEN: Ben34 55r, Ben35 23v, DaB 40r, Mc127 378, Mc540 86, Mc546 38, Mc.VII 9, McV 40r, Ott 50r, PuC 414.

375 RL: MRM (407, 422). SAC: Va (878). GREG: Ha (101, 107, 481, 689), Pa (80, 417, 664), Sp (1226). GEL8: En (146), Ge (132, 151, 155, 1074), Sg (134, 856). AM: Sb (1158). BEN: Ben33 (10r, 93v, 105v).

376 Is 45: 8. RL: GR (21), MRM (5, 13, 454). AMS 33a. BEN: Ben29 55r, Ben30 15v-16r, Ben34 55v, DaB 40r, Mc127 378-379, Mc540 86, Mc546 39, McV 40r, Ott 50r, PuL 68v, Ve 34v.

377 GREG: Ha 141. ES: F 265. BEN: Ben29 55r (m. v.), McO 271.

378 Is 7: 10. RL: MRM 324. LEC: Mu 21.4, CoP 537. BEN: Ben29 55r, Ben30 16r-v, DaB 40r, DaK 11v, Mc127 379, Mc540 87, McV 40v, PuC 418, PuL 69r.

379

GRADVALE Tollite portas.

380

TRACTVS ♪ Aue maria gratia plena dominus tecum. Benedicta tu inter mulieres. Et benedictus fructus uentris tui. ♪

381

EVANGELIVM [Lc 1: 26]. Missus est angelus.

382

OFFERTORIVM Aue maria gratia.

383

SECRETA Altario tuo domine superposita munera spiritus sanctus benignus assumat. qui hodie beate marie uiscera splendoribus sue uirtutis repleuit. per. in unitate eiusdem.

384

COMMVNIO Ecce uirgo concipiet.

---

380 *Vide Intro. p. 152*

---

379 Ps 23: 7. RL: GR (9-10), MRM (6, 454, 2: 190). AMS 33a. BEN: Ben29 55r, Ben30 16v, Ben34 55v, DaB 40r-v, Mc127 379, Mc540 87, Mc546 39, McV 40v, PuC 418, PuL 69-70.

380 Lc 1: 28. BEN: Ben29 55r, Ben33 17v, Ben34 55v, Ben35 23v-24r, DaB 40v, Mc127 379, Mc540 87, Mc546 39, McV 40v, Ott 50v, PuC 419, PuL 70, Ve 35r. Var. (melodia): RL: GR (459-461), ES: Syg 57, LS: Gs 183.

381 Lc 1: 26. RL: MRM 324. LEC: Mu 21.4, CoP 538. BEN: Ben29 55r, Ben30 17r-v, Ben33 17v, DaB 40v, DaE 22v, DaK 11v-12r, DaZ 347, Mc127 379, Mc540 87, McV 40v, PuC 420, PuL 70-71, Ve 35r.

382 Lc 1: 28. RL: GR 461, MRM 324. AMS 33b. BEN: Ben29 55r-v, Ben30 17v-18r, Ben33 17v, Ben34 56r, Ben35 24r, DaB 40v, DaZ 347, Mc127 379, Mc540 87, Mc546 40, McV 40v, Ott 50v, PuC 421, PuL 71v, Ve 35r.

383 GEL8: En 884, Ge 852, Sg 679. AM: Sb (84). ES: F 267. BEN: Ben29 55v, Ben30 18r, Ben33 17v, DaB 40v, DaZ 347, Mc127 379, Mc540 87, McV 40v, Ott 50v, PuC 422, PuL 71v.

384 Is 7: 14. RL: GR 462, MRM 325. AMS 33b. BEN: Ben29 55v, Ben30 18r, Ben34 56r, DaB 40v, DaZ 347, Mc127 379, Mc540 87, Mc546 40, McV 40v, Ott 50v, PuC 424, PuL 71v, Ve 35r.

385

POSTCOMMVNIO Gratiam tuam quesumus domine mentibus nostris infunde. ut qui angelo annuntiante christi filii tui incarnationem cognouimus. per passionem eius et crucem, ad resurrectionis gloriam perducamur. per.

IN SANCTI GEORGII.

386

♪ Protexisti me deus a conuentu malignantium alleluia. et a multitudine operantium iniquitatem alleluia alleluia. PSALMVS Exaudi deus orationem meam cum tribulatione. ♪

387

78v | ORATIO Tuus sanctus martir georgius nos quesumus domine semper letificet. ut dum eius merita in presenti festiuitate recolimus. patrocinia in augmentum uirtutum sentiamus. per.

388

SAPIENTIE [Sap 5: 1-5]. Stabunt iusti in magna constantia. ... sors illorum est.

---

388 angustiauerunt] angustaverunt *Vulgata* (5: 1)   intra] inter (5: 3)   angustia] angustiam (5: 3)   aliquando habuimus] habuimus aliquando (5: 3)   derisu] risu (5: 3)   ecce quomodo] quomodo (5: 5)

---

386 conuentu: dfd   *a²*: dB   mul*ti*tudine: e   o*peran*tium: ded   *alleluia²*: BdBdcdc   Ps.: GcBcdfedcAG

---

385 RL: MRM 325. GREG: Ha 143, Pa 385. GEL8: En 879, Ge 850, Rh 541. AM: Sb 890. BEN: Ben29 55v, Ben30 18r-v, DaB 40v, Mc127 379, Mc540 87, McV 40v, Ott 50v, PuC (812), PuL 71v, Ve 35r.

386 Ps 63: 3, 63: 2. RL: GR 478 (vide [15]-[16]), MRM 326. AMS 93a. ES: Vl4770 126v. BEN: Ben29 239v-240r, Ben33 91r, Ben34 153r, Ben35 88r, Ben38 70r, Ben39 59r, Ben40 51r, Mc127 380, McV 176v, Ott 248r, Ve 123v.

387 GEL8: En 915, Ge 884, Sg 710. AM: Sb 896. ES: F 856, Vl4770 126v. BEN: Ben29 240r, Ben33 91r, Mc127 380, McO 347 (m. v.), McV 176v, PuC 458.

388 Sap 5: 1-5. RL: MRM (418). BEN: Ben29 240r, Ben33 (93r).

389

♪ Alleluia. VERSVS Confitebuntur celi mirabilia tua domine et ueritatem tuam in ecclesia sanctorum. ♪

390

79v ♪ Alleluia. VERSVS Pretiosa |in conspectu domini mors sanctorum eius. ♪

391

SEQVENTIA SANCTI EVANGELII SECVNDVM IOHANNEM [15: 5-11]. In illo tempore. Dixit iesus discipulis suis. Ego sum uitis uos palmites. ... impleatur.

392

SEQVENTIA SANCTI SECVNDVM IOHANNEM [15: 1-4]. | In illo tempore. Dixit iesus discipulis suis. Ego sum uitis uera. ... in me manseritis.

393

SECVNDVM MATHEVM [Mc 13: 33-37]. In illo tempore. Dixit iesus discipulis suis. Videte, uigilate, et orate. nescitis enim quando tempus 80r sit. ... omnibus | dico uigilate.

---

391 arescet] aruit *Vulgata* (15: 6)   eum] eos (15: 6)   mittent] mittunt (15: 6)   ardebit] ardent (15: 6)

393 proficiscens] profectus *Vulgata* (13: 34)   uigilaret] vigilet (13: 34)

---

389 *Vide Intro. p. 155*

390 *Vide Intro. p. 155*

---

389 Ps 88: 6. RL: MRM 326. AMS 93a. ES: Schlager, *Katalog* F (D) 220. BEN: Ben29 240r, Ben33 (95v), Ben34 153r (163v), Ben38 (75v), Ben39 (68v), Ben40 (52r), Mc127 380, McV 176v, Ott 248r, PuC (476). Var. (melodia): RL: GR 478 (vide [16]), ES: Syg (171, 172), LS: Gs 216 (sine musica).

390 Ps 115: 15. RL: MRM (419). ES: Schlager, *Katalog* G 282. BEN: Ben29 240r, Ben33 (93r), Ben34 153r (164r), Ben35 (97r), Ben38 (75v), Ben39 (68v), Ben40 (52r), Mc127 380, McV 176v, Ott 248r. Var. (melodia): RL: GR ([19]-[20]), ES: Syg (218).

391 Io 15: 5-11. RL: MRM (418). BEN: Ben29 240r, Ben33 (138v), DaK 63v, Mc127 380-381.

392 Io 15: 1-4. RL: MRM (418). BEN: Ben33 (92v), DaE (94r), McV 176v, Ott 248r.

393 Mc 13: 33-37. RL: MRM (436, 440).

394

SEQVENTIA ♪ Ea caterua dicata tonanti summi prolis. Laudibus benignis reddite deuote silabis. ♪

395

OFFERTORIVM ♪ Confitebuntur celi mirabilia tua domine et ueritatem tuam in ecclesia sanctorum alleluia alleluia. ♪

396

SECRETA Tanto placabiles quesumus domine nostre sint hostie. quanto sancti martiris tui georgii. pro cuius sollempnitate exhibentur. tibi grata sunt munera. per.

397

COMMVNIO ♪ Ego sum uitis uera et uos palmites qui manet in me et ego in eo hic fert fructum multum alleluia alleluia. ♪

398

POSTCOMMVNIO Beati georgii martiris tui suffragiis exoratus. percepta sacramenti tui, nos uirtute defende. per.

---

394 *Vide Intro. p. 156*

397 *sum*: cA   *hic*: A   *fert*: GAcGF   *fructum*: AcB   *multum*: cdcA
alleluia[1]: BGAFAcBcA   *alleluia*[2]: AGBAGAGFGFGF

---

394 BEN: Ben38 (70v-71v), Ben39 (66r), Ben40 (46r-47r). Vide *Analecta hymnica* 53: 291-293.

395 Ps 88: 6. RL: GR 478 (vide [17]-[18]), MRM 326. AMS 93a. ES: Vl4770 127r. BEN: Ben29 240r, Ben33 91r, Ben34 153r-v, Ben35 88r-v, Ben38 70r-v, Ben39 59r-v, Ben40 (47r), Mc127 381, McV 176v, Ott 248r, PuC (478), Ve 123v.

396 SAC: Le (805). GEL8: En 916, Ge 886, Sg 711. AM: Sb 897 (inc. var.). ES: Vl4770 (127r). BEN: Ben29 240r, Ben33 91r, Mc127 381, McV 176v, Ott 248r, PuC 459.

397 Io 15: 5. RL: GR in Suppl. OSB (19-20), MRM (327). AMS (95). ES: Vl4770 (129v). BEN: Ben33 (93r), Ben34 (163r-v), Ben35 (97r), Ben38 (75r), Ben39 (68r), Ben40 51v-52r, McV (178r).

398 GREG: Pa (848). GEL8: En 918, Ge 888, Sg 713. AM: Sb 899. ES: F 860, Vl4770 127r. BEN: Ben29 240r, Ben33 91r-v, Mc127 381, McV 177r, Ott 248r, PuC 460.

IN SANCTI VITALIS.

399

Sancti nos uitalis domine quesumus natalicia uotiua letificent. et sui beneficii intercessione attolant. per.

IN SANCTI MARCI EVANGELISTE.

400

Protexisti.

401

Deus qui hunc diem beati marci apostoli tui et euangeliste. gloriose
80v passionis, lau|dabile roseo sanguine consecrasti rore perfusum. presta quesumus; ut ipse pro nobis aput te existat precipuus intercessor. qui unigeniti tui meruit fieri euangelicus predicaturo. per.

402

LECTIO [Sap 5: 1]. Stabunt iusti.

403

Alleluia. Pretiosa.

404

EVANGELIVM [Io 15: 1]. Ego sum uitis uera. et pater meus.

---

399 SAC: Va (1006). GEL8: En 919, Ge 922, Sg 723. ES: F 877, Vl4770 129v.

400 Ps 63: 3. RL: GR 478 (vide [15]), MRM 326. AMS (93a). ES: Vl4770 (129r). BEN: Ben29 241r, Ben34 (153r), Ben35 (88r), Ben38 70v, Ben39 (59r), Ben40 46r, Mc127 382, McV 177v, Ve 124r.

401 AM: Sacr. Aribert 664. ES: Vl4770 128v. BEN: Ben33 91v, McO 348, PuC 461 (m. v.).

402 Sap 5: 1. RL: MRM (418). BEN: Ben33 (93r), PuC (475), Ve (124v).

403 Ps 115: 15. RL: GR ([19]-[20]), MRM (419). BEN: Ben29 242r, Ben33 (93r), Ben34 (164r), Ben38 (75v), Ben39 (68v), Mc127 383, McV 178r.

404 Io 15: 1. RL: MRM (418). BEN: Ben29 242r, Ben33 (92v), DaE (94r), DaK 64r, Ott 248r.

405

OFFERTORIVM Confitebuntur.

406

SECRETA Munera quesumus domine tibi dicata sanctifica. et intercedente beato marco euangelista et martire tuo, per eadem nos placatus
intende. per.

407

COMMVNIO Ego sum uitis uera.

408

Sacro munere satiati, supplices te domine depcamur. ut quod debite
seruitutis celebramus officio. saluationis tue sentiamus augmento. per.

IN SANCTORVM PHILIPPI. ET IACOBI.

409

♪ Exclamauerunt ad te domine in tempore afflictionis sue et tu de celo exaudisti
eos alleluia alleluia. PSALMVS Gaudete iusti. ♪

---

409 *Ex*clamauerunt: E   *af*flictionis: C   *allelu*ia[1]: CEFEGF   *al*leluia[2]: CE
Ps.: FGAcAGFD

---

405 Ps 88: 6. RL: GR 478 (vide [17]), MRM 2: 193. AMS (93a). ES: Vl4770 (127r).
BEN: Ben29 242r, Ben33 (91r, 93v), Ben34 (153r-v), Ben35 (88r-v), Ben38 71v,
Ben39 67r, Ben40 47r, Mc127 383, McV 178r, PuC (478).

406 RL: MRM (411). SAC: Va (1290). GREG: Ha (492, 563, 626, 764), Pa (435, 512,
583, 769). GEL8: En (1165), Ge (966, 994, 1283), Rh (765), Sg (788, 1034). ES:
F (1161). BEN: Ben29 (242r-v), Ben33 (93r).

407 Io 15: 1. RL: GR in Suppl. OSB (19-20), MRM (327). AMS (95). ES: Vl4770
(129v). BEN: Ben29 242r, Ben33 (93r), Ben34 (163r), Ben35 (97r), Ben38 (75r),
Ben39 (68r), Ben40 (51v-52r), Mc127 383, McV 178r.

408 RL: MRM (325, 335). SAC: Le (793), Va (332). GREG: Ha (113, 462, 561, 647),
Pa (86, 395, 504, 606). GEL8: En (160, 562), Ge (166), Rh (127), Sg (146). AM:
Sb (225). BEN: Ben33 (11r, 119r).

409 2 Esdr 9: 27, Ps 32: 1. RL: GR 488, MRM 328. AMS 96. ES: Vl4770 129v. BEN:
Ben29 242v, Ben30 100r-v, Ben33 93r, Ben34 163v, Ben35 97r, Ben38 75v, Ben39
68v, Ben40 52r, Mc127 384, McV 178r, Ott 249v, PuC 473, Ve 124v.

410

ORATIO Deus qui nos annua apostolorum tuorum philippi et iacobi, solemnitate letificas. presta quesumus; ut quorum gaudemus meritis instruamur exemplis. per.

411

LECTIO [Sap 5: 1]. Stabunt iusti.

412

Alleluia. Pretiosa.

413

81r IOHANNEM [14: 1-13]. | In illo tempore. Dixit iesus discipulis suis.
81v Non turbetur cor uestrum neque formidet. ... | ... det uobis.

414

OFFERTORIVM Confitebuntur.

---

413 cum abiero] si abiero *Vulgata* (14: 3)   ueniam] venio (14: 3)   ibi et uos] et vos (14: 3)   ueritas] et veritas (14: 6)   cognoscetis] cognoscitis (14: 7) uidet ... uidet] vidit ... vidit (14: 9)   petieritis patrem] petieritis (14: 13) det uobis] hoc faciam (14: 13)

---

410 RL: MRM 328. GREG: Ha 479, Pa 415, Sp (1224). GEL8: En 927, Ge 930, Rh 559, Sg 731. AM: Sb (1155). ES: Vl4770 130r. BEN: Ben29 242v, Ben30 100v, Ben33 93r, Mc127 384, McV 178r-v, Ott 249v, PuC 474, Ve 124v.

411 Sap 5: 1. RL: MRM 328. LEC: Mu 81, CoP 206. ES: Vl4770 130r. BEN: Ben29 242v, Ben30 100v-101r, Ben33 93r, Mc127 384, McV 178v, Ott 249v-250r, PuC 475, Ve 124v.

412 Ps 115: 15. RL: GR ([19]-[20]), MRM (419). BEN: Ben29 242v, Ben30 101r, Ben33 93r, Ben34 164r, Ben35 97r, Ben38 75v, Ben39 68v, Ben40 52r, Mc127 384, McV 178v, Ott 250r.

413 Io 14: 1-13. RL: MRM 328. LEC: Mu 81, WuE 306, CoP 207. ES: Vl4770 130r-v. BEN: Ben29 242v-243r, Ben30 101r-102r, Ben33 93r-v, DaE 94v, DaK 51r-v, 64r, Mc127 384-385, McV 178v-179r, Ott 250r-v, PuC 477, Ve 124v-125r.

414 Ps 88: 6. RL: GR 489, MRM 328. AMS 96. ES: Vl4770 130v. BEN: Ben29 243r, Ben30 102r, Ben33 93v, Ben34 165r, Ben35 98r, Ben38 76r, 78v, Ben39 69v, Ben40 53r, Mc127 385, McV 179r, Ott 250v, PuC 478, Ve 125r.

415

SECRETA Munera domine que pro apostolorum tuorum philippi et iacobi; sollempnitate deferimus. propitius suscipe. et mala omnia que meremur auerte. per.

416

COMMVNIO ♪ Tanto tempore uobiscum sum et non cognouistis me philippe qui uidet me uidet et patrem alleluia non credis quia ego in patre et pater in me est alleluia alleluia. ♪

417

Quesumus domine salutaribus repleti misteriis. ut quorum sollempnia celebramus; eorum orationibus adiuuemur. per.

INVENTIO SANCTE CRVCIS.

418

91r ♪ Nos autem gloriari oportet in cruce domini nostri iesu | xpisti in quo est salus uita et resurrectio nostra per quem saluati et liberati sumus. PSALMVS Deus misereatur. ♪

---

418 *91r post 81v legendum est (vide App.)*

---

416 *tempore*: EFGFEFEDED   *et*[1]: C   *non*[1]: E   *philippe*: EFGFEFEDED
ui*det*[1]: AG   *non*[2]: EF   cre*dis*: EF   *pater*: FGF   alle*lu*ia[2]: E

418 glo*ri*ari: E   *in*[1]: GE   ie*su*: E   re*sur*rectio: E   *li*berati: GF   Ps.:
AGAFGAGE

---

415 RL: MRM 329. GREG: Ha 480, Pa 416, Sp (1225). GEL8: Ge 932, Rh 561, Sg 733. AM: Sb (1156). ES: Vl4770 130v. BEN: Ben29 243r-v, Ben30 102r, Ben33 93v, Mc127 385, McV 179r, Ott 250v, PuC 479, Ve 125r.

416 Io 14: 9-10. RL: GR 489, MRM 329. AMS 96. ES: Vl4770 130v. BEN: Ben29 243v, Ben30 102r, Ben33 93v, Ben34 165r, Ben35 98r, Ben38 76v, Ben39 69v, Ben40 53r, Mc127 385, McV 179r, Ott 250v, PuC 480, Ve 125r.

417 RL: MRM 329. SAC: Va (878). GREG: Ha 481, Pa 417, Sp (1226). GEL8: En (146), Ge (132, 151, 155, 1074), Sg (856). AM: Sb (1158). ES: Vl4770 130v. BEN: Ben29 243v, Ben30 102r, Ben33 93v, Mc127 385, McV 179r, Ott 250v, Ve 125r.

418 Gal 6: 14, Ps 66: 2. RL: GR 490-491, MRM 329. AMS 97*bis*. ES: Vl4770 131r. BEN: Ben29 243v, Ben33 93v, Ben34 165r (112v), Ben35 98v, Ben38 76v, Ben39 70r, Ben40 53r, Mc127 386, McV 179r, Ott 250v, PuC 482, Ve 125r.

419

ORATIO Deus qui in preclara salutifere crucis inuentione passionis tue, miracula suscitasti. concede. ut uitalis ligni pretio. eterne uite suffragia consequamur. per.

420

ALEXANDRI. EVENTI. ET THEODOLI. Presta quesumus omnipotens deus. ut qui sanctorum tuorum alexandri, euenti, et theodoli natalicia colimus. a cunctis malis imminentibus. eorum intercessionibus liberemur. per.

421

AD CHORINTIOS [Col 1: 26-28]. Fratres. Misterium quod absconditum ... perfectum. In christo iesu domino nostro.

422

GRADVALE Christus factus est.

---

421 notam] notas *Vulgata* (1: 27)   sacramentis] sacramenti (1: 27)   quem nobis] quem nos (1: 28)   corripientes omnes homines] corripientes omnem hominem (1: 28)   docentem] docentes (1: 28)   omni sapientia] in omni sapientia (1: 28)

---

419 RL: MRM 329. SAC: Va 869. GREG: Pa 421. GEL8: En 939, Ge 944, Rh 564, Sg 743. AM: Sb 905. ES: Vl4770 131r. BEN: Ben29 243v, Ben33 93v, Mc127 386, McO 356, McV 179r, Ott 250v, PuC 483, Ve 125r.

420 RL: MRM 2: 195. GREG: Ha 482, Pa 418. GEL8: En 936, Ge 941, Sg 740. ES: Vl4770 130v. BEN: Ben29 243v, Ben33 94r, Mc127 385-386, McV 179r, Ott 250v, Ve 126r.

421 Col 1: 26-28. BEN: Ben29 243v-244r, Ben33 93v, Mc127 386, McV 179r-v, Ott 250v-251r, PuC 484.

422 Phil 2: 8. RL: GR (196), MRM (157, 381, 453). AMS 97*bis*. BEN: Ben33 (64v), Ben38 (161r), Ben40 (123v), PuC (245).

423

91v ♪ Alleluia. VERSVS Dulce lignum dulces clauos dul|cia ferens pondera que sola
fuisti digna portare regem celorum et dominum. ♪

424

EVANGELIVM [Mt 13: 44]. Simile est regnum celorum thesauro abs-
condito in.

425

OFFERTORIVM ♪ Protege domine plebem tuam per lignum sancte crucis. ab
omnibus insidiis inimicorum omnium ut tibi gratam exibeamus seruitutem et
acceptabile tibi fiat sacrificium nostrum alleluia. ♪

426

Sacrificium domine quod immolamus, placatus intende. ut ab omni
nos exuat bellorum nequitie. et per uexillum sancte crucis filii tui; ad
conterendas potestates aduersariorum insidias. nos tue protectionis
securitate constitue. per eundem.

---

423 *Corr. neumae musicae, eadem manu*

---

423 *Alleluia*: EFAcBAcAdcB[*lac.*]cBAcAdcBAGF   *Dul*ce: FG   lig*num*: A
fe*rens*: B   *pon*dera: BAGAGcBAG   *que*: G   *so*la: Bcd   *digna*:
BAcBAB   por*tare*: cedcAdcBGAGFAGcBAGAG] sus*tine*re GR   *celo*rum:
GAGcBAG   domi*num*: G

425 *do*mine: CDEFEF   *li*gnum: EFGEGFEDEF   *omnibus*: DCFEFG-
DEFE   i*ni*micorum: CFE   *om*nium: D   exibe*amus*: GAFGFDEFE
sa*cri*ficium: D   al*le*luia: CDCDEDB'CD

---

423 RL: MRM 329. ES: Vl4770 131r. BEN: Ben29 244r, Ben33 93v, Ben34 165r-v,
Ben35 98v-99r, Ben38 77r, Ben39 70v, Ben40 53v, Mc127 386, McV 179v, PuC
485, Ve 125v. Var. (melodia All.): RL: GR 491-492, ES: Schlager, *Katalog* G (F)
242, Syg 174, LS: Gs 185.

424 Mt 13: 44. RL: MRM (313, 445). BEN: Ben29 244r, Ben33 93v-94r, DaE 96r,
Mc127 386, McV 179v, Ott 251r, PuC 486.

425 RL: GR (594), MRM (381, 454). BEN: Ben29 244r, Ben33 94r, Ben34 167r,
Ben35 100r, Ben38 78v-79r, Ben39 73r (var.), Ben40 55r-v, Mc127 386, McV
179v, PuC (659), Ve 126r.

426 RL: MRM 330. SAC: Va 871. GEL8: En 941, Ge 946, Rh 566, Sg 745. AM: Sb
907. ES: Vl4770 131v. BEN: Ben29 244r, Ben33 94r, Mc127 386, McV 179v, Ott
251r, PuC 488, Ve 126r.

427

COMMVNIO ♪ Per sanctam crucem tuamque gloriosam passionem. te xpiste rogamus exaudi nos ut ab antiqui hostis nos tuis famulis ♪ [*lac.*]

| VIGILIA SANCTI IOHANNIS BAPTISTE.

428

♪ Ne timeas zacharia exaudita est oratio tua et helisabet uxor tua pariet tibi filium et uocabis nomen eius iohannem et erit magnus coram domino et spiritu sancto replebitur adhuc ex utero matris sue et multi in natiuitate eius gaudebunt. PSALMVS Domine in uirtute. ♪

429

Presta quesumus omnipotens deus. ut familiam tuam, per uiam salutis incedat. et beati iohannis precursoris hortamenta sectando. ad eum quem predixit secura perueniat. per.

---

427 *lac. inter 91v-92r*

---

427 *Vide Intro. p. 157*

428 zacha*ria*: cdcBd   *nomen*: Bd   eius[1]: cdcA   e*rit*: B   *mag*nus: cA
*sanc*to: cd   *re*plebitur: c   *multi in*: AB   *nati*uitate: Bdc   Ps.: GcBcdfedcAG

---

427 BEN: Ben35 100v, Ben38 (132r), Ben40 55v.

428 Lc 1: 13, 15, 14, Ps 20: 2. RL: GR 521-522, MRM 340. AMS 117. ES: Vl4770 162r. BEN: Ben29 248v, Ben33 107v, Ben34 196r-v, Ben35 122r, Ben38 105v-106r, Ben39 108r-v, Ben40 85v, Mc127 398, Mc.VI 53, McV 184r, Ott 301v, PuC 543, Ve 161r.

429 RL: MRM 340. SAC: Le (241). GREG: Ha 568, Pa 520. GEL8: En 1024, Ge 1143, Rh 688, Sg 919. ES: Vl4770 162r. BEN: Ben29 248v, Ben33 107v, Mc127 398, Mc.VI 53, McO 384, McV 184r, Ott 301v, PuC 544, Ve 161r.

430

LECTIO YEREMIE PROPHETE [1: 4-10]. In diebus illis. Factum est
92v uerbum domini ad me dicens. Priusquam ... | ... et plantes. Dicit
dominus omnipotens.

431

GRADVALE ♪ Fuit homo missus a deo cui nomen iohannes erat hic uenit.
VERSVS Vt testimonium periberet de lumine et parare domino plebem perfec-
tam. ♪

432

INITIUM SANCTI EVANGELII SECVNDVM LVCAM [1: 5-17]. Fuit in diebus
93r-v herodis regis ... | parare domino plebem perfectam.

433

OFFERTORIVM Gloria et honore.

---

430 de uentre] de vulva *Vulgata* (1: 5)   et prophetam in gentibus] prophetam
gentibus (1: 5)   quia puer sum] quia *om. Vulgata* (1: 7)   uniuersa que]
universa quaecumque (1: 7)   ego sum tecum] tecum ego sum (1: 8)   dixit
michi] dixit Dominus ad me (1: 9)

432 uxor illius] uxor illi *Vulgata* (1: 5)   zacharias in ordine] in ordine (1: 8)
addextris] a dextris (1: 11)   oratio] deprecatio (1: 13)   helisabeth uxor
tua] uxor tua Elisabeth (1: 13)   siceram] sicera (1: 15)   incredibiles] incredulos (1: 17)

---

431 ho*mo*: FDFGFGDEDCD   *missus*: FAFGAcdcd   cu*i*: FA   no*men*:
AcBcAFG   *et*: cd   per*fectam*: cdcAGBAF

---

430 Ier 1: 4-10. RL: MRM 340. LEC: Alc 141, Mu 105, WuC 128, CoP 273. ES:
Vl4770 162r. BEN: Ben29 249r, Ben33 107v-108r, Mc127 398-399, Mc.VI 53, McV
184r-v, Ott 301v-302r, PuC 545, Ve 161r.

431 Io 1: 6-7. RL: GR 522, MRM 340. AMS 117. ES: Vl4770 162r. BEN: Ben29 249r,
Ben33 108r, Ben34 196v, Ben35 122r, Ben38 106r, Ben39 108v, Ben40 85v-86r,
Mc127 399, Mc.VI 53, McV 184v, Ott 302r, PuC 546, Ve 161r.

432 Lc 1: 5-17. RL: MRM 341. LEC: Mu 105, WuE 308, CoP 274. ES: Vl4770
162r-v. BEN: Ben29 249r-v, Ben33 108r, DaE 113v, Mc127 399-400, McV
184v-185r, Ott 302r-v, PuC 548, Ve 161r-v.

433 Ps 8: 6. RL: GR 522, MRM 341. AMS 117. ES: Vl4770 162v. BEN: Ben29 249v,
Ben33 108r, Ben34 197v, Ben35 122v, Ben38 107r, Ben39 110r, Ben40 86v,
Mc127 400, McV 185r, Ott 302v, PuC 549, Ve 161v.

434

SECRETA Munera domine oblata sanctifica. et intercedente beato iohanne baptista. nos per hec a peccatorum maculis emundet. per.

435

COMMVNIO Magna est gloria eius.

436

POSTCOMMVNIO Beati iohannis baptiste nos domine preclara commitetur oratio. et quem uenturum esse predixit. poscat nobis fieri placatum. per eundem.

NATALE EIVSDEM.

437

♪ De uentre matris mee uocauit me dominus nomine meo. et posuit os meum ut gladium acutum sub tegumento manus sue protexit me. posuit me quasi sagittam electam. PSALMVS Bonum est confiteri. ♪

438

ORATIO Deus qui presentem diem honorabilem nobis in beati iohannis natiuitate fecisti. da populis tuis spiritualium gratiam gaudiorum. et omnium fidelium mentes dirige in uiam salutis eterne. per.

---

437 ma*tris*: GAG   sagit*tam*: GFEFD   Ps.: FGAcAGFDCDCFGFDFEC-DED

---

434 RL: MRM 341. GREG: Ha 569, Pa 521, Sp (1100). GEL8: En (131), Ge (28, 136, 1029, 1069), Rh (115), Sg (123, 851). ES: Vl4770 162v. BEN: Ben29 249v, Ben33 108v, McV (185v), PuC 550, Ve 161v. Var.: BEN: McV 185r, Ott 302v.

435 Ps 20: 6. RL: GR 522, MRM 341. AMS 117. ES: Vl4770 162v. BEN: Ben29 249v, Ben33 (4v, 123v), Ben34 197v, Ben35 122v, Ben38 107r, Ben39 110r, Ben40 86v, Mc127 400, McV 185r, Ott 302v, PuC 551, Ve 161v.

436 RL: MRM 341. SAC: Le (240), Va 897, (906). GREG: Ha 570, Pa 522. GEL8: En 1028, Ge 1147, Rh 692, Sg 923. AM: Sb 960. ES: Vl4770 162v. BEN: Ben29 250r, Ben33 108v, Mc127 400, McV 185r, Ott 302v, Ve 161v.

437 Is 49: 1-2, Ps 91: 2. RL: GR 523-524, MRM 341. AMS 119. ES: Vl4770 163v. BEN: Ben29 250v, Ben33 108v, Ben34 197v-198v, Ben35 123r, Ben38 107v-108r, Ben39 112r, Ben40 87r, Mc127 401, Mc.VI 55, McV 185v, Ott 303v, PuC 553, Ve 162r.

438 RL: MRM 342. SAC: Le (251), Va 901. GREG: Ha 574, Pa 526. GEL8: En 1033, Ge 1152, Rh 694, Sg 928. AM: Sb (965). ES: Vl4770 163v. BEN: Ben29 250v, Ben33 108v, Mc127 401, Mc.VI 55, McO 385, McV 185v, Ott 304r, PuC 554, Ve 162r.

439

LECTIO YSAYE PROPHETE [49: 1-3, 5-7]. Hec dicit dominus. Audite
94r insule et atten|dite ... qui elegit te.

440

GRADVALE ♪ Priusquam te formarem in utero noui te et antequam exires de
uentre sanctificaui te. VERSVS Misit dominus manum suam et tetigit os meum et
dixit michi. ♪

441

94v ♪ Alleluia. VERSVS Multi gaudebunt sancti sicut sol ante dominum refulgen|ti-
bus in celum exultat ut cum domino astra sidera celique et maria collaudantes
deum in sede celestia regnant cum domino. VERSVS Ex utero senectutis et
sterilis. PROSA Iohannes baptista domini qui demonstrans digito ad iordanem.
Ecce agnus dicens. dei qui mundi sordes cunctas abluit et detergit. De quo
saluator factus est non mulierem maior natus est precursor domini. ♪

---

439 Et nunc hec dicit] hec *om. Vulgata* (49: 5)   Ut reducam ... convertendas
om. Dubr (49: 5-6)   Haec dicit Dominus ... Ad servum dominorum *om. Dubr*
(49: 7)   dominum deum tuum] propter Dominum quia fidelis est (49: 7)

---

440 *do*minus: dcAGABcd   *michi*: dcAFAGAGF

441 *Vide Intro. p. 145*

---

439 Is 49: 1-3, 5-7. RL: MRM 342. LEC: Alc 142, Mu 106, WuC 129, CoP 275. ES:
Vl4770 163v. BEN: Ben29 250v-251r, Ben33 108v, DaK 41r, Mc127 401, Mc.VI 55,
McV 185v-186r, Ott 304r, PuC 555, Ve 162r.

440 Ier 5: 1, 9. RL: GR 524, MRM 342. AMS 119. ES: Vl4770 163v. BEN: Ben29 251r,
Ben33 108v, Ben34 198v, Ben35 123r, Ben38 108r, Ben39 112r-v, Ben40 87r-v,
Mc127 401, Mc.VI 55, McV 186r, Ott 304r-v, PuC 556, Ve 162r.

441 Pr. *Multi gaudebunt*: ES: Vl4770 163v (cum *Iustus ut palma*), BEN: Ben39 113r
(m. v.), Ben40 88r (m. v.), cf. Corpus troporum 2/1 no. 40.5. All. *Ex utero*: ES:
Vl4770 163v, BEN: Ben29 251r, Ben38 108v, McV 186r, Ott 304v, cf. Schlager,
Katalog D 38. All. *Ex utero* cum Pr. *Iohannes*: BEN: Ben34 198v-199r, Ben35
123v-124r, Ben39 113r-v, Ben40 88r-v, cf. Corpus troporum 2/1 no. 16.1.

442

SECVNDVM LVCAM [1: 57-68]. In illo tempore. Helisabeth impletum est
95r ... | ... plebis sue.

443

OFFERTORIVM ♪ Iustus ut palma florebit sicut cedrus que in libano est
multiplicabitur. ♪

444

95v SECRETA Tua domine muneribus, altaria cumula|mus. illius natiuitatem
honore debito celebrantes. qui saluatorem mundi et cecinit affuturum.
et adesse monstrauit dominum nostrum iesum christum.

445

COMMVNIO ♪ Tu puer propheta altissimi uocaberis prehibis enim ante faciem
domini parare uias eius. ♪

446

POSTCOMMVNIO Sumat ecclesia tua deus beati iohannis baptiste generatione letitiam. per quem sue regenerationis cognouit auctorem.
Dominum nostrum.

---

442 patri sui] patris eius *Vulgata* (1: 59)   innuebant] innuebant autem (1: 62)
quis putas] quid putas (1: 66)   dominus deus] Deus (1: 68)

---

443 *in*: E   *multiplicabitur*: EFDGEFABAGAGFGEAGFGAGEGFE
445 *pu*er: AGAE   altissi*mi*: FGAD

---

442 Lc 1: 57-68. RL: MRM 342. LEC: Mu 106, WuE 308, CoP 276. ES: Vl4770
163v-164r. BEN: Ben29 251r-v, Ben33 109r, DaE 115r, DaK 41r-v, Mc127
401-402, Mc.VI 55, McV 186r-v, Ott 304v-305r, PuC 558, Ve 162r-v.

443 Ps 91: 13. RL: GR 525 (vide [41]), MRM 343. AMS 119. BEN: Ben29 251v,
Ben33 109r, Ben34 200v (25v-26r), Ben35 125v, Ben38 110r, Ben39 115r, Ben40
89r, Mc127 402, Mc.VI 55, McV 186v, Ott 305r, PuC 559, Ve 162v.

444 RL: MRM 343. SAC: Le 238, Va 903. GREG: Ha 575, Pa 527. GEL8: En 1035,
Ge 1154, Rh 696, Sg 930. AM: Sb (961). BEN: Ben29 251v, Ben33 109r, Mc127
402, Mc.VI 55, McV 186v, Ott 305v, PuC 560, Ve 162v.

445 Lc 1: 76. RL: GR 525, MRM 343. AMS 119. ES: Vl4770 164r (V¹ var.). BEN:
Ben29 251v, Ben33 109r, Ben34 200v, Ben35 126r, Ben38 110r, Ben39 115r,
Ben40 89r, Mc127 402, McV 186v, Ott 305v, PuC 562, Ve 162v.

446 RL: MRM 343. SAC: Va 904. GREG: Ha 576, Pa 528. GEL8: En 1037, Ge 1156,
Rh 698, Sg 932. ES: Vl4770 164r. BEN: Ben29 251v, Ben33 109r-v, Mc127 402,
McV 186v, Ott 305v, PuC 563, Ve 162v.

IN SANCTORVM IOHANNIS. ET PAVLI.

447

♪ Multe tribulationes iustorum et de his omnibus liberauit eos dominus. dominus custodit omnia ossa eorum unum ex eis non conteretur. PSALMVS Benedicam dominum. ♪

448

Quesumus omnipotens deus. ut nos geminata letitia. hodierne festiuitatis excipiat; que de beatorum iohannis et pauli glorificatione procedit. quos eadem fides et passio, uere fecit esse germanos. per.

449

LECTIO [Sap 3: 1]. Iustorum anime in manu.

450

82r GRADVALE ♪ Ecce quam | bonum et quam iocundum habitare fratres in unum. VERSVS Sicut unguentum in capite quod descendit in barbam barbam aaron. ♪

---

450 *N.B.: 82r post 95v legendum est (vide App.)*

---

447 D *inc.*] A *inc.* GR (F-*clavis*] c-*clavis trans.* GR *passim*)

450 *et*: FA   *quam*²: AGAF   *fra*tres: GAc   *unum*: AGcAGABFDECFA-GAGEFGFD   capi*te*: ABAGAcAcBAcGF   *bar*bam¹: AFAGABGFGFGA-FEFGFG   aa*ron*: AGAFDGFECDCDCDFDCDEFGFDED

---

447 Ps 33: 20-21, 33: 2. RL: GR 525 (vide 515-516), MRM 344. AMS 120a. ES: Vl4770 164v. BEN: Ben29 251v, Ben33 109v, Ben34 201r, Ben35 126r, Ben38 110v, Ben39 115r-v, Ben40 90r, Mc127 402, McV 186v, Ott 305v, Ve 162v.

448 RL: MRM 344. SAC: Le 269, Va 911. GREG: Ha 583, Pa 532. GEL8: En 1049, Ge 1168, Rh 705, Sg 943. AM: Sb (950). ES: Vl4770 164v. BEN: Ben29 251v-252r, Ben33 109v, Mc127 402-403, McO 387, McV 186v, Ott 305v, Ve 163r.

449 Sap 3: 1. RL: MRM (422). BEN: Ben29 252r, Mc127 403, McV 186v, Ott 305v.

450 Ps 132: 1-2. RL: GR 525 (vide 384), MRM 344. AMS 120b. ES: Vl4770 164v. BEN: Ben29 252r, Ben33 109v-110r, Ben34 201r-v, Ben35 126r-v, Ben38 110v-111r, Ben39 115v, Ben40 90r, Mc127 403, Mc.VI 56, McV 186v, Ott 305v, Ve 163r.

451

♪ Alleluia. VERSVS Hec est uera fraternitas que uincit mundi crimina xpistum secuta inclita tenent regna celestia. ♪

452

OFFERTORIVM ♪ Gloriabuntur in te omnes qui diligunt nomen tuum quoniam tu domine benedices iustum domine ut scuto bone uoluntatis tue coronasti nos. ♪

453

SECRETA Hostias tibi domine sanctorum martirum tuorum. iohannis et pauli dicatas meritis. benignus assume. et ad perpetuum nobis tribue prouenire subsidium. per.

454

82v COMMVNIO ♪ Et si coram hominibus tormenta passi sunt deus tempta|uit illos tanquam aurum in fornace probauit eos et sicut holocausta accepit eos. ♪

---

451 Alle*luia*: GcBdcBAGBcdcAcBAGAcABAG   *uera*: GcBdcBAG   fra-*ternitas*: AcB   *que*: GBcdcAcBAG   *mun*di: c   cri*mi*na: ABAGA   xpis-*tum*: dcABAcB   se*cu*ta: dG   *inclita*: GcBdcBAG   *tenent*: BAcBG   ce-le*stia*: GcBdcBAGcdcAcBAGAcABAG

452 no*men*: GcAc   domi*ne²*: BcBcGFG   *ut*: FGA   co*ro*nasti: GcAc

454 tor*menta*: cAG   *temptauit*: FDFGAGFE   *il*los: DEFEF   *sicut*: A] *quasi* GR   *eos*: DEFEF

---

451 RL: GR 525 (vide 495), MRM 344. BEN: Ben29 (270v), Ben34 (231v), Ben35 (145v), Ben39 (157r-v), Ben40 (120v).

452 Ps 5: 12-13. RL: GR 526, MRM 344. AMS 120b. ES: Vl4770 164v. BEN: Ben29 252r, Ben30 128r, Ben33 110r, Ben34 201v-202r, Ben35 127r, Ben38 111v, Ben39 116v, Ben40 91r-v, Mc127 403, Mc.VI 56, McV 186v, Ott 305v, Ve 163r.

453 RL: MRM 344. SAC: Le (104), Va (568). GREG: Ha 584, Pa 533, Sp (1130). GEL8: En (168, 1452, 1657), Ge (174, 1078, 1587, 1835), Rh (132), Sg (153, 860, 1300, 1485). AM: Sb (235). ES: Vl4770 164v. BEN: Ben29 252r, Ben30 128r, Ben33 110r, Mc127 403, Mc.VI 56, McV 186v, Ott 305v, PuC (773), Ve 163r, Vl10645 5r.

454 Sap 3: 4-6. RL: GR 526 (vide [25]), MRM 344. AMS 120b. ES: Vl4770 165r. BEN: Ben29 252r, Ben30 128r, Ben33 110r, Ben34 202r, Ben35 127r-v, Ben38 111v-112r, Ben39 116v-117r, Ben40 91v, Mc127 403, Mc.VI 56, McV 186v, Ott 305v, Ve 163r, Vl10645 5v.

455

POSTCOMMVNIO Sumpsimus domine sanctorum tuorum iohannis et pauli sollemnia celebrantes. sacramenta celestia. presta quesumus. ut quod temporaliter gerimus. eternis gaudiis consequamur. per.

VIGILIA APOSTOLORVM

456

♪ Dicit dominus petro cum esses iunior cingebas te et ambulabas ubi uolebas cum autem senueris extendes manus tuas et alius te cinget et ducet quo tu non uis hoc autem dixit significans qua morte clarificaturus esset deum. PSALMVS Celi ennarrant. ♪

457

Deus qui nobis beatorum apostolorum tuorum, petri et pauli, natalicia gloriosa preire concedis. tribue quesumus. eorum nos semper et beneficiis preueniri. et orationibus adiuuari. per.

---

456 *Di*cit: EGE   domi*nus*: FDF   *pe*tro: FGE   am*bu*labas: GE *au*tem[1]: GAG   *se*nueris: FD   exten*des*: B   *cinget*: GFED   *hoc*: E *dixit*: FGFGAG   *significans*: G   Ps.: AGAFGAGE

---

455 RL: MRM 344. SAC: Le (108), Va (821). GREG: Ha 585, Pa 534, Sp (1245). GEL8: En (154, 1642), Ge (159, 1048, 1774), Rh (638), Sg (832, 1470). AM: Sb (1084). ES: Vl4770 165r. BEN: Ben29 252r, Ben30 128r, Ben33 110r, Mc127 403, Mc.VI 56, McV 186v, Ott 305v-306r, Ve 163r, Vl10645 5v.

456 Io 21: 18-19, Ps 18: 1. RL: GR 530-531, MRM 345. AMS 121. ES: Vl4770 165r-v. BEN: Ben29 252r, Ben33 110r, Ben34 202r-v, Ben35 127v, Ben38 112r, Ben39 117r, Ben40 91v, Mc127 403, Mc.VI 57, McV 186v-187r, Ott 306r, PuC 564, Ve 163r-v, Vl10645 5v.

457 RL: MRM (300: var.). SAC: Va 915. GEL8: En 1059, Ge 1180, Rh 714, Sg 952. ES: F 1097, Vl4770 165v. BEN: Ben29 252r-v, Ben33 110v, Mc127 403, Mc.VI 57, McV 187r, Ott 306r, PuC 565, Vl10645 5v.

458

LECTIO ACTVVM APOSTOLORVM [3: 1-10]. In diebus illis. Petrus et
83r Iohannes ascendebant in templum ad horam orationis no|nam. ...
83v ex|tasi. in eo quod contigerat illi.

459

GRADVALE In omnem terram.

460

IOHANNEM [21: 15-19]. In illo tempore. Dixit iesus petro. Symon
iohannis diligis me plus his. ... esset deum.

461

OFFERTORIVM Michi autem nimis.

462

SECRETA Munus populi tui domine quesumus apostolica intercessione
sanctifica. nosque a peccatorum maculis emunda. per.

---

458 incipiens] incipientes *Vulgata* (3: 3)   dixit ad eum] dixit (3: 6)   eius
manu] ei manu (3: 7)

460 omnia nosti] omnia scis *Vulgata* (21: 17)

---

458 Act 3: 1-10. RL: MRM 345-346. LEC: Alc 143, Mu 108, WuC 130, CoP 279.
ES: Vl4770 165v. BEN: Ben29 252v-253r, Ben33 110v, Mc127 403-404, Mc.VI 57,
McV 187r, Ott 306r-v, PuC 566, Ve 163v, Vl10645 5v.

459 Ps 18: 5. RL: GR 531, MRM 346. AMS 121. ES: Vl4770 165v. BEN: Ben29 253r,
Ben33 110v, Ben34 202v, Ben35 127v, Ben38 112r-v, Ben39 117r-v, Ben40
91v-92r, Mc127 404, Mc.VI 57, McV 187r, Ott 306v, PuC (716), Ve 163v.

460 Io 21: 15-19. RL: MRM 346. LEC: Mu 108, WuE 309, CoP 280. ES: Vl4770
165v. BEN: Ben29 253r, Ben33 110v-111r, DaE 117r, Mc127 404, Mc.VI 57, McV
187r-v, Ott 306v, PuC 568, Ve 163v-164r.

461 Ps 138: 17. RL: GR 531, MRM 346. AMS 121. ES: Vl4770 165v. BEN: Ben29
253r, Ben33 111r, Ben34 203r-v, Ben35 127v-128r, Ben38 112v-113r, Ben39
118r-v, Ben40 92r-v, Mc127 404, Mc.VI 57, McV 187v, Ott 306v, PuC 569, Ve
164r.

462 RL: MRM 346. GREG: Ha 590, Pa 539, Sp (1244). GEL8: En (131), Ge (28, 136,
1029, 1069), Rh (623), Sg (123, 812, 851). ES: F 1099, Vl4770 165v. BEN: Ben29
253r, Ben33 111r, Mc127 404, Mc.VI 57, McV 187v, Ott 306v, Ve 164r.

463

COMMVNIO ♪ Symon iohannis diligis me plus his domine tu omnia nosti tu scis domine quia amo te. ♪

464

84r | Quos celesti domine alimento satiasti. apostolicis intercessionibus ab omni aduersitate custodi. per.

NATALIS APOSTOLORVM. PETRI. ET PAVLI.

465

♪ Nunc scio uere quia misit dominus angelum suum et eripuit me de manu herodis et de omni expectatione plebis iudeorum. PSALMVS Domine probasti me. ♪

466

ORATIO Deus qui hodiernam diem apostolorum tuorum petri et pauli martirio consecrasti. da ecclesie tue eorum in omnibus sequi preceptum. per quos religionis sumpsit exordium. per.

---

463 G *inc.*] F *inc.* GR (*trans. passim*)   *io*hannis: Gc

465 *Nunc*: EFDGFE   *quia*: B   *mi*sit: Bdc   *et*^{1}: E   eripuit: E   *et*^{2}: E   *ple*bis: GAGFGFEF   iude*o*rum: EGF   Ps.: AGAFGAGE

---

463 Io 21: 15, 17. RL: GR 531, MRM 346. AMS (122b: nat.). ES: Vl4770 166r. BEN: Ben29 253r, Ben33 111r, Ben34 203v, Ben35 128r, Ben38 113r, Ben39 118v, Ben40 92v, Mc127 404, Mc.VI 57, McV 187v, Ott 306v, PuC 571, Ve (165r).

464 RL: MRM 346. SAC: Va (850, 1261). GREG: Ha 592, Pa 541. GEL8: En 1063, Ge 1184, Rh 718, Sg 956. ES: F (111), Vl4770 166r. BEN: Ben29 253r, Ben33 111r, Mc127 404-405, Mc.VI 57, McV 187v, Ott 306v-307r, PuC 572, Ve 164r.

465 Act 12: 11, Ps 138: 1-2. RL: GR 532-533, MRM 347. AMS 122a. ES: Vl4770 166r. BEN: Ben30 128v, Ben33 111r, Ben34 203v-204r, Ben35 129r, Ben38 113v, Ben39 120r, Ben40 93v-94r, Mc127 405, Mc.VI 59, McV 187v, Ott 307r, PuC 573, Ve 164r.

466 RL: MRM 347. SAC: Le 280, (303, 357), Va 921. GREG: Ha 594, Pa 543. GEL8: En 1067, Ge 1188, Rh 721, Sg 960. ES: Vl4770 166r. BEN: Ben29 253v, Ben30 128v, Ben33 111r, Mc127 405, Mc.VI 59, McO 389, McV 187v-188r, Ott 307r, PuC 574, Ve 164r.

467

LECTIO. ACTVVM APOSTOLORVM [12: 1-11]. In diebus illis. Misit hero-
84v des rex manus ut affligeret ... | ... plebis iudeorum.

468

85r GRADVALE | ♪ Constitues eos principes super omnem terram memores erunt
nominis tui domine. VERSVS Pro patribus tuis nati sunt tibi filii propterea populi
confitebuntur tibi. ♪

469

♪ Alleluia. VERSVS Beatus es symon bar iona quia caro et sanguis non reuelauit
tibi sed pater meus qui in celis est. ♪

470

SECVNDVM MATHEVM [16: 13-19]. In illo tempore. Venit iesus in partes
85v cesaree ... | ... in celis.

---

467 in carcere tradensque] in carcerem tradens *Vulgata* (12: 4)   custodiendum]
custodire eum (12: 4)   esset eum] eum esset (12: 6)   excitauit] suscitauit
(12: 7)   caligas] gallicas (12: 8)   sequebatur eum] sequebatur (12: 9)

470 interrogauit] interrogabat *Vulgata* (16: 13)   alii heliam] alii autem Heliam
(16: 14)   dicit illis iesus] dicit illis (16: 15)   aduersus] adversum (16: 18)
solutum et] solutum (16: 19)

---

468 ter*ram*: AGBAGdcdcFGABcBA   *me*mores: BGBcd   *no*minis: cB
tu*i*: cB   *domine*: cBGFAGcdcAFAGAGF   *patri*bus: cBAcBGAFGAcA-
GAGFGAcdcdcdec   fi*li*i: F   propter*e*a: ABcdc   popu*li*: AcAGcABA
ti*bi*²: cGcABGFGF

469 *Vide Intro. p. 147*

---

467 Act 12: 1-11. RL: MRM 347. LEC: Alc 144, Mu 109, WuC 131, CoP 281. ES:
Vl4770 166r-v. BEN: Ben30 128v-130r, Ben33 111r-v, Mc127 405-406, Mc.vi 59,
PuC 575, Ve 164r-v.

468 Ps 44: 17-18. RL: GR 533, MRM 347. AMS 122b. ES: Vl4770 166v. BEN: Ben29
253v, Ben30 130r, Ben33 111v, Ben34 204r-v, Ben35 129r, Ben38 113v, Ben39
120r-v, Ben40 94r, Mc127 406, Mc.vi 59, McV 188r, Ott 307r, PuC 576, Ve 164v.

469 Mt 16: 17. RL: MRM 2: 206. AMS 122b. ES: Schlager, *Katalog* G 302, Vl4770
166v. BEN: Ben29 253v, Ben30 130r-v, Ben33 111v, Ben34 204v, Ben35 129r,
Ben38 113v-114r, Ben39 120v, Ben40 94r-v, Mc127 406, McV 188r, Ott 307r,
PuC 577, Ve 164v.

470 Mt 16: 13-19. RL: MRM 348. LEC: Mu 109, WuE 309, CoP 282. ES: Vl4770
166v. BEN: Ben29 253v, Ben30 130v-131r, Ben33 111v, DaE 118r, DaK 41v,
Mc127 406, Mc.vi 59, McV 188r, Ott 307r-v, PuC 578, Ve 164v.

471

OFFERTORIVM ♪ Constitues eos principes super omnem terram memores erunt nominis tui in omni progenie et generatione. ♪

472

SECRETA Hostias domine quas nomini tuo sacrandas offerimus. apostolica prosequatur oratio. per quam nobis expiari tribuis et defendi. per.

473

COMMVNIO ♪ Tu es petrus et super hanc petram edificabo ecclesiam meam. ♪

474

POSTCOMMVNIO Sumptis domine remediis sempiternis. tuorum mundentur corda fidelium. ut apostolicis petri et pauli natalis insignia. que corporalibus officiis exequitur. pia cordis intelligentia comprehendat. per.

---

471 Constitues: Bdc   omnem: AGBdcAG   terram: E   omni: AcBdcBcA
progenie: FAc   generatione: FABGA

473 edificabo: FGFDED

---

471 Ps 44: 17-18. RL: GR 534, MRM 348. AMS 122b. ES: Vl4770 166v. BEN: Ben29 253v-254r, Ben30 131r, Ben33 111v, Ben34 206v-207r, Ben35 131v, Ben38 115r-v, Ben39 126r-v, Ben40 98v, Mc127 406, Mc.VI 59, McV 188r, Ott 307v, PuC 579, Ve 164v.

472 RL: MRM 348. SAC: Le (368). GREG: Ha 595, Pa 544. GEL8: En (247), Ge 1190, Rh 723, Sg 962. AM: Sb (925). ES: Vl4770 166v. BEN: Ben29 254r, Ben30 131r-v, Ben33 111v, Mc127 406, Mc.VI 59, McV 188r, Ott 307v, PuC 580, Ve 164v.

473 Mt 16: 18. RL: GR 534-535, MRM 348. AMS (121: vig.). ES: Vl4770 166v. BEN: Ben29 254r, Ben30 131v, Ben33 112r, Ben34 207r, Ben35 131v, Ben38 115v, Ben39 126v-127r, Ben40 99r, Mc127 406, McV 188r, Ott 307v, PuC 582, Ve (164r).

474 SAC: Va 925. GEL8: En 1071, Ge 1193, Rh 725, Sg 964. AM: Sb (993). ES: Vl4770 166v. BEN: Ben29 254r, Ben30 131v-132r, Ben33 112r (m. v.), Mc127 406, Mc.VI 59, McV 188r, Ott 307v, PuC 583, Ve 165r.

| COMMEMORATIO SANCTI PAVLI APOSTOLI

475

♪ Scio cui credidi et certus sum quia potens est depositum meum seruare in illo die. PSALMVS Domine probasti me. ♪

476

ORATIO Deus qui multitudinem gentium beati pauli apostoli predicatione docuisti. da nobis quesumus. ut cuius natalicia colimus. eius apud te patrocinia sentiamus. per.

477

AD TIMOTHEVM [2 Tim 4: 1-8]. Karissime. Testificor coram deo. ... | ... aduentum eius.

478

GRADVALE ♪ Qui operatus est petro in apostolatu operatus est et michi inter gentes et cognouerunt gratiam dei que data est michi. VERSVS Gratia dei in me uacua non fuit sed gratia eius semper in me manet. ♪

---

477 imple sobrius esto] imple *Vulgata* (4: 5)   ego iam delibor] ego enim iam delibor (4: 6)   corona iustitie] iustitiae corona (4: 8)   in illo die] in illa die (4: 8)

---

475 Sci*o*: AG   *et*: EFD   *il*lo: ED   Ps.: FGAcAGFD

478 in*ter*: AGAc   *gra*tiam: ABcdc   michi^2: AGFG   *de*i: dcBcAcdcBcdA-FAcdcAcdcBcdAFABGABcdfedcd   *fu*it: AcAcBcBAGA   gratia^2: AGAcd-cAG   in^3: AG

---

475 2 Tim 1: 12, Ps 138: 1. RL: GR 535 (vide 417-418), MRM 348. AMS 123. ES: Vl4770 167r. BEN: Ben29 254r, Ben33 112r, Ben34 207v-208r, Ben35 132r, Ben38 116r, Ben39 127r, Ben40 100r, Mc127 407, Mc.VI 60, McV 188r, Ott 307v, Ve 165r.

476 RL: MRM 348. SAC: Va 927. GREG: Ha 604, Pa 548. GEL8: En 1073, Ge 1203, Rh 728, Sg 970. ES: Vl4770 167r. BEN: Ben29 254r, Ben33 112r, Mc127 407, Mc.VI 60, McO 391, McV 188r-v, Ott 307v, Ve 165r.

477 2 Tim 4: 1-8. RL: MRM (431, 439). BEN: Ben29 254r-v, Mc127 407, McV 188v, Ott 307v, Ve 165r.

478 Gal 2: 8-9, 1 Cor 15: 10. RL: GR 535 (vide 418-419), MRM 349. AMS 123. ES: Vl4770 167v. BEN: Ben29 254v, Ben33 112v, Ben34 208r, Ben35 132r, Ben38 116r-v, Ben39 127r-v, Ben40 100r, Mc127 407, Mc.VI 60, McV 188v, Ott 308r, Ve 165r-v.

479

♪ Alleluia. VERSVS Magnus sanctus paulus uas electionis uere digne est glori-
ficatus qui et meruit thronum duodecimum possidere. ♪

480

MATHEVM [19: 27-29]. In illo tempore. Dixit symon petrus ad iesum.
87r Ecce nos qui reliquimus omnia. ... | ... possidebit.

481

OFFERTORIVM Michi autem nimis.

482

SECRETA Ecclesie tue domine quesumus. preces et hostias; apostolica
commendet oratio. ut quod pro illius gloria celebramus. nobis prosit
ad medelam. per.

483

COMMVNIO ♪ Amen dico uobis quod uos qui reliquistis omnia et secuti estis
me centumplum accipietis et uitam eternam possidebitis. ♪

---

480 dixit eis] dixit illis *Vulgata* (19: 28)   quod uos qui reliquistis omnia et
secuti] quod vos qui secuti (19: 28)   generatione] regeneratione (19: 28)
reliquerit] reliquit (19: 29)

---

479 *Vide Intro. p. 148*

483 *uo*bis: AGAGFG   *uos*: FGEF   *qui*: D   e*ter*nam: GAGAG

---

479 ES: Schlager, *Katalog* D 47. BEN: Ben34 208r-v, Ben35 132r, Ben39 127v,
Ben40 100v, Ve 165v. Var. (melodia): RL: GR (419), LS: Gs (178), 189.

480 Mt 19: 27-29. RL: MRM 349. LEC: Mu 111, WuE 309, CoP 285. ES: Vl4770
167v. BEN: Ben29 254v, Ben33 112v-113r, DaE 118r, DaK 42v-43r, Mc127 407,
Mc.VI 60, McV 188v, Ott 308r, Ve 165v.

481 Ps 138: 17. RL: GR 535, MRM 349. AMS 123. ES: Vl4770 167v. BEN: Ben29
254v, Ben33 113r, Ben34 209v, Ben35 133v, Ben38 117v, Ben39 129r, Mc127
407, McV 188v, Ott 308r, PuC (719), Ve 165v.

482 RL: MRM 349. SAC: Le (318), Va (919). GREG: Ha 605, Pa 549. GEL8: En (239,
1065), Ge (235), Rh (168), Sg (218). ES: Vl4770 167v. BEN: Ben29 254v-255r,
Ben33 113r, Mc127 407, McV 188v, Ott 308r, Ve 165v.

483 Mt 19: 28, 29. RL: GR 535 (vide [47]), MRM 349. AMS 123. ES: Vl4770 168r.
BEN: Ben29 255r, Ben33 113r, Ben34 209v-210r, Ben35 133v, Ben38 117v, Ben39
129r, Mc127 407, McV 188v, Ott 308r, PuC (721).

484

POSTCOMMVNIO Perceptis domine sacramentis, beato paulo apostolo interueniente deprecamur. ut que pro illius celebrata sunt gloria. nobis proficiant ad salutem. per.

IN SANCTORVM. LAVRENTII. PETRI. ET ANDREE.

485

INTROITVS Sapientiam.

486

Deus qui hodiernam diem beatorum martirum tuorum laurentii, petri 87v et andree | passione decorasti. presta quesumus. ut eorum suffragia aput te sentiamus in celis. quorum pio amore ueneramur in terris. per.

487

SAPIENTIA [Eccli 44: 10-15]. Hi sunt uiri misericordie quorum iustitie obliuionem non acceperunt. ... ecclesia sanctorum.

488

GRADVALE Ecce quam bonum. VERSVS Sicut unguentum. *In sanctorum iohannis et pauli.*

---

487 iustitie obliuionem non acceperunt] pietates non defuerunt *Vulgata* (44: 10) cum semine eorum permanent] et cum semine ipsorum perseverat (44: 11) hereditas sancta nepotes eorum] hereditas nepotum illorum (44: 12) propter eos] propter illos (44: 13) generatio eorum] semen eorum (44: 13) corpora eorum] corpora ipsorum (44: 14) in secula] in generationes et generationes (44: 14) sapientiam eorum narrabunt omnes populi et] sapientiam ipsorum narrent populi (44: 15) pronuntiat omnis] nuntiet (44: 15)

---

484 RL: MRM 349. GREG: Ha 606, Pa 550, Sp (1223: var.). ES: Vl4770 168r. BEN: Ben29 255r, Ben33 113r (m. v.), Mc127 407, Mc.vi 60, McV 188v, Ott 308r, Ve 165v. Var.: SAC: Le (290), Va 930 (945), GEL8: En 1076, Ge 1207, Rh 730, Sg 972, AM: Sb (988).

485 Eccli 44: 15. RL: GR ([25]-[26]), MRM (419). AMS (113a, 125, 146, 156). BEN: Ben33 (105v, 113r, 123v), Ben34 (194v).

486 Non inveni.

487 Eccli 44: 10-15. RL: MRM (423). BEN: Ben33 (113r).

488 Ps 132: 1-2. RL: GR (384, 455-456), MRM (344). AMS (120b). BEN: Ben33 (109v-110r), Ben34 (201r-v).

489

Alleluia. VERSVS Hec est uera fraternitas.

490

[Lc 21: 9] In illo tempore. Dixit iesus discipulis suis. Cum audieritis prelia.

491

OFFERTORIVM Exultabunt sancti.

492

SECRETA Suscipe domine quesumus munera populi tui pro martirum tuorum festiuitate sanctorum. et sincero nos fac eorum natalicio interesse. per.

493

COMMVNIO Iustorum anime in manu dei.

494

POSTCOMMVNIO Vt accepta nos domine sancta uiuificent. sanctorum martirum tuorum laurentii, petri, et andree, merita gloriosa nos adiuuent. per.

IN SANCTE FELICITATIS CVM FILIIS SVIS.

495

Da nobis quesumus omnipotens deus. perpetue felicitatis esse partici-
88r pes. qua │ cum septem filiis suis fruitur beata felicitas. per.

---

489 RL: GR (495), MRM (344). BEN: Ben34 (231v).

490 Lc 21: 9. RL: MRM (428). BEN: DaE (143r).

491 Ps 149: 5. RL: GR ([28]), MRM (405, 429). AMS (114, 125, 159). BEN: Ben33 (105v, 113v, 115r, 124v), Ben34 (195r-v), PuC (749).

492 SAC: Le (397), Va (1118). GREG: Pa (834), Tc (3270). GEL8: En (223), Ge (216, 1822), Sg (203).

493 Sap 3: 1. RL: GR (505), MRM (429). AMS (93, 97, 112, 125, 129b, 159). BEN: Ben33 (94r, 113v, 124v), Ben34 (167v-168r), PuC (751).

494 Non inveni.

495 Non inveni.

IN SANCTE MARGARITE.

496

Deus qui beatam margaritam hodierna die ad celos per martirii palmam peruenire fecisti. concede nobis quesumus. ut eius exempla sequentes. ad te peruenire mereamur.

IN SANCTI HELIE PROPHETE.

497

INTROITVS Da pacem domine sustinentibus.

498

Deus qui mirabili dispensatione priscorum patrum glorificatione mundum coruscare sanxisti. concede propitius ut qui beati helie precursoris tui suffragium poscimus. eternitatis compendium interuentu eius assequi gaudeamus. per.

499

88v LIBER REGVM [3 Reg 17: 17-24]. In diebus illis. Egrotauit filius ... | ... uerum est.

---

497 Dominica XVII post pentecosten *add. alia manu beneventana in marg. dext.* Da pacem domine sustinentibus te. ut prophete tui fideles inuenientur et exaudi preces seruorum tuorum. et plebis tue israel. Letatus sum. *add. manu gotica in marg. inf.*

499 familias] familiae *Vulgata* (17: 17)   fortissimus] fortis nimis (17: 17) mulier ad heliam] ad Heliam (17: 18)   ad eam helias] ad eam (17: 19) posuit eum super lectum] posuit super lectulum (17: 19)   animam] anima (17: 21)   et exaudiuit] exaudiuit (17: 22)   et ait] et ait illi (17: 23)

---

496 LS: MWes 871.

497 Eccli 36: 18. RL: GR (372-373, [135]), MRM (290). AMS (193). BEN: Ben34 (259v).

498 BEN: Vl10645 6v.

499 3 Reg 17: 17-24. RL: MRM (110). BEN: Ben33 (50v), cf. Vl10645 6v (ref. ad Fr. 3 ebd. "de Samaritana," i.e., **3 Reg 17: 8-16** in Ben33 32r).

500

GRADVALE Iustus ut palma. VERSVS Ad annuntiandum. *Vigilia unius. apostoli.*

501

Alleluia. VERSVS Amauit eum dominus. *Vnius. martiris.*

502

LVCAM [4: 23-30]. In illo tempore. Dixerunt pharisei ad iesum.
89r Quanta audiuimus ... | ... per medium illorum ibat.

503

OFFERTORIVM Veritas mea et.

504

Accepta tibi sit domine oblatio nostri sacrificii. et oratio prohete helie nos apud te faciat munitos. per.

505

COMMVNIO Beatus seruus.

---

502 quia nemo ... in patria sua. In veritate dico vobis *om. Dubr per homeotel.* (4: 24-25)　　　ad nullam] et ad nullam *Vulgata* (4: 26)　　　in synagoga] in synagoga ira (4: 28)　　　precitarent] praecipitarent (4: 29)

---

500 Ps 91: 13, 3. RL: GR ([42]-[43]), MRM (403). AMS (13, 118a, 144, 154, 167). BEN: Ben33 (138v), Ben34 (23r).

501 Eccli 45: 9. RL: GR ([39]-[40]), MRM (434, 440). BEN: Ben34 (271v-272r).

502 Lc 4: 23-30. RL: MRM (87). ES: Vl4770 159v. BEN: Ben33 (40r), DaE 120r, Vl10645 6v.

503 Ps 88: 25. RL: GR ([6], [44]), MRM (415, 437, 440). AMS (22, 171, 171*bis*). BEN: Ben33 (9r, 16r, 114v), Ben34 (41v-42v).

504 Non inveni.

505 Mt 24: 46. RL: GR ([45]), MRM (437, 440). AMS (16b, 171, 171*ter*). BEN: Ben33 (6r, 16v), Ben34 (29r), PuC (761).

506

POSTCOMMVNIO Hodierna festiuitatis sacratissimi, prophete tui helie, officia domine persoluentes precamur clementiam tuam. ut hec sancta que in eius sollempnitate sumpsimus. sacrificia nobis tuis famulis proficiant ad remedium salutis eterne. per.

IN SANCTE MARIE. MAGDALENE

507

♪ Cognoui domine quia equitas iudicia tua et in ueritate tua humiliasti me. infige timore tuo carnes meas a mandatis tuis non me repellas. PSALMVS Beati immaculati. ♪

508

89v | Beate marie magdalene quesumus domine, suffragiis adiuuemur. cuius precibus exoratus quadriduanum fratrem uiuum ab inferis re-suscitasti. per.

509

YSAYE PROPHETE [61: 10-11, 62: 5]. Gaudens gaudebo ... deus tuus. Dicit dominus omnipotens.

---

509 uestimento] vestimentis *Vulgata* (61: 10)   letitie] iustitiae (61: 10) germinabit semen suum] semen suum germinat (61: 11)   cunctis] universis (61: 11)   iuuenis] iuvenis cum virgine (62: 5)

---

507 domi*ne*: B   *iudici*a: EFAFG   *tua*²: AGABA   *humili*asti: GAcB *infige*: GAcB   *ti*more: B   *tu*o: AcBA   man*da*tis: Bc

---

506 Non inveni.

507 Ps 118: 75, 120, 118: 1. RL: GR ([68]-[69]), MRM (441). AMS (145a). BEN: Ben34 (229v).

508 RL: MRM 354.

509 Is 61: 10-11, 62: 5.

510

GRADVALE ♪ Propter ueritatem et mansuetudinem et iustitiam et deducet te mirabiliter dextera tua. VERSVS Audi filia et uide et inclina aurem tuam quia concupiuit rex speciem tuam. ♪

511

90r | ♪ Alleluia. VERSVS Dilexisti iustitiam et odisti iniquitatem. ♪

512

SECVNDVM LVCAM [7: 36-50]. In illo tempore. Rogabat iesum quidam 90v phariseus. ut manducaret ... | ... uade in pace.

513

OFFERTORIVM Diffusa est gratia.

514

SECRETA Munera nostra quesumus domine beate marie magdalene gloriosa merita tibi reddant accepta. cuius oblationis obsequium 96r unigeni | tus filius tuus clementer suscepit impensum. per eundem.

---

512 et alius] alius *Vulgata* (7: 41)   diligit] diliget (7: 42)   hec unguento] haec autem unguento (7: 46)   remittuntur] remittentur (7: 47)

514 *96r post 90v legendum est (vide App.)*

---

510 *et*³: BA   dedu*cet*: ABGFG   mi*rabili*ter: AcBcBGFG   *dextera*: BGFEFGBcdcBcBGFDF   *in*clina: cd

511 *Vide Intro. p. 173*

---

510 Ps 44: 5, 11-12. RL: GR (620), MRM (445). AMS (140, 144*bis*). BEN: Ben34 (222v-223r), PuC (633).

511 Ps 44: 8. RL: MRM (444). ES: Syg (229: melodia var.). BEN: Ben40 (165v: vide Schlager, *Katalog* G 307).

512 Lc 7: 36-50. RL: MRM 354. BEN: Ben33 (56v-57r), DaE 120v, Mc540¹ 191, McV 294v, Ve 167r.

513 Ps 44: 3. RL: GR ([58]-[59]), MRM (446). AMS (28, 29b, 127). BEN: Ben33 (14v), Ben34 (49r-v), Mc540¹ 191, McV 294v, PuC (393).

514 RL: MRM 354. BEN: McV 294v (m. v.).

515

COMMVNIO ♪ Optimam partem elegit sibi maria que non auferetur hab ea in
eternum. ♪

516

POSTCOMMVNIO Sumpto domine uiuifico ac singulari remedio. corpore
scilicet et pretioso sanguine tuo. ab omnibus malis. quesumus beate
marie magdalene. patrociniis eruamur. per.

IN SANCTI APOLENARIS.

517

ORATIO Quesumus omnipotens deus. ut nostra deuotio que natalicia
beati apollenaris martiris tui atque pontificis celebrat. patrocinia nobis
eius acumulet. per.

VIGILIA SANCTI IACOBI APOSTOLI

518
Ego autem sicut.

519

ORATIO Concede nobis omnipotens deus. uenturam.

---

515 *Vide Intro. p. 173*

---

515 Lc 10: 42. RL: GR in Suppl. OSB (33: melodia var.), MRM (369).

516 RL: MRM 355. Cf. Ben: McV 294 (var.).

517 SAC: Va (969). GEL8: En (1634), Ge (1765), Rh (1030), Sg (1462). ES:
Vl4770 173v. BEN: Ben29 257v, Ben33 114v (m. v.), Mc127 412, Mc.VI 65, McV
190v, Ott 311r.

518 Ps 51: 10. RL: GR 558, MRM 2: 215. AMS (13, 154). BEN: Ben33 (4r), Ben34
(22v-23r), Mc127 412, McV 190v, Ott 311r.

519 GREG: Tc (3144, 3511, 3522, 3631). ES: F 1367. BEN: Mc127 (454).

520

EPISTOLA [Eph 1: 3]. Benedictus deus et pater domini.

521

LVCAM [Mc 10: 35-40]. In illo tempore. Acceserunt ad iesum iacobus
96v et iohannes ... | ... paratum est.

NATALE EIVSDEM

522
Michi autem nimis.

523

Esto domine plebi tue sanctificator et custos. ut apostoli tui iacobi
munita presidiis. et conuersatione tibi placeat. et secura mente de-
seruiat. per.

524
Nimis honorati sunt.

---

521 des] facias *Vulgata* (10: 35)   dicunt ei] et dixerunt (10: 37)   et dixit eis]
Iesus autem ait eis (10: 38)   baptismo] baptismum (10: 38)   et dixerunt] at
illi dixerunt ei (10: 39)   iesus autem dixit eis] Iesus autem ait eis (10: 39)
baptismo] baptismum (10: 39)   et sinistram meam] vel ad sinistram (10: 40)
dare uobis] dare (10: 40)

522 *Add. alia manu in marg. dext.*

524 *Add. alia manu beneventana*

---

520 Eph 1: 3. RL: MRM (404). LEC: Mu (117: nat.). Var.: BEN: Mc127 412 (Eccli
44: 25-27, 45: 2-4, 6-9 *Benedictio*), McV 190v, Ott 311r.

521 Mc 10: 35-40. BEN: Mc127 412, McV 190v-191r, Ott 311r-v.

522 Ps 138: 17. RL: GR 558, MRM 2: 215. AMS (160, 169). ES: Vl4770 161r. BEN:
Ben29 258r, Ben34 (235r), Mc127 412, McV 191r, Ott 311v, PuC (723), Ve 167v.

523 RL: MRM 356. SAC: Le (363), Va (1162). GREG: Ha (603). GEL8: En 1135, Ge
1247, Rh 754, Sg 1009. AM: Sb (989). ES: F 1137, Vl4770 161r-v, 174r. BEN: Ben29
258r, Ben30 148r-v, Ben33 115r, Mc127 412, Mc.VI 66, McO 401, McV 191r, Ott
311v, PuC 587, Ve 167v.

524 Ps 138: 17. RL: GR (644-645), MRM (300, 304, 2: 181, 246, 356). AMS (160,
168). BEN: Ben34 (235r-v), Mc127 412, McV 191r, Ott 311v, PuC (726).

525

SECVNDVM MATHEVM [20: 20-23]. In illo tempore. Accessit ad iesum mater filiorum zebedei ... a patre meo.

526

In omnem terram.

527

SECRETA Oblationes populi tui domine quesumus. beati apostoli iacobi
97r conciliet. et que nostris non apta sunt meritis. fiant | tibi placita eius deprecatione. per.

528

Amen dico uobis.

529

POSTCOMMVNIO Beati apostoli tui iacobi quesumus domine intercessione nos adiuua. pro cuius sollempnitate percepimus. tua sancta letantes. per.

---

525 orans] adorans *Vulgata* (20: 20)   dixitque ei] qui dixit ei (20: 21)   sinistram tuam] sinistram (20: 21)   sedere] sedere autem (20: 23)   sinistram meam] sinistram (20: 23)

526 *Add. manu beneventana*

528 *Add. alia manu in marg. dext.*

---

525 Mt 20: 20-23. RL: MRM 356. BEN: Ben29 258r, DaE 123r, Mc127 412, McV 191r, Ott 311v, Ve 167v.

526 Ps 18: 5. RL: GR 558, MRM 2: 215. AMS (160). BEN: Ben34 (236r-v), Mc127 413, McV 191r, PuC (4, 729).

527 RL: MRM 356. SAC: Le (286), Va (923). GEL8: En 1136, Ge 1248, Rh 755, Sg 1010. ES: F 1138, Vl4770 174r. BEN: Ben29 258r-v, Ben30 148v, Ben33 115r, Mc127 413, Mc.VI 66, McV 191r, Ott 311v, PuC 588, Ve 167v.

528 Mt 19: 28. RL: GR (101, 389, [47]), MRM (410, 437, 441). AMS (123). BEN: Ben29 (285r), Ben33 (113r), Ben34 (265r).

529 RL: MRM 356. SAC: Le (330), Va 864. GEL8: Ge 1250, Rh 757 (var.), Sg 1012. AM: Sb (158). ES: F 1140, Vl4770 161v (var.), 174r (var.). BEN: Ben29 258v, Ben30 148v, Mc127 413, Mc.VI 66, McV 191r, Ott 311v, PuC 589 (m. v.), Ve 167v.

VINCVLA SANCTI PETRI APOSTOLI.

530

Nunc scio uere.

531

ORATIO Deus qui beatum petrum apostolum a uinculis absolutum illesum abire fecisti nostrorum quesumus, solue uincula peccatorum. et omnia mala a nobis propitiatus exclude. per.

532

NATALIS MACHABEORVM. ORATIO Fraterna nos domine martirum tuorum corona letificet. et fidei nostre prebeat incitamenta uirtutum. et multiplici nos suffragia consoletur. per.

533

SECRETA Oblatum tibi sacrificium benignus assume. et intercedente beato petro apostolo tuo. aduersus omnium inimicorum insidias continuum presta pius auxilium. per.

534

POSTCOMMVNIO Deus qui angelico ministerio beatum petrum apostolum a uinculis carceris liberasti. eius intercedentibus meritis. ab omni nos quesumus tribulatione liberare digneris. per.

---

530 *Add. alia manu in marg. dext.*

---

530 Act 12: 11. RL: GR 563, MRM 359. AMS (122a). ES: Vl4770 176r. BEN: Ben29 259v, Ben33 111r (ref. ad Comm.), Ben34 (204r), McV 192r, Ott 312v, PuC (573), Ve 168v.

531 RL: MRM 359. GREG: Ha 622. ES: Vl4770 176r. BEN: Ben29 259v, Ben30 149r-v, Ben33 115v, Mc127 414-415, McO 403, McV 192r, Ott 312v-313r, Ve 168v.

532 RL: MRM 359. SAC: Va (1113). GEL8: En 1156, Ge 1277, Sg 1028. AM: Sb (1036: inc. var.). ES: F 1155. BEN: Ben29 259v, Ben30 148v-149r, Ben33 115v, Mc127 414, McO 404, McV 192r, Ott 312v, Ve 168v.

533 BEN: Ben29 260r-v (m. v.), Mc127 415, Ott 313v, McV 192v. Var. (inc. =): RL: MRM 359, GREG: Ha 623, Pa (67), Sp (1097), GEL8: En (116), Ge (116), Rh (100), Sg (108), AM: Sb (394), BEN: Ben30 149v, Ben33 115v, McV 168v.

534 BEN: Ben29 260v, Mc127 415, McV 192v, Ott 313v.

IN SANCTI STEPHANI PAPE.

535

Deus qui nos annua beati stephani martiris tui atque pontificis annua sollemnitate letificas. concede propitius ut cuius natalicia colimus. de eiusdem etiam protectione gaudeamus. per.

INVENTIO CORPORIS SANCTI STEPHANI.

536

97v Deus qui nos concedis | hodierna die reliquiarum sanctorum tuorum stephani, nichodemi gamalihelis atque abiba inuentionis sollemnia colere. tribue nobis quesumus in eterna letitia de illorum societate gaudere. per.

537

LECTIO [Eccli 44: 10]. Hi sunt uiri misericordie. *Require in sancti Laurentii. Petri. et Andree.*

538

SECVNDVM LVCAM [11: 47-51]. In illo tempore. Dicebat iesus turbis iudeorum. Ve uobis qui edificatis ... generatione.

---

537 Require ... Andree *add. alia manu in marg. sinist.*

538 qui effusus ... a generatione ista *om. Dubr* (11: 50)

---

535 RL: MRM 360. GREG: Ha 625, Pa 582. GEL8: En 1164, Ge 1282, Rh 764, Sg 1033. AM: Sb (876). ES: Vl4770 177v. BEN: Ben29 260v, Ben33 116r, Mc127 415, McV 192v, Ott 313v, Ve 168v.

536 RL: MRM (361, 421). GREG: Ha (633), Pa (588), Sp (1230). GEL8: En (1172), Ge (1290), Sg (1041). AM: Sb (1192). BEN: Ben29 260v, Mc127 415, McV 193r, Ott 314r, Ve 169r (inc. var.).

537 Eccli 44: 10. RL: MRM (423). BEN: Ben33 (113r).

538 Lc 11: 47-51. RL: MRM (427). BEN: Ben29 261r-v, Ben33 (122v), Mc127 416, McV 193r, Ott 314r-v.

539

SECRETA ORATIO Sacrificium domine laudis offerimus in tuorum commemoratione sanctorum. da quesumus, ut quod illis contulit gloriam. nobis prosit ad ueniam. per.

540

POSTCOMMVNIO Sumpsimus domine sanctorum tuorum, stephani. nichodemi. gamalhelis atque abiba, inuentionem celebrantes sacra-
98r menta celestia. presta quesumus. | ut quod temporaliter gerimus. eternis gaudiis consequamur. per.

IN TRANSFIGVRATIONE DOMINI.

541
Benedicta sit.

542

Deus qui hodierna die unigenitum tuum, mirabiliter transformatum celitus utriusque testamenti patribus reuelasti. da nobis quesumus. beneplacitis tibi actibus, ad eius semper contemplandam pertingere gloriam. in quo tue paternitati optime complacuisse testatus es. per eundem.

---

541 *Add. alia manu beneventana in marg. dext.*

---

539 SAC: Le (106). GREG: Ha (672), Pa (419, 638). GEL8: En (937), Ge (942), Rh (952: inc.), Sg (741). BEN: Ben29 261v, Mc127 416, McV 193r, Ott 314v.

540 SAC: Le (108), Va (821). GREG: Ha (585), Pa (534), Sp (1245). GEL8: En (154, 1642), Ge (159, 1048, 1774), Rh (638, 1036), Sg (832, 1470). AM: Sb (1084, 1171, 1661). BEN: Ben29 261v, Ben33 (110r), Mc127 416, McV 193v, Ott 314v, Ve 169r (m. v.).

541 **Tob 12: 6**. RL: GR (308), MRM (252, 450). AMS (172*bis*). ES: Vl4770 179v. BEN: Ben29 261v, Ben30 150v, Ben33 116v, Ben34 212v-213r, Ben35 135v-136r, Ben38 119v, Ben39 135v, Ben40 105r-v, Mc127 417, McV 193v, Ott 315r, PuC 590, Ve 169v.

542 RL: MRM 2: 220. ES: SVich 518, Vl4770 179v. BEN: Ben29 261v-262r, Ben30 150v, Ben33 116v, Mc127 417, McO 406, McV 193v, Ott 315r, PuC 591, Ve 169v (expl. var.).

543

LECTIO EPISTOLE BEATI PETRI APOSTOLI [2 Petr 1: 15-19]. Fratres. Dabo
98v autem opera ... | ... cordibus uestris.

544

SECVNDVM MARCVM [9: 1-8]. In illo tempore. Assumpsit iesus petrum
et iacobum et iohannem. et ducit illos ... resurrexerit.

545

SECRETA Suscipe domine sancte pater omnipotens munera que per
99r gloriosa filii tui transfiguratione deferi|mus. et concede propitius. ut
per hec a temporalibus liberemur incommodis. et gaudiis conectemur
eternis. per eundem.

546

POSTCOMMVNIO Deus qui hunc diem incarnati uerbi tui transfiguratione
tueque ad eum missa paternitatis uoce consecrasti. tribue quesumus ut
diuini pasti alimoniis. in eius mereamur membra transferi. qui hec in
sui memoriam fieri precepit. Iesus christus filius.

---

543 uos habere] habere vos *Vulgata* (1: 15)   in doctas] doctas (1: 16)
complacui ipsum audite] conplacui (1: 17)   lucentis] lucenti (1: 19)
caligoso] caliginoso (1: 19)   lucescat] inlucescat (1: 19)

544 solus] solos *Vulgata* (9: 1)   ait ad iesum] ait Iesu (9: 4)   nos hic] hic
nos (9: 4)   faciamus hic] faciamus (9: 4)   moysi unum] et Mosi unum (9: 4)
uiderunt amplius] amplius viderunt (9: 7)   quam] quae (9: 8)

---

543 **2 Petr 1: 15-19.** RL: MRM 2: 220. BEN: Ben29 262r, Ben33 116v, DaK 43r,
Mc127 417, McV 193v-194r, Ott 315r.

544 **Mc 9: 1-8.** ES: Vl4770 179v. BEN: Ben29 262r-v, Ben30 152r-v, DaE 125v,
Mc127 418, McV 194r, Ott 315v, Ott[1] 18, PuC 595, Ve 169v.

545 RL: MRM 2: 220-221. ES: SVich 518, Vl4770 180r. BEN: Ben29 262v, Ben30
153r, Ben33 117r, Mc127 418, McV 194r-v, Ott 315v, PuC 597, Ve 169v (expl.
var.).

546 RL: MRM 2: 221. ES: SVich 518, Vl4770 180r. BEN: Ben29 263r, Ben30 153v,
Ben33 117v, Mc127 419, McV 194v, Ott 316r, PuC 599.

BENEDICTIO VVE.

547

Bene✠dic domine hos fructus nouos uue. quos tu domine per rorem celi et inundationem pluuiarum. et temporum serenitatem. atque tranquillitatem. ad maturitatem perducere dignatus es. et dedisti ad usus nostros, cum gratiarum actione percipere. In ✠ nomine domini nostri iesu christi. per quem hec omnia domine semper bona ✠ creas.

VIGILIA SANCTI LAVRENTII.

548

♪ Dispersit dedit pauperibus iustitia eius manet in seculum seculi cornu eius exaltabitur in gloria. PSALMVS Beatus uir qui timet. ♪

549

99v   Adesto domine supplicationibus nostris. et intercessi|one beati laurentii martiris tui. perpetuam nobis misericordiam benignus impende. per.

550

SAPIENTIE [Eccli 51: 1-8, 12]. Confitebor tibi ... domine deus noster.

---

550 confitebor] confiteor *Vulgata* (51: 2)   persequentium] adstantium (51: 3) a rugientibus ... ad escam *om. Dubr* (51: 4)   de multis tribulationibus et a pressure flamme] de portis tribulationis quae circumdederunt me a pressura flammae (51: 5-6)   inferni] inferi (51: 7)   iniusta liberasti me] iniusta (51: 7) laudabit] laudavit (51: 8)   liberasti] liberas (51: 12)   manu angustie] manibus gentium (51: 12)

---

548 Dis*persit*: GBAGB   *pauper*ibus: ABABc   *iu*stitia: E   eius[1]: GcA-FABGF   *in*[1]: AG   *cornu*: Bc   *exal*tabitur: E   *glor*ia: GAGF   Ps.: GAcAGABG

---

547 RL: MRM 2: 302 (m. v.). SAC: Va 577, 1603. GREG: Ha 631, Sp 1462. GEL8: Ge 2833, Ph 1858, Rh 1263. AM: Sb 1526. ES: Vl4770 180v. BEN: Ben29 263r, Ben30 150r, Ben33 116v, Mc127 418-419, McV 194v.

548 Ps 111: 9, 111: 1. RL: GR 576, MRM 363. AMS 135. ES: Vl4770 181r. BEN: Ben29 263v, Ben33 118r, Ben34 216r-v, Ben35 138v, Ben38 121v-122r, Ben39 142v, Ben40 109v, Mc127 420, McV 195r, Ott 316v (ps. var.), PuC 600, Ve 170r.

549 RL: MRM 364. SAC: Le (758). GREG: Ha 639, Pa 597. GEL8: En 1187, Ge 1300, Rh 772, Sg 1055. AM: Sb (1022). ES: Vl4770 181r. BEN: Ben29 263v, Ben33 118r, Mc127 420, McO 409, McV 195r, Ott 316v, Ve 170r.

550 Eccli 51: 1-8, 12. RL: MRM 364. LEC: Alc 154, Mu 121, WuC 139, CoP 316. ES: Vl4770 181r. BEN: Ben29 263v-264r, Ben33 118r, Mc127 420, McV 195r-v, Ott 316v, PuC 602, Ve 170r.

551

GRADVALE ♪ Dispersit dedit pauperibus <iustiti>a eius manet in seculum
100r seculi. | VERSVS Potens in terra erit semen eius generatio rectorum benedice-
tur. ♪

552

EVANGELIVM [Mt 16: 24]. In illo tempore. Dixit iesus discipulis suis.
Si quis uult post me.

553

OFFERTORIVM ♪ Oratio mea munda est et ideo peto ut detur locum uoci mee
in celo quia ibi est iudex meus et conscius meus in eternum ascendat ad
dominum deprecatio mea. ♪

554

SECRETA Hostias domine quesumus quas tibi offerimus, propitius
suscipe. et intercedente beato laurentio martire tuo uincula peccatorum nostrorum absolue. per.

---

554 quas tibi] tibi quas *ante corr. in eadem manu*

---

551 *de*dit: cAcAGBGAB   secu*li*: dcdedcecefdcAGABcdcdededecABcA (*ut
vid.*)   *ter*ra: edcBcAGBGAcdedecefdcAGAcAGAdfefede   *er*it: fdefed
eius[2]: ecedcAcAcdedcedcdA

553 me*a*[1]: Bdc   *peto*: Bdcdc   e*ter*num: BdcdcBG] ex*cel*sis GR   domi*num*:
AF   depreca*tio*: cB

---

551 Ps 111: 9, 2. RL: GR 576-577, MRM 364. AMS 135. ES: Vl4770 181r. BEN:
Ben29 264r, Ben33 118r, Ben34 216v, Ben35 138v, Ben38 122r, Ben39 142v,
Ben40 109v, Mc127 421, McV 195v, Ott 316v, PuC 603, PuZ XVIII.b, Ve 170r-v.

552 Mt 16: 24. RL: MRM 364. LEC: Mu 121, WuE 312, CoP 317. ES: Vl4770
181r-v. BEN: Ben29 264r, Ben33 118r-v, DaE 126v, Mc127 421, McV 195v, Ott
316v-317r, PuC 604, PuZ XVIII.Ev, Ve 170v.

553 Iob 16: 20. RL: GR 577-578, MRM 364. AMS 135. ES: Vl4770 181v. BEN: Ben29
264r, Ben33 118v, Ben34 216v-217r, Ben35 138v, Ben38 122r-v, Ben39 143r,
Ben40 110r, Mc127 421, McV 195v, Ott 317r, PuC 605, PuZ XVIII.d, Ve 170v.

554 RL: MRM 364. GREG: Ha 640, Pa 598. GEL8: En 1190, Ge 1302, Rh 774, Sg
1057. AM: Sb (332). ES: Vl4770 181v. BEN: Ben29 264r, Ben33 118v, Mc127 421,
McV 195v, Ott 317r, PuC 606, PuZ XVIII.4, Ve 170v.

555

COMMVNIO Qui uult uenire.

556

POSTCOMMVNIO Quesumus domine deus noster. ut sicut beati laurentii martiris tui commemoratione temporali gratulamur officio. ita perpetuo letemur affectu. per dominum.

NATALE EIVSDEM.

557

♪ Probasti domine cor meum et uisitasti nocte. igne me examinasti. et non est inuenta in me iniquitas. -xaudi domine. ♪

558

100v | ORATIO Da nobis quesumus omnipotens deus, uitiorum nostrorum flammas extinguere. qui beato laurentio tribuisti tormentorum suorum incendia superare. per.

---

557 *Probasti domine*: GAFAGAcdc   *cor*: GABc   *meum*: cdc   *ui*sitasti: cdc   examina*sti*: B   *et*[2]: cBA   *non*: ced   *est*: dc   *inuen*ta: GcA Ps.: GcBcdfedcAG

---

555 Mt 16: 24. RL: GR 578, MRM 364. AMS 135. ES: Vl4770 181v. BEN: Ben29 264r, Ben33 118v, Ben34 217r, Ben35 138v, Ben38 122v, Ben39 143r, Ben40 110r, Mc127 421, McV 195v, Ott 317r, PuC 607, PuZ XVIII.e, Ve 170v.

556 RL: MRM 364 ("Da *quaesumus ... aspectu*"). SAC: Le (278). GREG: Ha 641, Pa 599, Sp (1229). GEL8: En 1192, Ge 1306, Rh 776, Sg 1059. AM: Sb (1195). ES: Vl4770 181v. BEN: Ben29 264r, Ben33 118v, Mc127 421, McV 195v, Ott 317r, Ve 170v.

557 Ps 16: 3, 16: 1. RL: GR (586-587), MRM (370). AMS (141). BEN: Ben29 264r, Ben30 153v, Ben33 118v, Ben34 217r-v, Ben35 139r, Ben38 122v, Ben39 143v-144r, Ben40 110v, Mc127 421, McV 195v, Ott 317r, PuC 611, PuZ XX.a.

558 RL: MRM 364. GREG: Ha 645, Pa 603. GEL8: En 1199, Ge 1311, Rh 777, Sg 1064. AM: Sb (1048). ES: Vl4770 181v. BEN: Ben29 264r, Ben33 (120v), Mc127 421, McO 411, McV 195v, Ott 317r-v, Ve 170v.

559

AD CORINTHIOS [2 Cor 9: 6-10]. Fratres. Qui parce seminat ... frugum iustitie uestre.

560

GRADVALE ♪ Probasti domine cor meum et uisitasti nocte. VERSVS Igne me 101r examinasti et non est inuenta in me | iniquitas. ♪

561

♪ Alleluia. VERSVS Laurentius bonum opus operatus est qui per signum crucis cecos illuminauit. ♪

562

SEQVENTIA SANCTI EVANGELII SECVNDVM IOHANNEM [12: 24-26]. In illo tempore. Dixit iesus discipulis suis. Amen amen dico uobis. Nisi granum ... pater meus qui in celis est.

---

559 in corde] corde *Vulgata* (9: 7)   enim] autem (9: 8)   et facere] facere (9: 8)   sufficientiam] omnem sufficientiam (9: 8)   seculum seculi] aeternum (9: 9)   ad manducabit] ad manducandum (9: 10)

562 in terra] in terram *Vulgata* (12: 24)

---

560 uisi*tasti*: AFABGF   *nocte*: FGFCDFEGABGABGFGAGAGABcBcA-BABGBABGFGFAGAGF   exami*nas*ti: cdcABAGAGFAcAFGAcdcAGA *inuenta*: cfdcAGAcdB   iniqui*tas*: cAcAcAFGAcdecAGBAF

561 *Vide Intro. p. 149*

---

559 2 Cor 9: 6-10. RL: MRM 364-365. LEC: Alc 155, Mu 122, WuC 140, CoP 318. ES: Vl4770 181v-182r. BEN: Ben29 264r-v, Ben30 154r-v, Ben33 118v, DaK 43r-v, Mc127 421-422, McV 195v-196r, Ott 317v, PuC 609, PuZ xx.Ep, Ve 170v.

560 Ps 16: 3. RL: GR 579, MRM 365. AMS 136. ES: Vl4770 182r. BEN: Ben29 264v, Ben30 154v, Ben33 118v, Ben34 217v, Ben35 139r, Ben38 122v-123r, Ben39 144r, Ben40 110v-111r, Mc127 422, McV 196r, Ott 317v, Ott[1] (37), PuC 614, PuZ xx.b, Ve 171r.

561 RL: MRM 365 (m. v.). ES: Schlager, *Katalog* G 284. BEN: Ben30 154v, Ben34 218r, Ben35 139v, Ben38 123r, Ben39 144r-v, Ben40 111r-v, McV (198v), Ott[1] (37), Ve 171r. Var. (melodia): RL: GR 579-580, ES: Syg 313, LS: Gs 194.

562 Io 12: 24-26. RL: MRM 365. LEC: Mu 122, WuE 312, CoP 319. ES: Vl4770 182r. BEN: Ben29 264v, Ben30 154v-155r, Ben33 118v-119r, DaE 126v, DaK 43v, Mc127 422, McV 196r, Ott 317v-318r, Ott[1] 20, PuC 616, PuZ xx.Ev, Ve 171r.

563

OFFERTORIVM ♪ Confessio et pulchritudo in conspectu eius sanctitas et magnificentiam in sanctificatione eius. ♪

564

101v   SECRETA Accipe quesumus domine munera dignanter obla|ta. et beati laurentii suffragantibus meritis. ad nostre salutis auxilium peruenire concede. per.

565

COMMVNIO ♪ Qui michi ministrat me sequatur et ubi ego sum illic et minister meus erit. ♪

566

POSTCOMMVNIO Conserua in nobis domine munus tuum quod te donante pro sollempnitate beati laurentii leuite percepimus, ut et salutem nobis prestet et pacem. per.

---

563 pul*chri*tudo: GBGA   *conspec*tu: EFAGAG   *eius*[1]: FGAGEFGAGA *et*[2]: FGE   *magni*ficentiam: FG   sanctificati*one*: EABAGAGE   *eius*[2]: FGA

565 *Qui*: G   mini*strat*: G   se*quatur*: cBcBcBG   *et*[1]: G   *ubi*: Gc *ego*: cGcdfef   *et*[2]: cBcAcAG   *minister*: FGEFD

---

563 Ps 95: 6. RL: GR 580, MRM 365. AMS 136. ES: Vl4770 182r. BEN: Ben29 264v, Ben30 155r, Ben33 119r, Ben34 219r, Ben35 140r, Ben38 124r, Ben39 145r-v, Ben40 112r, Mc127 422, McV 196r, Ott 318r, Ott[1] 21, PuC 617, Ve 171r.

564 RL: MRM 365. SAC: Le (759). GREG: Ha 646, Pa 604. GEL8: En (8, 137), Ge (17, 147), Rh (15), Sg (16, 129). AM: Sb (935). ES: Vl4770 182r. BEN: Ben29 264v, Ben30 155r, Ben33 119r, Mc127 422, McV 196r, Ott 318r, Ott[1] 22, Ve 171r.

565 Io 12: 26. RL: GR 581 (vide [15]), MRM 365. AMS 136. ES: Vl4770 182r. BEN: Ben29 264v, Ben30 155r, Ben33 119r, Ben34 219r, Ben35 140r, Ben38 124r, Ben39 145v, Ben40 112r, Mc127 422, McV 196r, Ott 318r, Ott[1] (41), PuC 619, Ve 171r.

566 AM: Sb 1053, D3-3 1086, STripl 2287.

IN SANCTI TIBVRTII.

567

Beati tiburtii nos domine foueat continuata presidia. quia non desinis intueri. quos talibus auxiliis concesseris adiuuari. per.

VIGILIA ASSVMPTIONIS SANCTE MARIE.

568

Dilexisti iustitiam et odisti.

569

Deus qui uirginalem aulam beate marie in qua habitares eligere dignatus es, da quesumus. ut sua nos defensione munitos. iocundos faciat sue, interesse festiuitati. per.

570

102r LECTIO LIBRI SAPIENTIE [Eccli 24: 21-31]. Ego quasi libanus ... | ... possidebunt.·,

571

GRADVALE Dilexisti iustitiam.

---

570 sancte spei] et sanctae spei *Vulgata* (24: 24)   est omnis spes] omnis spes (24: 25)   mel] melle (24: 27)   saluum] favum (24: 27)   audiunt ... confundentur] audit ... confundetur (24: 30)   possidebunt] habebunt (24: 31)

---

567 RL: MRM 365 (m. v.). GREG: Ha 649, Pa 609. GEL8: En 1208, Ge 1321, Sg 1073. AM: Sb (1050). ES: Vl4770 182v. BEN: Ben29 264v-265r, Mc127 422-423, McV 196v, Ott 318r, Ve 171r.

568 Ps 44: 8. RL: GR ([60]), MRM (441). AMS (3, 101, 169*bis*). ES: Vl4770 183v. BEN: Ben29 265r, Ben30 155v, Ben33 119r, Ben34 219v, Ben35 140v, Ben38 124v, Ben39 146r, Mc127 423, McV 196v, Ott 318v, PuC 621.

569 RL: MRM 367. GREG: Ha 658. ES: Vl4770 183v. BEN: Ben29 265r, Ben33 (120v), Mc127 423, McO 414, McV 196v, Ott 318v, Ve 171v.

570 Eccli 24: 21-31. RL: MRM 367-368 (Eccli 24: 23-31). BEN: Ben29 265v, Mc127 423-424, McV 196v-197r, Ott 318v-319r.

571 Ps 44: 8. RL: GR ([52]), MRM (444). AMS (3, 101, 127, 169*bis*). ES: Vl4770 184r. BEN: Ben29 265v, Ben30 156r, Ben34 219v, Ben35 (140v), Ben38 124v, Ben39 146r, Mc127 424, McV 197r, Ott 319r, PuC (769).

572

EVANGELIVM [Lc 1: 39]. Exurgens maria abiit in montana.

573

OFFERTORIVM Offerentur regi uirgines.

574

SECRETA Intercessio quesumus domine beate marie uirginis munera nostra commendet. nosque in eius tue ueneratione maiestati reddat acceptos. per.

575

COMMVNIO Diffusa est gratia in.

576

Sumptis domine sacramentis intercedente beata et gloriosa semperque uirgine dei genitrice maria. ad redemptionis eterne quesumus 102v profi|ciamus augmentum. per eundem.

---

572 Lc 1: 39. RL: MRM (8). ES: Vl4770 184r-v. BEN: Ben29 265v, Ben30 156r-v, Ben33 119v, DaE 127r, Mc127 424, McV 197r, Ott 319r, Ott¹ 24, PuC 624, Ve 172r.

573 Ps 44: 15. RL: GR (437, [54]), MRM (446). AMS (140: Assump.). BEN: Ben29 265v, Ben30 156v, Ben33 119v, Ben34 219v, Ben35 (140v), Ben38 124v, Ben39 146r, Mc127 424, McV 197r, Ott (320r), PuC 626, PuL (67v-68r), Ve 172r.

574 SAC: Va (820, 1004). GREG: Pa (622). GEL8: En (153, 1226, 1258), Ge (158, 1349, 1389), Rh (790), Sg (140, 1094). AM: Sb (1066). ES: Vl4770 184v. BEN: Ben29 (267r), Ben30 156v-157r, Ben33 119v, Mc127 (426), Ott¹ 26, PuC 627.

575 Ps 44: 3. RL: GR (559-560), MRM (446). AMS (3, 101, 169*bis*). ES: Vl4770 184v. BEN: Ben33 119v, Ben34 (5r), Ben35 (140v), Mc127 424, McV 197r, PuC 628.

576 RL: MRM (76, 276, 390). SAC: Va (1019). GEL8: En (1277, 1305), Ge (1330, 1406, 1432), Rh (829), Sg (1134, 1164). AM: Sb (334). ES: Vl4770 184v. BEN: Ben29 266r, Ben30 157r, Ben33 119v, Mc127 424, McV 197r, Ott 319r, Ott¹ 29, PuC 629.

ASSVMPTIO SANCTE. MARIE.

577
♪ Gaudeamus omnes in domino diem festum celebrantes sub honore marie uirginis de cuius assumptione gaudent angeli et collaudant filium dei. PSALMVS Eructauit. Gaudete iusti. ♪

578
ORATIO Concede quesumus omnipotens deus; ad beate marie semper uirginis gaudia eterna pertingere. de cuius nos assumptione ueneranda. tribuis annua sollempnitate gaudere. per.

579
LECTIO LIBRI. SAPIENTIE [Eccli 24: 11-13, 15-20]. In omnibus requiem
103r quesiui ... | ... odoris.·,

580
GRADVALE ♪ Propter ueritatem et mansuetudinem et iustiti<am.> et deducet te mirabiliter dextera tua. Audi filia et uide <et inclina> aurem tuam quia concupiuit rex <speciem> tuam. ♪

---

579 domini] eius *Vulgata* (24: 11)   mitte] ede (24: 13)   radicaui] et radicavi (24: 16)   partes] parte (24: 16)   *103r: frag.*   quasi palma] et quasi palma (24: 18)   aquas] aquam (24: 19)   balsamum] aspaltum (24: 20)

---

577 hono*re*: AG   assumptio*ne*: AG   *fi*lium: FGD

---

580 man*su*etudinem: FFF *ante corr. (ut GR),* AAA *post corr.*   *et*[3]: BA   de*du*cet: BABGFG   mi*rabili*ter: AcBcBGFG   *dextera*: BGFEFGBcdcBcBGFDF   con*cupi*uit: cd   tu*am*[2]: EFGAGFGAcAGFGAcGBAGFAGAGF

---

577 Ps 44: 2, 32: 1. RL: GR in Suppl. OSB (30-31), MRM 368. AMS (30). ES: Vl4770 184v. BEN: Ben30 (171r), Ben34 (49v-50r, 237r), Ve 172r.

578 GREG: Ha (494), Pa 621. GEL8: En 1225, Ge 1347, Rh 789, Sg 1092. AM: Sb 1065. BEN: Ben29 266r, Ben30 (155v), Ben33 (119r), Mc127 425, McV 197v, Ott 319r-v, PuC (622).

579 Eccli 24: 11-13, 15-20. RL: MRM 369. LEC: Mu 123. ES: Vl4770 184v. BEN: Ben29 266r-v, Ben30 157v-158r, Ben33 119v-120r, DaK 43v-44r, Mc127 425, McV 197v, Ott[1] 32, Ott 319v, PuC 632, Ve 172r-v.

580 Ps 44: 5, 11-12. RL: GR in Suppl. OSB (31), MRM 369. AMS 140. ES: Vl4770 184v. BEN: Ben29 266v, Ben30 158r-v, Ben34 222v-223r, Ben35 140v, Ben39 (149r-v), Ben40 115r, Mc127 425, McV 197v, Ott 319v, PuC 633, PuL (66r-v), Ve 172v.

581

♪ Alleluia. O quam beata es uirgo ma<ria que est prima inter> filias hierusalem quas cir<cumdant flo>res rosarum et lili<a conuallium.> ♪

582

103v | LVCAM [Lc 10: 38-42]. In illo tempore. Intrauit iesus, in quoddam castellum. ... [*cum lacunis*] ... ab ea.

583

OFFERTORIVM Offerentur.

584

SECRETA [*lac.*] munera nostra efficiat, [*lac.*] -atio. quam etsi pro conditionis <carnis migrasse> cognoscimus. in celesti gloria. <apud te pro nobis orar>e sentiamus. per eundem.

585

COMMVNIO Dilexisti iustitiam.

---

582 *103v: frag.*　　sola] solam *Vulgata* (10: 40)　　dominus dixit <illi>] dixit illi Dominus (10: 41)

---

581 *Vide Intro. p. 153*

---

581 ES: Schlager, *Katalog* G 373, Vl4770 184v-185r. BEN: Ben30 158v-159r, Ben33 120r, Ben34 223r-v, Ben35 140v-141r, Ben38 (126v), Ben39 149v-150r, Ben40 115v, Mc127 425, McV 198r, PuC 634.

582 Lc 10: 38-42. RL: MRM 369. LEC: Mu 123, WuE 313. ES: Vl4770 185r. BEN: Ben29 266v-267r, Ben30 159r-v, Ben33 120r, DaE 128r, DaK 44r-v, Mc127 425-426, McV 198r, Ott 319v-320r, PuC 635, Ve 172v.

583 Ps 44: 15. RL: GR (437, [54]), MRM (446). AMS 140. ES: Vl4770 185r. BEN: Ben29 267r, Ben30 159v, Ben33 120r, Ben34 226r, Ben35 143v, Ben38 (128r), Ben39 (152v), Ben40 117v, Mc127 426, McV 198r, Ott 320r, PuC 636, PuL (67v-68r), Ve 172v.

584 RL: MRM 369 (inc.: "Subveniat domine plebis tue dei genitricis oratio"). GREG: Ha 663 (inc. var.). BEN: Ve 172v (inc. var.).

585 Ps 44: 8. RL: GR ([71]), MRM (446). AMS 140. BEN: Ben29 267r, Ben30 159v, Ben33 120v, Ben34 226v, Ben35 144r, Ben(128r), Ben39 (153r), Ben40 118r, Mc127 426, McV 198r, Ott 320r, PuC 639, PuL (68r), Ve 173r.

586

SECRETA <Mense celestis> parti<cipes effecti> imploramus cle-
men<tiam tuam domine> deus noster. ut qui festa bea<te semper>
uirginis marie coli<mus a malis imminenti>bus eius intercessionibus
[*lac.*]

<COMMEMORATIO OMNIVM SANCTORVM>

587

104r [*lac.*] | [Mt 5: 15-16] sub modio. ... in celis est.

588

OFFERTORIVM ♪ Letamini in domino et exultate iusti et gloriamini omnes recti
corde. ♪

589

SECRETA Munera tibi domine nostre deuotionis offerimus. que pro
cunctorum tibi grata sint honore sanctorum. et nobis salutaria te
miserante reddantur. per.

---

587 *lac. inter 103v-104r*   supra] super *Vulgata* (5: 15)

---

586 RL: MRM 369. GREG: Ha 664. ES: Vl4770 185v. BEN: Ben29 267r, Ben30 160r,
Ben33 120v, Mc127 426, McV 198r, Ott 320r, PuC 640, Ve 173r.

587 Mt 5: 15-16. RL: MRM 396 (var.: **Mt 5: 1-12** *Videns Iesus turbas ascendit in
montem*). ES: Vl4770 206r. BEN: Ben29 279v-280r, Ben30 212r-v, Ben33 124r-v
(Mt 5: 2-16), DaE 134r (Mt 5: 1-12), DaK 48r-v, Mc127 445-446, McV 209r-v,
Ott 332r-v, PuC 679.

588 Ps 31: 11. RL: GR (415, 456), MRM (419, 429). AMS (24b, 92, 112, 116, 129b,
134, 146). ES: Vl4770 206r. BEN: Ben29 279v, Ben33 (11r, 107r, 117v), Ben34
(44r-v), Ben35 (150r), Mc127 446, McV 209v, Ott 332v.

589 RL: MRM 396. GREG: Ha (634), Pa (589), Sp (1231), Tc 3653. GEL8: En
(1173), Ge (1291), Sg (1042). AM: Sb (1193). ES: Vl4770 206r. BEN: Ben29 279v,
Ben30 212v-213r, Ben33 124v, Mc127 446, McV 209v, Ott 332v-333r, Ve 181r.

590

COMMVNIO ♪ Gaudete iusti in domino alleluia rectos decet collaudatio alleluia. ♪

591

POSTCOMMVNIO Omnipotens sempiterne deus; qui nos omnium sanctorum tuorum multiplici facis sollempnitate gaudere. concede quesumus. ut sicut illorum commemoratione temporali gratulamur officio. ita perpetuo letemur aspectu. per.

COMMEMORATIO OMNIVM DEFVNCTORVM.

592

104v | INTROITVS Requiem eternam dona eis.

593

ORATIO Omnipotens et misericors deus. clementiam tuam supplices exoramus. ut animas famulorum famularumque tuarum omnium fidelium defunctorum. intercedente beata maria semper uirgine cum omnibus sanctis; ad perpetue beatitudinis facias peruenire consortium. per.

594

105r AD CORINTHIOS [1 Cor 15: 51-57]. Fratres. Ecce misterium ... | ... christum.

---

594 canet enim tuba] canet enim *Vulgata* (15: 52)   incorruptionem] incorruptelam (15: 53)

---

590 *iusti*: CFAGFAGABAG   *in*: CDA   al*leluia*[1]: GFCDEFC   *rec*tos: FGCGAGcBABG   *alle*luia[2]: CFAGAFGFEGFGECDEFGFE

---

590 Ps 32: 1. RL: GR ([20]-[21]). AMS (92, 99). BEN: Ben33 (95v), Ben34 (153r), Ve 181r.

591 GREG: Tc 3656. AM: Sb 1639. ES: F 1401. BEN: PuC 684, Ve 181r-v.

592 4 Esdr 2: 34. RL: GR 94*, MRM (483). BEN: Ben34 265v, Ben35 169r, Ben38 153v, Ben39 193r, Ben40 156r, Ott 373v, PuC (147), PuL 28v.

593 Non inveni. Cf. RL: MRM (489: inc. var.).

594 1 Cor 15: 51-57. RL: MRM (484). BEN: PuL 31v-32r.

595

GRADVALE Conuertere anima meam. VERSVS Quia eripuit anima.

596

TRACTVS Absolue domine.

597

MATHEVM [25: 31-46]. In illo tempore. Dixit iesus discipulis suis.
105v Cum uenerit filius hominis ... | ... in supplicium [*lac.*]

106r | VIGILIA VNIVS APOSTOLI.

598

♪ Ego autem sicut oliua fructificaui in domo domini speraui in misericordia dei
mei et expectabo nomen tuum quoniam bonum est ante conspectu sanctorum
tuorum. Quid gloriaris. ♪

599

ORATIO Concede nobis omnipotens deus. uenturam beati apostoli tui
.illius. sollempnitatem congruo preuenire honore. et uenientem di-
gnam celebrare deuotionem. per.

---

597 quidem oues] oves quidem *Vulgata* (25: 33)   collegistis] collexistis (25: 35)
collegimus] colleximus (25: 38)   cooperuimus te] cooperuimus (25: 38)
sinistris eius] sinistris (25: 41)   preparatus] paratus (25: 41)   collegistis]
collexistis (25: 43)   carcerem] carcere (25: 44)   *lac. inter 105v-106r*

---

598 *autem*: ABAGABcB   *si*cut: B   fructi*fi*caui: AGE   miseri*cordi*a: GB
mei: AGFGABAG   expec*ta*bo: GcBc   *est*: DFDF   sanc*to*rum:
GcGcBAGA   Ps.: GABcAGABG

---

595 Ps 114: 7-8. BEN: Ben34 265v, Ben35 170r, Ben38 153v-154r, Ben39 193r,
Ben40 156r, Ott 373v, PuC (162).

596 RL: GR 95*-96*, MRM (485).

597 Mt 25: 31-46. RL: MRM (58). BEN: Ben33 (24r).

598 Ps 51: 10-11, 51: 3. RL: GR [1]-[2], MRM 403. AMS (13, 154). ES: Vl4770
215r. BEN: Ben29 284r, Ben33 (4r), Ben34 (22v-23r), DaZ (3), Mc127 454,
Mc426 (91), Mc546 97, McB 25v, McV 239v, Ott 341r, PuL 76r-v, Ve 183v.

599 GREG: Tc 3144 (Missa Alcuini). ES: F (1367). BEN: Ben29 284r, DaZ 1,
Mc127 454, McB 21r, McV 239v, Ott 341r, Ve 183v-184r.

600

LECTIO [Eccli 44: 25]. Benedictio domini super caput.

601

GRADVALE ♪ Iustus ut palma florebit sicut cedrus libani multiplicabitur in
106v domo domini. VERSVS Ad annuntiandum mane misericordiam | tuam. et
ueritatem tuam per noctem. ♪

602

SECVNDVM LVCAM [22: 24-30]. In illo tempore. Facta est contentio
inter discipulos iesu. ... israel.

603

108r OFFERTORIVM ♪ Gloria et honore coronasti eum et constitui|sti eum super
opera manuum tuarum domine. ♪

---

602 regno meo] regno *Vulgata* (22: 30)

603 *N.B.: 108r post 106v legendum est (vide App.)*

---

601 flo*re*bit: cAcAGBGAB   domi*ni*: dcdedcecefdcAGABcdcdedecABcB
*man*e: edcBcAGBGAcdedecefdcAGAcAGAdfefede   *mi*sericordiam: fdefed
*tu*am[1]: ecedcAcAcdedcedcdA

603 *coronasti*: FAGAGFAGAFcBAG   tua*rum*: EGAG

---

600 Eccli 44: 25. RL: MRM 403. LEC: Alc 52 (Suppl.). BEN: Ben29 (285r), DaZ
(3-5), Mc127 (455), McB 25v, McV 239v, Ott (342v-343r), PuC (697).

601 Ps 91: 13-14, 91: 3. RL: GR [2] (vide [42]-[43]), MRM 403. AMS (13, 118a,
144, 154, 167). ES: Vl4770 (216r). BEN: Ben29 284r, Ben33 (4v, 138v), Ben34
(23r), Mc127 454, Mc426 (100), Mc546 97, McB 25v, McV 239v-240r, Ott 341r,
PuL (78v-79r), Ve 183v.

602 Lc 22: 24-30. RL: MRM (355). BEN: Ben33 (114v), DaZ (5-7), Mc127 (458),
Ott (344v).

603 Ps 8: 6-7. RL: GR [2], MRM 403. AMS (13, 171*ter*). ES: Vl4770 (216r). BEN:
Ben29 284v, Ben33 (4v, 12r, 16v, 108r, 121v), Ben34 (23v-24r), DaZ 2, Mc127
454, Mc546 97-98, McB 25v-26r, McV 240r, Ott 341v, PuC (700, 739), PuL 77v,
Ve 183v.

604

SECRETA Accepta tibi sit domine nostre deuotionis oblatio. et ad apostolicam faciat peruenire festiuitatem. per.

605

COMMVNIO ♪ Magna est gloria eius in salutari tuo gloriam et magnum decorem inpones super eum domine. ♪

606

POSTCOMMVNIO Presta nobis eterne saluator. eius ubique pia oratione. cuius natalicia per hec sancta que sumpsimus. uotiuo preuenimus obsequio. per.

VIGILIA PLVRIMORVM APOSTOLORVM.

607

♪ Clamauerunt iusti et dominus exaudiuit eos. et ex omnibus tribulationibus eorum liberauit eos. PSALMVS Benedicam dominum. ♪

608

Concede quesumus omnipotens deus. ut sicut apostolorum tuorum .illius. et illius. gloriosa natalicia preuenimus. sic ad tua | beneficia promerenda. maiestatem tuam pro nobis ipsi preueniant. per.

108v

---

605 *ei*us: FGA   glo*ri*am: E   *su*per: GE   *e*um: FDFEDC

607 exau*di*uit: DFE   *om*nibus: DC   *e*os: CFCFEFDED   Ps.: CDCFGFDFECDED

---

604 GREG: Tc 3145 (Missa Alcuini). ES: F (1368). BEN: Ben29 284v, DaZ 2 (m. v.), Mc127 454, McB 21r, McV 240r, Ott 341v, Ve 184r.

605 Ps 20: 6. RL: GR [2], MRM 404. AMS (13, 31, 117, 155, 164, 177*bis*). ES: Vl4770 (216v). BEN: Ben29 284v, Ben33 (4v, 123v), Ben34 (24r), DaZ 2, Mc127 454, Mc426 (94), Mc546 98, McB 26r, McV 240r, Ott 341v, PuC (551, 741), PuL 78r.

606 GREG: Tc 3146 (Missa Alcuini). ES: F (1370). BEN: Ben29 284v (m. v.), DaZ 2, Mc127 454-455, McB 21r (m. v.), McV 240r, Ott 341v, Ve 184r.

607 Ps 33: 18, 33: 2. RL: GR (455), MRM (420). AMS (97, 112). BEN: Ben33 (15r, 94r, 115r), Ben34 (167v), Mc546 (100).

608 RL: MRM 404. SAC: Va 939. GREG: Tc 3168. GEL8: En (1435), Ge (1568), Rh (908), Sg (1283). AM: Sb (1141). ES: Vl4770 (215r-v). BEN: Ben33 (123v), DaZ 14, Ott 341v, Ve 184v.

609

PETRI APOSTOLI [1 Petr 1: 3-7]. Karissimi. Benedictus deus. ... in reuelationem iesu christi domini nostri.

610

GRADVALE ♪ In omnem terram exiuit sonus eorum et in fines orbis terre uerba
107r eorum. │VERSVS Celi enarrant gloriam dei et opera manuum eius annuntiat firmamentum. ♪

611

MATHEVM [10: 1-8]. In illo tempore. Conuocatis iesus discipulis suis.
107v ... │ ... gratis date.

612

OFFERTORIVM ♪ Michi autem nimis honorificati sunt amici tui deus nimis confortatus est principatus eorum. ♪

---

609 domini nostri] Domini nostri Iesu Christi *Vulgata* (1: 3)   uobis] in vobis
(1: 4)   probatio ... pretiosior] probatum ... pretiosius (1: 7)   auro] sit auro
(1: 7)   quod] quod perit (1: 7)   probatur] probato (1: 7)   et honorem et
gloriam] et gloriam et honorem (1: 7)

610 *N.B.: 107r post 108v legendum est (vide App.)*

611 infirmitatem in populo] infirmitatem *Vulgata* (10: 1)   iacobus] et Iacobus
(10: 3)   dicens] et dicens (10: 5)   ciuitate] civitates (10: 5)   appropinquabit regnum dei] adpropinquavit regnum caelorum (10: 7)

---

610 *ter*ram: cAcAGBGAB   exi*u*it: dcAGcAcdcA   or*bis*: cd   eo*rum*²:
dcdedcecefdcAGABcdcdededecABcA   e*nar*rant: edcBcAGBGAcdedecefdcA-
GAcAGAdfefede   *glo*riam: fdefed

612 *au*tem: FAG   *ni*mis¹: GcABGF   a*mi*ci: DEGE   *tui*: EGFEFGA-
BAGFGAG   conforta*tus*: A   *est*: GcAGAFAcGFDED

---

609 1 Petr 1: 3-7. RL: MRM (424: **1 Petr 1: 3-7, 4: 1-2**). LEC: Mu 162. BEN: Ben29
(286v-287r), Ben33 (109v: var.), Mc127 (456), McV 240r-v, Ott (342r-v).

610 Ps 18: 5, 2. RL: GR (629-630), MRM (408). AMS (121). ES: Vl4770 (215v).
BEN: Ben29 (287v), Ben33 (110v), Ben34 (202v), Mc127 (457), Mc426 (92),
Mc546 (98), McB (26r), McV 240v, Ott (343v), PuC (716).

611 Mt 10: 1-8. RL: MRM (2: 356).

612 Ps 138: 17. RL: GR (394), MRM (410). AMS (121, 123, 169). BEN: Ben33
(111r, 113r), Ben34 (203r-v), Mc127 (459), Mc426 (92), Mc546 (99), McV
242v, Ott (345r), PuC (719), Ve 185r.

613

SECRETA Muneribus nostris quesumus domine, apostolorum tuorum
.illius. et illius. natalicia precedimus. presta quesumus; ut que
conscientie nostre prepediuntur obstaculis. eorum meritis grata reddantur. per.

614

COMMVNIO ♪ Dico autem uobis amicis meis ne tereamini ab his qui uos
persequentur. ♪

615

POSTCOMMVNIO Quesumus domine salutaribus repletis misteriis. ut
quorum uenerando sollempnia preuenimus. eorum orationibus
adiuuemur. per.

NATALE VNIVS APOSTOLI.

616

Da nobis quesumus domine beati apostoli tui .illius, glorificatione
letari. ut eius semper et patrociniis ad [*lac.*]

---

614 tere*a*mini: F   *ab*: F

---

613 RL: MRM 405-406 (m. v.). SAC: Le (778), Va 940. GREG: Tc 3169. GEL8: En
(1436), Ge (1569), Rh (909), Sg (1284). BEN: Ben29 (288r: m. v.), McV (83r),
Ott 342r, Ve 185r.

614 Lc 12: 4. RL: GR ([28]), MRM (430). AMS (138). BEN: Ben33 (15v, 119r),
Ben34 (219v), Mc546 (109).

615 RL: MRM (407). SAC: Va (878). GREG: Ha (101, 107, 481, 689), Pa (80, 417,
664), Sp (1226). GEL8: En (146), Ge (132, 151, 155, 1074), Sg (134, 856). AM:
Sb (1158). ES: Vl4770 (618r). BEN: Ben29 (288r), Ben33 (93v, 105v: m. v.), DaZ
(21), Mc127 (459), McB (21r), McV 242v-243r, Ott (345v), PuL (79v, 83v), Ve
185v.

616 RL: MRM (304). SAC: Le (400), Va (1088). GEL8: Ge (1757), Rh (1024), Sg
(1456). AM: Sb (1159). BEN: Mc127 455, Mc426 91, Ott 342r, PuC 714 (m. v.).

\<NATALE PLVRIMORVM APOSTOLORVM\>

617

110r [*lac.*] |　♪ in omni progenie et generatione. ♪

618

SECRETA Munera domine que pro apostolorum tuorum .illius. et illius. sollempnitate deferimus. propitius respice. et mala omnia que meremur auerte. per.

619

COMMVNIO ♪ Vos qui secuti estis me dicit dominus sedebitis super sedes iudicantes duodecim tribus israhel alleluia alleluia. ♪

620

POSTCOMMVNIO Sumpto domine sacramento te supplices deprecamur ut intercedentibus beatis apostolis tuis .illius, et illius; quorum festa colimus; quod temporaliter gerimus, ad uitam capiamus eternam. per.

---

617 *lac. inter 107v-110r*　　N.B.: *110r post 107v legendum est (vide App.)*

---

617 *om*ni: BdcBcA　　*progen*ie: FAc

619 *Vide Intro. p. 175*

---

617 Ps 44: 18. RL: GR (534), MRM 410 (Ps 44: 17-18 *Constitues eos*). AMS: (122b). BEN: Ben29 288r, Ben33 (111v), Ben34 (206v-207r), Mc127 458-459, Mc426 96, Mc546 (99), McB 27r, McV 242v, Ott 345r, PuC (579), PuL (79v).

618 RL: MRM 406. GREG: Ha (480), Pa (416), Sp 1225, Tc 3177, Z6 XXXIV.2. GEL8: Ge (932), Rh (561), Sg (733). AM: Sb 1156. ES: Vl4770 (216r). BEN: Ben33 (93v, 123v), Mc127 459, Mc426 96, McB 21r, McV 242v, Ott 345v, PuC 730, PuL (79v), Ve (185v).

619 Mt 19: 28. RL: MRM 410. AMS (160). ES: Vl4770 (215v). BEN: Ben29 288r, Ben34 (236v), Mc127 459, McB 27r, McV 242v, Ott 345v, PuC 731, PuL 83v, Ve (185v). Var. (melodia): RL: GR (448, 588-589), ES: Syg (55), LS: Gs 203.

620 RL: MRM (406). SAC: Le (340), Va (941). GREG: Tc (3170). GEL8: Ge (1571), Rh (910), Sg (1286). AM: Sb (978). ES: Vl4770 216v-217r. BEN: Ott (342r), PuC 732 (m. v.), Ve (185r).

NATALE VNIVS MARTIRIS.

621

INTROITVS ♪ Letabitur iustus in domino et sperauit in eo et laudabuntur omnes recti corde. Exaudi deus orationem cum tribulatione. ♪

622

Deus qui hunc diem beati .illius. martirio consecrasti. tribue quesu-
110v mus, ut cuius annuo celebramus officio eius continuo │ foueamur auxilio. per.

623

ALIA ORATIO. Deus qui nos beati illius. martiris tui atque pontificis annua sollempnitate letificas. concede propitius, ut cuius natalicia colimus. de eiusdem etiam protectione gaudeamus. per.

624

LECTIO LIBRI SAPIENTIE [Sap 10: 10-14]. Iustum deduxit dominus per
109r uiam rectam. ... et men│daces ... eternam. dominus deus noster.

---

624 *N.B.: 109r post 110v legendum est (vide App.)*   fecit illum] illum fecit *Vulgata* (10: 11)   custodiuit eum] custodivit illum (10: 12)   tutauit illum] tutavit eum (10: 12)   et sciret] ut sciret (10: 12)   eum] illum (10: 13)   descenditque] descendit (10: 13)   illum] ipsum (10: 14)

---

621 domino: dc   omnes: cBcdcB   recti: cBAG

---

621 Ps 63: 11, 63: 2. RL: GR [12]-[13], MRM 415. AMS (27a, 142a, 147, 152). ES: Vl4770 217r. BEN: Ben29 288r-v, Ben33 (11v, 16v), Ben34 (45v), DaZ 25, Mc127 459, Mc426 102, Mc546 104, McB 27r, McV 243r, Ott 345v, PuC 733, PuL 86r, Ve 187r.

622 Var.: RL: MRM (347 + 383), SAC: Le (inc: 280, 303, 357), Va (inc: 921), GREG: Ha (594 + 701), Pa (543 + 675), GEL8: En (1067 + 1340), Ge (1188 + 1469), Rh (721: inc.), Sg (960 + 1199), AM: Sb (34: inc.).

623 RL: MRM 411. GREG: Ha (625), Pa (582). GEL8: En (1164), Ge (1282), Rh (764), Sg (1033). Var. (expl.): BEN: Ben29 288v, Ben33 (116r), McB 21r (m. v.), Mc127 459, McV 243r, Ott 346r.

624 Sap 10: 10-14. RL: MRM 412. GREG: Mu 161, Z6 xxxv.Ep. BEN: Ben29 288v-289r, DaK 52v, Mc127 460, Mc426 (111-112), McB 27r-v, McV 243v, Ott 346r-v, PuC 735, PuL 86r-v, Ve 187r.

625

SAPIENTIE [Eccli 14: 22, 15: 3-4, 6]. Beatus uir qui in sapientia ... illum. dominus deus noster.

626

GRADVALE ♪ Posuisti domine super caput eius coronam de lapide pretioso.
109v VERSVS Desiderium anime eius tribuisti ei et uoluntate labiorum eius | non fraudasti eum. ♪

627

GRADVALE Exaltent eum. VERSVS Confiteantur domino.

628

♪ Alleluia. VERSVS Posuisti domine super caput eius coronam de lapide pretioso. ♪

---

625 morabitur] sua morietur *Vulgata* (14: 22)   iustitia] iustitia sua (14: 22)
cibauit] cibabit (15: 3)   pane] panem (15: 3)   exaltabit] inaltabit illum
(15: 4)   et in medio ... super illum *om. Dubr* (15: 5-6)

---

626 *super*: AcAcdcAG] in GR   *caput*: AGAcAGAGF] capite GR   eius[1]:
AFGAcAcGFDCDFGAFEGAFE   *la*pide: A   Desi*derium*: DABAcAGA-
GEFGEFGBAGAFDEGAFEGAGFDFED   ani*me* eius[2]: AGFGA   e*um*:
AFAGAGFDGFECDGFGADCDEFGFDED

628 *Alleluia*:   CDCFGEDFEFDEDCDFGAGAFAGBAGEFDCDFGAFAGA-
FEDFD   *Po*suisti: CDEFG   *do*mine: FGAGAFAGBAGEFDCECEFG
eius: FAGABGFAFAFG   co*ronam*: AFABGFAGF   *pretioso*: CDEF-
GEDFEFDEDCDFGAGAFAGBAGEFD

---

625 **Eccli 14: 22, 15: 3-4, 6**. RL: MRM 412. LEC: WuC (189), CoP (467). BEN:
Ben29 289r-v, Mc127 461, Mc426 102-103, McB 28r, McV 244r, Ott 346v-347r,
Ve (186v).

626 **Ps 20: 4, 3**. RL: GR in Suppl. OSB (6-7), MRM 417. AMS (27b, 141, 148a, 152).
ES: Vl4770 217r (V. var.). BEN: Ben29 289v, Ben34 (45v-46r), DaZ 28, Mc127
461, Mc426 103, Mc546 105-106, McB 28r-v, McV 244v, Ott 347v, Ve (186v).

627 **Ps 106: 32, 31**. RL: GR [2¹]-[2²], MRM (320, 2: 172). BEN: Ben34 (244v-245r).

628 **Ps 20: 4**. RL: GR [17], MRM 417, 418. BEN: Ben29 289v, Ben33 (123r), Ben34
270r-v, Ben35 177v, Ben38 162v-163r, Mc127 461, McV 244v, Ott 347v, PuC
737, PuL 87r, Ve 187r.

629

♪ Alleluia. VERSVS Amauit eum dominus et ornauit eum stolam glorie induit eum. ♪ *usque ihc.*

630

TRACTVS ♪ Beatus uir qui timet dominum in mandatis eius cupit nimis. Potens
111r in terra erit semen eius generatio rectorum benedicetur. Gloria et diuitie | in domo eius et iustitia eius manet in seculum seculi. ♪

631

SECVNDVM LVCAM [9: 23-27]. In illo tempore. Dicebat iesus ad discipulos suos. Si quis uult post me uenire ... regnum dei.

632

OFFERTORIVM Gloria et honore.

---

629 usque ihc *add. alia manu*

630 N.B.: *111r post 109v legendum est (vide App.)*

631 semet] se *Vulgata* (9: 23)   perdet eam] perdet illam (9: 24)

---

629 Allelu*ia*:   ECDFDEFGEFDCDGEGAFGEFGFEDEDCDEFGAGFGFE
A*mauit*: DEDEFE   *eum*[1]: FEFE   *orna*uit: EGFGEFEDCEGFGEFED
glorie: GAFGEGAFGEFGFEDEDCDEFGAGFGFE   in*duit*: DEDEF-
GEFDC   *eum*[3]: DFE

630 *qui*: FG   *dominum*: BcAGFBAGAGAGcABGF   *mandatis*: FAcB-
GAGFGAcBc   *cupit*: FGBABAc   Po*tens*: B   *in*[2]: B   *terra*: BcB
erit: B   *semen*: B   *eius*[2]: cdcBAGAGABcBABcAG   *generatio*: FAcB-
GAGFG   be*ne*dicetur: GAF   Glo*ria*: B   *et*[1]: B   *diuitie*: BcB   *in*
domo: Bc   *eius*[3]: cdcBGAGABcBABcAG   *et*[2]: F   *iustitia*: FAcBGAGFG
ma*net*: GAF   secu*li*: cBcAGAG

---

629 Eccli 45: 9. RL: GR [39]-[40], MRM (434, 440). BEN: Ben29 289v, Ben34
271v-272r, Ben35 178r, Ben38 132r-v, Mc127 462, McB 28v, McV 245r, Ott 347v.

630 Ps 111: 2-3. RL: GR [8]-[9], MRM 2: 258. AMS (31*bis*, 32). BEN: Ben33
(15v-16r), Ben34 (52v), McV (258v).

631 Lc 9: 23-27. LEC: Mu 161. BEN: Ben29 290r, Ben33 (12r), DaZ 28-29, Mc127
464, McB 28v-29r, McV 245v, Ott 348r-v, Ve (186v).

632 Ps 8: 6. RL: GR [2], MRM 417. AMS (13, 171*ter*). ES: Vl4770 217r. BEN: Ben33
(4v, 12r, 16v, 108r, 121v), Ben34 (23v), Mc426 104, Ott 349r, PuC 739, Ve 187r.

633

In uirtute tua domine.

634

111v OFFERTORIVM ♪ Confessio et pulchritudo in conspectu e|ius sanctitas et magnificentia in sanctificatione eius. ♪

635

SECRETA Grata tibi sint domine hec munera, quibus sancti illius. martiris passio recolitur honoranda. per.

636

ALIA Vt nostre salutis munera oblata proficiant; sancti illius. martiris tui atque pontificis. quesumus domine. intercessio salutaris optineat. per.

637

COMMVNIO Magna est gloria.

638

COMMVNIO ♪ Qui uult uenire post me abneget semetipsum et tollat crucem suam et sequatur me. ♪

---

633 *Add. alia manu beneventana*

---

634 *conspec*tu: EFAGAF   *eius*[1]: FGAGEFGAGA   *et*[2]: FGE

638 *uult*: EF   *cru*cem: AGA   *sequa*tur: DFE   *me*[2]: D

---

633 Ps 20: 2. RL: GR [46]-[47], MRM 417. AMS (12, 31, 114, 118a, 137, 141, 142b, 144, 146, 161). ES: Vl4770 217v. BEN: Ben33 (108v, 138v), Ben34 (51v-52r), Mc127 464, Mc426 101, Mc546 108, McB 29r, McV 246v, Ott 349r, PuL 87v, Ve (186v).

634 Ps 95: 6. RL: GR (580), MRM (365, 2: 242). AMS (136). BEN: Ben33 (119r), Ben34 (219r), McV 247r, PuC (617).

635 Cf. GREG: Tc (3433: inc., Missa Alcuini). Var.: SAC: Le (700), Va (33), GEL8: Ge (44), Rh (40), Sg (43).

636 Non inveni.

637 Ps 20: 6. RL: GR [2], MRM 417. AMS (13, 31, 117, 155, 164, 177*bis*). ES: Vl4770 217v. BEN: Ben33 (4v, 123v), Ben34 (24r), PuC 741.

638 Mt 16: 24. RL: GR [12], MRM 417. AMS (27b, 135, 141, 149, 152, 161). ES: Vl4770 217r. BEN: Ben33 (12r, 118v, 121v), Ben34 (217r), Mc127 465, Mc426 104, Mc546 109, McB 29r, McV 247r, Ott 349v, PuC (607, 650), PuL 88r, Ve (186v).

639

POSTCOMMVNIO Tua sancta sumentes domine suppliciter deprecamur. ut beati illius martiris tui. cuius celebramus passionem. sentiamus protectionem. per.

640

ALIA POSTCOMMVNIO Presta quesumus domine. ut sacramenti tui uegetati participatione. sancti illius, martiris tui atque pontificis. patrociniis adiuuemur. per.

NATALE PLVRIMORVM MARTIRVM.

641

♪ Sapientiam sanctorum narrent populi et lau- [*lac.*]

<COMMVNE CONFESSORIS ET PONTIFICIS>

642

112r [*lac.*] | ♪ sacerdotii dignitas in eternum. Memento domine dauid. ♪

---

642 *lac. inter 111v-112r*

---

641 *Melodia ut* GR

642 *in*: DEFGEFGA

---

639 Var.: RL: MRM (356, 2: 215-216: expl. var.), SAC: Va (1002), GREG: Tc (3324), GEL8: En (1242), Ge (1365), Sg (1109), BEN: Mc426 (113).

640 SAC: Va (1015, 1072). GREG: Pa (821), Tc (3142). GEL8: En (1292, 1510), Ge (1422, 1643), Sg (1151).

641 Eccli 44: 15. RL: GR [25]-[26], MRM 419. AMS (113a, 125, 146, 156). ES: Vl4770 217v. BEN: Ben33 (105v, 113r, 123v), Ben34 (194v), Mc127 465, McV 247v, Ott 350r, Ve 188r.

642 Eccli 45: 30, Ps 131: 1. RL: GR [32] (*Statuit ei dominus*), MRM 430. AMS 171*ter*. Cf. ES: Vl4770 218v. BEN: Ben33 (9r), Ben34 (41r: ps. var.), Mc127 478, Mc546 109-110, McB 32r, McV 256v (ps. var.), Ott 358r-v, PuL 93v, Ve 189v.

643

Da quesumus omnipotens deus. ut beati .illius. confessoris tui atque
pontificis ueneranda sollempnitas, et deuotionem nobis augeat et
salutem. per.

644

ALIA ORATIO Deus qui beatum illum. pontificem tuum ad regna transtu-
listi celestia. da nobis per gloriosa eius merita. ad gaudia transire
perhennia. per.

645

SAPIENTIE [*cento* Eccli 44: 16-45: 20]. Ecce sacerdos magnus, qui in
diebus suis placuit deo. et inuentus est iustus. et in tempore iracundie
factus est reconciliatio. Non est inuentus similis illi. qui conseruaret
legem excelsi. Ideo iureiurando. fecit illum dominus crescere in
plebem suam. Benedictionem omnium gentium dedit illi; et testamentum suum confirmauit super caput eius. Cognouit eum in benedictio-
nibus suis. conseruauit illi misericordiam suam et inuenit gratiam
112v coram oculis domini. Magnificauit eum in conspectu regum. | et dedit
illi coronam glorie. Statuit illi testamentum sempiternum. et dedit illi
sacerdotium magnum, et beatificauit illum in gloria. Fungi sacerdotio,
et habere laudem in nomine ipsius. Et offerre illi incensum dignum in
odorem suauitatis.

646

EPISTOLA [Hebr 7: 23]. Fratres. Plures facti sunt sacerdotes secundum.

---

643 RL: MRM 430. SAC: Le (785), Va (968). GREG: Ha (79, 652), Pa (46, 612,
618), Sp 1233, Tc 3309. GEL8: En (85, 1189, 1346), Ge (73, 1476), Sg (73, 1205).
ES: Vl4770 218v (var.). BEN: DaZ 46, Mc127 478, Mc426 111, McB 22v, McV
257r, Ott 358v, PuL 93v, Ve 190r.

644 Non inveni.

645 Eccli 44: 16, 17, 20, 22, 25-27, 45: 2, 3, 6, 8, 19, 20. RL: MRM 433. GREG:
Z6 XXXVII.Ep, Mu 159, WuC 182, CoP 460. BEN: DaZ 46-48, Mc127 479, McB
32r-v, McV 257r, Ott 358v-359r, PuC (755), PuL 93v-94r, Ve 190r.

646 Hebr 7: 23. RL: MRM 433. LEC: Mu 159. BEN: Ben33 (15v), Mc127 480,
Mc426 (114), McB 32v-33r, McV 258r, Ott 360r, PuL (88v), Ve (192r).

647

GRADVALE ♪ Ecce sacerdos magnus qui in diebus suis placuit deo. VERSVS
Non est inuentus similis illi qui conseruaret legem excelsi. ♪

648

♪ Alleluia. VERSVS Inueni dauid seruum meum oleo sancto meo unxi eum. ♪

649

113r ♪ Alleluia. | VERSVS Elegit te dominus sibi in sacerdotem magnum in populo
suo. ♪

650

SEQVENTIA SANCTI EVANGELII SECVNDVM MATHEVM [25: 14-23]. In illo
tempore. Dixit iesus discipulis suis parabolam hanc. Homo quidam
113v peregre ... | ... intra in gaudium domini tui.

---

650 alia quinque] alia quinque talenta *Vulgata* (25: 20)   tradidisti michi] mihi
tradidisti (25: 20)   serue bone] bone serve (25: 21)   in pauca] super pauca
(25: 21)   supra multa] super multa (25: 21)   domini] domini tui (25: 21)
superlucratus] lucratus (25: 22)

---

647 *su*is: AGAcAFAGFGF   *placuit*: FGAGcABcBAGABAG   de*o*:
FDFGAGFEGAFAGAGF   il*li*: dcAcdcdcAcdfgfdecAcBdecedcedcBA

648 *Al*leluia: D   *Inue*ni: DFGAGFG   *da*uid: DFGAFDGFECDFDFDFC

649 *Vide Intro. p. 176*

---

647 Eccli 44: 16, 20. RL: GR [32]-[33], MRM 434. AMS (16a, 129a). ES: Vl4770
218v. BEN: Ben33 (6r), Ben34 (28v), DaZ 48, Mc127 480, Mc546 110, McB 33r,
McV 258r, Ott 360r, PuC 756, PuL 94v.

648 Ps 88: 21. RL: GR (514-515), MRM 434. AMS (16a, 170). BEN: Ben33 (6r),
Ben34 (212r), Ben38 164r, Mc127 480, Mc546 112, McV 258v, Ott 360v, PuL
94v, Ve 190v.

649 1 Reg 2: 28. AMS (132, 170). ES: Schlager, *Katalog* D 28. LS: Gs 223. BEN:
Ben34 (28v), Ben35 178v, Ben39 (174r), Mc127 480, Mc546 113, McB 33r, McV
258v, Ott 360v, PuC (757).

650 Mt 25: 14-23. RL: MRM 435. GREG: Z6 XXXVII.Ev, Mu 159. BEN: DaE 147v,
DaK 55r, Mc127 481-482, McB 33v, McV 259v-260r, Ott 361r, PuL (92r-93r),
Ve 190v.

651

MATHEVM [24: 42-47]. In illo tempore. Dixit iesus discipulis suis.
114r Vigilate ergo quia nescitis ... | dico uobis. quoniam; super omnia bona
sua constituet eum.

652

OFFERTORIVM ♪ Veritas mea et misericordia mea cum ipso et in nomine meo
exaltabitur cornu eius. ♪

653

OFFERTORIVM ♪ Inueni dauid seruum meum et in oleo sancto unxi eum manus
enim mea auxiliabitur ei et brachium meum confortabit eum. ♪

654

SECRETA Hostias quesumus domine quas in sancti .illius. cofessoris tui
atque pontificis sollempnitate sacris altaribus exhibemus. propitius
intende. ut nobis indulgentiam largiendo. tuo nomini, dent honorem.
per.

---

651 perfodi] perfodiri *Vulgata* (24: 43)   ideo] ideoque (24: 44)   nescitis qua
hora] qua nescitis hora (24: 44)   super] supra (24: 45)

653 in *add. alia manu*

---

652 *cornu*: EFGFE

653 *seruum*: BdcBc   *et in*: GA] *om. GR*   *sanc*to: cB   eum[1]: cdcB   *mea*:
AcAdcBcB   auxi*li*abitur: cB   bra*chium*: GAcBcB   me*um*[2]: BdcAGA

---

651 Mt 24: 42-47. RL: MRM 435. LEC: Mu 158. ES: Vl4770 218v. BEN: Ben33 (16r),
DaE 146v, Mc127 486-487, Mc426 112, McB 33r, McV 259r-v, Ott 360v, PuC
(758), PuL 94v-95r, Ve 191r.

652 Ps 88: 25. RL: GR [6], [44], MRM 437. AMS 171. ES: Vl4770 (219r). BEN:
Ben33 (9r, 16r, 114v), Ben34 (41v-42r), Mc127 483, Mc426 112, Mc546 113,
McB 34r, McV 260r, Ott 362r, PuL (93r).

653 Ps 88: 21-22. RL: GR [34], MRM 437. AMS (16a, 170). ES: Vl4770 218v. BEN:
Ben33 (6r, 116r), Ben34 (28v-29r), DaZ 49, Mc127 483, Mc546 113, McB
33v-34r, McV 260r, Ott 362r, PuC (759), PuL 95r, Ve 190v.

654 RL: MRM (274: m. v.). SAC: Va (1207). GREG: Pa (629), Sp (1166). GEL8: En
(1249), Ge (1372), Rh (796), Sg (1116). AM: Sb (1076). BEN: Mc127 483, McB
22v, McV 260r, Ott 362r.

655

SECRETA Sicut beati illius; confessoris domine atque pontificis. merita tibi sunt acceptabilia. ita eo optinente sacrificia nostra tibi sint placabilia. per.

656

114v COMMVNIO ♪ Domine quinque talenta tradidisti michi ecce | alia quinque superlucratus sum. euge serue fidelis quia in pauca fuisti fidelis supra multa te constituam intra in gaudium domini tui. ♪

657

COMMVNIO ♪ Fidelis seruus et prudens quem constituit dominus super familiam suam ut det illis in tempore tritici mensura. ♪

658

POSTCOMMVNIO Presta quesumus omnipotens deus. ut de perceptis muneribus gratias exhibentes. intercedente beato .illo. confessore tuo atque pontifice. beneficia potiora sumamus.

659

ALIA POSTCOMMVNIO Purificent nos domine sacramenta que sumpsimus. et intercedente beato .illo. confessore tuo atque pontifice. a cunctis efficiamur uitiis absolutos. per.

---

656 Domi*ne*: cA   tradi*di*sti: ede   *alia*: ede   superlu*cra*tus: Acd   *euge*: dfde   *consti*tuam: dcdede   gau*di*um: cB

657 *consti*tuit: dcde   famili*am*: B   *il*lis: cdA   *men*sura: B

---

655 Non inveni.

656 **Mt 25: 20-21**. RL: GR (396-397), MRM 437. AMS (22, 131, 151, 166). BEN: Ben33 (9v, 116r), Ben34 (42r-v), Mc127 483, Mc546 114, McV 260r, PuL 95v.

657 **Lc 12: 42**. RL: GR [34]-[35], MRM 437. AMS (32, 170). BEN: Ben33 (16r, 116v), Ben34 (52v), DaZ 50, Mc127 483, Mc546 114, McB 34r, McV 260r-v, Ott 362r.

658 RL: MRM 431. GREG: Ha (81, 711), Pa (48, 685), Z6 XXXVII.3, Sp 1235, Tc 3311. GEL8: En (77, 1367), Ge (75, 1496), Rh (70, 859), Sg (75, 1222). ES: Vl4770 (219r). BEN: Ben33 (6r), DaZ 50, Mc127 484, McB 22v, McV 260v, Ott 362r, PuL 95v.

659 RL: MRM (382). SAC: Va (1216, 1367). GREG: Ha (695), Pa (668), Tc (2515). GEL8: En (1334), Ge (1427, 1463), Rh (1314: var.), Sg (1193). BEN: Mc127 (465), McB (21v), McV (247v), Ott (349v).

NATALE CONFESSORIS QVI NON EST SACERDOS.

660

♪ Os iusti meditabitur sapientia. et lingua eius ♪ [*lac.*]

<COMMVNE VIRGINIS ET MARTIRIS>

661

115r [*lac.*] | ♪ letitia et exultatione. adduc<en>tur in templum regi domino. ♪

662

SEQVENTIA SANCTI EVANGELII SECVNDVM MATHEVM [13: 44-52]. In illo tempore. Dixit iesus discipulis suis. parabolam hanc. Simile est 115v regnum celorum. thesauro ... | ... uetera.

663

MATHEVM [25: 1-13]. In illo tempore. Dixit iesus discipulis suis. 116r parabolam hanc. Simile est regnum celorum decem uirginibus ... | ... neque horam.

---

661 *lac. inter 114v-115r*

663 lampades] lampadas *Vulgata* (25: 1)   cum] dum (25: 10)   nouissime autem (autem *add. inter lin.*)] novissime vero (25: 11)

---

660 *Melodia ut* GR

661 *Vide Intro. p. 176*

---

660 Ps 36: 30. RL: GR [42], MRM 438. AMS (20, 139, 155, 164). BEN: Ben33 (16v, 123r), Ben34 (40r-v), Mc127 484, Mc546 109, McB 34r, McV 260v, Ott 362r, PuC (753), Ve (191v).

661 Ps 44: 16. RL: GR [62]-[63] (*Audi filia*), MRM 2: 270-271 (*Audi filia*). BEN: Ben33 (11v: Tr. *Adducentur*), Ben34 (45r *Adducentur*), Ben35 (21r), McV 263r (*Adducentur*).

662 Mt 13: 44-52. RL: MRM 445. LEC: Mu 164, CoP 487. ES: Vl4770 220r. BEN: Ben33 (93v), DaE 150r, DaK 56v, DaZ 59-61, Mc127 488, Mc426 118-119, McB 35r-v, McV 263v-264r, Ott 365r-v, Ott[1] 49, PuC (771), Ve 193r.

663 Mt 25: 1-13. RL: MRM 445-446. LEC: Mu 164, CoP 488, Z6 xxxix.Ev. BEN: DaE 151r, DaK 56r-v, DaZ 55-57, Mc127 488-489, McB 35v, McV 263r-v, Ott 365r, PuC (781), Ve 192v.

664

Offerentur regi uirgines.

665

OFFERTORIVM ♪ Filie regum in honore tuo astitit regina addextris tuis in uestitu deaurato circumdata uarietate. ♪

666

SECRETA Sacris altaribus domine hostias superpositas. quesumus; ut sancta uirgo tua et martir. in salutem nobis prouenire deposcat. per dominum.

667

COMMVNIO ♪ Feci iudicium et iustitiam domine non calumnientur michi
116v superbi ad omnia man|data tua dirigebar omnem uiam iniquitatis hodio habui. ♪

668

POSTCOMMVNIO Adiuuent nos domine quesumus. et hec misteria sancta que sumpsimus, et beate .illius. uirginis et martiris tue intercessio ueneranda. per.

---

664 *Add. alia manu beneventana*

---

665 *regum*: cdcAcAc   *honore*: cdcdc   tu*o*: dededcd   *astitit*: AcdcBcB
tu*is* AcB   *deaura*to: AcAcGFGAGA   uari*etate*: cBdcBcAGFAGFGF

667 *et*: GF   iu*stiti*am: E   calum*nien*tur: AGAB   *omni*a: GFD
*man*data: D   *dirige*bar: GFEDEGF

---

664 Ps 44: 15. RL: GR [54], MRM 446. AMS (3, 16*bis*, 23*bis*, 25, 30, 101, 140, 153, 165b, 169*bis*). BEN: Ben33 (minor 119v, major 11v, 120r), Ben34 (minor 4v-5r, major 30r-v), Mc127 489, McB 35v, McV 264r, Ott 365v, PuC (772), Ve 192v.

665 Ps 44: 10. RL: GR [63]-[64], MRM 446. AMS (23b, 145b). ES: Vl4770 220r. BEN: Ben33 (9v, 15r), Ben34 (43r), DaZ 57, Mc127 489, Mc426 119, Mc546 119, McB 35v, McV 264r, Ott 365v, PuC 772.

666 RL: MRM (439). GREG: Pa (846), Tc (3300). GEL8: En (1123), Ge (1234), Rh (741), Sg (996). BEN: Mc127 489, McB 23r, McV 264r, Ott 366r.

667 Ps 118: 121-122, 128. RL: GR [59], MRM 446. AMS (23b, 165b). BEN: Ben33 (9v-10r), Ben34 (43v), Mc127 489-490, McV 264r, Ott 366r.

668 RL: MRM (2: 213). SAC: Va (828). GREG: Pa 843, Tc 3396. GEL8: En 1659, Ge 1837, Rh 1046, Sg 1487. ES: Vl4770 220r. BEN: DaZ 61 (m. v.), Mc127 490, McB 23r-v, McV 264v, Ott 366r, PuC (775), Ve 192v-193r.

NATALE VIRGINIS QVI NON EST MARTIR

669

Dilexisti iustitiam et odisti iniquitatem.

670

Deus qui nos beate uirginis tue .illius. annua sollempnitate letificas. concede propitius, ut eius adiuuemur meritis. cuius castitatis irradiamur exemplis. per.

671

GRADVALE ♪ Dilexisti iustitiam et odisti iniquitatem. VERSVS Propterea unxit te deus deus tuus oleo letitie. ♪

672

♪ Alleluia. VERSVS Diffusa est gratia in labiis tuis propterea benedixit te deus in eternum. ♪

---

671 *Cruces add. ante Gr. et V.*

672 *Cruces add. ante All. et V.*

---

671 Dile*xi*sti: DG   *iusti*tiam: DGFGABABc   iniquita*tem*: FGAEFDGFA-
cAG   *deus*[1]: GFGAEFD   letiti*e*: cdBcAGBcGAGFABcBGBABAG

672 Al*leluia*: AGAcBAcAcdcAGBcGAGFABcBGBABAG   *in*[1]: B   *la*biis: B
*tu*is: BcBGABFGBAGAG   *propterea*: AGB   *benedixit*: B   *te*: B
*de*us: cAcBGABAFBAGAcdecAcdBcdBcGAGBAGAF   *in*[2]:   AFGA
eternum: AcBcABcAGFAcABcBcBABGBABAG

---

669 Ps 44: 8. RL: GR [60], MRM 441. AMS (3, 101, 169*bis*). BEN: Ben33 (15r, 119r), Ben34 (4r), Mc127 490, Mc546 115, McB 34v, McV 264v, Ott 366v, PuC (766), Ve 192v.

670 RL: MRM (2: 213). GREG: Pa 840, Tc (3393). GEL8: En 1656, Ge 1834, Sg 1484. AM: Sb 1212, 1221. BEN: Mc127 490, McB 23v, McO 493 (m. v.), McV 264v-265r, Ott 366v (m. v.), PuC (767), Ve 193r (m. v.).

671 Ps 44: 8. RL: GR ([52]), MRM 444. AMS (3, 101, 127, 169*bis*). BEN: Ben33 (15r), Ben34 (4r-v), DaZ 55, Mc127 (487), Mc546 116, McV (262r), Ott (364v), PuC (769), Ve 192v.

672 Ps 44: 3. RL: GR (405), MRM 445. AMS (3, 199b). BEN: Ben33 (9v), Ben34 (4v), Ben35 179v, Mc127 490, Mc546 118, McB 35r, McV (262v), Ott (364v), PuC (770).

673

117r OFFERTORIVM ♪ Offerentur regi uirgines post eam proxime eius. of|ferentur tibi. ♪

674

SECRETA Hec hostia <domine> placationis et <laudis> quesumus; ut interueniente beata. <illa uirgi>ne tua. sua nos propitiatione <dignos> semper efficiat. per.

675

COMMVNIO ♪ Diffusa est gratia in labiis tuis propterea benedixit te deus in eternum. ♪

676

POSTCOMMVNIO Sanctificet nos domine quesumus tui <perceptio sa>cramenti. et intercessione <illius uirginis> tue tibi reddat acc<eptos. per.>

---

673 *Crux add. ante Off.*   *117r: frag.*

675 *Crux add. ante Com.*

---

673 *uir*gines: FGEFE   *ei*us: DEFEDC   offe*ren*tur[2]: FDFGFGEFGDC

675 e*ter*num: FGAGF

---

673 Ps 44: 15. RL: GR (437), MRM 446. AMS (3, 16*bis*, 23*bis*, 25, 30, 101, 140, 153, 165b). BEN: Ben33 (minor: 119v), Ben34 (minor: 4v-5r), DaZ 57, Mc127 490, McB 35r, McV 265r, Ott 366v, PuC (772), Ve 193r.

674 RL: MRM (400). GREG: Ha (752), Pa (752). GEL8: En (1499), Ge (1633), Rh (948), Sg (1344). AM: Sb (322). BEN: Ben33 (32r), Mc127 490, McB 23v, McV 265r, Ott 366v, Ve 192v.

675 Ps 44: 3. RL: GR (559-560), MRM 446. AMS (3, 101, 169*bis*). BEN: Ben33 (119v), Ben34 (5r), DaZ 57, Mc127 490, Mc426 120, Mc546 119, McB 36r, McV 265r, Ott 366v, PuC (774).

676 RL: MRM (300). SAC: Le (842). GREG: Ha (698, 765), Pa (839, 671, 770), Tc (3385). GEL8: En (1337), Ge (1466), Sg (1196). AM: Sb (1114). BEN: DaZ 57, 61, Mc127 490, McB 23v, McV 265r, Ott 366v.

\<PLVRIMARVM SANCTARVM VIRGINVM\>

677

Sanctarum uirginum .illius. et \<illius.\> quesumus domine supplicationi\<bus nos fo\>ueri. ut quarum u\<enerabilem sollem\>nitatem festiuo \<celebramus obsequio.\> earum intercessio\<nibus commendemur et\> meritis. per dominum [*lac.*]

678

Intende \<quesumus domine munera altaribus\> tu\<is\> [*lac.*]

679

117v | \<Supplices\> te rogamus omnipotens deus. ut \<interueni\>entibus sanctis uirginibus tuis. \<illa et illa\>. et tua in nobis dona multi\<plices\> et tempora nostra disponas. per.

IN DEDICATIONE ECCLESIE.

680

♪ \<Terri\>bilis est locus iste hic do\<mus dei\> est et portas celi et uocabitur aula dei. Dominus regnauit decorem. ♪

---

679 *117v: frag.*

---

680 por*tas*: FG ce*li*: FGFDED uocabi*tur*: DFCA'C Ps.] Quam dilecta GR (*eadem melodia*)

---

677 SAC: Le (26), Va (1059). GREG: Pa (837). GEL8: En 1654, Ge 1829, Sg (1089, 1339). AM: Sb (18). BEN: DaZ 57-58 (m. v.), Mc127 491, McB 23v, McV 265r, Ott 366v.

678 RL: MRM 442. SAC: Le (1200), Va (845). GEL8: Ge (239), Sg (222). AM: Sb (951). BEN: Mc127 491, McB 23v, McV 265r, Ott 366v-367r.

679 RL: MRM (401). SAC: Le (766). GREG: Ha (759), Pa (761). GEL8: Ge (1644), Sg (1353). BEN: Mc127 491, McB 23v-24r, McV 265r, Ott 367r.

680 Gen 28: 17, Ps 92: 1. RL: GR [71]-[72], MRM 447. AMS 100. ES: Vl4770 224v. BEN: Ben30 102r-v, Ben34 (172v), Ben35 104v, Ben38 84v, Ben39 80v-81r, Ben40 62v, DaZ 62, Mc127 491, Mc426 120, McB 36r, McV 265r, Ott 367r, PuC 789 (ps. var.), Ve 127r.

681

ORATIO <Deus qui in>uisibiliter <omnia conti>nes. et ta<men pro salut>e generis humani signa <tue potenti>e uisibiliter ostendis. tem<plum hoc pot>entie tue inhabita<tionis illustra et concede> ut omnes qui hic depre<caturi conueniun>t. ex quacumque tri<bulatione ad te c>lamauerint. con<solationis tue b>eneficia consequantur. per.

682

ORATIO <Deus qui nobis per singulos annos huius sancti templi tui>. conse<crationis reparas diem et sacri>s sem<per> [*lac.*]

118r | MISSA. IN HONORE SANCTE TRINITATIS.

683

♪ Benedicta sit sancta trinitas atque indiuisa unitas confitemini ei quia fecit nobiscum. misericordiam suam. Benedicamus patrem. ♪

684

ORATIO Omnipotens sempiterne deus. qui dedisti famulis tuis in confessione uere fidei eterne trinitatis gloriam agnoscere. et in potentia maiestatis adorare unitatem; quesumus. ut eiusdem fidei firmitate; ab omnibus semper muniamur aduersis. per te indiuidua.

---

682 *lac. inter 117v-118r*

---

683 Benedic*ta*: AF   *sancta*: GAcBA   *con*fitemini: GA   Ps.] Domine Deus noster GR (*eadem melodia*)

---

681 RL: MRM 447. GREG: Ha 817, Tc 4151. ES: Vl4770 223v. BEN: DaZ 62-63, Mc127 491, Mc426 120-121, PuC 790.

682 RL: MRM 447. GREG: Sp 1262, Tc 4163. GEL8: En 2162, Ge 2483, Ph 1520, Rh 1201. ES: Vl4770 224v-225r. BEN: Ben30 102v, DaZ 62, Mc127 491-492, McB 24r, McV 265r-v, Ott 367r, PuC 807, Ve 127r.

683 Tob 12: 6. RL: GR [84] (vide 308), MRM 450. AMS 172*bis*. ES: Vl4770 220r. BEN: Ben33 138r, Ben34 (212v-213r), Ben35 (135v-136r), Ben38 (119v), Ben39 (105r-v), Ben40 (119v), DaZ 102-103, Mc426 23, McB 24v, McV 238v, Ott 368v, PuC 231, Ve 193v.

684 RL: MRM 450. GREG: Tc 1806 (Missa Alcuini). AM: Sb 1255. ES: F 1779, Vl4770 220v. BEN: Ben33 138r, DaZ 103, Mc426 23, McV 238v, 268v, Ott 368v-369r, PuC 232, Ve 193v.

685

AD PHILIPENSES [2 Cor 13: 11, 13]. Fratres. Gaudete perfecti estote. ... uobis. Amen.

686

GRADVALE ♪ Benedictus es domine qui intueris abyssos et sedes super cheru-
118v bin. VERSVS Benedicite | deum celi et coram omnibus uiuentibus confitemini ei. ♪

687

♪ Alleluia. Benedictus es domine deus patrum nostrorum et laudabilis in secula. ♪

688

SECVNDVM IOHANNEM [15: 26-16: 4]. In illo tempore. Dixit iesus discipulis suis. Cum uenerit paraclitus ... dixi uobis.·,

---

685 spiritus sancti sit semper] sancti Spiritus *Vulgata* (13: 13)

688 perhibebitis] perhibetis *Vulgata* (15: 27)   se obsequium] obsequium se (16: 2)

---

686 *intueris*: cdcAGcdcABAGBAGdcdcGABcBA   a*bys*sos: BcdcBAB   *et*: F
sedes: Ac   *su*per: cB   *cherubin*: AGcdcAFAGAGF   V. Benedicite:
Vide Intro. p. 177

687 F *inc.*] G *inc.* GR (*trans. passim*)   Allelu*ia*: FGFGFGBAFGFGFGBA-
FAcBAGFGFGBAGFGF   Be*nedic*tus: FA   *domine*: Gc   *deus*: cBA
pa*trum*: A   nostro*rum*: FBABcBA   *et*: AG   *laud*abilis: B   se*cula*:
FAFGFGFGBAF

---

685 2 Cor 13: 11, 13. RL: MRM 450. BEN: Ben33 138r, DaZ 103-104, Mc426 24, McB 24v, McV 238v, Ott 369r.

686 Dan 3: 55. AMS 172*bis.* ES: V14770 220v. LS: Gs c. BEN: Ben33 138r, Ben34 (213r), Ben35 (136r), Ben38 (119v), Ben39 (135v-136r), Ben40 (105v), DaZ 104, Mc426 24-25, McB 24v, McV 238v-239r, Ott 368r, PuC 234, Ve 193v. Var. (V.): RL: GR [84] (vide 308-309), MRM 450, ES: Syg 260.

687 Dan 3: 52. RL: GR [84] (vide 309), MRM 450. AMS 172*bis.* ES: V14770 220v. BEN: Ben33 138r, Ben34 (213r-v), Ben35 (136r), Ben38 (119v), Ben39 (136r), Ben40 (105v), DaZ 104, Mc426 25, McB 24v, McV 239r, Ott 369r, PuC 235, Ve 193v.

688 Io 15: 26-16: 4. RL: MRM 450. ES: V14770 220v. BEN: Ben33 138r, DaE (100v), DaK 58r, DaZ 104-105, Mc426 25, McB 24v, McV 239r, Ott 369r, PuC 236, PuL 90r, Ve 193v.

689

119r OFFERTORIVM | ♪ Benedictus sit deus pater unigenitusque dei filius sanctus quoque spiritus quia fecit nobiscum misericordiam suam. ♪

690

SECRETA Sanctifica quesumus domine deus per tui sancti nominis inuocationem huius oblationis hostiam. et per eam nosmetipsos. tibi perfice munus eternum. per dominum.

691

COMMVNIO ♪ Benedicimus deum celi et coram omnibus uiuentibus confitebimur ei quia fecit nobiscum misericordiam suam. ♪

692

POSTCOMMVNIO Proficiat nobis ad salutem corporis et anime domine deus huius sacramenti susceptio et sempiterna sancte trinitatis confessio. per te.

---

689 *Benedic*tus: GAcBdc unige *nitus*que: BdcAGFAGAFGE sanc*tus*: AcGc *quo*que: cABAGA spi*ritus*: BdcBcA *quia*: FA no*bis*cum: BdcAG mi*sericordiam*: FABGA

691 *deum*: GF ui*uentibus*: GFGA con*fitebimur*: GFDFEDGFD *quia*: GF *fecit*: EGF nobiscum ... suam: c *inc. ante corr.*, A *inc. post corr. (ut* GR*)* no*bis*cum: cAGAB

---

689 Tob 12: 6. RL: GR [86] (vide 309-310), MRM 450. AMS 172*bis*. ES: V14770 220v. BEN: Ben33 138r. Ben34 (215r-v), Ben35 (137v-138r), Ben38 (120v-121r), Ben39 (137r-v), Ben40 (107r), DaZ 105, Mc426 25, McB 24v, McV 239r, Ott 369r, PuC 237, PuL 90r, Ve 193v.

690 MRM 451. GREG: Tc 1807 (Missa Alcuini). AM: Sb 1257. ES: F 1781, V14770 220v. BEN: Ben33 138r, DaZ 105, Mc426 25-26, McV 239r, 268v, Ott 369r, PuC 238, PuL 90r, Ve 193v.

691 Tob 12:6. RL: GR [86] (vide 310), MRM 451. AMS 172*bis*. ES: V14770 220v. BEN: Ben33 138r, Ben34 (215v), Ben35 (138r), Ben38 (121r), Ben39 (137v), Ben40 (107r), Mc426 27, McB 24v, McV 239r, Ott 369r-v, PuC 240, PuL 90v, Ve 193v.

692 RL: MRM 451. GREG: Tc 1809 (Missa Alcuini). AM: Sb 1259. ES: F 1784, V14770 220v. BEN33 138r, DaZ 105-106, Mc426 27, McV 239r, 268v, Ott 369v, PuC 241, PuL 90v, Ve 193v.

DE SANCTA CRVCE.

693

♪ Nos autem gloriari oportet in cruce domini nostri ihesu christi in quo est salus
119v uita et resurrec|tio nostra per quem saluati et liberati sumus. Deus misereatur
nobis. ♪

694

ORATIO Deus qui unigeniti filii tui domini nostri iesu christi pretioso
sanguine uiuifice crucis uexillum sanctificare uoluisti. cocede quesumus, eos qui eiusdem sancte crucis gaudent honore. tua quoque ubique
facias protectione gaudere. per eundem.

695

AD PHILIPENSES [2: 8-11]. Fratres. Christus factus est pro nobis
obediens ... patris.

696

GRADVALE ♪ Xpistus factus est pro nobis obediens usque ad mortem mortem
autem crucis. VERSVS Propter quod et deus exaltauit illum ♪ [*lac.*]

---

695 exaltauit illum] illum exaltavit *Vulgata* (2: 9)   dedit] donavit (2: 9)
nomen quod est super] nomen super (2: 9)   flectatur] flectat (2: 10)
terrestrium] et terrestrium (2: 10)   dominus noster] Dominus (2: 11)

---

693 glo*riar*: E   *in*[1]: GE   ihe*su*: E   re*sur*rectio: E   *li*berati: GF   Ps.:
AGAFGAGE

696 *ad*: GBAGA   *autem*: cABcBAGABAG   cru*cis*: FDFGAGFEGAFA-
GAGF   il*lum*: dcAcdcdcGcdfgfdecAcBdecedcedcBA[*lac.*]

---

693 Gal 6: 14, Ps 66: 2. RL: GR [104] (vide 490-491), MRM 453. AMS (97*bis*, 150).
BEN: Ben33 (63r, 93v), Ben34 (112v), Mc426[1] 19, McB 24v, McV 267v, Ott 369v,
PuC 242, PuL 195r.

694 RL: MRM 453. GREG: Tc 1835 (Missa Alcuini). ES: F 1837. BEN: Ben33 (122r),
Mc426 19, McV 268v, Ott 369v, PuC 243, Ve 195r.

695 Phil 2: 8-11. RL: MRM 453. BEN: Ben (122r), Mc426 20, McB 24v-25r, McV
267v, Ott 369v, PuC 244, Ve 195r.

696 Phil 2: 8-9. RL: GR [104] (vide 196), MRM 453. AMS (97*bis*, 150). BEN: Ben33
(64v), Ben34 (115r-v), Mc426 20, McB 25r, McV 267v, Ott 369v-370r, PuC 245,
Ve 195r.

<MISSA SANCTI SPIRITVS>

697

120r [*lac.*] | ♪ alleluia. ♪

698

SECRETA Munera domine quesumus, oblata sanctifica. et corda nostra sancti spiritus illustratione emunda. per eiusdem.

699

COMMVNIO ♪ Factus est repente de celo sonus aduenientis spiritus uehementis ubi erant sedentes alleluia. et repleti sunt omnes spiritu sancto loquentes magnalia dei alleluia alleluia. ♪

700

POSTCOMMVNIO Sancti spiritus domine corda nostra mundet infusio. et sui roris intima aspersione fecundet. per eiusdem.

---

697 *lac. inter 119v-120r*

699 *Crux add. ante Com.*

---

697 al*le*luia: AGAFBABGA

699 repen*te*: A uehemen*tis*: B se*den*tes: AcB al*le*luia[1]: AcB *magnali*a: cAcBABcAG *alleluia*[2]: GcBdc *al*leluia[3]: GAB

---

697 RL: GR [94] (Ps 67: 29-30 *Confirma hoc deus*), MRM 452. AMS (106, 172*ter*). BEN: Ben33 (99v, 102r, 104r, 105v), Ben34 (189v-190r).

698 RL: MRM 453. GREG: Ha (521, 527), Pa (461). GEL8: Ge (1029), Rh (623), Sg (812). BEN: Ben33 (98v), DaZ 131, PuC (539).

699 Act 2: 2, 4. RL: GR [94]-[95], MRM 453, AMS (106, 172*ter*). BEN: Ben34 (191r), PuC (541).

700 RL: MRM 453. SAC: Va (650). GREG: Ha (525, 531), Pa (465), Tc 1824. GEL8: Ge (1033), Rh (627), Sg (816). BEN: Ben33 (99v), DaZ 131, PuC (542).

AD HONOREM APOSTOLORVM.

701

ORATIO Exaudi nos deus salutaris noster. et apostolorum tuorum petri et pauli et andree; et omnium apostolorum nos tuere presidiis. quorum donasti fideles esse doctrinis. per.

702

SECRETA Munus populi tui domine quesumus apostolica intercessione sanctifica. nosque a peccatorum nostrorum maculis indesinenter emunda. per.

703

POSTCOMMVNIO Quos celesti domine alimento satiasti. beatorum petri et pauli et andree. atque omnium apostolorum tuorum intercessionibus; ab omni aduersitate custodi. per.

AD HONOREM VNIVS MARTIRIS

704

120v | Presta quesumus omnipotens deus. ut nos beati illius, martiris tui. interuentione gloriosa commendet. ut quod nostris actibus non meremur. eius precibus assequamur. per.

705

SECRETA Suscipe domine munera propitius oblata. que maiestati tue beati illius. martiris tui comendet oratio. per.

---

701 SAC: Le (337), Va (936). GREG: Ha (601), Pa (547), Tc (3171, 3185). GEL8: En (1083, 1444), Ge (1199, 1578), Rh (916), Sg (1292). AM: Sb (975). BEN: Ben33 (112r).

702 RL: MRM (346). GREG: Ha (590), Pa (539), Tc (2705). ES: F (1099). BEN: Ben33 (111r).

703 RL: MRM (346). SAC: Va (850, 1261). GREG: Ha (592, 597), Pa (541, 871). GEL8: En (1063, 1772), Ge (1184, 1952), Rh (718, 1094), Sg (956). BEN: Ben33 (111r), PuC (572).

704 BEN: McB 21r, Ott (346r).

705 RL: MRM (382). SAC: Va (962). GREG: Ha (694), Pa (667). GEL8: En (1169), Ge (1287), Sg (1038). BEN: Ben33 (116v), McB 21v, McV (247r), Ott (349v).

706

POSTCOMMVNIO Beati illius martiris tui domine intercessione placatus, presta quesumus. ut que temporaliter gerimus. perpetua saluatione capiamus. per.

AD HONOREM PLVRIMORVM MARTIRVM.

707

Infirmitatem nostram quesumus domine, propitius respice. et mala omnia que iuste meremur. sanctorum tuorum; illius. et illius. intercessione auerte. per.

708

SECRETA Purificent nos hec sancta misteria domine deus et intercedentibus sanctis martiribus tuis .illo et illo. ab omni semper iniquitate custodiant.

709

POSTCOMMVNIO Vt tuis domine semper possimus inherere seruitiis. intercedentibus sanctis martiribus illo. et illo. ab omni nos quesumus aduersitate defende. per.

AD HONOREM CONFESSORVM.

710

ORATIO Exaudi domine preces nostras; et interueniente beato .illo. confessore tuo supplicationes nostras intende placatus. per.

---

706 SAC: Va (1093). GREG: Ha (493), Pa (436). GEL8: En (150, 1691), Ge (154, 967, 995, 1796), Rh (124), Sg (137, 789). BEN: McB 21v, McV (247v), Ott (349v-350r).

707 GREG: Ha (687), Pa (662), Tc 1921, GEL8: En (1338), Ge (1467), Sg (1197).

708 GREG: Ha (951), Pa (911), Tc (2611). GEL8: En (1915), Ge (2830), Ph (1357), BEN: Ben33 (13v), McB 22r, McV (249v), Ott (357v).

709 BEN: McB 22r, McV (250v), Ott (358r).

710 RL: MRM (303, 389: m. v.). SAC: Le (380). GREG: Ha (729), Pa (708). GEL8: En (1400), Ge (1537), Sg (1255).

711

122r SECRETA | Hostias domine quas nomini tuo sacrandas offerimus. sancti illius. confessoris tui prosequatur oratio. per quam nos expiari tribuas et defendi. per dominum.

712

POSTCOMMVNIO Beati confessoris tui .illius. quesumus domine suffragiis exoratus. percepta sacramenti tui nos uirtute defende. per.

AD HONOREM SANCTARVM VIRGINVM.

713

Tribue nos quesumus domine. sancte .illius. supplicatione foueri. ut eius semper et intercessionibus commendemur et meritis. per.

714

SECRETA Hec hostia domine placationis et laudis. quesumus interueniente beata .illa. sua nos propitiatione dignos semper efficiat. per.

715

POSTCOMMVNIO Sanctificet domine quesumus tui perceptio sacramenti. et intercedente beata .illa. tibi nos reddat acceptos. per.

---

711 *N.B.: 122r post 120v legendum est (vide App.)* 112 *add. in marg. inf. manu recent.*

---

711 RL: MRM (321, 348:m.v.). SAC: Le (368). GREG: Ha (595), Pa (544). GEL8: En (247), Ge (244, 1190), Rh (172, 723), Sg (225, 962). AM: Sb (872, 925). BEN: Ben33 (15v, 16r: m. v.), PuC (405, 580: var.).

712 GREG: Pa (848), Tc (3302). GEL8: En (918, 1688), Ge (888, 1842), Sg (713, 1513). AM: Sb (899). BEN: McB 22v, McV (260v), Ott (362r).

713 Non inveni.

714 RL: MRM (73, 400). GREG: Ha (206, 752), Pa (178, 752). GEL8: En (373, 1499), Ge (360, 1633), Rh (226, 948), Sg (327, 1344). AM: Sb (322). BEN: Ben33 (32r), McB 23v, McV (265r), Ott (366v), Ve (192v).

715 Cf. supra **676**. RL: MRM (300). SAC: Le (842). GREG: Ha (698, 765), Pa (671, 770, 839). GEL8: En (1337), Ge (1466), Sg (1196). AM: Sb (1114). BEN: McB 23v, McV (264v), Ott (366v).

AD HONOREM OMNIVM SANCTORVM.

716

Concede quesumus omnipotens et misericors deus. ut sancta uirgo uirginum maria. omnesque ordines angelorum. atque omnes sancti et electi tui. nos semper et ubique adiuuent. ut quorum suffragia pariter poscimus. eorum iugiter precibus, ab omni aduersitate liberari. re-
122v missionemque omnium peccatorum consequi. | et ad tuam misericordiam peruenire mereamur. per.

717

SECRETA Munera tibi domine nostre deuotionis offerimus. que ut tuo sint grata conspectui. beate marie semper uirginis. omniumque ordinum angelorum atque omnium sanctorum, quesumus intercessionibus adiuuari semper et ubique mereamur. per.

718

POSTCOMMVNIO Maiestati tue nos quesumus domine. beate marie semper uirginis. et omnium ordinum angelorum simulque sanctorum omnium supplicatio sancta conciliet. ut qui cotidie grauiter offendimus. cotidiana eorum ueneratione. et assidua intercessione saluari. remissionemque omnium peccatorum consequi. et ad tuam misericordiam peruenire mereamur. per.

AD HONOREM PRO QVORVM RELIQVIE HABENTVR.

719

ORATIO Propitiare nobis quesumus domine famulis tuis. per horum sanctorum tuorum. qui in presenti requiescunt ecclesia merita gloriosa.

---

716 BEN: DaZ 108, Mc127 503, Mc426 30-31, McV 271v, Ott 370v-371r. Var. (inc. =): GREG: Tc (1870: Missa Alcuini).

717 RL: MRM (var.: 361, 385, 396, 421). GREG: Ha (634: var.), Pa (589: var.), Sp (1231: var.), Tc 1866 (var.). GEL8: En (1173), Ge (1291), Sg (1042). AM: Sb (var.: 1193, 1248). BEN: Ben33 (124v: var.), Mc127 503-504 (var.), Mc426 31, McV 271v, Ott 371r, DaZ 108-109.

718 GREG: Tc (1890, 3662: var.). BEN: DaZ 109, Mc127 504 (var.), Mc 426 31, McV 271v (m. v.), Ott 371r.

719 RL: MRM 449. GREG: Tc 1877 (Missa Alcuini).

ut eorum pia intercessione ab omnibus semper muniamur aduersis. per.

720

SECRETA Oblatis domine placare muneribus. et intercedentibus sanctis tuis. a cunctis nos defende periculis. per.

721

121r POSTCOMMVNIO Diuina libantes misteria domine quesumus. que | pro horum sanctorum tuorum ueneratione, tue optulimus maiestati. presta quesumus; ut per ea ueniam mereamur habere peccatorum. et celestis gratie donis reficiamus. per.

MISSA PLVRALIS.

722

ORATIO Pietate tua quesumus domine; nostrorum solue uincula omnium delictorum. et intercedente beata et gloriosa semperque uirgine dei genitrice maria. et beato illo. cum omnibus sanctis. nos famulos tuos et loca nostra in omni sanctitate et religione custodi. omnesque consanguinitate ac familiaritate. confessione et oratione nobis coniunctos. seu omnes christianos, a uitiis purga. uirtutibus illustra. pacem et salutem nobis tribue. hostes uisibiles et inuisibiles remoue. pestem repelle. incredulos conuerte. inimicis nostris caritatem largire. et omnibus fidelibus uiuis et defunctis in terra uiuentium. uitam pariter et requiem eternam concede. per.

---

721 *N.B.: 121r post 122v legendum est (vide App.)*

---

720 RL: MRM (340, 421, 459). GREG: Ha (135, 176, 566, 761), Pa (116, 147, 515), Sp (1244), Tc (1883). GEL8: En (319, 976), Ge (314), Rh (227, 573), Sg (287, 1125). AM: Sb (292). BEN: Ben33 (25r), PuC (297), Ve 195v.

721 RL: MRM 449. GREG: Sp (1306: var.), Tc 1880 (Missa Alcuini). BEN: PuC (59: expl. var.), PuL (var.: 32r, 40v).

722 RL: MRM 473 (m. v.). GREG: Tc 3130. BEN: DaZ 111-112, Mc127 502-503, McV 279v, Ott 377v.

723

SECRETA Deus qui singulari corporis tui. hostia totius mundi soluisti peccata. intercedente beata et gloriosa semperque uirgine maria. et 121v beato .illo. cum omnibus sanctis. hac obla|tione placatus. maculas omnium scelerum nostrorum potenter absterge. et omnium christianorum uiuorum et defunctorum peccata clementer dimitte. eisque et nobis premia uite eterne concede. qui uiuis.

724

POSTCOMMVNIO Sumpta sacramenta quesumus domine omnia crimina nostra detergant. omnemque prauitatem et infirmitatem. seu etiam hostilem rabiem atque subitam mortem. necnon et impugnationem uisibilium et inuisibilium inimicorum. meritis beate dei genitricis marie. et beato .illo. cum omnibus sanctis. a nobis procul repellant. et omnibus fidelibus uiuis et defunctis prosint ad ueniam. pro quorum tibi sunt oblata salute. per eundem.

MISSA PRO PASTORE.

725

Concede quesumus domine famulo tuo episcopo nostro. ut predicando et exercendo que recta sunt; exemplo bonorum operum animas suorum instituat subditorum. et eterne remunerationis mercedem, a te piisimo pastore percipiat. per.

726

SECRETA Suscipe quesumus clementer omnipotens deus munera oblationis. et per uirtutem huius sacramenti, famulum tuum episcopum nostrum, cum |

---

726 *fin. in media*

---

723 RL: MRM 473 (m. v.). GREG: Tc 3131. BEN: DaZ 112-113, Mc127 503, McV 279v, Ott 377v.

724 RL: MRM 473 (m. v.). GREG: Tc 3132. BEN: DaZ 113, Mc127 503, McV 279v, Ott 377v.

725 ES: F (2865). LS: MWes (2: 1152).

726 GREG: Tc (2256: Missa Alcuini). AM: STripl (2977).

Appendix

RECONSTRUCTION OF THE MANUSCRIPT

Catchwords, hairside/fleshside correspondences, and the presumed length of missing texts have provided the clues for the following reconstruction of the original state of the manuscript. The hypothetical original gatherings are represented by Roman numerals; the modern foliation has been used to identify the leaves, although it does not respect the original order of the manuscript. The foliation is accurate for the manuscript as it is bound, e.g., fol. 121r-v now precedes fol. 122r-v, but they were vice versa in the original binding. Damaged folios lacking portions of text are designated as "fragments" in the accompanying figures.

I. Lost gathering or gatherings containing the Sundays of Advent.

II. Fols. 1r-4v: damaged gathering (4 of 8 fols. survive) lacking the first mass of Christmas (before fol. 1r), parts of the third mass (between fols. 3v and 4r), and the end of the Sunday after Christmas (after fol. 4v).

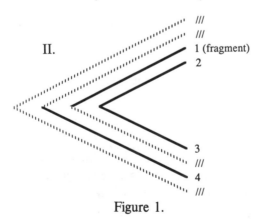

Figure 1.

III. Fols. 5r-11v: damaged gathering (7 of 8 fols. survive) lacking the beginning of the Marian mass within the octave of Christmas (before fol. 5r), but ending with the appropriate catchword "iustitiam" for the first folio of the following gathering (fol. 12r).

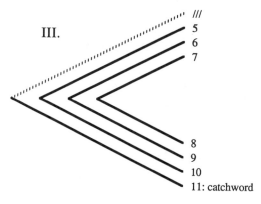

Figure 2.

IV. Fols. 12r-18v: damaged gathering (7 of 8 fols. survive) lacking part of Septuagesima (after fol. 18v).

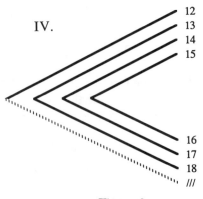

Figure 3.

V. Fol. 19r-21ᵃv: damaged gathering (4 of 6/8 fols. survive) lacking parts of Sexuagesima (between fols. 19v and 20r: probably no more than one folio lost containing the end of the epistle, the entire gradual and tract, and the beginning of the gospel for Sexuagesima), the end of Quinquagesima after the epistle, and the beginning of Ash Wednesday (between fols. 21v and 21ᵃr). Although the length of missing text suggests an irregular gathering of only six folios, the middle pair of folios (fols. 20r-v, 21r-v), which should open to the fleshside of the parchment in a gathering of three sheets, opens on the hairside, as one would expect in a regular gathering of eight folios. Thus, in a gathering of six folios, the missing folios between fols. 19v and 20r and fols. 21v and 21ᵃr would have been at variance with either the first or middle sheet in the otherwise standard progression of hairside and fleshside matches. For lack of further evidence, however, the textual and codicological conclusions must remain contradictory.

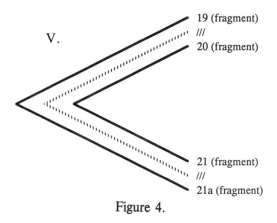

Figure 4.

VI. Fols. 22r-29v: regular gathering (8 fols.) with damage to fol. 22r-v and traces of a catchword (fol. 29v).

VII. Fols. 30r-35v: damaged gathering (6 of 8 fols. survive) lacking parts of the third Sunday in Lent (between fols. 31v and 32r) and parts of the fourth Sunday (between fols. 33v and 34r).

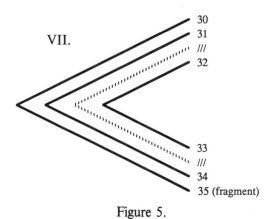

Figure 5.

VIII. Fol. 36r-v: damaged gathering (1 of perhaps 4 fols. survives) lacking the end of the fourth Sunday in Lent, the beginning of the Palm Sunday ceremony, including the incipit of the antiphon *Collegerunt* (before fol. 36r), and other blessings, exorcisms, and antiphons of Palm Sunday (after fol. 36v).

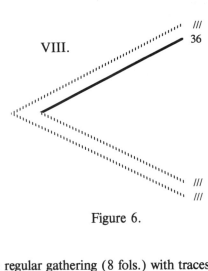

Figure 6.

IX. Fols. 37r-44v: regular gathering (8 fols.) with traces of a catchword (fol. 44v).

X. Fols. 45r-49v: damaged gathering (5 of 8 fols. survive) lacking parts of the Passion (between fols. 44v and 45r, and between fols. 46v and 47r) and the end of the mass of Holy Thursday (after fol. 49v).

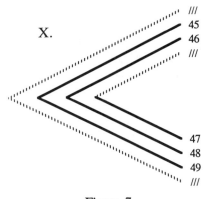

Figure 7.

XI. Fols. 50r-54v: damaged gathering (5 of 8 fols. survive) lacking the beginning of the Good Friday service (before fol. 50r) and the end of Holy Saturday (after fol. 54v).

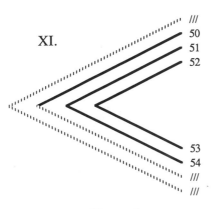

Figure 8.

XII. Lost gathering or gatherings containing Easter and the first to third Sundays after Easter.

XIII. Fols. 55r-60v: damaged gathering (6 of 8 fols. survive) lacking the beginning of the fourth Sunday after Easter (before fol. 55r).

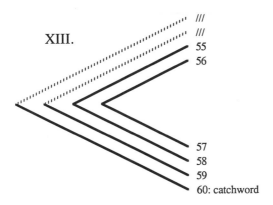

Figure 9.

XIV. Fols. 61r-66v: damaged gathering (6 of 8 fols. survive) lacking parts of Ascension (before fol. 61r).

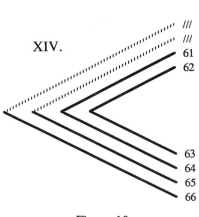

Figure 10.

xv. Fols. 67r-68v: damaged gathering (2 of 8 fols. survive) lacking the end of the first Sunday after Pentecost, all the fifth/sixth Sunday (before fol. 67r), the end of the seventh Sunday, and the start of the Sanctoral (after fol. 68v).

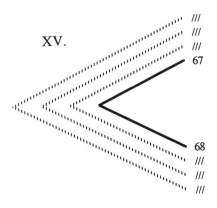

Figure 11.

xvi. Fols. 69r-71v: damaged gathering (3 of 8 fols. survive) lacking the beginning of the feast of Nicholas (before fol. 69r), the end of Nicholas, and other feasts of the Sanctoral before Christmas, including Thomas (between fols. 69v and 70r).

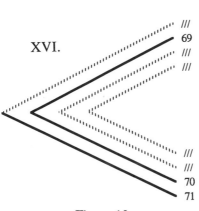

Figure 12.

xvii. Fols. 72r-73v, 74v-r: damaged gathering (3 of 8 fols. survive) lacking the feasts of Christmas week after Stephen (before fol. 72r), the end of the Conversion of Paul, and feasts before Blaise, including perhaps the Purification of the Virgin (after fol. 74v). Fol. 74r-v is bound in reverse, i.e., the text of the verso precedes the text of the recto.

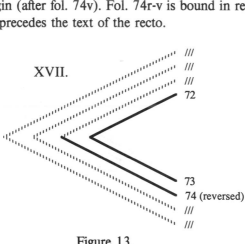

Figure 13.

xviii. Fols. 75r-81v, 91r-v: damaged gathering (8 of 9 fols. survive) lacking the start of the feast of Blaise (before fol. 75r). The added leaf (fol. 79r-v) presents some problems. Although it belongs at this point (the alleluia verse *Pretiosa* beginning fol. 79r carries over from fol. 78v and the gospel on fol. 79v carries over for two words onto fol. 80r), its contents are surprising (three gospels for the feast of George!) and its connections with the following folio not unambiguous, since fol. 80r begins on an erasure of three lines over which two words of the gospel from fol. 79v and the sequence *Eia caterua* have been written.

Could the scribe have originally written the conclusion of the alleluia verse *Pretiosa* and the incipit of a gospel on fol. 80r? Some confirmation of this possibility may be seen in an unerased custos in the right margin of fol. 80r, unsuitable for the present melody of the sequence but matching the final note of the alleluia (the custos in the manuscript was frequently used at the end of musical items as well as in its more usual position only at the ends of lines indicating the pitch of the first note of the next line: see the Introduction, p. 36). This arrangement was later modified: the alleluia verse and gospel incipits were erased, a new folio was added and the present texts written, including the end of the gospel on fol. 80r and the sequence. The sequence is unusual because it both follows the gospels and falls in the mass of George. It is proper to the feast of Mark in the three other codices in which it is found (Ben38, Ben39, Ben40). Perhaps fol. 79r-v was intended for the Common for a Martyr, and later adapted to its present position by some judicious erasing. Certainly the texts are appropriate, but the masses for a martyr and for a confessor in the manuscript are both complete at this point. If taken from another codex, it must have been by the same scribe, for the hand is indistinguishable. The hypothesis advanced in the Introduction (p. 138), that the gospels for George represent a Paschal Common, remains perhaps the most plausible explanation.

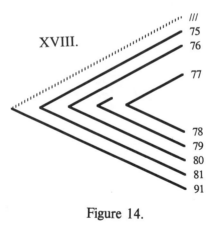

Figure 14.

XIX. Fols. 92r-95v, 82r-v: damaged gathering (5 of 7/8 fols. survive) lacking feasts between the Invention of the Cross and the vigil of John the Baptist, perhaps including the Invention of the Archangel, Barnabas, Bartholomew, and others (before fol. 92r). In the gathering, fol. 95r-v, though textually in order, is out of sequence in the otherwise regular arrangement of hairside and fleshside openings, suggesting that the folio was an added single leaf. The gathering, therefore, may have contained only seven folios originally with a lacuna of two folios at the beginning.

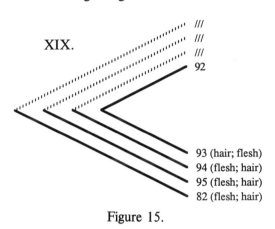

XIX.

/// /// /// 92

93 (hair; flesh)
94 (flesh; hair)
95 (flesh; hair)
82 (flesh; hair)

Figure 15.

xx. Fols. 83r-90v: regular gathering (8 fols.).

xxi. Fols. 96r-103v: regular gathering (8 fols.) with damage to fol. 103r-v.

xxii. Fols. 104r-105v: damaged gathering (2 of 8 fols. survive) lacking feasts between the Assumption of the Virgin and All Saints (before fol. 104r), and missing the feasts of November (after fol. 105v).

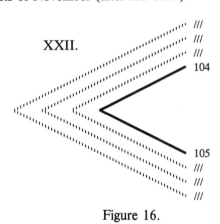

XXII.

/// /// /// 104

105 /// /// ///

Figure 16.

xxiii. Fols. 106r-v, 108r-v, 107r-v, 110r-v, 109r-v, 111r- v: damaged gathering (6 of 8 fols. survive) lacking most of the Common for an Apostle and the beginning of the Common for Apostles (between fols. 107v and 110r). The present binding and foliation confuses the original order of the gathering by placing the bifolium of 108r-109v inside the bifolium composed of fols. 107r-v and 110r-v; the foliation follows the modern, erroneous binding. Textual continuities indicate that the bifolia should be reversed, as is indicated in the following figure.

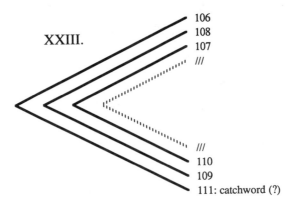

Figure 17.

xxiv. Fols. 112r-114v: damaged gathering (3 of 8 fols. survive) lacking most of the Common for Martyrs, the beginning of the Common for a Confessor-bishop (before fol. 112r), most of the Common for a Confessor-not-a-Priest, and perhaps other masses from the Common (after fol. 114v).

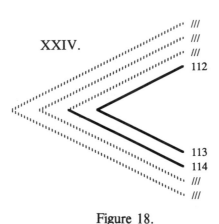

Figure 18.

xxv. Fols. 115r-119v: damaged gathering (5 of 8 fols. survive) lacking the beginning of the Common for a Virgin-martyr (before fol. 115r), and the mass for the dedication of a church (between fols. 117v and 118r).

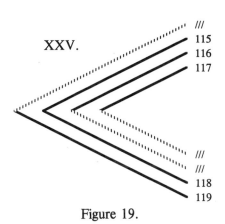

Figure 19.

XXVI. Fols. 120r-v, 122r-v, 121r-v: damaged gathering (3 of 8 fols. survive) lacking the end of the votive mass for the cross, the beginning of a mass for the Holy Spirit (before fol. 120r-v), and other votives (after fol. 121v); probably the last gathering of the original. The present binding and foliation does not respect the order of the texts: fol. 122r-v should precede 121r-v.

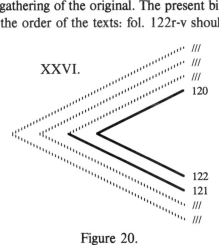

Figure 20.

Original Gatherings: I-IV^8, V$^{6/8}$, VI-VII^8, VIII$^{4(?)}$, IX-XVII^8, XVIII^9, XIX$^{7/8}$, XX-XXVI^8. Total: 202/205 fols.

List of Manuscripts Cited
(Including edited sources)

Altamura, Archivio Capitolare, Fondo pergamenaceo, cassetto A, Busta 3.
Angers, Bibliothèque Municipale, 92.
Arras, Bibliothèque Municipale, 230 (907).
Autun, Bibliothèque Municipale, 19 *bis.*
Avignon, Bibliothèque Municipale, 100.

Baltimore, Walters Art Gallery, W 6.
Bamberg, Staatliche Bibliothek, Lit. 53.
Bari, Archivio del Duomo, S.N. (rotulus: Benedictio fontis et ignis).
——, Archivio della Basilica di S. Nicola, S.N. (Proser of Sainte-Chapelle).
Benevento, Biblioteca Capitolare, 19 (= VI 19).
——, ——, 21 (= VI 21).
——, ——, 29 (see London, British Library, Egerton 3511).
——, ——, 30 (= VI 30).
——, ——, 33 (= VI 33).
——, ——, 34 (= VI 34).
——, ——, 35 (= VI 35).
——, ——, 38 (= VI 38).
——, ——, 39 (= VI 39).
——, ——, 40 (= VI 40).
Bergamo, Biblioteca di S. Alessandro in Colonna, 242.
Berlin, Deutsche Staatsbibliothek (Öffentl. Wissenschaftl. Bibl.), Phillipps 1667.
——, Staatsbibliothek Preussischer Kulturbesitz, Lat. fol. 920.
——, ——, Theol. lat. quart. 278.
Besançon, Bibliothèque Municipale, 184.
Brussels, Bibliothèque Royale, lat. 1960-1962.
——, ——, lat. 10127-10144.

Cambrai, Bibliothèque Municipale, 162-163.
——, ——, 164.
——, ——, 553.
Cambridge, Corpus Christi College, 286.
——, University Library, Nn.2.41.
Cologne, Bibliothek des Metropolitankapitels, 137.

Donaueschingen, Fürstlich Fürstenbergische Hofbibliothek, olim 192 (sold to an undisclosed buyer in 1982).
Dubrovnik, Franjevački Samostan Mala Braća, 5310/230/7, 8.
——, Dominikanski Samostan, Frag. (i).

Eichstätt, Bistumsarchiv, "Pontificale Gundecarianum II."
El Escorial, Real Biblioteca de San Lorenzo, R/III 1.
Exeter, Cathedral Library, 3502.

Florence, Biblioteca Medicea Laurenziana, Amiatinus 1.
——, ——, 29.8.
——, ——, 33.31.
Freiburg/Br., Universitätsbibliothek, 363.
Fulda, Landesbibliothek, Bonifatianus 1.

Geneva, Bibliothèque Publique et Universitaire, Comites latentes 195.
Göttingen, Universitätsbibliothek, Theol. 231.
Graz, Universitätsbibliothek, IV 9.
——, ——, IV 10.

Ivrea, Biblioteca Capitolare, 60.

Karlsruhe, Badische Landesbibliothek, Augiense 253.

Leningrad, Gosudarstvennaia ordena Trudovogo Krasnogo Znameni Publichnaia biblioteka imeni M. E. Saltykova-Shchedrina, lat. Q.v.I.16.
——, ——, lat. Q.v.I.41.
——, Sobrananie inostrannykh Rukopisei Otdela Rukopisnoi i Redkoi Knigi Biblioteki Akademii Nauk SSSR, F. no. 200.
Lille, Bibliothèque Municipale, 26 (olim 599).
London, British Library, Add. 12194.
——, ——, Add. 23935.
——, ——, Cotton Nero D.iv.
——, ——, Egerton 3511 (olim Benevento, Biblioteca Capitolare, 29).
——, ——, Royal 1.B.vii.
——, ——, Royal 2.B.iv.
Lucca, Biblioteca Capitolare, 606.
Lucerne, Stiftsarchiv S. Leodegar, 1912.

Macerata, Biblioteca Comunale Mozzi-Borgetti, 378.
——, ——, 1457, fasc. XII.
Madrid, Biblioteca Nacional, 52.
——, ——, 289.
——, ——, 678.
——, ——, 713.

——, ——, 715.
——, ——, 742.
Mainz, Seminarbibliothek, 1.
Milan, Biblioteca Ambrosiana, A 24*bis* inf.
——, ——, E 68 sup.
——, Biblioteca del Capitolo metropolitano, D 3-2.
——, ——, D 3-3.
Modena, Biblioteca Capitolare, O. I. 7.
Monte Cassino, Archivio della Badia, 127.
——, ——, 271.
——, ——, 318.
——, ——, 334.
——, ——, 361.
——, ——, 426.
——, ——, 451.
——, ——, 540.
——, ——, 546.
——, ——, Compactiones VI.
——, ——, Compactiones VII.
——, ——, Compactiones XXII.
Montpellier, Bibliothèque Universitaire (Faculté de Médicine), H 159.
Monza, Biblioteca Capitolare, c. 12/75.
——, ——, c. 13/76.
——, ——, f. 1/101.
——, Tesoro della Basilica s. Giovanni, 109.

Naples, Archivio di Stato, 4.
——, Biblioteca Nazionale, VI G 11.
——, ——, VI G 34.
——, ——, VI G 38.
——, ——, XVI A 19.

Oxford, Bodleian Library, Canon. Liturg. 325.
——, ——, Canon. Liturg. 333.
——, ——, Canon. Liturg. 342.
——, ——, Douce 222.
——, ——, Gough Liturg. 8.
——, ——, Misc. Lit. 366.
——, ——, Rawl. Liturg. e. 1*.

Padua, Biblioteca Capitolare, D 47.
Palermo, Archivio Storico Diocesano, 2.

Paris, Bibliothèque de l'Arsenal, 110.
——, ——, 160.
——, Bibliothèque Nationale, gr. 107.
——, ——, Coislin 186 (suppl. gr. 385).
——, ——, lat. 776.
——, ——, lat. 816.
——, ——, lat. 903.
——, ——, lat. 1084.
——, ——, lat. 1105.
——, ——, lat. 1118.
——, ——, lat. 2295.
——, ——, lat. 2301.
——, ——, lat. 7193 (see Vatican City, Biblioteca Apostolica Vaticana,
　　Reg. lat. 316).
——, ——, lat. 9433.
——, ——, lat. 9451.
——, ——, lat. 12048.
——, ——, lat. 12050.
——, ——, lat. 13246.
——, ——, lat. 17436.
——, ——, nouv. acq. lat. 1669.
——, ——, nouv. acq. lat. 2171.
——, Bibliothèque Sainte-Geneviève, lat. 111.
Parma, Archivio di Stato, Frammenti di codici 2.
Peterlingen, Comunalarchiv, S.N.
Prague, Knihovna Metropolitní Kapitoly, O. 83.

Rab, Nadzupski Ured, S.N.
Reims, Bibliothèque Municipale, 41.
Rome, Archivio Lateranense, 65.
——, Biblioteca Angelica, 123.
——, ——, F.A. 1408.
——, Biblioteca Casanatense, 614 (B III 7).
——, Santa Sabina, Archivio generale dell'Ordine Domenicano, XIV.L.1.
——, Biblioteca Vallicelliana, C 9.
——, ——, C 52.
——, ——, D 5.
Rossano, Biblioteca Arcivescovile, S.N. "codex Rossanensis."
Rouen, Bibliothèque Municipale, 274 (Y 6).

Sankt Gallen, Stiftsbibliothek, 348.
Split, Kaptolski Arhiv (Riznica Katedrale), D 624.

Trent, Museo Provinciale d'Arte, 1590.
Trogir, Kaptolski Arhiv (Riznica Katedrale), 2.
——, ——, 3.

Vatican City, Biblioteca Apostolica Vaticana, Vat. lat. 4770.
——, ——, Vat. lat. 5100.
——, ——, Vat. lat. 5319.
——, ——, Vat. lat. 6082.
——, ——, Vat. lat. 7231.
——, ——, Vat. lat. 7701.
——, ——, Vat. lat. 7818.
——, ——, Vat. lat. 10644.
——, ——, Vat. lat. 10645.
——, ——, Vat. lat. 10657.
——, ——, Vat. lat. 10673.
——, ——, Archivio S. Pietro, F 22.
——, ——, Barb. lat. 603.
——, ——, Barb. lat. 631.
——, ——, Barb. lat. 699.
——, ——, Borg. lat. 211.
——, ——, Ottob. lat. 145.
——, ——, Ottob. lat. 296.
——, ——, Ottob. lat. 356.
——, ——, Ottob. lat. 576.
——, ——, Pal. lat. 493.
——, ——, Reg. lat. 316.
——, ——, Reg. lat. 317.
——, ——, Reg. lat. 1997.
——, ——, Ross. 204.
——, ——, Urb. lat. 602.
Vercelli, Biblioteca Capitolare, 161.
Verona, Biblioteca Capitolare, 85 (80).
Vich, Museo Episcopal, 66.
Vienna, Österreichische Nationalbibliothek, 701.
——, Universität, Institut für Österreichische Geschichtsforschung, nr. 4.

Wolfenbüttel, Herzog-August-Bibliothek, Cod. Guelf. 112 Gud. Gr.
Würzburg, Universitätsbibliothek, M.p.th.f. 62.
——, ——, M.p.th.f. 68.

Zadar, Archiepiscopal Archives, S.N. "Codex monasterii S. Grisogoni"
    (missing since 1918).

——, Arhiv benediktinskog samostana sv. Marije, S.N. (Gregory I, *Moralia in Iob*).

——, Historijski Arhiv, Sv. 182, Poz. 4, list 4.

Zagreb, Metropolitanska Knjižnica (on deposit: Nacionalna i Sveučilišna Biblioteka), MR 166.

Zürich, Staatsarchiv, W 3 AG 19 (fasc. III).

——, Zentralbibliothek, C 43.

——, ——, Rh 30.

——, ——, Rh 80.

——, ——, Z XIV 4, nos. 1-4.

Bibliography

Acta sanctorum quotquot toto orbe coluntur, vel a catholicis scriptoribus celebrantur quae ex latinis et graecis, aliarumque gentium antiquis monumentis collegit, digessit, notis illustravit Joannes Bollandus (1600-1681). Ed. Jean Baptiste Carnandet. 2nd edition. 67 vols. Paris: V. Palmé, 1863-1925.

Altschul, Michael. "Conquests and Cultures, Norman and Non-Norman: Three Recent Studies." *Medievalia et Humanistica* ns 10 (1981) 217-222.

Amiet, Robert. "Un 'Comes' carolingien inédit de la Haute-Italie." *EL* 73 (1959) 335-367.

———. "La tradition manuscrite du missel ambrosien." *Scriptorium* 14 (1960) 16-60.

Amore, Agostino. "Dodici Fratelli." *Bibliotheca Sanctorum* (1964) 4: 669-670.

———. "Trifone e Respicio." *Bibliotheca Sanctorum* (1969) 12: 656-657.

Analecta hymnica medii aevi. Ed. Guido Maria Dreves, Clemens Blume, and Henry Marriott Bannister. 55 vols. Leipzig: O. R. Reisland, 1886-1922.

Andoyer, Raphaël. "L'ancienne liturgie de Bénévent." *RdCG* 20 (1912) 176-183; 21 (1913) 14-20, 44-51, 81-85, 112-115, 144-148, 169-174; 22 (1914) 8-11, 41-44, 80-83, 106-111, 141-145, 170-172; 23 (1919) 42-44, 116-118, 151-153, 182-183; 24 (1920) 48-50, 87-89, 146-148, 182-185.

Andreis, Josip. *Music in Croatia.* 2nd enlarged edition. Trans. Vladimir Ivir. Zagreb: Institute of Musicology, Academy of Music, 1982 (1st Croatian edition 1962).

Andrieu, Michel. *Le Pontifical romain au moyen-âge.* 4 vols. ST 86-88, 99. Vatican City: Biblioteca Apostolica Vaticana, 1938-1941.

———. *Les Ordines Romani du haut moyen âge.* 5 vols. Spicilegium Sacrum Lovaniense. Études et documents 11, 23, 24, 28, 29. Louvain: Spicilegium Sacrum Lovaniense, 1931, 1948, 1951, 1956, 1961.

Antiphonale sacrosanctae Romanae ecclesiae pro diurnis horis. Solesmes. No. 820. Paris, Tournai, Rome: Desclée, 1924.

Apel, Willi. *Gregorian Chant.* Bloomington: Indiana University Press, 1958.

"Aribonis De musica." See Gerbert.

Arnese, Raffaele. "Una notazione di derivazione beneventana esemplata nel codice musicale xvi-A 7 della Biblioteca Nazionale di Napoli." *Rivista delle Academie e Biblioteche d'Italia* 23 (1955) 263-269.

——. *I Codici notati della Biblioteca Nazionale di Napoli.* Biblioteca di Bibliografia Italiana 47. Florence: Leo S. Olschki, 1967.

Avagliano, Faustino. "I codici liturgici dell'Archivio di Montecassino." *Benedictina* 17 (1970) 300-325.

Avarucci, Giuseppe, Stefano Zamponi, Donatella Frioli, and Pietro De Leo. "Nuove testimonianze di scrittura beneventana." *Studi Medievali.* 3rd ser. 21 (1980) 423-452.

Avery, Myrtilla. *The Exultet Rolls of South Italy.* 2 vols. Princeton: Princeton University Press, 1936.

——. "The Beneventan Lections for the Vigil of Easter and the Ambrosian Chant Banned by Pope Stephen IX at Montecassino." *Studi Gregoriani* 1 (1947) 433-458.

Azevedo, Manuel de. *Vetus missale romanum monasticum Lateranense.* Rome, 1752-1754.

Babudri, Francesco. "Il Conte Amico di Giovinazzo: la sua impresa adriatica e la marineria apulo-normanna." *Archivio Storico Pugliese* 12 (1959) 87-137.

Bailey, Terence. *The Processions of Sarum and the Western Church.* Studies and Texts 21. Toronto: Pontifical Institute of Mediaeval Studies, 1971.

——. "Ambrosian Chant in Southern Italy." *Journal of the Plainsong and Medieval Music Society* 6 (1983) 1-7.

Balboni, Dante. "Il rito della benedizione delle palme (Vat. lat. 4770)." In *Collectanea Vaticana in honorem Anselmi M. Card. Albareda.* 2 vols. 1: 55-74. ST 219-220. Vatican City: Biblioteca Apostolica Vaticana, 1962.

Bannister, Henry Marriott. *Monumenti Vaticani di paleografia musicale latina.* Codices e Vaticanis selecti phototypice expressi, Series maior 12. Leipzig: O. Harrossowitz, 1913.

Baroffio, Bonifacio. "Liturgischer Gesang im Beneventanischer Raum." In *Geschichte der katholischen Kirchenmusik.* Ed. Karl Gustav Fellerer. Pp. 204-208. Kassel: Bärenreiter, 1972.

——. "Benevent." *MGG* 15: 643-656.

Baroffio, Bonifacio and Šime Marović. "Il sacramentario-rituale di Spalato e la tradizione eucologia latina." *EO* 4 (1987) 235-241.

Battelli, Giulio. "Il Lezionario di S. Sophia di Benevento." In *Miscellanea Giovanni Mercati.* 6 vols. 6: 282-291. ST 121-126. Vatican City: Biblioteca Apostolica Vaticana, 1946.

———. "L'orazionale di Trani." *Benedictina* 19 (1972) 271-287.

Benoît-Castelli, Georges. "Le 'Praeconium Paschale'." *EL* 67 (1953) 309-334.

Biblia sacra cum glossa ordinaria et interlineari ... et Postilla Nicholai Lyrani. 7 vols. Lyons, 1545.

Biblia sacra iuxta Vulgatam versionem. Ed. Robert Weber. 2nd revised edition. 2 vols. Stuttgart: Württembergische Bibelanstatt, 1975 (1st edition 1969).

Bibliotheca hagiographica Latina. See [Poncelet].

Bishop, Edmund. "The Litany of the Saints." In *Liturgica historica: Papers on the Liturgy and Religious Life of the Western Church.* Pp. 137-164. Oxford: Clarendon, 1918.

Blaise, Albert and Auguste Dumas. *Le Vocabulaire latin des principaux thèmes liturgiques.* Turnhout: Brepols, 1966.

Bloch, Herbert. "Monte Cassino, Byzantium, and the West in the Earlier Middle Ages." *Dumbarton Oak Papers* 3 (1946) 163-224.

———. "Monte Cassino's Teachers and Library in the High Middle Ages." In *La Scuola nell'occidente latino dell'alto medioevo.* Settimane di Studio del Centro italiano di studi sull'alto Medioevo, 15-21 aprile 1971. Pp. 563-605. Spoleto: Presso la sede del Centro, 1972.

———. *Monte Cassino in the Middle Ages.* 3 vols. Cambridge/Mass.: Harvard University Press, 1986.

Boe, John. "Rhythmic Notation in the Beneventan Gloria Trope *Aureas Arces.*" *Musica Disciplina* 29 (1975) 5-42.

———. "A New Source for Old-Beneventan Chant: The Santa Sophia Maundy in MS Ottoboni lat. 145." *Acta Musicologica* 52 (1980) 122-131.

———. "The Neumes and Pater Noster Chant of Montecassino Codex 426." In *Monastica. Scritti raccolti in memoria del XV centenario della nascita di S. Benedetto (480-1980).* 1: 219-235. Miscellanea cassinese 44. Monte Cassino, 1981.

———. "The Beneventan apostrophus in South Italian Notation, A.D. 1000-1100." *Early Music History* 3 (1983) 43-66.

———. "Old Beneventan Chant at Montecassino: Gloriosus Confessor Domini Benedictus." *Acta Musicologica* 55 (1983) 69-73.

Bonniwell, William R. *A History of the Dominican Liturgy.* New York: Wagner, 1944.

Bourque, Emmanuel. *Études sur les sacramentaires romains.* Pt. 1: *Les textes primitifs.* Studi di Antichità Cristiana 20. Vatican City: Pontificio Istituto di Archeologia Cristiana, 1948. Pt. 2: *Les textes remaniés.* 2 vols. 2.1: Québec: Presses Universitaires Laval, 1952. 2.2: Studi di

Antichità Cristiana 25. Vatican City: Pontificio Istituto di Archeologia Cristiana, 1958.

Brandi, Maria Vittoria, Cesarina Vighy, Maria Chiara Celletti, and Gian Dominico Gordini. "Biagio, vescovo di Sebaste in Armenia." *Bibliotheca Sanctorum* (1963) 3: 157-170.

Branner, Robert. "Two Parisian Capella Books in Bari." *Gesta* 8.2 (1969) 14-19.

Brett, Edward Tracy. *Humbert of Romans. His Life and Views of Thirteenth-Century Society.* Studies and Texts 67. Toronto: Pontifical Institute of Mediaeval Studies, 1984.

Brinktine, Johannes. *Sacramentarium Rossianum.* Römische Quartalschrift 25. Supplementheft. Freiburg/Br.: Herder, 1930.

Brou, Louis. "Les chants en langue grecque dans les liturgies latines." *SE* 1 (1948) 165-180; 4 (1952) 226-238.

———. "Étude historique sur les oraisons des dimanches après la Pentecôte dans la tradition romaine." *SE* 2 (1949) 123-224.

———. *The Monastic Ordinale of St. Vedast's Abbey Arras (Arras, Bibliothèque Municipale, MS. 230 [907], of the Beginning of the 14th Century).* HBS 86. London: Foundry Press, 1957.

Brown, Virginia. "The Survival of Beneventan Script: Sixteenth-century Liturgical Codices from Benedictine Monasteries in Naples." In *Monastica. Scritti raccolti in memoria del XV centenario della nascita di S. Benedetto (480-1980).* 1: 237-355. Miscellanea cassinese 44. Monte Cassino, 1981.

———. "A New Beneventan Calendar from Naples: The Lost 'Kalendarium Tutinianum' Rediscovered." *MS* 46 (1984) 385-449.

———. "A New Commentary on Matthew in Beneventan Script at Venosa." *MS* 49 (1987) 443-465.

———. "A Second New List of Beneventan Manuscripts (II)." *MS* 50 (1988) 584-625.

———. "*Flores psalmorum* and *Orationes psalmodicae* in Beneventan Script." *MS* 51 (1989) 424-466.

Brunner, Lance W. "A Perspective on the Southern Italian Sequence: The Second Tonary of the Manuscript Monte Cassino 318." *Early Music History* 1 (1981) 117-164.

Bruylants, Placide. *Les oraisons du Missel Romain. Texte et Histoire.* 2 vols. Études liturgiques 1, 2. Louvain: Mont-César, 1952.

Bryden, John R. and David G. Hughes. *An Index of Gregorian Chant.* 2 vols. Cambridge/Mass.: Harvard University Press, 1969.

Cagin, Paul. "Les évangiles de S. Nicolas d'Ossero." *Revue des Bibliothèques* 12 (1902) 41-73.

Cagin, Paul and Léopold Delisle. *Le sacramentaire gélasien d'Angoulême.* Angoulême: Société historique et archéologique de la Charente, 1919.

Cardine, Eugène. *Graduel neumé.* Solesmes: Abbaye Saint-Pierre, n.d.

Carraffa, Filippo and Maria Chiara Celletti. "Felicita e VII Figli, santi, martiri di Roma." *Bibliotheca Sanctorum* (1964) 5: 605-611.

Catalogus codicum hagiographicorum Bibliothecae Regiae Bruxellensis. 3 vols. Brussels: Polleunis, Ceuterick et De Smet, 1886-1889.

Cavallo, Guglielmo. *Rotoli di Exultet dell'Italia meridionale. Exultet 1, 2, Benedizionale dell'Archivio della cattedrale di Bari. Exultet 1, 2, 3 dell'Archivio capitolare di Troia.* Contributi sull'exultet 3 di Troia di Carlo Bertelli. Bari: Adriatica, 1973.

——. "Manoscritti italo-greci e cultura benedettina (secoli X-XII)." In *L'Esperienza monastica benedettina e la Puglia.* Atti del Convegno di Studio organizzato in occasione del XV centenario della nascita di san Benedetto, Bari, Noci, Lecce, Picciano, 6-10 ottobre 1980. Ed. Cosimo Damiano Fonseca. 2 vols. 1: 169-195. Università degli Studi di Lecce, Facoltà di Lettere e Filosofia, Istituto di Storia Medioevale e Moderna. Saggi e Ricerche 8-9. Galatina Congedo Editore, 1983, 1984.

Chavasse, Antoine. "Les plus anciens types du lectionnaire et de l'antiphonaire romains de la messe." *RB* 62 (1952) 3-94.

——. "Le calendrier dominical romain au VIᵉ siècle." *Recherches de science religieuse* 38 (1952) 234-246; 41 (1953) 96-122.

——. *Le sacramentaire gélasien (Vaticanus Reginensis 316). Sacramentaire presbytéral en usage dans les titres romains au VIIᵉ siècle.* Bibliothèque de Théologie, Série 4; Histoire de la Théologie 1. Tournai: Desclée, 1958.

——. "L'oraison 'Super sindonem' dans la liturgie romaine." *RB* 70 (1960) 313-323.

——. "Les fragments palimpsestes du Casinensis 271 (Sigle Z 6). A côté de l'Hadrianum et du Paduense, un collatéral, autrement remanié." *ALW* 25 (1983) 9-33.

——. "Cantatorium et antiphonale missarum. Quelques procédés de confection: dimanches après la Pentecôte. Graduels du sanctoral." *EO* 1 (1984) 15-55.

——. "Le sacramentaire de Monza (B. Cap. F 1/101)." *EO* 2 (1985) 3-29.

Chibnall, Marjorie, ed. and trans. *The Ecclesiastical History of Ordericus Vitalis.* 6 vols. Oxford: University Press, 1969-1981.

Codex diplomaticus regni Croatiae, Dalmatiae et Slavoniae. 17 vols. with revisions in progress. Zagreb: Jugoslavenska Akademija Znanosti i

Umjetnosti, 1874– . Vol. 1 (743-1100): revised edition by Marko Kostrenčić, Jakov Stipišić, and Miljen Šamšalović; Zagreb, 1967.

Codrington, Humphrey William. *The Liturgy of St. Peter.* LQF 30. Münster/W.: Aschendorff, 1936.

Coleti, Jacopo. *Illyrici sacri.* Vol. 6: *Ecclesia Ragusina cum suffraganeis, et ecclesia Rhiziniensis et Catharensis.* Venice, 1800.

Corbin, Solange. *Essai sur la musique portugaise au moyen âge, 1100-1385.* Collection portugaise 8. Paris: Les Belles Lettres, 1952.

——. "Neumatic Notations." *New Grove Dictionary* 13: 128-144.

Cornides, Augustine. "All Souls' Day." *NCE* 1: 319.

Costa, Eugenio Jr. "Tropes et séquences dans le cadre de la vie liturgique au moyen-âge." *EL* 92 (1978) 261-332, 440-471.

Cowdrey, H. E. J. *The Age of Abbot Desiderius. Montecassino, the Papacy, and the Normans in the Eleventh and Early Twelfth Centuries.* Oxford: Clarendon, 1983.

Creytens, Raymond. "L'Ordinaire des Frères Prêcheurs au moyen âge." *Archivum Fratrum Praedicatorum* 24 (1954) 108-188.

Crocker, Richard L. *The Early Medieval Sequence.* Berkeley: University of California, 1977.

Chronica monasterii Casinensis. See Hoffmann.

Dalton, John Neale. *Ordinale Exon. (Exeter Chapter MS. 3502 collated with Parker MS. 93) with two appendices from Trinity College Cambridge MS. B. XI. 16 and Exeter Chapter MS. 3625.* 2 vols. HBS 37-38. London: Harrison, 1909.

Décarreaux, Jean. *Normands, papes et moines. Cinquante ans de conquêtes et de politique religieuse en Italie méridionale et en Sicile (milieu du XIᵉ siècle-début du XIIᵉ).* Paris: Picard, 1974.

Décréaux, Joseph. *Le Sacramentaire de Marmoutier (Autun 19bis) dans l'histoire des sacramentaires carolingiens du IXᵉ siècle.* 2 vols. Studi di Antichità Cristiana 38. Vatican City: Pontificio Istituto di Archeologia Cristiana, 1985.

Delisle, Léopold. "Un livre du choeur normano-sicilien conservé en Espagne." *Journal des Savants* ns 6 (1908) 42-49.

Dell'Oro, Ferdinand. "Il Sacramentario di Trento." In *Fontes liturgici: Libri sacramentorum.* Ed. Ferdinando Dell'Oro et al. Pp. 1-416. Monumenta liturgica ecclesiae Tridentinae saeculo XIII antiquiora 2/a. Trent: Società Studi Trentini di Scienze Storiche, 1985.

Del Re, Niccolò and Maria Chiara Celletti. "Nicola (Niccolò), vescovo di Mira, santo." *Bibliotheca Sanctorum* (1967) 9: 923-948.

Demović, Miho. *Musik und Musiker in der Republik Dubrovnik vom Anfang des 11. Jahrhunderts bis zur Mitte des 17. Jahrhunderts.* Kölner Beiträge zur Musikforschung 114. Regensburg: Gustav Bosse, 1981.

Deshusses, Jean. *Le Sacramentaire grégorien: Ses principales formes d'après les plus anciens manuscrits.* 3 vols. SF 16 (2nd edition), 24, 28. Fribourg/S.: Éditions Universitaires, 1979, 1982.

——. "Hadrianum ex authentico ad fidem codicis Cameracensis 164." In *Le Sacramentaire grégorien: Ses principales formes d'après les plus anciens manuscrits.* 2nd edition. Vol. 1: Pars 1. SF 16. Fribourg/S.: Éditions Universitaires, 1979.

——. "Hadrianum revisum Anianense cum supplemento." In *Le Sacramentaire grégorien: Ses principales formes d'après les plus anciens manuscrits.* 2nd edition. Vol. 1: Pars 2. SF 16. Fribourg/S.: Éditions Universitaires, 1979.

——. "Gregorianum Paduense ad fidem codicis Paduensis D 47." In *Le Sacramentaire grégorien: Ses principales formes d'après les plus anciens manuscrits.* 2nd edition. Vol. 1: Pars 3. SF 16. Fribourg/S.: Éditions Universitaires, 1979.

——. "Additiones interpositae." In *Le Sacramentaire grégorien: Ses principales formes d'après les plus anciens manuscrits.* Vol. 1: Pars 4. Vols. 2-3. SF 16 (2nd edition), 24, 28. Fribourg/S.: Éditions Universitaires, 1979, 1982.

——. "Les messes d'Alcuin." *ALW* 14 (1972) 7-41.

Deshusses, Jean and Jacques Hourlier. "Saint Benoît dans les livres liturgiques." In *Le Culte et les reliques de saint Benoît et de sainte Scholastique.* Pp. 143-204. Studia Monastica 21. Montserrat: L'Abadia de Montserrat, 1978.

Deshusses, Jean and Antoine Dumas. *Liber sacramentorum gellonensis.* CCL 159-159A. Turnhout: Brepols, 1981.

Deshusses, Jean and Benoît Darragon. *Concordances et tableaux pour l'étude des grands sacramentaires.* 3 vols. (6 parts). Spicilegii Friburgensis Subsidia 9-14. Fribourg/S.: Éditions Universitaires, 1982-1983.

Devreesse, Robert. *Les Manuscrits grecs de l'Italie méridionale.* ST 183. Vatican City: Biblioteca Apostolica Vaticana, 1955.

Dirks, Ansgar. "De tribus libris manu scriptis primaevae liturgiae dominicanae." *Archivum Fratrum Praedicatorum* 49 (1979) 5-37.

——. "De liturgiae Dominicanae evolutione." *Archivum Fratrum Praedicatorum* 50 (1980) 5-21; 52 (1982) 5-76; 53 (1983) 53-145; 54 (1984) 39-82.

Dold, Alban and Anselm Manser. "Untersuchungsergebnisse einer doppelt reskribierten Wolfenbütteler Handschrift mittels der Fluoreszenz-Photographie." *Zentralblatt für Bibliothekswesen* 34 (1917) 233-250.

Dold, Alban. "Fragmente eines um die Jahrtausendwende in beneventanischer Schrift geschriebenen Vollmissales aus Codex Vatic. lat. 10645."
JLW 10 (1930) 40-55.

——. *Die Zürcher und Peterlinger Messbuch-Fragmente aus der Zeit der
Jahrtausendwende im Bari-Schrifttyp mit eigenständiger Liturgie.* Texte
und Arbeiten 25. Beuron: Beuroner Kunstverlag, 1934.

——. "Im Escorial gefundene Bruchstücke eines Plenarmissales in beneventanischer Schrift des 11. Jhs. mit vorgregorianischem Gebetsgut und
dem Präfationstitel 'Prex'." In *Spanische Forschungen der Görresgesellschaft.* 1st ser. Gesammelte Aufsätze zur Kulturgeschichte Spaniens.
Ed. Konrad Beyerle, Heinrich Finke, and Georg Schreiber. 5: 89-96.
Münster/W.: Aschendorff, 1935.

——. "Umfangreiche Reste zweier Plenarmissalien des 11. und 12. Jh. aus
Monte Cassino." *EL* 53 (1939) 111-167.

——. *Vom Sakramentar, Comes und Capitulare zum Missale: Eine Studie
über die Entstehungszeit der erstmals vollständig erschlossenen liturgischen Palimpsesttexte in Unziale aus Codex 271 von Monte Cassino.*
Texte und Arbeiten 34. Beuron: Beuroner Kunstverlag, 1943.

——. "Die vom Missale Romanum abweichenden Lesetexte für die Mess-
feiern nach den Notierungen des aus Monte Cassino stammenden Cod.
Vat. lat. 6082." In *Vir Dei Benedictus. Eine Festgabe zum 1400.
Todestag des heiligen Benedikt.* Ed. Raphael Molitor. Pp. 293-332.
Münster/W.: Aschendorff, 1947.

Dold, Alban and Leo Eizenhöfer. *Das Prager Sakramentar.* II. *Prolegomena
und Textausgabe.* Texte und Arbeiten 38-42. Beuron: Beuroner Kunstverlag, 1949.

Dold, Alban and Klaus Gamber. *Das Sakramentar von Monza.* Texte und
Arbeiten. Beiheft 3. Beuron: Beuroner Kunstverlag, 1957.

Douglas, David Charles. *The Norman Achievement 1050-1100.* London: Eyre
and Spottiswoode, 1969.

Drumbl, Johann. "Die Improperien in der lateinischen Liturgie." *ALW* 15
(1973) 68-100.

Duval-Arnould, Louis. "Un Missel du Mont-Cassin chez les chanoines du
Saint-Saveur de Bologne (Vat. lat. 6082)." *Rivista di Storia della Chiesa
in Italia* 35 (1981) 450-455.

Ebner, Adalbert. *Quellen und Forschungen zur Geschichte und Kunstgeschichte des Missale Romanum im Mittelalter. Iter Italicum.* Frei-
burg/Br.: Herder, 1896.

Falconi, Ettore. "Frammenti di codici in beneventana nell'Archivio di Stato
di Parma." *Bullettino dell'Archivio paleografico italiano.* 3rd ser. 2-3
(1963-1964) 73-104.

Farlati, Daniel. *Illyrici Sacri.* 8 vols. (vols. 1-5 by Farlati; vols. 6-8 by Jacopo Coleti.) Venice, 1751-1819. (See Coleti.)

Farmer, Hugh. "Tommaso Beckett, arcivescovo di Canterbury, santo, martire." *Bibliotheca Sanctorum* (1969) 12: 598-605.

Ferotin, Marius. *Le Liber Ordinum en usage dans l'église wisigothique et mozarabe d'Espagne du Ve au XIe siècle.* Monumenta Ecclesiae Liturgica 5. Paris: Firmin-Didot, 1904.

Ferrari, Filippo. *Catalogus Generalis Sanctorum qui in Martyrologio Romano non sunt.* Venice, 1625.

Fiala, Virgil. "Der Ordo missae im Vollmissale des Cod. Vat. lat. 6082 aus dem Ende des 11. Jahrhunderts." In *Zeugnis des Geistes. Gabe zum Benedictus-Jubilaeum 547-1947.* Pp. 180-224. Beiheft zur Benediktinische Monatschrift. Zur Pflege religiösen und geistigen Lebens 23. Beuron: Beuroner Kunstverlag, 1947.

Franz, Adolph. *Das Rituale von St. Florian aus dem zwölften Jahrhundert.* Freiburg/Br.: Herder, 1904.

——. *Die kirchlichen Benediktionen im Mittelalter.* 2 vols. Freiburg/Br.: Herder, 1909 (rpt. Graz: Akademische Druck- und Verlagsanstalt, 1960).

Frei, Judith. *Das ambrosianische Sakramentar D 3-3 aus dem mailändischen Metropolitankapitel.* Corpus Ambrosiano-Liturgicum 3. LQF 56. Münster/W.: Aschendorff, 1974.

Frere, Walter Howard. *Graduale Sarisburiense: A Reproduction in Facsimile of a Manuscript of the Thirteenth Century.* London: Bernard Quaritch, 1894 (rpt. Farnborough: Gregg, 1966).

——. *Bibliotheca musico-liturgica. A Descriptive Handlist of the Musical and Latin-Liturgical* MSS *of the Middle Ages Preserved in the Libraries of Great Britain and Ireland.* 2 vols. London: Bernard Quaritch, 1901, 1932 (rpt. Hildesheim: Georg Olms, 1967).

——. *Studies in Early Roman Liturgy.* II. *The Roman Gospel-Lectionary.* Alcuin Club Collection 30. Oxford, London: Oxford University Press, Humphrey Milford, 1934.

——. *Studies in Early Roman Liturgy.* III. *The Roman Epistle-Lectionary.* Alcuin Club Collection 32. Oxford, London: Oxford University Press, Humphrey Milford, 1935.

Frere, Walter Howard and Langton E. G. Brown. *The Hereford Breviary from the Rouen Edition of 1505 with Collation of* MSS. 3 vols. HBS 26, 40, 46. London: Harrison, 1904, 1911, 1915.

Gajard, Joseph. *Le Codex 10673 de la Bibliothèque Vaticane. Fonds latin (XIe siècle). Graduel bénéventain.* Paléographie Musicale 14. Solesmes: Abbaye Saint-Pierre, 1931.

——. *Le Codex VI.34 de la Bibliothèque capitulaire de Bénévent (XIe-XIIe siècle). Graduel de Bénévent avec prosaire et tropaire.* Paléographie Musicale 15. Solesmes: Abbaye Saint-Pierre, 1937.

——. "Le Chant de l'Exultet." *Revue grégorienne* 29 (1950) 50-69.

——. "Les récitations modales des 3e et 4e modes dans les manuscrits bénéventains et aquitains." *Études grégoriennes* 1 (1954) 9-45.

——. *Le Graduel romain.* 2 vols. (numbered 2 and 4). Vol. 2: *Les sources.* Vol. 4/1: *Le Texte neumatique. Le Groupement des manuscrits.* Vol. 4/2: *Le Texte neumatique. Les Relations généalogiques.* Solesmes: Abbaye Saint-Pierre, 1957-1962.

Gamber, Klaus. "Die mittelitalienisch-beneventanischen Plenarmissalien." *SE* 9 (1957) 265-285.

——. "Die Sonntagsmessen nach Pfingsten im Cod. VI 33 von Benevent." *EL* 74 (1960) 428-431.

——. "Väterlesungen innerhalb der Messe in beneventanischen Messbüchern." *EL* 74 (1960) 163-165.

——. "Das kampanische Messbuch als Vorläufer des Gelasianum: Ist der hl. Paulinus von Nola der Verfasser?" *SE* 12 (1961) 5-111.

——. "Das einsame 'Oremus' vor dem Offertorium." *Heiliger Dienst* 15 (1961) 22-23.

——. "Fragment eines mittelitalienischen Plenarmissale aus dem 8. Jahrhundert." *EL* 76 (1962) 335-341.

——. "Die kampanische Lektionsordnung." *SE* 13 (1962) 326-352.

——. "La liturgia delle diocesi dell'Italia centro-meridionale dal IX all'XI secolo." In *Vescovi e diocesi in Italia nel medioevo (sec. IX-XIII).* Atti del II Convegno di Storia della Chiesa in Italia, Roma, 5-9 settembre 1961. Pp. 145-156. Italia sacra: Studi e documenti di storia ecclesiastica 5. Padua: Antenore, 1964.

——. "Das Messbuch des hl. Paulinus von Nola." *Heiliger Dienst* 20 (1966) 17-25.

——. *Codices liturgici latini antiquiores.* 2nd edition. 1 vol. in 2 parts. Spicilegii Friburgensis Subsidia 1. Fribourg/S.: Éditions Universitaires, 1968 (1st edition 1963).

——. "Das altkampanische Sakramentar. Neue Fragmente in angelsächsicher Überlieferung." *RB* 79 (1969) 329-342.

——. "Das Basler Fragment. Eine weitere Studie zum altkampanischen Sakramentar und zu dessen Präfationen." *RB* 81 (1971) 14-29.

——. "Die griechisch-lateinischen Mess-Libelli in Süditalien." In *La Chiesa greca in Italia dal'VIII al XVI secolo.* Atti del Convegno Storico Interecclesiale, Bari, 30 aprile-4 maggio 1969. Ed. Michele Maccarrone, Gérard Gilles Meersseman, Alessandro Passerin d'Entrèves, and Paolo

Sambin. 3 vols. 3: 1299-1306. Italia Sacra 20-22. Padua: Antenore, 1972-1973.

——. "Fragmenta Liturgica v.29: Fragmente eines beneventanischen Missale in Montecassino." *SE* 21 (1972-1973) 241-247.

——. "Fragmente eines Missale Beneventanum als Palimpsestblätter des Cod. Ottob. Lat. 576." *RB* 84 (1974) 367-372.

——. "Benevento, Liturgy." *DMA* (1983) 2: 180-181.

Gamber, Klaus and Sieghild Rehle. *Manuale Casinense (Cod. Ottob. lat. 145).* Textus patristici et liturgici 13. Regensburg: Pustet, 1977.

——. "Fragmenta Liturgica vi.40: Fragmente eines Gregorianums in Split." *SE* 23 (1978-1979) 298-303.

[Gennadius of Marseilles]. *De viris inlustribus.* Ed. Ernest Cushing Richardson. In TU 14.1: 57-112. Leipzig: Hinrichs, 1896. (See also PL 58: 1059-1120.)

Gerbert, Martin. "Aribonis De musica." In *Scriptores ecclesiastici de musica sacra potissimum.* 3 vols. 2: 197-230. St. Blasien, 1784 (rpt. Milan: Bollettino bibliografico musicale, 1931).

Gjerløw, Lilli. *'Adoratio crucis': The Regularis concordia and the Decreta of Lanfranci.* Oslo: Norwegian Universities Press, 1981.

Gleeson, Philip. "Dominican Liturgical Manuscripts before 1254." *Archivum Fratrum Praedicatorum* 42 (1972) 81-135.

Glossa ordinaria. See *Biblia sacra cum glossa ordinaria.*

Gould, Karen. "The Sequences *De sanctis reliquiis* as Sainte-Chapelle Inventories." *MS* 43 (1981) 315-341.

Gozzi, Giorgio. *La Libera e sovrana Repubblica di Ragusa, 634-1814.* Rome: Volpe, 1981.

Graduale sacrosanctae Romanae ecclesiae de Tempore et de Sanctis ss. D. N. Pii X pontificis maximi iussu restitutum et editum ad exemplar editionis typicae concinnatum et rhythmicis signis a Solesmensibus monachis diligenter ornatum. cum *Missae propriae Ordinis S. Benedicti.* No. 696A. Paris, Tournai, Rome: Desclée, 1952.

Gräf, Hermann J. *Palmenweihe und Palmenprozession in der lateinischen Liturgie.* Veröffentlichungen des Missionpriester-Seminars St. Augustin Siegburg 5. Kaldenkirchen: Steyler Verlag, 1959.

Grégoire, Réginald. *Prières liturgiques médiévales en l'honneur de saint Benoît, de sainte Scholastique et de saint Maur.* Studia Anselmiana 54. Rome: Herder, 1965.

——. "Repertorium Liturgicum Italicum." *Studi Medievali.* 3rd ser. 9 (1968) 463-592; 11 (1970) 537-556; 14 (1973) 1123-1132.

——. "Le Mont-Cassin dans la réforme de l'Eglise de 1049 à 1122." In *Il Monachesimo e la riforma ecclesiastica (1049-1122).* Atti della quarta settimana internazionale di studio Mendola, 23-29 agosto 1968. Pp. 21-44. Miscellanea del Centro di Studi Medioevali 6; Publicazioni dell'Università cattolica de Sacro Cuore, ser. 3, var. 7. Milan: Editrice vita e pensiero, 1971.

Gregory I, Pope. *Dialogues.* See Vogüé, Adalbert de.

Guerrini, Francisco M., ed. *Ordinarium juxta ritum sacri Ordinis Fratrum Praedicatorum jussu Rev.mi Patris Fr. Ludovici Theissling eiusdem Ordinis Magistri Generalis editum.* Rome: Apud Collegium Angelicum, 1921.

Gunjača, Stjepan. *Ispravci i dopune starijoj hrvatskoj historiji.* 4 vols. Zagreb: Školska Knjiga, 1973-1978.

Gyug, Richard F. *An Edition of Leningrad, B.A.N., F. no. 200: The Lectionary and Pontifical of Kotor.* Diss. Toronto, 1983.

———. "A Pontifical of Benevento (Macerata, Biblioteca Comunale 'Mozzi-Borgetti' 378)." *MS* 51 (1989) 355-423.

Hänggi, Anton. *Der Rheinauer Liber Ordinarius (Zürich Rh 80, Anfang 12. Jh.).* SF 1. Fribourg/S.: Éditions Universitaires, 1957.

Hänggi, Anton and Alfons Schönherr. *Sacramentarium Rhenaugiense (Handschrift Rh 30 der Zentralbibliothek, Zürich).* SF 15. Fribourg/S: Éditions Universitaires, 1970.

Hardison, O. B., Jr. *Christian Rite and Christian Drama in the Middle Ages. Essays in the Origin and Early History of Modern Drama.* Baltimore/Md.: John Hopkins Press, 1965.

Haskins, Charles Homer. *Studies in the History of Mediaeval Science.* Cambridge/Mass.: Harvard University Press, 1924.

Heiming, Odilo. *Das Sacramentarium triplex (Die Handschrift C 43 der Zentralbibliothek Zürich).* Corpus Ambrosiano-Liturgicum 1. LQF 49. Münster/W.: Aschendorff, 1968.

———. *Das ambrosianische Sakramentar von Biasca (Die Handschrift Mailand Ambrosiana A 24 bis inf.).* Corpus Ambrosiano-Liturgicum 2. LQF 51. Münster/W.: Aschendorff, 1969.

———. *Liber sacramentorum Augustodunensis.* CCL 159B. Turnhout: Brepols, 1984.

Henderson, William G. *Missale ad usum percelebris ecclesiae Herefordensis.* Leeds, 1874 (rpt. Farnborough: Gregg, 1969).

[Hesbert, René-Jean.] "La tradition bénéventaine dans la tradition manuscrite." In *Le Codex 10673 de la Bibliothèque Vaticane. Fonds latin (XIᵉ siècle). Graduel bénéventain.* Pp. 60-465. Paléographie Musicale 14. Solesmes: Abbaye Saint-Pierre, 1931.

Hesbert, René-Jean. "La messe 'Omnes gentes' du VIIᵉ Dimanche après la

Pentecôte." *Revue grégorienne* 17 (1932) 81-89, 170-179; 18 (1933) 1-14.

——. "Le Répons 'Tenebrae' dans les liturgies Romaine, Milanaise et Bénéventaine." *Revue grégorienne* 19 (1934) 4-24, 57-65, 84-89; 20 (1935) 1-14, 201-213; 21 (1936) 44-62, 201-213; 22 (1937) 121-136; 23 (1938) 20-25, 41-54, 81-98, 140-143, 161-170; 24 (1939) 44-63, 121-139, 161-172.

——. *Antiphonale missarum sextuplex d'après le graduel de Monza et les antiphonaires de Rheinau, du Mont-Blandin, de Compiègne, de Corbie, et de Senlis.* Brussels: Vromant, 1935.

——. "Les dimanches de Carême dans les manuscrits romano-bénéventains." *EL* 48 (1934) 198-222.

——. "L'"Antiphonale missarum' de l'ancien rit bénéventain." *EL* 52 (1938) 28-66, 141-158; 53 (1939) 168-190; 59 (1945) 69-95; 60 (1946) 103-141; 61 (1947) 153-210.

——. *Le Prosaire de la Sainte-Chapelle (Manuscrit du Chapitre de Saint-Nicholas de Bari).* Monumenta Musicae Sacrae 1. Mâcon, 1952.

——. "L'Évangéliaire de Zara." *Scriptorium* 8 (1954) 177-204.

——. "Les Séquences de Jumièges." In *Jumièges.* Congrès scientifique du XIIIᵉ centenaire, Rouen, 10-12 juin 1954. 2 vols. 2: 943-958. Rouen: Lecerf, 1955.

——. "Un antique Offertoire de la Pentecôte, *Factus est repente.*" In *Organicae Voces. Festschrift Joseph Smits van Waesberghe angeboten anlässlich seines 60. Geburtstages (18. April 1961).* Pp. 59-69. Amsterdam: Instituut voor Middeleeuwse Muziekwetenschap, 1963.

——. *Corpus antiphonalium officii.* 6 vols. RED, Series maior, Fontes 7-12. Rome: Herder, 1963-1979.

Hiley, David. "The Norman Chant Traditions—Normandy, Britain, Sicily." *Proceedings of the Royal Musical Association* 107 (1980-1981) 1-34.

Hinnebusch, William A. *The History of the Dominican Order.* Vol. 1: *Origins and Growth to 1500.* Staten Island/N. Y.: Alba House, 1966.

Hoffmann, Hartmut. *Die Chronik von Montecassino/Chronica monasterii Casinensis.* MGH Scriptores 34. Hannover: Hahnsche, 1980.

[Hourlier, Jacques and Michel Huglo.] "Catalogue des manuscrits bénéventains notés." Pp. 51-69. "Étude sur la notation bénéventaine." Pp. 70-161. And "Notice descriptive sur le manuscrit." Pp. 162-175. In *Le Codex VI.34 de la Bibliothèque capitulaire de Bénévent (XIᵉ-XIIᵉ siècle). Graduel de Bénévent avec prosaire et tropaire.* Paléographie Musicale 15. Solesmes: Abbaye Saint-Pierre, 1937.

Hourlier, Jacques and Jacques Froger. *Le manuscrit VI-33 Archivio Arcivesco-*

vile Benevento. Missel de Bénévent (Début du XIe siècle). Paléographie Musicale 20. Bern, Frankfurt: Peter Lang, 1983.

Hudovsky, Zoran. "Missale beneventanum MR 166 della Biblioteca metropolitana a Zagrabia." *Jucunda laudatio* 3 (1965) 306.

Hughes, Andrew. *Medieval Music: The Sixth Liberal Art.* 2nd revised edition. Toronto Medieval Bibliographies 4. Toronto: University of Toronto Press, 1980 (1st edition 1974).

——. *Medieval Manuscripts for Mass and Office: A Guide to Their Organization and Terminology.* Toronto: University of Toronto Press, 1982.

Hughes, Anselm. *The Portiforium of St. Wulfstan.* HBS 90. London, 1960.

——. *The Bec Missal.* HBS 94. London: Faith Press, 1963.

Huglo, Michel. "L'invitation à la paix dans l'ancienne liturgie bénéventaine." In *La eucaristá y la paz.* Actas del Trigésimo quinto Congreso eucaristico internacional, 27 mayo-1 junio 1952. Sesiones de estudio. 3 vols. 1: 705-707. Barcelona, 1953.

——. "Fragments de Jérémie selon la Vetus latina." *Vigiliae christianae* 8 (1954) 83-86.

——. "Le chant 'vieux-romain'. Liste des manuscrits et témoins indirects." *SE* 6 (1954) 96-124.

——. "Les diverses mélodies du 'Te decet laus'. A propos du Vieux-romain." *Jahrbuch für Liturgik und Hymnologie* 12 (1967) 111-116.

——. "Te Deum." *NCE* 13: 954-955.

——. "Exultet." *New Grove Dictionary* 6: 334-336.

——. "L'ancien chant bénéventain." *EO* 2 (1985) 265-293.

Hunt, Richard W. *A Summary Catalogue of Western Manuscripts in the Bodleian Library at Oxford.* Vol. 1. Oxford: Oxford University Press, 1953.

Humbert of Romans. *Ordinarium.* See Guerrini.

Jacob, André. "L'Evoluzione dei libri liturgici bizantini in Calabria e in Sicilia dall'VIII al XVI secolo, con particolare riguardo ai riti eucaristici." In *Calabria Bizantina. Vita religiosa e strutture amministrative.* Atti del primo e secondo Incontro di Studi Bizantini. Pp. 47-69. Reggio Calabria: Parallelo 38, 1974.

Janini, José and José Serrano. *Manuscritos litúrgicos de la Biblioteca Nacional.* Madrid: Dirección General de Archivos y Bibliotecas, 1969.

Jesson, Roy. "Ambrosian Chant." In *Gregorian Chant.* By Willi Apel. Pp. 465-483. Bloomington: Indiana University Press, 1958.

[John the Deacon of Naples]. "Iohannis Diaconi Translatio sancti Severini." Ed. Georg Waitz. MGH Scriptores rerum Langobardicarum et Italicarum saec. VI-IX. Pp. 452-459. Hannover: Hahnsche, 1878.

[John the Deacon of Venice]. "Iohannis Diaconi Chronicon venetum." Ed. Georg Heinrich Pertz. MGH Scriptores 7: 4-38. Hannover: Hahnsche, 1846 (rpt. Leipzig: Hiersemann, 1925).

Jones, Charles Williams. *The Saint Nicholas Liturgy and Its Literary Relationships (Ninth to Twelfth Centuries).* With an essay on the music by Gilbert Reaney. Berkeley: University of California, 1963.

Jounel, Pierre. "Le culte de saint Grégoire le Grand." *EO* 2 (1985) 195-209.

Jungmann, Josef Andreas. *Missarum Sollemnia. Eine genetische Erklärung der römischen Messe.* 4th revised edition. 2 vols. Vienna: Herder, 1958 (1st edition 1948).

Kaeppeli, Thomas and Hugues V. Shooner. *Les manuscrits médiévaux de Saint-Dominique de Dubrovnik: Catalogue sommaire.* Institutum historicum Fratrum Praedicatorum Romae ad S. Sabinae: Dissertationes historicae 17. Rome: S. Sabina, 1965.

Kantorowicz, Ernst. "A Norman Finale of the Exultet and the Rite of Sarum." *Harvard Theological Review* 34 (1941) 129-143.

———. *Laudes Regiae. A Study in Liturgical Acclamations and Mediaeval Ruler Worship.* With a musical study by Manfred F. Bukofzer. Berkeley, Los Angeles: University of California Press, 1946.

Kelly, Thomas Forrest. "Montecassino and the Old Beneventan Chant." *Early Music History* 5 (1985) 53-83.

———. *The Beneventan Chant.* Cambridge: Cambridge University Press, 1989.

Kelly, Thomas Forrest and Herman F. Holbrook. "Beneventan Fragments at Altamura." *MS* 49 (1987) 466-479.

King, Archdale Arthur. *Liturgies of the Religious Orders.* Milwaukee: Bruce, 1955.

———. *Liturgies of the Primatial Sees.* London, New York: Longmans Green, 1957.

———. *Liturgies of the Past.* Milwaukee: Bruce, 1959.

———. "Rite of Benevento." *NCE* 2: 309.

Klauser, Theodore. *Das römische Capitulare evangeliorum.* I. *Typen.* LQF 28. Münster/W.: Aschendorff, 1935.

Kiseleva, Liùdmilla I. *Latinskie Rukopisi Biblioteki Akademii Nauk SSSR: opisanie rukopisei latinskogo alfavita x-xv vv.* Leningrad: "Nauka", Leningradskoe otdelenie, 1978.

Kniewald, Dragutin. "Zagrebački liturgijski kodeksi xi.-xv. stoljeća." *Croatia sacra* 10 (1940) 1-128.

Kottje, Raymund. "Beneventana-Fragmente liturgischer Bücher im Stadtarchiv Augsburg." *MS* 47 (1985) 432-437.

Krekić, Bariša. *Dubrovnik in the 14th and 15th Centuries: A City between East and West.* Norman: University of Oklahoma, 1972.

Ladner, Gerhart Burian. *The Idea of Reform: Its Impact on Christian Thought and Action in the Age of the Fathers.* Cambridge/Mass.: Harvard University Press, 1959.

Laurent, Vitalien. "L'Église de l'Italie méridionale entre Rome et Byzance à la vielle de la conquête normande." In *La Chiesa greca in Italia dall'VIII al XVI secolo.* Atti del Convegno Storico Interecclesiale, Bari, 30 aprile-4 maggio 1969. Ed. Michele Maccarrone, Gérard Gilles Meersseman, Alessandro Passerin d'Entrèves, and Paolo Sambin. 3 vols. 1: 5-23. Italia Sacra 20-22. Padua: Antenore, 1972-1973.

Legg, John Wickham. *Missale ad usum ecclesie Westmonasteriensis.* 3 vols. HBS 1, 5, 12. London: Harrison, 1891, 1893, 1897.

——. *The Sarum Missal Edited from Three Manuscripts.* Oxford: Clarendon Press, 1916.

Lentini, Anselmo and Maria Chiara Celletti. "Benedetto di Norcia, patriarca dei monaci d'Occidente, santo." *Bibliotheca Sanctorum* (1962) 2: 1104-1184.

[Leo of Ostia]. "Vita S. Mennatis". See Orlandi.

[Leo of Ostia and Peter the Deacon.] *Chronica monasterii Casinensis.* See Hoffmann.

Levy, Kenneth. "*Lux de luce:* The Origin of an Italian Sequence." *The Musical Quarterly* 57 (1971) 40-61.

Lippe, Robert. *Missale Romanum Mediolani, 1474.* 2 vols. HBS 17, 33. London: Harrison, 1899, 1907.

Loew [Lowe], Elias Avery. *The Bobbio Missal. A Gallican Mass-Book (MS. Paris. Lat. 13246).* 2 vols. in 3 parts. HBS 53, 58, 61 (with André Wilmart and Henry A. Wilson). London: Harrison, 1917-1924.

——. *Scriptura Beneventana: Facsimiles of South Italian and Dalmatian Manuscripts from the Sixth to the Fourteenth Century.* 2 vols. Oxford: Oxford University Press, 1929.

——. *The Beneventan Script. A History of the South Italian Minuscule.* 2nd edition prepared and enlarged by Virginia Brown. 2 vols. Sussidi Eruditi 33, 34. Rome: Edizioni di Storia e Letteratura, 1980 (1st edition 1914).

McNally, Robert Edwin. "Ember Days." *NCE* 5: 296-298.

Madan, Falconer. *A Summary Catalogue of Western Manuscripts in the Bodleian Library at Oxford.* Vols. 4 and 5 with corrections by Henry Marriott Bannister. Oxford: Clarendon, 1897, 1905.

Mallet, Jean and André Thibaut. *Les manuscrits en écriture bénéventaine de la Bibliothèque capitulaire de Bénévent.* 1. *Manuscrits 1-18.* Paris: Éditions du Centre National de la Recherche Scientifique, 1984.

Marcusson, Olof. *Corpus troporum.* Vol. 2: *Prosules de la messe.* Pars 1: *Tropes de l'alleluia.* Acta Universitatis Stockholmiensis, Studia Latina Stockholmiensia 22. Stockholm: Almqvist and Wiksell, 1976.

Martène, Edmond. *De antiquis ecclesiae ritibus.* 2nd edition. 4 vols. Antwerp, 1736-1738 (1st edition 1700-1702).

Martimort, Aimé-Georges. *La documentation liturgique de Dom Edmond Martène. Étude codicologique.* ST 279. Vatican City: Biblioteca Apostolica Vaticana, 1978.

——. "A propos du nombre des lectures à la messe." *Revue des sciences religieuses* 58 (1984) 42-51.

——. "Additions et corrections à la documentation liturgique de Dom Edmond Martène." *EO* 3 (1986) 81-105.

——. With Roger Béraudy, Bernard Botte, Noële Maurice Denis-Boulet, Bernard Capelle, Antoine Chavasse, Irénée-Henri Dalmais, Benoît Darragon, Pierre-Marie Gy, Pierre Jounel, Adrien Nocent, Aimon-Marie Roguet, Olivier Rousseau, and Pierre Salmon. *L'Église en prière: Introduction à la Liturgie.* Paris: Desclée, 1961.

——. With Robert Cabié, Irénée-Henri Dalmais, Jean Évenou, Pierre-Marie Gy, Pierre Jounel, Adrien Nocent, and Damien Sicard. *L'Église en prière: Introduction à la Liturgie.* Revised edition. 4 vols. Paris: Desclée, 1983-1984.

Mayer, Anton. "Catarensia." *Zbornik Historijskog Instituta Jugoslavenske Akademije* 1 (1954) 95-110.

Ménager, Léon Robert. "La 'byzantinisation' religieuse de l'Italie Méridionale (ixe-xiie siècles) et la politique monastique des Normands d'Italie." *Revue d'histoire ecclésiastique* 53 (1958) 747-774; 54 (1959) 5-40.

——. "Les fondations monastiques de Robert Guiscard, duc de Pouille et de Calabre." *Quellen und Forschungen aus italienischen Archiven und Bibliotheken* 39 (1959) 1-63.

Merolle, Irma. *L'Abate Matteo Luigi Canonici e la sua Biblioteca.* Rome, Florence: Biblioteca Mediceo-Laurenziana, Institutum Historicum Societatis Jesu, 1958.

Metzger, Max Josef. *Zwei karolingische Pontifikalien vom Oberrhein.* Freiburger Theologische Studien 17. Freiburg/Br.: Herder, 1914.

Missale s. Ordinis Praedicatorum auctoritate Apostolica approbatum et reverendissimi patris Fr. Martini Stanislai Gillet ejusdem Ordinis Magistri Generalis jussu editum. Rome: In Hospitio Magistri Ordinis, 1933.

Mitchell, J. B. "Trevisan and Soranzo: Some Canonici Manuscripts from Two Eighteenth-Century Venetian Collections." *Bodleian Library Record* 8 (1967-1972) 125-135.

[Mocquereau, André.] "Le Cursus et la psalmodie (1)." In *Le Codex 121 de la Bibliothèque d'Einsiedeln x^e-xie siècle. Antiphonale missarum s. Gregorii.* Pp. 25-204. Paléographie Musicale 4. Solesmes: Abbaye Saint-Pierre, 1893-1896.

——. *Le Codex 121 de la Bibliothèque d'Einsiedeln x^e-xie siècle. Antiphonale missarum s. Gregorii.* Paléographie Musicale 4. Solesmes: Abbaye Saint-Pierre, 1893-1896.

——. *Antiphonarium tonale missarum, xie siècle. Codex H. 159 de la Bibliothèque de l'École de Médicine de Montpellier.* 2 vols. Paléographie Musicale 7-8. Solesmes: Abbaye Saint-Pierre, 1901.

——. *Le Codex 903 de la Bibliothèque Nationale de Paris (xie siècle, Graduel de Saint-Yrieix).* Paléographie Musicale 13. Solesmes: Abbaye Saint-Pierre, 1925.

Moeller, Edmond. *Corpus benedictionum pontificalium.* 4 vols. CCL 162, 162A-C. Turnhout: Brepols, 1971-1979.

——. *Corpus praefationum.* 5 vols. CCL 161, 161A-D. Turnhout: Brepols, 1980-1981.

Mohlberg, [Leo] Kunibert [Cunibert]. *Radulph von Rivo. Der letze Vertreter der altrömischen Liturgie.* 2 vols. Louvain, Münster/W.: Bureaux de Recueil, Aschendorff, 1911-1915.

——. *Das fränkische Sacramentarium Gelasianum in alamannischer Überlieferung (Codex Sangall. No. 348).* 3rd edition. St. Galler Sakramentar-Forschungen 1. LQF 1-2. Münster/W.: Aschendorff, 1971 (1st edition 1918).

——. "Un sacramentario palinsesto del secolo VIII dell'Italia centrale." *Atti della Pontificia Accademia Romana di Archeologia* 3 (1925) 391-450.

——. *Missale Gothicum (Vat. Reg. lat. 317).* RED, Series maior, Fontes 5. Rome: Herder, 1961.

Mohlberg, Leo Cunibert, Leo Eizenhöfer, and Petrus Siffrin. *Sacramentarium Veronense (Cod. Bibl. Capitolare Veron. LXXXV [80]).* RED, Series maior, Fontes 1. Rome: Herder, 1956.

——. *Missale Gallicanum Vetus (Vat. Pal. lat. 493).* RED, Series maior, Fontes 3. Rome: Herder, 1958.

——. *Liber Sacramentorum Romanae aecclesiae ordinis anni circuli (Cod. Vat. Reg. lat. 316/Paris Bibl. Nat. 7193, 41/56).* RED, Series maior, Fontes 4. Rome: Herder, 1960.

Mohrmann, Christine. "Le latin liturgique." In *L'Ordinaire de la messe.* Ed.

Bernard Botte and Christine Mohrmann. Pp. 29-48. Études liturgiques 2. Paris, Louvain: Du Cerf, Mont Cesar, 1952.

———. *Études sur le latin des chrétiens*. 3 vols. Storia e Letteratura, Raccolta di Studi e Testi 65, 87, 103. Rome: Edizioni di Storia e Letteratura, 1956, 1965.

Moreton, Bernard. *The Eighth-Century Gelasian Sacramentary*. Oxford: Oxford University Press, 1976.

———. "Roman Sacramentaries and Ancient Prayer-Traditions." In *Studia patristica 15.* Papers presented to the Seventh International Conference on Patristic Studies, Oxford 1975. Pp. 577-580. TU 128. Berlin: Akademie-Verlag, 1984.

Morin, Germain. "Le plus ancien *Comes* ou Lectionnaire de l'église romaine." *RB* 27 (1910) 41-74.

———. "Liturgie et Basiliques de Rome au milieu du VII siècle d'après les listes d'évangiles de Würzburg." *RB* 28 (1911) 296-330.

Nitti di Vito, Francesco. *La Ripresa gregoriana di Bari (1087-1105) e i suoi riflessi nel mondo contemporaneo politico e religioso*. Trani: Vecchia, 1942.

Novak, Viktor. *Scriptura Beneventana s osobitim obzirom na tip dalmatinske beneventane. Paleografijska studija*. Zagreb: Tisak, 1920.

———. "La paleografia latina e i rapporti dell'Italia meridionale con la Dalmazia." *Archivio Storico Pugliese* 14 (1961) 145-160.

———. "Something New from the Dalmatian Beneventana." *Medievalia et Humanistica* 14 (1962) 76-85.

———. *Latinska Paleografija*. 2nd edition. Belgrade: Naučna Knjiga, 1980 (1st edition 1952).

O'Carroll, Maura. "The Lectionary for the Proper of the Year in the Dominican and Franciscan Rites of the Thirteenth Century." *Archivum Fratrum Praedicatorum* 49 (1979) 79-103.

Odermatt, Ambros. *Ein Rituale in beneventanischer Schrift. Roma, Biblioteca Vallicelliana, cod. C 32, Ende des 11. Jahrhunderts*. SF 26. Fribourg/S.: Éditions Universitaires, 1980.

Olivar, Alejandro. *El Sacramentario de Vich (Vich, Museo episc., 66)*. Monumenta Hispaniae Sacra, Serie litúrgica 4. Barcelona: Consejo Superior de Investigaciones Cientificas, Instituto P. Enrique Florez, 1953.

Opći Šematizam Katoličke Crkve u Jugoslaviji cerkev v Jugoslaviji, 1974. Zagreb: Biskupska Konferencija Jugoslavije, 1975.

Ordericus Vitalis. *The Ecclesiastical History*. See Chibnall.

Orlandi, Giovanni. "*Vita S. Mennatis*, opera inedita di Leone Marsicano." *Istituto Lombardo, Accademia di scienze e lettere: Rendiconti, Classe di lettere e scienze morali e storiche* 97 (1963) 467-490.

Ostojić, Ivan. *Benediktinci u Hrvatskoj i ostalim našim krajevima.* 3 vols. Split, 1963-64.

Ott, Carolus. *Offertoriale sive versus offertorium.* Paris, Tournai: Desclée, 1935.

Pächt, Otto and Jonathan J. G. Alexander. *Illuminated Manuscripts in the Bodleian Library Oxford.* 3 vols. Oxford: Clarendon, 1966-1973.

Paredi, Angelo. "Il Sacramentario di Ariberto." In *Miscellanea Adriano Bernareggi.* Ed. Luigi Cortesi. Pp. 329-488. Monumenta Bergomensia 1. Bergamo: Edizioni "Monumenta Bergomensia", 1958.

Paredi, Angelo and Giuseppe Fassi. *Sacramentarium Bergomense (Bergamo, Biblioteca di S. Alessandro in Colonna).* Monumenta Bergomensia 6. Bergamo: Edizioni "Monumenta Bergomensia", 1962.

Pecarski, Branka. "Testimonianze artistiche, letterarie e storiche sulla liturgia greca nella Dalmazia dall'VIII al XIII secolo." In *La Chiesa greca in Italia dall'VIII al XVI secolo.* Atti del Convegno Storico Interecclesiale, Bari 30 aprile-4 maggio 1969. Ed. Michele Maccarrone, Gérard Gilles Meersseman, Alessandro Passerin d'Entrèves, and Paolo Sambin. 3 vols. 3: 1237-1245. Italia Sacra 20-22. Padua: Antenore, 1972-1973.

Peirce, Elizabeth. *An Edition of Egerton MS. 3511: A Twelfth Century Missal of St. Peter's in Benevento.* Diss. London, 1964.

Pérez de Urbel, Justo and Atilano González y Ruiz-Zorilla. *Liber commicus.* 2 vols. Monumenta Hispaniae Sacra, Serie litúrgica 2-3. Madrid: Consejo Superior de Investigaciones Cientificas, 1950, 1955.

[Peter the Deacon and Leo of Ostia.] *Chronica monasterii Casinensis.* See Hoffmann.

Petrucci, Armando. *Codice diplomatico del monastero benedettino di S. Maria di Tremiti (1005-1237).* 3 vols. Fonti per la Storia d'Italia 98. Rome: Istituto storico italiano per il medio evo, 1960.

Pfaff, Richard W. *New Liturgical Feasts in Later Medieval England.* Oxford: Clarendon, 1970.

Pinell, Jordi M. "La benedicció del ciri pasqual i els seus textos." In *Liturgica Cardinali I. Schuster in memoriam.* 2 vols. 2: 1-119. Scripta et documenta 7, 10. Barcelona: Montserrat, 1956, 1958.

Plotino, Roberto and Justo Fernández Alonso. "Giacomo il Maggiore, apostolo, santo." *Bibliotheca Sanctorum* (1965) 6: 363-388.

[Poncelet, Albert.] *Bibliotheca hagiographica Latina antiquae et mediae aetatis.* 2 vols. with Supplement. Brussels, 1898, 1901 (rpt. 1949); 1911.

Pothier, Joseph. "Chant de la Généalogie à la nuit de Noël." *RdCG* 6 (1897-1898) 65-71.

Puniet, Pierre de. "Le sacramentaire romain de Gellone." *EL* 48 (1934) 3-65, 157-197, 357-381, 517-533; 49 (1935) 109-125, 209-229, 305-347; 50 (1936) 3-33, 261-295; 51 (1937) 13-63, 93-135, 269-309; 52 (1938) 3-27. Rpt. as Bibliotheca 'Ephemerides Liturgicae' 4. Rome: Ephemerides Liturgicae, 1938.

Radulph of Rivo (d. 1403). *De canonum observantia liber.* See Mohlberg.

Rehle, Sieghild. *Missale Beneventanum von Canosa (Baltimore, Walters Art Gallery, MS W 6).* Textus patristici et liturgici 9. Regensburg: Pustet, 1972.

——. "Missale Beneventanum (Codex VI 33 des Erzbischöflichen Archivs von Benevent)." *SE* 21 (1972-1973) 323-405.

——. "Zwei beneventanische Evangelistare in der Vaticana." *Römische Quartalschrift für christliche Altertumskunde und Kirchengeschichte* 69 (1974) 182-191.

——. "Missale Beneventanum in Berlin." *SE* 28 (1985) 469-510.

Reynolds, Roger E. "All Saints' Day." *DMA* (1982) 1: 176.

——. "All Souls' Day." *DMA* (1982) 1: 177.

——. "Odilo and the *Treuga Dei* in Southern Italy: A Beneventan Manuscript Fragment." *MS* 46 (1984) 450-462.

——. "A South Italian Ordination Allocution." *MS* 47 (1985) 438-444.

——. "South Italian *liturgica* and *canonistica* in Catalonia (New York, Hispanic Society of America MS. HC 380/819)." *MS* 49 (1987) 480-495.

——. "A South Italian Liturgico-Canonical Mass Commentary." *MS* 50 (1988) 626-670.

Revignas, Anna Saitta. *Catalogo dei manoscritti della Biblioteca Casanatense.* Vol. 6. Indici e Cataloghi ns 2. Rome: Istituto Poligrafico dello Stato, Libreria dello Stato, 1978.

Richter, Gregor and Albert Schönfelder. *Sacramentarium Fuldense saeculi X.* 2nd edition. With a bibliographic note by D. H. Tripp. Quellen und Abhandlungen zur Geschichte der Abtei und der Diözese Fulda 9. HBS 101. Farnborough: Saint Michael's Abbey Press, 1977 (1st edition 1912).

Saint-Roch, Patrick. *Liber sacramentorum Engolismensis (Manuscrit B.N. Lat. 816. Le Sacramentaire Gélasien d'Angoulême.)* CCL 159C. Turnhout: Brepols, 1987.

Salmon, Pierre. *Les manuscrits liturgiques latins de la Bibliothèque Vaticane.*

5 vols. ST 251, 253, 260, 267, 270. Vatican City: Biblioteca Apostolica Vaticana, 1968-1972.

Sauget, Joseph-Marie and Maria Chiara Celletti. "Marina (Margherita), santa, martire di Antiochia di Pisidia." *Bibliotheca Sanctorum* (1966) 8: 1150-1165.

Saxer, Victor. *Le culte de Marie Madeleine en occident des origines à la fin du moyen âge.* Cahiers d'archéologie e d'histoire 3. Ed. René Louis. Paris: Clavreuil, 1959.

——. "L'introduction du rite latin dans les provinces dalmato-croates aux xᵉ-xiiᵉ siècles." In *Vita religiosa, morale e sociale ed i concili di Split dei secc. X-XI.* Atti del Symposium Internazionale di Storia Ecclesiastica, Split 26-30 settembre 1978. Ed. Atanazie J. Matanić. Pp. 163-193. Medioevo e Umanesimo 49. Padua: Antenore, 1982.

Saxer, Victor and Maria Chiara Celletti. "Maria Maddalena, santa." *Bibliotheca Sanctorum* (1967) 8: 1078-1107.

Schlager, Karlheinz. *Thematischer Katalog der ältesten Alleluia-Melodien aus Handschriften des 10. und 11. Jahrhunderts, ausgenommen das ambrosianische, alt-römische und alt-spanische Repertoire.* Erlanger Arbeiten zur Musikwissenschaft 2. Munich: Walter Ricke, 1965.

——. "Ein beneventanisches Alleluia und seine Prosula." In *Festschrift Bruno Stäblein zum 70. Geburtstag.* Ed. Martin Ruhnke. Pp. 217-225. Kassel: Bärenreiter, 1967.

——. "Anmerkungen zu den zweiten Alleluia-Versen." *Archiv für Musikwissenschaft* 24 (1967) 199-219.

——. *Alleluia-Melodien.* I. *Bis 1100.* Monumenta monodica medii aevi 7. Kassel: Bärenreiter, 1968.

——. "Music of the Beneventan Rite." *New Grove Dictionary* 2: 482-484.

Schmidt, Hermann A. P. and Helmut Hucke. *Hebdomada sancta.* 2 vols. Rome, Freiburg/Br., Barcelona: Herder, 1956-1957.

Schramm, Percy Ernst. *Kaiser, Könige, und Päpste. Gesammelte Aufsätze zur Geschichte des Mittelalters.* 4 vols. in 5. Stuttgart: Hiersemann, 1968-1971.

Sindik, Dušan. "Pontifical kotorske biskupije u Leningradu." *Istorijski Časopis* 31 (Beograd, 1984) 53-66.

Snow, Robert J. "The Old-Roman Chant." In *Gregorian Chant.* By Willi Apel. Pp. 484-506. Bloomington: Indiana University Press, 1958.

Spadafora, Francesco. "Bartolomeo, apostolo." *Bibliotheca Sanctorum* (1962) 2: 852-862.

Stäblein, Bruno. "Evangelium." *MGG* 3: 1618-1629.

Stjepčević, Ivo. "Katedrale sv. Tripuna u Kotora." *Prilog Vjesniku za Arheologiju i Historiju Dalmatinsku* 51 (1930-1934) 1-101.

Stramare, Tarsicio, Francesco Spadafora, and Francesco Negri Arnoldi. "Elia, profeta." *Bibliotheca Sanctorum* (1964) 4: 1022-1039.

Stramare, Tarsicio and Antonietta Cardinale. "Giovanni Battista." *Bibliotheca Sanctorum* (1965) 6: 599-624.

Suñol, Gregório María. *Introduction à la paléographie musicale grégorienne.* Trans. André Mocquereau. Paris, Rome: Desclée, 1935.

Supino Martini, Paola. "Per lo studio della scritture altomedievali italiane: la collezione canonica chietina (Vat. Reg. lat. 1997)." *Scrittura e Civiltà* 1 (1977) 133-154.

Terrizzi, Francesco. *Missale antiquum S. Panormitanae ecclesiae (Palermo, Archivio Storico Diocesano, cod. 2).* RED, Series maior, Fontes 13. Rome: Herder, 1970.

Tolhurst, John B. L. *The Monastic Breviary of Hyde Abbey, Winchester (MSS. Rawlinson Liturg. e. 1.*, and Gough Liturg. 8, in the Bodleian Library, Oxford).* 6 vols. HBS 69-71, 76, 78, 80. London: Harrison, 1932-1942.

Tommasi, Giuseppe-Maria. "Lectionarius missae iuxta ritum ecclesiae Romanae ex antiquis MSS. cod. collectus." In *Opera omnia.* Ed. Antonius Vezzosi. Vol. 5. Rome, 1750.

"Translatio sancti Athanasii episcopi Neapolitani." See Waitz.

Väänänen, Vieko. *Introduction au latin vulgaire.* Bibliothèque française et romane, Série A: Manuels et études linguistiques 6. Paris: Klincksieck, 1963.

Van Dijk, Stephen J. P. "Three Manuscripts of a Liturgical Reform of John Cajetan Orsini (Nicholas III)." *Scriptorium* 6 (1952) 213-242.

——. *Handlist of the Latin Liturgical Manuscripts in the Bodleian Library Oxford.* Typescript on deposit in the Bodleian Library, Oxford. 1957.

——. "The Urban and Papal Rites in Seventh and Eighth-Century Rome." *SE* 12 (1961) 411-487.

——. *Sources of the Modern Roman Liturgy: The Ordinals by Haymo of Faversham and Related Documents (1243-1307).* 2 vols. Studia et Documenta Franciscana. Leiden: Brill, 1963.

Van Dijk, Stephen J. P. and Joan Hazeldean Walker. *The Origins of the Modern Roman Liturgy.* Westminster, Md.: Newman Press, 1960; London: Darton, Longmann, Todd, 1960.

——. *The Ordinal of the Papal Court from Innocent III to Boniface VIII and Related Documents.* SF 22. Fribourg/S.: Éditions Universitaires, 1975.

Vidaković, Albe. "I nouvi confini della scrittura neumatica musicale nell'Europa sud-est." *Studien zur Musikwissenschaft* 24 (1960) 5-12.

"Vita sancti Athanasii episcopi Neapolitani." See Waitz.

Vogel, Cyrille and Reinhard Elze. *Le Pontifical romano-germanique du dixième siècle.* 3 vols. ST 226-227, 269. Vatican City: Biblioteca Apostolica Vaticana, 1963, 1972.

Vogel, Cyrille. *Medieval Liturgy: An Introduction to the Sources.* Trans. and revised by William G. Storey and Niels Krogh Rasmussen. Washington: Pastoral Press, 1986 (1st French edition 1966).

Vogüé, Adalbert de, ed. and Paul Antin, trans. *Grégoire le Grand. Dialogues.* 3 vols. Sources chrétiennes 251, 260, 265. Paris: Du Cerf, 1978-1980.

Von Falkenhausen, Vera. "Il monachesimo italo-greco e i suoi rapporti con il monachesimo benedettino." In *L'Esperienza monastica benedettina e la Puglia.* Atti del Convegno di Studio organizzato in occasione del XV centenario della nascita di san Benedetto, Bari, Noci, Lecce, Picciano, 6-10 ottobre 1980. Ed. Cosimo Damiano Fonseca. 2 vols. 1: 119-135. Università degli Studi di Lecce, Facoltà di Lettere e Filosofia, Istituto di Storia Medioeval e Moderna. Saggi e Ricerche 8-9. Galatina Congedo Editore, 1983, 1984.

Waitz, Georg, ed. "Vita sancti Athanasii episcopi Neapolitani." and "Translatio sancti Athanasii episcopi Neapolitani." MGH Scriptores rerum Langobardicarum et Italicarum saec. VI-IX. Pp. 439-452. Hannover: Hahnsche, 1878.

Wellesz, Egon. *Eastern Elements in Western Chant: Studies in the Early History of Ecclesiastical Music.* Oxford, Boston: Byzantine Institute, 1947 (rpt. Copenhagen: Munksgaard, 1967).

Westerbergh, Ulla. *Anastasius Bibliothecarius. Sermo Theodori Studitae de sancto Bartholomeo Apostolo.* Acta Universitatis Stockholmiensis, Studia Latina Stockholmiensia 9. Stockholm: Almqvist and Wiksell, 1963.

White, Lynn T. *Latin Monasticism in Sicily.* Cambridge/Mass.: Medieval Academy of America, 1938.

Willis, G. G. *Essays in Early Roman Liturgy.* Alcuin Club Collection 46. London: S. P. C. K., 1964.

Wilmart, André. "Le *Comes* de Muhrbach." *RB* 30 (1913) 25-69.

——. "Prières médiévales pour l'adoration de la croix." *EL* 46 (1932) 22-65.

——. "Le Lectionnaire d'Alcuin," *EL* 51 (1937) 136-197. Rpt. as *Le Lectionnaire d'Alcuin.* Bibliotheca 'Ephemerides Liturgicae' 2. Rome: Ephemerides Liturgicae, 1937.

Wilson, Henry A., ed. *The Missal of Robert of Jumièges.* HBS 11. London: Harrison, 1896.

Zaninović, Antonin. "'Prophetia cum versibus' ou 'Epistola farcita' pour la 1re messe de Noël, selon deux manuscrits de Trogir." *Revue grégorienne* 20 (1935) 81-90.

Index of Musical Items
(Asterisks indicate texts without notation)

Omnes qui uidebant: 179 (Tr. V.)
Omnis terra adoret: 77 (Int.), 81 (All.)
Optimam partem: 515 (Com.)
Oratio mea: 553 (Off.)
Os iusti: 660 (Int.)

Pange lingua: 200* (Hymn.)
Passer inuenit: 153 (Com.)
Pater noster: 204* (Commune)
Pater si non potest: 183 (Com.)
Pax domini: 205
Pentecostes promissus: 269 (Pr.)
Per sanctam crucem: 427 (Com.)
Perfice gressus: 108 (Off.)
Petite et accipietis: 231 (Com.), 239* (Com.)
Popule meus: 196 (Improperia), 201 (Improperia Resp.)
Post partum uirgo: 29 (All.)
Posuisti domine: 626 (Gr.), 628 (All.)
Potens in terra: 551 (Gr. V.), 630 (Tr. V.)
Preceptis salutaribus: 204 (Commune)
Pretiosa in conspectu: 390 (All.), 403* (All.), 412* (All.)
Priusquam te formarem: 440 (Gr.)
Pro patribus: 468 (Gr. V.)
Probasti domine: 557 (Int.), 560 (Gr.)
Propter quod et deus: 189 (Gr. V.), 696 (Gr. V.)
Propter ueritatem: 28 (Gr. V.), 510 (Gr.), 580 (Gr.)
Propterea unxit te deus: 671 (Gr. V.)
Protege domine: 425 (Off.)
Protexisti me deus: 386 (Int.), 400* (Int.)
Psallite domino: 248 (Com.), 253* (Com.)
Puer natus est: 12 (Int.)
Pueri hebreorum tollentes ramos: 165 (Ant.)
Pueri hebreorum uestimenta: 166 (Ant.)

Quam bonus israhel: 178 (Gr. V.)
Qui biberit: 145 (Com.)
Qui confidunt: 140 (Gr.)
Qui gloria mundi spreuit: 304 (Gr. V.)
Qui habitat: 127 (Int. Ps.), 131 (Tr.)
Qui meditabitur: 124 (Com.)
Qui michi ministrat: 565 (Com.)

Tenuisti manum: 178 (Gr.)
Terribilis est locus: 680 (Int.)
Timebunt gentes: 90 (Gr.), 91 (All.)
Tolle puerum: 43 (Com.)
Tollite portas: 379* (Gr.)
Tu autem in sancto: 179 (Tr. V.)
Tu es petrus: 352 (Tr.), 356* (Com.), 473 (Com.)
Tu puer propheta: 445 (Com.)
Tui sunt celi: 18 (Off.)
Turba multa: 173 (Ant.)

Verba delictorum: 179 (Tr. V.)
Veritas mea: 503* (Off.), 652 (Off.)
Video celos apertos: 313 (All.), 317 (Com.)
Viderunt omnes fines: 16 (Gr.), 20 (Com.)
Vidimus stellam: 51 (All.), 55 (Com.), 71 (All.), 75* (Com.)
Vir dei benedictus: 366 (Int.)
Viri galilei: 250 (Int.), 251 (Off.)
Vltimo festiuitatis: 263 (Com.)
Vnus autem ex ipsis: 163 (Resp. V.)
Vocem iocunditatis: 214 (Int.)
Vos qui secuti: 619 (Com.)
Vsque modo non petistis: 218 (All.)
Vt testimonium: 431 (Gr. V.)

Xpistus *vide* Christus.

Index of Prayers and Benedictions

Index of Lections, Epistles and Gospels

Regum III
Egrotauit filius (17: 17-24): 499

Liber Sapientiae
Iustorum anime in manu (3: 1): 449
Stabunt iusti (5: 1-5): 388, 402, 411
Iustum deduxit dominus (10: 10-14): 624

Ecclesiasticus
Beatus uir (14: 22, 15: 3-4, 6): 625
In omnibus requiem quesiui (24: 11-13): 579
Ego quasi libanus (24: 21-31): 570
Iustus cor suum (39: 6): 368
Benedictio domini super caput (44: 5): 600
Hi sunt uiri misericordie (44: 10-15): 487, 537
Ecce sacerdos magnus (44: 16): 350
Ecce sacerdos magnus (44: 16, 17, 20, 22, 25-27; 45: 2, 3, 6, 8, 19, 20): 645
Ecce sacerdos magnus (50: 6-13): 303
Confitebor tibi (51: 1-8, 12): 550

Isaias
Locutus est ad achaz (7: 10): 378
Populus gentium qui ambulabat (9: 2): 27
Audite insule et attendite (49: 1-3, 5-7): 439
Propter hoc sciet (52: 6-10): 15
Surge illuminare ierusalem (60: 1-6): 49, 69
Spiritus domini super me (61: 1-2): 1
Gaudens gaudebo (61: 10-11, 65: 5): 509

Ieremias
Factum est uerbum domini (1: 4-10): 430

Ioel
Conuertimini ad me in toto corde (2: 12-19): 118

Matthaeus

Cum natus esset iesus (2: 1-12): 52
Defuncto herode (2: 19-23): 40
Venit iesus a galilea in iordanem (3: 13-17): 72
Ductus est iesus in desertum (4: 1-11): 132
Videns iesus turbas ascendit in montem (5: 1-16): 587
Cum ieiunatis nolite fieri (6: 16-21): 121
Conuocatis (10: 1-8): 611
Simile est regnum celorum thesauro (13: 44-52): 344, 424, 662
Venit iesus in partes cesaree (16: 13-19): 470
Si quis uult post me (16: 24): 552
Ecce nos qui reliquimus omnia (19: 27-29): 480
Simile est regnum celorum homini (20: 1-16): 102
Accessit ad iesum mater filiorum zebedei (20: 20-23): 525
Ecce ego mitto ad uos prophetas (23: 34-39): 314
Vigilate ergo quia nescitis (24: 42-47): 651
Simile est regnum celorum decem uirginibus (25: 1-13): 663
Homo quidam peregre (25: 14-23): 650
Cum uenerit filius hominis (25: 31-46): 597
Sciatis quia post biduum (26: 1—27: 66): 180

Marcus

Ingressus iesus in sinagogem sabbati et docebat (1: 21-34): 281
Cum egressus esset iesus ad mare omnis turba ueniebat (2: 13-17): 228
Cum sero esset factum (4: 35-40): 236
Assumpsit iesus petrum et iacobum et iohannem et ducit illos (9: 1-8): 544
Acceserunt ad iesum iacobus et iohannes (10: 35-40): 521
Videte uigilate et orate (13: 33-37): 306, 393

Lucas

Fuit in diebus herodis regis (1: 5-17): 432
Missus est angelus (1: 26): 381
Exurgens maria abiit in montana (1: 39): 572
Helisabeth impletum est (1: 57-68): 442
Pastores loquebantur ad inuicem (2: 15-20): 5, 30
Cum factus esset iesus annorum duodecym (2: 42-52): 62
Factum est autem cum baptizaretur (3: 21—4: 1): 45
Regressus iesus in uirtute spiritus (4: 14-22): 92
Quanta audiuimus (4: 23-30): 502
Rogabat iesum quidam phariseus (7: 36-50): 512
Cum autem turba plurima (8: 4-15): 105

Ad Corinthios I
Nescitis quod hi qui in stadio (9: 24-10: 4): 99
Conuenientibus uobis in unum (11: 20-32): 188
Si linguis hominum loquar (13: 3-8): 111
Ecce misterium (15: 51-57): 594

Ad Corinthios II
Fiduciam talem habemus (3: 4-7): 291
Deus qui dixit de tenebris (4: 6-10): 37
Qui parce seminat (9: 6-10): 559
Qui gloriatur in domino (10: 17): 341
Hortamur uos ne in uacuum (6: 1-10): 129
Gaudete perfecti estote (13: 11-13): 685

Ad Galatas
Quanto tempore heres paruulus est (4: 1-7): 24
Scriptum est quoniam abraham duos filios (4: 22-31): 157

Ad Ephesios
Benedictus deus et pater domini (1: 3): 520
Vnicuique uestrum data est gratia (4: 7-13): 243
Renouamini spiritus mentis uestre (4: 23-28): 301
Estote immitatores dei (5: 1-7): 149

Ad Philippenses
Hoc enim sentite (2: 5-11): 177
Christus factus est (2: 8-11): 695

Ad Colossenses
Misterium quod absconditur (1: 26-28): 421

Ad Thessalonicenses I
Rogamus uos et obsecramus in domino iesu (4: 1-7): 139

Ad Timotheum I
Testificor coram deo (4: 1-8): 477

Ad Titum
Apparuit benignitas et humanitas (3: 4-7): 3

Index of Rubrics